K H Blakes

January 1993

HYSTERIA AND RELATED MENTAL DISORDERS

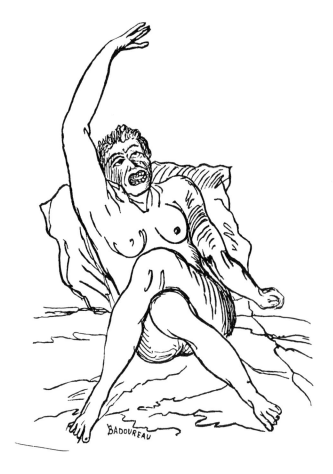

Hystero-epileptic attack. Period of contortions, showing the attitude of Charcot's patient, Ler, during the attack. (Facsimile of a sketch from nature.) *(Reproduced from 'Lectures on the Diseases of the Nervous System' by J. M. Charcot, 1879.)*

HYSTERIA AND RELATED MENTAL DISORDERS

AN APPROACH TO PSYCHOLOGICAL MEDICINE

By

D. WILFRED ABSE
MD, BSc (Wales), DPM (London), FAPA, FBPsS, FRC Psych

Clinical Professor of Psychiatry, University of Virginia, Faculty Member, The Washington Psychoanalytic Institute, and Attending Psychiatrist, St Albans Psychiatric Hospital, Radford, Virginia. Formerly Visiting Professor St Bartholomew's Hospital, London; Senior Psychiatric Consultant, David C. Wilson Hospital, Charlottesville, Virginia. Assistant, Department of Psychiatry, Charing Cross Hospital; Specialist in Psychological Medicine, R.A.M.C.; Deputy Medical Superintendent, Monmouthshire Mental Hospital, etc.

SECOND EDITION

WRIGHT
BRISTOL 1987

Published under the Wright imprint by
IOP Publishing Limited,
Techno House, Redcliffe Way, Bristol BS1 6NX

First edition, 1966
Second edition, 1987

British Library Cataloguing in Publication Data
Abse, D. Wilfred
  Hysteria and related mental disorders:
  an approach to psychological medicine. —— 2nd ed.
  1. Hysteria
  I. Title
  616.85′24   RC532

ISBN 0 7236 0811 3

Typeset by Activity Ltd, Salisbury, Wilts
Printed in Great Britain by The Bath Press, Lower Bristol Road,
Bath BA2 3BL.

Preface to the 2nd Edition

The first edition of this book drew largely on my experience as a military psychiatrist in Britain and India in World War II, an experience later amplified by work with American veterans of the wars in Korea and Vietnam. Following those wars, there were also many opportunities for me, as for others, to observe and to treat the effects of prolonged traumatic experiences of civilian survivors, as well as some severe neurotic problems which had arisen in the lives of survivors of massive destructive assault. At a regrettably high cost, modern warfare has facilitated the study of hysteria and hysteriform conditions. Emanuel Miller (1940),[1] during World War II, noted that the problems presented by functional diseases stand out in bold relief under wartime conditions. Similarly Arthur Hurst (1940)[2] asserted that World War I had provided a great opportunity of studying the varying manifestations of hysteria in soldiers. Hurst added: 'By the end of 1918 we had been able to demonstrate the hysterical nature of several conditions which had hitherto been regarded as organic.'

Widespread as hysterical conditions continue to be in peacetime, they are less readily recognized than in war. The science of medicine in its rapid technological development during the present century has found it more and more difficult to acknowledge the presence of hysteria in its protean forms, some of which are so easily confused with patterns of organic disease. Hysteria is the anomaly *par excellence* for a restricted 'medical model', an anomaly in the sense that it stubbornly resists assimilation into a prevailing paradigm.[3] None the less many serious investigators continue to try to fit it into a reductive paradigm of physico-chemical medicine, following the lead of F. L. Golla who declared in his Croonian Lecture of 1921 that a halt should be called to psychological investigations. He maintained that all the abnormalities evident in neurosis, including psychical reactions, were but symptoms of a disturbance of physical mechanisms — a failure of organic equilibrium.

Here it suffices to note that a one-sided approach to functional disorder can lead to serious iatrogenic problems. Certainly, often enough, a group of symptoms may be associated with a structural lesion, as, for example, when organic disease induces a regressive ego orientation with the activation of mental conflict; in such a case the symptoms express an exaggerated psychological reaction to the actual physical lesion. A more adequate medical model always takes psychological aspects into consideration, including those of the organic case, for diagnosis and prognosis and for management and treatment. Moreover, an adequate medical model avoids an either–or approach as is typified in the Croonian Lecture of 1921.

In peacetime, it has been possible to work in more prolonged intensive psychotherapy with patients suffering from hysteria and allied conditions, and to work with many of them in psychoanalysis. Since the first edition of this book, there have been numerous publications on the subject of hysteria and borderline character disorders of a hysteriform nature. Thus the concepts to be discussed now rest on a more ample clinical experience and theoretical foundation. However, there will be a continued emphasis here on the clinical methods by which a diagnosis of hysteria can be made in short-contact work. In this the differentiation of hysteria and hysteriform borderline disorder from organic disease and from schizophrenic psychoses is vital, since any lengthy delay in recognizing hysteria prejudices treatment outcome. Thus unduly prolonged physical investigation for the purpose of excluding organic disease may result in worsening of hysterical types of disorder.

The third edition of *The Diagnostic and Statistical Manual of Mental Disorders* (D.S.M. III)[5] of the American Psychiatric Association adopts several classifications which include many types of hysteria, such as Somatoform Disorders, Dissociative Disorders, Psychosexual Disorders and Personality Disorders. The attempt at clarification by earnest committees, or task forces, has instead too often resulted in obfuscation in relation to disorders of a hysterical nature, especially in its impact on the general practice of medicine and surgery. Whatever anti-therapeutic implication there may be in the label 'Hysteria', other labels often convey a false notion of encounter with a strange and unknown sickness. Moreover, in all forms of hysteria there are common processes of identification, of dissociation and of symbolism. These common processes need to be understood in order to form a diagnosis and an adequate treatment plan.

In elucidating the aetiology and psychopathology of hysterical conditions, I have continued to use examples from wartime as well as others from civilian life in peacetime. The military cases lend themselves as vivid illustrations of conflicts induced by stress and expressed in symptoms. As will be shown in the pages that follow, the emergence of concepts of dynamic psychiatry occurred under peacetime conditions, and these concepts were only later applied to problems of military psychiatry in World Wars I and II, in Korea and in Vietnam. However, these concepts were more readily accepted by more physicians under military conditions because their utility and their grounding in dramatic clinical manifestations were then so much more perspicuous.

Episodically in the decades following World War II, physicians in general have acknowledged the influence of emotional factors and mental conflicts in the pathogenesis of physical manifestations of disease. At other intervening times, they have generally denied or minimized their importance, often in association with temporary captivation by spectacular technical advances in pathophysiology and pharmacology.

The 1960s and the 1970s saw a renewed awareness among physicians, on both sides of the Atlantic, of the large incidence of behavioural and emotional problems in the general practice of medicine. The extent of psychiatric illness to be seen in general practice was clearly outlined by Michael Shepherd et al.[6] Later George Engel[7] emphasized the need for a broader medical model. The Whitfield and Winter Study[8] included an examination of the attitudes of general practitioners towards the psychiatric services in the United Kingdom which revealed considerable ambivalence. On the one hand, 43 per cent wanted further training in the management and treatment of neurotic disorder, on the other, only 33 per cent of these wanted a consultant psychiatrist to visit the practice at regular intervals. It would seem that to facilitate the integration of psychiatric and general medical practice a demystification of the conceptual framework of dynamic psychiatry is necessary. The adequate study of hysteria is the gateway to the whole field of psychological medicine, and it is hoped that this book will make a contribution towards a better understanding of the psychodynamic approach to psychiatry and psychological medicine.

Disappointment and dissatisfaction with the result of the more usual physical investigations and treatment, applied without adequate psychodynamic understanding, can be seen in the growth of a one-sided emphasis on 'ecological illness', embedded in so-called 'holistic medicine'. Certainly fatigue, vitamin deficiency, chemicals and allergies influence mood and both physical and mental functioning, and sometimes these physical causes are indeed ignored by modern physicians, but the extent to which such factors are responsible for sickness is vastly overstated in proportion to the degree that mental conflict and the power of the unconscious are underestimated. As von Mering[9] has shown, there is considerable coincidental psychopathology among chronic allergy sufferers, which argues for as much psychotherapeutic attention as dietary.

It is now nineteen years since the publication of the first edition of this volume. During this time there have been many new studies and further discussions of the matters it considered, so that revisions and amplifications have become necessary. This edition continues to focus on the problems of diagnosis and their bearing on management and treatment. In view of the continuing interest in and importance of ego psychology, the nature of disturbances of consciousness is explored further, with some regard for its increasing forensic relevance. Scrutiny is renewed of the relationship of language development to hysterical disorder, particularly regarding the importance of metaphor in linguistic development and related regressive events in the somatic conversion process, and the bridge consequently offered in psychotherapy from the conversion symptom to the strangulated affects. Finally, the evolution of the diffuse concept of dissociation has been re-examined, including recent notions of 'splitting' in relation particularly to borderline and psychotic personality disorders.

Recent emphasis on a variety of borderline conditions, including those comprising episodic depressive disorder, overshadows, and sometimes omits, their intimate relationship to hysteria. The impression often conveyed is that we are faced with new diseases. Such an impression is not justified by the study of history, whether ancient or more recent. Thus Freud,[10] writing to Jung, 30 December 1906, made the following remarks:

Perhaps you can make use of this observation in spite of its sketchiness. I have been called in as a consultant in the case of a woman of 26 who gave birth to her first child 6 weeks ago and whose condition set in about the middle of her pregnancy. According to the family doctor, who is not too familiar with our ideas, the woman's explanation of her severe depression is that she had turned herself into an 'imbecile' by the habit formed in childhood of retaining her urine so long that its discharge would provide her with sexual sensations. This she continued to do for some time after her marriage. Then she stopped (the illness probably began at that time). She married for love after an acquaintance of six years and a prolonged struggle with her family. She is very much in love with her husband (he is an actor) but has been totally anaesthetic in sexual intercourse. The patient adds that it has never occurred to her to blame her husband for her lack of satisfaction, that she is convinced it is her fault. Her depression was probably connected with her anxiety about impending delivery. She had kept insisting that she would not be able to give birth normally, and gloated when a forceps delivery was required: she had been right. She maintains quite seriously that her child is a hopeless 'imbecile'. She has made repeated attempts at suicide (always taking her precautions) and written her husband mournful letters of farewell. Once she actually left home, but only went as far as her sister's flat, where she played the piano. She has occasionally struck her baby. When asked if she loves the child, she says: 'Yes, but it's not the right one.'

States of manic excitation have been noted. One is struck by megalomaniacal statements in reference to her illness: her condition is unprecedented, the doctors will never be able to help her, and it would take them years to understand her. She argues very acutely, it is impossible to reason with her. She claims to have only the dimmest memory of her life or even of the things she accuses herself of. She says that her brain is affected by 'imbecility', that she cannot think clearly and is incapable of reflection, that only her illness is really clear to her. Though on the whole she gives an impression of dejection, there is an unmistakable affectation in her speech and movements. The family doctor says she behaves like an actress. And she does indeed accompany her speech with a perverse mimicry (eye-movements such as I have only seen in paranoia).

Formerly this would have been called 'masturbatory insanity', an abominable term. Don't you think it's Dementia Praecox? Don't you find this revelation of the aetiology so carefully kept hidden in hysteria interesting?

REFERENCES

1. Miller, E. (ed.) (1940). *The Neuroses in War*. London: Macmillan.
2. Hurst, A. (1940). *Medical Diseases of War*. London: Arnold.
3. Kuhn, T. (1962). *The Structure of Scientific Revolutions*. Chicago: Univ. Chicago Press.
4. Golla, F. L. (1921). 'The Objective Study of Neurosis', Croonian Lecture, London.
5. D.S.M. III (1980). *Diagnostic and Statistical Manual of Mental Disorders* (3rd ed.) Washington, D.C.: Am. Psychiat. Assoc.
6. Shepherd, M., Cooper, B., Brown, A. C. et al. (1966). *Psychiatric Illness in General Practice*. London: Oxford Univ. Press.
7. Engel, G. (1977). 'The need for a new medical model: a challenge to biomedicine'. *Science*, **196**, 129–36.
8. Whitfield, M. J. and Winter, R. D. (1980). Psychiatry and general practice: results of a survey of Avon G.P.'s. *Coll. Gen. Practit.*, **30** (220), 682–6.
9. Von Mering, U. (1972). The diffuse health aberration syndrome — a bio-behavioral study of the perennial outpatient. *Psychosomatics*, **13**, 293–303.
10. McGuire, W. (1974). *The Freud–Jung Letters: The Correspondence between Sigmund Freud and C. G. Jung* (Trans. (Freud) Manheim, R. and (Jung) Hull, R. F. C.). Princeton, NJ: Princeton Univ. Press.

Preface to the 1st edition

Fifteen years have passed since the publication of *The Diagnosis of Hysteria*, a book which I wrote based on war-time experience as a military psychiatrist. Meanwhile, interest, study, and discussion of the problems with which that volume dealt have become more wide-spread and sometimes more deep-reaching. My own studies and clinical and teaching experiences have led me to respond to this increasing interest by an amplification of the scope and purposes of that book. On the one hand, this volume deals more fully with problems of diagnosis and their bearing on management and treatment; on the other hand, in conformity with increased interest in ego psychology, the nature of disturbances of consciousness has been explored. An attempt has also been made to scrutinize the relationship of language development to hysterical disorder. In this tentative scrutiny particular attention has been paid to the importance of metaphor in linguistic development and related regressive events in the somatic conversion process. From the conversion symptom, metaphoric language offers a bridge in pyschotherapy to the strangulated affects. Freud's own contributions to language theory are fragmentarily scattered throughout his writings and are organically connected with development in his theory of mental functioning; without an understanding of this, linguistic studies cannot be adequately benefited. Finally, the evolution of the diffuse concept of dissociation has been examined and its present usefulness illustrated.

The adequate study of hysteria becomes a gateway to the whole field of psychological medicine. It is in this sense that this book is an introduction to the field; it is not confined to merely elementary considerations. It will become apparent to the reader that this book continues to follow pathways opened by Sigmund Freud, sometimes attempting to penetrate into contiguous and poorly explored sidetracks. At the same time there is consideration of contributions made by others, as long as these contributions are grounded in clinical experiences and related to clinical realities.

My wife, Elizabeth, has contributed a good deal to this book, including substantial editorial assistance and many useful suggestions based on her literary knowledge. Mrs. Glenna Wampler, whose husband recently qualified as a physician, loyally provided secretarial services. Thanks are also due to colleagues in the Department of Neurology and Psychiatry, University of Virginia School of Medicine, with whom many topics have been discussed. To Dr. Ian Stevenson especial thanks are due both for discussions and for his co-operation in administrative arrangements which provided time for the completion of this volume.

Although quotations from Freud are from earlier translations, for convenience references have been made to *The Standard Edition* (1953), as stated in the bibliography.

Charlottesville,   D. W. A.
Virginia.
February, 1966

Contents

CHAPTER 1

Hysteria and the Emergence of Dynamic Psychiatry

It is to the naturalistic outlook of the ancient Greek philosophers that hysteria owes its name, since they believed that otherwise unaccountable disorders of women were due to migration of the uterus *(hustera)* within the body. In this idiom, philophers and physicians among the Greeks from the time of Pericles recognized that some forms of bodily and emotional disorder in women were related to sexual disturbance. Plato's *Timaeus* contains a passage suggestive of 'male chauvinism' but which is at any rate an earnest effort to account for hysteria:

Of the men who came into the world, those who were cowards or led unrighteous lives may with reason be supposed to have changed into the nature of women in the second generation. And this was the reason why at that time the gods created in us the desire to have sexual intercourse, contriving in man one animated substance and in women another... Wherefore also in men the organ of generation becoming rebellious and masterful, like an animal disobedient to reason and maddened with the sting of lust, seeks to gain absolute sway; and the same is the case with the womb or matrix of woman; the animal within them is desirous of procreating children, and when remaining unfruitful long beyond its proper time, gets discontented and angry, and wandering in every direction through the body, closes up the passages of the breath, and, by obstructing respiration, drives to extremity, causing all varieties of disease.[1]

The ancient Greek attitude to women, as expressed above is a subject ably discussed in recent years by Philip Slater (1971).[2] Bodily or emotional disorders issuing from disturbances of sexuality were named by the Greeks in reference to their manifestations in women.

Hippocrates,[3] however, when writing *On the Sacred Disease*, as epilepsy was called, insisted that 'the brain is the cause of this affection,' and in early antecedence of modern knowledge about chemical and electrolyte imbalance, outlined a pathophysiology based on bodily intake and discharge of fluid and air. Scoffing at those who held supernatural views, he wrote:

...if they imitate a goat, or grind their teeth, or if their right side be convulsed, they say that the mother of the gods is the cause. But if they speak in a sharper and more intense tone, they resemble this state to a horse, or say that Poseidon is the cause. Or, if any excrement be passed, which is often the case, owing to the violence of the disease, the appellation of Enodia is adhibited; or if it be passed in smaller and denser masses, like bird's it is said to be from Apollo Nomius. But if foam be emitted from the mouth and the patient kicks with his feet, Ares then gets the blame. But terrors which happen during the night, and fevers, and delirium, and jumpings out of bed, and frightful apparitions, and fleeing away—all these they hold to be the plots of Hecate, and the invasion of the Heroes, and use purifications and incantations, and, as appears to me, make the divinity to be most wicked and most impious.

Hippocrates stoutly held to a naturalistic view of those priestesses allegedly afflicted with the 'sacred disease' who chanted their oracles after convulsing. In many of these cases, the sacred disease may well have been hysteria, for Hippocrates, like many a modern physician, found it difficult to distinguish convulsive hysteria from idiopathic epilepsy, as was noted by Gilles de la Tourette in 1895.[4]

In the second century A.D., Galen explained that kinds of mental and physical distress similar to those subsumed under the rubric of hysteria in women occurred in men; in these cases he assumed that the cause was retention of sperm (Veith, 1965).[5]

During the Middle Ages not only was the naturalistic viewpoint of the ancient Greek physicians and philosophers, and that later of Galen, largely disregarded, but also emphasis was placed more on diabolical possession than on any divine inspiration. Whereas the Greeks had often seen something supernatural in hysterical manifestations and connected them with prophetic power, people later came to regard them as loathsome evidences of the disturbed person's possession by evil spirits or the Devil himself. So firmly and widely was the latter belief adopted throughout Europe that it fostered an outbreak of persecution exceeded only by the recent Holocaust in Nazi Germany. In this connection we must appreciate the awesome power of modern mass communication to gain rapidly popular support for crass delusions.

From the thirteenth to the late seventeenth century, Europe was plagued by disease, and waves of bubonic, pneumonic and septicaemic infection due to rats, fleas and the *Bacillus pestis* added to the miseries of human existence. People often attributed such calamities to witches, thus largely absolving physicians of responsibility, although Ambroise Pare (Packard, 1926)[6] noted that they too were sometimes stoned to death. The so-called 'stigmata' of hysteria were relied upon in the medieval witch trials as proof of possession by the Devil. Accounts of the persecution of witches in Puritan New England indicate that those alleged to be witches—and often their 'victims' as well—suffered from hysteria. The tense atmosphere of the Salem trials, with their harsh judgements, no doubt fostered hysterical responses throughout the Massachusetts colony.

Szasz (1971)[7] has discussed witchcraft in relation to the struggle between professional and lay healers. He notes that the peasantry regarded witches as wise and gifted women who had many time-tested remedies to offer. As a matter of fact, many of their herbal medication still have a place in modern pharmacology; for example, ergot was used against the pains of childbirth at a time when the Church vigorously held to the view that pain in labour was God's punishment for Eve's sin. The witch with her empirical approach and her magic, was condemned by a Church that was deeply opposed to the empirical, that professed contempt for the material world, and that distrusted the senses as snares that would lead man away from faith and into carnality. According to Barbara Ehrenreich and Deidre English (1973):[8]

In the persecution of the witch, the anti-empiricist and the misogynist, anti-sexual obsessions of the Church coincide. Empiricism and sexuality both represent a surrender to the senses, a betrayal of faith. The witch was a triple threat to the Church. She was a woman, and not ashamed of it. She appeared to be part of an organized underground of peasant women. And she was a healer whose practice was based in empirical study. In the face of the repressive fatalism of Christianity, she held out the hope of change in this world.

The witch trials accused the 'possessed' of responsibility for all manner of misfortunes for which there was no other way to account. An appalling number of men, women and children were tortured and put to death for events with which they had no connection whatsoever. They were hung by their thumbs, starved in dungeons, stretched on the rack and broken on the wheel, often in their extremity confessing at last to impossible deeds.*

The application of exorcism as a cure for the possessed instead of their elimination for causing destruction marked a great advance in the treatment of the mentally deranged; and exorcism as a religious and compassionate rite, performed without punishment, was a further advance. Ellenberger (1970)[9] draws the line of progress from exorcism to magnetism, then to hypnotism, and, ultimately, to the dynamic psychiatry of our own time. During the seventeenth century medieval notions connecting hysteria with the supernatural gradually gave way again to naturalistic considerations. Ambroise Paré, like Hippocrates, wrote about 'suffocation of the womb'; Fernel differed from Galen who had denied that any movement of the womb produced hysteria (Havelock Ellis, 1911);[10] and Charles Lepois, physician to Henry II, insisted that hysteria could be seen in both sexes and occurred at all ages, and suggested that the seat of the disorder might well be the brain (Ellis, *op. cit.*).[10]

Two sixteenth century physicians had helped Western thought to emerge again from the morass of superstition. Henry Cornelius Agrippa, expelled from the University of Cologne in the early part of that century for inveighing against notions of witchcraft and for advocating humane treatment of people with disordered behaviour, underwent long imprisonment for his views (Atkinson, 1956).[11] At about the same time, Paracelsus (Theophrastus Bombastus von Hohenheim), often dubbed the father of therapeutics, also condemned the belief in witchcraft and challenged traditional Galenic medications, being especially critical of overmedication—as he might very well be today with respect to current abuse of synthetic chemicals. Denounced by his enemies, he was called an impostor and accused of sorcery; his flight and subsequent death demonstrates the dangers of originality in those days (Pachter, 1961).[12]

The struggle against medieval notions is well illustrated by Edward Jorden's 'Brief Discourse of a Disease Called the Suffocation of the Mother' written in 1603 (Brain, 1963),[13] the title of which reminds us of Plato's view of the

---

*The trials remind us that although modern man has ostensibly surmounted the fear of unseen malign forces lurking around and threatening Doomsday, yet we now contend with the fear of nuclear and chemical contamination, and of thermonuclear warfare, so that doomsday sturdily remains topical.

discontented uterus in the *Timaeus*. The discourse tells of a trial held in 1602, in which one Elizabeth Jackson was accused of having bewitched a 14-year-old girl into 'fittes so fearful, that all that were about her, supposed that she would dye. The girl had become 'speechless and blynde. Her necke and throat did swell. The lefte hand, arme and whole side were deprived of feeling and moving. Her belly showed certaine movings'. Two doctors at the trial ascribed the girl's problems to natural causes, but two took a more sinister view. The accused was imprisoned for a year and pilloried four times. Lord Brain (1963)[13] notes that Jorden

...in his rejection of a supernatural origin for the hysterical passion may for a time have reinforced the idea of its uterine origin, but Willis undermined that by attributing it to a discharge of animal spirits in the nervous system, the site of the discharge in his view differing from that which underlies the convulsions of epilepsy.

The year 1775 was critical in the evolution of dynamic psychiatry from exorcism. It marked the clash between Johann Joseph Gassner, noted exorcist and faith healer, and Franz Anton Mesmer, famous physician (Zimmermann, 1879).[14] Early in that year, hordes of people, rich and poor, nobles and peasants, swarmed to the small town of Ellwangen in Württemberg to see Father Gassner, whose reputation as a faith healer had spread far and wide. In the presence of physicians, noblemen of all ranks, members of the bourgeoisie and church authorities both Catholic and Protestant, and before sceptics as well as believers, he exorcized evil demons. His every word and gesture and those of his subjects were recorded by a notary public, and the official records of his activities were signed by distinguished eye witnesses. Although Gassner was but a modest country priest, as soon as he donned his ceremonial garments and had the subject kneeling before him, astonishing events took place. Ellenberger (1970)[9] quotes the account given by the Abbé Bourgeois:

The first patients were two nuns who had been forced to leave their community on account of convulsive fits. Gassner told the first one to kneel before him, asked her briefly about her name, her illness, and whether she agreed that anything he would order should happen. She agreed. Gassner then pronounced solemnly in Latin: 'If there be anything preternatural about this disease, I order in the name of Jesus that it manifest itself immediately.' The patient started at once to have convulsions. According to Gassner, this was proof that the convulsions were caused by an evil spirit and not by a natural illness, and he now proceeded to demonstrate that he had power over the demon, whom he ordered in Latin to produce convulsions (and other effects) in various parts of the patient's body; thus he called forth in turn the exterior manifestations of grief, silliness, scrupulosity, anger and so on, and even the appearance of death. All his orders were punctually executed. It now seemed logical that, once a demon had been tamed to that point, it should be relatively easy to expel him, which Gassner did. He then proceeded in the same manner with the second nun.

Even this short excerpt conveys to the psychoanalyst of two centuries later an impression of intuitive skill embedded in the idiom of demonology. Gassner clearly knew how to use institutional charisma and a sacred language; how to reinforce his personal prestige as a healer through impressive exhibitionism and the acclaim it evoked; and how to tame affects through his rituals. As a young priest Gassner had suffered from violent headaches and dizziness, attacks of which occurred—or worsened—as he celebrated the Mass, preached, or heard confession. The connection between the worsening of his physical state and the performance of his priestly duties led him to suspect that he was under attack from the Devil. When he resorted to churchly rituals of exorcism, his condition improved. He then began exorcizing rich people in his parish and had considerable success, word of which spread. He successfully exorcized a locally well-known hypochondriacal countess after which he was invited to perform similar cures in many distant places. His growing fame brought him many impassioned enemies, including various representatives of the Enlightenment. Rumour had it that cases of possession were sure to appear wherever a visit from Gassner was announced. An animated controversy about him erupted at the University and Medical School in Vienna. Among churchmen the chief critic of the belief in possession was Johann Saloman Semler (Zimmerman, 1879),[14] the founder of the new Protestant theology. If not the first, he was among the first Christian theologians to undertake a survey of the Bible from the historical point of view; he felt that the authors of the New Testament held ideas specific to their time. By 1767 he had concluded that a complete history of possession would contribute greatly to the destruction of what he held to be an anachronistic belief. He wrote:

If I desired to collect the thousands and thousands of stories of possessed persons and their cure, it would be a vast labour and would constitute a history of the devil in the Middle Ages. It would be of relatively large proportions, but would infallibly produce a happy, profound and lasting impression on all readers, inasmuch as they themselves, however simple-minded and credulous, would judge that it must be far from the truth. The frightful superstition which still brings forth many dark fruits would be very rapidly and generally weakened thereby. (Quoted in T. K. Oesterreich, 1974.)[15]

The opposition to Gassner, largely inspired in Europe by the new philosophy of the Enlightenment which proclaimed the primacy of reason over ignorance, superstition and blind tradition, was consolidated in commissions of inquiry. One such commission, appointed in Munich by the Prince of Bavaria, called Dr Mesmer, who claimed to have discovered a new principle called 'animal magnetism', to appear before it, thus bringing into confrontation with exorcism a representative of medicine. On 23 November 1775, Mesmer gave demonstrations in Munich which elicited in subjects the appearance and disappearance of various symptoms including convulsions. Ellenberger (1970)[9] writes:

Father Kennedy, the Secretary of the Academy, was suffering from convulsions, and Mesmer showed that he was able to bring them forth in him and dispel them at will. On the following day, in the presence of Court members and members of the Academy, he provoked attacks in an [alleged] epileptic and claimed he was able to cure the patient through animal magnetism. In effect, this amounted to Gassner's procedure, without involving the use of exorcism. Mesmer declared that Gassner was an honest man, but that he was curing his patients through animal magnetism without being aware of it. We can imagine that, upon hearing Mesmer's report, Gassner must have felt like Moses when the Egyptian wizards reproduced his miracles in the Pharoah's presence. But, unlike Moses, Gassner had not been permitted to witness Mesmer's performance or to reply to his report.

Gassner's fate was eventually sealed by an order of the Imperial Court requiring the Prince Bishop to banish him to the small community of Pondorf. After the investigation of Gassner's activities Pope Pius VI issued a decree stubbornly defending the practice of exorcism but insisting on discretion and strict adherence to Roman ritual. Ellenberger (1979)[9] notes that Gassner's absolute piety was never questioned and that his unpretentiousness and unselfishness were clear, but that he was caught up in the struggle between the new Enlightenment and the forces of tradition. His eclipse led to the honouring of a healing method without religious ties, one that would satisfy the requirements of an 'enlightened' time. As remains true today, fashions in treatment change rapidly or oscillate between one and another. It has never been enough to cure the sick—one must cure them by methods of which the community approves.

Mesmer, who lived from 1733 to 1815, was in time himself faced with the hostility of the medical community. Ilza Veith (1965)[5] has described the public clamour that arose in his defence, and notes the resultant appointment by Louis XVI of a Royal Commission to examine the validity of the concept of 'animal magnetism'. It is interesting that this commission included the then American Ambassador, Benjamin Franklin, expert concerning static electricity, the chemist Lavoisier and the astronomer Bailly, as well as other illustrious men of the time in France. Charged with determining whether such a phenomenon as 'animal magnetism' truly existed, it reported in the negative and attributed Mesmer's cures to the workings of the imagination. Like Columbus, who had discovered a new world the vast nature of which he did not fully grasp, Mesmer died a bitterly disappointed man. None the less, Mesmer is the link between magical methods of treatment and modern psychotherapy.

His clinic in Paris was unique. Patients entered a darkened room filled with soft music, and gathered around a low oaken tub or *baquet* in which iron filings were immersed in water. The patients applied iron rods that projected from the tub to ailing parts of their bodies. Then Mesmer would appear in a colourful silken robe, holding a large iron wand. The ecstatic or convulsive crises manifested by some of the patients no doubt impressed and encouraged the others. One now sees in these events an obvious form of suggestive group psychotherapy.

Puységur,[16] a disciple of Mesmer, subsequently found that instead of the usual types of mesmeric crisis a trance-like state could be induced during which the subject would be even more highly suggestible. This state of altered consciousness he termed 'somnambulism', and used it to further the cures. The Abbé Faria,[17] a Portuguese priest in Paris, showed that the mesmeric trance Puységur described was largely the result of the somnambulist's own expectations, and James Braid (1843),[18] a British physician, investigated the trance state energetically, concluding, as had the Royal Commission of Louis XVI, that no mysterious magnetic fluid was involved. He coined the word 'hypnotism' and used the term 'suggestion'. Liébault and Bernheim (Bernheim, 1884)[19] in Nancy, and Charcot (1882)[20] in Paris, later used hypnosis in the treatment of hysterical disorder. Incidentally, the word *psychothérapie* first became fashionable under the influence of disciples of

Professor Hippolyte Bernheim at the University of Nancy.

Armand Marie Jaques de Chastinet—the Marquis of Puységur—was the eldest of three brothers of French nobility who were among Mesmer's most enthusiastic disciples. He divided his time between his military duties and his castle in Buzancy, where his first patient was a 23-year-old peasant named Victor Race, whose family had been in the service of the Puységurs for several generations. Race suffered from periodic respiratory distress. He was easily magnetized, and while magnetized he had a peculiar crisis, going without the usual convulsions or jerking movements into an altered waking state of consciousness in which he was talkative and responsive to questions. His relationship to his 'magnetizer' was intensified in this condition, and his responsiveness was concentrated solely on him. He retained no memory of this experience. Puységur (1809) regarded this phenomenon as 'the perfect crisis', and because of its similarity to natural somnambulism suggested the term 'artificial somnambulism' for what was subsequently to be known as hypnotism. Soon there was a growing rift between orthodox mesmerists, who clung to the value of producing any sort of crisis and to the part played by a mysterious magnetic fluid, and the followers of Puységur, who concentrated on producing the special 'perfect crisis'. They held to a psychological theory instead of a literal view of 'animal magnetism'. With this shift Puységur and his followers were liberated from a disturbance of metaphoric symbolism in their thinking, inasmuch as they saw clearly that there was only an analogy to, and not an identity with, magnetism in the relation of hypnotist and subject.

Puységur soon had so many patients that, like Mesmer, he introduced collective treatment. Not far from the majestic castle of the Puységurs was the public square of the village of Buzancy, surrounded by trees and thatched cottages. In its centre, near a stream, stood a large and beautiful old elm now known as the Buzancy tree. Peasants were seated on stone benches beneath the tree with ropes hung from its branches attached to ailing parts of their bodies. They imagined they felt the magnetic fluid circulating through their bodies, though this misperception did not mislead Puységur. Sometimes the master would put one of them into a 'perfect crisis' and enthusiastic onlookers reported remarkable cures they had seen result from this special procedure. In this we recognize Puységur's exploitation of the primitive symbolism of sacred trees and springs in the folklore of the country people treated by the Marquis. Such magical notions are active to this day in the visiting of spas by the wealthy for treatment; and ancient myths often openly associate trees and springs with the healing gods.

Mesmer held that to effect healing a magnetizer must first establish rapport, a kind of psychic 'tuning in' to his patient, and Puységur understood and used this prerequisite. Although he did not share the illusions of his peasant clientele and did not organize his collective treatments around a *baquet* as Mesmer did with his wealthier patients, but rather around a tree he had 'magnetized', he saw what he did as a conscious scientific procedure that put popular beliefs and customs to therapeutic use.*

---

*Forests and sacred trees had been for so long considered divine by the Gauls that Christian missionaries and bishops had for centuries found difficulty in eradicating tree-worship among the peasantry. Sèbillot (1906),[21] in his monumental work *The Folklore of France*, describes how the sick attached themselves to trees with ropes to exchange their disease for the vitality (health) of these inexhaustible bearers of life.

Puységur's treatment of Victor during the phases of 'perfect crisis' often went beyond simply using rapport for direct suggestion. A dialogue between the magnetizer and the magnetized became possible when the latter was in the state of altered consciousness; its focus was on the thoughts and feelings of the patient, who made important contributions to it. Moreover, as Puységur's experience with Victor disclosed, a second, somnambulistic personality can emerge in this state—one less inhibited and more brilliant than the one normally belonging to the subject. The appearance of such a phenomenon in the trance state suggested a new model of the human mind based on a sequential duality of consciousness, and implied unconscious psychism, since one personality remained unconscious while the other became manifestly dominant.

The significance of the 'perfect crisis' can only be grasped in the context of an understanding of hypnoid states (*see* Chapter 10), some of which are characterized by this sort of heightened and narrowed form of attention, while most others demonstrate a diminished attention cathexis, with consequent vague ideation. Puységur's induction of a 'perfect crisis' rendered Victor Race capable of a type of therapeutic collaboration never previously achieved.

In reporting the first intimations of depth psychology such as this, one must take into account the increasing awareness and understanding of the phenomenon of multiple personality. The phenomenon of possession came to be understood as one variety of divided selfness. In 'lucid possession', the subject feels within himself two souls struggling for domination, and describes his conflict to his priest or physician. In the more regressive 'somnambulistic possession', which might follow 'lucid possession', an 'intruder' takes over the subject's body and shows in speech and behaviour a personality the subject knows nothing about when he returns to his normal state. As cases of possession became less common, case histories of other kinds of multiple personality disorders began appearing in mesmerist literature and other medical reports. Gmelin (1971)[22] published a case of 'exchanged personality' in which a 20-year-old peasant German woman, impressed by the influx of aristocratic French refugees into Stuttgart at the outset of the French Revolution, suddenly 'exchanged' her own personality for the manners and ways of a French lady, imitating them and speaking French perfectly, even speaking her native language with a French accent. These 'French' states recurred, and while in her French persona she had complete memory of all she had said and done during her previous French states, although as a German she knew nothing of her French personality. Gmelin could easily make her shift from one personality to the other by a motion of his hand. Reil (1803)[23] was greatly interested in this case, elaborated on it, and connected it with the duality sometimes evident in the sequence of waking consciousness and dream consciousness when the dreaming and waking personalities are felt to be in marked contrast.*

A more searching study of multiple personality was initiated in France by the publication in 1840 of the story of 'Estelle' by Antoine Despine (Père),[24] a general medical practitioner who sometimes used 'magnetic'

See the interesting footnote (No. 56) on p. 184 in Ilza Veith's *Hysteria: The History of a Disease* (1965).[5]

treatment. Eugene Azam (1887),[25] a professor of surgery at the Bordeaux Medical School, published another important early study, to which Charcot wrote an introduction, on his work over many years with the woman Félida X. The famous case of the Reverend Ansel Bourne considered by William James (1890)[27] was later published by Hodgson (1891–92).[26] Morton Prince later (1906)[28] wrote his monograph *The Dissociation of a Personality* about his patient, the now famous Miss Sally Beauchamp.

Theodore Flournoy's work is especially interesting in its demonstration of how the rigorous application of scientific method to parapsychology can yield useful concepts for the development of dynamic psychiatry. Flournoy (1900)[29] was enamoured of two maxims: 'Everything is possible,' and 'The weight of evidence must be in proportion to the strangeness of the fact'. He worked with the spiritistic mediums of Geneva, one of whom told him accurately about past events concerning his own family. A lengthy inquiry uncovered a long past relationship between the medium's parents and his own which might have made it possible for her to have heard about the events in question and then to have forgotten them. This medium, a woman named Catherine Muller but more widely known as Helene Smith, claimed in her 'second cycle' of three to be a reincarnation of Marie Antoinette; in her first, she re-enacted her supposed previous life as a fifteenth century Indian princess. Flournoy was able to trace much of the Hindu material she provided to a book she had read as a child. In the third or Martian cycle, she spoke and wrote in a strange tongue which she claimed to be that used on the red planet with some of whose inhabitants she was then apparently familiar. In brief, the results of Flournoy's five-year investigation showed her revelations to be romances of the subliminal imagination based on forgotten memories; they expressed wish-fulfilments. Her guiding spirit, Leopold, was an unconscious personality of her own. It was Flournoy who coined the term 'cryptomnesia' to help explain the caprices of memory. Helene Smith's cycles could clearly be explained by reversions of her personality to experiences she had had at different ages—early childhood, the age of 12 and the age of 16. Similarly, he demonstrated the psychological, albeit unconscious origin of some spiritistic messages. He was a pioneer in the exploration of mythopoetic functions of the unconscious, those unconscious tendencies to weave fantasies with which Freud grappled in his study of hysteria.*

In the nineteenth century, medical circles tended to emphasize anatomy and physiology, and to interpret all mental phenomena as diseased brain structure in accordance with a narrowed 'medical model' or paradigm. In this context, Briquet's (1859)[30] denial of any connection between hysteria and either the physical or psychic aspects of sex was influential and widely accepted. After 2000 years of debate about its cause and nature, hysteria came to be regarded as an organic disease of the brain rather than a mental ailment, and the role of sexual disorder in its pathogenesis was minimized. Nevertheless, in the 1870s and 1880s Jean-Martin Charcot (1889)[31] clung partly to a psychological

*Present day parapsychologists often seem to share their subjects' fantasies that are embedded in, or stimulated by, early forgotten experience. In the case of Catherine Muller (Helene Smith), the experiences of critical developmental periods of childhood, puberty and adolescence, with their frustrations and strains, and the use of grandiosity as a defence against feelings of helplessness, seem to have influenced her 'incarnations'.

approach, demonstrating that morbid ideas could produce hysterical manifestations, and that both pathogenic ideas and hysterical symptoms could be
influenced by hypnotism. Although he thus emphasized that hysteria was a
psychic disorder, he also maintained that neuropathic heredity was fundamental in the aetiology of the disease. With Marie he wrote (1892):[32]

> We do not know anything about the nature of hysteria, we must make it objective in
> order to recognize it. The dominant idea for us in the aetiology of hysteria is, in the
> widest sense, its hereditary predisposition. The greater number of those suffering from
> this affection are simply born *hystérisables* and on them the occasional cause acts
> directly, either through autosuggestion or by causing derangement of general nutrition
> and more particularly of the nutrition of the nervous system.

Charcot's contribution was to demonstrate the traumatic power of
emotional disturbance in provoking the manifestations of the disease, and to
show that mental influence by suggestion under hypnosis could result in the
disappearance of these manifestations. He denied that disorder of the sexual
organs was responsible for the disease and condemned extirpation of the
womb or ovaries as pointless and dangerous. This unfortunately led to a
general tendency to minimise sexual factors in the pathogenesis of the disease,
but his demonstrations opened the way for others to study the psychological
and sexual nature of the malady. He himself showed little further interest in
this aspect of the problem. As Freud (1925)[33] wrote:

> Even before I went to Paris, Breuer had told me about a case of hysteria which,
> between 1880 and 1882, he had treated in a peculiar manner which had allowed him to
> penetrate deeply into the causation and significance of hysterical symptoms. This was at
> a time, therefore, when Janet's words still belonged to the future. He repeatedly read
> me pieces of the case history, and I had an impression that it accomplished more towards
> an understanding of the neurosis than any previous observation. I determined to inform
> Charcot of these discoveries when I visited Paris, and I actually did so. But the great man
> showed no interest in my first outline of the subject, so that I never recurred to it.

The great influence of Janet's work on Freud should surely be acknowledged.* A few years Freud's junior, Pierre Janet of Paris was the first to
establish a twentieth century system of dynamic psychiatry, one to replace the
eighteenth and nineteenth century probings described above. Janet was aware
of his debt to the earlier explorers of the unconscious unlike most later scholars
of psychoanalysis. It was Janet[35] who in 1907 first examined the psychological
aspect of hysteria with care and sustained interest, concluding that it was 'a
malady of the personal synthesis'. He made a considerable descriptive
advance by emphasizing the retraction and dissociation of consciousness
evident in hysteria, but he did not penetrate as far into the meaning of its
symptoms as did Freud. These symptoms he considered, like Charcot, to be
chiefly due to an inherited 'preliminary ailing tendency'. He did, however,

---

*As Freud stated (1909)[34] in his Clark University lectures, 'it was his [Charcot's] pupil,
Pierre Janet, who first adopted a deeper approach to the peculiar psychical processes
present in hysteria and we [Breuer and Freud] followed his example when we took the
splitting of the mind and dissociation of the personality as the centre of our position'.

connect this predisposition with a mental inability under conditions of stress (toxic, exhaustive, or psychological) to prevent partial systems of thought splitting off from the main body of consciousness. His several studies of hypnotic suggestion, including the early article 'L'influence somnambulique et le besoin de direction' (1897),[36] were masterly, and related earlier studies of rapport to the later identification of 'transference' phenomena by Freud.

It was on his return to Vienna from Paris that Freud collaborated in Breuer's work on the latter's observation that the symptoms of hysterical patients are founded on highly significant but forgotten events in their past lives. Therapy based on this observation helped patients to remember and reproduce these events in a state of hypnosis; the process was named 'catharsis'.[37] This notion expressed anew the view of Aristotle that a 'purge' of the emotions could have a beneficial effect on the mind, though the ancient Greeks had not definitively related this to hysteria.

Yet there is evidence that Hippocrates paid attention to the dreams and sexual history of his patients who suffered from hysterical nervous disorder. Thus Brill (1936)[38] cites the episode of Hippocrates' cure of Perdiccas, King of Macedonia. The king suffered periodic fever, difficulty in concentrating, disturbed sleep and muscular weakness, and he would wander on lonely roads alone to find some ease for his distress. Following the failure of another physician to effect a cure, Hippocrates discussed the king's dreams with him, which led to his talking with emotion about his deceased father and his (the father's) erstwhile concubine Phila, once the playmate of Perdiccas in his youth but now the mistress of the palace. At the time Perdiccas was quite chaste, 'scorning slaves and prostitutes'. Hippocrates' diagnosis centered on love sickness. He told the king that he was ill from love of Phila, his father's voluptuous concubine who now 'radiated a sad warmth' (see also Baissette, 1931).[39] Witnessing the king's anger upon hearing his explanation, Hippocrates felt that his diagnosis was confirmed. The king's angry response was to smash a javelin he held in his right hand against a nearby rock and then to swear with upraised left hand that he never felt lust for Phila. Then he ran away and shut himself up in his quarters until the next day. However, he appeared at the hour of his appointment for his peripatetic psychotherapy with Hippocrates, and reluctantly and partially acknowledged then his feelings about Phila. He recalled that after she was 14 years of age she had been removed from him and ever since he had spoken to her with difficulty. In recalling Phila's beauty, he spoke of the anguish he had experienced. After several further discussions during daily walks he ran off to Phila one day and discovered the violence of his passion for her. This he communicated and found it reciprocated. Following a happy consummation, all his symptoms including the fever soon abated. Certainly the method of Hippocrates' intervention in this case resembled Freud's early type of investigative psychotherapy, which often precipitated the patient into action. In later work Freud became more interested in the resolution of internal conflict than in partial resolution and externalization.

Breuer and Freud collaborated in a preliminary paper (1893)[40] and then in a book on hysteria (1895).[37] From then on Freud continued the investigation alone, ultimately abandoning hypnosis as a means of treatment, partly because of its relative unreliability: he was not always able to induce hypnotic trance; moreover, it had turned out that patients improved by hypnosis often remained in the improved condition only as long as they kept in touch with the physician and on good terms with him. The improvement of patients treated by suggestion while in the waking state was often similarly impermanent.

Freud came to understand that the patient would confidently accept the therapist's propositions because the therapist was endowed in the patient's mind with prestige, through the *transference* to him of emotion pertaining to the prestige-endowed parental figures of the patient's past. The patient reverts mentally, while in the dependency relationship characteristic of hypnotic rapport, to the earliest few years of his life, during which he had seen his parents as omnipotent; thus he experiences a version of the lost omnipotence of his own earliest months in infancy. Hypnosis gives to the patient who has failed to master his problems through his own activity a type of passive–receptive mastery that also becomes available, although with less intensity, in other methods of suggestion. In sharp contrast to suggestive therapies and to persuasive therapies that use suggestion and reason, psychoanalysis is concerned with demonstrating to the patient the nature of his transference emotions and obtaining his collaboration in this investigation. In 1912 Freud[41] wrote:

In following up the libido that is withdrawn from consciousness, we penetrate into the region of the unconscious, and this provokes reactions which bring with them to light many of the characteristics of unconscious processes as we have learned to know them from the study of dreams. The unconscious feelings strive to avoid the recognition which the cure demands; they seek instead for reproduction, with all the power of hallucination and the inappreciation of time characteristic of the unconscious. The patient ascribes, just as in dreams, currency and reality to what results from the awakening of his unconscious feelings; he seeks to discharge his emotions regardless of the reality of the situation. The physician requires of him that he shall fit these emotions into their place in the treatment and in his life history, subject them to rational consideration, and appraise them at their true psychical value. The struggle between intellect and the forces of instinct, between recognition and strivings for discharge, is fought out almost entirely over the transference-manifestations. This is the ground on which the victory must be won, the final expression of which is lasting recovery from neurosis. It is undeniable that the subjugation of the transference-manifestations provides the greatest difficulties for the psychoanalyst; but it must not be forgotten that they, and they only, render the invaluable service of making the patient's buried and forgotten love-emotions actual and manifest; for in the last resort no one can be slain *in absentia* or *in effigie*.

By the eighteenth and nineteenth centuries, although the 'wandering womb' theory of the Greeks was discredited and the fear of witches, tinged as it was with sexual implications, had abated, many observers continued to find a connection between hysteria and sexual emotion. Villermay (Ellis, 1911) asserted in 1816, in spite of prevailing medical opinion to the contrary, that the most common causes of hysteria were deprivation of love's pleasures or menstrual disorders. Only a few courageous men before Freud had dared to study the peculiarities of sexual life; among those who did, Richard von Krafft-Ebing,[42] Iwan Bloch,[43] and Havelock Ellis,[10] were outstanding. Freud's first attempts to investigate Breuer's use of the cathartic method soon led to further revelations about sexuality. He wrote (1925):[33]

The theory which we had attempted to construct in the *Studien* remained, as I have said, very incomplete, and in particular we had scarcely touched upon the problem of aetiology, upon the question of the ground in which the pathogenic process takes root. I now learned from my rapidly increasing experience that it was not any kind of emotional excitation that was in action behind the phenomena of the neurosis but regularly one of a sexual nature, whether it was a current sexual conflict or the effect of earlier sexual experiences. I was not prepared for this conclusion and my expectations played no part in it, for I had begun my investigations unsuspectingly. While I was writing my *History of the Psychoanalytic Movement* in 1914, there recurred to my mind some remarks that had been made to me by Breuer, Charcot, and Chrobak, which might have led me to this discovery earlier. But at the time I heard them I did not understand what these authorities meant; indeed they had told me more than they knew themselves or were prepared to defend. What I heard from them lay dormant and passive within me, until the chance of my cathartic experiments brought it out as an apparently original discovery. Nor was I aware that in deriving hysteria from sexuality, I was going back to the very beginnings of medicine and following up a thought of Plato's.

In the *Studies on Hysteria*,[37] in Breuer's 'Theoretical Section', there is the following statement:

The sexual instinct is undoubtedly the most powerful source of persisting increases of excitation (and consequently of neuroses). Such increases are distributed very unevenly over the nervous system. When they reach a considerable degree of intensity the train of ideas becomes disturbed and the relative value of the ideas is changed; and in orgasm thought is almost completely extinguished. Perception too—the psychical interpretation of sense-impressions—is impaired. An animal which is normally timid and cautious becomes blind and deaf to danger. On the other hand, at least in males [sic!], there is an intensification of the aggressive instinct. Peaceable animals become dangerous until their excitation has been discharged in the motor activities of the sexual act'.

Early in their studies on hysteria (1895), Breuer and Freud[37] noted that sexual frustration, sometimes also associated with over-excitation, could lead to sex-linked anger. Later on in *The Interpretation of Dreams* (1900),[44] through dreams involving the death of a parent of the same sex (or a parent figure), Freud was able to trace memories belonging to the early years of childhood when boys regarded their fathers, and girls their mothers, as rivals in love. This passionate triadic involvement with the parents, now well-known as the Oedipus situation, is the culmination of complicated psychosexual development during infancy and childhood; because of inevitable associated conflicts it was found to be of central importance in the psychogenesis of neurosis.* Freud (1900)[44] associated disguised death wishes in dreams sometimes condensed with murderously hostile wishes concerning rivalrous siblings or their surrogates with Oedipal sexuality, and pre-Oedipal experience, evidence of which he invariably found in his hysterical female patients.

*From his correspondence with Fliess (Sigmund Freud, Letter 64 to Fliess, 31 May 1897, p. 206, and Letter 71, 15 October 1897, p. 221, in *The Origins of Psychoanalysis*,[45] it is clear that Freud had, by the summer of 1897, established the existence in childhood of the Oedipus complex. Although he described it in *The Interpretation of Dreams* (1900) he did not use the term 'Oedipus complex' until 1910 (Freud, S. 'A special type of choice of object made by men'. *The Standard Edition*, Vol. 11, p. 171. London: Hogarth Press (1910)).

When Sigmund Freud was on a travelling fellowship in Paris in 1885, he worked on *le service de Monsieur Charcot* at the Salpêtrière, the elegant seventeenth-century hospital built on the site of a former gunpowder factory. Freud, like Janet, drew much inspiration from his experience on Charcot's service. The earliest important work in the field of the neuroses to issue from this famous hospital in Paris was the *Traité clinique et thérapeutique de l'Hystérie* by Paul Briquet (1859).[30] This work, and others which followed it, prepared the ground for the studies on hysterical conditions being conducted at the time of Freud's visit.

There is now a pronounced tendency (shown, for example, by Guze and Perley)[47] to ignore, or crowd out, the vast advance made by the studies of Charcot and his associates, and his followers. There is a fallacy widespread, especially among neurologists, that Charcot remained exclusively focused on organic disease of the nervous system in these cases of hysteria; however, his lectures in 1889[31] show evidence of a broadening view in terms of 'functional' disease and psychodynamic causes. Janet (1907)[35] could thus reasonably assert that his mentor Charcot had held the view that hysteria had psychic origins. Owen[48] notes: 'What is surprising in Charcot's development is not his devotion to the organic and the material, but his emancipation therefrom—an orientation that more than the contributions of any other school opened the door to the era of psychological interpretation of the neuroses'.

Like Charcot himself, the hospital of the Salpêtrière occupies a unique place in the history of mental healing. The institution has come to be a presiding symbol of a revolution in the attitude of many physicians towards mental illness, and a refutation of both the demonological approach and that of a one-sided materialism. Since Graeco-Roman times the supernaturalistic and the naturalistic approaches had competed. The naturalistic concepts of the Corpus Hippocraticum did not reach the understanding of the overwhelming majority of the people of ancient Greece, who remained close to their gods. When troubled by physical and emotional disturbances they had recourse to the temples of Aesculapius, which were usually situated in places of considerable natural beauty conducive to rest and relaxation. After an initial period of expiatory sacrifices, ablutions and fasting, the patient was enjoined to rest on a couch in a small room. There the god would appear in a dream. Ilza Veith[5] writes:

A number of votive tablets found at the temple sites tell of the dreams and the visions the patients experienced during their temple sleep. In most cases, it seems Aesculapius appeared to them and brought about their recovery by words alone or manipulation at the site of the malady. The god carried a staff and was often accompanied by one or more of the large snakes which abounded in the temples. Sometimes the patients felt they were touched or licked by these snakes. According to the tablets, cure was the almost invariable result of these dreams. It was a distinctly psychotherapeutic atmosphere in which these cures were undertaken with rudiments of many of the procedures that were to endure through the millenia to the present day. Even the couch, of a fame then scarcely foreseeable, was in evidence.

At the Salpêtrière, the polar categories of 'organic' and 'functional' replaced notions of the ancient 'supernatural' and the medieval 'demonologi-cal'. These categories (organic/functional) were, however, well within the naturalistic realm of thinking in early élite and scientific medicine in Greece. As I have shown elsewhere[49] the conceptual framework of the ancient Greek physicians conflated the psychological and anatomical, on account of a defect in metaphoric symbolism. This was to a considerable extent remedied in Paris towards the end of the nineteenth century by Charcot and his associates. It must be added that while at first these polar categories of 'organic' and 'functional' were clarifying they also soon became a source of error as some physicians took a crude 'either–or' view of nervous disease, which obscured further conceptual development, and led to a rigid one-sided approach to treatment. Charcot himself avoided this pitfall. Indeed, he insisted that central nervous pathways were always involved in functional diseases, even if these pathways were, he acknowledged, sometimes unknown at the time of his investigations.

Henri Ey,[50] emphasizing the emotional perturbations precipitating hysterical disorder, quotes Pitres' five propositions defining mental and physical disturbances of an hysterical nature:*

1. They are functional disturbances of the nervous system.
2. They are labile and can be suddenly brought on, modified or suppressed.
3. They rarely exist in isolation, and generally occur with other manifestations of a neurotic condition.
4. They develop irregularly.
5. They do not cause deterioration of the general physical condition.

Hysterical neuroses and related mental disorders fulfil these criteria, except that very often they do cause deterioration of the general physical condition especially when associated with alcohol and drug abuse.

At the time of Freud's work with Charcot in Paris, with the early expansion of industry in France and the increasing organization of the working class, physical injuries resulted in claims for compensation. Similarly, with the spread of railways across North America and Europe, accidents on them resulted in claims for damages and there was, as there now is, much legal dispute. Charcot held that nervous disorder often derived from 'psychonervous commotion', even when the victim sustained little or no physical injury, and he found that such a disorder was produced or occasioned by mechanical accident even if its appearance was delayed. Later, in World War I (1914–1918), there was considerable incidence of 'battle neuroses' in soldiers of all the nations involved. Valiant attempts were made to provide some respectable organic explanation for the curious phenomena which occurred with such frequency. The term 'shell shock' was coined implying general medical belief that in some way these conditions were the result of structural disturbance. Some physicians, notably in Great Britain Sir Arthur Hurst (1940),[51] demonstrated the functional nature of several conditions that had hitherto been regarded as organic, including paralyses, contractures, abnormal postures and gaits, tremors, seizures, disorders of speech, vomiting, deafness, blindness, stupor, amnesia and 'soldier's heart', all of which were differentiated from 'true shell-shock'. The latter diagnosis Hurst reserved for

*See Pitres, A. and Regis, E. (1902). *Les Obsessions et les Impulsions*. Paris: Doin.

cases where the patient had been exposed 'to the forces generated by the explosion of powerful shells in the absence of any visible injury to the head or spine'. 'In such cases', he added, 'there is an organic basis, which consists of the more or less evanescent changes in the central nervous system resulting from the concussion caused by aerial compression, to which is often added concussion of the head or spine caused by the sandbags of a falling parapet or by the patient being blown into the air and falling heavily on to his head or back. On this organic basis hysterical or anxiety symptoms are often superposed.'

The three physicians whose works most influenced psychiatrists at the beginning of World War I were Hermann Oppenheim, Jean-Martin Charcot and Sigmund Freud. Oppenheim (1911),[52] who studied many patients suffering nervous *sequelae* of physical injuries caused by industrial accidents, recognized four conditions: hysteria, neurasthenia, organic syndromes and traumatic neurosis. Hurst[51] based his view of 'true shell-shock', noted above, on Oppenheim's opinion that the aetiology of traumatic neurosis resided in molecular disturbances 'due to electrical changes in the central nervous system'. Charcot[31] had dissented from this view, emphasizing psychogenesis; he noted that some of the symptoms of traumatic neurosis such as alterations of consciousness resembled those observed in hypnosis, and that some symptoms could be removed by hypnotic suggestion. He held the view that 'nervous shock' in accident cases caused an alteration of consciousness which included an exceptionally heightened suggestibility since autosuggestion could readily produce symptoms. He used the phrase *'une condition séconde'* which Eugene Azam (1887)[25] first employed in his study of the successive states of Félida X. Breuer and Freud[37] agreed with Charcot that the altered state of consciousness was related to the hypnotic trance and called it the hypnoid state. At that time, they concluded that it was from the emotions generated and suggestions conveyed during this state that neurosis developed. As regards the traumatic neuroses of war, following in this path were W. H. R. Rivers,[53] and William McDougall,[54] as well as Freud's followers: Ferenczi, Abraham, Simmel, and Jones[55] and Eder.[56]

Charcot himself refused to admit an essential distinction between traumatic neurosis comprising conversion phenomena, and conversion hysteria without a history of a recent, evident, and severe traumatic event or, for that matter, of prolonged antecedent traumatic stress. Later Freud and others showed that adult psychoneuroses were associated with forgotten traumatic situations in childhood, and now there is much controversy as to the aetiologic roles of actual trauma and associated fantasies and of self-generated fantasy in early life masquerading as memories of psychic trauma. In any case, as Fenichel (1945)[57] insists, there is no traumatic neurosis without psychoneurotic complications. He writes:

After the individual has experienced too much influx, he is afraid, cuts himself off from the external world and therefore blocks his discharges; and experience of a trauma creates fear of every kind of tension, sensitizing the organism in regard even to its own impulses. If, on the other hand, discharges are blocked (psychoneurotic defence) a little influx, otherwise harmless, may have the effect of one much more intense, creating a flooding. A neurotic conflict creates fear of temptations and punishments and also sensitizes the organism in regard to further external stimuli. 'Trauma' is a relative concept... .

Following World War I there were many victims of chronic traumatic neurosis and Abram Kardiner (1947)[58] explored the discombobulations of ego function evident in these chronic cases. He emphasized the attempts at adaptation and the attempts of the organism to achieve psychic equilibrium after trauma. He wrote:

The traumatic experience can precipitate any of the well-known types of neurotic or psychotic disorders. However, irrespective of the nature of the resulting clinical picture, the distinctive features of traumatic neurosis are always present.

This view is in accord with that expressed more recently by Krystal (1968) and Niederland,[59] who recognized a syndrome resulting from massive psychic trauma and characterized by persistence of symptoms of withdrawal from social life, insomnia, recurrent nightmares, chronic depressive and anxiety reactions and far-reaching somatization.

In war neurosis the aetiological emphasis is generally on the role of the immediate stress and the actual conflict engendered by it, whereas in peacetime neurosis the emphasis is on unsettled infantile and childhood situations. Case examples from World War II in the next chapter will illustrate the fact that there is always an aetiological constellation of conditions within the field of medical observation. In one case, the relevant conditions may obtain more in constitution or in developmental maladjustments, and in another, in the degree of recent stress to which a person was subject. Psychoanalytic work has revealed that the amount and type of stress which can be tolerated without symptoms of illness depends in large measure on individual experiences and reactions during the early years of life.

In discussing the war neuroses, Freud (1921)[60] referred to 'parasitic doubles of the super-ego' which for a time could usurp the power of regulation of the super-ego acquired in childhood. Not only does a 'war super-ego' permit the expression of impulses otherwise forbidden, but it may even enjoin conduct which the reinstated super-ego of peacetime may find difficulty defending against.

Both Jung (1928)[21] and McDougall (1920)[62] point out the limited therapeutic value of abreaction in the traumatic neuroses engendered in the unique psychic atmosphere of the battlefield. The dramatic rehearsal of the traumatic moment, its emotional recapitulation in the waking or in the hypnotic state certainly often has a beneficial therapeutic effect. On the other hand, McDougall points out that in quite a large number of cases simple abreaction can worsen the patient's neurotic disturbance. He argues that in such refractory cases, an essential factor, that of dissociation, has been overlooked. It is this dissociation in the psyche and not only the existence of a highly charged affective complex that has to be reckoned with in treatment, and the therapeutic task must include the facilitation of integration. As Jung (1928)[61] observed: 'the typical traumatic affect is represented in dreams as a wild and dangerous animal—a striking illustration of its autonomous nature when split off from consciousness'. Abreaction is itself partly an attempt to reintegrate the autonomous complex, but this attempt at incorporation and belated mastery, by reliving the traumatic situation repeatedly, often can be effective only with the active support and in the presence of the doctor; and as Jung insists this curative process in many cases requires something more than a feeble rapport. These considerations amply demonstrate the application of key concepts forged during the decades of psychotherapeutic work from before World War I. The work of the therapist in such instances may be stated figuratively thus: his supportive attention to the patient enables them both to face those terrible moments and this serves to exorcize their lingering traumatic power while acknowledging their powerful roles in shaping what we become.

At the onset of World War II, the concepts of dynamic psychiatry were much better understood and accepted, and further studies such as those of Grinker and Spiegel (1945)[63] extended our knowledge of the effects of trauma upon the ego. Moreover the effects of prolonged traumatic experiences were later explored. In their account of clinical observations on the survivor syndrome, Krystal and Neiderland[59] show that the problems of survivors of massive destructive assault are many and complex. They describe far reaching disturbances of personality which can be directly traced to the oppressive and/or threatening milieu in which the survivors were forced to dwell for so long. An identification with the bad image attributed to them by their oppressors ('devil-identity') may become a life-long burden—or a reversal and reprojection may sometimes take place as in the 'white devils' theory of the American Black Muslims. Commonly, however, the victim assumes a 'slave' identification or a 'slave house-boy' identity. The former involves a constriction of human capabilities, the latter an ambivalent ingratiating stance associated with a turning against fellow sufferers. These authors discuss the consolidated masochistic and paranoid character deformations engendered by the need to maintain repression of reactive hostility, including murderous rage, towards their oppressors for a prolonged period. Krystal and Niederland[59] further introduce consideration of the dimension of social pathology, especially the formation later of abnormal families and communities. For besides such symptoms as hypervigilance, conversions, phobias, sleep disturbances, disorders of memory, spells of disorientation, dreams merging into hallucinosis and dream-like experiences in the waking state, muscle tensions and other psychosomatic disorders, much serious schizoid and paranoid and depressive disorder was engendered in these survivors of prolonged stress, and their families and communities were later adversely affected. Robert Jay Lifton (1970)[64] also emphasizes social pathology, including the dehumanization of both invaders and those invaded in war. It is obvious that the concepts developed from the historically early treatment of individual traumatic neuroses can only convey some hints of what may be necessary for people who have been exposed to extreme situations for long periods, often *en masse*, including 'death immersion'. Of course, wars between nations now create conditions that quickly facilitate collective regressive attitudes—dehumanization of the enemy, disowning projections on to him, rationalizations and licence to murder him. In the ensuing peace some of these regressive mental changes stick with many of the survivors with distressing social consequences.

Van Patten and Emory (1973)[65] discussed, and gave case histories to illustrate, the earlier ignoring of traumatic neuroses in Vietnam returnees. These patients, because they reject authority and mistrust institutions, came for medical help to the Veterans' Hospital only out of desperation, years after discharge from service. Explosive aggression, 'flashbacks' of combat scenes, and phobic problems of a paranoid type had led to mistakes in diagnosis such as psychomotor epilepsy, schizophrenic disorder, or attribution entirely to substance abuse. Such patients in my experience have not received early effective treatment with emphasis on cathartic psychotherapy. On the contrary, they received, while in Vietnam, treatment which involved massive psychotropic medication, followed by the crowding out with sundry recreational activities of any focus on their essentially traumatic and pathogenic experiences. Such temporarily suppressive treatment invited the reinforcement of dissociation, though it may have worked for a period, while the soldier was in active service overseas. Van Patten and Emory[65] rightly insist that early recognition of the syndrome is really essential. Even in those cases with delayed recognition of combat neurosis, appropriate treatment resulted in much genuine improvement. As they state,

> The current emphasis on the 'here and now' in psychotherapy, in conjunction with the combat veteran's reluctance to discuss his traumatic experiences and the therapist's wish to be done with the war, may easily create a tacit agreement between therapist and veteran to avoid the subject, although desensitization through abreaction may be more helpful.

Hendin, Pollinger, Singer and Ulman[66] have shown that the individual 'meanings of combat' require to be elucidated in an adequate psychotherapy. Two veterans, for example, had similar experiences of witnessing a prisoner of war pushed to his death from a helicopter. For one, the event aroused an identification with the helplessness of the victim; for the other, a sense that he could have prevented it. Obviously eventually to secure adequate psychotherapeutic leverage these meanings would require an understanding of their connections by both therapist and patient. Harvey Schwartz[67] has shown that in such cases of post-traumatic stress disorder, the building of a trusting relationship with the patient is achieved only by great patience and quiet perseverance. These patients suffer from deep-seated guilt related to the unconscious mobilization of primitive, destructive fantasies and they are apt to disown and project the wish to destroy upon the therapist, making the handling of the transferences a difficult but not usually insurmountable problem. Only as a more and more positive dependent transference is achieved can the patient gradually recover memories of traumatic events and discuss their meanings for him and his feelings and notions about his own involvement, with progressive integration.

REFERENCES

1. Plato. *Timaeus*. In: *Great Books of the Western World* (ed. Hutchins, R. M., Adler, M. J. et al.), Vol. 7. London: Encyclopedia Britannica (1952).
2. Slater, P. E. (1971). *The Glory of Hera*. Boston: Beacon Press.

3. Hippocrates. *On the Sacred Disease.* In: *Great Books of the Western World* (ed. Hutchins, R. M., Adler, M. J. et al.), Vol. 10. London: Encyclopedia Britannica (1952).
4. De la Tourette, G. G. (1895). *Traité clinique et thérapeutique de l'Hystérie.* Paris: Plon, Nourritt.
5. Veith, I. (1965). *Hysteria: The History of a Disease.* Chicago and London: Univ. Chicago Press.
6. Packard, F. R. (1926). *The Life and Times of Ambroise Paré* (2nd ed.). New York: Hoeber.
7. Szasz, T. (1971). The witch as healer. In: *The Manufacture Of Madness.* New York: Delta Books.
8. Ehrenreich, B. and English, D. (1973). *Witches, Midwives and Nurses: A History of Women Healers.* New York: The Feminist Press.
9. Ellenberger, H. F. (1970). *The Discovery of the Unconscious: The History and Evolution of Dynamic Psychiatry.* New York: Basic Books.
10. Ellis, H. (1936). *Studies in the Psychology of Sex.* New York: Random House.
11. Atkinson, D. T. (1956). *Magic, Myth and Medicine.* New York: World Publishing Co.
12. Pachter, H. ? ! . (1961). *Paracelsus: Magic into Science.* New York: Collier Books.
13. Brain, W. R. (1963). The concept of hysteria in the time of William Harvey. *Proc. R. Soc. Med.* **56**, 317.
14. Zimmerman, G. A. (1897). *Johann Joseph Gassner, der berumte Exorzist.* Kempton: Jos Kösel.
15. Oesterreich, T. K. (1921). Possession and exorcism among primitive races. In: *Antiquity, the Middle Ages, and Modern Times* (trans. Ibberson, D.). Causeway Books.
16. Chastenet de Puységur, A. M. J. (1809). *Suite des Mémoires pour servir à l'Histoire et à l'Etablissement du Magnétisme animal* (2nd ed.). Paris: Cello.
17. Faria, Abbé de (1819). *De la Cause du Sommeil lucide.* Paris: Madame Horiac.
18. Braid, J. *Neurypnology, or the Rationale of Nervous Sleep, Considered in relations with Animal Magnetism.* London.
19. Bernheim, H. (1884). *De la Suggestion dans l'Etat hypnotique et dans l'Etat de Veille.* Paris: Doin.
20. Charcot, J.-M. (1882). Sur les divers états nerveux déterminés par l'hypnotisation chez les hystériques. *C. r. Hebd. Séances Acad. Sci.* **XCIV.**
21. Sébillot, P. (1906). *Le Folk-lore de France.* Paris: Guilmoto.
22. Gmelin, E. (1791). *Materialen für die Anthropologie.* Tübingen: Cotta.
23. Reil. J. C. (1803). *Rhapsodien über die Anwendung der psychischen Curmethode auf Geisteszerruttüngen.* Halle: Curt.
24. Despine, A. Sr. (1840). *De l'Emploi du Magnétisme animal et des Eaux minérals dans le Traitement des Maladies nerveuses suivi d'une Observation très curieuse de Guérison de Neuropathie.* Paris: Germer, Ballière.
25. Azam, E. E. (1887). *Hypnotisme, double Conscience et Altération de la Personnalité.* Preface de J. M. Charcot. Paris: Ballière.
26. Hodgson, R. (1891–2). A case of double consciousness. *Proc. Soc. Psychic. Res.* **VII**, 221–55.
27. James, W. (1890). *Principles of Psychology.* New York: Dover (1950).
28. Prince, M. (1906). *The Dissociation of a Personality.* New York and London: Longmans, Green.
29. Flournoy, T. (1900). *From India to the Planet Mars: A Study of a Case of Somnambulism with Glossolalia.* New York and London: Harper.
30. Briquet, P. (1859). *Traité clinique et thérapeutique de l'Hystérie.* Paris: Ballière.
31. Charcot, J.-M. (1889). *Clinical Lectures on the Diseases of the Nervous System.* London: New Sydenham Society.

32. Charcot, J.-M. and Marie, P. (1892). Hysteria. *Dictionary of Psychological Medicine* (ed. Tuke, D. H.). London: Churchill.
33. Freud. S. (1925). An Autobiographical Study. In: *The Standard Edition of the Complete Psychological Works of Sigmund Freud* (ed. Strachey, J.), Vol. XX. London: Hogarth Press (1955).
34. Freud, S. (1909). *Five Lectures on Psychoanalysis*. In: *The Standard Edition*. Vol. XI. London: Hogarth Press (1955).
35. Janet, P. (1907). *The Major Symptoms of Hysteria*. New York: Macmillan.
36. Janet, P. (1897). L'influence somnambulique et le besoin de direction. *Rev. Philos.* **XLIII** (I), 113–43.
37. Breuer, J. and Freud, S. (1893–5). *Studies on Hysteria* (trans. and ed. Strachey, J. in collaboration with Freud, Anna, assisted by Strachey, A. and Tyson, A. In: *The Standard Edition*, Vol. II. London: Hogarth Press (1955).
38. Brill, A. A. (1936). Anticipations and corroborations of the Freudian concept from non-analytic sources. *Am. J. Psychiat.*, **92**, 1127–35.
39. Baisette, G. (1931). *Hippocrate*. Paris: Grasset.
40. Breuer, J. and Freud, S. (1893). On the psychical mechanism of hysterical phenomena: preliminary communication. *Studies in Hysteria*. In: *The Standard Edition*, Vol. II. London: Hogarth Press (1955).
41. Freud, S. The Dynamics of Transference. In: *The Standard Edition of the Complete Works of Sigmund Freud* (trans. Strachey, J., Freud, Anna, Strachey, A. and Tyson, A.) Vol. XII, pp. 107–8. (The translation of 'Zur Dynamik der Übertragung' differs somewhat from Joan Rivière's translation in *Collected Papers*, Vol. 2. pp. 312–22.)
42. Krafft-Ebing, R. von (1886). *Psychopathia Sexualis*. New York: Physicians and Surgeons Book Co. (1931).
43. Bloch, I. (1933). *Strange Sexual Practices*. New York:
44. Freud, S. (1900). *The Interpretation of Dreams*. In: *The Standard Edition*, Vols. IV and V. London: Hogarth Press (1955).
45. Bonaparte, M., Freud, A. and Kris, E. (eds) (1954). *The Origins of Psychoanalysis*. London: Imago Publishing Co.
46. Freud, S. (1910). A Special Type of Choice of Object made by Men. In: *The Standard Edition*, Vol. XI. London: Hogarth Press (1955).
47. Guze, S. B. and Perley, M. J. (1903). Observations on the natural history of hysteria. *Am. J. Psychiat.*
48. Owen, A. R. G. (1971). *Hysteria, Hypnosis and Healing: The Work of Jean-Martin Charcot*. New York: Garrett.
49. Abse, D. W. (1971). *Speech and Reason*. England: Wright; Charlottesville, Va: Univ. Press Virginia.
50. Ey, H. (1982). History and analysis of the concept of hysteria. In: *Hysteria* (ed. Roy, A.), Chap. I. Toronto: Wiley.
51. Hurst, Sir A. (with the cooperation of Ross, T. A.) (1940). *Medical Diseases of War*. London: Arnold.
52. Oppenheim, H. (1911). *Text Book of Nervous Diseases*. New York: Stechert.
53. Rivers, W. H. R. (1924). *Instinct and the Unconscious*. London: Cambridge Univ. Press.
54. McDougall, W. (1926). *Outline of Abnormal Psychology*. New York: Scribner.
55. Ferenczi, S., Abraham, K., Simmel, E. et al. (1921). *Psychoanalysis and the War Neuroses*. London: Internat. Psychoanal. Press.
56. Eder, M. D. (1917). *War Shock*. London: Heinemann.
57. Fenichel, O. (1945). *The Psychoanalytic Theory of Neurosis*. New York: Norton.
58. Kardiner, A. (1947). *War, Stress and Neurotic Illness*. New York: Hoeber.
59. Krystal, H. (ed.) *Massive Psychic Trauma*. New York: Internat. Univ. Press.
60. Freud, S. (1921). Introduction to: *Psychoanalysis and the War Neuroses* (ref. 55

above). London: Internat. Psychoanal. Press.
61. Jung, C. G. (1928). The therapeutic value of abreaction. In: *Contributions to Analytical Psychology*. London: Baillière.
62. McDougall, W. (1920) in: Discussion of: 'The revival of emotional memories and its therapeutic value', by William Brown. *Br. J. Psychol.* Medical Section.
63. Grinker, R. and Spiegel, J. P. (1945). *Men under Stress*. Philadelphia: Blakiston.
64. Lifton, R. J. (1970). *History and Human Survival*. New York: Random House.
65. Van Patten, T. and Emory, W. H. (1973). Traumatic neuroses in Vietnam returnees: a forgotten diagnosis. *Arch. Gen. Psychiat*, **29**.
66. Hendin, H., Pollinger, A., Singer, P. and Ulman, R. B. (1981). Meanings of combat and the development of post-traumatic stress disorder. *Am. J. Psychiat.*, **138**, 11.
67. Schwartz, H. (1982). Vietnam veteran: handle with care. *Medical Portfolio for Psychiatrists*, **3**, No. 1.

CHAPTER 2

Aetiology and Psychopathology of Hysteria

Preliminary Definition

The term 'hysteria' is a capacious rubric just because hysterical conditions assume so many forms. These varieties of form make definitions so difficult for some theorists that the diagnosis of hysteria completely eludes them. Thus Szasz[1] has pronounced it the most mythical of mental illnesses, whereas even those psychiatrists whose orientation is predominantly organic have recognized it as the most psychogenic of all physical illnesses. Lewis[2] in this vein acknowledged that hysteria 'tends to outlive its obituarists'. The protean forms it assumes lead to such absurdities as the acknowledgement of Conversion Disorders while claiming them to be 'relatively uncommon' but simultaneously making a different category for Psychogenic Pain Disorder, and another for Atypical Somatoform Disorder (D.S.M. III) 1980.[3] These more recent obscurations are partly due to the limitations of the usefulness of symptom-observation without regard for an understanding of the unconscious processes involved in symptom-formation, and partly, as with the current plethora of chemical tests, due to an effort to win a spurious respectability within the ambit of a narrow medical model. Of course, informed symptom-observation, as we will see, despite limitations, is useful in diagnosis provided the observer is alert to processes of identification, of dissociation and of symbolism. Since hysteria and hysteriform disorders are manifested in many different forms, many of which can be readily confused with organic disease, it is necessary for accurate diagnosis not only to understand the characteristics of hysteria, but also to be familiar with the manifestations of organic disease. Hysteria may be seen in pure culture; or a disturbance that is predominantly hysterical may present features of psychosis, organic disease, borderline character disorder, or some other neurosis. The possibility of a compound clinical picture necessitates careful discrimination.

The typical clinical features of hysteria are:

i. A group of physical symptoms without an ascertainable structural lesion;

ii. Complacency in the presence of gross objective disability (Janet's *'la belle indifférence'*;[4] and/or

iii. Episodic disturbances in the stream of consciousness when an ego-alien (dissociated) homogeneous constellation of ideas and emotions occupies the field of consciousness. This may altogether exclude the normative stream of consciousness in the individual so affected.

The term *Hysterical Personality* is used to describe an habitual pattern of behaviour which includes excessive attention-seeking and dramatic hyperbolic descriptions of complaints and past symptoms, and constitutes a predisposition to develop periodically functional physical disorder and/or pathological alterations of consciousness (dissociative reactions).

It is characteristic of hysteria that whatever the result of dissociation, be it a localized muscular paralysis or an alternate personality, the operative mental function is a homogeneous whole; affect and ideation are not utterly incongruous, and there is no primary thought disorder, as in schizophrenia. In hysteria, the splitting (or dissociation) of the personality is molar—not, as in schizophrenia, molecular. Some cases evince a transition from hysterical disorder to schizophrenia. In transitional phases, it may be difficult to predict whether the movement will be a reaching back to reality that is accompanied by a consolidation of hysterical symptoms, or will be a deepening withdrawal accompanied by molecular disintegration, or will be a favourable integrative progression. The direction of change often depends largely upon management and psychotherapy. From consideration of these clinical features, the diagnostic differentiation of hysteria from organic disease on the one hand, and from schizophrenia on the other, is clearly a crucial concern.

The term 'hysteria' is often loosely applied to a wide variety of sensory (or more properly, perceptual), motor and psychic disturbances exhibiting the typical clinical features listed. These disturbances may either appear in the absence of any known organic pathology, or accompany organic illness and grossly exaggerate its effects. In the latter event, the *somatic compliance* may be in a partly damaged organ that presents a *locus minoris resistentiae* for the incubating hysteria. The term 'hysteria' is also used to describe certain forms of group excitement (mass hysteria). Hysterical phenomena such as convulsions, pareses and sensory disturbances often appear among participants in frenetic religious, political, or erotic group activity. Although the term usually designates (in this as in other contexts) a type of psychoneurotic disorder, many persons who exhibit transient hysterical phenomena during the course of group excitement may also show evidence at this time, if not later, of psychotic disorder, including paranoid delusions. Related terms are 'hysteriform' and 'hysteroid', which are often used for the sake of greater precison, the former usually to designate conditions that in some respects suggest the hysterical type of psychoneurosis but in others suggest psychotic disorder; the latter, to indicate a general resemblance to hysteria (Fenichel, 1934).[5]

In clinical practice, as noted, hysterical symptoms may be found associated with other kinds of neurotic disturbances, or may occur together with florid manifestations of psychosis.[6] Hysterical symptoms appear often among males, children and elderly people, as well as among young women; many soldiers suffer hysterical disorder when faced with the stresses of war, while in peacetime hysterical symptoms are most common among young women. The designation 'hysterical' is often used in disparagement. Various forms of excessive psychic excitement or of undue inhibition are often designated as 'hysterical' in the vernacular, and frequently in disparagement. This common usage may coincide with psychiatric classification, but is often also applied to other nervous disorders mistakenly.

In accordance with the first clinical feature listed, the physician will often diagnose hysteria by ruling out the presence of any physical condition that could account for the symptoms presented. The positive aspect of a psychiatric diagnosis, however, rests on an understanding of the fact that a patient has a mental conflict, and of the psychological connection between this conflict and the symptoms he exhibits, as Freud (1917)[7] emphasized in *The Paths to the Formation of Symptoms*. Freud (1896)[8] had already pointed to two conditions the presence of which requires that the patient's symptoms be considered as the consequence of psychological disturbance: the *traumatic power* of the disturbance in question must be strong enough to be held accountable; and its *determining quality* must be appropriately related to specific symptoms exhibited.

In *conversion hysteria* there are dramatic somatic symptoms into which the patient's mental conflict is 'converted', whereas in *dissociative mental reactions* the patient, at the cost of disturbed memory and stream of consciousness, attempts to avoid mental conflict. In conversion hysteria there may be gross paralytic, spasmodic, or convulsive motor disturbance, or perversion of sensation; a loss of sensation may occur and lead to dumbness, deafness, or blindness; sometimes pain is experienced. In dissociative mental reactions, amnesia, fugue, or somnambulism may be the first symptoms to attract attention. Any of these symptoms may occur together, although when this is the case they tend to cluster in characteristic patterns; or one symptom may appear by itself, or in alternation with others. Flamboyant symptoms often subside temporarily in response to equally dramatic modalities of magical or magico-religious treatment (*see* Chapter 1).

As already noted the words 'hysteria' and 'hysterical' are used to designate excessively histrionic, sexually provocative, and overly manipulative behaviour patterns in those personalities apt to develop hysterical symptoms. Hysterical characters are also described as readily suggestible, and subject to irrational emotional outbursts and dramatic, even chaotic behaviour. They may have a tendency to mendacity, an extreme form of which is known as *pseudologia phantastica*. However, there are other antecedent behavioural patterns in the regressive personalities liable to have hysterical symptoms (Fenichel,[9] Rangell,[10] Chodoff and Lyons[11]).

The invariable role of mental conflict in the pathogenesis of conversion reactions is discussed in the next section. As will be outlined, Freud (1905)[12] draw attention to conversion symptoms having roots in unconscious phallic–Oedipal conflict. In 1959 Rangell[10] broadened the notion of conversion to include conversion reactions that expressed pregenital conflicts, recognizing a spectrum of personality backgrounds ranging from the hysterical patient who develops a somatic symptom in his struggle with Oedipal conflicts organized at the phallic level to the catatonic schizophrenic for whom a somatic symptom expresses a defensive struggle against primitive cannibalistic wish-fantasies. Rangell found support for his view in the study by Chodoff and Lyons[11] in 1958, to be discussed later (*see* Chapter 7). Easser and Lesser (1956)[13] differentiated the 'hysteroid' from the category of hysterical personality, and remarked on the painful masochistic fantasies the hysteroid patient exhibits. This classification overlaps the 'hysteriform'. The hysteriform or hysteroid character resorts to severe dissociative reactions and depersonalized states more often than the hysterical character. The combined presence of massive denial, flight into hyperactivity or complete passivity, projective distortion and pathological lying—sometimes amounting to *pseudologia phantastica*—often indicates the more damaged ego-functioning of the hysteriform character.

Pieter C. Kuiper (1967)[14] has emphasized 'ungenuineness' as one of the main character traits of the hysterical personality; the patient expresses his feelings in an ungenuine way, but not with conscious intent to deceive others. Ungenuineness may infiltrate the interpersonal relations of the hysterical patient; when this is carried to an extreme such patients have been described as hysterical psychopaths (Menninger, 1959).[15] In hysterical personality the ungenuineness is a fixed reaction pattern, formerly adapted in childhood to the expectations of the adult entourage but rooted in anxiety that prevents the development of soundly integrated individuation. Kuiper (1967)[14] noted that 'the danger of being genuine is menacing to all of us, and there are innumerable shades between a really genuine attitude and an ungenuine one.' Dostoevsky (1864)[16] carried this view further in his declaration in *Notes from Underground* that in an urban society 'we're all cripples to some degree.' His novel confronts the problem of authentic identity, a major theme in modern literature. A demand for the solution of this very problem is what many patients bring to their initial interviews with a psychiatrist; and the problem is inseparable from the 'malady of personal synthesis' (Janet, 1907[17]) that constitutes hysteria.

In the *Diagnostic and Statistical Manual of Mental Disorders* published by the American Psychiatric Association (D.S.M. II, 1968)[18] hysterical neurosis is briefly defined under the rubric of neuroses (300) as

characterized by an involuntary psychogenic loss or disorder of function. Symptoms characteristically begin and end suddenly in emotionally charged situations and are symbolic of the underlying conflicts. Often they can be modified by suggestion alone.

This definition is in accordance with the considerations outlined here, as is the even briefer definition offered by the neurologist Brain (1933):[19]

A neurosis characterized by mental dissociation leading in severe cases to multiple personality and amnesia, but more often to somatic symptoms such as convulsions, paralysis, and sensory disturbances.

Mental Conflict and Symptom Formation

The term 'hysteria' is sometimes loosely applied, on the basis of characteristic perceptual, motor and psychic disturbances, to various forms of mental disorder that share similar surface manifestations. The usual order of the events is that the patient undergoes a physical examination because of his somatic symptoms, but the findings are negative; or as is often the case, the extent of somatic dysfunction is much greater than can be explained by the identifiable physical lesion that is discovered. An example of the latter situation is the soldier with a small, superficial gunshot wound, but whose presenting complaint is paralysis of an entire limb. After a thorough physical examination, such a patient is often referred to a psychiatrist as a case of hysteria, or as a case of dysfunctional overlay of concomitant conversion reaction.

A psychiatric diagnosis rests on positive findings. Cases labelled 'hysteria' in the negative (eliminative) process just described sometimes turn out to be suffering from a different type of mental illness. Hypochondriasis is common in the early phases of schizophrenia, and a patient with this disease may complain to his doctor of physical symptoms, as might a patient with melancholia. Such cases imperfectly diagnosed in a largely negative manner should, from a purist point of view, be referred without a definitive psychiatric label. What is more important for practical purposes is that when mental or emotional disturbance is suspected, early psychiatric investigation should be secured, since elaborate and protracted physical examination can result in iatrogenic reinforcement of the patient's conviction that he has a 'purely' physical disease and is 'uncontaminated' by mental conflict and emotional disturbance.

A searching examination that includes many laboratory tests is often made when diagnosis is unclear, and when this is conducted by a physician scornful of psychological influences or cautiously dedicated to 'defensive medicine', it may adversely affect subsequent psychotherapy. The proliferation of iatrogenic illness is also now associated with toxic effects (side effects) of the triumphant extension of medical techniques, including the use of psychotropic drugs. Sometimes, indeed, the patient who observes other patients and notes the medications they are taking, will, when given the same medication himself, unconsciously mimic the side effects from which they suffer, especially when these are movement disorders. This topic is discussed more fully in Chapter 19.

It has been noted that Freud (1917)[7] emphasized as positive grounds for the diagnosis of hysteria the perception and understanding of mental conflict and of its connection with the symptoms. Two patients illustrate this; one was a young, single Englishwoman seen in wartime Britain (1943), and the other a young American matron seen in peacetime in Virginia. Both suffered from blindness. Hysterical amblyopia may, like other hysterical affections, take various forms such as loss of visual acuity, a loss of colour vision, or diminution in the visual field. The characteristic form of the visual field in such cases of hysteria is either a spiral contraction or an extreme concentric limitation.

Case 1. The girl, 17 years of age, was referred for a psychiatric opinion on account of complete blindness. She had been in the A.T.S. for about four months and had at first been quite happy and efficient. During the week prior to her admission to hospital she

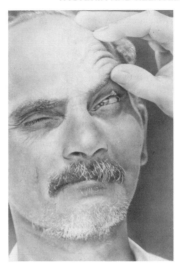

Fig. 1. Hysterical blindness with blepharospasm in an Indian male patient.

suffered from blurring of vision, and the condition had rapidly deteriorated until she lost her sight. Examination by the ophthalmic specialist revealed nothing abnormal, and general physical examination was equally unilluminative. On psychiatric examination she denied any outstanding domestic or other worries, apart from her anxiety about her eyesight. She was intelligent (S.G.2 on the progressive matrices test), and gave a good general account of herself. In civilian life she had worked in a Ministry of Food office as a shorthand typist. At home she had lived a sheltered existence and, as an only child, had come in for a good deal of attention. A spirit of adventure and a patriotic urge had caused her to enlist despite parental discouragement. She had, she said, enjoyed her work and liked the life in the A.T.S. Moreover, she did not see what this had to do with her illness, and plainly stated that she resented being sent to the doctor 'who looked after mad people'.

It was first of all necessary in this case, as regrettably it is in so many, to allay the patient's anxiety and resentment at being referred for a psychiatric examination. Unfortunate remarks made, perhaps jestingly, by those around her when it became known that she was to be seen by an 'alienist' had not had by any means a good effect. (Such unnecessary facetious comments to the candidate for psychiatric interview are not uncommon and are often made in ignorance of their unfavourable influence on the patient.) It was necessary to explain to her that those around her did not consider her mad, and that the duties of a psychiatrist are not limited to the examination of the insane. It was further pointed out that it was because emotional disturbance was capable of causing bodily disorder that her doctors had referred her for examination, having been quite unable to find any other cause. The patient was able to grasp this intellectually as a general statement of possibility, so some degree of rapport was at last achieved, and she began to speak a little more freely about herself, ending up with the statement that whether or not the doctors could find a cause, the sad fact remained that she was blind.

It was explained to her that seeing is an active process, and so is hearing. If she were not now listening to me, she would not comprehend my statements; she might not even hear me at all. It must have frequently happened to her that she did not hear conversation around her when she was not paying attention. In the same way it was necessary to look in order to be able to see (cf. Hurst, 1940[20]). At this point the patient protested that she was trying hard to see but could not do so, so that this state of affairs did not apply to her case. The reply to this was that in her case there was a kind of blocking in the active process of seeing, but that if she set about actively looking, with my help she would be able to see. For this purpose I required full cooperation from her, and she had to do exactly as I asked. Though sceptical, she stated that she was prepared to try anything if there was a chance of regaining her vision.

So it was that she was gently persuaded to relax, and quite simply, her confidence having been sufficiently gained, she was lightly hypnotized. Under the light hypnosis she was urged to tell her worries. She then gave the following story:

She had done something very wrong. Her parents had shown objection to her intention to enlist. Until she was 18 years of age she could not enlist without their permission. She had not informed them of this fact, as she had felt certain that they would not allow her to join. So she had secured the necessary papers and had not only signed her own section but had also filled in her parents' signatures in the appropriate place. This deception had worried her, even more so when, after enlistment, she was thoroughly enjoying her new life.

It was clear that here was an essential conflict; she had deceived her parents and was enjoying herself. *Her sense of duty to her parents was in conflict with her rebellious desire to enjoy herself away from their constricting influence.* The conflict had been conscious and had hardly been far from consciousness at any stage, so that its avowal was easily recovered under light hypnosis. [This question of the degree of conscious formulation that a conflict has is, of course, of the very first importance, and will later receive more attention. That this one had its roots in unconscious over-dependence upon the parents and countermanding insistence on her independence from them need not now be elucidated.] How, then, was this particular conflict related to the blindness of the patient?

Deeper hypnosis was induced, and the patient was asked about fears relating to her eyes. In response to this, a vague and poorly formulated story of an attack of loss of clear vision at the age of three years was eventually obtained. As far as could be gathered from her description of this frightening episode, she had had some trouble with her eyes (possibly conjunctivitis), found it difficult to open them and when she did so could make out only a blur. She could not see her mother, but could hear her calling her. After this occurrence she had always entertained fear of the dark.

By this time there was sufficient information to understand the symptom formation in some measure. I then suggested that when she awakened she would look and she would see. This suggestion, made on the basis of my former conversation with her, was reiterated for several minutes while she remained under hypnotic rapport. After about 15 minutes she was awakened. Her first reaction was to grasp my spectacles and to exclaim, 'You are wearing glasses!' She then kept remarking, 'It is coming and going,' referring to her visual impressions. There was a map on the wall, and she was made to look at this while her geographical location and that of her parents was pointed out—a topic of obvious affective moment in view of the conflict disclosed. Later she was seeing quite clearly and followed me without groping, constantly exclaiming that she could see, until we reached the medical ward some distance away.

The following day discussion revealed that she experienced a pressing need to make some sort of reparation to her parents (cf. Klein and Riviere, 1937[21]). After a few further discussions it was arranged that she would return home to wait until she reached the age of 18 when she would be able to re-enlist legitimately. In these interviews her duties and obligations, as well as her rights and privileges, had been duly considered by both of us.

From all this the nature of the girl's mental conflict and its connection with her symptom should be sufficiently obvious. In fact, the patient had punished herself for deceiving her parents, and she had done so in a manner which accorded with a fear based on a temporary loss experienced in early childhood. That is, of course, only the gist of the connection, but it illustrates sufficiently clearly the psychological connection of conflict and symptom; except that it is particular to be noted that the psychopathology was worked out on *an unconscious plane.* She had forgotten the temporary loss of sight in childhood, and had no awareness of its connection with her symptom, and the outstanding current conflict had been temporarily excluded in an *ad hoc* repression, while its connections were quite out of the realm of her awareness prior to the hypnotherapy. (Cf. Brenman and Gill, 1944;[22] Gill and Brenman, 1961;[23] Reiff and Scheerer, 1959;[24] West, 1963.[25]) Certainly it will be clear that from the existential viewpoint this patient had felt inwardly trapped within the confines ordered by her parents, despite her rebellious effort to break free.

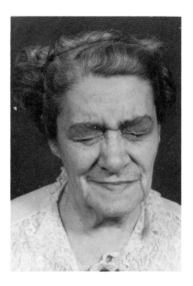

Fig. 2. A recent case of hysterical blepharospasm presenting in the ophthalmological department (patient of Dr As'ad Masri, Resident in Psychiatry on consulting service). Compare with *Fig.* 1.

Case 2. This case was first brought to my notice by the patient's father, a physician, who telephoned me from a distant large city. His daughter was in a metropolitan hospital suffering from partial blindness. He insisted that she was emotionally disturbed. At first I attempted to guide him back towards the physicians, including psychiatrists, and ophthalmic surgeons under whose care his daughter was being investigated. But it became apparent that it was from these psychiatrists that he had at last obtained my name. He was dissatisfied with their view, shared with the neurologists and ophthalmologists, that her emotional disturbance had followed the onset of blindness. On the contrary, he felt from his observations, that she was calmer now that she had been for some months. Further conversation revealed that the doctors found she had absolute central scotomata, and that the differential diagnosis to date had been retrobulbar neuritis, or multiple sclerosis; or since she had been having severe headaches recently before the onset of the partial blindness, a sequel of severe migraine.

I explained that in cases of hysterical amblyopia there was a concentric diminution of vision, and that on this account, I did not think it likely that his daughter had the type of case where sight would be recovered following hypnotherapy, about which he had asked me pointedly. He replied that that was what he had already been informed, but he would let me know more about his daughter if I would be good enough to talk with him again. In a few days he telephoned again. He stated that though there seemed to be a consensus that there was a pallor of the discs and that she was probably suffering retrobulbar neuritis, he would like me to examine his daughter. He called yet again in a couple of days to tell me that his daughter was now totally blind, and that he wanted her admitted under my care into the psychiatric ward of the University of Virginia Hospital. This was later accomplished.

During several distributive discussions with this 36-year-old mother of three, it became clear that she had indeed been very disturbed for some months, and increasingly so, before experiencing defects of central vision. Her husband, an ophthalmic surgeon, was, she thought, having an affair with the nurse who assisted him in the operating room. He came home very late at night much more frequently than hitherto, and some nights she paced around the house after the children were in bed and fretted about his tardiness. Many times she had prepared a special meal for him after his long day's work, but he did not reach home until midnight. She wept and railed, and especially reviled the nurse assistant of whom she was very jealous.

Following several such sessions there was some slight improvement in her vision. At this time, especially in view of the central scotomata and the possibility that hysteria and organic disease were both operative factors in her illness, I considered hypnotic investigation with her. The residents in psychiatry who were working with me assisted in this enterprise. We had previously obtained a neurologist's report, which also noted some pallor of the discs. Under hypnosis she was able to recall the evening before the onset of her blindness, when she had prepared another gourmet meal for her husband, looked forward to his return home, and then received the message that she was detained at work. Pacing around the house, she went into his study. On his desk was a medical textbook open at the section of retrobulbar neuritis, which she read. She thought he was worried about just such a case. All of this and other details were certainly edifying for me, and for the residents in training, and I proceeded to make suggestions that she would look and she would see. She recovered her full vision, and remained in the hospital for several weeks before discharge for outpatient psychotherapy with a psychiatrist in the city where she lived. In the meantime her husband visited her, and during his visit we three discussed the marital situation productively.

This case study will indicate that in this patient disappointment in her love life with her husband resulted in rage against him, which conflicted with her continued desire for his love. Also, in our discussions it became evident that in accordance with her 'liberated woman' ideas and ideals her pride was in conflict with her wish to castigate him and the nurse. These related painful conflicts led to her wish to ignore the whole business of her husband's sexual digression (not to see it), and this wish was symbolized in her symptoms of blindness. At the same time she wanted to punish him, to castrate him, and to puncture his 'omnipotence' for she knew that he was vexed by cases which were not curable by his surgical or other interventions. In this process she also punished herself, as was true also of the patient in the previous case of hysterical blindness. The symptoms thus *condensed* her resentful wishes with punishment fantasies.

Here is another case history with sufficient detail to illustrate the existence of a mental conflict and its connection with the symptoms. Incidentally, it illustrates too that insomnia may have a hysteroid structure.

Case 3. In 1944, at a time when I had acquired some facility in Urdu, an Indian patient complained that he could not sleep, and observation in hospital confirmed the fact that he was sleepless. He explained that for the past two months the power of sleep had been taken away from him. Questioning revealed that two months earlier his mother had died. Owing to his absence from home in the Army he had been unable to carry out the appropriate religious ceremonies. He felt he had 'insulted his mother', and that in consequence the divine power had rendered him incapable of sleep. Only by returning home and seeing the local religious doctor could he hope to regain the power of sleep. He did not know what particular treatment would be prescribed for him, but in discussing this he gave some indication of the type of treatment meted out; as, for example, immersion in medicated oil for several hours every morning on a local hillside with a sacred reputation, perhaps for 48 days. During the immersion process the healer would pronounce certain magic mantra. The patient went on to say that the healer whom he wished to consult was 100 years old and had had experience in three villages. Further, he hinted that it was possible to learn much from this gifted centenarian.

Despite this initial display of prejudice against youth in regard to choice of doctor, it was possible for me to engage the interest of this patient, and with his cooperation he was hypnotized. Under hypnosis it became apparent that his wish to return home was activated not only by a sense of guilt in regard to his religious defection, but that he also strongly desired to be with his wife. Moreover, it was elicited that this same symptom of loss of sleep had occurred to a relative when he had neglected his religious duties. Suitable suggestions were proferred following which he was able to sleep, and he awakened convinced of the efficacy of his treatment. He slept every night thereafter, as suggested. He was granted leave before having to return to his military duties.

There were various reasons for this patient's wanting to go home, and the conflict of his desire to do so with what the Army demanded of him caused him to emulate, through identification, a relative who had been unable to sleep because of having neglected his religious duties. Also, this patient's inability to sleep made him unfit for military duty, and he knew that the authorities eventually sent the unfit home. He was homesick, and additionally distressed by his mother's death. He attributed his distress entirely to the forced neglect of religious obligations. As in the first case cited, symptoms served a purpose; this patient's inability to sleep rendered him unfit for military duty as did the first patient's blindness. In each of these cases the home-seeking purpose is clear.

As Fairbairn (1943)[26] emphasized, *in war neurosis there is often nostalgia in the beginning, and in conversion hysteria this is followed by flight into illness.* Nostalgia is common enough among soldiers obliged to leave much that is important to them behind, without any inevitable appearance of physical symptoms, so that it seems clear that the conjunction of homesickness and physical symptoms is by no means pathognomonic of neurosis. A positive psychiatric diagnosis must be based on an evaluation of the economics and dynamics of the neurosis, i.e. of the specific conflictual trends in the particular individual, and the psychological connections with his particular symptoms. Without such dynamic understanding, definitive diagnosis may be inappropriate.

Fig. 3. Hysterical 'bent back', a manifestation of conversion hysteria. Case of
Dr J. Lyle and Dr J. B. Rioux. *(Reproduced by courtesy of Dr J. Lyle and Dr J.
B. Rioux. US Army Photograph.)*

In these examples of monosymptomatic hysteria, there is intrapsychic
conflict. The patient was unaware, or only partially aware, of the meaning of
the symptom and its connection with conflict. In the third case, the Indian
soldier did understand that his difficulties arose from the need to leave his
home. Since World War II, most of the cases in Indian military hospitals were
obviously due to the provoking stress of leaving home and separation from the
familiar way of life in the village where enlistment had taken place. The soldier
was in direct conflict with his strange environment. Yet, however much of the
struggle was evident on the surface, the conflict had deep roots. Bent back
(camptocomia) in soldiers may be taken as an example *(see Fig.* 3).

First described by Souques in 1915, this disorder was often encountered
among soldiers during the massive slaughter of World War I (Simons,
1964[27]). When questioned, a soldier with this complaint would state that his
back was diseased or broken. Probed further, he would say that his condition
made him unfit for the Army, that his back was broken, and he would be better
off at home. Such statements reverse in a primitive way—as sometimes occurs
in dreams—the true state of affairs: it is the longing to go home which led to the
back being 'broken' and his becoming useless as a soldier. The conflict is at the
surface inasmuch as the soldier is in direct conflict with his strange

environment and adopts a massive defence against it. This defence is worked out, however, on an unconscious plane. He does not deliberately hold his back in this abnormal posture.

To understand the significance of 'bent back' as an expression of distaste for and fear of army service it is necessary to consider the primitive type of indirect means of representation (similar to dream symbolization) that a patient may unconsciously use (cf. Jones, 1916[28]). We have all heard about people who 'lack backbone' or are 'spineless', and we understand by this metaphoric language that such people lack courage, stability and the power to stand up for themselves. It is precisely this—their powerlessness—that the hysterical 'bent-back' patients are dramatizing, though the metaphor is submerged. Sometimes in the history of such cases one finds that there had been minor injury to the back, and that this experience of trauma had provoked the onset of frank neurosis and had partially determined the choice of body language employed. More often no such history of trauma is forthcoming. The most primary type of symbolism is the equating of one part of the body with another (Ferenczi, 1913[29]), and the spine is often a phallic symbol, as close psychiatric examination of patients with 'bent back' has shown. For separated as they are from their ordinary means of satisfaction, and unable as they have found themselves to adjust to their strange new milieu with any degree of emotional satisfaction, they feel themselves to be psychologically castrated, to lack all the qualities of the combative and active males that they see all around them. In these patients unconsciously (cryptophorically) the spine is a phallic symbol, and at a metaphoric level (see Chapter 16), a symbol of power. The symptom of 'bent back' expresses very eloquently their feelings of incapacity to cope with service in the Army, and at the same time provides a means of escape from it.

It is true that here there is little ego resistance against a very regressive form of expression. But to maintain, as is sometimes done, that such patients are deliberately persisting in such a posture with the clear idea of thus evading military service is in general to ascribe strength where there is weakness and to ignore the more deeply placed psychological connections of the symptom.

This question, as to whether the conflict is mainly intrapsychic or not, is of importance as it raises the problem of malingering (Norris, 1945[30]). Where there is a regressive form of expression as in 'bent back', and when this is perpetuated, it can usually be safely assumed that the patient is not deliberately feigning illness, even though there may be some collaboration from the side of consciousness. More than this, when there has been no history of a severe traumatic experience, it is an even safer proposition that the patient is of no military value and is a burden to the Army. It is an unsatisfactory state of affairs from the military point of view, especially because firm disciplinary management often only drives the patient deeper into his neurosis.

The following account of an Indian solider serves to illustrate another aspect of the matter:

Case 4. An adult Muslim, 25 years of age, was unable to speak. He had been examined by the ear, nose and throat specialist, with negative findings. Psychiatric investigation had to be carried out by allowing the patient to write down his replies. It was elicited that two months earlier he had been performing a religious rite when he felt some strong spirit playing on him. He rolled beneath the bed under the influence of this spirit, and lost consciousness. A friend returned him to the bed. In the morning, when he awakened, he found that he had lost the power of speech. He explained further that he had previously dedicated his belongings to God, but had afterwards offered some of them to his friend; this he considered to be a sin. No improvement was secured during or after sodium pentothal intravenous injection and forceful persuasion to speak. The patient made unavailing but apparently desperate attempts to produce sound, and his repeated efforts were equally unsuccessful. He felt that he could be cured only by returning to his home, where the local *hakim* would be able to deal with his illness, though he thought that even this would take a long time. When seen again, some days later, he continued to be quite unable to say a word. Thus, while under observation in one hospital for over two months, and under treatment with sodium pentothal for one week in another, he had not uttered a single audible sound. He was told firmly that he would have to remain in hospital until he spoke freely and easily, and that he was in fact capable of speech. He gesticulated excitedly and wrote down that he was trying his best without success, and that it was useless to keep him any longer in hospital. The reply was that he was to stay in hospital until he spoke; and the advice was added that he had better pray to God to grant him the power of speech soon, as it would be a long time before reconsideration otherwise. The patient went away, protesting in the language of gesture. While others were being interviewed a note from the patient arrived in which he besought his discharge from hospital. This request was again refused, and he was once more advised to seek for the return of his speech through suitable prayers.

The following morning, after a sleepless night of prayer, the patient was able to speak freely. Conversation then revealed that he was very eager to return home to visit his four wives. Sick leave was later granted to him.

As a rule it is not possible to reduce symptoms in hysteria this way. Furthermore, the fact that firm handling is efficacious is not to be taken as evidence that the patient has been malingering. In this case, for example, the essential conflict in the soldier's mind centred around his fears of involvement in passive homosexuality but his difficulties were not formulated in these terms at all. To understand hysteria it is necessary to penetrate into the psychopathology of the disease, for even in short-contact work the accuracy of diagnosis depends on a grasp of its basic dynamics. The therapist with considerable experience and perspicacity will know when and how to apply a disciplinary technique, which is worse than useless in the majority of cases of conversion hysteria, contrary to popular expectations; when inappropriately used it can drive the patient deeper into his neurosis, from which he may later be extricated only with great difficulty, if at all.

The Importance of the *Vita Sexualis*

Freud[31] wrote in 1925:

> The theory which we had attempted to construct in the *Studien* remained, as I have said, very incomplete, and in particular we had scarcely touched upon the problem of aetiology, upon the question of the ground in which the pathogenic process takes root. I now learned from my rapidly increasing experience that it was not any kind of emotional excitation that was in action behind the phenomena of the neurosis, but regularly one of a sexual nature, whether it was a current conflict or the effect of earlier sexual experiences.

The following case history illustrates how a current sexual conflict can occasion the outbreak of neurosis and determine the form of the symptom (Freud, 1896,[8] 1898[32]):

Case 5. In 1944 the patient, a British soldier, was first examined by a dermatologist, Capt. S. C. Gold, RAMC, who later wrote the following account.
'Patient admitted to hospital in Delhi complaining of a small localized area of excessive sweating on the left wrist. This had developed some six weeks before and had been gradually getting worse. On examination he revealed no obvious skin lesion. It appeared that these attacks of hyperhidrosis were sporadic, generally lasting an hour. He was unable to say what caused them to start or stop. During an attack there was an area, about two inches by three inches, over the ulnar styloid process on his left hand which was covered with sweat. The edge of this abnormal patch was clearly defined and during the sweating attack it was hyperaemic. On wiping the sweat away, it was possible to see beads form and rapidly coalesce to drops. In thirty seconds there was a channel of sweat running from this wrist. Palms, soles, groins and axillae showed no hyperhidrosis. There was no history of injury, no evidence of local or general organic nervous disease. As he was a clerk, it seemed likely that he had developed a chemical contact sensitivity with some ink, varnish, etc. Patch tests of the common inks were negative. He was worried about his condition and feared it going to involve a greater part of his body.
'Several forms of local treatment had been tried: ten per cent formalin, formaldehyde powder, aluminium acetate, and finally galvinism. Before X-ray applications were ordered he was shown at a clinical meeting, and the psychiatrist expressed a desire to look into the case. The result of his treatment was dramatic.'
In the medical conference at Delhi, to which allusion is made in this report, discussion first centered around 'contact dermatitis'. When hysteria was first suggested it was conceded that the complaint was a depressing one, but conversation slid away to a discussion of 'rational therapeutics'—the use of aluminium acetate or X-ray, for example, and it was then that I expressed a desire to interview the patient.
He expressed surprise at being seen by a 'nerve specialist' but admitted that he was depressed, and he assumed he was to be treated for 'nervous depression'. It was not difficult to point out that he had been depressed before the appearance of his skin disorder. He thoughtfully agreed with this, but complained that his affliction had considerably worsened his depression, and that if only his skin trouble would respond to treatment he would have a chance of becoming more cheerful. So far the disorder was spreading rather than receding in spite of treatment.
A distributive discussion about his home. his devotion to his wife, his homesickness following separation from his family, and his occupation followed. In the course of this discussion he was asked whether he had had anything to do with women in India. He protested with some heat, 'Certainly not!' Thereupon he was asked why he was so definite about this. This brought to his mind a resolution he had made after disembarkation at Bombay. The medical officer had delivered a lecture about venereal disease, during which he stated that 90 per cent of the population of India was so affected. It was mentioned that this was, of course, a gross exaggeration. He replied that anyway he was determined to go home 'fit and clean'. I agreed that this was a laudable notion, and questioned him about the exact nature of his resolution. He replied that it was to have absolutely nothing to do with any woman in India, regardless of colour or race.
I said that this was a very heroic resolution, one that reminded me of the resolution of a teetotaller. He responded to this at once, saying he was not 'TT'. He felt such abstemious people were afraid that they would not know when to stop once they began indulging. He saw the point when I said that this was the reason for my comparison. I then asked him what he knew about venereal disease. His ideas on this subject seemed very restricted; he knew that it was associated with a 'discharge', and thought it might result in impotence, or be communicated to his wife.

Then I asked him about the office in which he was employed. He explained that he worked under good conditions, that there was a fan nearby, which was a very good thing, as he dreaded the heat. I asked whether were any women working in the office, and the reply was affirmative. At this juncture I told him that there was one working on his left side. This assertion surprised him and he agreed that there was. In further conversation I asked whether he had anything to do with her. At first he denied this strongly, but when I suggested that he did have a little to do with her, he agreed that in the course of work he had to point out certain things in the book in which she wrote. I then rose and walked around to his side of the table, stood on his right side, and placed my left arm over his shoulder, pointing with my right and to the area of table immediately in front of him.

I said, 'You did this with the young lady at your side when you pointed into her book.' And I showed him that as I bent over him with my left arm lightly across his left shoulder the lower part of the ulnar region of my forearm was in contact with the spine of his scapula.

By this time the patient was ready to receive an explanation of his 'contact dermatitis'.

The conflict in this case was between digressive heterosexual impulses and devotion to his wife. He unconsciously felt that contact with another woman would give rise to a discharge—and so it did by means of that 'mysterious leap from mental to bodily' characteristic of conversion hysteria (Ferenczi, 1919[33]). His symptoms made it impossible for him to be useful at his work; it was *as if* he were assuming that, were he at home with his wife and not in a tropical place far away from her, he would not be exposed to temptation. After a few further discussions he made a quick recovery, although at first his discharges increased remarkably in frequency and intensity *pari passu* with a heightening of his resistances, then becoming less in amount and occurring less frequently. As Freud (1893–5)[34] noted, during the psychotherapy of a patient with hysteria, symptoms that are capable of increasing or decreasing in intensity—or of returning after disappearing—are apt to 'join in the conversation'. He wrote:

The problematical symptom re-appears, or appears with greater intensity, as soon as we reach the region of the pathogenic organization which contains the symptom's etiology, and thenceforward it accompanies the work with characteristic oscillations which are instructive to the physician.

Finally, a week after this patient was first seen, the involved area of his skin became quite normal. Consideration of this case shows how necessary it is to know about the psychosexual life of the emotionally disturbed patients, and, more than this, to have some understanding of his thoughts and fantasies in the erotic sphere. In the casual phrase attributed to Charcot (Freud, 1914),[35] 'Mais, dans des cas pareils c'est toujours la chose génitale, toujours.'

However, Dosuzkov (1975)[36] has reported on the psychoanalysis of a patient in whom excessive sweating first appeared at the age of 27, and whose disorder of skin function related to pregenital conflicts. Dosuzkov firmly concluded that his disorder was a special form of pregenital conversion. Bernard Lerer (1977)[37] concludes in a review of essential hyperhidrosis that empirical observation has established a definite link between the condition and emotional disorder, and that controlled psychodiagnostic assessment of hyperhidrotic subjects may provide answers to questions about the scope and extent of the psychopathology involved.

Psychocutaneous Medicine

The problems of psychological medicine are exhibited, though with important differences, in all organ systems. Diseases of the integument illustrate these problems in specific ways. It is convenient at this point, following consideration of *Case* 5 above, to outline a preliminary view of the larger arena in which conversion hysteria has its particular place.

The simple sign of dermographia, indicating a lability of skin capillaries, is sometimes readily elicited in constitutionally hypersensitive types lacking in varying degrees an adequate 'stimulus barrier' (cf. Escalona, S. K., 1968).[39] Similarly, the simple symptom of anxious excessive sweating also demonstrates that the reactivity of the skin is influenced by the emotional state of the organism. Cutaneous disorder is indeed often characterized by vasomotor instability and excessive sweating and is clearly related to emotional disturbance as in *Case* 5 above. The facts are:

1. The function and state of the skin in general depends heavily upon variations in its vascular supply and in the activity of the sweat glands.

2. The vessels and sweat glands respond to nervous impulses and chemical stimuli generated by the autonomic nervous and endocrine system. Thus psychic and emotional factors must be considered in relation to the aetiology of all skin diseases (*see* Figure opposite).

Sydenham[40] described angioneurotic oedema as early as 1681, in his discussion of 'hysterical diseases'; and in 1726 Turner[41] attributed a woman's rosacea to emotional problems resulting from her husband's death. Clearly, the concept that emotional factors play a part in the aetiology of cutaneous disorders is not new; indeed, it is part and parcel of the folklore of all cultures, old and new, where it is usually embedded in magical and superstitious thinking so that facts are exaggerated and distorted. Thus the 'King's touch' was widely believed during the Middle Ages to cure leprosy. This belief hints at the fact that suggestion can so alter a patient's emotional state that his skin disorder may temporarily—or permanently—improve.

As Chapter 17 will clarify, it is necessary to take metaphoric symbolism, as well as more primitive forms of symbolism, into account in the pathogenesis of hysterical conversion symptoms. Metaphor is of basic importance in the development of thought and language, and English like other tongues, has many expressive figures of speech referring to the skin. We have 'sweating it out', 'no skin off my back', 'itching for a fight', 'fond of his own skin', 'burning with shame', 'by the skin of my teeth', 'I blush for you', and so on. There are, in fact, several fundamental bases for dermatoses of psychogenic origin, and for those in which emotional factors constitute an important element. These may be briefly summarized as follows:

1. The skin as the outermost layer of the body is a boundary between the self and the outer world. In the development of the body image, which is the psychic representation of one's body and a core part of the mental ego, the

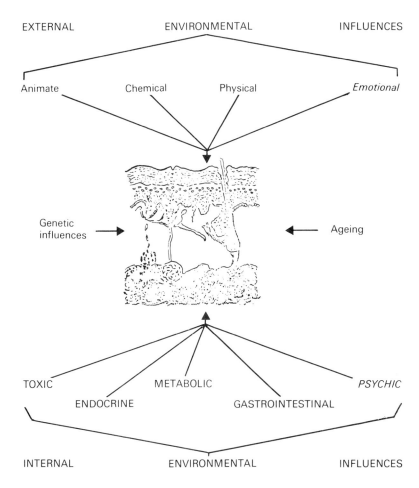

EXTERNAL   ENVIRONMENTAL   INFLUENCES

Animate   Chemical   Physical   *Emotional*

Genetic
influences   Ageing

TOXIC   METABOLIC   *PSYCHIC*

ENDOCRINE   GASTROINTESTINAL

INTERNAL   ENVIRONMENTAL   INFLUENCES

Aetiology of skin diseases. (From: Wittkower, E. and Russell, B. (1953).
Emotional Factors in Skin Diseases, p. 17. New York: Hoeber.)[38]

texture of the body's outer layer as well as its contours has considerable emotional importance (*see* Chapter 13).

Thoughts and feelings about the self may be particularly compelling during crises of individual development, as in adolesence and young adulthood. The problem of acne vulgaris requires consideration on this account. Wittkower's (1953)[38] work has shown that sexual conflict often aggravates this disorder, and von Plenck's opinion (Comrie, 1922[40]), voiced in 1783, that satisfaction of sexual needs may cure it is still widely believed. Arrsted sexual development due to inner conflict in which a fearful asceticism plays a part must first be resolved. Maximilian Obermayer (1955)[41] has written:

> Psychosomatic aspects of acne vulgaris involving factors not so directly related to sexual matters have been widely investigated. Their consideration in relation to acne during adolescence must include appreciation of the dynamic changes that constitute puberty and their forceful psychological impact. Sexual maturing and the development of sexual desire create problems of adaptation; not only are personal, physiological and psychological changes confronted, but the world of childhood is left behind. Different social patterns must be coped with—as well as responsibilities assumed—at home, at school and at play. A prominent manifestation of the psychological and physiological changes of adolscence is the accentuated concern with physical appearance; hence the exaggerated shame and embarrassment suffered because of the blemish of acne. The pimples, blackheads and oily shine of acne vulgaris constitute a real threat to adolescent poise—precarious at best. I entirely agree with Sulzberger and Zaiden's[42] statement 'that there is probably no single disease which causes more psychic trauma, more maladjustements between parents and children, more general insecurity and feelings of inferiority, and greater sums of psychic suffering than does acne vulgaris.'

2. The skin as a covering layer has a generally protective function that may become inappropriately exaggerated in response to threats emanating from fantasies within which are then projected. For example, Bartemeier (1938)[43] reported a psychoanalytical study of a patient with a chronic exudative dermatitis who had raised plaques on his hand. The analysis uncovered a severe castration anxiety from which the patient was thus inappropriately protecting himself. The symptom also served as a means of self-punishment for his own sadistic castrating wishes. The skin condition abated with reduction of anxiety and guilt in the analytic psychotherapy (a two year analysis in this case).

3. The skin is an important erogenous zone. Havelock Ellis (1936)[44] wrote:

> We are accustomed to regard the skin as mainly owing its existence to the need for the protection of the delicate vessels, nerves, viscera and muscles underneath. Undoubtedly it performs, and by its tough and elastic texture is well fitted to perform, this extremely important service. But the skin is not merely a method of protection against the external world; it is also a method of bringing us into sensitive contact with the external world. It is thus, as the organ of touch, the seat of the most widely diffused sense we possess, and, moreover, the sense which is the most ancient and fundamental of all—the mother of the other senses.

As the organ of touch the skin is one of the most important conveyors of stimuli that influence tumescence and direct sexual choice. Long before the erogeneity of the skin is associated with adult sexual enjoyment, however, the experiences of touching and of feeling differences of temperature provides erogenous pleasure that is a basic component of *infantile sexuality*. The displeasure of feeling cold, and the pleasure of feeling warm again are as old as the displeasure of being hungry, and the pleasure of being again well fed. Spitz (1951)[45] has attempted a classification of the psychogenic diseases of infancy based on the kind and amount of physical and emotional contact existing between mother and child. He has pointed out the primary importance of the mother's serving as an 'external ego' for the infant while his own ego is being formed and organized. Some disturbed mother–infant relationships are of a 'psychotoxic' kind; others, due to *insufficient* amounts of mothering, produce 'emotional deficiency' diseases of infancy. Infantile neurodermatitis was found to be associated with a manifestly anxious mother who, as investigation revealed, had an unusual amount of repressed hostility in her relation with her own infant.

There are people who grow up in a number of ways but never grow up in others; they basically and unconsciously have an oral fixation because of deprivation or over-indulgence in infancy. The excessive amount of narcissistic supplies such people demand includes not only food, warmth and body contact, but other symbolically related sources of supply, and these demands may be frustrated. Pain may be a source of erogenous cutaneous pleasure because of the experience of having often been beaten in childhood. In such personalities the stage is set for frustration to lead to some form of dermatitis.

4. According to Fenichel (1945)[9] 'The skin as the surface of the organism is the part which is externally visible; this makes it the site for the expression of conflicts around exhibitionism.' These conflicts may complicate frustrated needs for narcissistic supplies, and augment psychological inclination toward dermatitis.

5. Skin reactions may be anxiety equivalents; sympatheticotonic reactions of vessels in the skin may represent unacknowledged anxiety that the patient does not overtly experience.

As Alexander (1950)[46] noted, the similarity between hysterical conversion symptoms and vegetative responses to emotions lies in the fact that both are reactions to psychological stimuli. We will discuss later the problems of differential diagnosis, including the differentiation of conversion hysteria from psychophysiologic autonomic disorder (*see* Chapter 19). This general discussion of psychocutaneous medicine can serve meanwhile as a paradigm that points to the multifactorial basis of functional disorder in all organ systems.

The stress of experience in battle sometimes highlights cutaneous psychosomatic reactions—and the limitations of our knowledge—as the following case illustrates.

Case 6. The military dermatologist reported on this case as follows: 'Bombardier, L. D., admitted British Military Hospital, Delhi from Dehra Dun with the following history. He had suffered no previous skin disease until August 1942, when he was in N. Africa. Then during the Battle of El Alamein, he noticed the sudden appearance of 'spots on his legs and wrists'. These caused intense irritation and persisted all throughout the battle. He was not in a position to report sick and had to wait till the end of the action. When his unit was relieved and moved out of the front line his skin condition disappeared with no treatment.

He thought nothing more about it until 18 months later when he found himself in the Arakan. Now the same rash appeared, again on his legs and wrists. The irritation was worse than during the previous attack. He was later diagnosed as lichen planus (LP) and evacuated to base. Sleepless nights were frequent because of irritation.

'On examination he presented a typical picture of the hypertrophic type of LP. Flat-topped, polygonal, violaceous papules with Wickham's striae were profuse over his shins and dorsal surface of both feet. Lesions also on wrists, forearms (ventral surface) up to the flexure of the elbows. There were also a few isolated papules on the buccal mucosa of both cheeks. Over the right ankle there was a confluence of papules to form a sheet, 3″ by 2″ of lichen.

'Treatment: He was given Hydrarg: perchlor and liquor arsenicalis by mouth, daily. A simple calamine and phenol lotion applied locally, was all that seemed necessary. In view of the history he was referred to the psychiatrist.

'He made a very rapid recovery and was discharged in thirty days looking and feeling a different being. The lesions had not entirely disappeared but were very much less evident.'

In the course of the first psychiatric interview this patient became very anxious. His pupils were dilated, and there was pronounced digital tremor. It became apparent to both of us that he was frankly frightened of returning to the Arakan, where he had suffered from repeated bombing attacks during which he could do nothing but lie immobile in a slit trench. In speaking of his terrifying experiences he interrupted himself several times, repeating that he felt he should be 'with his mates'. He declared that were it not for his skin trouble causing loss of sleep he could have 'stood up to it all'.

In skin disorder following severe stress, it is my experience that leading conflicts are near the surface mentally just as they are so represented physically. Often anxiety is not overtly evident at first, as in this case, but it soon becomes apparent as the recent conflictual basis is broached. Indeed, as in this case, such patients often wear a mask of imperturbability and display considerable self-control which is in marked contrast to the considerable anxiety aroused even in the most tactfully conducted interview. Usually, it is not difficult to arrive intuitively at a 'panpsychic' Groddeckian (Groddeck, 1950[47]) interpretation of the actual type of organic lesion. In this case, for example, it seemed to me that the bombadier, necessarily passive during a long-drawn-out life-threatening bombing situation, was unconsciously attempting to don a defensive armour: that is to say a pachydermatous regression was provoked within by the pathoplastic forces of the unconscious.

The Oedipus Complex and the Role of the Actual Conflict

As Freud (1925)[31] pointed out, one looks not for just any kind of emotional excitation to account for the phenomena of neurosis, but for excitation of a sexual nature—sometimes a current sexual conflict, and sometimes the 'effect of earlier sexual experiences'. Beginning with his *Contributions to the Psychology of Love* (1912)[48] he elaborated the view that the 'earlier experiences' in question occurred during the first five years of life and were critical in the subsequent formation of the character of the individual, and his fate. During these early years the child passes through a complicated psychosexual development that is accompanied by a greatly heightened imagination, anxiety and other dysphoric affects, including grief and anger. This culminates in a now widely recognized Oedipus situation in which the boy regards his father as a rival since he loves his mother and wants to have his father's privileges. The girl also passes through this phase, but is seized by a powerful sexual attraction to her father, and looks on her mother as a rival; the rivalry is the second stage of the Oedipal plight, which has been called the 'Electra situation' in reference to the Greek myth (Freud, 1933[49]). Childhood sexuality has now reached a stage that begins to correspond to the later, genital, sexual life of the adult, and the child is on the slippery threshold of more adequate relationships of the self with others. The Oedipus situations of the boy and girl as described are complicated by subsidiary attitudes of a quite conflicting nature, as will be considered more fully later. Meanwhile, we must note the hating feelings towards the same-sexed parent as an accompaniment of loving feelings towards the parent of the opposite sex.

There is no easy solution to this problem. Sexual wishes are surrendered at this stage of the child's life in moving to a moratorium known as the latency period, during which there is a more or less affectionate aim-inhibited relationship to the parents. The operative factor involved in this momentous transition to desexualization and moderation of instinctual demands is a fear of the possible result of incest as conceived in the imagination of the child. Henceforward a taboo on incest is present (Freud, 1916,[50] 1917[51]). During adolescence, infantile wishes are reactivated on another plane (Jones, 1922[52]) as a result of a resurgence of instinctual energy resulting from hormonic changes and other bodily alterations. Subsequently, a solution is found by displacing these sexual impulses to a socially legitimate love object. These facts, constantly confirmed by analytic investigation, seem astonishing at first, partly because the early period of life is lost to the individual in a massive amnesia.

One of the most characteristic features of the psychoanalytic approach to psychopathology is the genetic viewpoint summarized already in 1895[53] in the aphorism: 'hysterics suffer from reminiscences'. As Freud's and his co-workers' experience and knowledge increased, it became evident that this genetic viewpoint illuminated the origins of neurosis not only in the recent past of the patient but also in that of his adolescence and, earlier, his childhood. With the publication in 1905 of 'Three Essays on the Theory of Sexuality' Freud[54] showed that successive psychic developmental phases of childhood unfolded spontaneously and were dependent upon an innate emergent or epigenetic programme as well as on facilitating or inhibiting environmental events. The early stages of genital sexuality within the Oedipus situation noted above sometimes lead to a partial impasse instead of an adequate transition, as is illustrated in a case of selective impotence briefly reported below. Freud (1912)[48] had pointed out that disturbances of genital potency are quite common hysterical symptoms, and this case is reported here because of its value as a collective paradigm. Certainly such a case constitutes a cliché, a run-of-the-mill experience for the clinician. None the less it starkly places emphasis on the traumatic power of unconscious fixation in the Oedipus complex.

Case 7. A married man sought treatment because of impotence with his wife, although he had no such difficulty with other women. His wife was eight years older than he, and they were devoted to one another, as shown by the fact that the marriage had lasted for four years despite his persistent symptom and his wife's longing for a child. The youngest of a large family, he had been greatly indulged by his mother in childhood, and had never adequately emancipated himself from her influence. The source of his trouble was found to be deep-seated. His wife had eventually been chosen on the model of his mother, and then after a protracted courtship. This 'anaclitic-type' choice, based on his over-dependent need for mothering, was associated with an unconscious identification of his wife with his mother, resulting in selective impotence with her (Flugel, 1921[55], Chapter X). As long as he was refuelled, as it were, in his day-to-day emotional life with his wife, he presented an aggressive attitude outside the home in his business affairs and in his occasional affairs with other women, with whom he had orgastic sensual pleasure in coitus. This patient had, it became apparent, compounded his difficulties by marrying a woman closely resembling his mother, as this had helped him to solve the severe problem of eventually redirecting his strongly mother-bound tender feelings. The conflict between his sexual urge and his sense of guilt remained unconscious, and was itself the result of an unconscious provocation. The neurosis was referable to an unsettled Oedipus situation in early life, as became increasingly clear in analytic psychotherapy. Moreover, pronounced oral dependency problems had to be worked through in the treatment before the selective impotence abated. Anxious and jealous emotions related to the possibility of his wife's becoming pregnant emerged; he was especially afraid of a baby's deflecting her attention from him—after all, he insisted he was 'her boy'. Most important, the unconscious identification of mother and wife had activated the incest taboo, and this resulted in an inhibition in sexual function in marriage (Flugel, 1921[25], Chapter X).

Comparison with *Case* 5, that of hyperhidrosis of the wrist, yields obvious differences. In that case the actual or current conflict was that between the patient's notions of devotion to his wife and his promiscuous sexual desires. This actual conflict led to the onset of his neurosis. When at home, he had been symptom-free, and he was not in any way responsible for his posting to India. The stress to which he was subject was brought about by circumstances quite outside his personal control. At the same time, it is notable that in this case he was unaware of the actual conflict, and part of the work of therapy was to make this conscious, and also to make conscious the connections between this current conflict and the symptoms.

In war neurosis in general the emphasis is on the role of the actual conflict; whereas in peacetime neurosis the emphasis is on unsettled childhood situations. This is a difference to be taken into consideration when treatment is being planned. It is, as stated, a question of emphasis, for in no case is it possible to assume a solitary cause of illness. There is always an aetiological constellation of conditions within the field of medical observation (Halliday, 1943[55]). In one case, the relevant conditions may obtain more in constitution or in developmental maladjustments, and in another in the degree of stress to which a person is subject. Psychoanalytical work has revealed that the amount and type of stress which can be tolerated without symptoms of illness will depend in large measure on individual experiences and reactions during the early years of life; it has thus brought into prominence a hitherto much neglected field of medical observation.

Case 8 is a peacetime account of spasmodic torticollis in a civilian, when the actual current conflict played a major role. Then a case of war neurosis, predominantly dependent on unresolved childhood conflicts, is cited (*Case* 9). These are exceptions to the general rule given above, and will serve to indicate that hysteria is essentially the same in war and peace.

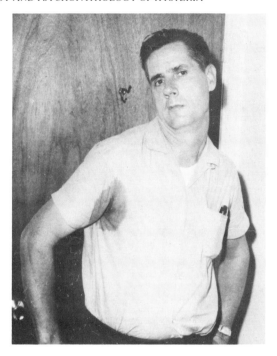

Fig. 4. A case of spasmodic torticollis, conversion reaction, in treatment at the University of Virginia Hospital (patient of Dr David Kruger, Chief Resident in Psychiatry). At first the severe postural deformity, including that of the trunk, led to thorough neurological investigation to exclude the possibility of dystonia musculorum deformans, perhaps postencephalitic or due to vascular disease. Later, in psychotherapy, the patient showed improvement. As can be seen in the illustration, the neck muscles remain in spasm, with continued milder postural deformity, an anxious painful facies, and hyperhidrosis. The patient continues to improve in prolonged psychotherapy with Dr Kruger. In this case chronic otitis media constituted somatic compliance which partially determined symptom choice and required operative intervention. A variety of spontaneous metaphoric verbal productions, including expression of the feeling of having his neck wrung like a chicken's and imagery concerned with restraining a wild horse, led to the elucidation of severe guilt concerning at first frustrated sexual wishes in his marriage and hostile feelings at first connected with his employer.

Case 8. A man aged 44 was suffering from severe spasmodic torticollis. The condition had been present for a year and had gradually worsened. During this time he had received thorough physical investigation, including radiographic and neurological examinations, with negative findings. He presented a pathetic picture. The head and neck would twist to the right about eight times a minute, the neck appeared swollen, and his facies wore an anxious, pained expression. In conversation he complained bitterly of the pain and the impossibility of his attending to his work as chief clerk in a large office. A careful history showed the following facts.

His illness had begun at a time when he was greatly worried about his son, aged 14 years. The boy had been ill with acute appendicitis and had been removed to hospital. Following appendectomy his life hung in the balance. His father frequently telephoned to the hospital to ask about his condition, and he persisted in this when the boy was already out of danger and after he had been repeatedly assured of his recovery. It was indeed at this time that the patient's neck movements commenced; he was working at his desk in the office when he found that his head moved to the right so that he could not keep his eyes on his work. It was further elicited that his marriage presented certain difficulties. At first, in the early days of his marriage, he had enjoyed passionate happiness, but after the birth of his only child his wife's attitude had changed. She had, for example, informed him that they now had something serious to occupy their attention, and that the 'nonsense' of their mode of life must now cease. She renounced sexual intercourse, and in consequence he had been sexually abstinent since.

From this it will be clear that the patient had been subject to protracted stress, and that his illness had crystallized in response to further stress. The psychopathology underlying his illness will be more fully considered on p. 48.

Case 9. A young Air Force officer came to psychiatric interview on account of persistent headache for which no physical basis was discoverable. It was thought to be due possibly to 'flying stress'. In fact, investigation showed that he had joined the service and had volunteered to go abroad out of rebelliousness against his father, whose second marriage, to the housekeeper who had been largely responsible for his upbringing after his mother's death, he vigorously condemned. He felt that he never wished to return home again, and that he would make his life in the future outside his native country. He was contemplating a marriage in India, one which would consolidate his desire to remain in the Far East, when his headache commenced. It became apparent in psychotherapy that his illness was largely due to his unresolved hostility against his father and his dependence on his mother or substitutes for her, and that these emotional difficulties in adult life were a hangover from an unsettled Oedipus situation in early life.

From these two cases it can be understood that there is no rule of thumb by which neurotic disturbance in war can be diagnostically distinguished from that occurring under peacetime conditions. In both, the role of the actual conflict is variable, and often it is itself unconsciously provoked; but in general it does assume a greater importance in wartime.

The Disturbance of Repression

There is a common analogy, proximately useful though ultimately inadequate, that compares the mind to an iceberg. In the case of an iceberg a small fraction lies above the surface, the greater portion occupying the space below the water level; this state of affairs accounts for its danger to navigation. The greater part of the psychic life is also below the level of immediate awareness, and belongs to the sphere of the Unconscious. It is easy enough, in a general way, to appreciate the reality of subliminal psychic life; the physician has no need to allow himself to become confused by hair-splitting philosophies or tortuous academic definitions. If, for example, the question were posed: 'What did you have for dinner last night?' the chances are that this would not be difficult to recall. Ideas not in the field of consciousness would become temporarily placed in this field. In some form they existed before; since they were not conscious before, we say that they were previously unconscious. There is much that freely enters the field of consciousness in this manner and, for the sake of convenience, is termed 'preconscious'. There is much more that has no such free access to the field of consciousness, and this belongs to the unconscious proper (Freud, 1912[57]).

In hysterical amnesia it may happen that a person is not able to recall the events of the day before. In other words, what is normally freely accessible to consciousness (preconscious) has become blocked. We can describe this state of affairs by stating that what was previously preconscious has become relegated to the unconscious proper. We would then be describing the process of *repression* (Freud, 1915[58]).

Hysteria is essentially the result of a disturbance in the process of repression.

Case 10. In 1943 a soldier was brought in for psychiatric interview after having been picked up by the military police in a seaside resort. Although he was unable to give an account of himself, or even to recall his name, investigation revealed that he had been very homesick for a long time, and that in a state of confusion he had left his unit and caught the train for home. The place where he had been picked up by the military police was not on the route to his home. It appeared that he had changed trains at a junction and made for this seaside resort, which had many pleasant associations: he had spent his honeymoon there and he and his wife had returned there for their annual holidays.

Where was the disturbance in the process of repression? It was in fact distributed over several nodal points in the whole episode of fugue followed by amnesia. The soldier's periodic desire to go home was in conflict with his sense of duty. In the course of time it became very urgent; the accumulated energy with which it was invested was due to frustration of unconscious instinctual pressures. Its urgency brought about anxiety; what would happen to this man if in fact he succumbed to it, and what about his self-respect in that case? The desire therefore had to be excluded from consciousness—that is, repressed. However, it had been too powerful and too highly charged, so it became necessary for him to act it out. The behaviour he then exhibited was out of touch with his current reality and gave evidence of his being in a state of altered consciousness. He did not, in fact, go home, but tried in fantasy to recapture his happy days of peace and security. The disturbance of consciousness characteristic of fugue was essential if he were to have no realization of his duties and the danger from authority he was running. He had no memory of the fugue state later; the whole episode was repressed (cf. Janet, 1907, Chapter III[59]).

First, the desire to go home acquired a forbidden character because of the anxiety provoked by its urgency. It was then repressed. Secondly, there was a partial breakdown in the process of repression when the wish found some conscious expression, albeit with a clouding of consciousness. Lastly, massive repression followed. *The fugue state was initiated by a partial breakdown in the process of repression, when a forbidden wish found access to consciousness.* Hypnoid alterations of consciousness, including fugues and somnambulisms, will be discussed in Chapter 10. These often occur in hysteriform borderline personalities who also readily suffer dissociative reactions under stress—that is, failure of repression readily leads to gross splitting mechanisms as a secondary, more primitive, defence. Obversely, one might say that such psychic splitting saves the cost of continued efforts to repress, especially when they demand renewed energy because of external stimuli that are provocative (e.g. sexually tempting and forbidden situations, or the suffering of narcissistic injuries that evoke rage).

We may recall that in *Case* 8, because of the neurotic attitude of his wife after the birth of a son, the patient felt he had to accept sexual abstinence. His submission to this situation was largely due to activation of his unresolved Oedipus complex. His wife had in fact become a mother, and his unconscious complex resonated to her reinforcement of sexual taboo. Thus his desire for sexual intercourse with her was suppressed and then repressed. This was difficult to sustain, and he had to support this repression by another defence mechanism.

For many years he had had trouble getting to sleep. As he lay beside his wife he would unprofitably review office problems. He prided himself on keeping his mind on his responsibilities at work, but it became apparent that taking this preoccupation to bed was a heroic effort to keep out of his consciousness any ideational representation of his sexual impulse. From this defence in rumination we can gather that his repression was held only tenuously in operation over the fourteen years before he exhibited the spasmodic torticollis. This symptom was due to a partial breakdown in his repressive resistances brought about by the illness of his son. Analysis revealed that he had unconsciously resented the appearance of this unwelcome intruder, who had so upset the affectionate relationship he had formerly enjoyed with his wife. Indeed, unconsciously he wanted his own son out of the way, and this desire was also excluded from his consciousness; its exclusion was assisted by yet another defensive mechanism known as 'reaction formation' (Anna Freud, 1936[60]). He had always been over-anxious about the health and welfare of his son, but the severe illness of his son resulted in a partial breakdown in the process of repression. The *unconscious* sadistic wish came near to realization in reality, and his anxiety about the boy became so heightened that he made a nuisance of himself, questioning the surgeon even when the boy was out of any real danger. His mind was not filled with sexual and sadistic thoughts, because these were objectionable on logical, aesthetic and ethical grounds, and on this account in conflict with both the demands of conscience and his sense of reality, as well as with his love for his son. The repressive resistances were by no means overthrown. Instead, he suffered the outbreak of his symptom (cf. Garnett and Elberlik, 1953[61]).*

Closer investigation revealed that this symptom was a disguised expression of his unconscious wish, and that the repressive resistance had been

---

*Spasmodic torticollis may sometimes result from organic disease of the nervous system, especially when the corpus striatum is implicated; in these instances it is sometimes part of torsion spasm (dystonia musculorum deformans). In the series (9 cases) treated by Garnett and Elbirlik there was no evidence of organic disease; 2 cases were of a hysterical nature and were relieved of the symptom in brief psychotherapy; other cases, in which the symptom represented more of a compulsive act in a schizoid personality, were considerably improved in brief psychotherapy.

sufficiently overcome to permit this disguised expression. The movements of his neck were of a auto-erotic nature; that is to say, he had pleasurable sensations on account of them. The neck had come to represent the erected genital organ, was a symbol for it; vasomotor disturbances resulted in swelling, and the rhythmic movements aped those in coitus. This kind of displacement 'from below upwards' is not uncommon (Jones, 1916[28]). But the symptom represented more than this. It was also an expression of the other side of the psychological field, of his conscience and sense of guilt; for in fact he also suffered periodically from considerable pain. In short, he was punishing himself, unconsciously for the disguised expression of his forbidden wish, and the fury of this punishment had the quality of his own deep-seated hostility against his son. *He was turning his aggression against himself* (Anna Freud, 1936[60]).

The symptom indeed was a compromise formation between the two sides of his unconscious conflict. It was more than this, for it had an attention-attracting function; it was an expression of his wish for sympathy in his appalling psychological situation, a wish at first directed toward his wife. Here we see what a complex state of affairs is covered by a flight into illness, and what complexities are uncovered by analysis. The symptoms of hysteria must be treated with respect, for they represent a deep disturbance in the psychic life of the sufferer (*see* Fig. 4).

Points of Fixation and Regression

Freud's grasp of the psychology of the neuroses deepened when with Breuer he recognized that 'hysterics suffer from reminiscences' (Breuer and Freud, 1895[53]). He first concluded that his hysterical patients had been exposed to traumatic sexual seduction in childhood, and he tried to identify the intrinsic characteristics that could make such traumatic experiences pathogenetic. He conjectured that in hysteria the primary early sexual overstimulation had been experienced passively, and that it had been accompanied by fright and revulsion, whereas in obsessional neurosis, sexual acts had been initiated by the patients themselves with pleasure during their childhood. He saw the recurrent pathological ideas that later plagued such obsessional patients as transformed self-reproaches that had re-emerged from repression, and that were related to this early forbidden and pleasurable sexual activity. According to these conjectures (relative to the polarities of passivity–activity) he cited the greater incidence of hysteria in women, and of obsessional neurosis in men (Freud, 1896[8], 1898[32]). These tentative formulations, including sexual aggression as the core aetiology of obsessional neurosis, were made at the time when Freud took his patients' 'recollections' literally, before he discovered that childhood fantasies, reawakened in the process of investigative psychotherapy, infiltrated memories and remodelled them, often exaggerating and distorting actual events. Then he grasped the importance of unfolding infantile and childhood sexuality as a spontaneous instinctual basis for these misrepresentations.

In 1896 Freud[8] had put forward the view that many of his patients who suffered hysterical symptoms had been violently abused sexually—mostly women patients seduced by their fathers. His later doubts and partial repudiation of this aetiology led to his momentous discoveries of the power of wish-fantasy, for the most part unconscious, and of the Oedipus complex. There are great difficulties in getting to know retrospectively the actual transactions in the early life of the child. In my experience of analytic psychotherapy with severely sick patients, a substantial proportion of hysterical and hysteriform disorders, especially frequently in women, continue to reveal an aetiological constellation which includes actual sexual seduction in childhood. There is, of course, as Freud repeatedly stated, a complementary series of causative factors which ultimately issues in symptom-formation. In cases of severe hysteroid dysphoria, that is to say, hysteriform conditions with depressive disorder, the nature of the actual traumatic events of early childhood is often very difficult to elucidate. We certainly should beware of ascribing all to fantasy formation without any basis in actuality. Of course, the fantasies regularly allude to actual experiences of fulfilment and frustration, and of conflict and of trauma.

J. M. Masson[62] attempts to show that Freud suppressed the seduction theory, and gave up his traumatic theory in this regard as erroneous, in order to participate again in a medical society that had earlier ostracized him. In point of fact, Freud's doubts that actual incest had occurred in the childhood of his women patients led him to his central theory, even more unconventional and shocking to his total social milieu, namely, that small children have active sexual imaginations, the phases of which are keys to the personality development of all human beings. Masson[62] does expertly outline Freud's doubts and oscillations concerning this important matter (for which he has eagle eyes) as Freud continued to investigate the neuroses by his evolving method. However, he comes close to a preposterous inference which impugns Freud's veracity.

Jung (1954)[63] called attention to the striking analogy that exists between the development of a human child and a butterfly, infancy being comparable to the nutritive caterpillar stage, the latency period resembling the chrysalis, and puberty the imaginal butterfly. Human sexuality has a complex development, one only possible to discern by means of psychological techniques. As it announces itself in the adult years of an individual it is very different from what it was in its early beginnings. Just as the first naturalist who observed the genesis of a butterfly must have found surprising a phenomenon that we now take for granted, people were surprised to learn what Freud (1917)[64] revealed about the phased development of the sexual instinct in human beings after he devised a special means of observing it.

The human individual first attains satisfaction in his own body, as an infant, in what is known as the auto-erotic phase. Stimulation of almost any part of the body surface but especially certain erotogenic zones provides a pleasurable feeling. First, the mouth area is given sensuous pleasure when stimulated, and this is normally a source of gratifying experience to some degree throughout life; in the early oral phase the sensuous pleasure is related to breast-feeding. Then the anal zone assumes greater importance, and this is related to the sphincter control which the child develops and is induced to attain. Later, in the phallic phase, the pleasure-giving possibilities become largely located in the genital region. It is not only in regard to zone, but also in regard to the object toward which the sexual urge (libido) is directed that development takes place. In the auto-erotic phase this urge attains satisfaction exclusively in the body of the individual himself. With increasing consciousness there follows a narcissistic phase of self-love. This is succeeded by a homosexual phase, when the object of the sexual instinct becomes another individual of the same sex. The heterosexual phase, when the object becomes an individual of the opposite sex, follows later. Each phase subsists in some measure, but loses some of the psychic energy with which it is invested as progress occurs. The subsistence of each phase is recognizable analytically at a later date in the outlets obtained in sublimations and character formations, apart from more direct gratification (Abraham, 1921,[65] 1924,[66] 1925[67]). Development with regard to zone proceeds *pari passu* with change of object. The ultimate result is usually a predominance of genital and heterosexual components in the sexual instinct. Development may, however, become arrested (fixated) at any phase, due to constitutional and external factors; in this case, one of the erotogenic zones may continue to afford sexual pleasure to as great an extent as, or greater than, the genital zone. The development with regard to object may be similarly fixated; perhaps, for example, predominantly at the homosexual phase.

The climax of childhood sexuality, the Oedipus situation has already been briefly considered. It is in the phase of early genital predominance that this situation, as we have described it, takes form. *This climax is that phase of organization of the instinctual life of the child to which hysteria is definitively related* (Freud, 1917[68]).*

The phases that antedate this, the pregenital phases, have been adumbrated above. Fixation at any phase may result in later years in a regression to this phase under psychological stress. The form of psychic illness depends in large measure on the phase to which regression takes place. Another important factor in the form of illness is the predominant type of defensive technique (Anna Freud, 1936[60]). In hysteria we have seen that there is disturbance in the process of repression.

To sum up: in the subjects of hysteria, the fixation is on a childhood love object at the phase which most nearly corresponds to the genital sexual life of the adult, and the most important defensive technique is that of repression. In the illness itself, regression to the characteristic point of childhood fixation in the instinctual life occurs and the defensive formations are disturbed.

These bares bones of psychic growth can be fleshed out in some measure here with reference to one developmental line which has received attention from psychoanalysts ever since Freud's early analytic work with hysteria when he was confronted with the intense love cravings and dependency strivings of his patients. This is the sequence that leads from the human newborn's utter dependence on maternal care to the young adult's emotional and material self-reliance. The successive stages of libido development (oral, anal, phallic) constitute the innate maturational base for the shift from overdependency to adequate self-reliance; and to mature adult relationships. These include

---

*Multiple fixation points, pregenital as well as phallic, are of importance in hysteriform conditions. Oral dependency problems are anyway often prominent, and set the stage for later intensified Oedipal problems and liability to hysterical disorder (*see* p. 217, Chapter 10).

interdependency, and, in marriage, a mutuality of nurturance and responsibility. Anna Freud (1965) has listed steps along this way that are now well documented from the analyses of adults and children as well as from direct observation of infants and children. These steps may be summarized as follows:

1. The biological unity of the mother-infant couple, beginning with the nursing couple, a 'narcissistic milieu' (Hoffer, 1952[70]) that has been subdivided by Margaret Mahler (1952,[71] 1969[72]) into the autistic, symbiotic, and separation-individuation phases, with significant danger points for developmental disturbances lodged in each phase.

As Abse and Ewing (1960)[73] pointed out, the symbiotic phase when prolonged beyond its time becomes a *dyssymbiosis* inasmuch as psychological growth is impeded though psychological survival may be facilitated. When there is only a very fragile ego foundation (Speers and Lansing, 1965[74]), the budding ego is threatened by the alternative danger of engulfment while escaping the dangers of annihilation involved in separation. A later propensity to hysteria is present in cases in which the dyssymbiosis is mild, whereas when it is more severe the likelihood of subsequent schizophrenia is increased; and grounds for later obsessional, phobic, and borderline conditions will be found along the middle of the spectrum. Severe dyssymbiosis results in the need-fear dilemma of the adult schizophrenic, with primitive splitting and object redefinition, as described by Donald L. Burnham, Arthur I. Gladstone, and Robert W. Gibson (1969).[75]

The vital importance of the quality of mothering has been emphasized in recent decades, notably by Winnicott (1958[76] and 1965[77]). The infant is usually sufficiently well equipped to thrive in an average 'good enough' maternal 'holding' environment such as the average mother will supply.

2. The healthy infant is endowed with a rooting reflex, or breast-seeking sequence of orientating movements, and a sucking reflex which attaches him to the mother's breast or preferred bottle. Soon a need-fulfilling anaclitic relationship to a 'part-object' (Melanie Klein 1948)[78] develops as step two. This relationship is based on the urgency of need and is intermittent and fluctuating, interest being withdrawn when satisfaction is achieved.

3. Next the stage of object constancy is reached. This signifies the development of the ability to maintain a psychic inner image of the object whether satisfied or not.

4. The ambivalent relationship of the pre-Oedipal, anal-sadistic stage next develops, and this is characterized by ego attitudes of clinging, torturing, dominating and controlling the love objects.

5. The object-centered phallic Oedipal phase is the next step in the forward thrust of libido development. This is characterized by possessiveness of one parent and jealousy and rivalry with other, as discussed above. In this phase, protectiveness, curiosity, bids for admiration and exhibitionistic attitudes are common; in girls a phallic-Oedipal (masculine) relationship to the mother precedes the Oedipal relationship to the father. This complication of female development will be outlined in greater detail as it relates especially to the liability of young women to hysterical disorder (*see below*).

6. The post-Oedipal lessening of drive urgency results in the latency period with much displacement of libido to coevals, teachers and sublimated

interests. Fantasies give evidence of dillusionment with the parents (family romance type fantasies are common).

7. There is a pre-adolescent prelude to the well-known adolescent revolt phase. This prelude comprises a partial return to a dependent need-fulfilling part-object and to severe ambivalence (steps 2 and 4 above).

8. Next arrives the adolescent struggle for independence—loosening the ties with the parents, defending against pregenitality, and finally establishing genital supremacy with libidinal cathexis transferred to objects of the opposite sex outside the family.

To find a flexible optimal distance from others, to be at once individual and in relation, is to achieve what Margaret Mahler (1975)[79] has called 'psychological birth'. As Winnicott (1965)[77] stated, ambiguously, 'there is no such thing as a baby.' Of course we see a separated physical entity before the baby knows itself to be one. The process of separation and individuation, according to Mahler (1975),[79] is especially active in the first two-and-a-half years of life. The infant gradually acquires a sense of identity mainly through his early relationship with his mother. During the long period of symbiosis noted above, he sees her as a part of himself, the mothering part of the symbiotic dyad. At last he comes to a terrifying awareness of her separateness, and, in the 'rapprochement crisis', experiences intense ambivalence. He longs to return to the comfort of symbiosis, but knows that this would mean denial of the tenuously emerging sense of self. He wishes to be independent, but has an endopsychic perception of vulnerability. Unresolved conflicts originating in this period characterize both the schizoid individual and the hysteric personality; these conflicts are less intense in the latter, and the defensive formations differ (*see* Chapter 7).

According to Freud (1920[80]), there are two broad groups of instincts: (1) the life instincts (Eros), directed toward the building up of living matter; and (2) the destructive instincts (Thanatos), directed toward the breaking down of living matter to a previous inorganic state. Most instinctive manifestations contain a fusion of the two; thus there are sadistic and masochistic elements in sexual relationships. Aggression is normally at the service of the ego, fused with the life instincts that direct it to the aims and objects of self or of sex in the external world. Instinctual defusion occurs in disease: that is, the deeper the regression, the more split off from the life instincts aggression becomes. Its fate is then variable; it might turn back from the external world on to the ego itself, producing self-punishment. In many of the clinical cases of hysteria described here we infer this happening; frustration results in regression and in rage turned against the self.

The Castration Complex

It has been noted that the hysteric has had particular difficulties at that period of psychosexual development subsumed under the term 'Oedipus situation'—when the child arrives at the transition to the genital-heterosexual phase of the libidinal organization. Such difficulties are extensions of earlier ones and are related, for example, to the difficulty of being weaned from the mother's breast. Examples may make clearer the special difficulties experienced by the hysteric in displacing object libido from the parents to others. We will later direct closer attention to this background, its derivative over-dependent attitudes as reflected in attempts at external adjustment, and its usual accompaniment of psychological 'growing pains' made evident in neurotic traits (Flugel, 1921[55]). It has been further noted that conflict in the real world, such as compels the attention of the individual in wartime, may activate these deep-seated dependency problems.

It is now necessary to consider the peculiar difficulties encountered by the individual in the Oedipus situation. It is to be remembered that we all have to face the problems involved in the process of growing up; there is only a difference in degree between the 'normal' and the 'pathological' in the relative resolution of the Oedipus complex. To restate the essential feature of this phase of the male individual's psychic growth—genital primacy is beginning to be established and the boy longs for exclusive possession of his mother and regards his father as an unwelcome rival. Hostile feelings against the father are aroused by the frustration inherent in this situation. The child, of course, is not powerful or competent enough to take the place of the father in relation to his mother, and yet he longs to do so. Were he to strike a blow to usurp his father's position, as well he might in fantasy, he would lay himself open to severe punishment by a physically superior and enraged father. In his fantasy the child projects his own jealousy and hostile impulses onto his father, seeing him as a 'bad object', however gentle and kind a man he may be in reality. Anxiety results, and fear of retribution from the imagined ogre. In this phase of his development the child envisions himself becoming the victim of talion punishment. He has projected his own fierce impulses on to his father, creating an evil, castigating father-figure, who will in turn deprive him of his means of satisfaction (Freud, 1933[81]), i.e. castrate him.

The formulation of his wishes and their concomitant fear is beyond the comprehension of the child himself, but the wishes (for sexual possession of the mother and the lasting absence of the father) and the fear (of castration) are concrete facts of experience for the child at this stage of his life. This is repeatedly confirmed in individual cases by anamnestic analysis, and more directly by the play technique of child analysis (Melanie Klein, 1932[82]). The castration fear leads to repression of the child's wishes (Freud, 1926[83]), and it is this exclusion from consciousness, carrying with it as it does associated happenings, that draws a veil over the psychic events of early life, and initiates the period of latency.

In the case of the girl, who also passes through a phallic-Oedipal stage, there ensues a complicated series of events, the chronological relationships of which show considerable individual variability. The attainment of the feminine position requires an additional change of libidinal object, from the mother to the father; and another erotogenic zone, the vagina. Moreover, as Freud (1933)[49] elucidated, there is a difference between the sexes in the relation of the Oedipus situation to castration anxiety. The boy's Oedipal strivings develop directly out of the phase of phallic sexuality. The threat of castration results in a more decisive repression of these strivings than happens with a girl, and a severe superego is inwardly established as the heir to the rivalrous relationship with the father. In contrast, with the girl the castration complex, including penis envy, paves the way from the first stage of phallic-Oedipal attachment to her mother to an intensified positive relationship with the father, that is, to the second stage of the Oedipus situation, in which she is apt to remain indefinitely. This move from the first to the second stage of the Oedipus situation requires the abandonment of the notion that all human beings possess a penis; the acceptance of its absence in females, including herself; and acceptance of substitutes for it, including a baby. The phase dominance of the phallic (clitoridal) stage involves a heightened cathexis of the organ, soon, however, to encounter a chagrined estimation of its 'inferiority' compared to that of a boy. This early narcissistic injury contributes to the abandonment of the intense positive attachment to the mother, who is indeed blamed for not equipping her adequately. On the other hand, as Freud (1931)[84] stated, the rivalry with the father for the affection of the mother during the early phallic-Oedipal attachment never reached the intensity that characterizes the boy's Oedipal plight, so the minor 'inverted' positive attachment to the father in the first stage is readily heightened to become the intense positive attachment to him in the second stage.* There are in sum several interrelated significant changes in the move from the first to the second stage of the Oedipus situation in the typological ideal of normal feminine development, namely, changes of object (mother to father); beginnings of integration of sensations of the clitoridal area with those of the vagina; change from active masculine sexual position to passive receptive aims; reduction of penis envy; the achievement of suitable feminine identifications; and diminution of anxieties concerning penetration in sexual intercourse through decreased vehemence of sado-masochistic fantasies of coitus. Nagera (1975[85]) describes the girl's sexual life as one deprived of a definitive executive organ beyond the time of puberty, until the time when vaginal sensations become integrated with those of the clitoridal area.

The complications which beset the development of a woman, in childhood and following puberty, are responsible for her greater liability to hysteria, which not infrequently remains on the plane of specifically sexual disability (Abraham, 1920[86]).

Attention has been drawn to the castration complex here because of its universality among humans, and especially because of its importance in the study of hysteria, a disease encountered around the world in many different guises, some of which are culture-specific. The castration complex is the outcome of earlier anxieties about separation and the loss of love, just as the phase of early genital primacy is the outcome of earlier organized drives. The cases of hysteria cited can be reviewed with reference to this complex.

The events described as an inevitable part of childhood development have a nightmarish quality. They may activate memories of the more gruesome fairy tales. This is not surprising since the nightmare is the disguised expression of the wishes and intense anxieties of the childhood period through which we all must pass. John E. Mack (1974)[87] notes that:

Returning to Ernest Jones' monumental survey of the nightmare from the perspective gained by the lapse of nearly sixty years, one is struck now, not so much by the varied

---

*Nagera's terminology in his book, *Female Sexuality and the Oedipus Complex* (1975)[85], as, for example, represented in his figures 1 and 2, seems to me questionable. 'Negative' should refer, I think, to the hate aspects of the triadic relationships represented in each box; then there would be a *minor* inverted (so-called 'negative' in Nagera's account) as well as a *major inverted* (so-called 'inverted' in his account).

nature of the demons that cause oppression in these dreams or by the symbols of sexuality that can be found in them, as by the objective reality people of earlier centuries attributed to these visions.

Jones (1910)[88] had pointed out that society and the church gave support from the earliest period of Christianity to the belief that the devils, werewolves, and witches that troubled people in their sleep were actually present at the bedside. He also pointed out that fairy tales are based on infantile fantasies of magic and omnipotence, and the child's wish to overcome the anxieties experienced within the life of the family. It is fortunate that the anxieties that are represented in hysteria are often easier to approach than those of other mental disorders in which regression goes deeper.

It will now be clear that Case 7 above exemplifies an open expression of castration anxiety with inhibition of function. An unconscious identification of wife and mother revived the incest taboo, and his impotence kept the patient from committing the 'sin' that would expose him to imagined paternal threat; it was also punitive in punishing the patient for having contracted what he unconsciously felt to be an improper marriage. Since the same situation did not prevail with other women, he was potent with them.

The marriage relations of the patient in Case 5 had no such psychic illegitimacy, but the prospect of extramarital relations had the threat of taboo since the patient's fear of veneral disease was old castration anxiety updated (Freud, 1933[81]). It is notable in this case that it was another part of the body that was affected; largely on account of external happenings, the wrist became eroticized and thus a symbol for the phallus (Freud, 1917[50]). After this genitilization it became the site of a discharge. *It frequently happens that castration fear, as well as the defensive measures against it, is transferred to other organs, while genital potency may be undiminished.* For example, one patient defended against severe castration anxiety by a studied preoccupation with developing arm and chest muscles through excessive weight-lifting exercises, although he had no difficulty with genital potency.

The treatment given to the patient in Case 4, who was unable to speak, was a 'covering' variety. His more deep-seated complexes were not uncovered by any form of psychological analysis. However, can we explain his illness along similar lines? As a matter of fact, from knowledge of similar cases, and the record of events, it is easy to make certain assumptions. That he had never been securely poised heterosexually is indicated by his need for several women in order to insist upon his masculinity (as in the erotomanic defence against latent homosexuality, seen more clearly in the Don Juan character type).*
After his separation from his womenfolk his sexual life was assuming a homosexual direction. He felt that offering presents to his friend was a sin, and this, it will be recalled, immediately antedated his illness. Losing his speech prevented him from uttering words that might have led to sexual approach. A sublimated function was becoming sexualized, and this preceded its loss. Passive homosexual aims are felt to lead to castration unconciously and this

---

*In the case discussed here, this vulnerability of heterosexual adaptation is a subcultural 'modal personality' phenomenon.

was his fear (Abraham, 1911[106]). The symptom was enabling him to escape from the intolerable homosexual atmosphere.

Lastly, let us reconsider *Case* 1, in which hypnosis resulted in 'uncovering' sufficient information to enable us to make a positive psychiatric diagnosis, and treatment by suggestion under hypnosis was adequate to the task of restoring the patient's vision. Analysis would have been far more revealing. Here again on the basis of our knowledge of the psychology of women, we can make out certain common difficulties. The patient's rebelliousness was an expression of her protest against the passive-feminine role in her life, of her desire to be a tomboy. Penis envy, and the defence measures to compensate for and overcome it, occupy an important place in the unconscious psychic life of women (Freud, 1933[49]). It might be mentioned too that eyes not only serve to guide our footsteps, but are also at the service of the sexual 'lust of the eye' (Freud, 1933[49]).

The nuclear position of the Oedipus situation and its inevitable conflicts should be evident from this short survey, necessarily an oversimplification, especially in respect to 'ambivalence'—the simultaneous occurrence of love and hate in unstable object relationships. Ambivalence is, however, more marked in states of deeper regression than occur in hysteria, in disorders in which instinctual defusion is more pervasive (Freud, 1923,[89] Chapter IV).

It may be mentioned here that the ancient Greek notion of a 'wandering uterus' issuing in bodily or emotional disorders (thus expressing a disturbance of female sexuality) and their naming the disease on this basis as discussed in Chapter 1, was peculiarly one sided. It is evident from the case of torticollis (*Case* 8) and that of hyperhidrosis (*Case* 5), and will be evident from other vignettes in this volume, that the sexual–symbolic aspect of hysterical conversion symptoms, the 'genitalization', is not confined to the female sex organs. The disease might just as well have been named in terms of a peregrinating penis as a wandering womb.

We will later take more fully into account the influence of multiple fixation points, especially in connection with *hysteriform* conditions and certain concepts of hysteria itself (Lampl-deGroot, 1963[90]; Arlow, 1963[91]). We will also discuss the more recent attempts to differentiate hysterical character neurosis from borderline and narcissistic personality disorders, especially as they refer to primitive internalized object relations, and ego weakness that results in the use of splitting and other primitive defences (Volkan, 1976[92]; Giovacchini, 1975[93]; Kernberg, 1975[94]). (*See* Chapter 7.)

Convulsive Hysteria and the Significance of the Epileptiform Seizure

In his *Traité de l'Hystérie* Paul Briquet (1859)[95] included statistics that indicated that nearly three-quarters of his hysterical patients had convulsive attacks. In Paris in the last decades of the nineteenth century Charcot's patients also had convulsions so commonly that he divided hysteria into two types, the convulsive and the non-convulsive (1873).[96] *Table I* shows that among Indian soldiers in 1944 convulsive attacks were usually accompaniments of hysteria, although *Table II* indicates the comparative absence of hysterical fits among the British military. Later statistics from the Policlinique Psychiatrique Universitaire, Lausanne (Schneider et al.,

Table I. An Analysis of Psychiatric Cases seen at the Indian Military Hospital, Dehli, in 1944

Number of Psychiatric Cases during the Year:—

Remained from 1943		82
New cases in 1944		562
	Total	644

Number of Cases in Different Clinical Groups:—
1. *Psychoneuroses*
   Hysteria   370
   Anxiety states   80
   Other neuroses   5
2. *Psychoses*
   Mania   37
   Depression   21
   Schizophrenia   56
   Toxic-infective psychosis   3
3. *Mental deficiency*   31
4. *Psychopathic personality*   41

Relative Frequency of the Occurrence of Predominating Symptoms in the Cases of Hysteria:—

	No. of Cases		No. of Cases
Fits	188	Vomiting	6
Pains in the abdomen	83	Contracture	5
Amnesia	25	Sciatica	5
Aphonia	12	Headache	3
Deafness	11	Speech defect	3
Paralysis	10	Enuresis	3
Blindness	7	Anaesthesia	2
Tremors	7		

1964[97]), show only a small number of hysterical patients suffering *hystero-épilepsie*.

Convulsive hysteria may closely simulate idiopathic or symptomatic epilepsy, and is always involved, though not necessarily on an either–or basis, in the differential diagnosis of partial seizures with complex symptomatology (impairment of consciousness, dysmnesic and ideational disturbances, affective storms and automatisms). Difficulties in the differential diagnosis and in the degree to which hysteria contributes an overlay or a parallel aspect of basically patho-physiologic aetiology had already been recognized and discussed by Charcot (1877[98]). These problems have been confronted more recently with the use of electroencephalography by F. Rabe (1970)[99] and F. E. Dreifuss (1975).[100] For practical purposes hysteria may be suspected at once if: the patient is not completely unconscious during the attack; the attack occurs only in the presence of onlookers; the patient does not fall in a dangerous situation; the corneal, pupillary and deep reflexes are present; the patient does not bite his tongue or urinate; he becomes red in the face rather

Table II. An Analysis of 669 Psychiatric Cases Examined at the Military Hospital, Chester, during the period June–October 1943

Number of Cases in Different Clinical Groups:—

1. *Psychoneuroses*	
Hysteria	161
Anxiety states	331
Obsessional neurosis	7
2. *Psychoses*	
Mania	2
Depression	26
Schizophrenia	15
Toxic-infective psychosis	1
Paranoid state	8
3. *Mental deficiency*	46
4. *Psychopathic personality*	42
5. *Miscellaneous, including epilepsy,*	8
migraine, and post-traumatic	
personality change	
6. *No gross psychiatric disorder*	22

Predominating Symptoms in the Cases of Hysteria:—

	No. of Cases		*No. of Cases*
Headaches	44	Spasmodic movements	4
Pains and paraesthesiae		Insomnia	4
(stomach, feet, 'rheumatic',		Vomiting	3
chest, and back)	43	Tremors	3
Enuresis (nocturnal)	17	Deafness	2
Paresis (mainly difficulty		Blindness (and blurring	
in walking)	11	of vision)	2
Amnesia	10	Speech defect	2
Fits	7	Weakness and fatigue	2
'Black-outs'	6	Sleep-walking	1

than blue or white; he resists attempts to open his eyes; pressure on the supraorbital notch causes withdrawal of the head. However, hysteria is manifest in many forms, some of which very closely imitate organic disease of the nervous and other systems, so symptoms can be misleading without the distinctive marks of the aetiology and psychopathology of hysteria itself.

Where epilepsy is associated with abnormal brain rhythms the EEG will help differentiate it from convulsive hysteria, although it is necessary to be cautious since reliance on one test is often insufficient to eliminate the diagnosis of hysteria altogether, or for that matter, to eliminate functional nervous disease other than epilepsy. A clinical experience will illustrate the limits of present medical knowledge, and the difficulties of medical semantics.

Case 11. A resident in neurology with some experience on the psychiatric service called my attention to a patient in his care whom neurologists had diagnosed as having 'continuous epileptic seizures'. He stated that although the case seemed similar to one of catatonic stupor he had once examined with me, the patient's EEG showed spike and

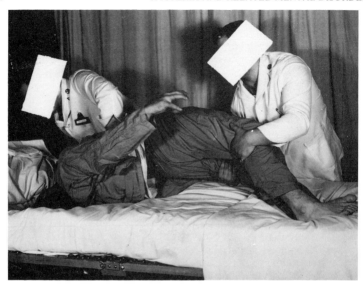

Fig. 5. 'La grande hystérie'; a patient being restrained during a hysterical attack. Case of Dr J. Lyle and Dr J. B. Rioux. *(Reproduced by courtesy of Dr J. Lyle and Dr J. B. Rioux. US Army Photograph.)*

wave patterns typical of epilepsy. After examining the black 17-year-old boy I was convinced that the diagnosis was indeed catatonia. Since he was quite mute and unresponsive I interviewed his mother and older sister when they visited the hospital later that day. They disclosed that the patient had been rejected by a girl with whom he was in love, and that he had complained bitterly about this to his mother and sister shortly before going to his room and suddenly falling into the resistive stupor from which it was impossible to rouse him. On the basis of knowing the severe narcissistic injury the patient had suffered I talked to him at length again on that day and the following day. His face and eyes moved slightly as I spoke, especially at any mention of the girl's name. A few hours after I had left the ward he got out of bed. He was immediately taken to have the EEG repeated; the results were within normal limits. He soon left the hospital for what comfort family and friends could provide. There seemed no possibility of a mistake in his EEG records.

It is usually held that hysterical convulsive attacks are less common in the United States than their reported incidence in Paris a century ago. My experience is that if a fallacious 'either–or' dichotomy is avoided, hysteria contributes frequently to convulsive attacks in the USA. Sometimes the presence of hysteria is accurately identified. For example, N. R. Bernstein (1969)[101] reported case histories from the Massachusetts General Hospital of adolescent girls who presented to the neurologists their complaints suggestive of epileptic disorder. However, their symptoms were found to be the outcome of their struggles with sexual pressures accompanied by severe anxiety, and served as an angry dramatization of their plight. Bernstein[101] noted that many types of conversion reaction, such as those of these adolescent girls, were reported by psychiatrists in the community and in general hospitals. In these

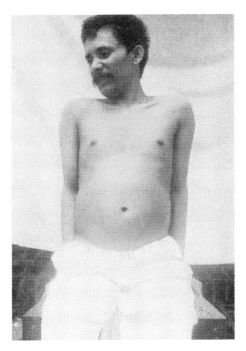

Fig. 6. A case of hysterical pseudocyesis (patient of Capt. N. N. Sinha, IAMC). The patient had deserted when his wife was pregnant; later apprehended and returned to the Army, when he suffered swelling of the abdomen. The swelling was reduced under pentothal narcosis.

cases, the symptoms turned out to be psychogenic (cf. F. P. McKegney, 1967[102]). The incidence of convulsive hysteria may be obscured by changes in neurological definition following increasing though imperfect knowledge of the participation of temporal lobe and limbic neural structures in the elaboration of symptoms, and be a fallacious 'either–or' attitude to the problems of organic versus hysterical disease. As Charcot (1873)[96] recognized, functional changes must be present in neural substrates and pathways in hysterical disorders, although at the time he did not know anything about some substrates and pathways that have been discovered and investigated since, and could not then demonstrate such postulated changes.

An attack consisting of loss of consciousness accompanied by incoordinate movements seems at first sight far removed from other manifestations of hysteria. In one case of conversion hysteria of predominantly motor type (spasmodic torticollis, *Case* 8, pp. 48–9) the essential psychopathology was briefly discussed. It was found that these automatic movements, over which the patient could exercise little volitional control, had an individual significance which it was possible to uncover. Between this type of motor hysteria and the fully developed convulsive attack there is only a difference of degree. In order to appreciate this difference it is necessary to consider the mechanisms of condensation and displacement which comprise the *primary process*, in contrast to the *secondary process* (Freud, 1911[103]). The example of spasmodic torticollis cited serves to illustrate that a single element in a neurosis may express several thoughts or trends which are thus *condensed*. The rhythmic movements were found to be essentially an indirect representation (or symbol) of both his frustrated erotic desire and his need for punishment on account of it, besides representing his craving for sympathy and flight into illness. Moreover, displacement is evident as well as condensation; frustrated genital tension is displaced upwards and seeks discharge in the rhythmic movements of the neck.

Condensation and displacement are fundamental characteristics of unconscious mentation, and often invade conscious thought and behaviour as well. For example, the individual infuriated over something said or done by his superior at work must discharge his passion somehow; since it is clearly dangerous to confront his superior in a rage, the worker finds someone else to 'take it out on' and inappropriately makes a victim of someone—an underling at work, perhaps, or his wife at home—who has done nothing to deserve his ill temper. Such a person is *displacing* his emotion. Condensation and displacement, difficult to identify in the neurotic individual, may become more readily accessible in his dreams (Freud, 1900[104]). Under usual circumstances, the ideas of an individual while awake are subject to strict conditions, and are more or less appropriate to the occasion and logically related under the sway of the 'secondary process'. The derivatives of those instinctual and impulses that originate in the unconscious are formulated and expressed through its mediation—unless they are altogether repressed and thus withheld from consciousness. Freud (1911)[103] thus considered that mental energy has two forms; it is 'unbound' in the primary process when displacement and condensation occur freely, and 'bound' in the secondary process when such freedom is surrendered for the sake of clarity, and for the purpose of dealing adequately with external realities. 'Bound' and 'unbound', it must be added, are relative and not absolute concepts.

When the typical epileptic attack is considered from this point of view it becomes apparent that the process of 'binding' has in this case failed almost entirely; tension is released in the discharge of the convulsive attack, the only condition being that such discharge takes place within the body of the patient himself—although in epileptic furore it may also involve outwardly directed and indiscriminate violence. Indeed, it is from these paroxysmal attacks that sometimes replace the convulsive seizure and which are known as psychic equivalents that we gain insight into the nature of the tension being released. Such psychic equivalents are episodic disturbances of consciousness associated with automatic motor acts; they often involve criminal violence.

The hysterical fit is also essentially a rage reaction; it may be replaced by a temper tantrum. Aroused hostility, generated in this case by frsutration of instinctual genital trends, thus finds release. There is often evidence of erotic discharge also in the *form* of the attack, in *attitudes passionnelles*, ecstatic poses, etc. The following case provides an illustration:

Case 12. A 19-year-old woman was referred for psychiatric examination because of having frequent 'fits'. These took place at half past six every evening as she listened to the radio,* which she had been in the habit of doing with a young man with whom she had been in love but from whom she was now separated. He had appeared at her house at about this hour each evening, and they would sit side by side listening to the radio. Her fits were preceded by painful sensations in her right side where she had formerly had the pleasurable awareness of the close proximity of her boyfriend's body. This patient said at first that she did not care at all about her friend's defection, but this defence of pretended indifference served her adequately during only part of the day; the convulsive attacks provided a needed outlet for her outraged feelings.

It is clear from all this that the difference in degree between motor hysteria with spasmodic movement and hysterical convulsion is a difference in the degree to which the secondary process has been abrogated. In *Case* 8 (spasmodic torticollis) both displacement and condensation occurred to an extent altogether impossible for logical thought, but there is a 'binding' in the symptom, so the secondary process is by no means entirely eluded. In the convulsive attack there is almost complete abrogation and the tension is freely discharged.

Janet (1907)[17] traced the connection between convulsive attacks and somnambulisms, and showed that convulsive attacks were merely degraded forms of somnambulism where the outer expression of somnambulistic idea in physiognomy, attitude, and act was no longer clear. Under the conditions of an abrogation of the secondary process, it is of course no longer possible for clarity and definition to emerge (cf. Augusta Bonnard, 1958[105]). As Janet (1907)[17] insists, however, hysterical convulsive attacks have the same 'moral causes' as somnambulisms or other expressions of hysteria; and, he writes, these hysterical accidents, like others 'begin on the occasion of particularly affecting events, genital perturbations, sorrows, fears, etc.' Where the secondary process is constitutionally inefficient, as in mental dullness, convulsion is more liable to occur as an expression of hysteria than a more individual spasmodic pattern.

The following account of a soldier suffering convulsive attacks shows many typical features:

Case 13. In early June 1945, a gunner, aged 22, was admitted to hospital following the observation of three epileptiform fits during the course of two hours at his unit. Immediately before the onset of the attack he had drunk a little gin, and after the fits he was escorted to the hospital in a condition of violent exictement requiring restraint. In the hospital he was given a sedative that night, and after a sound sleep was more thoroughly examined by the medical officer, in the morning.

The patient gave the medical officer a history of head injury two years previously, following which he had suffered occasional 'black-outs'. Examination revealed no gross signs apart from an abrasion of the right hand sustained during the fits, and his behaviour was apparently normal. All this was duly noted by the medical officer, who transferred him to a neurological centre with a note querying the possibilities of post-traumatic

---

*Such hysterical attacks are sometimes confused with 'musicogenic epilepsy', but this is often a mistaken diagnosis (the term refers to the pattern of *meaningless* sound that serves as a provocative stimulus).

epilepsy or subdural haematoma. On admission to the neurological centre the following day, he was noted to be semi-comatose, slowly obeying simple commands if they were forcefully given; the medical officer considered that he was gradually recovering from *status epilepticus*. He remained drowsy for another day and was then thoroughly investigated physically during the next fortnight. Towards the end of the first week of this period investigations reached something of a climax with the insertion of a spinal needle into the cisterna magna. After this diagnostic operation he showed partial palsy of the right 6th nerve and some weakness of the right leg. The day after this he went again into status epilepticus, when eight convulsions were observed and controlled by administration of pentothal. Investigations were energetically pursued with an encephalogram. However, X-rays, lumbar puncture and serological and neurological examinations, even after repetition, proved essentially negative. Then he told the medical officer that he had had 'faints' before the accident. So he was referred for psychiatric examination.

The following relevant facts were ascertained during interview. He had been a nervous child and had feared the dark until the age of 12. As a child he had frequent temper tantrums that brought him into conflict with his father. He was a poor scholar, and after leaving school was employed as a farm labourer. At this time he suffered frequent 'dizzy' attacks. Later he volunteered for the Army and signed on for 7 years with the colours and 5 reserve, although his parents objected. Both before and after the accident of July 1943, when he fell out of a train and suffered concussion, he had in the Army suffered attacks of dizziness without falling down. In December 1944 he heard of his father's death, and since that time had come to be worried about his mother, who was in poor health, and his two younger siblings, both of whom required institutional treatment on account of nervous disorder. At this time (December 1944) and until April 1945, he was on active service in Burma and was exposed to considerable enemy shelling. ('Though I was very shaky at the time, it used to cheer me up when we sent it back to them.') His regiment was pulled out in April 1945 for re-equipment. As a lot of the men were due for repatriation, return into action was delayed for the purpose of training reinforcements. It was in May 1945 that he had his first 'black-out' during which convulsions were observed, as already noted, and he was then admitted to the hospital. It was learned that on the occasion of this first convulsive seizure he was confined to barracks on account of absence, and that he had two small gins from someone while in barracks.

To convey a picture of the impression created by this patient during interview the following remarks are recorded. These remarks were made after his confidence had been gained; at first he had displayed a truculent attitude:

1. *Describing his childhood:* 'If I didn't want to lose my temper I'd have to walk out, and often have to take it out on my kid brother and hit him with all my strength. Then there'd be trouble with my father who'd hit me in the face... .'

'I used to like carpentry at school but often had to smash the wood. Then I'd get the cane. My temper has been my trouble all my life.'

2. *Describing his present situation in life:* 'I sometimes can't stand other people. It's a damn sight more pleasant in action than in hospital. Just the same with the girl (his most recent attachment in England). When I'm writing I just have to hurt her and let it go. Might do something I'm sorry for if I marry. A normal girl wouldn't bother with me.' 'If I have to suppress my feelings [language borrowed from me] and you keep me in hospital, I'll finish up in the "cage". I'll have to slosh somebody.'

In this case there is a personality background suggestive of unresolved sadistic trends. The onset of the convulsive attacks immediately followed his withdrawal from front-line action when he was becoming very homesick. Such a temporal connection between the onset of convulsions and 'particularly affecting events' is typical of hysteria. During his sojourn in hospital under psychiatric observation this patient suffered from one convulsive attack, following which he lapsed into coma. While comatose he kept repeating, 'Let me out!'. This outcry pointed to the crux of the situation. As with so many people of very aggressive inclination, he was excessively fearful of aggression. His experience in action led to a desire to go home, rationalized and reinforced by feelings of guilt relating to his family and his father's death. His conflict between his desire to get out and his view of himself as a fighting man was connected with the onset of convulsive seizures. Following discussions the attacks ceased, and he was returned to duty in a lower medical category after lengthy observation.

Here are the notes of another case of later vintage treated at the University of Virginia Hospital by Drs Linda Thompson and Richard Oliver in consultation with myself. The notes are condensed from the discharge summary, and illustrate the problems of differential diagnosis of partial seizures with complex symptomatology as outlined by F. E. Dreifuss (1975[100]).

Case 14. A 17-year-old white boy from the city of R. entered the hospital at the suggestion of his neurologist in R. following a three-month period of symptoms which progressed to include headache, somnolence, atypical seizure disorder and amnesia.

Present illness: This high school football player practised for one week at the beginning of the season. After one morning practice he ate lunch and became nauseated, vomited and passed out. He was taken to a local doctor's office, where he became combative and from which he was admitted to a local hospital for a two-day neurological evaluation which revealed nothing abnormal. Following discharge, he continued his football practice but had headaches in the vertex of his head which were followed by spells of somnolence at any time of the day. He saw Dr D. in R. who, on neurological evaluation, found occipital spiking indicative of a seizure disorder. It was suggested that the patient stop football, to which he reacted negatively, and two days later he developed an amnesia for his entire lifetime up to the time of the present football season. He dropped out of school, began taking Dilantin and phenobarbital, and in October of this year was admitted to a hospital in R. for an eight-day neurological evaluation. During this hospitalization he exhibited strange seizure disorder characterized by an atypical thrashing around. It was suggested at this time that he see a psychiatrist, and he was scheduled for admission here for evaluation. During this interval he remained amnesic as before. After discharge from the R. hospital and before admission here, he visited his school; but was unable to remember the names of friends or any of those in his class.

Family history: The patient had three older siblings, two female and one male; and two younger siblings, both male. There was no history of family disease, and both parents were alive and in good health.

Social history: The patient dated occasionally, but had no steady girlfriend. His parents described him as being moderately extroverted, with average academic achievement. He had recently been preoccupied with football at the expense of everything else.

Past history: He had no allergies. He was taking Dilantin and phenobarbital, but no other medication. At the age of six he had had an operation on his left eye for the removal of a foreign body. He had had no medical illnesses, and did not use cigarettes or alcohol.

Physical examination: On admission his blood pressure was 120/80, his pulse 75, respirations 16. Examination of the head revealed no trauma. Eyes, ears, nose and throat were within normal limits. The thyroid was normal in size. The lungs were clear to P & A. Examination of the heart disclosed a regular rhythm and no murmurs. The abdomen was normal, and both testes had descended. Peripheral pulses were strong and symmetrical. The neurological examination showed deep tendon reflexes, cranial nerves, cerebellar functioning, Romberg and sensory motor system intact.

Mental state examination: He was orientated to all spheres and his mood was normal and appropriate. There was no retardation evident in his stream of talk, the content of which was limited to the three months just before admission, complete amnesia prevailing for the time before that. His recent memory was normal, but his remote memory very incomplete. His fund of knowledge was greatly decreased, and his insight was felt to be very poor. He was not suicidal nor did he have hallucinations or delusions.

Laboratory examination: Showed normal urinalysis, white count of 4700, hematocrit of 48. Two-hour post-prandial sugar was 65. BUN was 26. Uric acid was 6.3. VDRL was negative.

Psychological testing: On the MMPI the patient failed to cooperate sufficiently, not answering 70 of the questions. However, in the questions answered, schizophrenia, paranoia and hypomanic scales were high. IQ estimation by the WAIS was estimated to be in the clinically average group. With regard to sexuality and its control, panic and confusion were found to be scattered throughout the content of the Rorschach. The examiner reports, 'One gets the feeling that the patient is a passive–aggressive type.' Neurology consultation showed no abnormality.

Hospital course: A few days after admission to the hospital, the patient's amnesia totally reversed itself so that he became amnesic for the last three months and remembered his entire life prior to that. It is interesting that this reversal took place two days following the termination of his home town's football season.

The patient was evaluated by Dr Abse, who diagnosed him as having a primitive hysterical disorder with many schizoid features. The patient gave the staff the distinct feeling that he was being uncooperative, by verbalized resistance to therapy, wanting to be discharged and feeling at first that he had no illness that needed to be treated. This seemed greatly to reduce the possibility of long term follow-up. Because he had insurance for only a one-month period it was necessary to discharge him. Immediate follow-up was, however, arranged. The patient had an EEG while in the hospital which showed no abnormality; that is, no occipital focus of seizure. For this reason the Dilantin and phenobarbital were discontinued.

Impression: Hysterical neurosis, dissociative type.

As outlined in the report above, this young man who fainted after performing vigorously in a football trial, could later remember little about many years prior to the beginning of the football season; when this gross gap in memory was filled again, he could remember nothing of the short segment of time during which he had tested his athletic prowess at this level of increased competition. As he gradually recalled his fanatical yearnings and hope during early high school years for fame as a football player, and his energetic and pleasurably successful practice during that time, there was a curious reversal of amnesia. He became amnesic for the most recent months of time, but remembered his entire life before that. These three months included the final strenuous time of testing of the prepared metal in the fire. It was later apparent that during this time he had feared that severe injury might result from his fanatically aggressive efforts, as indeed his worried father had warned him. At the same time, he had wanted to think of himself as unafraid. It was this enmeshment in conflict and associated painful feelings, including those evoked by threatened loss of self-respect, that he was seeking to exclude from consciousness by means of repressive forgetting. Later psychotherapy revealed that his precarious self-respect had become dependent upon an exaggerated ego-ideal compounded of elements which included a counter-phobic type of machismo.

REFERENCES

1. Szasz, T. S. (1961). *The Myth of Mental Illness.* New York: Dell.
2. Lewis, A. (1975). The survival of hysteria. *Psychol. Med.*, **5**, 9–12.
3. D.S.M. III (1980). *Diagnostic and Statistical Manual of Mental Disorders*, 3rd ed. Washington, D.C.: Am. Psychiat. Assoc.
4. Janet, P. (1901). *The Mental State of Hystericals: A Study of Mental Stigmata and Mental Accidents.* New York: Putnam.
5. Fenichel, O. (1934). *Outline of Clinical Psychoanalysis.* New York: Norton.
6. Noble, D. (1951). Hysterical manifestations in schizophrenic illness. *Psychiatry*, **14**, 153–160.
7. Freud, S. (1917). The Paths to the Formation of Symptoms. *Introductory Lectures on Psycho-analysis.* In: *The Standard Edition*, Vol. XVI. London: Hogarth Press (1953).
8. Freud, S. (1896). The aetiology of hysteria. In: *The Standard Edition*, Vol. III. London: Hogarth Press (1953).
9. Fenichel, O. (1945). *The Psychoanalytic Theory of Neurosis.* New York: Norton.
10. Rangell, L. (1959). The nature of conversion. *J. Am. Psychoanal. Assoc.*, **7**, 632–62.
11. Chodoff, P. and Lyons, H. (1958). Hysteria, the hysterical personality and 'hysterical conversion'. *Am. J. Psychiat.*, **114**, 734–40.
12. Freud, S. (1905). Fragment of an Analysis of a Case of Hysteria. In: *The Standard Edition*, Vol. VII. London: Hogarth Press (1955).
13. Easser, B. R. and Lesser, S. R. (1965). Hysterical personality: a re-evaluation. *Psychoanal. Quart.*, **34**, 390–405.
14. Kuiper, P. C. (1967). *On Being Genuine and Other Essays.* New York and London: Basic Books.
15. Menninger, K. A. (1959). Recognising and renaming psychopathic personalities. In: *A Psychiatrist's World: Selected Papers.* New York: Viking Press.
16. Dostoevsky, F. M. (1864). *Notes from Underground.* trans. (MacAndrew A. R.). New York: New American Library (1961).
17. Janet, P. (1907). *The Major Symptoms of Hysteria.* New York: Macmillan (1920).
18. D.S.M. II (1968). *Diagnostic and Statistical Manual of Mental Disorders*, 2nd ed. Washington, D.C.: Am. Psychiat. Assoc.
19. Brain, W. R. (1933). *Diseases of the Nervous System.* London: Oxford Univ. Press.
    20. Hurst, A. (1940). *Medical Diseases of War.* London: Arnold.
21. Klein, M. and Riviere, J. (1937). *Love, Hate and Reparation.* London: Hogarth Press.
22. Brenman, M. and Gill, M. M. (1944). *Hypnotherapy.* New York: Josiah Macy Jun. Foundation.
23. Gill. M. M. and Brenman, M. (1961). *Hypnosis and Related States: Psychoanalytic Studies in Regression.* New York: Int. Univ. Press.
24. Reiff, R. and Scheerer, M. (1959). *Memory and Hypnotic Age Regression.* New York: International University Press.
25. West, L. J. (1963). Hypnosis in medical practice. In: *The Psychological Basis of Medical Practice* (ed. Lief, H. J., Lief, V. F. and Lief, N. R.). New York: Harper and Row.
26. Fairbairn, W. R. D. (1943). The war neuroses, their nature and significance. *Br. Med. J.*, **1**, 183.
27. Simons, R. C. (1964). A case of camptocormia (conversion) in a schizophrenic process. *Arch. Gen. Psychiat.*, **11**, 277.
28. Jones, E. (1916). The theory of symbolism. In: *Papers on Psycho-analysis.* London: Ballière, Tindall and Cox (1938).

29. Ferenczi, S. (1913). The ontogenesis of symbols. In: *Contributions to Psycho-analysis*. Boston: Badger (1916).
30. Norris, D. C. (1945). Malingering. In: *Rehabilitation of the War Injured*. New York: Doherty and Runes.
31. Freud, S. (1925). An Autobiographical Study. In: *The Standard Edition*, Vol. XX. London: Hogarth Press (1955).
32. Freud, S. (1898). Sexuality in the Aetiology of the Neuroses. In: *The Standard Edition*, Vol. III. London: Hogarth Press (1955).
33. Ferenczi, S. (1919). The phenomena of hysterical materialization. In: *Further Contributions to the Theory and Techniques of Psychoanalysis*. London: Hogarth Press (1926).
34. Freud, S. (1895). The Psychotherapy of Hysteria. Breuer, J. and Freud, S. *Studies on Hysteria*. In: *The Standard Edition*, Vol. II. London: Hogarth Press (1955).
35. Freud, S. (1914). A History of the Psycho-analytic Movement. In: *The Standard Edition*, Vol. XIV. London: Hogarth Press (1955).
36. Dosuzkov, T. (1975). Idiosophobia: a form of pregenital conversion. *Psychoanal. Quart.*, **44**, 253–65.
37. Lerer, B. (1977). Hyperhidrosis: a review of its psychological aspects. *Psychosomatics*, **18** (5), 28–31.
38. Wittkower, E. and Russell, B. (1953). *Emotional Factors in Skin Diseases*. New York: Hoeber.
39. Escalona, S. K. (1968). *The Roots of Individuality*. London: Tavistock Publications,
40. Comrie, J. D. (1922). On the hysterical affections, In: *Selected Works of Thomas Sydenham*. New York: Wood.
41. Obermayer, M. E. (1955). *Psychocutaneous Medicine*. Springfield, Ill.: Thomas.
42. Sulzberger M. B. and Zaidens, S. H. (1948). Psychogenic factors in dermatologic disorders. *Mayo Clin. N. Am.*, **32**, 669.
43. Bartemeier, L. (1938). A psychoanalytic study of a case of chronic exudative dermatitis. *Psychoanal. Quart.*, **7**, 216.
44. Ellis, H. (1936). *Studies in the Psychology of Sex*, Vol. II, Part I. New York: Random House.
45. Spitz. R. A. (1951). The psychogenic diseases in infancy. In: *The Psychoanalytic Study of the Child*, Vol. VI, p. 255. New York: Internat. Univ. Press.
46. Alexander, F. (1950). *Psychosomatic Medicine*. New York: Norton.
47. Groddeck, G. W. (1923). *The Book of the It*. New York: Funk and Wagnalls (1950).
48. Freud, S. (1912). On the Universal Tendency to Debasement in the Sphere of Love. *Contributions to the Psychology of Love*. In: *The Standard Edition*, Vol. XXI. London: Hogarth Press (1955).
49. Freud, S. (1933). Feminity. *New Introductory Lectures*. In: *The Standard Edition*, Vol. XXII. London: Hogarth Press (1955).
50. Freud, S. (1916). The Sexual Life of Human Beings. *Introductory Lectures on Psycho-analysis*. In: *The Standard Edition*, Vol. XVI. London: Hogarth Press (1955).
51. Freud, S. (1917). The Development of the Libido and the Sexual Organisations. *Introductory Lectures on Psycho-analysis*. In: *The Standard Edition*, Vol. XVI. London: Hogarth Press (1955).
52. Jones, E. (1922). Some problems of adolescence. In: *Papers on Psycho-analysis*. London: Ballière, Tindall and Cox (1938).
53. Freud, S. (1895). *Studies on Hysteria*. In: *The Standard Edition*, Vol. II. London: Hogarth Press (1955).
54. Freud, S. (1905). Three Essays on the Theory of Sexuality. In: *The Standard Edition*, Vol. VII. London: Hogarth Press (1955).

55. Flugel, J. C. (1921). *The Psycho-analytic Study of the Family*, Chap. 10. London: Hogarth Press (1939).
56. Halliday, J. L. (1943). Principles of aetiology. *Br. J. Med. Psychol.*, **19**, 367.
57. Freud, S. (1912). A Note on the Unconscious in Psycho-analysis. In: *The Standard Edition*, Vol. XXII. London: Hogarth Press (1955).
58. Freud, S. (1915). Repression. In: *The Standard Edition*, Vol. XIV. London: Hogarth Press (1955).
59. Janet, P. (1907). *The Major Symptoms of Hysteria*, Chap. 3. New York: Macmillan (1920).
60. Freud, Anna (1936). *The Ego and the Mechanisms of Defence*. London: Hogarth Press (1937).
61. Garnett, R. W. and Elbirlik, K. (1953). Torticollis: its dynamics and therapy. *South. Med. J.*, **46**, 892.
62. Masson, J. M. (1984). *The Assault on Truth*. New York: Farrar, Strauss and Giroux.
63. Jung, C. G. (1954). *The Development of Personality*. London: Routledge and Kegan Paul.
64. Freud, S. (1917). The Development of the Libido and the Sexual Organisations. *Introductory Lectures on Psycho-analysis*. In: *The Standard Edition*, Vol. XVI. London: Hogarth Press (1955).
65. Abraham, K. (1921). Contributions to the theory of the anal character. In: *Selected Papers of Karl Abraham*. London: Hogarth Press (1927).
66. Abraham, K. (1924). The influence of oral erotism on character-formation. In: *Selected Papers of Karl Abraham*. London: Hogarth Press (1927).
67. Abraham, K. (1925). Character-formation on the genital level of libido-development. In: *Selected Papers of Karl Abraham*. London: Hogarth Press (1927).
68. Freud, S. (1917). Some Thoughts on Development and Regression–Aetiology. *Introductory Lectures on Psycho-analysis*. In: *The Standard Edition*, Vol. XVI. London: Hogarth Press (1955).
69. Freud, Anna (1965). *Normality and Pathology in Childhood: Assessments of Development*. New York: Internat. Univ. Press.
70. Hoffer, Willie (1952). The mutual influences in the development of ego and id: earliest stages. In: *The Psychoanalytic Study of the Child*, Vol. VII, pp. 31–41.
71. Mahler, M. S. (1952). On child psychosis and schizophrenia: austistic and symbiotic infantile psychoses. *The Psychoanalytic Study of the Child*, **7**, 286–305.
72. Mahler, M. S. (1969). *On Human Symbiosis and the Vicissitudes of Individuation*. London: Hogarth Press.
73. Abse, D. W. and Ewing, J. A. (1960). Some problems in psychotherapy with schizophrenic patients. *Am. J. Psychother.*, **14**, 505–19.
74. Speers, R. and Lansing, C. (1965). *Group Therapy in Childhood Psychosis*. Chapel Hill: Univ. North Carolina Press.
75. Burnham, D. L., Gladstone, A. I. and Gibson, R. W. (1969). Foreword: Cohen, R. A. *Schizophrenia and the Need–Fear Dilemma*. New York: Internat. Univ. Press.
76. Winnicott, D. W. (1958). *Collected Papers*. London: Tavistock.
77. Winnicott, D. W. (1965). *The Maturational Process and the Facilitating Environment*. New York: Internat. Univ. Press.
78. Klein, M. (1948). *Contributions to Psycho-analysis*. London: Hogarth Press.
79. Mahler, M. S., Pine, F. and Bergman, A. (1975). *The Psychological Birth of the Human Infant*. (Symbiosis and Individuation.) New York: Basic Books.
80. Freud, S. (1920). Beyond the pleasure principle. In: *The Standard Edition*, Vol. XVIII. London: Hogarth Press (1955).
81. Freud, S. (1933). Anxiety and Instinctual Life. *New Introductory Lectures on Psycho-analysis*. In: *The Standard Edition*, Vol. XXII. London: Hogarth Press (1953).

82. Klein, M. (1932). *The Psycho-analysis of Children*. London: Hogarth Press.
83. Freud, S. (1926). Inhibitions, Symptoms and Anxiety. In: *The Standard Edition*, Vol. XX. London: Hogarth Press (1955).
84. Freud, S. (1931). Female Sexuality. In: *The Standard Edition*, Vol. XXI. London: Hogarth Press (1955).
85. Nagera, H. (1975). *Female Sexuality and the Oedipus Complex*. New York: Aronson.
86. Abraham, K. (1920). Manifestations of the female castration complex. In: *Selected Papers of Karl Abraham*. London: Hogarth Press (1927).
87. Mack, J. E. (1974). *Nightmares and Human Conflict*. Boston: Houghton Mifflin.
88. Jones, E. (1910). *On the Nightmare*. London: Hogarth Press (1931).
89. Freud, S. (1923). *The Ego and the Id*, Chap. IV. In: *The Standard Edition*, Vol. XIX. London, Hogarth Press (1955).
90. Lampl-deGroot, J. (1963). Symptom formation and character formation. *Internat. J. Psycho-anal.*, **44**, 1–11.
91. Arlow, J. A. (1963). Conflict, regression and symptom formation. *Internat. J. Psycho-anal.*, **44**, 12–22.
92. Volkan, V. (1976). *Primitive Internalised Object Relations*. New York: Internat. Univ. Press.
93. Giovacchini, P. L. (1975). *Psychoanalysis of Character Disorders*. New York: Aronson.
94. Kernberg, O. (1975). *Borderline Conditions and Pathological Narcissism*, Chap. 7. New York: Aronson.
95. Briquet, P. (1859). *Traité Clinique et Thérapeutique de l'Hystérie*. Paris: Boillière.
96. Charcot, J.-M. (1873). *Leçons sur les Maladies du Système Nerveux faites à la Salpêtrière*. Paris: Delahaye.
97. Schneider, P. B., Assal, G., Vigil, C. et al. (1965). *Contribution à l'Étude de l'Hystérie*. Paris and Lausanne: Masson.
98. Charcot, J.-M. (1877). *Lectures on the Diseases of the Nervous System* (trans. Sigerson, G.). London: New Sydenham Society.
99. Rabe F. (1970). Diagnostische Problems bei der Unterscheidung von hysterischen und epileptischen Anfaellen. *Nervenarzt*, **41**, 271–74.
100. Dreifuss, F. E. (1975). The differential diagnosis of partial seizures with complex symptomatology. In: *Advances in Neurology* (ed. Perry, J. K. and Daly, D. D.), Vol, II, Chap. 9. New York: Raven Press.
101. Bernstein, N. R. (1969). Psychogenic seizures in adolescent girls. *Behavioural Neuropsychiat.*, **10**, No. 4. 68–83.
102. McKegney, F. P. (1967). The incidence and characteristics of patients with conversion reactions. *Am. J. Psychiat.*, **124**, 542–5.
103. Freud, S. (1911). Formulations on the Two Principles of Mental Functioning. In: *The Standard Edition*, Vol. XII. London: Hogarth Press (1955).
104. Freud, S. (1900). *The Interpretation of Dreams*. In: *The Standard Edition*, Vols. IV and V. London: Hogarth Press (1955).
105. Bonnard, A. (1958). Pre-body-ego types of (pathological) mental functioning. *J. Am. Psychoanal. Assoc.*, **6**, 581–611.
106. Abraham, K. (1911). Notes on the psychoanalytical investigation and treatment of manic-depressive insanity and allied conditions. In: *Selected Papers*. London: Hogarth Press.

CHAPTER 3

Hysteria and Sexual Disorder

Preliminary Considerations

One of the most illuminating of Freud's books, his *Three Contributions to the Theory of Sex*,[1] is concerned with the deviations of sexual instinct as these relate to the healthy development of adult sexuality, both from the elementary excitations of infancy and the later changes that come about at the time of puberty. The psychoanalytic investigations that Freud initiated led him to views that were first outlined in this book, namely, as we have noted (Chapter 2), that sexual development is complicated: beginning in infancy, reaching a climax about the age of four or five, halting then and resuming at puberty, when further development ensues. He showed how the final stage of genital primacy is reached only through many evolutionary changes in the elementary components that comprise the beginnings of sexuality. These changes are influenced by both the inborn sexual constitution and the experiences of life, especially early life, and they are thus subject to many inhibitions, fixations and deviations in the course of development.

Havelock Ellis[2] had earlier published a series of histories of sexual development that revealed in great detail the varied nature of prepubertal sexuality in both boys and girls. Anal and oral eroticism, sadism and masochism, masturbation, exhibitionism and voyeurism, homosexual and heterosexual incest, zoophilia—all described as adult perversions in Krafft-Ebing's *Psychopathia Sexualis* in 1886[3]—were reported as having been present long before puberty in the patients whose histories Ellis elicited. Freud's theory of sexual development maintained that small children are 'polymorphously perverse', and that 'perversions' in adults are essentially symptoms of immaturity.

In another early essay which we have already remarked upon, Freud[4] reported his clinical findings in cases of men with disturbances of potency. He stressed the importance of infantile fixations, the barrier of the incest taboo and the later sexual privations during adolescence as aetiological factors. The common difficulty encountered in these cases was that of fusing feelings of tenderness, which are emphatic toward the loved mother, with sensual urges. These patients regarded tender feelings and sensual urges as incompatible, and Freud asserted that the difficulty they encountered in fusing them is common throughout our civilization. Indeed, he thought that no civilized man is completely potent in the sense of being able to enjoy a fully developed love relationship with maximal sensual pleasure. He held that respect for the partner inhibits sensual pleasure in varying degrees, and that in consequence many men are capable of intense physical pleasure in sex only with a woman socially, morally or aesthetically of a lower order. Certainly in the southern United States this difficulty is often broached by men who, for one reason or another, apply for psychiatric consultation. It seems clear also that the question of adolescent frustrational relationships requires consideration, along with the issue of providing contraception to the unmarried, especially since today's adolescent mores emphasize early and sustained pairing.

It is significant in this connection that the Kinsey group[5] reported a high correlation between a woman's premarital sexual experience and the frequency of orgasm in her marital coitus. This effect of premarital experience remained discernible a decade or more after her marriage. From their data they inferred that the early experience of orgasm does more to promote a full responsiveness in intercourse subsequently engaged in with a spouse than any kind of therapy instituted to correct unsatisfying marital coitus can offer to a woman without such experience.

Nearly 20 years after writing the essay on male sexual potency mentioned above, Freud[6] again expatiated on this theme in a contribution to sociological thought that had wide implications then and even wider implications now in the presence of societal disintegration and the fear of nuclear holocaust. He saw civilized society as being perpetually menaced by disintegration because of the primary hostility of men toward one another. Society erects barriers against man's aggressive and sexual instincts, and these are reinforced by policies that drive men to identifications and aim-inhibited love relationships with other men which deplete the libido available for their wives. When men knew no form of common life except that provided by family, the ever-present conflict between love and hate expressed itself early in the Oedipus complex, which created feelings of guilt and generated the conscience. When man tries to institute wider forms of communal life, as he is more and more obliged to do, the conflict between love and hate is intensified, and society foments an ever-increasing sense of guilt in order to check aggressiveness within the closely knit mass it hopes to achieve. A vicious circle is thus established in which the sense of guilt becomes insupportably strong for the individual and for the peace of society as a whole. The socially induced unconscious oppression of guilt and the need to suppress aggressiveness combine to disable the sexual life of modern man.

The difficulty in fusing tender and sensual feelings that Freud found so common among his male patients was often expressed in disturbed potency in the marital bed, whereas extramarital sensual satisfaction was generally obtained. This difficulty was related also to the ascendancy of the ascetic Christian ideal in the Western World, as indeed it is to other similar monastic ideals in the Orient.*

---

*Many of the Oriental religious systems revolve around the axis of detachment from the world of the senses, rather than directly discountenancing the physical impulse of sex. In the more extreme forms, or advanced stages, of the religious process, the obsessive concern with detachment is translated into a more massive withdrawal from and participation in the external world, a dilemma beautifully portrayed in the Celestial Poem of the Bhagavad-Gita. In the poem Krishna elucidates the view that detachment and participation are not necessarily in conflict.

The view of celibacy as the *summum bonum* in a hierarchic value system reinforced the antisexual forces of the psyche. Jung[7] gave particular attention to the regular recurrence in history of those polar attitudes toward the world identified by Nietzsche as Apollonian and Dionysian. Nietzsche describes the former as measuring, numbering, limiting and mastering all of the savage and hitherto untamed aspects of life and the latter as freeing unmeasured instinct and liberating the unbridled dynamics of the animal and divine nature. Thus Dionysian man is a *satyr*, god above and beast below. The Dionysian represents horror at the annihilation of the principle of individuation and at the same time rapturous delight at this destruction. The Dionysian posture is comparable to frenzy; individuality is suspended in orgies of exuberant sexual licence and in religious mysteries that provide ecstasies. Jung discussed the battle of the early Christian Church against sensual pagan practices and against the *gnosis*, a passion for thought, contrasting the characters of Tertullian and Origen, the influential fathers of the second century. Tertullian was a pagan who yielded himself to the lascivious life of his city until about his 35th year when he became a Christian and created the Church Latin that has lasted for more than a thousand years. The passion of his thinking was so inexorable that his ethical code was bitter in its severity. He commanded martyrdom to be sought, not shunned; he permitted no second marriage and required the permanent veiling of women. He attacked with unrelenting fanaticism the philosophy of the *gnosis*, including early science. To him is ascribed the sublime confession: *Credo quia absurdum est* (I believe because it is against reason). The self-mutilation achieved by Tertullian in the *sacrificium intellectus* led him to the complete rejection of philosophy and science. In contrast to Tertullian, Origen remained a philosophical theologian but before A.D. 211 actually castrated himself. Christianity encountered in Origen a type whose bedrock foundation was his relation to other people. His self-castration was thus the expression of the sacrifice of his most valuable function. It is characteristic of Tertullian that he should perform the *sacrificium intellectus*, whereas Origen was led to the *sacrificium phalli*, since the Christian process at that time demanded a complete abolition of the sensual hold upon the object.

The anti-sensual direction taken by the early church in its battle with paganism was augmented in the Middle Ages when the ascetic ideal flourished and monasticism became the refuge of many of the finest minds. As a consequence, there came into being a conception of woman as the supreme temptress, the most dangerous of all obstacles in the way of salvation. At the same time ambivalence became manifestly heightened in a counterdoctrine of the superiority of women, an adoration of the Virgin in Heaven, of the lady upon earth. (The latter resulted in the ideals of chivalry.) As Trethowan[8] has emphasized, the persecution of witches is attributable to the ferocious asceticism, a complex distortion largely a result of the redirection of the sexual urge away from its natural context. It was believed that certain women had given up their immortal souls to the Prince of Evil for the privilege of enjoying the services of his demons. In particular witches were accused of hindering husbands from performing the sexual act and wives from conceiving. The most ardent persecutors of witches were, of course, men sworn to celibacy.

Innocent VIII, elected to the papacy in 1484, became sincerely alarmed at the profusion of witches. In his celebrated Bull of 1488 he called upon the nations of Europe to rescue the Church, then imperilled by the arts of Satan, and set forth the horrors that were rampant, including the blighting of the marital bed. Sprenger and Kramer shortly thereafter published the *Malleus Maleficarum*, or *Hammer to Knock Down Witches*[9], in which they laid down a regular form of trial and appointed a course of examination by which inquisitors might best discover the guilty. Mackay[10] gives a detailed account of the ensuing exacerbation of the witch mania all over Europe, a vivid example of group hysteria.

In both the *Malleus* and the later *Compendium Maleficarum* (Guazzo, 1608) there is a classification of impotence which Trethowan[8] points out is in certain respects related both phenomenologically and psychodynamically to modern knowledge. Both works give evidence of some appreciation of the part played by the inner (unconscious) mental process, which by deceiving the senses can give rise to the illusion of genital deprivation, a phenomenon that can probably be equated with castration anxiety and conviction. Trethowan[8] sums up as follows:

> Viewed retrospectively, the persecution of witches in medieval times seems to have stemmed from several sources. Because Ritual Witchcraft represented the persistence in Europe of the pre-Christian pagan religion or Dianic cult, those who practised it were regarded as heretics. Further impetus was given to this persecution by knowledge of certain sexual rituals probably akin to primitive fertility rites. This in the setting of misogyny attendant upon the Christian ascetic ideal, led to the emergence of a delusional belief that witches had power to interfere with sexual relationships.

Male Potency Disturbances

Kinsey[10] points out that many men of lower socioeconomic levels take it as a matter of course that ejaculation should be reached quickly and that the female's response need have no special consideration. On the other hand, sexologists usually indicate that a man suffers from premature ejaculation if he is frequently unable to maintain coital contact with penile erection long enough to provide a climax for a partner who is capable of orgastic response. It is a widely held clinical impression, derived from experience with patients of all classes and subcultures, that the average duration of genital intercourse is from one to five minutes from the action of insertion to the completion of orgasm (see for example, Eisenstein[11]). Ejaculation is usually accomplished following some 30–50 frictional movements during approximately three minutes. Although it is not possible to use a time-standard rigorously because of wide variations in time taken for joint orgastic experience by different couples, premature ejaculation is usually characterized by the fact that although erection is attained, ejaculation and detumescence occur either before penetration of the vagina or within a minute after intromission. Premature ejaculation is a common potency disorder; it may be only a transient manifestation denoting no serious pathology in orgastic potency or it may be persistent. Sometimes there is a history of furtive adolescent sexual activity occurring hastily in great excitement and fear of detection and with accompanying feelings of guilt. Some of these cases yield in quite brief and superficial psychotherapy, whereas others are more firmly anchored in deeper sources of guilt and require more prolonged analytic work. It is said that Freud was once consulted by Gustav Mahler in 1910. In a few hours during a walk through the park, Freud enabled Mahler to understand how his potency disturbance was due to an unconscious confusion of his wife with his mother, noting incidentally that both were named Marie (cf *Case* 7, Chapter 2, p. 43). After this single peripatetic psychotherapeutic session Mahler recovered his full potency. Other cases require numerous sessions.

Case 15. A married man, aged 40, usually without potency disturbance, returned from a ten-day business conference on the West Coast of America and two months later sought an appointment. While away, he explained in an interview, he had attempted intercourse with a prostitute and had failed—he had ejaculated before intromission. After he returned home, the same thing had occurred with his wife on several occasions and since then he had refrained from intercourse. This led to complications with his wife, who was now loudly demanding to know what had upset him during his trip. The patient, who had at first appeared calm in the interview, became progressively more excited, demanding a cure before there was more trouble for him with his wife. He had gone to his own doctor several times. The physician had referred him for psychiatric consultation after medication failed to relieve the precocious ejaculation. In the course of several interviews it became evident that he feared he might have contracted venereal disease as a punishment for his sexual digression. Following an examination which included the usual laboratory tests by another specialist to whom I referred him, he was firmly reassured and sent back to discuss this matter further with me.

In the course of ensuing interviews—which included discussion of his restrictive upbringing in childhood, of his excursions to a brothel with other college students and the later development of a steadfast devotion to his church, like his father's—the patient came to fear my disapproval. This, it became increasingly clear, was partly the result of a transference-projection upon me of his own conscience insofar as this had been formed on the model of his father's. This too was brought into the field of discussion, so that it became possible to reduce his castration-anxiety and to alleviate his sense of guilt. At this time the patient was able to discuss his secret struggle with masturbation during adolescence and his fear and anger against his father during high school and college years. Shortly, the patient recovered his potency with his wife and showed no further desire to continue in investigative psychotherapy, which anyway he regarded as too expensive—although he insisted upon his gratitude in terminating therapy.

Complete impotence denotes the inability to attain or to maintain an erection during an attempt at intercourse. This may also be transient and may occur only as a result of special conditions that evoke an acute mental conflict of an hysterical nature. Goethe[12] notes in his diary the events of a delay that overtook him while travelling and necessitated an overnight stay in an inn where he flirted with a pleasing chambermaid and arranged for a midnight rendezvous in his room. However, at the critical time his sexual excitement subsided and he became altogether impotent. Baffled, he recalled the enjoyment he had always had with his wife, and his thoughts caused a strong erection which promptly disappeared once he tried again to approach the chambermaid. The girl fell asleep, and Goethe[12] wrote the following words to his wife in his diary:

I was approaching my home, when the last hours threatened to move me away from you, my beloved. But then, in a peculiar place, and under peculiar circumstances, I found back my faithful heart. You may not understand this and the following inference, beloved, but note the mysterious final verse: Often it is illness that helps preserve our health.

When psychogenic impotence is persistent, however, it betokens more serious neurotic disorder. When the patient is a young man this symptom requires early psychiatric consultation. In such cases secondary depression is often severe and there is a risk of suicide. This situation contrasts markedly with its counterpart of persistent frigidity in young women, which is so often accepted without severe depressive reaction, as will be discussed later.

Case 16. A young man of 22 who had attempted suicide by hanging was in treatment in hospital for severe depression, and this treatment was continued on an outpatient basis for a further 18 months with sessions four times a week. The son of a wealthy businessman, he had dropped out of college despite his high intelligence and had spent a good deal of his time racing around the country in his sports car, keeping his parents anxious and intimidated. His father had attempted thrashing and severe coercion during his defiant early adolescence but had later not found it possible to control him. Psychiatric evaluation indicated that he had not yet emerged from late adolescence. In addition to hysterical disorder, there was evidence of obsessive and pronounced schizoid problems. Early in the treatment of his depression, I had discovered the suicide attempt had followed a sexual fiasco and that he had attempted intercourse many times previously without success, his sexual disability varying at different times from precocious ejaculation to complete impotence. The ensuing intensive analytically orientated psychotherapy revealed a severe castration anxiety defended against by attempted identification with a brutal, sadistic father, an identification which was, however, shattered by his experiences in a number of sexual involvements with different women. Moreover, as part of his apparent strong attachment to his mother, it shortly became clear that his hostility toward her was so severe that this too impeded his relationship with other women. In particular there was an unconscious equating, represented in fantasy, of ejaculation with defecation and urination.

In the work with this patient, problems of acting out were particularly difficult to deal with. His more openly expressed hostility to his parents at home resulted in his father's attempting to control the therapy both by threats of terminating (he paid the bills) and by trying to bribe me by means of increasing my fees. At a later stage in therapy, the patient, without bringing it to my notice for a long time—at this time he was compliantly remembering details of his childhood—seduced his father's secretary (an attractive woman in her 40s who was his father's mistress, as he knew) and became deeply involved in a love affair with her during the course of which he discovered his potency. During the further course of the therapy he sadistically rid himself of this woman but later began an attachment to a younger woman and made good progress in therapy.

Treating this individual was a hair-raising experience for the therapist, both because of the patient's reckless driving in which he expressed his self-destructive trends and because of his brinkmanship with his father's mistress. The handling of the defiant and guilt-ridden father transference was thus an especially thorny problem.

This vignette draws attention to the severe underlying problems sometimes encountered in dealing psychotherapeutically with potency disturbances. In less severe cases the potency disturbances are often built on impeded developmental foundations and are symptoms of a hysterical neurosis. Adequate treatment in such cases must thus be directed not to the sexual symptom itself but to the underlying neurotic problems which even in young men may require several years of psychoanalysis. On the other hand, many potency disturbances are often readily responsive in brief psychotherapy consisting of distributive discussions. In the course of these discussions it is necessary to elucidate the leading mental conflicts and to provide an adequate opportunity for the patient to ventilate his feelings. Certainly the sexual disorder of a single man should be treated before marriage is contemplated; marriage should never be recommended as a deliberately therapeutic step.

From the foregoing, it is evident that sexual impotence has varying bases and refers to a number of symptoms all of which are characterized by some disturbance, transient or more permanent, in performing the act of intercourse with orgasm. *Case* 7 (discussed in Chapter 2, p. 43) concerned a marriage marred by persistence of impotence and the wife's unmet longing for a child in consequence. The husband had no such sexual problem in extra-marital relations. The designation in such a case could be altered to *selective potency*. Some men indeed are potent only when certain specific, and sometimes bizarre, conditions are fulfilled. A total lack of interest in the sexual act may have its basis in a secondary depression, or in an underlying incipient depressive or other psychotic disorder.

A longstanding lack of interest may indicate a compulsive neurotic basis. In such cases, investigative psychotherapy may reveal a secret 'chastity clause' by which the individual wards off guilt. This chastity commitment may have been forged in adolescence as an attempted solution to the struggle against masturbation, and later forgotten. Strong incestuous attachments are always involved in such instances, and sometimes actual incestuous relations have occurred with a sister in childhood or youth. The sacrifice of interest in sexual intercourse is often a self-punishing device that satisfies the sense of guilt sufficiently for moderate success and enjoyment in other areas of living. Abstinence in marriage may be a source of considerable cruelty, however, unless the wife is otherwise accommodated or is in collusion because she too fears sexual intercourse. It may indeed be 'the most distressing of perversions', as Robert Latou Dickinson dubbed it in his book *A Thousand Marriages*.[13]

Fetishism

Some men are aroused sexually by an object such as a shoe, a handkerchief or some particular article of lingerie; sexual arousal may also concern a part of the woman's body—the foot, the ankle, the nose, the breasts or the neck. Whenever sexual excitement is brought about by such an object or such a body part *and is associated with the avoidance of actual genital intercourse instead of promoting the movement toward it* we recognize fetishism exhibited as a perversion.

Freud[14] found the fetish to be a symbolic substitute for the penis that the little boy once believed his mother had, and which 'for reasons familiar to us—he does not want to give up.' The 'familiar reasons' are those that impel the boy to defend himself against a terrible fear by denying the possibility of castration. Probably no male human being escapes the fear occasioned by his early glances at the female genitalia; some may fend it off by creating a fetish, some may retreat to homosexuality. The last impression registered before the uncanny and traumatic event of seeing the female genitalia effects the imprinting of a fetish; the foot or shoe is so often preferred as a fetish because the little boy peered at the genitals from below and saw the woman from her feet up. Fur and velvet are substitutes for the sight of pubic hair that comes before the anticipated phallus; an item of underclothing may crystallize the moment the woman undressed before displaying the unexpected and startling vision—the last moment in which the woman could still be regarded as phallic and in which the frightening possibility that some beings lack penises could be disregarded. Freud showed that the fetish contains elements of the affirmation of castration in spite of the fact that it was constructed chiefly to disavow castration. Although the fetishist maintains the child's assumption that women have penises, he knows at the same time that they do not.

The following excerpt from a case reported by Sandor Ferenczi[15] illustrates the complex connection between foot-fetishistic fixation and potency disturbance in a man struggling to overcome his guilt-ridden inhibitions and succeeding in doing so only with expert psychoanalytic help.

A 32-year-old workman had never achieved a sustained erection in sexual intercourse despite innumerable attempts and despite a physician's attempts at treatment with electrical stimulation. At the time of consultation, the patient wished to marry, having become seriously attached to a suitable young woman. Although the coitus mechanism failed completely at the critical moment in actuality, the patient indulged in daydreams which comprised sexual situations; during these fantasy elaborations, he experienced intense erections which subsided at the moment when he imagined intromission. The patient also had nocturnal sexual dreams in which he was often with a corpulent woman whose face he never saw, and with whom at the critical moment he was unable to bring about sexual union. On the contrary, instead of intromission, as might have been expected in the dreaming consciousness, he would be overtaken by acute dread and would wake up in alarm with such thoughts as 'This is impossible!' and 'This situation is unthinkable'. After such anxiety dreams he would feel exhausted, be bathed in sweat and suffer palpitations and usually then have nervous symptoms throughout the day.

The fact that in the dream he never saw the woman's face stirred Ferenczi to entertain the hypothesis, in line with Freud's dream theory, that the omission served the purpose of making the person towards whom the libidinous dream-wish was directed unrecognizable in dreaming consciousnesss, and the waking in alarm signified that it was nevertheless beginning to dawn in his consciousness how 'unthinkable this situation was' with the woman hinted at by the dream.

As Ferenczi[15] wrote, 'The anxiety attack is the affective reaction of consciousness against a wish fulfilment of the unconscious... '

On one of the following days, the patient had a peculiar hypnagogic hallucination: in going to sleep he felt as if his feet were rising in the air while his head sank down, and he started up in intense dread. Ferenczi, who had already learned something of the patient's fetishistic attitude to feet from his daydreams and had learned too about his having an obese sister whom he disdained, obtained the patient's free associations to the theme of the 'swinging' sensation in the anxiety-arousing hypnagogic hallucination. The following memory images emerged, which he had long forgotten and which were most painful to him.

The corpulent sister whom he 'couldn't stand' and who was ten years older than the patient, used to undo and do up the shoes of the then three-year-old brother, and it also frequently happened that she would let him ride on her naked leg (covered only by a short stocking) whereupon he used to experience a voluptuous sensation in his member... When he wanted to repeat this later on, his sister, now 14 or 15 years old, rebuffed him with the reproach that such conduct was improper and indecent. Later the patient recollected that in his youth (from the 15th to the 18th year) he selected this childhood experience with his sister to elaborate sexual images and fantasies during masturbation. Indeed, it was the dread of his conscience after self-gratification of this kind that made him finally give up masturbation altogether; from that time the childhood experience had never occurred to him until the discussion of his dreams.

This case serves to illustrate the profound influence of memories of childhood, especially forgotten experiences and related wish-fantasies of an incestuous type, on adult sexual performance. More than half a century ago psychoanalysts recognized incestuous fixation of the libido as a frequent cause of psychosexual impotence. Because of persistent unconscious incest wishes, the dread of castration is aroused, and intense anxiety and guilt inhibit the development of adequate sexual responses in heterosexual genital inter-course. In such instances the woman partner becomes unconsciously forbidden and is identified partly with the mother or sister in the drive organization of memory.

The phenomenon of fetishism, as Wilhelm Stekel[16] emphasized, is normatively represented in the contributory attractions at work in the healthy love-life of most people. For many persons a particular sensual effect or several such effects take on a dominating importance. A way of walking, a tone of voice or a special odour can become the basis of powerful attraction or contrarily of insurmountable repulsion. Such fetishistic attractions are the homologues in humans of imprinting in animals—that is to say, learning that occurs only during an early critical period and possibly as a result of only one brief experience. Such imprinted patterns of sexual response in humans are apt to encounter impediments related to the taboo of incest. Freud was clearly impressed with the connection of fetishism and pleasurable odours; again in recent decades psychoanalysts have become interested in the pregenital and more primitive aspects of object-relatedness incorporated in fetishistic regressions and fixations. In the sexual aberration of fetishism, the fetish replaces the sexual partner, and the tendency to repeat the forbidden infantile pleasure sometimes leads to impulsive acts including kleptomania and the secret collection of sacred objects—a kind of substitute harem cult accom-panying the depreciation of real women.

In all the manifestations of male potency disturbances so far noted there is an underlying castration anxiety or, more exactly, an unconscious apprehen-sion of injury to the penis in some instances equated with or reinforced by the fear of death. Associated with this underlying anxiety are a number of other psychodynamic factors that have different degrees of importance in different cases. Always primary is the influence of the individual's character structure as it is related to the pregenital organization of his libido—that is to say, the relative dominance of oral, anal, urethral, dermal and other body areas in the childhood sexual history. This history includes both the actual experiences and the fantasies with which early sexual theories are associated. These often have a profound influence on the later development and manifestations of the sexual drive. They usually consist of notions of birth by the bowel and a sadistic misconception of coitus.

Female Frigidity

We noted in Chapter 2 (p. 51) that Karl Abraham (1920)[17] pointed out that the intricacies of normative female psychosexual development left in their train a legacy of vulnerability to hysterical disorder and that this, not infrequently, remained on the plane of specifically sexual disability. However, there are other primary causes besides those primarily psychogenic ones for functional female frigidity. Thus Sherfey (1973)[18] insists that inadequate erotic stimulation is the most frequent cause of vaginal frigidity. Even so, just as male potency disturbances are often the expression of neurotic problems, frigidity in women is often also an hysterical affliction.

The general term *frigidity* has been applied to a number of symptoms of female sexual disability. Impairment of a woman's capacity to enjoy heterosexual genital intercourse may be partial or total, and partial impairment is a common symptom. In 1912 Freud[4] wrote that the adult sexual life of women, as that of men, was adversely affected by the prevalent conditions of upbringing in civilized society. He emphasized that the strong incestuous fixations of childhood and the frustrations of adolescence which impaired the sexual life of men also affected women. Moreover, women were strongly affected by the sharp contrast between the 'mother' and the 'harlot' projected by the attitude of men. This was especially the case when a woman shared this splitting. Commonly the outcome had a different emphasis from that in men. Freud[4] stated this as follows:

> In my opinion the necessary conditions of forbiddenness in the erotic life of women holds the same place as the man's need to lower his sexual object. Both are the consequences of the long period of delay between sexual maturity and sexual activity which is demanded by education for social reasons. The aim of both is to overcome the psychical impotence resulting from the lack of union between tenderness and sensuality. That the effect of the same causes differs so greatly in men and women is perhaps due to another difference in the behaviour of the two sexes. Women belonging to the higher levels of civilisation do not usually transgress the prohibition against sexual activities during the period of waiting, and thus they acquire this close association between the forbidden and the sexual. Men usually overstep the prohibition under the conditions of lowering the standard of object they require, and so carry this condition on into their subsequent erotic life.

As noted above, the Kinsey group[5] found that unresponsiveness in marital coitus seemed to be related to sanctions against earlier sexual genital experience and its consequent postponement. Because of this condition of forbiddenness women often desire to keep even legitimate sexual relations secret for a long time, and some women who are frigid in legitimate relations recover the capacity for full sensation when the condition of prohibition is restored in a secret intrigue with a lover. The commonly reported partial frigidity in marriage often owes something to this paradoxical need for the 'forbiddenness' that promotes maximal sensual pleasure by its correspondence with fantasy; should the 'forbiddenness' become unduly strong, however, frigidity reappears.

The following case illustrates a problem often brought to the psychiatrist.

Case 17. A 30-year-old married woman was referred for psychiatric consultation by a gynaecologist who had found no physical reason for the frigidity of which she complained. Since the birth of her baby two years earlier she had felt an increasing aversion to sexual intercourse, enjoying it less and less until she was overtaken by total vaginal anaesthesia a year before consulting the gynaecologist. She had reacted well to motherhood; there had been no problems with the pregnancy and delivery. Sexual life during the first few years of her marriage had been active and had given her pleasure. Pregnancy had been delayed by contraception since the couple were busy establishing a reasonable economic security. The patient had helped her husband in his haulage business as a bookkeeper and yard supervisor, and she continued to do the bookkeeping at home. The business prospered and took more and more of her husband's time.

After a second interview this attractive and intelligent woman arranged for three psychotherapeutic sessions a week; after four months she was treated once a week for two months more. She confessed early in treatment that she was involved with a young employee of her husband's whom she had been in the habit of seeing when she worked in the yard. Their flirtation then was conversational, and often carried on in her husband's presence. On occasional visits to the yard after the birth of her child she saw the young man again, at times when her husband was absent. Although he also was married he expatiated on how much he had missed her during her pregnancy; soon he began driving his truck to her home on various pretexts, and he finally appeared in the park where she took her baby. Romantic protestations and lovemaking that fell short of actual intercourse became the pattern, and although she was thrilled with her secret assignations she was worrying about them. It was clear to both of us that the advance of this affair was coincidental with her increasing aversion to sexual intercourse with her husband and the onset of vaginal anaesthesia.

The anamnesis in psychotherapy centred around her attachment to a formidable father who had found her an amusing and enjoyable child. In spite of having been acutely ambivalent towards her mother during adolescence, the patient pictured her as a warm and affectionate woman with whom she had identified. The transference to me became erotically tinged; in discussing this her adolescent erotic fantasies relating to her father were remembered. She saw that her husband's preoccupation and success in his business was like her father's and that he deserved credit for his achievement, although she missed his being playful with her now that his limited time for relaxation focused on his child.

As her transference to me developed further, her interest in meeting with the young man subsided. She decided to end her involvement and did so after talking with him. Her curiosity and erotic fantasies about me were uncovered following analysis of defensive inhibited silences that recurred in our sessions. Indeed, she became more concerned about her relationship with me than with the sexual problem in her marriage. The blushing, embarrassed silences were replaced by tearful sessions in which we came to discuss the stringencies of the doctor–patient relationship and its relatedness to the sensual barriers between her and her father. We also discussed at this time the equating of the psychotherapeutic sessions with forbidden and secret assignations; these were brought into conscious connection with the games she had played with her father and with her elaboration of them in fantasy. Shortly the sexual incapacity with her husband diminished, although it fluctuated as we discussed cutting down on the therapeutic hours and ultimately terminating them. Six months after terminating therapy the patient brought me a small gift and reported a happy relationship with her husband.

In this analytically orientated brief psychotherapy of a woman of basically sound personality afflicted with an hysterical type of frigidity disorder, the factors Freud called outstandingly important were obvious—the incestuous fixation in childhood, the postponement of sexual experience in adolescence and the need for a certain degree of replicated 'forbiddenness'. Equally obvious were her need for love and her anxiety about enjoying my approval as well as her father's. This need was utilized without being analyzed in this brief psychotherapy. This anxiety in women (that is, fear of the loss of love) corresponds to castration anxiety in the man, and the patient's frigidity in intercourse with her husband was related to self-punishment for the extramarital involvement about which she felt guilty and which she felt should cost her her husband's love. His reactions to her becoming a mother also played an important part in the ensuing daily marital interactions that led to total vaginal anaesthesia. In the brief psychotherapy of this case no obtrusive problems of penis envy found conscious expression. The hints of these problems that were evident to me were not interpreted at all.

In more intense degrees of frigidity than the example discussed above, anxiety results in dyspareunia (painful intercourse) in which the vaginal sphincter muscle closes tightly and obstructs or partially obstructs the entry of the penis into the vagina (severe vaginismus). This, too, may be merely transient, however. When it is more permanent the basic significance is usually associated with deep-seated guilt as well as anxiety; the guilt is connected with repressed sadistic impulses, such as revenge upon the penis and the man, and the anxiety connected with masochistic anticipations of genital injury. Even this severe form of frigidity, though often exhibited in relation to any sexual partner, is sometimes dissociated inasmuch as it occurs within the marriage, the marital partner having assumed incestuous meaning and having absorbed the greater force of reactions to penis envy; whereas extramarital affairs may yield a measure of satisfaction. Some guilt-ridden and vindictive women induce the husband to perform lengthy manual stimulation of the clitoris or oral-genital contact or both and in these and other ways demand excessively prolonged forepleasure to enable them, they rationalize, to become more receptive to the act of penetration itself. Often enough these rationalizations have been initiated or reinforced by reading, and often misinterpreting, 'enlightened' instructions about sexual technique in manuals. Analysis, however, reveals that *inter alia* these excessive demands are motivated by an attempt to disparage the penis as a pleasure-giving organ and that the rationalizations serve an unconscious hostility to and envy of men. My clinical experience supports the statement of Bergler[19] that:

> The opinion is false that the man must have a certain technique or even knowledge of perverse tricks to produce orgasm in the woman. The healthy woman only permits coitus if she loves tenderly too... It is true that the graph of excitement in coitus shows a more rapid rise and fall in the man than in the woman, so that pre-pleasurable acts are in many cases necessary, but this implies by no means that special subtleties are required.

The husband is in some instances further humiliated by his wife's infidelity becoming known to him, if it is not directly announced by the wife, whereupon she insists upon the sexual satisfaction obtained with the other man and blames him for his sexual incompetence. Abraham[17] described this type of woman, the revengeful or vindictive type, who encounters so many difficulties in erotic life, and he emphasized the neurotic manifestations of penis envy, perhaps to some extent overlooking other contributory earlier experiences of jealousy within the family drama which lend a paranoid tendency, or hostile world outlook, to the entire personality.

Involuntary contractions of the vagina are a sequel to pleasurable sensation and characteristic of full orgasm. The current obsessional concern of some women about experiencing a more diffuse rather than sharply focused orgasm is, however, often a disguised expression of unsurmounted penis envy which is misleadingly reinforced by some sexologists. An eminent woman analyst[20] has stated:

> The road to the feminine woman as a sexual object leads through the psyche, and all the four fundamental factors...must be taken into account if her conditions are to be met. Her inhibition can be strengthened by her narcissism, masochism, tie to former objects and motherliness; and each of these four factors, if present to an excessive degree, can become a source of frigidity. Especially in favour of the last-named component does the feminine woman often renounce orgastic gratification, without the least suffering in her psychic health. But even if motherliness is not involved, she often tolerates her own sexual inhibition without losing her all-embracing warmth and harmony.

While I would not agree that such renunciation of orgastic satisfaction is accomplished without a price to psychic and physical health, this statement does confront the unproductive and self-defeating querulousness of some of these women suffering from unsurmounted penis envy.

Helena Wright, the English gynaecologist, has helped many such women with precisely detailed and authoritative instructions.[21] These instructions include a mental preparation for a conscious intention to enjoy sexual stimulation which resembles the preparation advocated by Theodoor Hendrik van de Velde[22] and the 'sensate focus' more recently advocated by Virginia Johnson.[23] Wright and van de Velde both emphasize the importance of emotional rapport and foreplay. Helena Wright's instructions for genital stimulation are designed for the eventual enjoyment of vaginal as well as clitoral stimulation. Dr Wright insists that without adequate rhythmic friction no sexual satisfaction is possible for either man or woman. It is frequently the case that a man has learned his preferred rhythm in the course of masturbating and in previous experiences of copulation; the wife, cautions Dr Wright, must follow his example, discover her own pattern of rhythmic friction and then teach it to her husband. To accomplish this, the husband places his hand over the wife's clitoral region, keeping it relaxed and flexible. The wife can then put her hand over his and move his fingers in any way she likes. It is not necessary for her to think or plan, the clitoris and the surrounding sensitive area respond to touch. The wife is instructed in this situation to move her husband's fingers 'instinctively and freely' and to go on with the movements for as long as she feels pleasurable sensations.

Dr Wright insists that every wife who has learned that her clitoral region gives pleasure when suitably stimulated finds it easier to believe that 'one day her vagina might also come alive'. Edward M. Brecher[24] guesses that the cure rate is much higher among those women who are able and willing to follow Dr

Wright's guidance than among those whose masturbation taboo is so deeply rooted that they balk. Brecher notes that:

> Even more important, perhaps, Dr Wright with all of her moral and medical authority is assuring her patients and readers that sexual response to clitoral stimulation is licit—even in the presence of a man and at his touch. These indirect psychic effects of the procedures Dr Wright prescribes, I strongly suspect, are as important as the direct physical effect of rhythmic stimulation of the clitoris—though the importance of the latter should certainly not be underestimated.

Many women are afraid to lose control, to let go, and Dr Wright's procedures seem also calculated to enable such women to feel in control to a considerable degree, certainly until they have experienced the intense pleasure and beneficial feelings actually induced through full orgasm, following which there is more likelihood of sexual surrender.

On account on the one hand of misconceptions commonly employed in argument against Freud's libido theory and, on the other, of notions of imperfection, often heavily defended against, when genital discharge is not regularly achieved, it is useful to point out that the significance of orgastic experience, or its absence, has to be evaluated in its individual context. Actually, orgastic experience can occur under conditions of psychic disturbance, and certainly for both men and women it does not necessarily denote psychic health. Thus Phyllis Greenacre[25] discussed the automatic vaginal orgasm of 'latent psychotic' patients as part of a revival of an intense polymorphous perverse period. In early life the incapacity of the weak infant to endure overstimulation to which it is subjected can cause a discharge through many channels, including the genitals; and later vaginal orgasm may be readily elicited. One borderline psychotic patient in treatment with me for a number of years for symptoms other than sexual, and for whom sexual acting out was a problem, had intense orgastic experience in sexual intercourse. Besides oral deprivation, her childhood history included a vehement struggle between her mother and her constipation; she had been overstimulated by frequent enemas. In a paper which discussed defence against anxiety by means of libidinization, Fenichel[26] gives an account of a cyclothymic woman who used sexuality, as did the patient just mentioned, in defence against anxiety. One hysterical woman patient required only the sight of a married man with whom she was infatuated to trigger an orgasm. When he entered a room in which she was socially engaged with other people, the sight of him, walking in her direction, was sufficient to release an orgastic experience, interpreted by others as a swoon.

It is difficult or impossible to distinguish physiologically between the so-called true orgasm and counterphobic types of orgastic experience. Before drawing conclusions in regard to sexual normalcy, the context in which heterosexual intercourse takes place as well as the history and psychic life in general of the individual require careful and detailed study. Then it is possible to decode, as it were, the manifest sexual behaviour that becomes a further key to the understanding of the total defence and adaptive struggle of the patient.

Freud (1932)[27] pointed out that the girl's development into womanhood is more difficult and complicated than the boy's move into manhood. The girl has two unique burdens; the change to decisive femininity requires that the clitoris, the dominant erotogenic zone in the phallic phase, surrender its sensitivity to the vagina in part; and the first love-object, the mother, must be in a large measure relinquished in favour of the father in the Oedipal phase. The boy is required to make no such change in emphasis in erotogenic zone or first object-cathexes after the phallic phase. The husband of a neurotic woman, who inherited his position vis-à-vis his wife from her father, often comes in the course of time to inherit the mother's position as well, so that the conflicts of the wife's pre-Oedipal attachment to her mother are re-enacted in the marriage. Thus in many instances the later part of a woman's life is taken up with a struggle against her husband just as a shorter earlier part was occupied with rebellion against her mother. If the man himself is neurotically burdened with sadomasochistic problems, the consequent interactive hostility, partly displayed in sexual conflict, may come to resemble a Strindberg play staged on the domestic scene. Often in reality hidden from any audience and often enough 'expressionistic', since the emotions at work are inadequately represented in words or objective situations, the drama further unfolds in the psychiatrist's office with the complaint of frigidity. Therese Benedek[28] tersely describes an important aspect of this situation:

> Since the social and emotional significance of frigidity is different from that of impotence, women can use the suppression of their own sexual needs as a weapon against their husbands.

This behaviour is the obverse of the current preoccupation with orgastic deficits with which many women connect inferiority feelings; both of these polar attitudes (feelings of inferiority and the attribution of inferiority to the husband) may sometimes be elucidated in the first psychiatric consultation.

The Human Sexual Response and Psychoanalysis

Much recent work has been directed towards obtaining a fuller knowledge of the anatomical and physiological foundations of sexual responses, and some of these studies have focused particularly on the sequence of physiological events that culminate in orgastic satisfaction. These valuable investigations throw new light on human sexual experience and on the satisfactions and frustrations connected with it which are so important in clinical practice. Such anatomical and physiological studies must be integrated with the psychological aspects of human development and personality organization, however, before one accepts the conclusions to which some modern marriage manuals have jumped. Masters and Johnson[29] state:

> From an anatomic point of view, there is absolutely no difference in the response of the pelvic viscera to effective sexual stimulation regardless of whether stimulation occurs as a result of clitoral area manipulation, natural or artificial coition, or, for that matter, from breast stimulation alone... The human female's physiological responses to effective sexual stimulation develop with consistency regardless of the source of the psychic or sexual stimulation.

In clinical practice the effort to help achieve sexual satisfaction must also deal with mental conflicts related to problems of psychosexual development and object-choice and with the aesthetic and ethical preferences similarly related. Freud distinguished between two kinds of orgasm: one retaining features from solitary masturbation, and the other, more fully related to coitus, being promoted by vaginal stimulation. This distinction remains psychologically valid despite the objective findings of Masters and Johnson that all orgasms are physiologically alike whatever the sources of stimulation.

Socio-ideological Rationalization

It is necessary to draw attention to the destructive effect of a deep-seated, unconscious sense of guilt. Considerations of the momentous findings of psychoanalysis incorporated in Freud's *The Ego and the Id*[30] might serve to modify some of the sanguine assertions made in discussions of adult sexual difficulties. Freud postulated, on the basis of intensive studies of neurosis and of melancholia, that within the ego there is a differentiating grade that is 'less firmly connected with consciousness' which he called the 'ego-ideal' or 'super-ego'. He was concerned with the persistence of certain self-critical faculties within the mind, especially those not readily influenced by the current realities in the individual's life. Indeed, he saw the core of the super-ego as not only unconscious but more or less completely removed from the conscious conscience and often quite irrationally remote from the actual demands of adult reality. Freud[30] showed that the super-ego is formed largely on the basis of early personal relationships into which a child inevitably enters in the course of normal development. He wrote:

The super-ego is, however, not simply a residue of the earliest object-choices of the *id*; it also represents an energetic reaction-formation against those choices. Its relation to the ego is not exhausted by the precept: 'you *ought* to be like this (like your father) [or mother]'. It also comprises the prohibition: '*you may not be* like this (like your father) [or mother]—that is, you may not do all that he [or she] does; some things are his [or her] perogative.' This double task of the ego-ideal derives from the fact that the ego-ideal has the task of repressing the Oedipus complex; indeed it is to that revolutionary event that it owes its existence.*

Besides accounting for the connection of the super-ego with the Oedipus complex, Freud saw the super-ego as founded in the prolonged helplessness and dependence of the human child.

There can be no doubt but that we are in the midst of a complex sexual revolution. Sexual needs and problems are very much more freely and adequately discussed than in the past. Physicians, psychiatrists, social scientists and religious leaders express newly permissive views in publications and lectures which reach a public eager for information and receptive to tolerant views. The change has been so great that some claim that today there is less hypocrisy about sex than about money. The archaic punitive core of the super-ego nevertheless must be reckoned with; *this resists change stubbornly*, however readily the more conscious and evolved layers of the super-ego or conscience undergo metamorphosis. Thus many people, and certainly many of

*It might be noted that this double task is often the foundation for the 'double-bind' in the attitude towards sex.

those who seek psychiatric help, are unconsciously possessed by attitudes far different from those they may express, perhaps even in anonymous responses to a poll or questionnaire. Investigative psychotherapy, particularly psychotherapy that is analytically oriented, will uncover the persistence of attitudes (childhood attitudes) that have been verbally disavowed under other circumstances.

Case 18. A young married woman suffering depression came into psychiatric treatment complaining of frigidity with her husband, although she occasionally enjoyed sexual satisfaction to orgasm with other men. She had enjoyed intercourse with her husband at first but had become averse to sexual relations with him, and indeed had had less and less satisfaction from other men. She had become profoundly depressed. The couple belonged to an avant-garde group of intellectuals with a free and permissive life-style, and they scoffed at first at the notion that the sexual behaviour they rationally endorsed would involve any inner conflict. The patient felt that her marital frigidity, and reduction of pleasure in her extramarital connections, indicated the onset of physical disease; she accounted for her depression on the grounds of the loss of sexual pleasure.

It became clear in therapy that she hated her mother, who had in fact shown her little affection when she was a child and who had become as time went on so addicted to alcohol that her daughter despised and pitied her. As a child the patient had had a close relationship with her father, but she subsequently alienated him by her extramarital affairs. Her depression tempted her to drink too much, like her mother, and she sought psychiatric help on account of the unacceptability of this solution. Her mother, who had seemed to her daughter to be little interested in sex, had given her no sexual information. On the other hand, her father had discussed his lady friends with her when she was an adolescent and had explained that he needed such relationships because of his wife's coldness. Moreover he had early given his child every opportunity to see his body, often roaming the house in the nude and leaving the bathroom door open when he was urinating. He had also fondled and excited her in other ways during her childhood. In brief her childhood experiences had been both over-exciting sexually (father) and guilt-provoking (mother, especially) before and after the development of her individual Oedipal drama. The development and fate of the Oedipus complex had certainly been influenced by such childhood experiences, and the result was a conscious investment in the ideals of sexual freedom accompanied by a savagely puritanical but unconscious conscience that operated unceasingly and relentlessly beneath this veneer and negatively influenced first her life in general and ultimately her sexual life in particular.

This situation illustrates that that part of the super-ego based on early experiences and fantasies in infancy and childhood often becomes quite dissociated from later modifications of the super-ego. This archaic part is always only loosely connected with consciousness and is highly resistant to change, whereas the later acquisitions of the super-ego are less stable than the ego itself and generally more malleable and fluid.

We often discover in dealing with severe frigidity within a marriage that we are dealing with a partial regression in the super-ego (cf. Kelly, 1965[31]) and that this is largely responsible for the sexual inhibition and is associated with a masochistic character disorder. Basically these patients resist change, even in spite of their protests about having an enlightened attitude toward sex; in such cases nothing but deep-reaching psychoanalysis is likely to effect any considerable psychosexual change. It should be said also that some of the more severe masochistic character neuroses may be considerably helped by psychoanalysis without its having an appreciable concomitant influence on the patient's frigidity (cf. Deutsch 1944).[20]

Other Aspects of Frigidity

Since the term 'frigidity' has been applied to a number of symptoms of sexual disability in women, considerable semantic confusion exists about its use. Some authors have even used the term to point to the absence of focused and felt orgastic activity of the vagina when orgasm does occur and does convey pleasure. Such a loose definition has sometimes given rise to unnecessary concern; as a matter of fact, one may not always assume that sexual stimulation that falls short of orgasm makes coitus unpleasant or unsatisfactory. Some women report having been married for ten years or more and having experienced during that time few orgasms or none at all, yet they describe intercourse with their husbands as enjoyable. Others do acknowledge a sense of frustration or unpleasant tension when coital arousal fails to reach orgasm, and such cases may safely be considered to exhibit partial frigidity. Women who have some satisfaction in coitus in the absence of orgasm may be deriving gratification from giving sexual pleasure to their husbands or they may be denying their own feeling of sexual inadequacy. Such reactions may represent an adjustment to frigidity when it is present, and such a woman is likely to consult a psychiatrist only if other neurotic symptoms appear; then she may have an opportunity to ventilate her feelings of sexual inadequacy and acknowledge her lack of sexual satisfaction.

Case 19. A middle-aged professional woman who was unable to continue working complained bitterly in therapy about being frigid. The elder of two sisters, she had sought zealously throughout childhood and adolescence to please her parents—her compulsive mother by her compliance and her intellectually ambitious father by her school achievement. During her school-days she felt her father would have preferred a son, and she tried to console him by doing well in her studies. Though greatly upset at his apparently greater appreciation of the rebellious sister who concentrated on social charm, she continued trying to please him, even to the point of marrying a man whose professional accomplishment her father admired.

Shortly after her father's death she felt unable to work and saw her life as meaningless. Her husband, watching her withdraw as she mourned, compulsively increased his sexual demands; becoming aware of the 'as if' nature of his marriage, he responded with neurotic disturbances and insisted on frenetic sexual experimentation with his wife, trying to arouse her in all the sexual postures described in the manuals and initiating oral-genital contact, which disgusted her. It became evident in her psychotherapy that her life had collapsed with the death of her father, whom she had continued trying to please by her compliance as a wife and for whose favour she had competed with her mother and sister. Her husband's pleas for love while she was in treatment reinforced her contempt for him; he sought psychotherapy also.

Even this fragmentary account demonstrates that if a woman's background is such as to promote in her marriage the display of hostility and resentment towards men, sexual chaos can result. This patient's fixation to her father and ramifications of penis envy were significant elements in working with her. As her treatment went on it was clear that she fantasized herself as a sleeping beauty capable of being aroused only by her therapist, who in the transference replaced a grandiose image of the father. Her husband had some intuition of what the situation was when he unsuccessfully essayed the role of superman. Faced with the complex situation of a mourning wife who felt that through dying her father had finally failed her, he had at his peril consulted manuals on sexual performance. Unfortunately in this as in other similar situations the sexual impasse is but one part, however critical, of a more comprehensive personality disturbance that cannot be remedied simply by prescribing more exciting sexual ingredients.

This patient complained of frigidity in the course of treatment already undertaken for depression and inability to work. In contrast, many patients who present themselves with complaints of frigidity soon relegate this problem to the background as they discuss more basic problems, often generated in the distant past. Many parents cast long and even ugly shadows over their children's subsequent marital happiness; often frigidity is relieved by resolving early anxieties and guilts instead of by concentrating only on the present symptom itself. Thus a patient undergoing prolonged psychotherapy came to recall how as a child she had initiated sexual explorations with the little boy next door in spite of parental taboo and how discovery of these explorations had provoked an awesome punitive uproar in both families who had, she felt, labelled her a wicked temptress. These unconsciously active memories of a time when her Oedipal wishes were strongest had led to a great fear of taking any sexual initiative, even in appropriately feminine ways, and had brought about a passivity in her present sexual relations which precluded the activation of uninhibited responses that would allow excitement to reach plateau, trigger orgasm and be resolved.

It is necessary to discuss how much the male partner contributes to female frigidity in marriage. It would not be so difficult to determine this if one could take as a constant an ideal wife who had adequately dealt with all of her developmental problems, including pre-Oedipal and Oedipal conflicts, her bisexuality, her culturally reinforced feminine masochism and every other source of inhibition, including the fear of pregnancy. As McGuire and Steinhilber[32] write:

> Characteristically, the male achieves orgasm before the female and may refuse to continue or may have difficulty maintaining sufficient erection to bring the female to orgasm if considerable disparity in orgastic times exists. Three-quarters of males in the Kinsey sample reached coital orgasm in less than 2 minutes, while that same proportion of females had not achieved orgasm until beyond 5 minutes, with 12 per cent requiring beyond 10 minutes coital stimulation. Certainly some men fail to understand that the adequate stimulation of erogenous areas would lead to a readier sexual response on the part of the wife as Sherfey (1973)[18] indicates. However, in the case of the strongly inhibited woman such manipulations might evoke shame and guilt and hence further impair responsiveness. In clinical practice the psychiatrist will, of course, also take into account neurotic interactions between husband and wife in areas of the common life other than the sexual.

Organic Disease and Sexual Disorder

The above discussion places emphasis on the psychogenic aspects of impairment of sexual potency and of frigidity. These aspects are too often disregarded, and the hysterical nature of most sexual disturbances ignored. There are, however, not only psychosomatic sequences but somatopsychic sequences, and these may both occur in a dynamic circular system so that in any individual case organic factors of a primary or secondary, or of a contributory nature require evaluation. Even mild systemic physical illness, exhaustion and fatigue or pain from organic disease can cause transient sexual inhibition. Surgical operations, not only because of the mobilization of mutilation fantasies, are often responsible for transient impotence or frigidity. It is especially important to keep in mind that the phases of the menstrual cycle strongly affect the intensity of sexual desire, sexual behaviour itself and the degree of gratification it yields. Benedek and Rubinstein (1942)[33] made a detailed collaborative study of the relationship between endocrine function and psychological processes in women. Heterosexual interest is generally stronger during the pre-ovulatory phase of the cycle when oestrogen levels are relatively high than during the post-ovulatory phase when progesterone exerts its effects which include a shift of emotional concern to the body and its welfare consistent with the somatic preparation for pregnancy. The decline of progesterone production that is characteristics of the premenstrual phase brings about a regression of psychosexual integration conducive to hysterical disorder which, often enough, takes the form of conversion reaction.

Premenstrual Tension Syndrome
Many women have one or more of a broad range of symptoms, presently to be described, which persist for a week or so and usually cease abruptly or become mild discomfort at the onset of the menses. These molimina consist of bloating sensations, some cramping, acne, swelling of hands and feet, and heightened emotional tension. In some women these symptoms are much more severe, and nervousness amounting to agitation is present with irritability, temper tantrums and insomnia, succeeded soon by fatigue, lethargy and depression. Abdominal bloating and cramps and sometimes nausea and vomiting, increase in these women, disabling them and curtailing their activities. Headache may be severe; also vertigo and paraesthesias of the hands and feet may be complained of. Consistent with the decline of progesterone production characteristic of the premenstrual phase of the cycle, Dalton[34] has advocated therapeutic intervention by injection of progesterone (100 mgm daily) or progesterone administered by suppository (400 mgm daily). Sometimes, in very severe cases of premenstrual tension elimination of cyclic ovulatory changes may be beneficial, and this can be accomplished by intramuscular injection of a long-acting progestin.

In many cases the administration of analgesics, of diuretics and of pyridoxine may also be helpful symptomatically. The gynaecologist Eleanor B. Easley[35] has stated:

For dealing with cases of premenstrual tension, I have adopted the following procedure: first, I make the briefest possible statement about the normality of physiological changes related to the menstrual cycle; second, I state that premenstrual tension always indicates serious difficulty in adjusting to some kind of problem; third, I invite the patient to tell me her problems. After that, it is usually hard to get a patient to stop talking.

Easley came to understand that these cases were victims of the 'Rejection of Feminity Syndrome' in greater or lesser degrees. Similarly, Somers Sturgis et al.[36] presents evidence that emotional factors are invariably present in both functional dysmenorrhoea and premenstrual tension (often both occur in the same patient); he found that there are more profound psychopathological disturbances in severe premenstrual tension than in severe dysmenorrhoea, when these occur singly.

From these considerations it will be clear that psychotherapy is necessarily of primary importance in the adequate treatment of the Premenstrual Tension Syndrome and of severe dysmenorrhoea.

The widespread occurrence in present Western society of the more severe forms of premenstrual tension and dysmenorrhoea and their association with psychopathology of an hysterical nature shows:

i. at the least there is an overlay of hysteria compounding a psychosomatic problem;

ii. that such statements as the one quoted below by Ilza Veith[37] mar scholarly work insofar as this touches upon the present incidence and prevalence of hysteria:

It may not be too paradoxical to state that it was the intensified understanding of the cause of hysteria by leading psychiatrists during this century that contributed to the near disappearance of the disease.

In fact, east and west, hysteria continues unabated in various guises. It has merely been disguised in our society in new symptoms expressed through such occurrences as industrial and road accidents. Also many neurological illnesses mask hysteria which often remains undiagnosed, and this includes many seizure disorders. Moreover, as is evident from the incidence of hysteria in gynaecological disorder, this psychic disorder melded with somatic compliance was not so named by the ancient Greeks without an empiric foundation. Psychogenic pelvic pain varies from 5 per cent to 25 per cent of gynaecological patients according to different authorities in the USA.

Finally here it is necessary to note the present scourge of *Herpes genitalis*, so often looked upon as divine castigation for sexual digression, especially by young women. In my experience they often express as much hysterical type over-reaction as their parents, guardians and teachers, and require adequate counselling on this account, including reality orientations to the problem which is so often compounded by morbid apprehensions arising from exuberant punitive fantasies.

REFERENCES

1. Freud, S. (1905). Three Essays on the Theory of Sexuality. In: *The Standard Edition*, Vol. VII. London: Hogarth Press (1955).
2. Ellis, H. (1903). *Studies in the Psychology of Sex*. New York: Modern Library.
3. Krafft-Ebing, R. von (1886). *Psychopathia Sexualis*. New York: Physicians and Surgeons Book Co. (1931).

4. Freud, S. (1912). The Most Prevalent Forms of Degradation in Erotic Life. *Contributions to the Psychology of Love*. In: *The Standard Edition*, Vol. XXI. London: Hogarth Press (1950).
5. Kinsey, A. C., Pomeroy, W. B., Martin, C. E. et al. (1953). *Sexual Behaviour in the Human Female*. Philadelphia and London: Saunders.
6. Freud. S. (1930). *Civilisation and its Discontents*. In: *The Standard Edition*, Vol. XXI. London: Hogarth Press (1961).
7. Jung, C. G. (1921). *Psychological Types*. New York: Harcourt Brace (1923).
8. Trethowan, W. H. (1963). The demonpathology of impotence. *Br. J. Psychiat.*, **109**, 341–7.
9. Sprenger, J. and Kramer, H. I. (1486). *Malleus Malleficarum*. New York: Dover (1971).
10. Kinsey, A. C., Pomeroy, W. B. and Martin, C. E. (1948). *Sexual Behaviour in the Human Male*. Philadelphia and London: Saunders.
11. Eisenstein, V. W. (1956). Sexual problems in marriage. In: *Neurotic Interaction in Marriage* (ed. Eisenstein, V. W.), pp. 101–24. New York: Basic Books.
12. Goethe, J. W. von (1833). *Dichtung und Wahrheit*.
13. Dickinson, R. L. and Beam, L. (1932). *A Thousand Marriages*. Baltimore: Williams and Wilkins.
14. Freud, S. (1927). Fetishism. In: *The Standard Edition*, Vol. XXI. London: Hogarth Press (1961).
15. Ferenczi, S. (1908). The analytic interpretation and treatment of psychosexual impotence. *Sex in Psycho-analysis (Contributions to Psycho-analysis)* (trans. Jones, E.). New York: Dover.
16. Stekel, W. (1930). *Sexual Aberrations*. London: Bodley Head.
17. Abraham, K. (1920). Manifestations of the female castration complex. *Int. J. Psychoanal.*, **3** (1), 1–29 (1922).
18. Sherfey M. J. (1973). On the nature of female sexuality. In: *Psychoanalysis and Women* (ed. Miller, J. B.). New York: Brunner/Magel.
19. Bergler, E. (1946). *Sexual Conflict in Marriage. Unhappy Marriage and Divorce: A Study of Neurotic Choice of Marriage Partners*. New York: Int. Univ. Press.
20. Deutsch, H. (1944). *The Psychology of Women: A Psychoanalytic Interpretation*, Vol. 1, Chap. 5, pp. 185–218. New York: Grune and Stratton.
21. Wright, H. (1959). *More about the Sex Factor in Marriage*, 2nd ed. London: Williams and Norgate.
22. van de Velde, T. H. (1930). *Ideal Marriage: Its Physiology and Technique*. New York: Covici, Friede.
23. Masters, W. H. and Johnson, V. (1970). *Human Sexual Inadequacy*. Boston: Little Brown.
24. Brecher, E. M. (1969). *The Sex Researchers*, Boston: Little Brown.
25. Greenacre, P. (1952). Special problems of early female sexual development. In: *Trauma Growth and Personality* (ed. Greenacre, P.), pp. 237–58. New York: Norton.
26. Fenichel, O. (1952). Defense against Anxiety, particularly by Libidinisation. In: *The Collected Papers of Otto Fenichel. First Series*, Vol. 27. New York: Norton (1953).
27. Freud, S. (1932). Feminity. In: *The Standard Edition* Vol. XXII. London: Hogarth Press (1964).
28. Benedek, T. (1959). Sexual functions in women and their disturbance. In: *American Handbook of Psychiatry* (ed. Arieti, S.), Vol. 1, pp. 540–5. New York: Basic Books.
29. Masters, W. H. and Johnson, V. E. (1966). *The Human Sexual Response*. Boston: Little Brown.
30. Freud, S. (1923). *The Ego and the Id*. In: *The Standard Edition*, Vol. XIX. London: Hogarth Press (1961).

31. Kelly, W. (1965). Regression of the Superego. *Bull. Philadelphia Psychoanal.*, pp. 224–35.
32. McGuire, T. H. and Steinhilber, R. M. (1964). Sexual frigidity. *Mayo Clin. Proc.*, **39 (6),** 416–26.
33. Benedek, T. and Rubinstein, B. B. (1942). *The Sexual Cycle in Women.* Psychosomatic Medical Monographs, Vol. III, Nos. I. and II. Washington, D.C.: National Research Council.
34. Dalton, K. (1977). *The Premenstrual Syndrome and Progesterone Therapy.* London: Heinemann.
35. Easley, E. B. (1964). Marriage problems and gynaecologic illness. In: *Marriage Counseling in Medical Practice. A Symposium* (ed. Nash, E. M., Jessner, L. and Abse, D. W.). Chapel Hill, N.C.: Univ. North Carolina Press.
36. Sturgis, S. H., Meniger-Benaron, D. and Morris, T. A. (1962). *The Gynaecological Patient: A Psychoendocrine Study,* Chapters 2 and 3. New York: Grune and Stratton.
37. Veith, I. (1965). *Hysteria: The History of a Disease,* Chap. XI, p. 274. Chicago and London: Univ. Chicago Press.

DIAGNOSIS I

CHAPTER 4

Differentiation of Conversion Hysteria from Organic Disease

Approach to Diagnosis

Classic accounts of the major symptoms of hysteria such as Pierre Janet's (1907)[1] include somatic disorders and personality disturbances like those in some of the vignettes in the preceding chapters. These helped illustrate the aetiological importance of mental conflict in precipitating the manifestations of the disease, this mental conflict then being related both to the symptoms in question and to important aspects of psychopathology. Investigators since Janet have sought to limit themselves to descriptions of symptoms, then have tested empirically in follow-up studies the reliability and validity of the diagnosis so based (cf. Ziegler and Paul, 1954[2]; Guze, 1967[3]). Actually, Janet himself went far beyond mere description. An approach limited to phenomenology, however sophisticated the methods employed in follow-up, can result in misleading conclusions. As Alan Krohn (1978)[4] writes:

> Some descriptive approaches are limited to descriptions of symptoms, some to descriptions of personality traits found in the hysterical character; still others try to embrace both.
> The descriptive approach has liabilities. First, the descriptions are often, in actuality, rather vague. Second, the omission or under-emphasis of a theory of the dynamics which lie at the root of the behaviour described can lead to the error of assuming that two patients who manifest the same overt behaviour have the same ego structures and internal conflicts.

The positive diagnosis of hysteria requires an understanding of the aetiology and psychopathology of the disease, as well as of its symptoms; the relationship of symptom to leading conflicts and, more generally, to unconscious psychopathology must be elucidated. We will later consider more fully the communicative purpose of symptoms in hysteria, and the view long entertained that hysteria is a communicative disorder. It is, indeed, because the somatic symptoms and personality disturbances strive to communicate that they are often dramatic, presenting themselves to those around the patient and attempting to involve them. Gross paralytic spasmodic, and convulsive motor disturbances, exaggeration, diminution or perversion of sensation, or dumbness, deafness, or blindness may dominate the clinical picture in *conversion hysteria*. Amnesias, fugues and somnambulisms may occur along with somatic disturbances or apart from them in *dissociative*

a   *b*

Fig. 7. A case of conversion hysteria in an American soldier. On admission to hospital the patient emphasized his inability to perform his duties because of paralysis of the right hand. He complained: 'I cannot salute and I cannot handle a gun with this hand; it has to be treated.'
    a: The patient on admission to hospital. *b*: The patient on recovery, ready for duty as an infantryman.
    Case of Dr J. Lyle and Dr J. B. Rioux. *(Reproduced by courtesy of Dr Lyle and Dr J. B. Rioux. US Army Photograph.)*

reactions, as illustrated in the cases described in the last chapter. Typically, the clinically presenting features of hysterical neuroses may be subsumed as:

1. A group of clinical symptoms without an ascertainable structural lesion.

2. Complacency in the presence of gross objective disability (the celebrated *belle indifférence*).

3. Episodic disturbances in the stream of consciousness when an ego-alien homogeneous constellation of ideas and emotions occupies the field of consciousness and excludes the normative stream of consciousness.

A group of symptoms may be associated with a structural lesion. Organic disease can induce a regressive ego orientation and reawaken conflict when part of the personality combats the regression; in such a case the symptom may express exaggerated psychological reaction to the actual physical lesion. These cases serve to warn the physician not to adopt an 'either–or' frame of reference in distinguishing hysteria from organic disease. Anxiety may be overt in *anxiety-hysteria* when the conversion defence reduces but fails to obviate anxiety altogether. Sometimes anxiety residues may result in 'affectualization' (Bibring et al., 1961[5]; Valenstein, 1962[6]). This often is an episodic response to strengthen defence; feelings are intensified in the service of dramatizing the appeal for help and of avoiding rational understanding. Sometimes depression will arise as a secondary phenomenon. Such considerations indicate the impropriety of the view that symptom observation alone is enough to establish a diagnosis of hysteria.

On the other hand, Menninger et al. (1963)[7] seem to take an extreme position when they write:

> Diagnosis has gradually become a matter less of seeking to identify a classical picture and give it a name than of understanding the way in which an individual has been taken with a disability, partly self-imposed and partly externally brought about.

To 'understand the way' is certainly to take a big step in the direction of a positive diagnosis of hysteria, and when a classical picture is not evident, this assumes even more importance. When a classical picture does appear it provides the clue because some symptoms readily betray the inner nature of the disease if the observer is prepared to make relevant inferences concerned with identification, dissociation and symbolism. Moreover, the symptoms wax and wane and shift in response to changes in the life situation, especially when in psychotherapy they 'join in the conversation' (Freud, 1895[8]).

Charcot's (1892)[9] diagnosis of hysteria was based on the characteristic assemblages of symptoms seen in Europe in his time. He showed the impossibility of identifying a neurological *lesion* as the anatomical locus of the disease, although he clung to the notion of *functional* neurophysiological disorder. As the inner nature of hysteria is so conspicuously geared to psychodynamic processes, whatever the neurophysiological correlates, one would expect these processes to have an influence on the form as well as on the content of the symptoms. Since *pathological identification* is the process that may be involved, the symptoms are especially apt to mimic prevalent organic or other diseases, including other cases of hysteria in that particular time and place; indeed, as Babinski showed (1908)[10] some characteristic symptoms have been suggested to sick patients by their doctors. It is this readiness of hysterical patients to adopt symptoms that led to Babinski's (1901)[11] famous dictum that 'entre l'hystérie et la fraude il n'y a qu'une différence d'ordre morale'. He had not then quite grasped the full significance of unconscious dynamics, and was too much impressed with the patient's apparent wilfulness. Heightened suggestibility itself is, of course, related to pathological forms of unconscious identification.

Suggestibility based on identification results in a considerable variation of symptomatic form according to the time and place. Moreover, there are variations from one subculture to another, as can be seen within the United States. La Barre's (1962)[12] description of the snake-handling cults of Appalachia serves to show that hysterical behaviour is extensively and intensively shaped by the local culture. Even minicultures such as the Army basic training camps, not only increase the incidence of hysterical phenomena but determine the form they will take, as Rabkin (1964)[13] found among recruits suffering conversion reactions.

The fact that hysteria appears under so many guises, in different syndromes at different times and in different places, does not mean that the label 'hysteria' lacks precision. However dangerous it may be to use a label that does not take the progressive potentials into account, without its use the manifestations in question would no doubt give rise to the notion of a strange and unknown sickness. As it is, many cases of conversion hysteria continue under care in the neurological wards of general hospitals without being brought to the attention of a psychiatrist.

More specifically characteristic symptoms such as hysterical astasia–abasia (the inability to stand or walk although the legs are under control when the patient lies down) or the inability to speak one familiar language while being able to speak another, in themselves betray dissociative psychodynamic aspects that point to the probability of hysterical disorder.

Kraepelin (1913)[14] and Bleuler (1911)[15] showed that certain constellations of symptoms are characteristic of schizophrenic disease and provide reliable grounds for diagnosis. In schizophrenia, regression is more total and reaches deeper than in hysteria. There is a more distant and distorted object relatedness than in hysteria which to a considerable extent, cetainly in florid cases, disengages the person from current social and cultural moulding pressures. On the basis of these earlier investigations of Kraepelin and Bleuler, Kurt Schneider (1959)[16] identified 'symptoms' of the first rank that pertain to schizophrenic disease. Even so, using standard techniques of clinical examination and recording of symptoms, Wing, Cooper and Sartorius (1974)[17] found that only two-thirds of a group of patients diagnosed as having schizophrenia or paranoid psychosis had experienced symptoms belonging to a central schizophrenic syndrome; also the symptoms in this defined syndrome were not confined to Schneider's 'symptoms of the first rank'. Thus there are problems with the diagnosis of schizophrenia when the criteria are limited to surface manifestations considered definitely pathognomonic by any one group of psychiatrists. In two extensive international studies in which standardized techniques were used to describe and classify the symptoms of patients admitted to psychiatric clinics in many parts of the world, it was found that some syndromes were labelled as schizophrenic even when the defined central syndrome was altogether absent (Wing, 1978[18]). In diagnosing hysteria such difficulties of establishing a consensus on the basis of visible symptoms without adequate regard for psychogenetics and psychodynamics are multiplied.

Nevertheless, despite limitations, symptom observation is useful in diagnosing hysteria if the observer understands processes of identification, dissociation, and symbolism, in which case he will be led to engage in a diagnostic psychiatric interview.

Diagnostic Psychiatric Interview

The painstaking investigation of the history of the patient's present illness will reveal the aetiological importance of mental conflict in precipitating its manifestations. Carried further, the patient's history can convey some idea of his personality background, and in hysteria this will show characteristic features related to the essential psychopathology of the disease. It is necessary to relate chronologically the onset, perpetuation, exacerbation, and disappearance of each patient's symptoms with changes in his life situation, for it is such changes that evoke conflicts responsible for and connected with symptom formation. It must be emphasized that life changes are brought about not only by external events but also by the passage of time, which moves each of us from one phase of life to the next. It is necessary to recognize, however, that somatic disorders occurring in response to changes in the life situation are not necessarily indicative of hysterical conversion; and that psychogenic somatic disturbances not *primarily* conversion reactions can ultimately be caught up in hysterical symptom formation. An example will illustrate:

Case 20. A man had a compulsive need to clear his throat. It was learned from this patient, suffering with obsessional neurosis, that he had developed this habit at a time when he longed for the departure of his mother-in-law, who was making a lengthy visit to her daughter. After several weeks of habitually clearing his throat he began to suffer from pharyngitis, no doubt because of the drying and repeated minor irritation of the pharyngeal mucosa.

His pharyngitis was thus the physical result of an attitude toward his mother-in-law the full extent and intensity of which he was unaware, due to his habitual defensive isolation of strong feelings from conscious representation. It should be noted that his pharyngitis was not sought, consciously or unconsciously, and had no effect on the length of time his mother-in-law stayed in his home, irritating him. Although as much psychogenic as histogenic in origin, it was not a conversion phenomenon and in no way represented a translation of a specific fantasy into 'body language'. In this case we are concerned with a stirring up of a chronic affective attitude by the *visitation* of a mother-in-law, with no concomitant discharge of his resentment. The compulsive cough had unconscious magical meanings, including repeated but actually ineffective attempts to rid himself of his mother-in-law; but the resulting pharyngitis had no such meaning. Somatic symptoms are sometimes created more directly by aroused affects held in check short of being fully experienced—so-called 'affect equivalents'; for example, cardiac organ neurosis often begins as an anxiety equivalent although it may become conversion hysteria. In all these instances of psychogenic somatic disorder we are concerned with the reactions of a patient to changes in his life situation. The following case in an example of this:

Case 21. A patient came to interview in India referred by the medical specialist with a diagnosis of a 'paroxysmal tachycardia'. He had been first examined by a doctor when in an attack, and the doctor had carefully recorded the rapid pulse rate, the blood pressure and position of the apex beat, etc. Moreover, he had recorded response to pressure on the left carotid sinus (effective in lowering blood pressure and steadying the pulse rate); and he had recorded many negative findings. After this the patient underwent X-ray examination and laboratory tests such as urea clearance estimation. The doctor also advised a psychiatric consultation although the patient showed no overt anxiety except during the actual attack, and seemed to have a cheerful attitude towards life, as several other doctors involved in an attempt to diagnose his difficulty had observed. They had all noted, too, that the attacks began when the patient was 15, that they became more frequent for nearly a year when he was 17, then over a period of two years they occurred only about once in two months; after the patient came to India they increased in frequency, intensity and duration.

In psychiatric interview it was learned that when the patient was 15 his invalid elder brother had died from rheumatic cardiac disease, and when he was 17 his father had also died of a heart disease. His attacks had not increased in frequency in India until he was sent on active service.

All these facts were recalled by the patient himself, although his attention had not previously been directed to the coincidental connection of these happenings in his life with the onset and exacerbation of his symptoms. Of course, much more than this was uncovered in the interview, and the patient was able to make more than these merely temporal connections.

Such temporal connections between events significant to the patient and their emotional and bodily repercussions do, however, contribute to diagnosis and have value in treatment as well, since the patient immediately gets some useful hints from them. It is often necessary to ask oneself and the patient what it was that occurred at this or that time to affect him adversely; the question is usually posed indirectly to the patient, who may be unaware of any connection between his emotional disturbance and the appearance of symptoms. Such 'unawareness' is not fortuitous but part of the necessary structure of the illness, which may at one time or another have been the only possible emotional solution the patient had.

It should be added that such connections may be more cryptic that the ones described here; and the patient may be amnesic for the critical events involved. Often only apparently trivial events are at issue, but they have activated fantasy. A reconstruction may not always be easy, and may require considerable time or some special technique such as narcoanalysis or hypnosis. However, conversation with the patient often elicits enough information about the connections between changes in his life situation and the symptoms he exhibits to facilitate diagnosis. A patient who has come for medical help naturally wants to tell about his suffering. In diagnostic psychiatric interview it is usually wise to allow him to tell about his present illness and then to point out a correlation between whatever stress or traumatic experience he has undergone, and the appearance of his symptoms. This is done by tactfully engaging his co-operation in working out such a correlation, after which his general personality background may be evaluated.

As stated in Chapter 2, the predisposition to acquire hysteria is laid down in the early years of childhood. It is likely, however, that the patient will have almost completely forgotten his early emotional difficulties and struggles, and what he does remember may consist in unconscious falsifications or 'cover memories', especially in regard to those early and critical love-and-hate relationships with parents and siblings. To reach these more adequately, lengthy analysis is necessary. However, *the status and degree of satisfactory resolution of these inevitable early conflicts are represented throughout later life by derivative attitudes*, and we can more easily study the type and extent of independence achieved by the individual—the 'dependent aspects' (Flugel, 1921[19]) of his personality background as these have been shown in his development and attitude toward life since his schooldays.

The developmental process is beset with intrinsic difficulties even under conditions of optimum economic, familial and social security. At the beginning the child must be weaned from the breast, then learn control of his sphincters, become able to walk and talk, and to co-operate with others and make appropriate concessions to them. All of this involves progressively more self-control and self-reliance. He may resist to some degree what is required of him, and show this resistance in his behaviour—in anxiety or defiance, in a failure or delay of achievement. After infancy and early childhood, emotional adjustments to peers and teachers and more demanding intellectual achievements are required at school, and these demands may in some measure be resisted in similar ways. The process of 'growing up' culminates, in health, in a good adjustment to the three central aspects of life—social, occupational and sexual (Adler, 1929[20]). But resistance to development may be evident here also. Events occurring since one's schooldays are more or less easily recollected, and are readily available for a personality survey in the psychiatric interview. The nature of the patient's current and recent interpersonal relationships, and his occupational, social and sexual adjustments, provide evidence of the extent to which he has attained maturity. If he is encouraged to speak further of his past, the way in which he has met, circumvented, or avoided the successive problems of life will become apparent, and more light will be thrown on the dependence aspects of his personality background.

Even under optimum conditions, the process of development is one of recurring adjustments to ever-new demands, but in general it is necessary to study these adjustments (or maladjustments) against a background that deviates from the ideal; and it is necessary to study the deviations, too, which may not only take the form of economic or social insecurity, but also involve educational or parental policy.

The predisposition to hysteria arises very largely from undue emotional attachment to one or both parents and subsequent difficulty in displacing this attachment later. Over-dependence on parents or their surrogates is usually demonstrated clearly enough in the hysteric's 'style of life' (Adler, 1929[20])—in his ways of dealing with life's problems, and in his habits. For instance, he may not make friendships easily, find enjoyment, or secure independent occupation outside the family circle. His opinions may be largely dependent on his family's. Such difficulties may have found intense expression at school, and later they may be evident in a characteristically restricted choice of sexual partner or occupation, or by strong dependent desires. The patient's history may point to over-anxious or over-protective parents, or to early rejection as reasons, at least in part, for the over-dependence characteristic of the hysteric. There is usually little need to give the patient much direction in revealing his dependence; as far as possible he is allowed to tell about himself in his own way. It is well to avoid stereotypy in taking a history since it defeats the object of inquiry by disturbing rapport. The psychological tendency of the patient to repeat behaviour patterns in response to different problems in the course of his development often makes it possible to assess his independence from a sample; such assessment may be refined later by asking questions about critical phases. Although basic conative and affective factors may remain obscure in an early conversational interview, developmental success can be appreciated by the degree of independence achieved. Sometimes even the basic dependent and unsettled emotional relations to the parents are also clear enough in interview.

In the process of personality development there are interacting forces of correlated psychical and physical maturation and outer environmental factors. According to its own schedule, maturation inexorably follows an endoge-nously unfolding program. As Hartmann (1939)[21] has noted, in any culture complex there is an 'average expectable environment' that unfolds an exogenous programme of more and more differentiated expectations of integrated behaviour. Also unfolded are more and more differentiable opportunities for the various directions personality development can take.

During the time when the human infant and growing child remains helpless and dependent his need of protection and stimulation to facilitate the endogenous maturational program is startlingly great. An index of this is the fact that, in health, birth weight is doubled within the first six months, and trebled in a year. Correspondingly, the psychic demands of the oral phase, with which this period of rapid incorporation of physical substance is associated, are considerable, and the supplies to meet these demands must be as appropriate for the particular individual, with his own innate physical and temperamental qualities, as is his food. When these psychic demands are inappropriately met in early life, succeeding phases of development are beset with more difficulties, as is especially evident at critical periods.

The following case illustrates the way in which the personality background as elicited from the history offers clues about the nature of later maladaptation in adult life:

Case 22. An unmarried man of 35 was referred by his medical officer because of nervous symptoms. He complained of pains in the head and neck, and feelings of suffocation while lying in bed. It was elicited that these symptoms had followed talk of overseas service in his unit. As a child he was of a nervous type, and during his schooldays he did not go out alone after dark because of fear. He was timid with strangers, and did not mix very well at school. He was, and remained, very much attached to his mother. Because of trouble with his father, he left home at the age of 14, but he shortly returned. At the time of interview he continued to express definite distaste for his father. After leaving school he took employment as a shop assistant, and remained at home and employed nearby until he enlisted. He was circumcised at 21 because he thought this was 'healthy'. At that time he was given an anaesthetic. His symptoms of headache and muzziness, especially when in bed, were like the sensations he had experienced during the induction of anaesthesia 14 years earlier.

In this case the emotional dependence upon the mother and unsettled resentment against the father were clear. His restricted life and constant opposition to 'growing up' were exemplified at the significant age of 21 when he invited symbolic castration. He remained with his mother and opposed change but when war came he enlisted. When his fear of separation from her was again aroused by threat of overseas service he dramatized his impotence and dependence again.

In many cases of hysteria the dependent pattern of the personality background is often not so simple or obvious in the first few psychiatric interviews. We will later discuss more fully the views of Chodoff and Lyons (1958)[22], which challenge the close relationship adduced between conversion phenomena and the hysterical personality by others. Meanwhile, in order to begin to understand deviations from such a pattern it is necessary to take into account that the evident achievements in external adjustment may have the character of 'over-compensation' (Adler, 1929[20]). In such cases the patients have displayed heroic insistence on independence prior to the outbreak of frank neurosis—an insistence that avoided the mature acceptance of the interdependence and emotional mutuality necessary for optimum adult psychic health. Sometimes this over-striving for independence has totally alienated the individual from his family and led to similar problems with his reference group. In other instances, the patient has remained with his primary family group but has become the mainstay of the home; in many such cases it is clear that the surprising efforts at independence are over-compensation for basic over-dependence, motivated by deep-seated anxiety on account of the intense unconscious dependence, itself related to early oral deprivation or over-indulgence. Such patients remain unconsciously fixated on the early infantile object, the mother, in fantasy or in fact, and are vigorously defending themselves against this (Jones, 1913[23]). It is when the defensive formation is overthrown by events in the external world that decompensation and illness begin.

Case 23. A 30-year-old man began suffering from pains in his stomach after enlisting in the Army, and later had trouble with his eyes, especially when riding his motorcycle. He could not keep his eyes open, and complained that they kept 'screwing up'. An aggressive man, he had often performed in fairgrounds on the 'wall of death', demonstrating his skill on a motorcycle and earning considerably more money than his father did. He had always been a dare-devil, and amateur motorcycling had been his hobby from an early age. He was employed as a butcher and was the mainstay of his home. He was greatly attached to his mother and had never entered any continuing relationship with another woman. In conversation he made it clear that he was ready for anything in the Army, and could perform wonders on his motorcycle were it not for the trouble with his eyes.

It is this basic over-dependence, whether masked or evident, that makes the patient vulnerable to intense nostalgia when separated from his family, and this is often the beginning of a severe neurosis or psychosomatic disorder. In the case of the motorcyclist, regression to dependence in hysterical neurosis followed the disruption of a conspicuous defence in 'identification with the aggressor' (Anna Freud, 1936[24]), which, together with other counterphobic defences, had formerly protected him from the emergence of castration anxiety. This anxiety was all the more intense because of its genetically earlier relation to his unresolved dependence on his mother.

Alfred Adler (1924)[25] emphasized that the subjective significance of events depends very much on the individual's lifestyle and the ways in which he adapts in order to achieve his goals. He maintained that in neurosis these ways become excessively saturated with techniques for securing power over others and thus militate against social cooperation. He found that, in general, a lifestyle is formed by the manifold techniques the individual uses to handle the special problems of his early experience in the family. He routinely asked each of his patients to report his earliest memory, which always revealed his lifestyle. This information could then be supplemented by additional early memories concerning the parents and siblings. Thus considerations of the patient's lifestyle in general, and of his earliest available memories, are important in the diagnostic interview. Adler (1924[26]; 1917[27]) emphasized, moreover, that the patient often had a specific organ vulnerability because of the inferiority of an organ of his body, and that this deficiency was elaborated in his self-image; it gave rise to the notion of defective functioning of a body part, and led to attempts at compensation. Over-compensation occurred in neurosis, and could be discerned in the lifestyle; sometimes, indeed, notions of defective function were expressed in hysterical conversion reactions. In emphasizing the 'over-compensation' of neurosis, and in suggesting reaction formation and the turning of aggression against the self, Adler pioneered the exploration of ego defence mechanisms that were more systematically investigated later in the main stream of psychoanalysis. In the hysterical character, feelings and fantasies related to severe dependency and inferiority are inextricably intertwined and sometimes over-compensated for in grandiose histrionics; and a notion of the inferiority of one part of the body may provide the focus for a hysterical flight into illness.

David Shapiro (1965)[28] considered ways of thinking and perceiving, and of experiencing emotions, modes of subjective experience in general, and modes of activity that are associated with various pathologies. He described the hysterical style as impressionistic and global; that is, the cognitive experience of the hysteric is not one of sharply observed facts and developed judgements, but of quick hunches and impressions. People with this style are suggestible and easily carried away by their impressions. The relative insufficiency of complex cognitive integration seen here has a parallel, according to Shapiro, in the immediacy and peremptoriness of affect, which can appear in veritable explosions of emotion. His description of the hysterical style—the global perceptual manner, the impressionistic grouping of constructs, and the experience of being periodically at the mercy of emotions—is complementary to the earlier descriptions of the defence mechanisms of denial and faulty repression by Breuer and Freud (1895)[29] and other psychoanalysts. Moreover, the same mode of inadequate integration of cognitive and emotional experience only too readily becomes a prelude to the more marked alterations of consciousness known as hypnoid states, which may be identified as the vagaries of the hysterical personality's history unfolds. Shapiro's work on the vague hysterical cognitive style indicates that the hysterical personality thus handles unacceptable thoughts and feelings by regarding himself as being visited by them. Krohn (1978)[4] interprets this as an active ego strategy promoting a 'myth of passivity'. Similarly, Leslie Farber (1966)[30] maintains that the hysteric feels that he is being acted upon, and thus absolves himself of wilful interest although his actual behaviour is overwhelmingly wilful. Farber thus recognizes the same paradox of the hysterical ego that Shapiro and Krohn described. He writes:

> Returning to seduction, once the partner commits himself sexually, he will find another goal in fending off that commitment. The will's nimbleness in shifting goals has been aptly called 'teasing', the organ prefix depending on the sex of the partner.

It is possible in diagnostic interview to enlarge understanding of the patient and of his illness by a consideration of the neurotic traits he has evinced during the developmental process. These may be considered as merely underlining the resistance to growing up and becoming more self-reliant, with more self-control and initiative at certain periods of life. The patient may draw attention to these traits himself, especially if they have given him trouble; or he can be asked directly about them after he has completed his story. The neurotic traits commonly encountered in hysteria as well as in other frank neuroses are:

1. Fear of the dark.
2. Nail-biting.

3. Nightmares.
4. Bed-wetting.
5. Sleep-talking, bruxism; teeth grinding.
6. Sleepwalking.
7. Temper tantrums.
8. Stammering.
9. Faints.
10. Phobias about animals, crowds, inanimate objects, places, special situations, or fights.
11. Somatic reactions such as headaches, stomach aches, skin trouble, asthmatic attacks, etc.
12. Proneness to experience delirium with common infections.
13. Excessive auto-erotic activity such as masturbation, or tics.
14. Excessive day-dreaming.

These may be marked behaviour patterns during childhood and adolescence and even persist into adult life. It is the prominence or persistence of some of these psychological growing pains in the anamnesis of the patient that lends support to a diagnosis of hysteria. Any one of them may at one time have assumed great importance, becoming symptoms of a definitive neurosis.

It is desirable to elicit from the patient as far as he is able to reconsider it the history of any previous frank neurosis. A previous illness, of which he may speak in the most general terms, may be quite obviously evidence of neurosis, and a report of it may lead to fuller investigation along psychological lines of the present illness. An example:

Case 24. A patient with backache and restricted movement of his spine had undergone very thorough physical examination. X-rays showed evidence of arthritis and the patient grew progressively worse after being told about this. A preliminary interview disclosed that the patient had had temporary loss of sensation in his hand and wrist. Managed psychologically, he showed remarkable improvement. In this case the deleterious effect of iatrogenic suggestion was only too obvious; since he was able to gain full movement of his spine, and freedom from pain, the arthritic spicules shown in his X-ray had little pathogenic significance. That such was the case was first suggested by his account of 'glove' anaesthesia.

The patient's family and hereditary history are important in diagnosis. A family history of nervous instability is undoubtedly important in the weighing of probabilities that goes into the establishment of a clinical diagnosis, but this statement needs qualification because the inquiry and its reply are in this connection somewhat different from the usual medical question and answer. First, as noted, the view the patient retains of his parents and siblings can help in diagnosis; his attitude toward their diseases or death, for example, may be very complex-ridden indeed, so the doctor would often be ill-advised to accept the patient's notion of a legacy of woe. It often happens that this aspect of the history is more cogent than any theory of constitution, and the patient's identifications in hysteria may have a decisive effect on the way his neurotic conflict is expressed. At the start of this chapter I described a patient whose symptoms involved the heart, and whose brother and father had both died of organic cardiac disease.

As already noted in Chapter 1, however, Charcot and Marie (1892)[9] emphasized the geno-genic origins of vulnerability to hysterical disorder, writing frequently of morbid inheritance. According to Eysenck (1982)[31], hysterics typically score high on the personality dimensions of extraversion and neuroticism as measured by psychodiagnostic tests. Linford Rees (1973)[32] found that both male and female hysterics usually show the typical extravert body-build (eurymorph). Since physique is strongly determined by geno-genic factors, this finding strengthens the view linking hereditary predisposition, extraversion and hysteria. It is of course necessary to transcend the early nineteenth century disputes between the *Somatiker* and the *Psychiker*, as the two main psychiatric trends were designated in Germany. This was already accomplished early on in regard to hysteria by Moritz Benedikt (1892)[33] who restated his theory of hysteria in 1892, maintaining that its basis consisted of an inborn and acquired vulnerability of the nervous system, but that its actual cause in both men and women was either a psychic trauma or a functional disturbance of the genital system or the sexual life. As far as women were concerned, Benedikt reported that they carefully kept their sexual life secret from their relatives and their family doctors and on this account required special efforts in psychotherapy.

The Table opposite gives a résumé of the requirements in history-taking for the diagnosis of hysteria. No scheme can be rigidly followed, nor should it be, but the data required for diagnosis are indicated. A diagnostic interview may, of course, have to be fragmented, and more than one distributive discussion may be needed to elicit the data needed. The Figure opposite represents some major aspects of the psycho-dynamics involved in hysteria, and may be useful as a frame of reference in history taking when the possibility of conversion reaction is in question.*

The following account of a case shows how the diagnosis of hysteria can sometimes be established on positive grounds from a point of view that relates symptoms, aetiology and psychopathology.

Case 25. The patient, aged 59, complained of paralysis of the left leg and weakness of the left arm. His left upper and lower limbs were slightly spastic, and when he was encouraged to flex the left thigh at the hip joint, the antagonistic muscles went into increased spasm. The patient was next required to raise himself into the sitting position in bed, his arms being folded and his legs separated. Under these conditions the paralysed left leg remained firmly on the bed (Babinski's 'second sign' negative). The plantar reflex was flexor (Babinski's sign negative), and the tendon reflexes were present on both sides, and equal.

It was ascertained in discussion that his illness began during the bombing of London and necessitated his leaving the city and giving up his work. He said that he had been very fearful during the bombing, but that giving up his work had been quite a serious matter as he was approaching the time for retirement on a full pension. It was disclosed that his father had died in his eighties of cerebral thrombosis with left-sided paralysis. No further information was obtained in distributive discussion as he remained convinced that his illness was organic, and that further discussion along psychological lines was

---

*For further study of the initial evaluation of the patient the reader is referred to the work of Drs Ian Stevenson and William Sheppe (1959) on the interview in the *American Handbook of Psychiatry*, p. 34.

Table 4.1. Directive Scheme for History-Taking in Diagnostic Interview*

1. Present illness:
   a. Consideration of chronological correlations of onset and exacerbation of symptoms with changes in life situation (or traumatic experiences).
   b. Consideration of conflicts evoked by such changes in life situation. The connections of these conflicts with particular symptoms as far as can be consciously disclosed in discussions by the patient when his attention is directed thereto.
2. Personality background:
   a. Dependence aspects:
      i. Nature of current interpersonal relationships, especially family and affianced.
      ii. Current occupational, social, and sexual adjustment, including recreational and cultural interests.
      iii. Employment and school record and achievement.
   b. Neurotic traits:
      Predominant type, time of appearance, disappearance, or persistence.
   c. Previous nervous breakdown: type, correlation with life situation at that time.
3. Family and hereditary history, and the patient's view of it.

*Reproduced by permission of the publishers, from D. W. Abse, *The Diagnosis of Hysteria.* Bristol: Wright (1950).

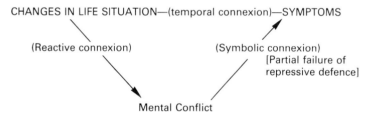

CHANGES IN LIFE SITUATION—(temporal connexion)—SYMPTOMS

(Reactive connexion)   (Symbolic connexion)
                            [Partial failure of
                            repressive defence]

Mental Conflict

Predisposing personality background, including basic over-dependence, neurotic traits, and other disturbances in individuation.

(Other associative connexions)

Arousal of childhood conflicts, especially those of Oedipal phase of development, and of early experiences and fantasies.

Fig. 8. Diagram representing some important aspects of psychodynamics in hysteria. The symptoms are a regressive expression of the conflicts aroused in autoplastic symbolic language. The contents of the conflicts, specific sexual and aggressive wishes, and counter forces of conscience with associated fantasies, are condensed in the symptoms.

valueless. However, he admitted feeling depressed and ascribed this feeling to his physical disability. Later, having made no progress, he was interviewed again, and he then consented to the use of sodium amytal, given intravenously, for psychological exploration. Under narcosis he prayed for forgiveness of his sins, and told about using contraceptives during his married life since the birth of his second son 25 years earlier; doctors had advised against having further children because of his wife's ill health, so although contraception was against his religious convictions and those of his father, he practised it. He also spoke of struggling with masturbation before he married, and wept bitterly. It became clear that he felt that he had committed grave sins for which he felt he should be punished, and that he did not feel entitled to enjoy his retirement as his father had enjoyed his. During the bombing he felt convinced that retribution was at hand. In further discussions without narcosis, he at first denied any sense of having done wrong, and defended his conduct during his marriage on the grounds that he had to think of his wife's health, and that in any case he was quite satisfied with two boys, etc. He appeared quite reasonable in his attitude toward his sexual problems. He admitted having spoken in public against contraception in any form, however, and went on to talk of the moral dangers involved.

An interview with his wife disclosed his great dependence on her in all respects, including his incapacity for making decisions without her. Moreover, she reported that on their honeymoon 30 years earlier her husband's worry about the possibility of having cancer had marred their happiness.

In this case the symptoms were characteristic of hysteria; there was a temporal connection between the onset of the patient's paralysis and the stress of bombing. A conflict of a sexual nature evoked by this stress was uncovered, and the meaning of the symptoms became clear. Moreover, his personality background showed evidence of over-dependence and neurotic traits, the latter presenting briefly in the form of hypochondriasis at the time of his marriage, which, incidentally, he had postponed for some time.

Differentiation from Organic Disease

After this discussion of the clinical psychiatric methods by which it is usually possible in short-contact work to establish a diagnosis of hysteria, the differentiation of the disease from organic disease now requires consideration.

Hysteria is a great imitator, and in order to avoid confusing it with organic disease it is necessary to grasp its characteristics, as well as to be familiar with organic disease patterns. As noted, the characteristics of hysteria are usually elicited readily in the taking of an adequate history. Thus, hysterical spasm of abdominal muscles can be detected whether it simulates pregnancy (pseudocyesis), new growth (phantom tumour), or other organic abdominal conditions. Besides, in such cases the results of physical investigation either are negative or yield discrepant data, so even if only a cursory history is obtained at first, it is likely to be amplified and refined later by adequate psychological investigation, provided that the possibility of hysteria and/or psychosomatic disturbance is borne in mind. Differentiation may be more difficult in other cases, examples of which will be discussed. But it is first necessary to remark on the fact that hysteria and/or psychosomatic disturbances and organic disease may be simultaneously present and have determinants that are only partially separable. Often there is a definite inter-relationship, as the following case will demonstrate.

Case 26. During World War II a middle-aged suburban housewife came for interview at the psychiatric outpatient department of a London hospital. She complained of progressive loss of weight, breathlessness on exertion, depression and other symptoms. She explained that she had no one else for whom to cook since her husband and son went away on service, and that consequently she had eaten little over a long time. She believed that she was tolerating the absence of her husband as well as did other women similarly placed, and that her depression was secondary to her physical ill health. However, discussion disclosed that her explanation of losing interest in food since the departure of her menfolk only partly accounted for her condition, and that her loss of appetite was an expression of her feelings of depression from the beginning. Since she had been obese, the weight loss was not a serious matter, but the pallor of her face and conjunctivae suggested the advisability of taking a blood count. This showed a secondary microcytic anaemia, and some of her symptoms such as breathlessness and anaemia were definitely related to this. In this case the symptoms of her anaemia confirmed her hypochondriacal fears and enabled her to transpose her problem to the physical sphere more completely, and to disguise from herself her inability to live up to a stoical ideal. She was medicated with an iron preparation and appropriate psychotherapy was initiated. This included encouragement to take up some active interest outside her home, and she improved considerably.

A severe case such as this, designated anorexia nervosa, is often found in young women with the ostensible desire to lose weight for cosmetic reasons, a desire that covers a deeper one to remain a child and to resist the changes of form associated with a young woman's growth (Jessner and Abse, 1960[35]). In one case, for example, it became necessary to administer intravenous glucose-saline to correct a severe acidosis; and in severe cases of anorexia nervosa multiple nutritional deficiencies may supervene and require medical correction.

In all such cases the physical changes are essentially secondary to the mental disturbance, as adequate anamnesis in interviews invariably discloses. In other cases the physical disease is primary, and secondary mental disturbance results in an overlay of hysteria. For example, it often happens that the mental stress of disability from disseminated or multiple sclerosis* results in super-added hysterical symptoms. In this disease symptoms are often more than can be accounted for by the extent of the lesions actually present.

The Multiple Sclerosis-Conversion Hysteria Complex

The literature of neurology abounds with references to the observed close association of multiple sclerosis and hysteria. According to Gowers (1893)[36], this association had been recognized since Charcot. Oppenheim (1911)[37] stated that disseminated sclerosis* was often mistaken for hysteria: he noted Westphal's recognition of a general neurosis that cannot be distinguished

---

*It does not seem to me that the newer term 'multiple sclerosis' replacing 'disseminated sclerosis' is an improvement. The adjective 'disseminated' designates more adequately the way the lesions are scattered in the central nervous system, and includes the notion of 'multiple'.

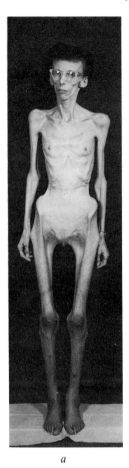 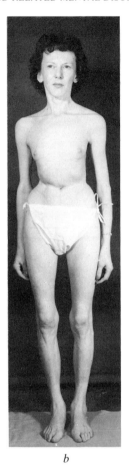

           a   *b*

Fig. 9. A case of anorexia nervosa. *a*: Shortly after admission to hospital; *b*: Following psychotherapy in hospital (patient of Dr Ian Stevenson at University of Virginia Hospital). Behaviour therapy, with operant conditioning techniques, was also employed in the psychotherapy. (*See* Bacharach, Erwin and Mohr (1965) in *Case Studies in Behaviour Modification* (ed. Ullman and Krasner). New York: Holt, Rhinehart and Winston, Inc.)

either in symptoms or course from the most common type of multiple sclerosis. Wilson (1940)[38] termed the early stages of this kind 'pre-disseminated', and drew the following picture:

> Experience has led me to recognize what may be termed a 'pre-disseminated' type, whose symptoms are still chiefly, if not solely, subjective, and where a superficial though perhaps natural diagnosis of hysteria is apt to be made. Complaints include parasthesiae of this and that kind, 'losing the use' of a limb or limbs, giddiness, fatigability; perhaps

also headache, imperfect vision, general shakiness. Examination discloses no single unequivocal sign of 'organic' nervous disease; heightened deep reflexes do not help should cutaneous be unaltered. But an abdominal reflex that can be tired, nystagmoid jerking, perhaps a few 'kicks' in the endeavour to elicit ankle clonus, and absence of defective antagonist inhibition in tests for muscular weakness, combine to arouse suspicion of a structural basis; and when with these a smiling cheerfulness co-exists, an early phase of insular sclerosis becomes probable. 'Formes frustes' of this kind are frequent in England, and numerous examples have been followed to a stage where diagnosis becomes certain.

Charles D. Aring (1965)[39] comments:

My quite personal experience including rounds with Wilson, makes for the observation that an undue impatience with emotional problems sometimes gets in the way of compassion. It is not for the understanding of psychology that we honour Wilson. Generally, neurologists become impatient with psychiatric patients... Those who have lived with these patients whom Wilson classed as a 'predisseminated' type are likely to consider relevant the publications of Langworthy [1941[40]; 1948[41]; 1950[42]; 1952[43]] and his colleagues. Rather than establishing a dichotomy between multiple sclerosis and hysteria, as implied by most authors, they posited a relationship between them. In their studies they noted the basic hysterical personality structure of certain patients with multiple sclerosis long before they developed signs of the neurological disease. A therapeutic programme was processed accordingly.

Langworthy (1948)[41] wondered if the origin of multiple sclerosis comes from the same emotional sources as those from which conversion hysteria derives. The florid symptoms of the conversion state are often not unlike those of multiple sclerosis, and they may somehow gell into signs.

Aring (1965)[39] stated that though it is not possible to say with certainty that multiple sclerosis develops with greater facility in persons with conversion hysteria, the association merits careful consideration. In any case, he contends that whatever the nature of multiple sclerosis, there is little now to offer the patient save the doctor–patient relationship. In this context Langworthy (1945[41]; 1950[42]) has engaged in insight therapy with a limited number of multiple sclerosis–hysteria patients. Aring notes that Langworthy's method, which he has partly followed, was non-directive, allowing the patient adequate time to express his feelings about the disease and whatever else came to his mind. Most of these patients keep anxiety well hidden, but as they learn to trust the physician they may be assisted in working out emotional problems with which they have been unable to cope. Aring comments:

Personal re-orientation toward their situation is one goal. Of course this does not preclude the judicious use of medicaments or physical techniques.

He gives an interesting and important account of his own experience with such patients.

The flagrant symptoms in this particular group of patients very nearly have to be ignored to keep oneself in equilibrium. In a sense one judiciously joins the patient in one of his defences, that of denial. In following patients with multiple sclerosis–hysteria over the years, I saw them frequently early in the course of their disorder. Later contacts with them were on a demand basis, the patient coming in when he felt the need for it. Parenthetically, some of these people know the term by which their disease goes, others have been carried along under another appellation. Giving patients a name for disease is judged according to whether it will be of help to them. Generally they inquire diffidently about this or that symptom or they may say little about signs that are quite obvious. I lay on hands in all later desultory consultations with a survey neurological examination. The neurological findings remain remarkably constant from examination to examination, although fading or accentuation of signs has been seen.

Once I have garnered a grasp on the psychological dynamics, I don't press for material. If it arises spontaneously well and good. With as humorous an approach as is warranted, I am accepting of everything said about relationships with key people in everyday living. Generally these people avoid discussion of sexual matters. They need assurance, the main assurance being that there is no one better versed in the treatment of their disorder than their general physician... My remarks are calculated to arouse little, if any, anxiety. I infer that their course is about what is expected. In summary, after I have learned who the patient is, his formative years, where he fits in the family hierarchy, his psychosocial functioning, and his previous physical health, I adopt what might be thought of as a neurological approach. It is gratifying to note that persons with multiple sclerosis–hysteria usually hold to an equilibrium that allows them to function adequately for many years.

Aring quotes and then criticizes a paragraph by McAlpine et al. (1965),[44] which is taken from the chapter entitled 'The Problem of Diagnosis':

A hysterical overlay in multiple sclerosis is by no means uncommon. It should be suspected if a degree of unsteadiness or apparent weakness of the limbs, accompanied by an unwillingness to walk without support, cannot fully be accounted for by the physical signs. This situation may arise in the early stage of the disease either because the patient, knowing the nature of the complaint, anticipates its downward course, or from the anxious over-protection frequently shown by parents, relatives, and friends. The detection of this overlay is important, since a simple rational explanation followed by persuasion and walking exercises often results in marked improvement.

Aring comments on this:

I would criticize two points particularly in this statement. The term 'overlay' has become a cliché generally applied by those unable or unwilling to look 'beneath'. And while 'rational explanation followed by persuasion' may be useful in the context of a secure patient–physician relationship, it will fail the usual practitioner. The secure relationship is the point, and not the method. As the statement stands, it is inferred that the patient is in control of the symptom. This is no more the case than that he is in control of any other symptom regardless of its origin.

One can agree in general with such lucid criticism, especially as it is informed by knowledge of the complexity of the relation of multiple sclerosis to the stress of protracted and repressed mental conflicts. Yet, however often clichés were abused—and this can frequently be the case in oversimplification—sometimes their reference to some aspects of reality has to be respected. Often in disseminated sclerosis, the symptoms are much more than can be accounted for by the extent of the lesions actually present. The following is an example of such 'hysterical overlay' in another disease:

Case 27. In regard to this case there was an initial error for which in extenuation the lack of time because of the pressure of the situation in which we were both involved. A soldier suffering from paralysis of the lower limbs was referred for psychiatric examination. This man was obviously grossly disturbed emotionally, being tearful and anxious. It was possible to allay his anxiety in conversation, and to persuade him to relax, and from this I went on promptly to induce hypnosis. Under hypnosis, suggestions were given that he move his legs. The doubt in my mind grew as it became clear that some muscle groups were not moving though others were, and that the extent of the movement was limited. It was equally clear, however, that this was not an organic paralysis *en masse*. Later investigation, including more thorough physical examinations, lumbar puncture and a more detailed history, showed that he was suffering from poliomyelitis. After a lengthy period he showed considerable improvement before evacuation home.

In this case the emotional disturbance was largely *post hoc*, and resulted in some degree of hysterical overlay that complicated the clinical picture of infective disease (Prange and Abse, 1957[45]). Under ideal conditions it is extremely unlikely that such psychotherapeutic interference would have been countenanced, for there would have been no chance of establishing a diagnosis apart from the infective disease. This would have been positively diagnosed on the grounds of a history of pyrexia followed by the clinical signs of a lower neuron lesion. Certainly enough would have been determined to justify a lumbar puncture, whereupon the diagnosis would have been clinched—as it was later in the actual event. In this case the hypnosis, although superfluous for this purpose, indicated the existence of organic disease accompanied by an hysterical overlay. It was at first a paralysis *en masse*, and subtraction of disability under hypnosis revealed it as one of individual muscle elements.

In general, an organic lesion of *lower* motor neuron type is one of individual muscle elements,* whereas hysterical paralysis is a paralysis *en masse* (Freud, 1883[46]), so there is little chance of confusion save in a case such as the one just described, or in the case of hysterical contracture of isolated muscles. It may be difficult to differentiate hysterical muscular contraction from organic disease, especially in the presence of injury in the vicinity of peripheral nerves. Hysterical contracture is not uncommon in children, and may be sometimes preceded by minor physical trauma inconsistent with the extent and configuration of the contracture. This usually occurs in a disturbed domestic atmosphere with quarrelling parents. Stanley Gold (1965)[48] gave an account of six such cases, stressing the importance of early recognition and prompt institution of psychotherapy in order to prevent iatrogenic reinforcement of symptoms by orthopaedic procedures. However, the possibility of positive diagnosis along psychological lines needs careful checking. In hysteria there is usually deviation from the facts of known anatomical necessity. In regard to this, it must be admitted that there is sometimes a tendency to segmental distribution as, for example, in an injury that results in reversible organic damage but is overlaid by hysterical perpetuation (the refusal to get well since the illness provides a solution of emotional conflict). Often a conspicuously extensive sensory loss is seen in hysteria, and sometimes this is in a 'glove and

---

*Of course, when there is a sufficiently extensive lesion affecting the lower motor neurons, paralysis *en masse* occurs. This is not often the case.

stocking' distribution. However, the patient may have special medical knowledge, or may pick up suggestions unconsciously conveyed by the doctors who examine him.

I have often encountered the expression of resentful feelings when investigating a case of hysterical contracture which is related to the muscular spasm psychologically. The following case is illustrative:

Case 28. A British soldier had a congenital supernumerary thumb, which 'got in the way', especially in the Army, and was often injured. He became excessively conscious of this anomaly and complained about it to his medical officer, who referred him to the surgeon, who agreed to remove it. The cosmetic result was excellent, but then the 'normal' thumb refused to move. The soldier was assured that movement would shortly return to the extent that had formerly obtained; it had always been slightly restricted in its movement because of a degree of malformation. Yet three months later it not only remained paralysed but assumed the position shown in *Fig.* 12. Since there was now no possible organic explanation for this the patient was referred for psychiatric interview. It was necessary to be tactful in getting his history since he was taciturn and depressed.

He had been a driver during the greater part of his time in the Army, and one day the truck he was driving collided with a car driven by a brigadier. He was blamed and assigned to other duty. He felt that the officer had been responsible for the accident and that he himself had been dealt with unjustly. It was after the accident that he worried increasingly about his extra thumb, and had the operation performed, with the contracture following. He had to be handled with care in the interview since by this time his dislike of officers included those in the Royal Army Medical Corps, but as soon as good rapport was achieved he began to speak freely and bitterly. After considerable abreaction of his resentment against authority for alleged injustice, he offered an explanation on a superficial level. He was interviewed again on the following day, and again he abreacted voluminously, showing considerable resentment again at the way officers had treated him. Suggestions were made about his returning to driving when he should recover, but there was no movement of his thumb or change in its position, although his general attitude was greatly improved, particularly towards me. On another occasion he was lightly hypnotized, and after this he improved to the point that within a week his thumb had regained its full potential of movement, and was no longer held in an abnormal position.

The deprivation of his usual work as a driver had resulted in feelings of loss of power and of resentment, and his changed situation had evoked an ambivalent conflict with authority that was symbolized in the typically hysterical contracture of his thumb. In my experience with Indian patients hysterical contracture concealed such strong resentment that it was often insurmountable, and it was seldom as amenable to treatment as in the case described.

In general, however, as noted, paralysis occurs *en masse* in hysteria, whereas an organic lower motor neuron lesion is usually so localized that the resultant paralysis is one of muscle elements. Observation of the affected part and its motility is usually enough to rule out hysteria in the case of an organic lower motor neuron lesion. Since it is movements that are represented in the motor cortex, an upper motor neuron lesion often results in a paralysis that superficially resembles that occurring in hysteria. The two conditions are then not so easily differentiated.

In cerebral paralysis, however, there are important common points that often clearly differentiate it from hysteria, as Freud (1893)[46] emphasized. Thus lower face paresis is common in cerebral paralysis, and is said not to occur in hysteria.

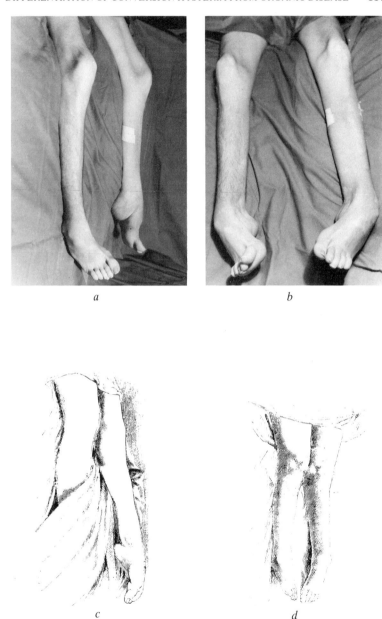

Fig. 10. *a, b:* Hysterical contracture of lower limbs of middle-aged woman, photographed for comparison with Charcot's illustrations *(c, d)*.

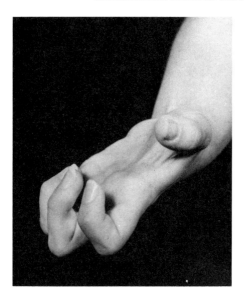

Fig. 11. Problematic contracture of hand. The 27-year-old woman whose hand is shown had painful contractions and fluctuating spasms of the left shoulder and arm for 4 years following the birth of her third child. Several weeks before this she had suffered a mild whiplash injury when she had driven her car into the rear of another. She had experienced some neck pains for a week after this, but this cleared up until after the birth of the third child when the symptoms became severe. Ten months prior to admission the 7th cervical intercostal nerve on the left was found to be compressed by a fibrous band arising from the first rib, and this band was resected with subsequent improvement of paravertebral and shoulder pains. However, after 3 months the symptoms recurred in full intensity. Lack of neurologic deficit led the neurological service to refer her for psychiatric evaluation and treatment.

It is noteworthy that as a baby she had frequent dislocation of the left shoulder, during adolescence had noted painful paraesthesiae and clenching of the left fist whenever under stress, and that she had been under increasing marital stress before the birth of her third child. Outstanding features of her personal history: her rearing in a family extremely solicitous about illness and marked dependence on her mother. (Patient of T. R. Johns, MD, Neurologist-in-Chief, University of Virginia Hospital.)

The same holds for hemianopia, as the hysteric is obviously unlikely to have had any understanding of the optic chiasma, any more than another individual without a medical education. Circumduction of the leg at the hip is also held not to occur in hysteria; it does occur in the case of an upper motor neuron lesion on account of the fact that extension and plantar flexion in the leg recover more completely than flexion and dorsiflexion. This makes it difficult for the patient to lift the leg off the ground, so circumduction occurs. The hysteric, on the other hand, usually drags the leg.

It is with these facts in mind that the following exceptionally difficult case is

Fig. 12. A case of hysterical contracture. The muscles of the thenar eminence are contracted. If the thumb is abducted against resistance by the application of 'force' it returns to the abnormal posture immediately after the 'force' is relinquished. Both the posture and movement are entirely outside the sphere of the patient's conscious control and volition.

discussed. A certain conclusion was not possible in the circumstances, but discussion shows the difficulties that can arise, and ventilates those points of value in discriminating between an organic upper neuron lesion and motor hysteria.

Case 29. A 40-year-old sergeant-major was referred for psychiatric interview, complaining of loss of vision on the right side, and weakness of the right upper and lower limbs. He had been examined earlier by an ophthalmologist, whose report was in his record; it told of a lengthy examination that had revealed no evidence of optic atrophy, but established that when suggestion were made under sodium pentothal narcosis, the defect of vision largely cleared up for a short time. Moreover, the patient's reactions to visual tests, including the use of coloured lenses, made the ophthalmologist suspect that the patient was malingering. A physician's report indicated the following:

'This Warrant Officer, aged 40 years, has had 17½ years' service and has been in France, Madagascar and Burma. Three months ago he had a moderate blurring of vision and was treated at Bangalore. He noticed some weeks ago a weakness of right side of face, weakness of right arm, and clumsiness of the finer movements of the right hand—e.g. in writing, in using a fork—and a dragging of the right leg.

'Personal history: Nothing of note but admits frequent extra-marital coitus. On examination: Well nourished but untidy individual. Plulse 70, vessel wall palpable; B.P. 110/70. Heart, lungs, abdomen, nothing abnormal discovered. CNS, pupils small, equal—no nystagmus; right palpebral fissure widened; paresis, right side of face, arm, and leg, with a degree of hypertonus of muscles of arm and leg. Deep reflexes

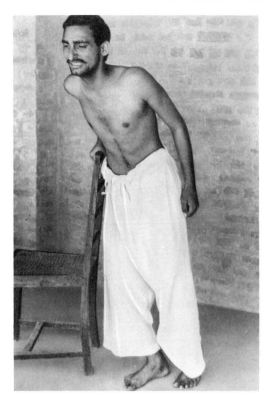

Fig. 13. Hysterical hemiparesis.
The whole musculature of the left side of the body is hypertonic.

exaggerated right side. Plantar reflex extensor response (R). No intention tremor, no Rombergism, no sensory changes. Gait, semicircular swinging movement right leg.

'Conclusion—in my opinion this Warrant Officer is suffering from the effects of a cerebral thrombosis (left internal capsule) producing a hemiparesis of the right side.' There was a further report by a neurologist, an extract of which read:

'... This patient shows: 1. Pathological pallor of the right disc; 2. Right-sided organic hemiplegia, with an exaggeration of deep reflexes also on left side. Right, PR ↑ ; left, ↑ ↓ . There is no detailed report on CSF. In the absence of headaches, the likeliest diagnosis is disseminated sclerosis.'

Later, cerebrospinal fluid showed no abnormality, and the Wassermann and Kahn reactions in blood and cerebrospinal fluid were negative.

On the basis of these reports the following considerations arise. One is entitled to doubt the accuracy of the ophthalmologist's tentative view based on tests with coloured lenses since it is a well-known psychiatric finding that the same incompatibility with organic disease is exhibited in hysteria. For example, Freud (1893)[47] observed total aphasia, motor and sensory, for a given language in a case of hysteria in which the patient had no difficulty at all in speaking and understanding another tongue with which he was familiar; this is a phenomenon unheard of in organic aphasia. Such dissociation is also exemplified to a ludicrous extent in hysterical astasia–abasia, in which the patient can move his limbs while he is lying down but is unable to stand and walk. (He is, of course, expressing in body language his childlike dependence and inability to 'stand on his own feet'.) A malingerer would not be likely to think of such behaviour, known to the clinician as characteristic of hysteria; on the contrary, he would surely imitate more nearly the picture of organic disease, and malingering would have to be detected in some other way. A dissociation of visual acuity with differently coloured lenses might well occur in hysteria; the patient might, for example, see better through a blue glass than through a red one. In fine, on the sole basis of the ophthalmologist's report of the absence of organic changes, alteration in vision following suggestion, and evidence of dissociation, we might well entertain the possibility of hysteria.

Since, as already noted, lower face paresis, hemianopia and circumduction of the hip are usually definite indications of an organic upper motor neuron lesion, these symptoms would be enough to make us sceptical of the possibility of hysteria. However, it happened that before the physician noted these features in his report the patient had been seen by another psychiatrist whose short report seemed to establish adequately enough for practical purposes her diagnosis of hysteria. Moreover, the neurologist added to the confusion by finding further signs on the left side. Such an extension of hypertonus would, of course, be possible in disseminated sclerosis, the diagnosis he made: but so would it be in hysteria.

On the evidence submitted so far, perhaps we would be prepared for a compromise in this case based on organic disease plus a hysterical overlay. In view of the low blood pressure, and the indication in the history that the patient awakened one morning after a deep sleep that followed a period of exhaustion, one would be inclined to assume that the organic element was a cerebral thrombosis.

It is an unpopular but established fact that human fallibility is especially clamant in observation. We so often see what we expect, not to mention what we want to see, and unfortunately this is sometimes true of the clinician seeking to establish a diagnosis. For the most part we reduce the possibility that we have subjectively distorted our observation by allowing for the refracting influence of our expectations; we try to eliminate error by repeating examinations, seeking consultation, and engaging in discussion about the evidence. The evidence so far outlined was therefore treated with considerable caution: the reader will be equally cautious about the observations I now bring forward.

In the first place, when I saw the patient he certainly had a facial paresis, but when on repeated occasions I saw him walk, he *dragged* his leg. In regard to the hemianopia, the first report caused doubt. At first I was concerned about the facial paresis. Was it possible for this too to be part and parcel of a hysterical representation paralysis? Conversation directed towards this possibility revealed that this soldier had been a nursing orderly for a lengthy period in a hospital, and that he had often seen cases of hemiplegia. This, of course, was not conclusive, but it gave one confidence to pursue investigations along psychological lines, especially in view of the previous suggestive psychiatric report and the conflict of other evidence.

Here is the report later submitted, with only non-essential military details excluded:

Patient aged 40 years. Service 14½ years. Recent service in India 10 months. Complains of loss of vision laterally on the right side. Relevant history: His present illness began in August, 1944, when on leave in Bangalore. The onset was sudden with blurring of vision amounting at times to blindness. For about two months prior to this he had been on active service, once running into an ambush when 10 of his men were killed, 12 wounded, and the captain seriously wounded too. At the British Military Hospital, Bangalore, a diagnosis of optic atrophy was provisionally made and the patient transferred to X hospital. There his disability improved to a large extent following treatment by suggestion, and examination revealed no basis for his symptoms, but the patient's reaction to visual tests, including the use of coloured lenses, led the specialist in ophthalmology to suspect malingering.

Gross insecurity in childhood on account of a drunken father; and later, when the patient was 10 years of age, his mother died and he was sent to an orphanage. At 16 years he ran away to his father's new home: again ran away at 17 years, this time to sea. After reaching South America he joined an irregular platoon which helped the Bolivians against Paraguay (the Murderous Chaco War). During this time he was hit by a sniper and still bears the scar of a bullet wound on his right forehead. After many months he got a ship to Canada, and later to Newfoundland, where he obtained a job as steward, and so returned to Scotland. He continued to work in the Merchant Navy until 26 years of age, when he joined the British Army. Shortly after this he married, his wife being then 16 years of age, and as he puts it 'properly broken in', so that he would have a home in later years. Service in India from 1929 to 1936, during which time his wife came out for four years. He now has five children. He was on the beaches of Dunkirk, and went through a 'rough and hungry' time. Returned to the United Kingdom in 1940 and volunteered to be trained as a commando. Later volunteered to come to India and came out in December 1943.

Altogether he has led a wild life, including much drinking and womanizing, but he has sought to be a useful fighting soldier. He has felt guilty about his conduct in relation to this wife, and its effects on his children—to such an extent that he has deemed it a good thing to die on the battlefield, when his family would secure a pension and he a glorious death. This idea has been active since the beginning of this war. It has felt that if he were to survive and return home he would never become able to settle down, but would be burdensome to his family on account of his lack of emotional control. Moreover, he dreads the onset of old age and likes to feel that he is still young and active, and as capable physically as men in their twenties.

Present condition: Of pyknic habitus with right-sided facial paresis. Slovenly in his dress and in his manner, with a suspicious attitude at first, of rather dull mentality, but when roused displays considerable aggression and his conversation is not without colour. Keeps insisting that he should be returned to the fighting line with his unit, and elusive in psychotherapeutic discussion largely on account of a primitive psychotic defence of denial in fantasy. He does not accept his illness as a fact very easily. Prolonged conversation reveals a conflict between an intense urge to make a heroic sacrifice in action (this to allay his sense of guilt) and his desire to survive. It is difficult to approach an understanding of fear with this patient, as he is so afraid to be afraid that his defences are heavily consolidated.

Opinion: My opinion coincides with that expressed by Major Sinha, I.A.M.C. This is a case of conversion hysteria in a soldier who has shown considerable personality disturbance for many years. In this case 'covering' treatment and management is necessary, as he would not benefit by, and would not be able to co-operate in, insight psychotherapy. He requires firm management and encouragement and should be made to carry on usefully in spite of residual symptoms. However, he should not be allowed to go into front-line action where his judgement would be likely to be disturbed (and this might bear unfavourably upon others) and where he would be likely to have a relapse (if he did not get himself killed). His medical category should be lowered to C on psychiatric grounds, and he should be posted to a training battalion and given light employment. In this way the onus of responsibility would be taken from his shoulders, despite his protests to be allowed to go into front-line action. Thus, the intrapsychic conflict would be less intense, and he would be able to make such reparation as is practicable for him.

Lastly, it may be added that there is no evidence of malingering, and such evidence as was apparent was misinterpreted.

The report concluded with a recommendation that in the absence of symptomatic deterioration he should not be confined to hospital. It was felt that he would improve after being discharged from hospital.

The reader will observe that positive reasons for a diagnosis of hysteria are adumbrated in this report: there was a conflict with deep-seated connections; his compulsion to expose himself to danger was of suicidal intensity and was countered by a massive defence in illness which made it impossible for him to sight along his rifle and fire it and which at the same time inflicted severe disability. The compulsion to expose himself to danger had resulted in his being sent back by his officers, who had good reason to see him as a danger to his men. Moreover, the outbreak of symptoms had occurred when he was energetically trying to enjoy himself while on leave. (He had been travelling about in search of a woman.) Lastly, his personality background was of such a psychopathic nature as to make hysteriform disease a likely possibility; indeed, it showed psychotic trends of a cyclothymic type also. In fact, any attempt to interfere too rapidly with his symptoms resulted in an exacerbation of his depressive notions of suicide, and when he was enabled to walk with some success this resulted in his hitting his head against every available obstacle on the blind right side. This was the reason for the mention in the report of his unsuitability for 'uncovering' methods of treatment. It was my opinion that were his symptoms countered too energetically, he would commit suicide—assuming that such a subtraction of symptoms was possible. Many of my colleagues, however, were unconvinced of any psychogenesis, and the patient was exhibited by a physician at a clinical meeting as a case of cerebral thrombosis.

No doubt in this case there is an *element* of organic disease. Even so this was a case of major conversion reaction, and it was hardly possible for me to accept the easy conclusion that there was a simple overlay of hysteria. The chronological correlations would make this extremely unlikely; while fate's providing him with a cerebral thrombosis just as he was building up for an emotional crisis that would require him to save his life by a heroic defensive illness would have seemed the utmost coincidence.

There is, however, another view more in accord with modern knowledge about psychosomatic processes. Sometimes in severe psychotic depression the blood pressure is lowered. At such a time, especially after exhaustion as a result of preceding psychomotor overactivity, thrombosis would be more likely. This may have occurred in some measure and was then utilized by the 'incubating hysteria'; and thus would account for some of the neurological anomalies. Far-fetched as this may seem, and incomplete as such an explanation must remain, it is less unlikely than that thrombosis should suddenly occur in a healthy man of 40 with no demonstrable organic disease. At this time I produced for the edification of my colleagues at a clinical meeting a case of hysterical hemiplegia of readily reversible type, the patient being an Indian soldier. The sergeant-major was examined, and his case discussed. The alteration in the deep reflexes, the sign of Babinski, and the sustained ankle clonus were elicited and held to be absolutely pathognomonic of extensive thrombotic catastrophe in the left capsule. The doctors were then invited to examine my Indian patient, whom I had selected from a large group at a neighbouring hospital because of the apparent clinical similarity of his condition with the sergeant-major's. In his case there was alteration of the deep reflexes, the affected side, as is the case in hysterical *hypertonic* paralysis, showing an exaggerated knee- and ankle-jerk. He also had ankle clonus but this was ill-sustained. The plantar reflex response was flexor. The doctors were impressed by the tendon reflexes and even in some measure by the ill-sustained ankle clonus. However, the consensus of opinion was that doubt would have led them to refer the patient to a psychiatrist. It will be noticed that discussion centred around the paralysis of the lower limb, and that the sign of Babinski became the last stronghold of immunity from considerations of psychopathology. Although I explained that it would not be wise to remove the sergeant-major's paralysis rapidly, since at present the illness was the only practical solution for his difficulties, and that any sudden freedom from symptoms would be fraught with danger, no one was impressed.

Feeling challenged, on the following day, after further investigation of the sergeant-major, I invited the doctors to a demonstration of hypnosis. Under hypnosis the sergeant-major relaxed his right limb and moved it freely in their presence. When this occurred, the doctors found *they could no longer elicit ankle clonus or Babinski's sign.* When the patient was awakened, he got up and walked back to the ward unaided and much more freely. Shortly thereafter he was sent to the United Kingdom from hospital, so I had no further opportunity of pursuing investigation of his case.

Discussion of this case shows the difficulties sometimes encountered. It is true that psychological investigation sometimes reaches the bedrock of the organic and is in a region where our knowledge is insecure. On the other hand, absolute reliance on changes in the tendon reflexes to establish organic disease is unjustified, though combined with other findings they are of course of very great importance. Further, clonus, though impressive, is even more unreliable in distinguishing organic from functional illness. As for Babinski's sign, there is doubt as to its *absolute* value as an index of an organic lesion; further careful research in regard to this is indicated (Lassek, 1944[47]). Finally, the apparent reversibility of physical signs, or the removal of symptoms by any method of suggestion, is not in itself a proof of the absence of a physical lesion (Mapother and Lewis, 1942[48]).

Myasthenia Gravis
Mackenzie and associates[49] found that 7 of 25 randomly selected myasthenic

patients recognized that their disease had commenced when they were under considerable stress. It would seem that similar considerations as those outlined above concerning the onset of disseminated sclerosis appertain to myasthenia gravis. Emery and Szymanski[50] discussed a case showing psychological symptoms for several months before reaching the diagnosis of myasthenia gravis, and regarded as 'an unresolved issue' whether the patient's considerable difficulties with her husband and mother contributed to the development of myasthenia. Usually the early symptoms of myasthenia gravis are those of drooping eyelids and swallowing difficulties. However, muscle weakness may not be evident at first in the eyes and face, or in swallowing, but may start with muscle weakness in the legs or feet, and cramping and weakness in these or other muscles. It is now well-known that antibodies in the blood of these patients interfere with the acetyl choline which mediates neuromuscular functioning. As with curare poisoning, the site of the defect is thus in the neuromuscular junction. Edrophonium chloride (Tensilon) is dramatically useful for the differential diagnosis of myasthenia, being a powerful temporary anticholinesterase. However, as in other autoimmune diseases, concomitant conversion reactions and considerations relating to psychogenesis strongly indicate that besides medication with durable anticholinesterase agents and corticosteroids and/or thymectomy, or other necessary physical measures, psychotherapy should play a part in adequate treatment.

As already noted, convulsive hysteria may simulate idiopathic or symptomatic epilepsy. Sometimes hysteria may be suspected on the following grounds: during the attack the patient is not completely unconscious; the attack occurs only in the presence of onlookers; the patient does not fall in a dangerous situation; the corneal, the pupillary, and deep reflexes are present; the patient does not bite his tongue or micturate; he becomes red in the face rather than blue or white; attempts to open the eyes are resisted; pressure on the supraorbital notch causes withdrawal of the head. However, it requires restatement here that hysteria and hysteriform conditions are manifest in many forms, some of which closely imitate organic disease of the nervous and other systems, so that symptom observations alone may be misleading. Where epilepsy is associated with the development of abnormal rhythms in the cerebral cortex, the electroencephalograph can be useful in differential diagnosis. There are cases with cerebral dysrhythmia that are hysteriform, as an adequate psychiatric examination will disclose. Since nature does not always provide sharp boundaries (Hill, 1963[51]; Kiloh, 1976[52]) between various conditions, pharmacotherapy and psychotherapy are complementary procedures in such cases.

Additional difficulties in the differential diagnosis between hysteria and organic brain lesions are sometimes posed when these lesions are situated in the so-called 'silent areas'. Parietal disease may result in bizarre alterations of body image, hallucinations of touch and spatial sense disorder, and may be accompanied by a denial of illness (Critchley, 1964[53]; Weinstein and Kahn, 1955[54]).

We will discuss psychosomatic disorder later. Here it is relevant to observe, as Ging et al. (1964)[55] confirmed, that some patients complaining of multiple physical symptoms have an associated abortively paroxysmal electroencephalogram. Such patients may be described as having an unstable nervous system, and they are peculiarly liable to psychogenic autonomic disturbance, with gastro-intestinal, head, and chest pains, and black-out spells. Apart from the EEG findings there is no evidence of organic disease in such patients, but they sometimes elaborate hysterically their periodic malaise, ultimately presenting with a *hysteriform disorder*, which will be discussed later.

Iatrogenic Suggestion and the Stigmata

It will be clear from the previous section that the nosological separation of hysteria from organic disease is sometimes a complex problem, and that hysteria and organic disease may be present concomitantly. The customary methods employed in the past to diagnose hysteria—namely, elimination of an adequate physical basis by means of thorough physical examination, and, more positively, the discovery of so-called 'stigmata', although useful, are often not only insufficient but may, when abused, even aggravate the disability. As Bleuler (1916)[56] stated:

> Not entirely unimportant, unfortunately, is the iatrogenic origin of neurotic manifestations. The physician solemnly diagnoses 'enlargement of the heart', whereupon the patient is frightened and breaks down until the X-ray photograph resorted to by another physician relieves him of his nightmare.

Here is the story of a patient, written out by himself on request, that will surely convey conviction of the possible hazards of a psychophobic attitude:

Case 30. Before joining the Army in 1941 I enjoyed perfect health and never lost any time at work through sickness. In April 1941 I reported sick with severe pains in my left hand and forearm. I was given medicine to drink twice daily. After a few days I lost all sense of feeling in my hand and wrist and the pains in the forearm and elbow became more acute. I reported to the Medical Officer again, and thinking I was trying to get off duty, he pricked my hand with a needle till the blood dropped off my finger-tips. He then sent me to see a specialist who ordered me to have heat treatment and massage. After about four weeks my hand and arm were good enough to allow me to report back for duty and very soon were as good as ever.

In April 1942 I was posted abroad to India and in the first few days of July I caught a fairly severe cold and when I reported sick was told to take some aspirin and a hot drink when going to bed at night. I did this for a few nights and the cold lifted but it left me very deaf. I was posted to a new station at this time and reported to the Medical Officer at my new station. Here I had my ears syringed out twice daily and drops put in. The Medical Officer contacted the local British Military Hospital to make an appointment with the ear specialist and by this time my hearing had improved quite a lot. The specialist asked a few questions and tested my hearing. No report was ever forwarded to my Medical Officer and as my hearing was almost quite normal again I stopped having treatment, and although my hearing is not as keen as it once was I feel lucky that I can hear as well as I can.

About the end of 1942 I was troubled with dizzy spells and almost complete black-outs and generally felt washed out. I reported sick again, and, after answering all the Medical Officer's questions, I was told to lie down and rest in a back room. After about half an hour the Medical Officer took my blood pressure. I was then told I would have to go to the British Military Hospital, but as we were very short of staff and had a lot of work to do, I asked to be allowed to go back to work. The Medical Officer got quite annoyed and so I went to hospital. The Medical Officer instructed me to tell the Ward

Medical Officer to 'phone him as he wanted to talk to him about my case'. I gave this message to the ward doctor. He came back from the 'phone and, looking excited to me, he made the ward boy double to find his instruments. He then took my blood pressure and said there was nothing to get worried about, to which I replied that he was the only one who had got excited. He then told me that the next time I saw my unit Medical Officer I was to tell him to get his instruments tested.

When I delivered the message I heard enough to make my ears burn for hours afterwards. My blood pressure was supposed to have been 220 at the first reading and 175 at the second reading. Now I am told that it is almost normal and I am told that blood pressure does not jump up and down like a jack-in-the-box. When after a few more days in the British Military Hospital I saw that there was supposed to be nothing the matter with me I asked to be discharged and was discharged the following day. Shortly after this work eased off a bit and I managed to get some leave which helped me a lot. Although I have had very slight attacks since, I never troubled and they always wore off on their own.

The next trouble I had was pains in my back. I can't be certain when they started. Sometime about November 1944. These pains gradually grew worse as time passed on, but thinking I had twisted my back sometime and not noticed at the time, I kept putting off reporting sick. In December we had a few more British other ranks added to our staff and I started training one of these to do my job. A little later on more officers were posted too, and when both officers and other ranks had a fairly good idea of the procedure and I could endure the pain no longer, I reported sick. This was about the middle of March. The Medical Officer gave me medicine to take internally and something resembling cream paint to rub on my back. This treatment was tried with no improvement for two weeks. I was then sent to the British Medical Hospital and had my back X-rayed. I was then told to report for a Medical Board, on 9 April. The Board down-graded me from A1 to C1 temporarily for three months. I then asked if I was going to get any treatment in the meantime, and was told no as I had arthritis in my spine and nothing could be done for me. Three majors and two captains saw the X-rays and all agreed. I reported back to work on 10 April which was Saturday. I carried on during the following week and with the pain in my back and the thought ever present in my mind of what the doctors had told me I felt bad with the prospect of going through life a pain-racked cripple, or practically so. I reported back to the specialist on Monday, 19 April, and told him that I couldn't carry on. There was another Medical Officer present whom I hadn't seen before. He asked to see the X-ray and after talking a few minutes to the specialist I was told to come into the hospital the next day.

I have been X-rayed here and after examination by the specialist it is found I have very little arthritis wrong with me, as only a faint trace is shown on the X-ray. I have been having heat treatment and massage here and at present I feel almost fit again and hope to get back to work soon. I have had the pleasure of having a few talks with the psychiatrist here. I didn't look forward with any pleasure to our first talk but after the first I looked forward to the second. I don't know whether the massage department or the psychiatrist deserves the most credit for my feeling so fit today. Soon I expect to feel as fit as ever, and I hope never to have to enter a British Military Hospital at any time in the future.

Little comment is needed except to say that the effects of iatrogenous suggestion were countered in my discussion with this patient after he had told me all about his wife and family; and that the 'massage department', as is often usefully the case in 'covering' treatment, was utilized in the suggestion therapy. Active movements, which he failed to mention in the above report, were the chief means employed in the psychotherapy.

It often happens that the doctor, in his efforts to find a satisfactory physical diagnosis, sends the patient deeper into illness by suggestion. Even if this lopsided 'physical' attitude is adopted, it is possible for the patient to get well, if the doctor is prepared to listen to his patient so the latter will develop a 'will to health' in order to please the doctor and show gratitude for his efforts. However, it happens that those who expect always to find a physical lesion are not ready listeners: moreover, prolonged investigations by a puzzled doctor confirm the patient in his belief in an exceptional illness.*

It is pointed out here again that a psychiatric opinion at an early stage may be an advantage in doubtful cases, and that a diagnosis of hysteria can often be made on positive grounds.

With regard to painful muscular dysfunction in such cases outlined by the voluble patient (*Case* 30 above), physiotherapy is usefully combined with psychotherapy. Sometimes this can be accomplished through 'Bio-energetic therapy'.[58]

Trygve Braatöy (1952)[59] explains in an important paper that on close analysis there is no opposition between psychology and anatomy in certain muscular disorders. A combined neurophysiological and psychological approach elucidates that occupational myalgias, the result of sustained static strain induced by particular work situations, are often also partially determined by emotional factors, as happens, for example in the 'arm neurosis' of office workers. The posture of such patients is often complicated by a long-sustained primitive 'startle pattern' that mobilizes the same muscles already overburdened from static causes; static and emotional factors thus overlap. On the other hand, sustained attitudes that make the typical 'soldier posture', and that involve overactivity of the latissimi dorsi muscles, counteract the complex of movement that the 'startle pattern' evokes in shoulders, back and upper extremities. This hypertension of the latissimi dorsi muscles, among other tensed muscles, thus imprisons primitive anxiety reactions, but may itself result in restricted movements and pain. Braatöy shows that physiotherapeutic treatment requires attention to both the local symptoms and the more comprehensive emotional problems of the patient. Massage and other influences on movements and posture may indeed result in unwonted talkativeness and a release in affective expression, just as the psychoanalyst's verbal analysis exerts an influence on the patient's motor apparatus and posture and thereby on his emotions and respiration. A sustained and physiologically inexpedient posture is often a reflection of character armour that includes counterphobic defences. These chronic postural alterations of the organism in cosmos are comparable to the suppression of acute anxiety reactions by gritting the teeth, clenching the fists, and holding the breath. Darwin's theory of emotional expression (to be considered later) includes the 'principle of antithesis', which helps to explain the postural alterations attempting to negate a readiness for anxiety in both an acute and chronic way.

The traditional positive grounds for the diagnosis of hysteria are certain anomalies held to be characteristic and designated on this account 'stigmata'. Those usually described are:

---

*On the other hand, the physician who habitually approaches the sick patient with a rigid, dogmatic, omnipotent attitude may sooner or later easily become involved with the hysteric in a mutually frustrating and anti-therapeutic interpersonal relationship (Casson, 1949[57]; Prange and Abse, 1957[45]).

1. Concentric contraction of the field of vision.
2. A feeling of having a lump in the throat (globus hystericus).
3. Pharyngeal anaesthesia, sometimes with anaesthesia of the gums.
4. Hyperaesthetic spots, especially over the lower abdomen and more particularly over the ovaries.
5. Sometimes the absence of reflex closure of the eye when the conjuctiva or cornea are touched.
6. Localized reduction or absence of cutaneous sensation (Mapother and Lewis, 1942[48]). Further, in status hystericus and certain hysterical attacks, usually convulsive, pressure on a particular part of the body sometimes checks the episode—so-called 'hysterofrenic pressure'. Also, in some hysterical patients pressure on some part of the body, usually a hyperaesthetic spot, will induce a paroxysm; this part of the body is called a 'hysterogenic area'.

Babinski (1908)[10] and Babinski and Froment (1916)[60] came to regard the stigmata as caused by suggestion. Babinski coined the word 'pithiatism', maintaining that everything that is hysterical may be caused by suggestion, or, literally, by forceful persuasion, just as he also maintained that forceful persuasion would remove hysterical phenomena, temporarily at any rate. Certainly, sometimes from the physician's expectation, injudicious conversation, and the general style of examinations, the patient becomes a victim of iatrogenic suggestion. In other cases the stigmata occur independently of the doctor and accompany other symptoms of hysteria. Ferenczi (1919)[61] showed that the stigmata occur on body sites peculiarly adapted for the representation of unconscious fantasies, and he believed on this account that they were characteristic anomalies.

In support of this view he cited the fact that hemianaesthesia is often left-sided in right-handed invididuals. The right side of the body in such people is more active and more under conscious control, a condition that led Hughlings Jackson to call the left cerebral hemisphere the more objective and voluntary, and the right more automatic. When the repressive process is failing in such right-handed individuals, the unconscious fantasies find their representation more easily on the left side of the body, presumably on the principle of the *pars resistentiae minoris*. In the same way, the central part of the field of vision engages the attention more actively, so the outer part of the field is more easily affected. It is thus that more weakly ego-invested parts of the body image are sometimes more easily dissociated or sometimes fall victim to unconscious distortion. On the other hand, as with hyperaesthetic spots (which may also be hysterogenic or hysterofrenic), if parts of the body are given more than usual prominence in the body image, due to autogeneous displacement or to heterosuggestion, they then too readily acquire fantasy endowment. Similarly, sometimes as a result of organic disease a part of the body acquires prominence, so altering the *Gestalt* of the body image and readily attracting fantasy elaboration, a condition known as 'somatic compliance'.

We will later discuss more fully the relations of the body language of conversion hysteria to word language, relations that are important in the understanding of hysteria as a disorder of communication. Meanwhile, in connection with the stigmata, globus hystericus requires consideration. In terms of conscious experience, many will recall a transient sensation of having a lump in the throat under certain emotional conditions, perhaps when reminiscing about loved things and people now lost. Tennyson wrote:

Tears, idle tears, I know not what they mean
Tears from the depth of some divine despair,
Rise in the heart and gather to the eyes,
In looking on the happy autumn fields,
And thinking of the days that are no more.

When such tears are *suppressed* by someone who is very homesick, he is likely to get a lump in his throat and wonder whether perhaps he is ill and suffering from an obstruction. The external conditions under which this transformation into thoughts of inside bodily obstruction occurs often coincide with a real obstruction in circumstances that the enactment of a sickness might begin to solve. Thus, in the cases presented during military service overseas, globus hystericus, with other symptoms, occurred in connection with a real obstruction to returning home. It can occur in any frustrating circumstance when the rememberances of happier situations throng the mind. A discussion of the present frustrating conditions, with an abreaction of emotion, even actual weeping, can be helpful in getting rid of such a lump in the throat. Of course, efforts to suppress tears in frustrating circumstances do not necessarily lead to globus hystericus, which occurs only if there is the total process of an 'incubating hysteria'; then the lump in the throat begins to re-acquire archaic meanings through regression, following attempts at repression that are only partly effective.

It is important to note that the suppression of tears in frustrating circumstances can lead to disorder other than hysterical conversion. Consider this case of a military patient stationed in the Far East who suffered from angioneurotic oedema of the eyelids that resembled a symptom seen in nephritis. The personality background of this patient could be summarized as one of compulsive character disorder with prominent defences of isolation of affect from ideation, and excessive insistence on emotional control. This patient was suffering from a psychogenic disorder related to suppressed tears; the path of emotional expression in tears was blocked, as it were, at the penultimate appropriate body area. As has been noted, an 'affect equivalent' may come about when aroused affect is blocked in a person with a chronically defensive attitude toward affective expression; the ideas connected with his feelings of frustration and anger are often consciously elaborated and given verbal expression, i.e. they are not *repressed* (ineffectively) as is characteristic in hysterical disease. Freud (Breuer and Freud, 1895[29]) mentioned this difference between hysteria and obsessive neurosis—that in the former, ideas are more excluded than affects from 'preconscious' connections with words, whereas in obsessional neurosis affects are defended against more vigorously than ideas.

Primarily from the studies of Darwin (1872)[62] we have learned that emotionally expressive movements and secretions, such as those of physiognomy, are a widely diffused phenomenon, so consistent in character as to be readily recognized by all mankind, whatever the language, culture, or education, and demonstrable in typical guise even in the congenitally blind.

He wrote about tears as follows:

The fact of tears not being shed at a very early age from pain or any mental emotion is remarkable, as, later in life, no expression is more general or more strongly marked than weeping. When the habit has once been acquired by an infant, it expresses in the clearest manner suffering of all kinds, both bodily pain and mental distress, even though unaccompanied by other emotions, such as fear or rage. The character of the crying, however, changes at a very early age, as I noticed in my own infants—the passionate cry differing from that of grief ... (Tears are restrained) ... at a more advanced age, under most circumstances excepting grief ... With adults, especially of the male sex, weeping soon ceases to be caused by, or to express, bodily pain. This may be accounted for by its being thought weak and unmanly by men, both of civilized and barbarous races, to exhibit bodily pain by any outward sign. With this exception, savages weep copiously from very slight causes, of which Sir J. Lubbock has collected instances. A New Zealand chief cried like a child because the sailors spoilt his favourite cloak by powdering it with flour. I saw on Tierra del Fuego a native who had lately lost a brother, and who alternately cried with hysterical violence, and laughed heartily at anything which amused him. With the civilized nations of Europe there is also much difference in the frequency of weeping. Englishmen rarely cry, except under the pressure of the acutest grief, whereas in some parts of the Continent the men shed tears much more readily and freely.

And he writes later in the book of his belief...

...That the chief expressive actions, exhibited by man and by the lower animals, are now innate or inherited... So little has learning or imitation to do with several of them that they are from the earliest days and throughout life quite beyond our control; for instance, the arteries of the skin in blushing, and the increased action of the heart in anger. We may see children, of two or three years old, and even those born blind, blushing from shame; and the naked scalp of a very young infant reddens from passion. Infants scream from pain directly after birth, and all their features then assume the same form as during subsequent years. These facts alone suffice to show that many of our most important expressions have not been learned; but it is remarkable that some, which are certainly innate, require practice in the individual, before they are performed in a full and perfect manner; for instance, weeping and laughing. The inheritance of most of our expressive actions explains the fact that those born blind display them...equally well with those gifted with eyesight. We can thus understand the fact that the young and the old of widely different races, both with man and animals, express the same state of mind by the same movements.

Darwin (1872)[62] further emphasized his view that the communicative function of such emotional expression was based on an immediate biological utility, *or* an association with. *or* remnants of, movements possessing such utility, as, for example, the showing of the teeth in anger. In this way he suggested an evolutionary interpretation of the changes of feature and posture that are characteristic of the major emotions.

The study of communicative disorder is illuminated by these views. It becomes apparent that certain psychogenic somatic disorders, i.e. the so-called 'affect equivalents', have a *symbolic function* inasmuch as they cryptically represent a state of feeling, and, like the overt expression of major emotion, they are often the remnants of movements that possessed biological utility (like the baring of teeth in anger). This last example of overt emotion employs the kind of symbolism that makes the part-reaction (the showing of the teeth) represent the whole reaction (biting the offender). Although it falls somewhat short of representing the whole reaction in full force it none the less quite definitely refers to the state of feeling that would lead to and accompany such biting. It will be clear that the distinction between conversion reaction and psychosomatic disorder sometimes offered—namely, that the first has a symbolic character and that the second is asymbolic—often fails to stand up under close scrutiny. The difference between hysteria and hysteriform conditions from psychosomatic disorder will be discussed later more fully.

As regards globus hystericus it is often the precursor of other hysterical symptoms. The patient suffering from this condition has usually been confronted with an unacceptable situation in his life just before, or at the time of, his first becoming aware of a contraction in his throat. It is as if he senses, rather than states in words, that he 'cannot swallow' this or that; as indeed one might say in colloquial English without experiencing such a sensation. Already the contraction of the throat is both an affective symbol referring to his inner reactions and a symbol of his ideas about the external situation insofar as these ideas have to do with its unacceptability. As the contraction becomes a persistent lump in the throat we move into that reliable 'stigma' of hysteria, globus hystericus. Ferenczi (1919)[61, 63] found that deeper analysis in the established condition showed that, like other stigmata, this has regressively become a materialization of more deeply placed unconscious fantasies; in globus fantasies of fellatio have become activated.

So globus hystericus comes to appear as a regressive expression of being forced into a passive sexual role after being unable to achieve an active wish. Here, as elsewhere in hysteria, we reach a genital symbolic level. In the autoplastic body language of hysteria, that part of the origin of speech which is sexual is to a large extent recovered. The leading fantasies in soldiers suffering from globus hystericus had to do with their feelings of being 'screwed'; in psychotherapy they ventilated these in colloquial English. These fantasies were thus of an undesired homosexual kind. The common globus hystericus of women in civilian life is often related to forbidden incestuous wishes.

Case 31. During the course of the analysis of a 30-year-old American woman it emerged that the first time globus hystericus had occurred as a definite symptom was in her late 'teens, when she was on a prolonged trip to the West Coast in the company of her beloved father. After they had travelled together for some days, the father became sexually interested in a woman encountered on a train. His daughter described this woman as being middle-aged, attractive and 'tackily dressed'. Her father quickly cultivated her acquaintance and soon left his daughter to carouse with her. Such incidents were repeated on their trip, and at first the daughter felt sensations of contraction in her throat. Soon, as her father's defections continued, she felt a lump in her throat, and finally her inability to eat led father and daughter to seek medical advice. Caught up in this turn of events, her father became more and more attentive to his daughter, and his sexual interest in other women subsided. As her life situation became more acceptable, her symptoms abated. It was marital discord later in her life that again brought on globus hystericus.

This case, as others, suggests that the stigmata have to be considered in the setting of the individual's total psychological situation. Although the diagnosis of hysteria may be suggested by these anomalies insofar as it becomes apparent that the patient is having recourse to a regressive form of expression, the absence of such anomalies does not indicate the absence of hysteria. We may use the same language and yet cry out with different words! Moreover, the same words may, under different circumstances, or at another time, require another meaning.

Hemi-anaesthesia may sometimes be right-sided in a right-handed individual. If, in general, as Ferenczi supposed, the left side of the body in right-handed people may come to represent the unconscious, and the more active and more controlled right side to represent the conscious ego, this would then require explanation along other lines.

Case 32. One patient had paralysis of dorsiflexion of the right foot, which puzzled the surgeons for a long time. This localized paralysis caused him to adopt a curious gait, and prevented him from attending dances. It was found during treatment that although he urgently wanted the society of women he had an obverse and equally strong fear of them on account of an activation of the castration complex, including *vagina dentata* fantasies. His foot had become 'genitalized', and he was unable to lift it in order to dance; then this limitation in movement was extended to locomotion in general. It was his right foot that was affected, and the relevant point here is that the right side of his body had come to represent the masculine, and the left side, the feminine side of his bisexuality. It would seem that this may more generally obtain, so that the bilateral configuration of the human body is capable of giving representation to more that one mental bipolarity.

From this it is clear that the so-called stigmata have a relationship to the experience and problems of the patient in the same way as other symptoms in conversion hysteria. The only justification for the continued use of such a word would be that it should denote a frequency, if not a regularity, of occurrence in hysteria. Moreover, the word is a persuasive definition of something socially reprehensible, as one might expect from its history in superstitious beliefs about witchcraft.* Such a censorious attitude is not conducive to the study of emotional disturbance and its expression in body language.

*Illis (1964)[64] discussed the ancillary belief in werewolves that often accompanies a belief in witches and witchcraft. The most consistent picture of the werewolf includes the following stigmata: the skin is pale with a yellowish or greenish tint, with numerous excoriations, and a red mouth. The eyes are unsteady. A man—or, occasionally a woman or child—with these physical characteristics wanders about at night, and shows other evidence of abnormal behaviour. Illis points out that the rare disease congenital porphyria may have given some purchase in reality to the myth of the metamorphosis of man into wolf, for there is a remarkable relation between the symptoms of this rare disease and many accounts of werewolves through the centuries. A congenital porphyric, because of photosensitivity and the resulting disfigurement, may choose to wander about only at night. The pale, yellowish, excoriated skin is explained by the haemolytic anaemia, jaundice and pruritus. These features, along with hypertrichosis and pigmentation, fit well with the descriptions of werewolves in the older literature.[65] Of course such a person is or easily becomes, mentally disturbed, especially when the physical and social treatment he receives is based on explanations of his odd appearance in terms of witchcraft or Satanic possession.

REFERENCES

1. Janet, P. (1907). *The Major Symptoms of Hysteria*, 2nd ed. New York: Macmillan (1920).

2. Ziegler, D. and Paul, N. (1954). On the natural history of hysteria in women. *Dis. Nerv. System*, **15**, 301–6.
3. Guze, S. B. (1967). The diagnosis of hysteria: what are we trying to do? *Am. J. Psychiat.*, **124**, 491–8.
4. Krohn, A. (1978). *Hysteria: The Elusive Neurosis*. New York: Int. Univ. Press.
5. Bibring, G. L., Dwyer, T. F., Huntington, D. S. et al. (1961). A study of the psychological processes in pregnancy and of the earliest mother–child relationship. In: *The Psychoanalytic Study of the Child*, Vol. 16, pp. 9–72. New York: Int. Univ. Press.
6. Valenstein, A. F. (1962). The psycho-analytic situation, affects, emotional reliving and insight in the psycho-analytic process. *Int. J. Psychoanal.*, **43**, 315–23.
7. Menninger, K., Mayman, M. and Pruyser, P. (1963). *The Vital Balance*. New York: Viking Press.
8. Freud, S. (1895). The psychotherapy of hysteria. *Studies on Hysteria*, Chap. 4. In: *The Standard Edition*, Vol. II. London: Hogarth Press (1955).
9. Charcot, J.-M. and Marie, P. (1892). Hysteria. In: *A Dictionary of Psychological Medicine* (ed. Tuke, D. H.). Philadelphia: Blakiston, (1928).
10. Babinski, J. (1908). My conception of hysteria and hypnotism (pithiatism). *Alienist and Neurologist*, **9**, 1–29.
11. Babinski, J. (1901). Définition de l'hystérie. *Rev. Neurolog.*, **9**, 1074–80.
12. La Barre, W. (1962). *They Shall Take Up Serpents*. Minneapolis, Ma: Minnesota Univ. Press.
13. Rabkin, R. (1964). Conversion hysteria as social maladaptation. *Psychiat.*, **27**, 349–63.
14. Kraepelin, E. (1913). *Text Book of Psychiatry* (trans. Barclay, R. M.). Edinburgh: Livingstone (1919).
15. Bleuler, E. (1911). *Dementia Praecox or the Group of Schizophrenias* (trans. Zinkin, A.). New York: Int. Univ. Press (1950).
16. Schneider, K. (1959). *Clinical Psychopathology* (trans. Hamilton, M. W.). New York: Grune and Stratton.
17. Wing, J. K., Cooper, J. E. and Sartorius, N. (1974). *Measurement and Classification of Psychiatric Symptoms*. London and New York: Cambridge Univ. Press.
18. Wing. J. K. (1978). *Schizophrenia: Towards a New Synthesis*. London: Academic Press; New York: Grune and Stratton.
19. Flugel, J. C. (1921). *The Psycho-analytic Study of the Family*. London: Hogarth Press (1939).
20. Adler, A. (1929). *Problems of Neuroses*. New York: Cosmopolitan Book Corp. (1930).
21. Hartmann, H. (1939). *Ego Psychology and the Problem of Adaptation* (trans. Rapaport, D.). New York: Int. Univ. Press (1958).
22. Chodoff, P. and Lyons, H. (1958). Hysteria, the hysterical personality, and hysterical conversion. *Am. J. Psychiat.*, **114**, 734–40.
23. Jones, E. (1913). The god complex. In: *Essays in Applied Psychoanalysis*. London: Hogarth Press (1951).
24. Freud, Anna (1936). *The Ego and the Mechanisms of Defense*. London: Hogarth Press (1937).
25. Adler, A. (1924). *Understanding Human Nature*. New York: Greenberg (1927).
26. Adler, A. (1924). *Individual Psychology*. New York: Kegan, Trench and Trubner.
27. Adler, A. (1917). *Study of Organ Inferiority and its Psychical Compensation; A Contribution to Clinical Medicine*. New York: Nervous and Mental Diseases Publishing.
28. Shapiro, D. (1965). *Neurotic Styles*. New York: Basic Books.
29. Breuer, J. and Freud, S. (1895). The Psychotherapy of Hysteria. *Studies on Hysteria*. In: *The Standard Edition*, Vol. II. London: Hogarth Press (1955).

30. Farber, L. H. (1961). Will and willfulness in hysteria. In: *The Ways of the Will*, pp. 99–117. New York: Basic Books (1966).
31. Eysenck, H. J. (1892). A psychological theory of hysteria. In: *Hysteria* (ed. Roy, A.), Chap. 6. Toronto and New York: Wiley.
32. Rees, L. (1973). Constitutional factors and abnormal behaviour. In: *Handbook of Abnormal Psychology* (ed. Eysenck, H.). London: Pitman.
33. Benedikt, M. (1892). Ueber Neuralgien und Neuralgische Affectionen und deren Behandlung. *Klinische Zeit und Streitfragen*, **VI** (3), 67–106.
34. Stevenson, I. and Sheppe, W. M. (1959). The psychiatric examination. In: *American Handbook of Psychiatry* (ed. Arieti, S.). New York: Basic Books.
35. Jessner, L. and Abse, D. W. (1960). Regressive forces in anorexia nervosa. *Br. J. Med. Psychol.*, **33**, 301–12.
36. Gowers, W. (1893). *A Manual of Diseases of the Nervous System*, 2nd ed., Vol. II, pp. 543–58, New York: Stechert.
37. Oppenheim, H. (1911). *Textbook of Nervous Diseases*, 5th ed., Vol. I, pp. 332–50. New York: Stechert.
38. Wilson, S. A. K. (1940). *Neurology*, Vol. I, P. 156. Baltimore: Williams and Wilkins.
39. Aring, C. D. (1965). Observations on multiple sclerosis and conversion hysteria. *Brain*, **88**, 663–74.
40. Langworthy, O. R., Kolb, L. C. and Androp, S. (1941). Multiple sclerosis. *Am. J. Psychiat.*, **98**, 243.
41. Langworthy, O. R. (1948). Multiple sclerosis. *Arch. Neurol. Psychiat.*, **59**, 13.
42. Langworthy, O. R. (1950). Multiple sclerosis. *Res. Publ. Ass. Nerv. Ment. Dis.*, **28**, 598.
43. Langworthy, O. R. and LeGrand, D. (1952). Multiple sclerosis. *Am. J. Med.*, **12**, 586.
44. McAlpine, D., Lumsden, C. E. and Acheson, E. D. (1965). *Multiple Sclerosis*, pp. 174–5. Baltimore: Williams and Wilkins.
45. Prange, A. J. and Abse, D. W. (1957). Psychic events accompanying an attack of poliomyelitis. *Br. J. Med. Psychol.*, **30**, 75–87.
46. Freud, S. (1893). Some points in a comparative study of organic and hysterical paralysis. In: *Collected Papers*, Vol. I. London: Hogarth Press (1924).
47. Lassek, A. M. (1944). The human pyramidal tract: X, The Babinski sign and destruction of the pyramidal tract. *Arch. Neurol. Psychiat.*, **52**, 484.
48. Mapother, E. and Lewis, A. (1942). Hysteria. In: *A Text Book of the Practice of Medicine*, 6th ed. (ed. Price, F. W.). London: Oxford Univ. Press.
49. Mackenzie, K. R., Martin, M. J. and Howard, F. M. (1969). Myasthenia gravis: psychiatric concomitants. *Can. Med. Assoc. J.*, **100**, 989–91.
50. Emery, E. J. and Szymanski, H. von (1981). Psychological symptoms preceding diagnosed myasthenia gravis. *Psychosomatics*, **22**, 993–5.
51. Hill, D. (1963). The E.E.G. in psychiatry. In: *Electroencephalography* (ed. Hill, D. and Parr, G.). New York: Macmillan.
52. Kiloh, L. G. (1976). Electroencephalography. In: *Encyclopaedic Handbook of Medical Psychology*. London and Boston: Butterworths.
53. Critchley, M. (1964). Psychiatric symptoms and parietal disease: differential diagnosis. *Proc. R. Soc. Med.*, **57**, 442.
54. Weinstein, E. A. and Kahn, R. L. (1955). *Denial of Illness: Symbolic and Physiological Aspects*. Springfield, Ill.: Thomas.
55. Ging, R. J., Jones, E. and Manis, M. (1964). Correlation of electroencephalograms and multiple physical symptoms. *J. Am. Med. Assoc.*, **187**, 579.
56. Bleuler, E. (1916). *Text Book of Psychiatry*. New York: Macmillan (1930).
57. Casson, F. R. C. (1949). Some interpersonal factors in illness. *Lancet*, **2**, 681.
58. Lowen, A. (1958). *Physical Dynamics of Character Structure*. New York: Grune and Stratton.

59. Braatöy, T. (1952). Psychology versus anatomy in the treatment of arm neuroses with physiotherapy. *J. Nerv. Ment. Dis.*, **115**, 215.
60. Babinski, J. and Froment, J. (1916). *Hysteria*. London: London Univ. Press (1918).
61. Ferenczi, S. (1919). An attempted explanation of some hysterical stigmata. In: *Further Contributions to the Theory and Technique of Psychoanalysis*. London: Hogarth Press (1926).
62. Darwin, C. (1872). *The Expression of the Emotions in Man and Animals*. London: Murray.
63. Ferenczi, S. (1919). The phenomena of hysterical materialisation. In: *Further Contributions to the Theory and Technique of Psychoanalysis*. London: Hogarth Press (1926).
64. Illis, L. (1964). On porphyria and the aetiology of werewolves. *Proc. R. Soc. Med.*, **57**, 23.
65. Baring-Gould, S. (1865). *The Book of Were-wolves. Being an Account of a Terrible Superstition*. New York: Causeway Books (1973).

CHAPTER 5

Conversion Hysteria Within the Context of the Family

The term 'conversion' was originally applied by Breuer and Freud[1] to the transformation of psychic anxiety into bodily expression. Freud came to understand more deeply the relationship of this anxiety to the conflicting forces within the psyche. Conversion then came to be seen as a symbolic physical expression of contending unconscious elements. These would have continued to be attended by anxiety had they remained in the psychic sphere, and would be the cause of renewed gross anxiety were they to regain access to consciousness without skilled help. We have already noted that it is in the context of consideration of early events within the family, and of the style of family life, that we can more easily decipher the deeper cryptic meanings related to anxiety-laden mental conflict embodied in symptoms.

Paul Schilder in 1939[2] stated that hysterical phenomena in children show, with marked clarity, the continuous interaction between the attitudes of the patient and the parents. He gives an account of a 13-year-old girl, Jenny, observed on the children's ward of the Bellvue Psychiatric Hospital in New York.

Jenny's hysterical phenomena all related to body sensations. She had periods when she felt that she was shrinking; at other times she felt dizzy, or hot all over, or else she experienced sensations of being pierced by pins and needles. Sometimes her vision became blurred; at other times, her hearing failed. One or other of these phenomena was observed after the visits of her mother, and the child could quickly be relieved of them, settling down to a fairly normal adjustment until she was again disturbed by her mother. The mother had exhibited at different times dramatic hysterical phenomena which some of Jenny's behaviour closely resembled. Moreover, the family history was filled with sickness and operations. Jenny herself had had a necessary operation for the correction of strabismus at the age of 10.

From such clinical observations as well as from the study of retrospective accounts in investigative psychotherapy of adults, Schilder maintained that childhood experience of over-concern about physical sickness within the family is an important predisposing factor to the development of conversion symptoms in the adult individual under stress and that hysterical persons are skilful identifiers. He emphasized that experience of organic ailment in childhood is of fundamental importance in the development of the typical psychology of the adult hysteric who under the stress of mental conflict takes a flight into physical illness. The childhood experience of organic illness may reinforce an underlying masochistic attitude, and the adult regressive flight into illness reinstates the helplessness and increased dependence of the sick child on the love and protection of his parents. It is thus obvious that attitudes which later lead to hysterical conversion symptoms are promoted by actual organic disease or by over-concern about physical illness within the primary family. Schilder[2] noted that people with such ingrained attitudes of dependence and masochism when later frustrated in the erotic sphere or when in need of social help, developed hysterical conversion symptoms in the absence of actual organic disease or at such times when organic disease was not too severe. About the latter cases he wrote:

> In general, it [hysteria] will be found in chronic disease, or at the beginning or decline of an acute disease. If the organic disease is at its height or completely incapacitating, the individual will get the full social recognition for it without hysterical symptoms.

That is to say the symbolic hysterical form may be rendered unnecessary by severe organic disease.

At this point it is worthwhile to consider *growing pains*. This expression for recurrent physical pains in childhood is common but its use is ambiguous: for some it means that physical growth causes pain; others assume that physical growth is not in itself painful but 'emotional growth can hurt like hell'.[3] Two points may be stressed:[4] so-called 'growing pains' are not at their commonest when growth is most rapid and the usual sites of the pain do not tally with the sites of maximum growth. In 1958, J. Apley,[5] showed that recurrent childhood pains in limbs, head and abdomen are interrelated, often interchangeable, and are usually associated with emotional disturbance.

Naish and Apley,[6] restricting the term 'growing pains' to intermittent limb pains recurring over a period of months and not specifically located in the joints, found that among 213 such cases in children only seven had an organic disease—one with rheumatic heart disease, two with congenital heart disease, two with primary tuberculosis and one with Osgood–Schlatter disease (limping caused by apophysitis of the tubercle of the tibia).

As far as the physical disease aspect of 'growing pains' is concerned it is apparent that the diagnosis of 'subacute rheumatism' is very imprecise and that acute rheumatism can be ruled out by the general and cardiac examination and a normal erythrocyte sedimentation rate. Congenital heart disease with a defective circulation to the limbs must also be ruled out before childhood hysteria is considered. The possibility of occult infection should be investigated in the case of a child who is not thriving, and is complaining—chest X-ray, urinary examination and culture, etc. Orthopaedic disability or osteochondrosis are usually readily diagnosed. Recurrent pains may of course be caused by leukemia or Henoch–Schönlein purpura.

The diagnosis of conversion-reaction-type pains associated with emotional or family disturbances has been discussed by Apley and R. C. MacKeith[7]. Such a diagnosis in children is based on two complementary findings. First, the physician should exclude organic disease, though without going to unreasonable lengths. Secondly, he should find positive evidence of emotional disturbance.

In my experience, the background of many adult patients suffering conversion hysteria shows a sharp contrast between the parents' general emotional neglect of the patient as a child and remorseful attention whenever the child was afflicted with physical disease or distress. Usually, these patients were to a very large extent ignored by their parents except when physically sick. This background is an obvious determinant, among others, of a readiness for a flight into illness, a flight to which much unconscious effort may be devoted, when the adult is confronted with frustration and conflict in later life.

In contrast to the sort of childhood background of severe chronic organic illness and/or of excessive parental concern which prepares the way for a hysterical flight into illness, the more usual behavioural reactions of children to common minor illness warrant note. Mattsson and Weisberg[8] observed 35 pre-school children during minor physical illness at home while they were cared for by their mothers. These children came from one paediatrician's private practice and had no history of chronic illness or of hospital admission. A total of 76 periods of illness were observed. During the acute phase of illness all children showed some temporary loss of age-appropriate behaviour. Particularly striking were the changes in the children's relationships with their mothers. These changes were of two types related to age. Reaction 1, predominant among the ill two-year olds, was characterized by the child's clinging, whining dependence, while children over the age of three tended to show Reaction 2—a self-contained, rather undemanding state. During convalescence all children demonstrated a few days of irritable, impatient behaviour. Altogether the pre-school child's reactions to acute illness at home appear to change in an orderly continuum towards self-contained, rather independent behaviour. Mattson and Weisberg[8] also note that minor illness has a role in promoting the young child's reality-sense and responsibility for the care of his own body. The realization of his mother's relative helplessness during his illness is one factor which challenges the growing child's attempts to reach for more independence.

The behavioural changes seen in all these children during their convalescence appear similar to those found by H. Shrand.[9] His report noted anxious behaviour in many children after illness at home, behaviour which when shown by children who have been nursed in hospital is attributed to physical separation. Mattsson and Weisberg[8] write:

> In our study there was a frequent appearance of separation fears during convalescence among the group of children who during the acute phase of the illness had shown undemanding, self-contained behaviour. It seemed as if these children had experienced 'emotional separation' from their mother during their state of relative withdrawal. This may partly explain their anxious, controlling behaviour which emerged as they improved and resumed interaction with the family...

Love Overload

In order to penetrate more deeply into the family contribution to the psychogenesis of hysteria, we must look anew at several aspects of the psychopathology already discussed. It has been repeatedly confirmed since Freud's classic work that when traced to its roots hysteria in all its forms is predominantly related to that climax of early developing sexuality, the Oedipus situation, which is concerned with the child's struggle to surmount incestuous genital-sexual and hostile strivings towards his parents. It is recognized that a certain type of hysteric personality, liable to a flight into illness, is likely to have been the victim in childhood of an emotional overloading of the filio-parental tie. The hysterical character is, in general, basically, even when not overtly, characterized by strong parental attachment, and the attachment to the parent of opposite sex is usually ascendant. It happens that widowers, widows, those who are unhappily married, or parents with an only child, frequently display a more than normal degree of attachment to their offspring. The children receive in addition to the love that would ordinarily fall to their share, the displaced affection which would otherwise find its outlet in the love of spouse or other children. A decade ago, Jacob Arlow[10] discussed the problems of an only child, including his more than usual fear of moving out of the protective family unit into a world of sibling substitutes. This exaggerated anxiety is the result in some cases of early fantasies about his 'only' situation. Regardless of what he learns in this context he blames himself for being an only child, elaborating unconsciously the notion that he destroyed potential rival siblings. He then is apt to fear retaliatory encounters.

The tie between widowed parents, those unhappily married or parents with an only child and their children is apt to be more than usually close, as J. C. Flugel[11] pointed out more than 60 years ago in his masterpiece, *The Psycho-analytic Study of the Family*. Moreover, such a close attachment might become less than usually aim-inhibited, with sensual nuances, which provoke precocious sexual stimulation and undue fixation. In my own psychotherapeutic experience, and as Schilder and others have reported, the attachment to the parent of opposite sex is often remembered as connected with genital sensations or even genital activity. In some cases, more-or-less close genital contact of the girl with the father has been reported. In one example reported by Schilder,[2] there were early sex relations with the father. Clinical experience shows that early actual sexual stimulation results in a traumatic situation which sows the seeds of later hysteria. In other cases, and these are more frequent, there is an emotional overloading of the filio-parental tie with unconscious incestuous undertones and fantasy formations only clearly revealed retrospectively in analytic psychotherapy, that is, in the treatment of established cases of hysterical symptom neurosis. In these cases, the struggle is to win sexual emancipation through the resolution of the unconscious Oedipus complex with its attendant guilt and anxiety.

Seidenberg and Papathomopoulos[12] point out that daughters who tend their fathers for a long time when they are sick are often later vulnerable to hysterical sickness themselves. Such a nursing situation facilitates the return of repressed strivings and feelings related to the 'family romance' of early childhood. In the nursing activity previously taboo bodily contacts become mandatory. The daughter is often exposed to, and is the object of, severely regressed behaviour of an aged and chronically sick father. Under such stressful conditions, pathological forms of over-identification may readily issue from healthy compassion. Thus the daughter may take on the sufferings of her father to relieve aroused guilt, or later the sufferings may be enlisted to cope with loss and separation. Seidenberg and Papathomopoulos[12] also draw attention to chronic reactions of bitterness in many cases with resentful feelings concerned with having been exploited. Sacrifices may, of course, have been actually entailed with forsaken ambition and loss of chances of marriage. On the other hand, the daughter may welcome her 'enslavement' in the nursing situation, thus finally winning out over her mother and having father for herself; and she may also thus hide from the possibility of marriage on account of having been impounded in the Oedipal struggle. Sometimes the nursing situation results in the arousal of an ambivalent unconscious mixture of welcoming and going against the grain. Moreover, sometimes the daughter may have a supervalent hostile, revengeful motive: as expressed by Seidenberg and Papathomopoulos[12]:

Here, the girl, harbouring lifelong anger and revengeful desires toward the dominating male in the family may find secret gratification in being a witness to his demise.

Such a case may develop from a very early close relationship with the father which was abandoned at puberty.

Seidenberg and Papathomopoulos[12] are impressed with the recurrent theme of hysteria in young women following the illness and death of a father whom they had actively nursed such as the earliest case histories of Breuer and Freud (1895) show. They cite Anna O., Dora and Elisabeth von R. in this regard. They also make a literary survey which includes some of Balzac's and Tolstoy's novels, Shakespeare's and Ibsen's plays and the Sophoclean trilogy, of which, *Antigone* and *Oedipus at Colonus* are concerned with faithful daughters who supported a banished and enfeebled father.

Love Deprivation

Flugel[11] pointed out that even if children come to regard their parents as obstacles to the full attainment of their own desires and as unwelcome causes of interference with their most cherished activities, then parents have at least equal reason for complaint against their children. There are bound to be sacrifices involved in parenthood. The effort, responsibility and anxiety involved in rearing children diminish very considerably the time and energy available for other occupations and ambitions. Herbert Spencer[13] saw antagonism between individuation and procreation as a general biological law. He neglected the positive aspect of parenthood as a stimulus to personal development, to the process of individuation, a proposition to which Therese Benedek[14] has devoted an enlightening paper. The negative aspect, however, is that the hostile feelings of some parents towards their children which stem from resentment of sacrifice are often enormously amplified by their unconscious identification of the child with their own parent (the child's grandparent). This tendency to identify child with grandparent is deeply implanted in the human mind. Indeed in many parts of the world grandparents are supposed to become reincarnated in their grandchildren—a belief which is probably responsible for the widespread practice of naming a child after a grandparent; for example, the eldest son after the paternal grandfather. At any rate, when combined with a violent parent hatred, such unconscious identification of children with their grandparents may take on tragic proportions and lead to neurotic consequences in the child. The affection which should be forthcoming from the parent to the child may thus be subverted and the child may be left with an ambivalent fixation to the parent, one which is displaced to surrogate figures in later life. The outcome may be a love-craving which is unconsciously and intrinsically doomed to repeated guilty re-enactment, with failure to achieve a stable pairing intimacy in adult life, an hysterical fate-neurosis, one which is often punctuated by sensory and motor conversion phenomena at times of frustration and heightened inner conflict.

Marmor[15] has emphasized that, in many cases of hysteria, fixations in the Oedipal phase of development are themselves the outgrowth of pre-Oedipal fixations, chiefly of an oral nature. He writes:

> The kind of parent whose behaviour keeps a child at an 'oral' level is apt to be the kind of parent whose behaviour favours the development of a strong Oedipus complex. The pre-Oedipal history of most of the hysterias I have seen has revealed one of two things—either intense frustration of their oral-receptive needs as a consequence of early defection or rejection by one or both parent figures, or excessive gratification of these needs by one or both parent figures...

The concept of multiple points of fixation (and, in particular, in hysteria, of the importance of oral as well as Oedipal fixation), explains psychodynamically the clinical associations noted in many cases between hysteria and schizophrenia, hysteria and depressive disorder, and hysteria and addiction, especially alcoholism. Where the oral fixation factor is of greater importance, the ego-integrative capacity is weaker and psychotic regression is more likely to occur. In less easily defined cases where oral-narcissistic fixation is of importance, certain hypnoid disturbances of consciousness may periodically be evident: at times self-observation is deleted, ideation is affect-charged, restricted and vague. In such alterations of consciousness, the ideational and verbal performance becomes quite inadequate. The process of symbol-making may depart considerably from the denotational to saturation with connotational fantasies.

These and other psychic disturbances, including dysmnesic and other dissociative reactions—states of depersonalization, fugues, somnambulisms and multiple personality disorder—may occur in patients whose ungratified oral phase of libidinal development results in a fragile ego fundament. It is these patients who usually exhibit in the most exaggerated form Pierre Janet's view of hysteria as 'a malady of the personal synthesis'. These psychic disturbances will be considered in later chapters. Here it is to be noted that they may accompany conversion phenomena, and indicate a severe form of hysterical neurosis or of borderline disorder.

The important role of identification in the sociology of the body-image is amply discussed by Schilder,[16] who emphasized that the image of the body is not static but is in constant flux, changing according to reactions to circumstances. There is a continuous process, underlying the evident changes of experience—a process of construction, dissolution and reconstruction of the body image. Unconscious processes, including regression, identification, projection and condensation, are of considerable importance in bringing about such changes. Thus, as we mentioned earlier, the 13-year-old child Jenny at the Bellvue Hospital sometimes felt after a visit by her mother that she was shrinking. In this instance, the mother's infantilizing influence is symbolized, whereas in other instances, such as the pins-and-needles and pains all over, the child's sensations resembled the dramatic complaints her mother had earlier displayed.

It is indeed a notorious fact that hysteria is a great imitator and this may be an awkward trap for the unwary medical diagnostician. The sensations or movements constituting the conversion symptoms may partly relate to observations of others made by the patient. For example, Freud's patient Dora[17] developed a cough which was found to be a traceable to her observations of Mrs K's coughing attacks. Unconsciously, she wished to put herself in Mrs K's position as the wife of Mr K, but felt guilty about her rivalry. She selected Mrs K's affliction as the point of identification; thus her forbidden and envious wishes were masochistically distorted in the service of self-punishment. This aspect of the dynamics as revealed in the case of Dora may serve to indicate that identification is often part of a complex pathogenetic process. Schilder also draws attention to Freud's patient Dora. He thought her coughing attacks also expressed genital wishes and their punishment by being infected and thus she was taking the place, in fantasy, of her mother who had vaginal catarrh. Bonnard[18] has drawn attention to the peculiar gestures of some very disturbed children and their meaning as partial identifications with both an aggressor and a victim. These children had been exposed repeatedly to the severe quarrelling, including physical combat, of their respective parents. Their uncontrollable gestures testified mimetically to the violent scenes to which they had been exposed though they said nothing for some time about these sadomasochistic performances witnessed at home.

Many events of traumatic power that affect the children within a family are concerned with the family pets or other domestic animals on the family scene. It is well known that children do not make adequate differentiation between animals and humans, and this applies also to some adults, whereas most adults, despite the facts of evolution, make altogether too large a gap between human beings and other animals.

Case 33. This young married woman of 23 years had symptoms including frigidity. The frigidity had developed following spontaneous abortion during her second pregnancy. Despite reluctance on her part she had gone along with unusually vigorous genital sexual intercourse which her husband had initiated, and noted with alarm the next day that she was spotting. The situation soon led to the abortion of a consciously desired pregnancy. Later investigation came to reveal, among other important childhood events, a distorted memory (or very vivid fantasy) of her witnessing at the age of six years an older brother having sexual intercourse with a hen. This hen was found dead shortly afterwards. It became evident that side by side with normal wishes for pleasurable sexual intercourse, which had for so long before prevailed, the patient had aversive feelings based on fantasies of the destructiveness and painfulness of genital intercourse. Unconsciously there had been an identification with the ill-fated hen, and the spontaneous abortion had incurred a recathexis of the memory of bestiality (with re-repression and the partial failure of repression until further de-repression in analytically orientated psychotherapy). The unconscious identification with the hen in the setting of farmyard behaviour generally as well as in the culminating incident when she witnessed her brother pretending to take the place of the cock, was not consciously accepted in the way of a psychotic delusional formation, that is, she did not believe she was a hen; but neither was it quite simply figurative (rather than literal), as it first came out in psychotherapy.

Fenichel[19] states that identification is the very first type of reaction to another person. All later object-relationships may, under certain circumstances, regress to identification. The hysterical identification is characterized by the fact that it does not involve the full amount of cathexis available. It is often possible through study of the types of identification the patient has made, and of the correlative fate of the object-relationships involved, to evaluate how far from psychosis a particular case of hysteria or hysteriform disorder may be. We will later consider such assessments in relation to borderline disorder. Here we will consider some aspects of hysteria as they reflect communicative disorder within the family.[20]

As outlined in Chapter 2, the symptomatic changes in physical function which constitute conversion unconsciously give distorted expression to the instinctual strivings (sexual and hostile) that had been previously more fully repressed. At the same time, the symptoms indirectly represent the defensive force in conflict with the derivatives of instinctual impulses and the retribution or punishment for these forbidden wishes. Freud found that the symptoms are substitutes for both the ideational representation of these strivings and of the forces opposing them, and that, accordingly, the symptoms could gradually be translated into word language from their 'body-language', with accompanying affective expression of the mental conflict. The following example illustrates.

Case 34. Mrs X, a 35-year-old, white, married and physically very attractive woman, was admitted to the medical wards of a large university hospital, referred by her family physician for repeated fainting attacks and complaints of severe pain in the neck. At the time this patient was first interviewed, she was in bed, constrained by an ingenious traction apparatus which pulled on her neck muscles. There was considerable spasm of these muscles, though exhaustive physical examination had failed to reveal any basic organic pathology. The patient complained that despite the apparatus and the various medications she still had a severe pain in the neck. She proceeded to say that before admission to the hospital, in addition to this neck pain which had progressively worsened, she had had alarming 'black-outs'. She was asked what she meant by a 'black-out', and the patient, looking puzzled by my apparent ignorance of the vernacular, explained about her faints. It was indicated that this was understood, but attention was directed to the phrase 'black-out' and inquiry was made as to whether she herself had thought of using this expression. It seemed the patient was not at all sure as to the first application of this term to her faints whether by her husband, herself, or one of the doctors. She was then asked whether when she was 'out' in the faint did she see black. Hesitating a moment, the patient stated thoughtfully, 'No, in fact, I pass out and see red.' In further conversation she gave a restrained account of her widowed mother-in-law who was living at her home. The patient's husband was this woman's only offspring and there ensued a talk about the close attachment of this woman to her only son, and the possible difficulties this might have led to. The conversation became increasingly animated, and at one point the patient was told that despite her conciliatory and laudably understanding attitude towards her mother-in-law, in fact this lady had begun to give her a pain in the neck, and the first occasions when she had seen her mother-in-law breakfasting alone with her husband had made her see red.

As the emergency psychotherapy progressed in later interviews with this patient, more adequate affective expression of her rage against and jealousy of her mother-in-law became clearly evident, as well as expressions of guilt feelings. These strong feelings were the affect indicators of strong and conflicting conative trends, which had roots, it was later revealed in analytic psychotherapy, in her early family drama with a tyrannical mother who excluded her even from everyday communication with her father as she was growing up.

In the case of this married woman who suffered a severe pain in the neck and who saw red in her fainting attacks, it became evident that her wish for her mother-in-law to live elsewhere, if she were to live at all, came into conflict with her sense of duty. When the attempt to translate her symptoms into affect-laden metaphorical language began, she protested that she ought to be able to get along with her mother-in-law whom she respected, though the presence of this lady disturbed her feelings of well-being. She soon acknowledged that she herself had thought what a pain in the neck the good woman was, and that sometimes she had made her see red. Thus, this translation of her symptoms into word-language was but a re-translation back to the unspoken language of her own thoughts, thoughts which had later become forbidden. Later this conflict was found to have many ramifications, including the fact that it was but a re-edition of an older, unresolved conflict with her own mother.

As discussed elsewhere,[20] the acquisition of discursive language, with its power of generality and abstraction, is the result of a complicated series of developments. From primitive naming, that is, basic phonetic symbolic representation, there is a semantic movement through metaphor and the fading of metaphor. We are concerned here, however, with the earlier sort of metaphoric symbolism whose function is largely to convey feelings, and whose adequacy depends on how well it performs this function. Often in the preliminary retranslation of hysterical somatic symptoms to word-language, it performs this function vividly and only less dramatically than the symptoms themselves. The essential messages in a conversion reaction are embodied cryptically in the somatic symptoms, which do not involve primarily any words at all, and only relatively infrequently the laryngeal apparatus. Word language is reduced and compressed in inaudible symbols of a more primitive character, in such a way that the subject is unaware of their essential meaning, and very likely misleads his reference group. We have, of course, the concepts of repression and of the unconscious (of the repressed unconscious) as well as of regression to aid us in our quest for understanding. The disorder of expression and of communication, internal and external, is indeed a function of pathological disturbance in repression and regression, as we have learned from Freud.

Besides the messages readily translatable to a verbal metaphorical symbolic level, other messages are couched, as we have shown in Chapter 2, in a more primitive (cryptophoric) symbolism. And as we will later discuss more fully in Chapters 16 and 17, there are six interrelated communicative aspects of motor and sensory phenomena in conversion reactions:

1. Sexual symbolic references couched in cryptophoric symbolism.
2. Distorted affect expressions, e.g. of appeal, of resentment, of weeping, of joy, etc.

3. Condensation of identifications, to which we have alluded here in the context of the family.

4. Associated connotations relating to conflicting fantasies—wish-fulfilling and punitive.

5. Denotative propositional pantomimic movements—often truncated, or with reversals in sequence, or other disguises.

6. Metaphorical embodiments, as illustrated in the last case discussed with symptoms including fainting attacks and severe pain in the neck.

We live in an era of considerable velocity of cultural change including a wider dissemination of education, a decrease in prudery and secrecy about sex and even an increase in understanding that physical symptoms can result from emotional disturbance. Now physiological expressions of emotional disturbance often reach discharge through the autonomic nervous system with excessive stimulation of innervated visceral structures. When the attempted symbolic resolution of an emotional conflict in bodily malfunction begins to communicate nearly as much as word language to the patient himself as well as to those in his particular life space, the attempt may immediately become abortive. It is then that re-repression is supplemented by deeper partial regression and dissociation, as will be later elucidated in the chapter in psychophysiologic disorder (Chapter 19). The unresolved tension thus reaches discharge through the autonomic system with damaging physical results. In this way, an increased incidence of psychophysiologic disorder may occur in the upper and middle urban classes of the population, replacing the classic hysterical forms of neurosis observed and described by Charcot in Paris in the last decades of the nineteenth century.

A. B. Hollingshead and F. C. Redlich,[21] in their study of the relationship of social class to the prevalence of mental disorders, found more psychotics and fewer neurotics among the lower classes in the USA than among the upper classes. However, hysterical reactions, unlike the other neurotic disorders, showed an inverse relationship with class position in this painstaking study.

My experience has shown that classic forms of hysteria continue in quite heavy incidence in the lower socioeconomic classes of the urban populace and in rural areas. Examination of such instances of classic hysteria often reveals that the familial style of life, including sleeping arrangements, results in the relatively frequent early observation by the children of sexual scenes between the adults. This 'primal scene' exposure is associated with heightened difficulty in surmounting the Oedipus complex, and a later vulnerability to frustration, with the occurrence of major classic hysterical attacks, including convulsive disorder and hypnoid spells.

Towards the end of the nineteenth century, Jean Martin Charcot[22] studied 'accident hysterias' in which the illness followed a physical trauma. He observed that the patient's symptoms (anaesthesia, paresis, tremor, etc.) were connected with the specific accident situation. Under hypnotic revival of this traumatic situation, it became clear that in cases of hysteria ideas entertained during this period were of more pathogenic significance than the physical injury itself. Thus a patient in hypnosis who had been a passenger during a train collision was worried about getting his legs crushed immediately after the railway accident, though in fact he was only shaken up physically. This patient then developed the fixed idea of having lost the power of movement in his legs, which was represented in his non-hypnotic state by hysterical paresis and anaesthesia.

Nowadays, there is much more to be concerned with in regard to 'spontaneous' hypnoid states which develop before accidents, so-called 'highway hypnosis'. A man or woman especially predisposed to the development of hypnoid states on account of hysterical character background is apt to act out in an altered state of consciousness with the aid of an automobile. Thus it is often clear in analytic anamnesis that a car accident which, say, resulted in a fracture of the leg, had followed a disturbed and conflicted state of mind engendered during a quarrel with a spouse, or other family member. In such a case the incubating hysteria has run its course without 'conversion' for this has been accomplished by actual physical force. Such 'accident hysterias' are today of frequent occurrence, and are but one category among the worldwide consequences of our emotional involvement with the automobile.

While Freud's work on the meaning of hysteria, together with the work of other medical pioneers, notably Havelock Ellis, led to less prudery and hypocrisy about sex, the work had other important lessons, still to be learned by many, for mental hygiene. In particular, it is evident that early exposure to sexual scenes, or for that matter to sexual instruction, *before readiness has developed for this in the developing ego*, leads to damaging rather than helpful effects. Premature sexual excitation stimulated by adult behaviour can have a traumatic effect and can establish the soil out of which further emotional excitation in later years will produce more or less intensive morbid hysterical phenomena. These possibilities should be brought to the notice of both 'enlightened' parents and 'progressive' psychotherapists, some of whom are over-anxious to stimulate the curiosity of children. There is also of course a need to improve the housing conditions of the less educated and less sublimated members of the community. There is also a probability that exposure of a child to repeated scenes of sexual violence on television is conducive to later hysterical attacks. These are important aspects of the promotion of healthy development of children and the prophylaxis of adult neurosis.

Schilder[2] stressed that attitudes that may later lead to hysterical conversion reactions under stress are more likely to develop by actual experience of bodily disturbance as a result of organic disease in childhood or by an atmosphere of over-concern with the possibilities of physical illness within the primary family group. In my experience, as noted above, there is also frequently a childhood background situation in cases of adult conversion hysteria of a sharp contrast between being well-nigh ignored by parents when physically well and excessively anxious care by them when physically sick.

As elaborated by J. C. Flugel, emotional overloading of the filio-parental tie, either through gross neglect or by overindulgence, aggravates the problems of the Oedipus complex and increases the chances of adult neurosis. Overly close attachment of one parent is often associated with neglect by the other and sometimes by precocious sexual stimulation. A frequently observed pattern of childhood experience includes one parent's overly close attachment, the other's physical or emotional absence, and precocious sexual stimulation. This is especially conducive to later hysterical symptom formation.

Another aspect of disturbed filio-parental attachment is often that of the parental identification of the child with his or her parent. This results readily in the parent's unconscious revisitation of Oedipal problems, with his or her child as a captive and dependent participant in a replayed earlier pathogenic family drama, one which is repeated in essentially noxious features; or else adverse features are a result of exaggerated reaction formations. In these families, it is difficult for any one individual in a particular generation to escape the situation and this is sometimes only achieved through psychoanalysis. On the other hand, it frequently happens in families of lower socioeconomic class, and sometimes in others, that if an individual is to change sufficiently so that he is not easily liable to recurrence of hysterical symptoms, the context in which he lives must also change. In the event that the patient cannot be extricated from the family soup as it were, the soup must be doctored. There is in many instances insufficient basic individuation and socialization and excessively deep collective family dependency, so that only temporary improvement results from individual or even from group psychotherapy—when the group is not composed of the family itself. Family therapy is thus an important modality of treatment. When there are children in the family they may be best excluded from some of the sessions, and included in others.

Contrasting patterns of regulation at critical phases of the child's development by different members of the family may lead to incompatible introjects. In extreme instances, super-ego cleavage may later be manifest as alternating hysterical personality malfunction, as will be discussed in the chapter on multiple personality (Chapter 11).

We have discussed briefly only some events of traumatic power as these affect the children within the family. Overtly displayed marital sadomasochistic interaction and severe physical punishment of the child are especially conducive to later convulsive forms of hysteria. Other events of traumatic power may be generated by siblings, neighbours and by animals in the childhood milieu. Adequate prosexual communication by the parents at appropriate phases of the child's development, without overstimulation, is a basic requisite for later healthy psychosexual maturity, and a lessened liability to hysteria. However, it is useful for the psychiatrist to keep in mind Moebius's[23] dictum: 'Every human being is a little hysterical.' After all, it is a part of the complex human condition to be liable to hysterical types of disorder.

REFERENCES

1. Breuer, J. and Freud, S. (1893–5). *Studies on Hysteria*. In: *The Standard Edition*, Vol. II. London: Hogarth Press (1955).
2. Schilder, P. (1939). The concept of hysteria. *Am. J. Psychiat.*, **95**, 1389–413.
3. Apley, J. (1970). Clinical Canutes. *Proc. R. Soc. Med.*, **63**, 479–84.
4. Editorial (1972). Growing pains. *Br. Med. J.* 365.
5. Apley, J. (1958). Common denominator in the recurrent pains of childhood. *Proc. R. Soc. Med.*, **51**, 1023–4.
6. Naish, J. M. and Apley, J. (1951). Growing pains. *Arch. Dis. Child.*, **26**, 134–40.
7. Apley, J. and MacKeith, R. C. (1968). *The Child and His Symptoms*, 2nd ed. Oxford: Blackwell.

8. Mattsson, A. and Weisberg, I. (1970). Behavioural reactions to minor illness in preschool children. *Pediatrics*, **46**, 604–10.
9. Shrand, H. (1965). Behaviour changes in sick children nursed at home. *Pediatrics*, **36**, 604.
10. Arlow, J. (1972). The only child. *Psychoanal. Quart.*, **41**, 507.
11. Flugel, J. C. (1921). *The Psycho-analytic Study of the Family*. London: Hogarth Press.
12. Seidenberg, R. and Papathomopoulos, E. (1966). Daughters who tend their fathers: a literary survey. In: *The Psychoanalytic Study of Society*, Vol. 2, pp. 135–60. New York: Int. Univ. Press.
13. Spencer, H. (1864). *Principles of Sociology*. New York: Appleton (1925).
14. Benedek, T. (1959). Parenthood as a developmental phase. *J. Am. Psychoanal. Assoc.*, **7**, 389–417.
15. Marmor, J. (1953). Orality in the hysterical personality. *J. Am. Psychoanal. Assoc.*, **1**, 656–71.
16. Schilder, P. (1950). *The Image and Appearance of the Human Body*. New York: Int. Univ. Press.
17. Freud, S. (1905). Fragment of an Analysis of a Case of Hysteria. In: *The Standard Edition*, Vol. VII. London: Hogarth Press (1955).
18. Bonnard, A. (1957). *Testificatory Gestures of Children*. (Lecture.) Chapel Hill, N.C.: Univ. North Carolina Press.
19. Fenichel, O. (1945). *The Psychoanalytic Theory of Neurosis*. New York: Norton.
20. Abse, D. W. (1971). *Speech and Reason*. Charlottsville, Va.: Univ. Press of Virginia; Bristol: Wright.
21. Hollingshead, A. B. and Redlich, F. C. (1958). *Social Class and Mental Illness: A Community Study*. New York: Wiley.
22. Charcot, J. M. (1873). *Leçons sur les Maladies du Système Nerveux*. Paris: Delahaye.
23. Moebius, P. J. (1894). Über Astasie–Abasie. In: *Neurologische Beiträge*, Vol. 1. Leipzig: Meiner, Barth.

CHAPTER 6

Neurosis, Psychosis and Borderline States

Neurosis and Psychosis

The following fragment of a case history will illuminate the starting point of a neurosis:

Case 35. A patient presented himself for psychiatric interview with the complaint that he could not concentrate on his work adequately, and that he suffered from feelings of tension by day and disturbance of sleep at night. A dentist by profession, involved as an assistant in a busy practice, he amplified his account by stating that often during the day his concentration on work was disturbed by a train of thought accompanied by a series of mental images. The intrusive train of thought, suffused with unpleasant affect, essentially consisted of the question whether life was worth while. He then felt doubtful about the answer. Soon his mind was occupied by an image of a locked door that he would unlock with a key only to be confronted by an image of another locked door which again he fancied he opened, only to be confronted again with a locked door, and so on. Usually he counted five such doors and broke off the series with the last unlocked, following which he experienced a definitive feeling of ill-being and disinterest in his immediate task. The patient said that he felt that these ideas and images were 'quite silly', but they obtruded themselves against his will and he sometimes feared he was 'going mad'. Later work with this patient disclosed that the images symbolized a series of obstructions that he had had to surmount in his progress through life.

He had had to contend with opposition from his father in going to the university. Later he had had to surmount the difficulty of lack of money to make his way through dental school. As a consequence of this he had been delayed in the school before he went on to take the final qualifying examinations. After this he had found it necessary to enlist in the Army, and it was with great relief that he eventually found himself demobilized. In attempting then to establish himself in civilian practice, by necessity he had taken a position as assistant, though his desire was to be his own master in individual private practice. However, owing to family responsibilities, he now found himself, after two years of this, unable to proceed to risk the final step—the realization of his ambition. During many discussions of the series of frustrations, and his recent further discouragement, he came to ventilate much anger. He ranted and railed against family responsibilities, his chief, and impeding social and economic forces. The symptoms, including the thoughts and images abated.

Thus a frank neurosis, in this instance an obsessional neurosis, followed frustration, with symptoms that directly showed the patient's emotional disturbance or else indirectly represented (symbolized) his feelings of frustration. Other neuroses, and functional psychoses also, have their *starting point in frustration*, however this may be brought about, whether by gross difficulties in external reality, or because of the pressure of strongly charged wishes which, by their very nature, cannot be satisfied; sometimes the frustration is brought about by a combination of difficulties in reality and the pressure of wishes which in themselves are difficult to satisfy in usual circumstances. Frustration is the common starting point of a frank psychosis in some people and of a frank neurosis in others.

We have noted that in conversion hysteria there may be bland affect—*la belle indifférence*—where the defence in conversion is quite consolidated. However, in anxiety-hysteria or phobia, anxiety may be intense, often limited to the phobic situation but sometimes more diffuse. These cases are in many respects intermediate between conversion hysterias and obsessive compulsive neuroses. In the case just briefly described anxiety was kept within limits by means of isolation of affect, and reaction-formation also supported the repression of resentment and anger prior to psychotherapy. It is evident that this patient came for treatment because he understood that he was sick. Unlike the conversion hysteric who also pronounces himself sick but in his body, this patient knew that his own mind was disturbed, and that this was responsible for his diminished capacity to work and to enjoy himself. In neurosis in general the patient knows that he is suffering from a sickness, whereas in psychotic disturbance such *objective insight* may be absent. In this neurotic disturbance, the patient was also quickly capable in psychotherapeutic work of developing *psychodynamic* insight (Schilder, 1938[1]). He was, for example, easily able to appreciate the significance of the intrusive images which he had previously regarded as 'quite silly' when the relationship between them and his account of his frustrations was pointed out. Of course, this matter of insight is one of degree and depth. It is in general the case that the patient suffering neurosis retains a greater degree of objective insight than the sufferer from psychosis. It is also generally the case that such patients are more readily amenable in psychotherapy and have the capacity to understand how their conflicts are represented in their symptoms by developing psychodynamic insight. In contrast, here is a vignette to depict the plight of a patient suffering from a major psychosis.

Case 36. A patient confined within a mental hospital periodically showed disorder in his behaviour; this occurred whenever anyone came into mildly forceful bodily contact with him, even in a friendly and playful way. On these occasions the patient would suddenly become violent and assaultive, though he otherwise conducted himself quietly. When this problem was explored, it was found that the patient believed that his body was not composed of the usual human substances but was compounded of a glass-like substitute. As a result of this, the patient reasoned, he could not bear the usual stresses engendered by forcible contact with other people without danger of his body breaking into pieces. Consequently, if anyone brushed against him he became acutely fearful and excited and would run away, and sometimes he would hurl nearby articles at the supposed offender. The false belief or delusion concerning his body chemistry distorted reality to such an extent that his reactivity or behavioural response under some conditions was decidedly eccentric, and made others think of him as dangerous and requiring supervision and restraint.

In psychosis there is often a gross distortion of reality to an extent not found in neurotic disturbance. This patient was lacking in objective insight. He did not think that his mind was in anyway disturbed; on the contrary, he felt that his enemies had chemically engineered a change in his body that made him vulnerable to quite slight injuries, and that he needed to take elaborate precautions in order to survive. It is notable that the hypochondriacal concerns here take a bizarre form, unlike the morbid body image distortion exhibited in conversion hysteria. Study of such cases has revealed, among other dynamic and genetic factors, pronounced homosexual urges which are consciously quite unacceptable (Freud, 1911[2]). This patient's delusion crystallized his feelings of being vulnerable to sexual excitation by bodily contact with other men, his fantasies and fears of this, and his need to defend himself against homosexual stimulation. Of course, in this regard he possessed no psychodynamic insight; the very thought of homo-erotism was so abhorrent that he could in no way connect it with himself. The delusion was a device whereby the homosexual danger was disguised in such a way that he could find a reason to keep himself away from contact with others, and that, in the event of such contact occurring none the less, he could vent his fury. Freud (1911)[2] explored the psychopathology of such paranoid conditions in the autobiography of a former judge of the appeal court in Dresden, Daniel Paul Schreber, who detailed a florid delusional system in an obvious attempt to deny his homosexuality. The denial formula of 'I do not love him, I hate him' was transformed to 'He hates me' by means of unconscious disowning projection and reversal. This was further developed by rationalizations to the effect 'I hate him because he hates and persecutes me'.

One difficulty in establishing a workable transference relationship with many of those patients suffering from psychotic disturbance is their withdrawal from reality on a massive scale. In neurotic disturbance there is no such massive withdrawal. The frustrations encountered in real life are met by withdrawal from it into a world of fantasy which becomes moulded in a way that attempts gratification of the inner needs of the patient. Such attempts are met with opposition, however, from partial personality systems in conflict with these particular inner needs, so that the reconstructions become complex. Here again, of course, the withdrawal, like the distortion of reality which accompanies or follows it, needs to be appraised in respect of its degree and persistence. For instance, in regard to degree, the day-dreams of the adolescent comprising his erotic and ambitious fantasies may to a considerable extent be disconnected from his contemporary reality, but they might have connection with real future possibilities; and in regard to persistence, they may only temporarily disconnect him from active participation in the real world. Dreams often show an extreme degree of disconnection from reality, for they occur in sleep, which is a rhythmic but none the less massive withdrawal from the outer world. However, the neurotic sleeper awakes to adjust to the contingencies of real life; whereas the withdrawal from and distortion of reality of the psychotic persists during wakefulness.

Corresponding to the much more considerable scope of the loss of foothold in reality, certain symptom complexes occur in psychotic disorder which are not present in neurosis. These are delusions, hallucinations, illusions, generalized automatizations, language disorder, incongruities of affective expression and ideation, and severe affective alterations (elation, depression). Usually several of these symptoms occur together and the distinctive symptom complex or clinical picture provides the psychiatrist with the most proximate differentiating feature of the patient's illness. It is the purpose here, however, to emphasize the central importance of the persistent and severe disturbance of the sense of reality which characterizes psychosis, and which is reflected in the clinical manifestations, whether the psychosis is of organic reaction type or so-called 'functional type'.

In his book on the group of schizophrenias Bleuler (1911)[3] wrote:

> However, schizophrenia is characterized by a very peculiar alteration of the relation between the patient's inner life and the external world. The inner life assumes pathological predominance (autism) ... The most severe schizophrenias, who have no more contact with the outside world, live in a world of their own. They have encased themselves with the desires and wishes (which they consider fulfilled) or occupy themselves with the trials and tribulations of their persecutory ideas; they have cut themselves off as much as possible from any contact with the external world. This detachment from reality, together with the relative or absolute predominance of the inner life, we term autism. In less severe cases, the affective and logical significance of reality is only somewhat damaged. The patients are still able to move about in the external world but neither evidence nor logic has any influence on their hopes and delusions. Everything which is in contradiction to their complexes simply does not exist for their thinking and feeling.

As Bleuler, stresses, autism is not necessarily easy to detect. Sometimes even severely and chronically schizophrenic patients show quite good contact with their environment with regard to the relatively impersonal aspects of everyday life. Bleuler was also aware of the paradox of schizophrenia, the fluctuating attention to the environment, despite some appearances to the contrary:

> Particularly in the beginning of their illness, these patients quite consciously shun any contact with reality because their affects are so powerful that they must avoid everything which might arouse their emotions. The apathy towards the outer world is then a secondary one springing from a hypertrophied sensitivity.

Many studies have shown how much and in what ways the personal environment deeply affects the psychotic patient; the studies of Stanton and Schwartz (1954)[4] and of Freeman, Cameron, and McGhie (1958)[5] especially demonstrate the influence of nurses and attendants.

Freud (1933)[6] has familiarized us with the concept of the ego which struggles to mediate between the claims of id, super-ego, and outer world. All three masters need to be served simultaneously, and it is this situation which leads us to feel the 'difficulties of life'. The most important difference between neurosis and psychosis is a psychogenetic one. Neurosis is the result of conflict between the ego and the id, whereas psychosis is the analogous outcome of conflict between ego and outer world. In neurosis, in the service of super-ego and outer reality, the ego battles with the id. In psychosis the ego ruptures relationship with the outer world and then attempts a distorted reconstruction of it. The ego is overwhelmed by unconscious forces in psychosis and is thus torn from reality in the beginning (Freud, 1924[7, 8]). However, even this genetic difference really applies only to a decisive crisis. For example, in *Case*

36 the delusion of being composed of a glass-like substance, based on the patient's struggle with homosexuality, was preceded by a protracted intrapsychic conflict in which the ego attempted to mediate without recourse to psychosis.

Against the background of this short discussion of some of the salient differential features of neurosis and psychosis some qualifying statements are required. A patient suffering some forms of psychotic depression may preserve objective insight to the extent that he realizes that he is suffering from sickness of mind, however much objective insight is impaired in other respects. Then again, remarkable flashes of psychodynamic insight are sometimes evinced by schizophrenic patients. Indeed, residual healthy ego function in psychotic disorder may fluctuate, so that at different times, even within minutes, insight is alternately present and absent. This kind of bewildering shift only becomes understandable as dissociation in the form of gross splitting comes to be seen as a conspicuous characteristic of the schizophrenic personality. Similarly in manic-depressive psychosis at one hour of the day, the patient may discuss his illness with objective insight, and at the next hour, overwhelmed by depressive feelings, he is self-rebuking and denigrates himself on the basis of trivial events, with delusions of unworthiness, of bodily disease and of poverty.

These considerations serve to emphasize the need for close and prolonged observation and study of many psychiatric patients before diagnosis is established. The old psychiatric adage 'rest them, feed them, observe them' retains its force with regard to patients newly admitted to hospital with mental disturbance. On the basis of our observations we have to rely on inferences concerned with some of the dynamics briefly discussed above. Especially important are the extent and depth of regression, particularly as this is reflected in the status of object relations. In psychosis with the deeper regression there is severe instinctual defusion and the predominating deployment of primitive defences such as projection, introjection and denial.

At the end of Chapter 5 it was noted that Moebius (1894)[9] had maintained that under some circumstances 'everyone is a little hysterical.' Von Feuchtersleben (1838)[10] had previously gone further in his opinion that everyone 'harbours the seed of insanity'; he later (1845)[11] used the term 'psychosis' to denote disorder of personality. Almost 60 years later Dubois (1904)[12] wrote of 'psychoneuroses' to denote those personality disturbances which he found amenable to persuasive psychotherapy. Thus in general, historically, the differentiation of the psychoneuroses from psychotic disturbance was effected on the basis of accessibility in a treatment process that emphasized an appeal to the patient's reason, as well as utilizing suggestion. Nowadays, on account of increasingly frequent recognition of borderline states, the sharp differentiation between psychoneurosis and psychosis is giving way to an assessment of the patient's mental illness in both dimensions, including a scrutiny of his ego assets, especially his capacity to relate in one way or another to the therapist.

Borderline States

It was, and is, a common experience of psychiatrists and psychoanalysts in this century, since the well-known classification of disorders of personality functioning into the two dimensions of psychotic and psychoneurotic, to see and treat in open sanatoria or in office practice, many patients whom they regard as not fitting into either large category satisfactorily, yet seeming to fit into both in part. The categories of psychotic and neurotic are not precisely circumscribed by boundary limits but are nominated by central criteria; not by what these categories strictly exclude, but what they include. Often borderline states and personality disorders have been previously diagnosed as severely psychoneurotic and have been found to have been refractory in treatment. Many patients previously diagnosed as suffering from severe obsessive-compulsive disorder, some victims of intractable phobias and others exhibiting the major symptoms of hysteria, when examined more adequately and more frequently over a longer period of time, reveal themselves as involved in psychotic distortions and aberrations of conduct. It may be a question of a severe degree of depression and suicidal preoccupation, or of the extent and ominousness of paranoid trends, or of the perils, social or physical, repeatedly courted by inappropriate actions. Freud (1913)[13] alerted psychoanalysts to the possibility of psychosis sometimes even underlying a psychoneurotic picture of lenity in his warning:

> Often enough, when one sees a case of neurosis with hysterical or obsessional symptoms, mild in character and of short duration (just the sort of case, that is, which one would regard as suitable for the treatment) a doubt which must not be overlooked arises whether the case may not be one of incipient dementia praecox, so-called [schizophrenia according to Bleuler: paraphrenia, as I prefer to call it], and may not sooner or later develop well marked signs of this disease.

Knight (1954)[14] pointed out that as a result of various combinations of the factors of constitutional tendencies and of traumatic events involving disturbed human relationships, 'the ego of the borderline patient is labouring badly'. Ego functions of integration, concept formation, judgement, realistic planning, and of defending against eruption into consciousness of id impulses and their fantasy elaborations, are gravely impaired. Other ego functions, such as conventional adaptations and superficial maintenance of personal relationships, may exhibit varying degrees of intactness. Still others, such as memory, calculation and habitual routines, may seem unimpaired.

The neurotic defences and relatively intact adaptive ego functions may be misleading without repeated, and more thoroughgoing psychiatric interviews concerned with the patient's total ego functioning. The face-to-face psychiatric interview provides a relatively structured situation in which conventional devices of avoidance, evasion, denial, minimization, changing the subject, concealment of emotion, may be deployed relatively easily by patients who seek help but do not communicate fully their strong feelings towards relatives or friends, and their autistic preoccupations. In the course of several interviews, Knight[14] cites certain findings: occasional blocking, peculiarities of word usage, obliviousness to obvious implications, contaminations of idioms, arbitrary inferences, inappropriate affect and suspicion-laden behaviour and questions, as clues to an unwitting betrayal of ego impairment of psychotic degree. In addition to these microscopic evidences of ego weakness in respect to id eruptions in borderline cases, Knight outlines macroscopic manifestations: lack of concern about his life predicament, grossly inappropriate treatment proposals, multiple complaints viewed as due to malevolent influences, lack of achievement over a long period accompanied by some degree of disintegration of self-care, vagueness in planning, bizarre dreams with insufficient contrast between dreaming and waking experiences.

Knight[14] sometimes utilized the free-association interview as a diagnostic tool with the patient on the couch, changing the fairly well-structured situation of the face-to-face interview into a relatively unstructured one, so the patient could not rely on his usual defensive and conventionally adaptive devices to maintain his front. Borderline patients under these conditions are likely to show in bolder relief the various microscopic and macroscopic signs of schizophrenic illness. They may block completely with mounting anxiety; or their verbalization may show a high degree of autistic content, with many peculiarities of expression; or their inappropriate affect may become more obvious. Knight[14] writes:

> The diagnosis is aided by the couch-free association technique, but the experience may be definitely anti-therapeutic for the patient. Definitive evidence of psychotic thinking may be produced at the expense of humiliating and disintegrating exposure of the patient's naked pathology.

It is evident that clinical judgement might foreclose resort to such a free-association tactic. Indeed, haste should be avoided in the quest to reach an accurate diagnosis. In this quest, however, psychodiagnostic testing can be valuable. The clinical use of projective techniques which are geared primarily to the exploration of the patient's inner world facilitate psychodynamic assessment when borderline personality disorder is suspected.

REFERENCES

1. Schilder, P. (1938). *Psychotherapy*. New York: Norton.
2. Freud, S. (1911). Psychoanalytic Notes upon an Autobiographical Account of a Case of Paranoia (Dementia Paranoides). In: *The Standard Edition*, Vol. XII. London: Hogarth Press (1953).
3. Bleuler, E. (1911). *Dementia Praecox or the Group of Schizophrenias*. New York: Int. Univ. Press (1950).
4. Stanton, A. H. and Schwartz, M. S. (1954). *The Mental Hospital*. New York: Basic Books.
5. Freeman, T., Cameron, J. L. and McGhie, A. (1958). *Chronic Schizophrenia*. London: Tavistock.
6. Freud, S. (1933). The dissection of the mental personality. *New Introductory Lectures on Psycho-analysis*. In: *The Standard Edition*, Vol. XXII. London: Hogarth Press (1953).
7. Freud, S. (1924). Neurosis and Psychosis. In: *The Standard Edition*, Vol. XIX. London: Hogarth Press (1953).
8. Freud, S. (1924). The Loss of Reality in Neurosis and Psychosis. In: *The Standard Edition*, Vol. XIX. London: Hogarth Press (1953).
9. Moebius, P. J. (1894). Über Astasie–Abasie. In: *Neurologische Beiträge*, Vol. 1. Leipzig: Meiner, Barth.

10. von Feuchtersleben, E. F. (1838). *Zur Dialetik der Seele*, 23rd ed. Vienna: Gerold (1861).
11. von Feuchtersleben, E. F. (1845). *The Principles of Medical Psychology*. London: Sydenham Society (1847).
12. Dubois, P. (1904). *The Psychic Treatment of Mental Disorders*. New York: Funk and Wagnalls (1909).
13. Freud, S. (1913). Further Recommendations in the Technique of Psycho-analysis: I. On Beginning the Treatment. In: *The Standard Edition*, Vol. XII. London: Hogarth Press (1953).
14. Knight, R. P. (1954). Borderline states. In: *Psycho-analytic Psychiatry and Psychology* (ed. Knight, R. P.), Vol. 1. New York: Int. Univ. Press (1956).

CHAPTER 7

The Hysterical, Borderline and Narcissistic Personalities

The Hysterical Personality

Human beings interact, communicate and form relationships, and their ways of doing so reveal enduring patterns of perceiving and thinking about their surroundings and themselves. These patterns in an individual constitute his long-term character traits and they are exhibited in his particular social reference group and more widely in the society in which he dwells. When these character traits are inflexible and maladaptive and cause substantial impairment in social, educational, occupational and sexual adjustment, and subjective distress in consequence, they constitute a personality disorder.

The second edition of the *Diagnostic and Statistical Manual of Mental Disorders* of the American Psychiatric Association (DSM II, 1968)[1] makes the following behavioural observations concerning 'Hysterical Personality (Histrionic Personality Disorder)':

> These behavioural patterns are characterized by excitability, emotional instability, overreactivity, and self-dramatization. This self-dramatization is always attention seeking and often seductive, whether or not the patient is aware of its purpose. These personalities are also immature, self-centered, often vain, and usually dependent on others (p. 43).

In the third edition of the *Diagnostic and Statistical Manual of Mental Disorders* (DSM III, 1980)[2] the terse remarks of DSM II are considerably amplified as follows:

Histrionic Personality Disorder
The essential feature is a personality disorder in which there are overly dramatic, reactive and intensely expressed behaviour and characteristic disturbances in interpersonal relationships.

Individuals with this disorder are lively and dramatic and are always drawing attention to themselves. They are prone to exaggeration and often act out a role, such as the 'victim' or the 'princess', without being aware of it.

Behaviour is overly reactive and intensely expressed. Minor stimuli give rise to emotional excitability, such as irrational, angry outbursts or tantrums. Individuals with this disorder crave novelty, stimulation and excitement and quickly become bored with normal routines.

Interpersonal relationships show characteristic disturbances. Initially, people with this disorder are frequently perceived as shallow and lacking genuineness, though superficially charming and appealing. They are often quick to form friendships; but once a relationship is established they can become demanding, egocentric and inconsiderate; manipulative suicidal threats, gestures or attempts may be made; there may also be a constant demand for reassurance because of feelings of helplessness and dependency. In some cases both patterns are present in the same relationship. These people's actions are frequently inconsistent, and may be misinterpreted by others.

Such individuals are typically attractive and seductive. They attempt to control the opposite sex or enter into a dependent relationship. Flights into romantic fantasy are common; in both sexes overt behaviour often is a caricature of femininity. The actual quality of their sexual relationships is variable. Some individuals are promiscuous; others, naive and sexually unresponsive; but still others have apparently normal sexual adjustment.

In other classifications this category is termed Hysterical Personality.

Associated features: Individuals with this disorder often experience periods of intense dissatisfaction and a variety of dysphoric moods, usually related to obvious changes in external circumstances, such as a breakup with a lover. They may make suicidal gestures or attempts.

Usually these individuals show little interest in intellectual achievement and careful, analytic thinking, though they are often creative and imaginative.

Individuals with this disorder tend to be impressionable and easily influenced by others or by fads. They are apt to be overtly trusting of others, suggestible and show an initially positive response to any strong authority figure who they think can provide a magical solution for their problems. Though they adopt convictions strongly and readily, their judgement is not firmly rooted, and they often play hunches.

Frequent complaints of poor health, such as weakness or headaches, or subjective feelings of depersonalization may be present. During periods of extreme stress, there may be transient psychotic symptoms of insufficient severity or duration to warrant an additional diagnosis.

When the disorder is present in men, it is sometimes associated with a homosexual arousal pattern.

Impairment: Interpersonal relations are usually stormy and ungratifying. In extreme cases there is gross inability to function.

Complications: A common complication is Substance Use Disorder, particularly in women. Additional complications include Major Depression, Dysthymic Disorder, Brief Reactive Psychosis, Conversion Disorder, and Somatization Disorder.

Predisposing factors: No information.

Prevalence and sex ratio: The disorder is apparently common, and diagnosed far more frequently in females that in males.

Familial pattern: The disorder is apparently more common among family members than in the general population.

Differential diagnosis: In Somatization Disorder complaints of physical illness dominate the clinical picture, although histrionic features are common. In many cases Somatization Disorder and Histrionic Personality Disorder coexist.

Borderline Personality Disorder is also often present; in such cases both diagnoses should be made.

Diagnostic criteria for Histrionic Personality Disorder

The following are characteristic of the individual's current and long-term functioning, are not limited to episodes of illness, and cause either significant impairment in social or occupational functioning or subjective distress.

A. Behaviour that is overly dramatic, reactive and intensely expressed, as indicated by at least three of the following:

    (1) self-dramatization, e.g., exaggerated expression of emotions;
    (2) incessant drawing of attention to oneself;
    (3) craving for activity and excitement;

    (4) overreaction to minor events;

    (5) irrational, angry outbursts or tantrums.

B. Characteristic disturbances in interpersonal relationships as indicated by at least two of the following:

    (1) perceived by others as shallow and lacking genuineness, even if superficially warm and charming;

    (2) egocentric, self-indulgent, and inconsiderate of others;

    (3) vain and demanding;

    (4) dependent, helpless, constantly seeking reassurance;

    (5) prone to manipulative suicidal threats, gestures, or attempts.

In DSM III above, the rubric 'predisposing factors' is followed by the remarkable statement: 'No information'. We have already discussed the influences in the family which predispose towards the later development of hysterical personality, with a proneness under stress to take flight into illness (Chapter 5). These influences were briefly considered in the two categories of 'love overload' and 'love deprivation'. As mentioned, often enough there is a paradoxical mixture of such influences. Thus in cases of adult conversion hysteria developing out of a matrix of hysterical personality disorder, there is frequently a background childhood situation of being well-nigh ignored by parents when physically well and cared for with excessive anxiety when physically sick. As discussed here, the predisposition to acquire hysteria is heightened by traumatic experiences in the early years of childhood. These experiences consist of an array of pathogenic factors, any one of which, or several together, culminate in an adult propensity to deploy hysterical modes of defence and maladaptation under stress. Sometimes there is a discrete trauma which sows the seed for the later development of hysteria, for example sexual overstimulation, sometimes with actual seduction, or sudden loss of a parent, or parental surrogate, during or following the Oedipal period. Such a loss at this time often generates fantasies concerned with fulfilment of and punishment for rivalrous wishes, sometimes with an intensified identification with the deceased; sometimes there is a lifelong search for replacement of the loss. Krohn 1978[3] writes:

> The timing of an influence in terms of the psychosexual modality, the balance between self—and object—cathexis, and the flexibility of the ego, all work together to determine whether this or that trauma, this or that set of regular environmental pressures, will prove to be pathogenic.

Thus to revert to the example of the child's experience of lack of solicitude when well and oversolicitude when sick, we find such parental behaviour patterns have often been preceded by an earlier very overprotective anxious coddling during the toddler phase which results in an impediment in the developmental line from egocentricity to companionship (Anna Freud[4]).

Commensurate with the powerful influence of parental rearing policies and attitudes, heredo-constitutional factors are of importance in predisposition to develop hysterical personality and hysterical neurosis, as was emphasized by Charcot and numerous other investigators (*see* Chapter 1). Though the evidence is against the existence of significant genetic factors *specific* to hysterical neurosis, there is evidence for their role in the pathogenesis of abnormal personalities, including those psychopathic personalities who are at increased risk of developing hysterical symptoms (hysterical psychopaths, as designated by Karl Menninger 1938[5]). The wavering confines of what is to be designated 'psychopathic personality' certainly include some features which overlap with those of hysterical personality disorder, as well as the common feature of antisocial behaviour. Schulsinger (1972)[6] included these within the 'psychopathic spectrum' in his adoption study of psychopathy. According to Cloninger, Reich and Guze (1975)[7] hysteria and sociopathy are part of the same disease for which they claim a polygenic inheritance. James Shields (1982)[8] has described several genetic investigations beginning with that of the Estonian psychiatrist Kraulis (1931)[9] and including the studies mentioned above, during this past half-century.

Charcot (1892)[10] emphasized the role of heredo-constitutional factors in the pathogenesis of hysterical neurosis and might thus have proceeded to a detailed investigation of the inborn characteristics of the personality of those suffering hysterical symptoms. However, he directed his interest to the classification of symptoms and the differentiation of hysteria from organic neurological disease, so that apart from drawing attention to the unstable nervous system and the exaggerated suggestibility of those suffering hysterical symptoms, he did not offer a more detailed analysis of the behavioural or anamnestic characteristics of his hysterical patients. At this time, the known aetiological field consisted of constitutional factors and of environmental factors which were not especially related to early emotional transactions in childhood. The important role of the early personal environment was largely hidden from the view of clinicians before Freud's investigations. Freud was in fact also impressed with the importance of heredo-constitutional factors in the aetiology of the neuroses, but in unravelling the meaning of symptoms in terms of the patient's experience, he penetrated the amnesia for events in early life, and recognized also the crucial formative importance in personality development of those early happenings. More attention thus came to be paid to the personality characteristics of patients suffering from symptom neuroses.

The first psychoanalytic contribution to characterology was Freud's paper in 1908[11] on the anal character. As it became apparent that the optimal goal of therapy went beyond the relief of symptoms to resolving the need for symptom formation, psychoanalytic characterology increasingly assumed clinical importance. Reich (1933),[12] in his book on character analysis, attempted to depict the character structures in symptom neuroses, including hysteria. He described the behaviour of the hysterical character as obviously sexualized, including coquetry in women and softness and effeminacy in men. Even locomotion, he considered, was sexualized so that movements are soft, graceful and sensually provocative. As the sexual behaviour came closer to attaining its apparent goal, apprehensiveness became evident. Reich also described unpredictability, strong suggestibility, sharp disappointment reactions, imaginativeness, lack of conviction, compliance readily giving way to depreciation and disparagement, compulsive need to be loved, overdependency on others for approval, powerful capacity for dramatization, and somatic compliance. He attempted to explain these features as being determined by fixation in the early genital phase of infantile development with incestuous attachment, but as we have noted (Chapter 2), Marmor (1954)[13] and others have with more cogency related some of these features to pronounced orality in the hysterical personality.

Chodoff and Lyons (1958)[14] challenge the close relationship adduced by others between conversion phenomena and the hysterical personality. Of 17 patients with unequivocal conversion reactions, only 5 satisfied the criteria (similar to those of Reich's description above) they laid down for the diagnosis of the hysterical personality. They therefore concur with Kretschmer (1926)[15] and Bowlby (1940)[16] in the opinion that conversion reactions do not occur, by any means, solely in patients who present the characteristics of the designated hysterical personality. They suggest that instead of conversion hysteria there may be substituted one of the three more precisely defined diagnoses: conversion reaction, hysterical personality, or hysterical personality with conversion reaction, whichever may be appropriate. In the 1968 edition of the *Diagnostic and Statistical Manual of Mental Disorders* (DSM II), authorized by the Council of the American Psychiatric Association, 'Hysterical Neurosis, Conversion-Type', 'Hysterical Neurosis, Dissociative-Type', and 'Hysterical Personality (Histrionic Personality Disorder)', are separately listed—a manoeuvre which enables adequate classification without at any time separating conversion reaction from its venerable association with hysteria, but with the option of either separating conversion-type hysteria from the hysterical personality, or citing them together. As noted above, DSM III, 1980, also acknowledges that 'in many cases, Somatization Disorder and Histrionic Personality Disorder coexist', thus also allowing for the same option though in tampered terminology.

In regard to Chodoff and Lyons' divorce of conversion reactions from 'hysterical personality', the following comments are appropriate. Freud (1916)[17] noted that instances of neurotic illness fall into a complementary series within which the two factors of type of personality and adverse experience (discussed as the fixations of the libido and frustration) are represented in such a manner that if there is more of the one, there is less of the other. As stated above, some of the features of the hysterical personality belong to derivatives of pregenital points of fixation, and where these are absent it might be expected that the aetiological role of the actual conflict would be more emphatic. Secondly, while the predisposition to acquire hysterical illness is built up very largely from undue emotional attachment to one or both parents, with difficulty of later displacement of this attachment, the dependent and other correlative patterns of personality are often not so simple and obvious. To understand deviations from such a pattern it is necessary to study the total repertoire of unconscious defences and to take into account that the evident achievements in external adjustments and independence may show the marks of overcompensation. Basically, such patients remains unconsciously dependently fixated on the infantile object (in fact or in fantasy), and are vigorously defending themselves against this fixation. We previously noted in Chapter 4 (*Case* 18), an example of such counterphobic overcompensation which may be briefly summarized here:

Following enlistment in the army, the patient, aged 30, developed pains in the stomach. Later, he began to suffer trouble with his eyes, especially when riding his motorcycle. He could not keep them open and complained they kept 'screwing up', which, indeed, they did. He was of a very aggressive character-type. Prior to enlistment, he often performed in fairgrounds on the 'wall of death', demonstrating his skill and daring on a motorcycle, and was proud to be earning much more money than his father. He had always been a dare-devil, amateur motorcycling being his hobby from an early age. His usual employment was that of a butcher, and he was the mainstay of the home. He had never taken up a sustained relationship with any woman other than his mother, to whom he remained closely attached. In discussions he made it clear that he was ready for anything in the army and could perform wonders on his motorcycle—were it not for the spasms of his eyes.

In this case, both the unconscious underlying overdependency and passive homosexual strivings were vigorously countermanded by character defences. These gave an appearance of remarkable and heroic virility and independence, with others depending upon him, prior to his separation from his mother and the onset of symptoms, including conversion reaction.

Brody and Sata 1967[18] had suggested prior to DSM III that a semantic solution could be achieved by using the term 'histrionic personality' to describe that type of hysterical personality background identified by Reich and by Chodoff and Lyons. They gave the following useful clinical description:

> The people described in this manner are vain, egocentric individuals displaying labile, and excitable, but shallow affectivity. Their dramatic, attention-seeking, and histrionic behaviour may encompass lying and pseudologia phantastica. They are conscious of sex and appear provocative, but they may be frigid and are dependently demanding in interpersonal situations. They have a life-long history of seriously disturbed relationships with others. The loss of a parent through divorce, desertion, or death is often reported.
> Histrionic personalities under stress may exhibit impaired reality testing, intensive fantasy production, and convictions about the motives of others bordering on delusion. In moments of repose, they are characteristically vague and imprecise about emotionally significant matters. They cannot express their inner feelings with accuracy and often utilize bodily action for communicative purposes.
> Although histrionic personalities may exhibit conversion reactions, the latter can occur in association with almost any type of character structure. Histrionic character features occur more frequently in Western society among women. They are, indeed, considered feminine by our societal standards, and male histrionic characters are frequently described in this way.

In a transcultural survey of 21 female patients, 7 from San Francisco, 7 from London and 7 from Copenhagen, Blinder (1966)[19] found that they all exhibited the characteristics of hysterical personality adumbrated above. A picture emerged of a group of women, often the youngest children in their families, born of mothers who seem to have had scant time or talent for serving as models for identification and of fathers even less able to interact favourably with their growing daughters. These women exhibited a significant number of persistent childhood neurotic traits, and their medical histories revealed an uncommonly high incidence of abdominal surgical procedures. Particularly in the sexual sphere, they were strikingly underdeveloped or inhibited.

Blinder was impressed with their superficially cheerful childlike manner, their emotional lability, their dramatic use of overstatement, or of stoic understatement when this could be used for dramatic effect, the incongruence of their verbal communication with their actual behaviour, their emphasis on feminine characteristics to the point of caricature, and their widespread use of denial.

Both in the East and West there are in fact 'histrionic personality disorders' suffered by men and women who are liable to conversion-type hysterical neurosis. However, there are other character structures not so well or so frequently discussed in the literature, and the soldier described briefly above is an example. Such men do not exhibit 'softness and effeminacy' as described by Reich. On the contrary, character traits of persistent insistence on being the strong man, of exaggerated exhibition of sadistic masculinity, are anamnestically revealed prior to hysterical symptom formation. It is indeed remarkable that Reich (1933)[12] omitted a discussion of the consolidated reactive defence (including identification with the male aggressor) against unconscious feminine identification of these men who are liable to hysterical attacks and symptoms. Some of them, though by no means the majority, pursue women vigorously, are hyperactive, even athletic, sexually, thus feverishly countermanding castration anxiety and remaining busy a large part of their time constructing and reconstructing a 'he-man' image for themselves, and to purvey to others.

Many women liable to hysterical attacks and symptoms are quite overtly inhibited sexually. On account of deep-seated guilt and anxiety, related to incestuous fantasies which continue to saturate their sexual strivings unconsciously, they strenuously avoid sexual provocation and sexual contact, dress drably, and far from being aggressively exhibitionistic, are excessively modest and masochistic in their style of life. When symptom formation occurs, the sexual symbolic references are ample.

It will be recalled that the same Oedipus who eventually killed his father and married his mother began life by being exposed on a mountain, deprived of maternal care. While the final stages of the Oedipus drama are more representative of one broad category of hysterical character disorder and neurosis, one generally accessible to psychoanalysis of relatively limited duration, there is a second broad category for which the beginnings of the legend are more pertinently parabolic. This second broad category contains those with pronounced oral character traits, sometimes also undergirded by severe narcissistic ego disorder. These latter cases may often be better considered as hysteriform borderline personalities. In the course of treatment psychotic problems may become apparent. It has been noted by Reichard (1956)[20] that 2 of the 5 patients reported in the *Studies on Hysteria* showed schizophrenic features. Easser and Lesser (1965)[21] differentiate 'hysteroid' from hysterical characters and especially remark on the painful masochistic elements in the fantasies of these more pregenitally orientated patients. Alan Krohn (1978)[3] contends that the terms 'hysteria' and 'hysterical personality' should be reserved

for relatively mild or moderate forms of neurotic and/or character disturbance, characterized by a relatively intact ego, mild to moderate incapacity to handle life responsibilities, and phallic-Oedipal (as opposed to pregenital) levels of fixation.

He further states:

The recent contributions on the borderline personality strongly suggest that such terms as 'hysteroid' (Easser and Lesser, 1965) and 'hysteriform' (Abse, 1966) be discarded, and that such patients be considered as borderline personalities.

He also points out that the so-called 'hysteroid', or 'hysteriform' personality disorder includes such traits as erratic impulsive behaviour, failure to sustain enduring relationships, feelings of detachment and isolation, paranoia-like trends, primitive fear of being engulfed and overwhelmed, and limited capacity for delay of gratification as well as the dramatic, romantic, sexualized and childish traits of the hysterical personality. The additional characteristics, Krohn insists, reflect profound pervasive differences from the 'true hysteric' (Zetzel, 1968[22]), and describes a personality racked with more severe pathology. Thus he concludes:

> It is confounding to consider them in any way in the same category.

Certainly, there are differences in these two types in their respective capabilities of regulating impulse, maintaining differentiated object represen-tations, and taming primitive affective storms, but not only do they share some characteristics, they also shade one into the other so that I would amplify the descriptive label as 'hysteriform borderline personality disorder' for the more severely afflicted forms.

Mardi Horowitz (1977)[23] emphasizes the disordered perceptual, cognitive and verbal communication patterns of the hysterical personality. Shapiro (1965)[24] and Gardner et al. (1959)[25], sharing the general ego-psychological approach of Hartmann,[26] had earlier put forward the view that individuals possess relatively stable cognitive structures which influence their form or style of ego functioning, whatever their motives or needs. Shapiro (1965) outlined the global perceptual style of processing and organizing information, the impressionistic groupings of constructs and the shallow repertoire of memories utilized by hysterical personalities, a way of being complementary to their regularly deployed defence mechanisms of denial and repression. Besides the 'long-order' patterns of interpersonal relations and the 'medium-order' patterns consisting of the character traits, already noted above, Horowitz (1977)[23] focuses on the 'short-order' patterns of the hysterical patients' information processing style. Within small time intervals, it is possible to observe

> unclear verbal statements, use of language for effects on others rather than for meaning, choice of global rather than specific labels for experience, and shallowness (in the sense of failure to understand ideational implications) ...

He analyses the changes in a hysterical personality during the course of psychoanalytic treatment, adding:

> the cognitive and object-relations point of view of contemporary psychodynamics to classical metapsychological formulations.

He examines changes in style of thought, emotion and defensive process, and changes in inner models of self and others in a representative case. During an analysis of four years, Horowitz's patient learned to attend to details appropriately rather than to attend to wholes overmuch, to pay attention to her own acts rather than to be selectively inattentive to them, and to pick up clues concerning her own and others' motives without being dominated by stimuli relevant to her own wishful and fearful fantasies. In regard to the latter domination, Jung (1906)[27] had pointed out that in both hysteria and schizophrenia, word association reactions are characterized by an abnormally strong complex which the psyche cannot overcome; thinking along the lines dominated by a complex was designated 'katathymic' (Bleuler, 1911[28]).

The representative patient whose case Horowitz chooses to illustrate the cognitive and object-relational issues had lived through the frequently encountered constellation of an early experience of parsimonious nurturance in infancy soon followed by an early turning to the father for narcissistic supplies. Hollender (1971)[29] commented:

> The crucial turning point developmentally is that young girls who become hysterical personalities turn to their fathers or mother's father as substitute mothers.

Tracing this crucial precocious turning away from the mother to the father, Blacker and Tupin (1977[30]) point out that the girl often finds that she can only extract an early sufficient nurturing interest from the father through the exhibition of coy, seductive, flirtatious behaviour. Then as genital sexual strivings and feelings and thoughts being to stir in the nascent Oedipus situation, the anxiety engendered instigates their repression. Yet the coy, seductive, flirtatious, and anxious behaviour persists and is rewarded, resulting in a consolidated split between behaviour and fantasies which remains characteristic. Horowitz maintains that the interaction between a thought style centered on a lack of awareness and core schemata of self and others based upon such adverse experiences of childhood and cognate 'fantasy images' results eventually in the formation of the hysterical personality.

In analysis Horowitz's patient used enactive (bodily) and imaging modes of representation and she inhibited translation of these into words whenever conflictual mental contents were approached. Her enactive representations included body movements indicative of sexual interest, but her awareness of this was quite limited. Horowitz wrote (1977)[23]:

> She did not know she behaved provocatively and could not label her posture, gesture, or facial expression with specific words describing meaning.

The verbal nature of the analytic situation, maintained by the analyst through his lexical help in meeting the implicit demand for translation of experience into words, led to detailed reports, eventually far beyond her habitually vague and global descriptions. Later she was able to reach further clarity concerning her transference experiences which became amenable to transference interpretation. Horowitz gives a vivid account of the modifications and revisions of self-and object-schemata subsequently achieved. The patient was able to approach new experience more rewardingly, particularly her love life, without perceptual distortions subtended by embedded schemata derived from her painful experiences in disturbed relationships with the members of her family. More importantly the defectiveness of her parents as models and mirrors which had interfered so much with her personality development no longer exerted devastating traumatic power. Stereotypic modes of disruption of current relationships in her life-space diminished and she became able to enjoy companionship.

Horowitz thus affords an account of an analysis which reveals the gradual mitigation of such core descriptors of hysterical personality as exaggerated aggressive behaviour, inundating and unstable emotionality, sexual problems, persistent inexpedient obstinacy, inappropriate exhibitionism, excessive egocentricity, habitual and indiscriminate sexual provocativeness and over-dependency in relations with others, in addition to the progressively more adaptive alterations in cognitive style.

Table 7.1 opposite charted by Blacker and Tupin (1977)[30] usefully outlines the diagnostic features of the hysterical personality in both genders. They write:

Not only is there a make-believe quality to the sexual identity of hysterics but there is also a similar 'as if' quality in other aspects of their behaviour. Thus maturity is more apparent that real—a pseudo-adult facade as is suggested by the term child-woman ... There is both a distortion of gender role and a false maturity. The 'little girl' quality of some female hysterics is well recognized. A similar 'little boy' quality in the male hysteric is frequently seen when illness or injury intervenes, and a break occurs in the shell of the counterphobic bravado.

In analysis of the hysteric personality, Zetzel (1973)[31] contended that there were four sub-groups to be considered. The first group, the 'true good hysterics', retain the capacity to recognize and tolerate internal reality and internal conflicts, and to distinguish internal reality from external reality. This is a major criterion of analysability inasmuch as it entails the patient's capacity to perceive the difference between therapeutic alliance and transference neurosis. The second group, the 'potential good hysterics' have a major difficulty in establishing a stable analytic situation; fearful of dependent strivings, they may respond with a flight into health or by plunging into a regressive transference neurosis before a therapeutic alliance can be established. The third group comprises women who present with manifest hysterical symptoms which mask an underlying depressive character structure. The fourth group, the 'so-called good hysterics', consists of women whose social façade masks pregenital and pre-Oedipal developmental failures. Meissner (1973)[31] writes:

The last group of hysterics, Zetzel's 'so-called good hysterics' usually have a floridly hysterical symptomatic picture. In treatment they prove incapable of tolerating a genuine triangular conflict.

They have too a considerable difficulty in establishing the requisite therapeutic alliance for analysis, and in distinguishing it from the transference neurosis. Meissner allows, however, that such patients may profit from psychotherapeutic efforts other than 'traditional psychoanalysis'.

Lazare (1971)[32] pointed out that Zetzel's first group 'the true good hysterics' come from relatively intact families with adequate early mothering whereas, along a spectrum, he finds increasingly chaotic family backgrounds with

Table 7.1

Pseudo-feminine expression	Diagnostic descriptors	Pseudo-masculine expression
Subtle, indirect manipulation, competitive with males, dominant, easily angered, argues, sarcastic, pouts but controlled, provokes guilt in others	Aggression	Direct, threatens others with verbal or physical fights, fights to prove self, bombastic, resists dependency
Poor emotional control, sentimental, romantic, cries easily, behavioural and emotional overreaction, intense emotional response, calms quickly, diffuse, shallow, labile	Emotionality	Impulsive, transient, superficial affect, may deny feelings or be sentimental
Frigid, avoids sexual encounters, surprise at men's response to sexual provocativeness	Sexual problems	Sexual exploitation, Don Juanism, hypermasculine
Stubborn, will not give in on 'rights'–feminine prerogatives	Obstinacy	Stubborn on masculine issues, for example, independence and non-dominance by females
Dress, cosmetics, posture and gait, or any attribute including defects or needs used to attract attention	Exhibitionism	Show of strength, bravery or tolerance of pain, dress attracts attention, flashy cars or gadgets
Own needs first, sensitive to critical remarks, vulnerable to slights	Egocentricity	Self-interest first, body image very important, uses others, vulnerable to slights
Flirtatious, cat-and-mouse games with men, romantic, coy, coquettish	Sexual provocativeness	Flirtatious, frequent affairs of fact or fantasy, conquest important
Protests for independence but rarely acts, may abuse drugs or alcohol	Dependency	Pseudo-hypermasculinity, disabled with relatively minor illnesses and injuries

*From Blacker, K. H. and Tupin, J. P. (1977). Hysteria and Hysterical Structures: Developmental and Social Theories. In: *Hysterical Personality* (ed. Horowitz, M.J.), Chap. 2. New York: Aronson (1977).

mothers who were often absent, seriously depressed and who offered poor models for identification. In the good hysterics, Lazare finds, that the symptoms are more clearly ego-alien, that sexual difficulties are at a genital level and secondary to inhibition, and the behaviour more modulated. They have a history of more success at school, at work, socially and in psychotherapy. He suggests the separation of an hysterical character disorder by recognition of its more pathological object relations, ego-syntonic maladaptive patterns, and more primitive libidinal orientation from patients with hysterical personality traits. In an earlier study, Lazare and Klerman (1968)[33] had emphasized the psychopathic aspects of hysterical personality disorder. They found that often the fathers of lower class women were periodically drunk and then brutally intrusive, evoking fears of sexual attack in the women of their families. Their daughters became afflicted with severe hysterical character disorder. Their histories showed relatively frequent non-psychiatric physical attention in hospitals, especially for gynaecological surgery, reflecting tendencies to invite medical treatments involving the genitals and to relapse into invalidism. My own experience coincides with these statistical findings, and I have often drawn the inference of determining unconscious pathogenic masochistic fantasies and fears, and more conscious wishes to be rescued, in individual cases.

In one extreme example, the woman had had the gallbladder, the appendix, the uterus, ovaries and tubes removed and subsequently on account of complaints of irritation, the vagina. Continuing to complain of itching she had finally had a vulvectomy before referral for psychiatric evaluation. Her history was one of a chaotic family milieu and background, including a periodically drunk and abusing father in her childhood, and including her own addiction to alcohol and analgesics.

As we approach the more pathological end of the hysterical spectrum, we encounter types with crude seductiveness as an habitual part of their behaviour, sexual promiscuity, marked masochistic and/or sadistic tendencies, weaker ego-integrative functions (and a less integrated super-ego) with a propensity towards addiction, severe depression and psychotic regression.

The 27 male inpatients studied by Louisada, Peele, and Pittard (1974)[34] seem to lie at this end of the spectrum; some perhaps come within the hysteriform borderline disorder to be discussed below. The majority of them had a history of suicidal threats, many had a family history of mental illness, usually alcoholism. Fathers had been emotionally or physically absent in their childhood. Few of them had stable marriages, and many of those who were married had older wives. All had disturbed sexual relationships, sometimes including unhappy homosexual experiences. The majority abused alcohol and drugs and had criminal records for disorderly conduct when inebriated or for assaultive robbery. Striking effeminacy was noted in four patients and hypermasculinity in two. While physical complaints were common, there were no indications of overuse of surgery. There was much acting out antisocially, as noted.

Hysteriform Borderline Personality Disorder

The fact is that in many other cases only in more prolonged clinical evaluation can an adequate psychoanalytically informed diagnosis be made—that is, one that is then a useful guide to treatment beyond immediate rest, support, and observation. These cases constitute the nosological category called borderline, already briefly considered (Ch. 6, p. 154). David Beres[35] has made a distinction between a mere label and a deeper-reaching diagnosis. Certainly, besides mere labelling a psychoanalytic diagnosis demands a formulation of the basic psychodynamics in the individual case: the conflicts, the unconscious

wishes and fantasies, the defences, the adaptive capacities, and the possible origins of the problem.
Already in 1891 George M. Beard (1891)[36] had written:

> In a recent series of essays in the New York *Medical Record*, I applied this term—border-liners—to that very large class of nervous persons—sometimes hypochondriacal, sometimes neurasthenic, sometimes hysterical, sometimes epileptic, sometimes inebriate, sometimes several of these united—who are almost insane at times, or all the time, and yet who never really become insane; whose mental responsibility is impaired by disease, more or less, but not seriously enough impaired to justify at any time the diagnosis of insanity; but who are usually able at most times, if not at all times, to maintain a measure of respect and good sense in their relations to the external world, and who are never driven by their disease to any kind of crime, though they may and do very often, indeed, cause life-long distress to their relatives, dependents and friends. These neurasthenics very often become border-liners; they come so near to the border that the question arises frequently whether they have not crossed it; whether restraint is not needed; whether their mental responsibility is not impaired so as to require separation from home and friends; but, as a rule, the worst cases of this kind—and I see the very worst cases possible—do not cross the borderline, although they may do so; and that possibility is to be considered in extreme cases; for I have seen them take that last step before my eyes, while I was doing my best to prevent them.

This eloquent early description remains familiar. As Beres[35] insists, to deal more productively with such patients one must give *comprehensive* scrutiny to the total personality and mental functioning of each one. As noted (Ch. 6, p. 155), this is what Robert Knight insisted upon, showing that the diagnostic criteria customarily used in the past—the emphasis on a break with reality, the concept that neurosis and psychosis are mutually exclusive, and a one-sided dependence on libido theory—can be inadequate and misleading in the determination of the therapy to be recommended. Knight (1954)[37] advocated psychodiagnostic testing in addition to face-to-face psychiatric interviews, pointing out that suitable psychological tests combine the advantages of support from a visible and interested professional, with those of the diagnostically significant unstructured situation of the free association session on the couch.

Otto Kernberg (1967)[38] attempted a more general systematic account of the symptomatic, structural and genetic-dynamic aspects of the borderline personality. He noted that transient psychotic episodes may develop in patients with borderline personality organization when they are under severe stress or under the influence of alcohol or other drugs. Such psychotic episodes usually remit with relatively brief but well-structured treatment approaches. According to Kernberg (1967)[37]

> When classical analytic approaches are attempted with these patients, they may experience a loss of reality testing and even develop delusional ideas which are restricted to the transference.

Thus they develop a transference psychosis rather than a transference neurosis. These patients usually maintain their capacity for reality testing, except under the special circumstances of severe stress, regression induced by alcohol or drugs, or a transference psychosis. In clinical interviews the formal organization of the thought processes of these patients appears intact. Psychological testing, particularly with the use of non-structured projective tests, will often reveal the tendency of such patients to use primary process functioning.

Kernberg (1967)[38] emphasizes that these patients have a relatively stable pathological organization, and that most of them do not fluctuate between neurosis and psychosis. My experience leads me to emphasize rather that some of these patients may in fact have rapid shifts in behaviour, the result of a sudden cathexis of a previously dissociated ego nucleus organizing a different and contrasting drive and affect state, usually with regressively charged object relatedness. Indeed, it is on this account that I would also qualify Beard's original descriptive definition of borderliners inasmuch as I would emphasize that some of them are *sometimes* driven by their disease to crime, including murder, while in an altered state of consciousness, perhaps abetted by drugs.

Kernberg (1967)[38] has outlined a schematic point of view that is perhaps excessively Procrustean; thus in his structural analysis he discusses as one 'non-specific' manifestation of ego weakness the 'lack of developed sublimatory channels'.

However, in my experience there is, on the contrary, often an unusual strength in some sublimatory channels. Sometimes treated in analysis were highly creative and oustandingly successful writers, artists and scientists who were undoubtedly 'borderliners'. None the less, Kernberg's generalizations are of challenging value. He enumerates specific defensive operations at the level of borderline personality organization, namely splitting, primitive idealization, early forms of projection (especially projective identification), denial, and omnipotence with devaluation of others. He rightly emphasizes the characteristic instinctual vicissitudes of borderline personality organization, which include a particular pathological condensation of pregenital and genital drives under the overriding influence of strong pregenital aggressive needs.

Malcolm Pines (1975)[39] describes the case of an attractive intelligent girl who broke down in her second year at university and could not complete her exams:

> The university scene has forced her to face her great social and sexual anxieties and her inability to cope and adapt has led to regression. She begins to withdraw into sleep for up to 20 out of 24 hours, to sit staring at the wallpaper and ceiling which take on animate shapes, or else sits by the river for long hours contemplating suicide. Her sense of her own reality alters and she feels like an empty shell possessed by her mother whom she constantly telephones yet quarrels bitterly with when they are together. She hates everyone around her and feels poisoned by her hate. She has a violent hatred of men and sees sex as a battle for possession of the helpless victim; she never takes off her jacket as it serves to hold her together and to ward off sexual attention and she hates the other girls who spread rumours that she is a cold fish.
>
> In analysis she goes into malignant regression, pouring contempt and hatred over the analyst and the analytical situation, but nevertheless clings desperately to it. The sessions are filled with a Berlin Wall of silence and she begins to write of her despair, her rage and of her impossible love. She is utterly ruthless and possessive which gives her great suffering. At times she is driven to physical attacks on the therapist, kicks him with

her ugly black boots. The only escape for both patient and therapist is for her to fall into a deep slumber from which she wakes more accessible and accepting.

She experiences her 'self' as filled with poison; maggots and cockroaches infest her stomach and eat her mother's poisoned food; ten million red-hot ants bite into her brain; unuttered screams threaten to emerge from her tears and her eyes devour cannibalistically; she becomes terrified to be in the street as she fears to be attacked from behind; she clings to the consulting room as a temporary haven from the terror that awaits her outside that she will collapse into a heap of garbage that will be swept up into a refuse collection van where she will be pulverized. Her body is torn by the pains of severe life-long constipation that lead her to tear out impacted faeces with her fingers; her menstruation terrifies her by its pain and ferocity.

She is the youngest of three children, the only natural child of the three, the older two being adopted. She fell asleep at the breast, developed massive constipation at the age of one, but was an intelligent and quite active child, though sensitive and quarrelsome and with her scarcely older adoptive brother she often behaved savagely and wildly. The children were left for 9 months by the parents when she was about 9 years old which has turned out to be an important precipitant of later illness (cf. Masterson, 1971[77] as quoted in Pines, 1975[39]). Her family was originally Jewish, but both parents converted to Roman Catholicism and she was given convent education of a rather strict sort. Her father died when she was 15 and for the year prior to his death she dreamt about his being ill and dying which greatly reinforced her magical thinking. She has evidently not completed normal mourning and remains tied to the bad father image, behaving as if she had become the tyrannical, hateful, powerful one, and constantly fears his re-emergence to haunt and persecute her. Occasionally she dreams of incestuous relationships with him.

Her mother is seen as a witch, vampire, spider, cat; all that is malevolent and dangerous. She feels poisoned by her mother's food, invaded by her voice yet cannot separate from her. She fears homosexual fantasies and dreams about her mother.

The transference reveals all the primitive fears and impulses. She would ruthlessly possess the analyst, rob him of his wife and children by murder, keep him shackled and torture him endlessly to make him share and understand her pain and feel for a moment the triumph of revenge. She would also like to be inside him to feel protected and to wear him as a cloak when she leaves the session. Without him she is lost in an endless sea of confusion and hopelessness. She can take nothing from him, his words are meaningless garbage, yet only he can comfort and protect her from the anxiety that explodes inside and spins her like a spinning wheel.

The sessions are almost unremittingly painful and tense. Yet now she holds down a responsible part-time job, has friends, often has fun with them, now she can begin to care for her sister's children, for a boy whom she teaches, and for her dog. Her sexual life remains masturbatory, the fantasies probably primitive, and sadistic and secret ...

The initial symptomatic disturbance in this case, namely aprosexia, the inability to sustain and concentrate her attention in order to prepare for examinations, is, of course, a common neurotic complaint made by university students. It is to be noted that this student had reached a level in her schooling which indicates a considerable capacity to sublimate her energies into intellectual channels, before the regressive events, following social and sexual stresses, took a sinister direction. The severity of ego regression in this case, is much greater than in the run-of-the mill aprosexia usually encountered. In these borderline cases, the fragility of the capacity for sublimation (which paradoxically may be much greater than average) is distinctive. Anyway the strength of the autonomy of the ego is, in my opinion, over-rated by many psychoanalysts and psychologists; the autonomous functions are only too readily disrupted in people when conflict is generated. In borderliners, the *resilience* of ego functions is more impaired than in similar psychoneurotic inhibitions, though less so than in schizophrenia.

Kernberg (1967)[38] rightly emphasizes the poor integration of the self, partially separable from ego integration in general, as a characteristic feature of borderline personality defect. The following excerpt of a case illustrates this problem of self-definition:

Case 37. A young woman of 25 years had a history of bulimia with frequent food binges, use of vomiting or laxatives to purge the food eaten, a feeling of being out of control, and low self-esteem, often accompanied by depression. Following a suicidal attempt through overdosage of anti-depressant medication prescribed by the family physician, she had been admitted to the hospital. During her latency period she became 'the fat girl' and was ridiculed by the other children in the school. At that time she progressively became enormous and later in high school came to weigh 350 lbs, and was for the most part ridiculed, though pitied by some of her coevals. None the less, she did well at her studies. In childhood, when she was 4 years of age her father had deserted her mother, herself and her older brother and younger sister, for another more agreeable woman than her argumentative mother. The mother and three children moved into her grandmother's house. The patient had had a close relationship with her father and but little attention from her mother. Following the father's abandonment, the patient became the grandmother's favourite, and the grandmother expressed her affection by feeding her up overmuch so that she became a fat girl, doted upon by her grandmother. At this time the mother found herself a job and later another husband. The couple moved away and at 7 years of age the patient with her siblings joined them in another city. The patient became progressively fatter through severe eating disorder and as stated, became the wretchedly overweight fat girl, reaching dimensions suitable for show at a circus. In her 'teens she had fantasies of dating like the other students in the coeducation high school, and at that time she began to make efforts to reduce her food intake and to exercise more. In addition, she got into laxatives and the ancient Roman technique to combat weight gain. Though she lost weight, her problem with depression escalated. Moreover whenever she approached 180 lbs she began to suffer from depersonalization. She became confused about herself and had perplexity reactions. She did not know who she was. In the ensuing psychotherapy this became a central problem. It became clear that as she approached what she considered to be normality, the bulimia escalated, and even in hospital her compulsive eating could not be easily controlled. It became evident that she felt she had no impact on the world as she lost weight to approach 'normality' and that anyway she was afraid she would be rejected by young men. Her sense of selfness was encoiled in being the wretched huge fat girl who as such was noticed even if ridiculed and loved even if condescendingly. In this masochistic role, her ego boundaries were established so that she could be a separate being in the world, otherwise she felt she was threatened by disintegration. She reiterated at crucial phases of psychotherapy that she was afraid she would go to pieces—and indeed incipient symptoms of psychotic distortion, including a paranoid notion of being swallowed up, made their appearance at these times. It became clear that this was not a simple matter of hysterical hyperbole.

Gunderson and Singer (1975)[40] point out that depersonalization among their six basic features of the borderline syndrome may be helpful in establishing a differential diagnosis. In a later sophisticated statistical study, Gunderson and Kolb (1978)[41] sharpened the focus on those characteristics of borderline patients which are the best overall discriminators for use in differentiating them from schizophrenic patients, neurotic depressed patients and from other patients with affective and personality disorders. Their results support the view of Grinker and associates (1968)[42] and (1977)[43] that a definitive syndrome exists which is characterized by:

1. *Low achievement* in the two years before hospital support became necessary.

2. *Impulsivity*, often involving a pattern of alcohol and drug abuse, sometimes associated with promiscuity, or with sexual deviancy.

3. *Manipulative suicide*, especially gestures designed to exact rescue from a significant person.

4. *Heightened affectivity*, especially anger. (There is absence of flat affect; satisfied feelings are also relatively absent.)

5. *Mild psychotic experiences* including derealization and episodic paranoid ideation.

6. *High socialization*, due to intolerance of being alone and often compulsive in character.

7. *Disturbed close relationships*. In regard to this Gunderson and Kolb (1978)[41] write:

Devaluation, manipulation, dependency and masochism characterized and caused instability in the intense attachments of borderline patients.

These patients usually vacillate between brief, superficial relationships and others characterized by an intense, demanding dependency. Apparently socially adapted, and showing for a long time before decompensation a good school or work record, appropriate manners and strong social awareness, these patients often mimic, one after another, those in their reference group with baffling changes in attitudes. These manoeuvres of changing superficial identifications cloak problems of achieving consolidated identity. But then under stress, and sometimes associated with resort to alcohol or other drugs, self-destructive acting out becomes melodramatic:

Turning and turning in the widening gyre
The falcon cannot hear the falconer;
Things fall apart; the centre cannot hold;
Mere anarchy is loosed upon the world ...

Janet, as already noted, considered hysteria to be 'a malady of the personal synthesis', and, as such, 'characterized by the retraction of the field of personal consciousness and a tendency to the dissociation and emancipation of the systems of ideas and functions that constitute personality' (1907)[45]. Due to what Charcot has postulated as an 'inherited ailing tendency', a nervous vulnerability, Janet considered that under conditions of emotional and/or toxic stress there occurred 'an exhaustion of the higher functions of the encephalon', an '*abaissement de niveau mentale*', following which partial systems of personality split off from one another, including sometimes (in conversion hysteria) 'morbid modifications of the body that are caused by mental representations.' He states: 'Man, all too proud, figures that he is the master of his movements, his words, his ideas and himself', but that 'it is perhaps of ourselves that we have the least command. There are crowds of things which operate within ourselves without our will' (1984).[46]

Janet emphasized *passive* splitting, helpless fragmentation beyond one's control, whereas Freud put the emphasis on active splitting 'from a motive of defence' (1895)[47]. It must be acknowledged, however, that this notion of active defence was adumbrated by Janet. For example, in the case of Achilles (1894)[46] it became evident to Janet that his identification with the devil, preceded by inability to speak by day and dreaming of Satan by night, all followed the patient's attempt to forget an incident of marital infidelity six months earlier. When accomplished actively unconsciously and defensively, splitting of various kinds involves momentary or permanent countercathexes against unacceptable and unwanted perceptions and feeling. In *Inhibitions, Symptoms and Anxiety* Freud (1926)[48] singled out repression as a special method of defence, and advanced the notion that there was an intimate connection between repression and hysteria. Repressive forgetting might be regarded as a form of dissociation or splitting but as is evident in Janet's case of Achilles it is very different from the primitive splitting which follows and which issues in demoniacal possession (see Chapter 13: The Concepts of Dissociation and Splitting).

Kernberg (1967)[38] has usefully and successfully addressed the kind of splitting which occurs defensively at the level of borderline personality organization. He writes:

> One essential task in the development and integration of the ego is the synthesis of early and later introjections and identifications into a stable ego identity. Introjections and identifications established under the influence of libidinal drive derivatives are at first built up separately from those established under the influence of aggressive drive derivatives ('good' and 'bad' internal objects, or 'positive' and 'negative' introjections). This division of internalized object relations into 'good' and 'bad' happens at first simply because of the lack of integrative capacity of the early ego. Later on, what originally was a lack of integrative capacity is used defensively by the emerging ego in order to prevent the generalization of anxiety and to protect the ego core built around positive introjections (introjections and identifications established under the influence of libidinal drive derivatives).
>
> *This defensive division of the ego, in which what was at first a simple defect in integration is then used actively for other purposes ...*

Besides this kind of splitting, Kernberg (1967)[38] elaborates on the deployment of other developmentally early ego-states as regressive defences in borderline cases, namely projective identification, massive denial, preservation of narcissistic omnipotence with devaluation of others and primitive idealization. It is my view that the diagnosis of *hysteriform borderline disorder* should be applied to those cases where the above mentioned defences are prominent so that episodes of hypnoid alterations of consciousness, sometimes including depersonalization, have been frequent and where often symptoms of conversion hysteria are present. This diagnosis draws attention to both the hysterical and borderline character of the disorder, and distinguishes it from other borderline personality disorders of which there are several, as enumerated by Michael H. Stone (1983)[49]. The combined presence of massive denial, a flight into activity or complete passivity, projective distortion of objects in the environment, and pathological lying is often indicative of the more psychotic ego processes found in hysteriform borderline disorder. Sometimes in the analytic psychotherapy of borderline patients hypnagogic experiences of the kind described by Isakower (1938)[50] are reported; and sometimes too the phenomenon of the dream screen may be disclosed. This phenomenon in the dreams of such patients is related to the revival of severe traumatic infantile experience (Abse, 1977[51]).

Narcissistic Personality Disorder and Hysteriform Borderline Personality Disorder

Though there remain considerable doubts and problems in separating the narcissistic personality disorder category from borderline personality disorder, the third edition of the *Diagnostic and Statistical Manual of Mental Disorders* (DSM III) of the American Psychiatric Association goes along with the current fashionable mode, especially in Chicago, and lists it as a distinct character disorder. Waelder (1925),[52] reporting in detail on an egregiously egotistical patient, characterized 'narcissistic personalities' as in general displaying condescending superiority, intense focus on maintaining self-esteem and social prestige, and marked obliviousness to the needs of others, but nevertheless achieving adequate external relationships. The lack of empathy is revealed saliently in sexual relationships. In extreme cases, such as the one detailed by Waelder, there is a libidinization of thinking with over-valuation of it. Moreover, sensitivity to minor slights borders on the edge of paranoid distortion. Waelder (1925)[52] considered his patient to be suffering from a muted variant of schizophrenic disorder.

Annie Reich (1960)[53] discussed the narcissistic pathology, correctly in my opinion, as a means to undo feelings of inferiority based on severe early narcissistic injury. Such over-compensatory ego-inflation was discussed exhaustively by Alfred Adler (1929)[56]. He pointed out that this pathology was an exaggeration of the normative core of egoism necessary for human beings' attempts to dominate and master their environment. Kohut (1971)[55] posits a separate developmental sequence in the balance of narcissistic and object-libido, independent of object-relations determined by libido and aggression. In this part of his theory, his writings bear a remarkable resemblance to those of Alfred Adler, though, of course, he does not abandon drive theory, but decants narcissism off from drive-determined conflicts. In this respect his theoretical position is challenged by Kernberg (1975)[56] who views pathological grandiosity as defensive and related to drive-determined conflicts rather than as a halt in normal development unrelated to these conflicts. Kernberg portrays aggression, especially infantile oral rage, as the inciting agent in the deformation called narcissistic personality disorder. Here his view too is in accord with that of Alfred Adler (1909)[57] who, however, took a much more one-sided approach to the problems of neurosis, psychosis and criminosis. Insofar as his partitive approach was original and contributed a great deal to our understanding of human nature, the attempt to integrate his findings into psychoanalytic theory remains a worthy task. The Kohut-Kernberg controversy is usefully discussed by Salman Akhtar and J. Anderson Thomson (1983).[58]

Akhtar and Thomson have also attempted a synthesis of present views of the diagnostic criteria requisite for the designation of narcissistic personality disorder. *Table* 7.2 outlines the clinical features as overt and covert character-

*Table 7.*2 Clinical features of the narcissistic personality disorder

Clinical features	Overt characteristics	Covert characteristics
Self-concept	Inflated self-regard; haughty grandiosity; fantasies of wealth, power, beauty, brilliance; sense of enlightenment; illusory invulnerability	Inordinate hypersensivity; feelings of inferiority, worthlessness, fragility; continuous search for strength and glory
Interpersonal relations	Shallow; much contempt for and devaluation of others; occasional withdrawal into 'splendid isolation'	Chronic idealization and intense envy of others; enormous hunger for acclaim
Social adaptation	Social success; sublimation in the service of exhibitionism (pseudosublimation); intense ambition	Chronic boredom; uncertainty; dissatisfaction with professional and social identity
Ethics, standards, and ideals	Apparent zeal and enthusiasm for moral, sociopolitical, and aesthetic matters	Lack of any genuine commitment; corruptible conscience
Love and sexuality	Seductiveness; promiscuity; lack of sexual inhibitions; frequent infatuations	Inability to remain in love; treating the love object as extension of self rather than as separate, unique individual; perverse fantasies; occasionally, sexual deviations
Cognitive style	Egocentric perception of reality; articulate and rhetorical; circumstantial and occasionally vague, as if talking to self; evasive but logically consistent in arguments; easily becoming devil's advocate	Inattention to objective aspects of events, resulting at times in subtle gaps in memory; 'soft' learning difficulties; autocentric use of language; fluctuations between being overabstract and overconcrete; tendency to change meanings of reality when self-esteem is threatened

From Akhtar, S. and Thomson, J. A. (1983). Narcissistic Personality Disorder. In: *New Psychiatric Syndromes*, Chap. 2. New York and London: Aronson.

istics; that is, those features readily observable and those which are partially masked though consciously apprehended and thus less easily noticed.

Bursten (1973)[59] and Volkan (1976)[60] have noted that narcissistic individuals overlap in some characteristic features with those in the category of hysterical personality. Both types tend to be demonstrative, exhibitionistic and, at times, seductive. Akhtar and Thomson (1983)[58] state:

However, the narcissistic patient's exhibitionism and seductiveness have a haughty, exploitive, and cold quality; the hysterical persona is more human, playful and warm. Indeed both obsessional and hysterical individuals, unlike narcissistic individuals, retain the capacity for empathy, concern, and love for others.

Therese Benedek (1956)[61] outlined the dynamic circular processes involved within the primary unit of mother–child. She showed that the feeling of confidence is originally an intrapsychic precipitate of positive libidinal processes of the symbiotic phase of the mother–child relationship. On the other hand, she revealed the transactional processes of the ambivalent relationship between mother and child which can disrupt the development of stability of confidence and hope. If the early potential to develop confidence is impeded, the result is persistently excessive feelings of inferiority, enormous hunger for acclaim and a continuous search for strength and glory as is evident in narcissistic personality disorder. Of course, there are other exogenous and endogenous factors involved and other possible outcomes of early disturbances in the primary unit. Some narcissistic concerns in hysterical patients undoubtedly have their origin in disturbances in very early development. However, the feelings of inadequacy and sensitivity to criticism frequently found in the hysterical personality may be more related to narcissistic injuries during the Oedipal phase. As Krohn (1978)[3] observes:

> While this phase is correctly viewed predominantly in terms of conflicts between libidinal instinctual drives and the fear of castration or loss of love, the Oedipal-phase child suffers significant narcissistic assaults because he really is smaller, less competent, and generally less powerful than the parents, and really is incapable of consumating a sexual relationship ... The impossibility of such a relationship is a very significant assault on the child's phallic narcissism ... These phallic-Oedipal narcissistic assaults, like depressive affects and anxiety, can trigger conflict. They may lead to an unconscious fantasy of phallic grandiosity, including, for example, a body-phallus equation. An adult hysteric may have an unconscious self-image of being a little child, and a defensive need then for continual assertion of phallic superiority. These narcissistic concerns in hysterical patients may have entirely phallic-Oedipal, not pregenital sources.

In this connection, it is notable that some forms of psychoneurotic depression in women may not have fundamentally anaclitic roots, but may stem from childhood difficulties in accepting the lack of a penis as part of their bodily configuration with fantasies concerned with castration conviction. Thus the depression sometimes associated with female hysteria is often connected with phallic conflicts at the Oedipal period. On the other hand, characterological narcissistic defences may be embedded to ward off this kind of depression and may be part of a strident and aggressive 'masculine protest' comparable with that exhibited by men with a high potential of castration anxiety who are actively domineering and cruel. Adler (1929)[54] had applied the term to both men and women who harboured fixed assumptions that the masculine aspect of individuality represents the highest standard of human potency and that the feminine aspect is to be relegated to an inferior position. There are hysterical personalities of both sexes whose regulation of self-esteem is based unconsciously on such chauvinistic assumptions. Though not necessarily avowed, the behaviour is rationalized on confrontation and generally dissociated. Among women, there are variants of the hysterical personality who sometimes achieve leadership roles which caricature those of men, in contrast to the more usual hysterical personality which is a caricature of femininity.

A conspicuous feature of hysteriform personality disorder, in contrast with narcissistic personality disorder, is an outspoken fear of being alone. Moreover, as already noted, during times of stress and anxiety, including loss or other forms of separation from people on whom they had been dependent, there is evidence of katathymic thinking, that is, thinking heavily determined along complex-ridden paths which grossly disturbs perception, judgement and logical order. These features are reflected in the course of treatment by peculiarities of behaviour and by reported subjective experiences. Thus during a short break in psychotherapy of ten days, a patient came to inquire of the secretary whether I had returned after three days, although she had had plenty of time to assimilate the fact of my projected absence for the longer period. The secretary, of course, confirmed the actualities. Yet the patient came in several times in later days before my expected and actual arrival and sat quietly in the waiting room for about 20 minutes. Later she reported that this was 'a calming experience'. She had repeatedly become very anxious in my absence. Waiting quietly she conjured up my face and voice very vividly on these several occasions and then felt calm and departed to her home to resume her care of her children. This patient was both a talented homemaker and musician and of high intelligence and education.

Robert and Tova Spiro (1980)[62] discuss borderline phenomena in relation to performance on the Rorschach test. They report of two patients that their performance on the WAIS was articulate, competent and flexible:

> Cognitive functioning was smooth and well-regulated, and reasoning was precise, with no intrusions, personalized associations or peculiar thinking noted. While these patients' performance reflected intact and high level functioning on the highly structured WAIS, it progressively deteriorated with a loosening of structure. Thus, their Rorschach performance revealed the presence of both fabulations and fabulized combinations and illustrated the typical borderline picture by confirming the essential role of structure in the emergence [and recession] of their pathology. Their difficulties were similarly observed throughout the clinical course of treatment during times of stress, anxiety and fear of loss and separation.

Spiro and Spiro[62] then discuss their performance on the Rorschach with respect to their intense preoccupation with being alone. The striking finding was the significant number of responses in which faces were seen on both records. This led the Spiros to compare the Rorschachs of 20 additional patients, ten borderline and ten schizophrenic, to determine if the key issues identified for the borderline patients were also reflected in the records of the schizophrenics. They write:

> The results were surprising. While concerns and content having to do with boundaries, separation, and disintegration appeared equally distributed among all patients, the seeing of faces clearly and significantly differentiated these two groups. Faces were seen in every borderline record while their presence was unusual, and often not-existent in the Rorschachs of schizophrenics.

According to the Spiros, faces were of central importance to the borderline patients. In times of stress they were recalled and then functioned as transitional consoling objects. They cite the work of Spitz (1965)[63] and Mahler et al. (1975)[64] as suggestive of the developmental importance of the mother's face. The mother's face is influential in organizing the infant's first social smiling response and in constructing the first libidinal tie. They write:

> The actualization of the infant's capacity to smile signals his emergence from relative isolation into a mutual, need-satisfying relationship that is sustained at optimal levels by reciprocal, face-to-face contact. The importance of this contact in mutually regulating the fit between mother and child is at a peak during the symbiotic period. Therefore, it is not unreasonable to assume that for these individuals whose pathology can be traced to this phase of development, difficulties with the processes of the subsequent phase (separation-individuation) as well as the content (faces) would permeate the overall character structure in later years.

John Frosch (1964)[65] has pointed out that in borderline disorder, the ego position vis-à-vis reality is impaired (*a*) in the relationship to reality; (*b*) in the feeling of reality; and (*c*) in the capacity to test reality, just as occurs in psychosis. However, in contrast to psychosis, the impairment is predominantly in the first two areas with relatively less impairment in the third. That is, there is a *relative* preservation of the capacity to test reality in these patients. This capacity, however, may be lost transiently under stress because it is defective, though less so than in psychotic patients. Frosch (1964)[65] proposes that these ego defects so similar to those encountered in psychotic patients render the term psychotic character disorder preferable to other appellations. To illustrate the similarities with and differences from psychotic disorder he gives a brief account of a woman patient who while at a concert suddenly felt the floor tremble. She thereupon asked the people beside her whether they felt this too, but they had not. She stated: 'I was puzzled by this. I concluded, therefore, that this was a projection of my own vaginal orgasm.' Frosch[65] comments:

> Now this certainly reveals a closeness to the id which raises suspicions of psychosis. The perception of the trembling of the floor reflects some disturbance in the relationship to reality; but when two other persons did not perceive the trembling, the patient was able to realize that the experience was derived from herself.

Even when there is a disturbance in the capacity to test reality, as well as in the relationship to and feeling of reality, it is but temporary. There is a capacity for reversal. Moreover, Frosch maintains that though the psychotic character remains fundamentally at an infantile level of object relations there has been developmental progression 'to the point of recognition of need-gratifying objects', and, in contrast to psychosis, the resurgence of more archaic psychotic-like manifestations of object relations are rapidly reversed.

One of Frosch's patients who showed a propensity to de-differentiate and fuse with her environment became very disturbed when both she and her daughter wore pink dresses. The common colour led to a moment of fusion and loss of her identity. She became frightened and pulled herself back to realize that she was a separate being and her child another.

In his discussions in 1960[66] and 1964[65], Frosch emphasizes the disturbance in the sense of external reality. Earlier, Deutsch (1942)[67] had discussed a series of cases in which in addition to impoverishment of emotional relationship to the outside world an impoverishment of the sense of selfness is experienced and defended against by means of adopting an 'as if' personality. Deutsch found weak object-cathexis in these patients beneath apparently normal relationships with others. She wrote:

> The apparently normal relationship to the world corresponds to a child's imitativeness and is the expression of identification with the environment, a mimicry which results in an ostensibly good adaptation to the world of reality despite the absence of object cathexis.

It was mentioned above in connection with the varieties of hysterical personality that some women repeatedly display behaviour patterns more in accord with a caricature of men, rather than of feminity, and that some of these achieve leadership roles in diverse areas of social life, including politics, athletics and the stage. In several such instances, following symptom-formation and in the course of treatment, partial arrest of libidinal development at a tomboy phase, often encouraged by the father's attitude, became evident, with a line of overly one-sided ego development issuing from this. Sometimes such women became impounded in lesbianism. Others married overly passive men. In such marriages, there is a currently socially reinforced emphasis of unisex, a minimization of gender differences, physical and mental. In analysis, this emphasis is traceable to defences against castration anxiety in the man or against castration conviction in the woman. These defences of denial and minimization were evoked originally by early recognition of the notable anatomical difference between the sexes in childhood. There result two ego tracks, one which acknowledges in terms of perceptional organization and another which disavows, in opinion as well as in behaviour, the fact that there are penis-less human beings. Krohn (1978)[3] insists that the phallic-narcissistic character type should be clearly distinguished from the hysterical personality. Acknowledging that both types present fixations at the phallic-Oedipal level, he points out that the hysterical personality manifests a triangular Oedipal conflict whereas the emphasis in phallic-narcissism is more with an underlying sense of genital or body inferiority. The phallic-narcissistic type is more organized around overt wishes to exhibit and be admired, and fear of shame and humiliation, whereas the hysteric struggles more with guilt related to incestuous wishes and fantasies, inwardly and unconsciously. This is an important distinction which, however, must in practice remain one of emphasis rather than be clear cut clinically, except in some instances. In these extreme instances, in women, adverse situational events which issue in puncture of the myth of a penis, and concomitantly of narcissistic omnipotence, are followed by severe depressive disorder. In treatment, the 'as-if' nature of the pre-psychotic adaptation becomes apparent, and one is led to an accompanying diagnosis of hysteriform borderline personality disorder.

We have already noted (Chapter 2) the emphasis which Pieter C. Kuiper (1967)[68] placed upon 'ungenuineness' as a character trait of the hysterical personality. Ungenuineness may infiltrate the interpersonal relations of the patient with hysteriform personality disorder and cause him or her extreme distress. This distress may be absent in those described by Menninger (1959)[5] as hysterical psychopaths, but in many borderliners there is much subjective distress. This becomes especially evident in the psychoanalytically orientated psychotherapy of these patients. Feelings of victimization or of being especially elevated, or both, adhere to the basic identity of the patient and only with these adherent feelings does he (or she) feel himself to be somebody. Ego-feeling is entangled with fantasies and emotions which allude to the actualities of early childhood trauma due to maternal lovelessness and the patient is afraid of being nothing. It is more difficult for human beings to feel ignored than to feel rejected. Erik H. Erikson (1968)[69] asks: 'Is the sense of identity conscious? At times, of course, it seems only too conscious.' 'One of these times', he writes, '[is] when we are about to enter a crisis and feel the encroachment of identity confusion.' Such a time occurs in the course of achieving a corrective emotional experience in psychotherapy. Erikson noted that an optimal sense of identity is experienced as a sense of psychosocial well-being, a feeling of being at home in one's body, a sense of direction, and an inner assuredness of anticipated recognition from those who count with one. This position is arrived at only with great difficulty by the patient with hysteriform personality disorder in intensive prolonged analytically orientated psychotherapy.

Richard D. Chessick (1974)[70] notes that both psychoanalytic clinical research and clinical descriptive research strongly support the presence of a large group of borderline disorders which are clearly distinguishable from the schizophrenias and other psychoses on the one hand and from the neuroses on the other. He cites Stern (1938)[71] who originally characterized these patients as 'traumatized pre-Oedipal children' whereas Chessick maintains (1974[70]) 'the classical neuroses are based primarily, although not entirely, on disasters during the Oedipal period of development'. The presence of genetic and biochemical factors in the aetiology of these disorders has been much less investigated than in schizophrenia.

Michael H. Stone (1983)[72] points out that current European definitions of borderline incline toward either the schizophrenic spectrum of disorder (Benedetti, 1965[73]) or the inclusion of organic cases with perinatal damage (Aarkrog, 1981[74]). On the other hand the American definitions mostly comprise borderline affective disorder. Since the advent of lithium therapy, there is a tendency in the USA to put in the manic depressive category those patients who apparently respond favourably to this treatment. Stone's studies (1977)[75] and (1981)[76] of patients diagnosed as borderline by Kernberg's criteria highlighted the frequency with which their first-degree relatives exhibited either frank manic-depressive or some related milder disorder.

REFERENCES

1. DSM II (1968). *Diagnostic and Statistical Manual of Mental Disorders*, 2nd ed. Washington, DC: Am. Psychiat. Assoc.
2. DSM III (1980). *Diagnostic and Statistical Manual of Mental Disorders*, 3rd ed. Washington, DC: Am. Psychiat. Assoc.

3. Krohn, A. (1978). *Hysteria: The Elusive Neurosis*. New York: Int. Univ. Press.
4. Freud, Anna (1965). *Normality and Pathology in Childhood: Assessments of Development*. New York: Int. Univ. Press.
5. Menninger, K. A. (1959). Recognising and renaming psychopathic personalities. In: *A Psychiatrist's World: Selected Papers*. New York: Viking Press.
6. Schulsinger, F. (1972). Psychopathy: heredity and environment. *Int. J. Ment. Hlth*, **1**, 190–206.
7. Cloninger, C. R., Reich, T. and Guze, S. B. (1975). The multifactorial model of disease transmission. III. Familiar relationship between sociopathy and hysteria (Briquet's syndrome). *Br. J. Psychiat.*, **127**, 23–32.
8. Shields, J. (1982). Genetical studies of hysterical disorders In: *Hysteria* (ed. Roy, A.), Chap. 5. New York and Toronto : Wiley.
9. Kraulis, W. (1931). Zur Vererbung des Hysterischen Reactions weise. *Zeitschrift für die Gesamte Neurologie und Psychiatrie*, **136**, 174–258.
10. Charcot, J. M. and Marie, P. (1982). Hysteria. In: *A Dictionary of Psychological Medicine* (ed. Tuke, D. H.). Philadelphia: Blakiston.
11. Freud, S. (1908). Character and Anal Erotism. In: *The Standard Edition*, Vol. IX. London: Hogarth Press (1959).
12. Reich, W. (1933). *Character Analysis* (trans. Wolfe, T.), 3rd ed. New York: Orgone Institute Press (1949).
13. Marmor, J. (1954). Orality in the hysterical personality. *J. Am. Psychoanal. Assoc.*, **1**, 656–71.
14. Chodoff, P. and Lyons, H. (1958). Hysteria, the hysterical personality and hysterical conversion. *Am. J. Psychiat.*, **114**, 734–40.
15. Kretschmer, E. (1926). *Hysteria, Reflex and Instinct* (trans. Baskin, V. and Baskin, W.). New York: Philosophical Library (1960).
16. Bowlby, J. (1940). *Personality and Mental Illness*. London: Kegan Paul, Trench, Trubner.
17. Freud, S. (1916). Some thoughts on development and regression—Aetiology. *Introductory Lectures on Psycho-analysis*, Lecture 22. In: *The Standard Edition*, Vol. XVI. London: Hogarth Press (1963).
18. Brody, E. B. and Sata, L. S. (1967). Personality disorders: trait and pattern disturbances. In: *Comprehensive Textbook of Psychiatry*, Chap. 25. Baltimore: Williams and Wilkins.
19. Blinder, M. G. (1966). The hysterical personality. *Psychiat.*, **29**, 227–35.
20. Reichard, S. (1956). A re-examination of studies in hysteria. *Psychoanal. Quart.*, **25**, 155.
21. Easser, B. R. and Lesser, S. R. (1965). Hysterical personality: a re-evaluation. *Psychoanal. Quart.*, **34**, 390–405.
22. Zetzel, E. (1968). The so-called good hysteric. *Int. J. Psychoanal.*, **49**, 256–60.
23. Horowitz, M. (1977). Structure and the processes of change. In: *Hysterical Personality* (ed. Horowitz, M.). New York: Aronson.
24. Shapiro, D. (1965). *Neurotic Styles* (foreword by Knight, R. P.). New York: Basic Books.
25. Gardner, R., Holzman, P. S., Klein, G. S. et al. (1959). Cognitive controls: a study of individual consistencies in cognitive behaviour. *Psychological Issues*, **1**, 1–186.
26. Hartmann, H. (1958). *Ego Psychology and the Problem of Adaptation*. New York: Int. Univ. Press.
27. Jung, C. G. (1906). *The Psychology of Dementia Praecox*. New York: Nervous and Mental Disease Publ. Co. (1936).
28. Bleuler, E. (1911). *Dementia Praecox or the Group of Schizophrenias*. New York: Int. Univ. Press (1950).
29. Hollender, M. H. (1971). Hysterical personality. *Comments Contemp. Psychiat.*, **1**, 17–24.

30. Blacker, K. H. and Tupin, J. P. (1977). Hysteria and hysterical structures: developmental and social theories. In: *Hysterical Personality* (ed. Horowitz, M. J.). New York: Aronson.
31. Zetzel, E. and Meissner, W. W. (1973). *Basic Concepts of Psychoanalytic Psychiatry*. New York: Basic Books.
32. Lazare, A. (1971). The hysterical character in psychoanalytic theory—evolution and confusion. *Arch. Gen. Psychiat.*, **25**, 131–7.
33. Lazare, A. and Klerman, G. L. (1968). Hysteria and depression: the frequency and significance of hysterical personality features in hospitalised depressed women. *Am. J. Psychiat.*, **124**, 48–56.
34. Louisada, P. V., Peele, R. and Pittard, E. A. (1974). The hysterical personality in men. *Am. J. Psychiat.*, **131**, 518–21.
35. Beres, D. (1974). Character pathology and the 'borderline' syndrome. Paper delivered to Study Group (New York).
36. Beard, G. M. (1891). *Sexual Neurasthemia*. New York: Trent.
37. Knight, R. P. (1954). Borderline states. In: *Psychoanalytic Psychiatry and Psychology*, Vol. 1. New York: Int. Univ. Press (1956).
38. Kernberg, O. (1967). Borderline personality organisation. *J. Am. Psychoanalyt. Assoc.*, **15**, 641–85.
39. Pines, M. (1975). Borderline personality organisation. *Psychother. Psychosom.*, **25**, 58–62.
40. Gunderson, J. G. and Singer, M. T. (1975). Defining borderline patients: an overview. *Am. J. Psychiat.*, **132**, 1–10.
41. Gunderson, J. G. and Kolb, J. E. (1978). Discriminating features of borderline patients. *Am. J. Psychiat.*, **135** (7), 792–6.
42. Grinker, R. R. sen., Werble, B. and Drye, R. C. (1968). *The Borderline Syndrome: A Behavioural Study of Ego Functions*. New York: Basic Books.
43. Grinker, R. R. and Werble, B. (1977). *The Borderline Patient*. New York: Aronson.
44. Yeats, W. B. (1921). *The Second Coming*. In: *The Collected Poems* (1933). New York: Macmillan.
45. Janet, P. (1907). *The Major Symptoms of Hysteria*, 2nd ed. New York: Macmillan (1920).
46. Janet, P. (1894). Un cas de possession et l'exorcisme moderne. *Bull. Univ. Lyon*, **VIII**, 45–57.
47. Freud, S. (1895). The Psychotherapy of Hysteria. Breuer, J. and Freud, S. *Studies on Hysteria*, Chap. IV. In: *The Standard Edition*, Vol. II. London: Hogarth Press (1955).
48. Freud, S. (1926). Inhibitions, Symptoms and Anxiety. In: *The Standard Edition*, Vol. XX. London: Hogarth Press (1955).
49. Stone, M. H. (1983). Borderline personality disorder. In: *New Psychiatric Syndromes: DSM III and Beyond* (ed. Akhtar, S.), Chap. 1. New York: Aronson.
50. Isakower, O. (1938). A contribution to the patophsychology of phenomena associated with falling asleep. *Int. J. Psychoanal.*, **19**, 331–45.
51. Abse, D. W. (1977). The dream screen phenomenon and noumenon. *Psychoanal. Quart.*, **46**, 256–86.
52. Waelder, R. (1925). The psychoses: their mechanisms and accessibility to influence. *Int. J. Psychoanal.*, **6**, 259–81.
53. Reich, A. (1960). Pathological forms of self-esteem regulation. *Psycho-Anal. Study of the Child*, **15**, 215–32.
54. Adler, A. (1929). *Problems of Neuroses*. New York: Cosmopolitan Book Corp. (1930).
55. Kohut, H. (1971). *The Analysis of the Self*. New York: Int. Univ. Press.
56. Kernberg, O. F. (1975). *Borderline Conditions and Pathological Narcissism*. New York: Aronson.

57. Adler, A. (1909). *The Neurotic Constitution: Outlines of a Comparative Individualistic Psychology and Psychotherapy* (trans. Glueck, B. and Lind, J. E.). New York: Books for Libraries Press (1972).
58. Akhtar, S. and Thomson, J. A. (1983). Narcissistic personality disorder. In: *New Psychiatric Syndromes: DSM. III and Beyond* (ed. Akhtar, S.), Chap. 2. New York: Aronson.
59. Bursten, B. (1973). Some narcissistic personality types. *Int. J. Psychoanal.*, **54**, 287–300.
60. Volkan, V. D. (1976). *Primitive Internalised Object Relations*. New York: Int. Univ. Press.
61. Benedek, T. (1956). Toward the biology of the depressive constellation. *J. Am. Psychoanal. Assoc.*, **4** (3), 389–427.
62. Spiro, R. H. and Spiro, T. W. (1980). Transitional phenomena and developmental issues in borderline Rorschachs. In: *Borderline Phenomena and the Rorschach Test*. New York: Int. Univ. Press.
63. Spitz, R. A. (1965). *The First Year of Life; A Psychoanalytic Study of Normal and Deviant Development of Object Relations*. New York: Int. Univ. Press.
64. Mahler, M. S., Pine, F. and Bergman, A. (1975). *The Psychological Birth of the Human Infant*. New York: Basic Books.
65. Frosch, J. (1964). The psychotic character: clinical psychiatric considerations. *Psychiat. Quart.*, **38**, 81–96.
66. Frosch, J. (1960). A specific problem in nosology. The psychotic character disorder. In: An examination of nosology according to psychoanalytic concepts. *J. Am. Psychoanal. Assoc.*, **8**, 544–8.
67. Deutsch, H. (1942). Some forms of emotional disturbance and their relationship to schizophrenia. *Neuroses and Character Types*, Chap. 20, pp. 262–81. In: Deutsch, H. (1965). *Clinical Psychoanalytic Studies*. New York: Int. Univ. Press.
68. Kuiper, P. C. (1967). *On Being Genuine and other Essays*. New York and London: Basic Books.
69. Erikson, E. H. (1968). *Identity: Youth and Crisis*. New York: Norton.
70. Chessick, R. D. (1974). The borderline patient. In: *American Handbook of Psychiatry*, 2nd ed. (ed. Arieti, S. and Brody, E. B.), Chap. 36, pp. 808–19. New York: Basic Books.
71. Stern, A. (1938). Psychoanalytic investigation of and therapy in borderline group of neuroses. *Psychoanal. Quart.*, **7**, 467–89.
72. Stone, M. H. (1983). Borderline personality disorder. In: *New Psychiatric Syndromes: DSM III and Beyond* (ed. Akhtar, S.), Chap. 1. New York: Aronson.
73. Benedetti, G. (1965). Psychopathologie und Psychotherapie der Grenzpsychose. *Report of the Dikemark Seminar*, pp. 1–29. Norway: Dikemark Sykehuset.
74. Aarkrog, T. (1981). The borderline concept in childhood, adolescence and adulthood. *Acta Psychiat. Scand. Suppl.*, **64**, 293.
75. Stone, M. H. (1977). The borderline syndrome: evolution of the term, genetic aspects and prognosis. *Am. J. Psychother.*, **31**, 345–65.
76. Stone, M. H. (1981). Borderline Syndromes: A Consideration of Subtypes and an Overview, Directions for Research. *Borderline Disorders* (ed. Stone, M. H.), Chap. 1. Philadelphia: Saunders.
77. Masterson, J. (1976). *The Psychotherapy of the Borderline Adult*. New York: Bruner-Mazel.

CHAPTER 8

Schizophrenia

The Symptoms

Schizophrenia is one of many kinds of personality disturbance. It is manifest in symptoms that may be similar in different varieties of personality disturbance, so the presence of a particular symptom is not necessarily indicative of schizophrenic disorder, but may be a manifestation of a quite different disturbance, even one of fleeting character due to fatigue, arousal of strong emotion, excessive ingestion of alcohol, or a combination of such factors. Therefore when we describe a symptom commonly encountered in schizophrenic disease, even one encountered in a florid variety of schizophrenia, it must not be assumed that its occurrence implies the presence of this disorder. Thus a persistent and grave symptom of personality disturbance may be due to a tumour of the brain. Such questions of differential diagnosis can be settled only by *physical investigation*.

Certain varieties of schizophrenic personality disturbance are manifested by *characteristic patterns of symptoms*, so the study of symptoms immediately assumes importance, although we always must bear in mind this problem of differential diagnosis. There is a difficulty of another order, too, and that is as to what is recognizable as 'symptomatic' of severe personality disturbance. This may be best elucidated in a discussion of a particular symptom not uncommon in schizophrenia, i.e. the symptom of delusion.

A delusion is a false belief, false inasmuch as it does not correspond to ascertainable fact, and is unamenable to correction by appeal to reason. If this were all, delusion in the sense of being a symptomatic expression of personality disturbance would indicate that mankind is generally disturbed. Indeed, writers have often pungently stated this very conclusion. The outstanding literary figure of the eighteenth century, François Arouet, better known by his adopted name of Voltaire (1763)[1], in the course of his long continued war against superstition and intolerance in Europe (which he attacked under the slogan *Écrasez l'infâme!*) repeatedly made the scornful observation that this planet is inhabited by dangerous lunatics. In the nineteenth century Kierkegaard (1849)[2] more mildly and tolerantly expressed his position thus:

> Just as the physician might say that there lives perhaps not one single man who is in perfect health, so one might say perhaps that there lives not one single man who after all is not to some extent in despair, in whose inmost parts there does not dwell a disquietude, a perturbation, a discord, an anxious dread of an unknown something.

In our time, Walter J. Garre (1976)[3] has propounded the view that as man evolved in the animal kingdom, he gained dominion over other species through tools and weaponry. Thus he overcame feelings of helplessness that were partly rooted in the actualities of his existence, especially in childhood, and developed more and more notions of grandiosity. Because they countermanded persistent feelings of helplessness, these notions resulted in magical thinking of a delusional kind that infiltrates a variety of socially accepted forms of 'insanity'.

The diverse miracles, prophecies and mysteries of fabulous religion vouched for by different groups of men must largely be inventions falsely believed in—falsely, if only on the logical grounds of their mutual incompatibility, though these beliefs may function to alleviate the disquietude described by Kierkegaard. Such shared beliefs of the kind embodied in traditional religions or folklore are usually in harmony with the individual's education and social milieu. Though these may be studied and interpreted psychoanalytically and with reference to the modal personality function of a particular group, these are not the beliefs or delusions with which we are more immediately concerned in schizophrenia or other definitive mental disorder.

The simple definition of delusion as a false belief unshaken by rational argument, or even by demonstration of evidence to the contrary, is thus too wide for our clinically more restricted purpose. Reflection would convince us that most of our acquaintances 'suffer' in this way, and that few, except perhaps ourselves, are free from irrational beliefs. Thus to indicate disease, pathological delusion must announce itself in a certain context, part of which is comprised of accompanying symptoms, the whole presenting a symptom pattern or a more or less typical clinical picture. Emotional enthusiasms expressed as grotesque metaphor in the context of daily life by asymptomatic people need not, for example, be taken into account. When at breakfast a friend who has risen early for a brisk swim announces that he 'could eat an ox' he is simply using florid metaphor; we need feel no concern about his grasp of reality.

The more common delusions expressed in schizophrenic disease may be classified as those of persecution, grandeur and hypochondria, and in any given case these may be to some degree combined. Thus a schizophrenic patient who expresses the view that he is 'King of All the World' might feel that his just claim to the privileges to which this pre-eminence entitles him is being thwarted, and in ways that indicate jealous enemies bent on his destruction. In such a case, the primary grandiose delusion is closely followed by delusions of persecution. Or an individual may proclaim that he is under malevolent supervision that puzzles him until he finds the solution—that he is an important person with a great mission, and that this is why he has been the object of such attention. Here a delusion of persecution has been followed by grandiose notions. Rational connections of this kind often link delusions, although in schizophrenia in general such rationalization is often weak as compared with the rationalization seen in other paranoid disorders.

Hypochondria consists in the belief that one has a physical disorder when this conclusion is supported by no physical evidence. It occurs in many kinds of mental and emotional disturbance and is often closely connected with disordered bodily sensations. In schizophrenia, hypochondriasis often assumes a bizarre form; a patient may complain persistently of abdominal pain, and insist that he has two stomachs, one male and the other female, and that his pains are the result of a periodic fierce struggle between the two. Such delusions of persecution, grandeur, and hypochondriasis are the superficial indications of deep-seated and widespread disorder. Any superficial connections they may have are due to secondary processes, a common origin being hidden from immediate view.

Hallucination is often a symptom in schizophrenia, and may be defined simply as a sense perception in the absence of external stimulus. One may thus distinguish hallucination from illusion, which is mistaken perception, i.e. in illusion the stimulus is present but is misinterpreted. Although in hallucination there is no external object, the mental impression of an object occurs with full sensory vividness. This is, of course, normal in dreams during sleep, and some people have so-called 'hypnagogic' hallucinations as they drop off to sleep, or 'hypnopompic' hallucinations as they awaken. Visual or auditory hallucinations experienced in the waking state have been reported by a number of historical personages, Joan of Arc and Martin Luther among them, and a recent Pope spoke of having a vision. However one may interpret such phenomena, hallucination in the waking state is rarely compatible with mental health. As a rule, a vision of the Angel Gabriel or an awareness of hearing the voice of Satan usually occurs in a setting of accompanying symptoms, and the total symptom pattern may be typical of a form or phase of schizophrenia.

Impulsivity is sometimes another symptom; a notion is suddenly translated into action at a time and place in which such activity is inappropriate and generally unexpected, sometimes even by the patient himself. A patient who seems cheerful and friendly may suddenly tear the buttons off his clothes; or he may clap a chamberpot on his head. There may be an outburst of fury that is inexplicable to the observer, to whom the reasons later advanced seem grossly inadequate. Such impulsive acting out sometimes occurs in response to auditory hallucination in which a 'voice' told the patient to act as he did. Impulsivity is not usually a presenting symptom in the sense that it is the primary manifestation to bring a patient with other symptoms in his background to a doctor. However, this can be the case, as was true of a man repeatedly arrested for car theft. The authorities did not initially obtain psychiatric examination for him, although they were puzzled both by the fact of the theft being out of character in a man always quiet and submissive, and by his indifference to concealing his crime and his inability to make any excuse for it. It turned out that he was haunted from time to time by a voice that demanded he steal cars; and although the man was unwilling to do so, he felt unable to resist these commands. He was secretly grappling with this partial personality system split off from his ego, but did not feel that he could discuss this with the authorities. It is not always easy to achieve adequate rapport with a man in this frame of mind although he might discuss rationally and freely topics unrelated to his personal life. In some forms and phases of schizophrenia, indeed, such 'dyssymbole' (Skottowe, 1939[4]; Thomas, 1940[5]) is indeed a typical symptom; the patient is unable to discuss topics of a personal nature, and any approach to them is met by an anxious effort to change the subject or to withdraw into silence, if not literally to run away.

Although there are many other symptoms, it must be emphasized that those discussed here are often absent or capable of detection only by the skilful, although they are perhaps of the kind popularly expected of mental disorder. Eugen Bleuler (1911)[6] categorized such symptoms as 'accessory,' and gave the first adequate account of those he considered 'fundamental'—disturbances of the association of ideas, disorders of feeling and divorce from reality leading to autism. We will shortly discuss these, but before doing so it will be useful to recall a simple frame of reference originally provided by Immanuel Kant (1790),[7] which marks the beginnings of method and system in the observation of mental symptoms.

Kant categorized three aspects of mental process as knowing, feeling, and striving; or, to use the words of modern psychology, cognition, affect and conation. Cognitive processes are concerned with awareness and thought affective processes with feeling and emotion and conative processes with willing and striving. To illustrate this we can dissect a simple instinctive process into its components:

I see a tiger (Cognition)
I feel afraid (Affect)
I run away (Conation)

Cognition denotes those activities that answer the question: 'What do you know, or think, about it?' Affect denotes those that answer the question: 'What do you feel about it?' Conation refers to those that answer the question: 'What do you want to do about it?' Of course, these three aspects do not occur apart from one another, and are not separate activities of the mind, since it is virtually impossible to think of anything without feeling something about it and experiencing some degree of impulse towards it.

Nevertheless, mental symptoms more emphatically belong to one or another category when closely observed. Disturbances of the association of ideas first and most obviously involve a deficiency in organizing awareness of the world, the self and the body. Faced with a patient whose conversation exhibits greatly disturbed association of ideas, we recognize major deviation from health in the evident impairment of cognition.

It is to be noted that all the disturbances of association of ideas, as they occur in schizophrenia and as they have been described by Bleuler, may range from complete confusion to a state in which the departure from the usual is likely to be detected only by a skilled psychiatrist.

Before discussing the fundamental symptom of 'primary thought disorder' that Bleuler emphasized as a cardinal feature of schizophrenia, it may be well to pursue certain other psychological considerations.

One of the oldest theories in psychology was known to Plato, and was formulated by Aristotle in language that persists in modern textbooks. It is an attempt to account for the totality of thought and conduct on the basis of laws of association of ideas. There are two such laws as originally stated by Aristotle; that of similarity (or opposition or contrast), and that of contiguity. The first states that one idea tends to call up another if there is either resemblance or opposition between the two; and the second law holds that one idea tends to follow another if the two have been connected in the past either in time (simultaneously or successively) or in place. James Mill (1829)[8] gives an example of this second law in his *Analysis of the Phenomena of the Human Mind*. He writes:

> I see a horse: that is a sensation.* Immediately I think of his master: that is an idea. The idea of his master makes me think of his office: he is minister of state: that is another idea. The idea of a minister of state makes me think of public affairs: and I am led to a train of political ideas.

In its simplest form associationism makes of the mind an elaborate machine responding to the environment in a causally determined manner. After initial response to the environment, ideas are linked together passively and mechanically according to the laws of similarity and contiguity. It happens that this is far from being the whole truth, but it is a part of it. James Mill's 'analysis' was built on this part of the truth, and represents the extreme denial of activity in mind characteristic of classical associationism. The associations are studied in regard to their difference in strength according to frequency, recency and vividness of the experiences in which they are formed and renewed.

At about the same time that Mill was exploring classical associationism within the confines of its closed circle, J. F. Herbart (1816)[9] began to expand basic concepts, stressing the activity of mind, and extending the conception of it beyond the realm of the conscious. He recognized three degrees of consciousness:

1. Focal ideas clearly in consciousness.
2. Marginal ideas dimly present.
3. Ideas forced out of consciousness.

He held the view that ideas were dynamic entities struggling to enter consciousness, sometimes against one another and interacting quantitatively. Thus those ideas forced out of consciousness sometimes return as a result of the weakening of opposite ideas or as a result of cooperating with allied ideas.

Herbart's departure from classical associationism has proved amply rewarding and especially significant for clinical psychology in that part of its task that is concerned with disturbance of the association of ideas. The notion of conflict, of psychic elements excluded from consciousness and struggling to re-enter it, is one with which Freud has since made us familiar. Freud developed these concepts from clinical experience and systematic observation of his patients during years of laborious investigation. He clearly showed the reason for opposition to reside in the conative-affective sphere; thus certain urges are incompatible with other dominating forces within the psyche and for this reason are banished to the unconscious. For Freud, mental energy is evinced in striving and feeling. Ideas are effective insofar as they arouse or modify desires, or determine the steps to be taken in reality to gratify wishes.

Study of the disturbances of association in schizophrenia indicates that although cognitive impairment may be immediately apparent, the source of the disturbance in association of ideas is in the conative-affective sphere—in other words, in the individual's emotional life. I do not therefore agree with

---

*What Mill designates 'sensation' here would now be called 'perception', a more organised unit than sensation, or sensation to which meaning has become attached.

Bleuler, that the thought disorder is primary, but rather that it is secondary to emotional disturbance, as will be more fully discussed later. However, he did not always imply by the word 'fundamental' a genetic significance in regard to the origin of symptoms; rather, the connotation was of basic symptoms that clearly indicated the presence of schizophrenia. With this connotation one can more easily agree. It must be remembered that Bleuler remained in some measure tied to a notion of toxic organic cerebral disorder as fundamental in schizophrenia, which may indeed, as it is noted below, apply in the course of development of schizophrenia. As he stated, there is a group of diseases with similar symptoms that can be identified as 'schizophrenic'. However, there remains considerable doubt as to whether all schizophrenic reactions should be considered as manifestations of one disease entity.

FUNDAMENTAL SYMPTOMS

Thought Disorder, Affect Disorder and Ambivalence, and Autism

As it is well known, Freud introduced into psychotherapy a technique known as 'free association', which consists of obtaining the patient's cooperation in expressing himself freely as he reclines comfortably; in his telling everything that comes into his mind, whether trivial, embarrassing, or apparently irrelevant or illogical. By implication the patient is asked to suspend the selective criticism instinctively exercised towards incoming thoughts, and to verbalize them. In practice, although the 'normal neurotic' may consciously strive to cooperate in this way, and quite often goes a long way towards accomplishing it, the process is interrupted by transgressions that express instinctive resistance, and which are themselves scrutinized in the developed technique of psychoanalysis. The patient shares in the scrutiny from time to time, switching off from attempts at free association in order to understand aspects of himself revealed in the total process. What concerns us here is that the actual verbalizations of some schizophrenic patients resemble the so-called free associations produced under special conditions. In other words, in the waking state and without invitation to do so, schizophrenic patients behave as though they have little control over incoming thoughts, do not make the usual selection of them, and verbalize apparently illogically and irrelevantly. Up to this point then there is this resemblance; however, the kind of habitual looseness of association spontaneously displayed in the language of schizophrenic patients is an indication of the loss or impairment of the usual selective and synthetic functions of the ego.

This does not mean, however, that the schizophrenic patient's associations usually fail to observe the laws of association partially formulated by Aristotle and emphasized by the classical associationist psychologists. On the contrary, in general they give confirmation of these laws, and an even more emphatic view of the mind as a passive piece of machinery responding to inner and outer stimuli without intervening selection, choice, or decision. Important exceptions may be characterized as 'skidding' and 'blocking'. In skidding, there is a sudden break in the associations, which then go off into an apparently disconnected chain of ideas. In blocking there is a sudden interruption that may be of short or long duration.

As Bleuler (1911)[6] pointed out, only the goal-directed concept can weld the links of the associative chain into logical thought. The goal-directed concept is not just one single idea, but a complicated hierarchy of ideas. For example, in writing at this time on the theme of schizophrenia, the first goal is a paragraph, which again will be subordinate to a chapter, and so forth. To quote Bleuler (1911):[6]

Even where only a part of the associative threads is interrupted, other influences, which under normal circumstances are not noticeable, become operative [in schizophrenia] in the place of logical directives.

Ideas under usual circumstances and in waking consciousness are subject to more or less strict conditions, and are more or less logically related and appropriate. This 'secondary process' is a property of waking consciousness, whereas the so-called 'primary process' dominates dream life. Freud (1911)[10] demonstrated that mental energy exists in two forms, 'bound' and 'unbound'—unbound in the primary process, when condensation and displacement occur freely, and bound in the secondary process, when such freedom is surrendered for the purpose of clarity in dealing more adequately with external realities. In schizophrenia, primary process thinking intrudes or even dominates, and is partly reflected in a loosening of the association of ideas. The primary process is a property of the unconscious, and in schizophrenic disorder the ego is overwhelmed to a greater or less degree by unconscious strivings and affects, and the ideation associated under these conditions partakes of the properties of the unconscious.

Carl Gustav Jung (1918),[11] Bleuler's assistant, gave his attention to the unconscious influences that distort the association of ideas in controlled association experiments. Instead of using the free association technique he gave his patients a list of words. He would read out one of the words, and the patient was expected to say as rapidly as possible the first word that occurred to him in response. The reaction time between the utterance of the control word and the patient's offering of the associated word was measured each time with a stop watch. A sample of the hundred words on his list is: Head, Green, Water, Sing, Dead, Long, Ship, Make, Woman, Friendly, Love. Jung heard many different reactions to the stimulus word, since some patients would give a rhyming word, a synonym or antonym, or refer the word to himself or merely repeat it, and so on. Then again the reaction time may be prolonged or shorter than usual. Jung's work was in this way a development of word association experiments conducted earlier by Galton (1883)[12] and Wundt (1896),[13] and he applied this technique to the study of schizophrenia. In studying a number of these experiments it was found that inappropriate reactions and prolonged or unduly fast reaction times in any particular case pointed up emotionally heavily loaded constellations of ideas, or 'complexes' as Jung termed them. Since similar experiments with neurotic patients had already demonstrated the disturbing effects of so-called 'complexes', Jung thus demonstrated that this was the case in schizophrenia too; and further that psychotic symptoms had meaning in terms of these complexes just as in neurosis.

At the time, the significance of this lay in the demonstration of important meaning in the apparently meaningless association of the ideas of schizophrenic patients. For example, a woman who repeated the name 'Socrates' in her verbal response was found to mean that she was ill-treated and unjustly imprisoned like the great philosopher. This repeated utterance was found to be a condensation of this complex of ideas relating to her feelings of being victimized. The difficulty in comprehending the speech of some schizophrenic patients was, in general, found to be partly due to excessive condensation. It will be noticed that this condensation obeys the law of association of ideas by similarity, however illogically and unrealistically.

Logic does not enter into all the phenomena of mental activity, although it provides forms that an argument must exhibit to be legitimate, certain tests by which fallacy may be detected, and certain barriers against ambiguity in the use of language. In *The Organon* Aristotle dealt with the laws of syllogistic logic and showed how, in the process of reasoning, these laws provide a framework the abandonment of which results in sophistical faulty thinking. In general, much normative thinking departs from this Aristotelian logic, but this departure is much more obvious and widespread in schizophrenic thought disorder. Von Domarus (1944)[14] illustrates this by the following examples:

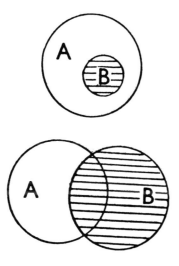

In the figure the area A designates 'All men are mortal', and Area B, 'Socrates is a man'. Following the so-called 'Mode of Barbara' in logical thinking, the correct conclusion is: 'Socrates is mortal'. The conclusion is justified when the major premise contains the minor one.

In the diagram that follows, A designates, 'Certain Indians are swift', and B, 'Stags are swift'. The area of intersection of A and B symbolizes the common element of swiftness. Illogical thinking may reach the conclusion, 'Certain Indians are stags'. Everything that lies outside the area of intersection is ignored, and A is thus identified with B, and an identity of subjects is assumed from a common single predicate.

Jung[11] first showed that such disturbances in logical thought were due to the operation of 'complexes', and that a meaning for such departures from logical thought could be found in specific unconscious motivations. In schizophrenic disturbance these motivations are so strong and overwhelming that there is a generalized retreat from logical thinking, and the resultant kind of thinking may often be of the type shown in von Domarus's second example. Formal logic is often largely abandoned in schizophrenic thought disorder, though the association of ideas is none the less often in accord with classical laws. Sometimes this is crudely expressed by the statement that the schizophrenic is at the mercy of his complexes. It happens that the skidding that sometimes takes place is largely due to the sudden arousal of another complex. This then dominates with peculiar abruptness the content of thought, and at the point of transition a dissociation or break with the usual laws of association is apparent. However, this phenomenon is more apparent than real, for it can sometimes be shown that a chance outer stimulus that escaped the observer's attention was responsible for the sudden transition or break in the continuity of thought, or that a tangential association served as a bridge in arousing another complex to dominate thought. Later we shall review dissociative phenomena in general from the psychodynamic viewpoint, when their meaning in terms of ego disorder will be more fully explored.

Turning from cognitive impairment to the evidences of affective disorder, we are confronted by manifold phenomena. Emotional deterioration is obvious in some forms and phases of schizophrenia. Chronic schizophrenics may sometimes be seen to sit around for years with expressionless faces, without spontaneity and vivacity, apparently emotionally unresponsive alike to supportive efforts on the part of their attendants and to occasional injuries inflicted upon them by other disturbed patients. This apathy may, however, alternate with extreme irritability and an abnormally heightened responsiveness in some cases, especially in regard to therapeutic efforts to invade their distinctive private worlds. Bleuler[6] pointed out that the apparently sustained apathy exhibited in these cases suffering from severe emotional deterioration did not of itself entitle us to the view that the psychic capacity to produce affects has disappeared in chronic schizophrenia; and he emphasized in general the important role of affectivity in schizophrenic disorder.

As a fundamental symptom the forms of affective disorderliness should be described further. There is sometimes a striking incongruity between affect and ideation, instead of the simple lack of adequate affective expression. Some patients will tell cheerfully, even with laughter, of torturing hallucinations or delusions of victimization. Thus a woman who claimed to be a witch gave an account of her arm and hand changing and becoming hairy, with long claws, partially turning her into a werewolf; she laughed in a weird way about this admittedly frightening experience. The odd impression created may be heightened by a dissociation in the component mechanisms of emotional expression: for example, the eyes wrinkled in an expression of gloom when the mouth expresses happiness. In acute phases of the disease, rapid alternations of affective expression may appear: a patient may switch within seconds from angry agitation to an exaggeratedly happy eroticism, and then turn tearful and sad for perhaps only a moment before another switch occurs.

The phenomenon of ambivalence bestrides both the affective and conative aspects of the psychic activity in schizophrenia. The hesitation between one feeling and its opposite, for example, the wavering between feelings of love and hate, shows the ambivalence of the emotions. Two opposite feelings may be simultaneously entertained toward the same object. Bleuler found this symptom in some form or another in every schizophrenic disorder he encountered, and since he introduced the concept of ambivalence its reference in neurosis has been explored also.

The ambivalent affective attitude may be accompanied by ambivalence of will ('ambi-tendency'). Thus the patient may wish to eat and at the same time wish to refrain from eating. He begins to feed himself by bringing the spoon to his mouth, but hesitates to complete the act. Or he announces his demand to leave the hospital and then resists discharge when his wish is granted. Ambivalence of the will shows every kind of gradation. In extreme forms of negativism, as encountered in catatonic forms of schizophrenia, the patient will switch to a negative attitude as soon as help is secured in regard to a request. It is not uncommon for such a patient to ask to get up out of bed, and then, when helped to do so, to resist the process. One patient, after making such a request, would resist the nurses' attempts to help him rise, and only when they reversed their efforts in gentle manual pressure to keep him in bed would he force himself out.

We have already discussed (Chapter 6) the fundamental symptom of autism, which may be manifested externally. Not only do some schizophrenic patients remain apparently unconcerned with anything around them, but they sit with faces constantly averted, or shut off their sensory portals by drawing a skirt or their bedclothes over their heads. Indeed, formerly, when patients were abandoned to their own devices, they could often be found in a bent-over, squatting position in an indication that they were trying to restrict as much as possible of the sensory surface area of their skin from contact with outer environment.

First Rank Symptoms

Many further attempts have been made to clarify in detail symptomatic criteria diagnostic of schizophrenia. One such attempt was made by Kurt Schneider (1959)[15] with first and second rank symptoms. The presence of first rank symptoms indicates a schizophrenic process. These include: the hearing of one's own thoughts spoken aloud (thought echo); hallucinated voices in the form of statement and reply; auditory hallucinations that comment on one's behaviour; the experience of thoughts being controlled; the spreading of one's thoughts to others (thought broadcasting); thought insertion and thought utterance beyond the control of the will; bodily passivity experiences; delusional perceptions; the experience of having one's actions influenced from the outside; the attribution of important self-reference to an actual perception; and all impressions of being controlled in movement, speech and drive.

Second rank symptoms include other forms of hallucinosis: perplexity; depressive and euphoric disorders of affect; and emotional blunting. According to Schneider, second rank symptoms alone do not justify a diagnosis of schizophrenic psychosis. His list of allegedly inconclusive symptoms, however, includes some that Kraepelin and Bleuler regard as fundamental. Fish (1966)[16] acknowledges that Schneider's scheme is not entirely satisfactory, though it is none the less usually highly discriminatory for schizophrenia.

Kurt Schneider and his school elaborated the comparison of the schizophrenic state with the dream. This comparison had been previously made by a number of philosophers, including Kant (1764),[17] who held that 'the lunatic is a dreamer in the waking state.' Schneider (1959)[15] maintains that the basic mechanism of reality sensation is the same in schizophrenia as in the dream; one can seldom recognize during the dream, but always on awakening from it, that one has gone through one's own mental process as though through reality. The schizophrenic is not in a position to awaken from his pathological realities, but lives with them and mixes them with life's realities, and falsifies both.

Federn (1952)[18] pointed out that in a sense there is gain rather than loss in some kinds of schizophrenia inasmuch as mere *thought* becomes reality, so that the loss of reality is a consequence of this rather than its cause. Freud (1915)[19] discussed one aspect of this increment in the sensation of reality in his essay on 'The Unconscious', namely that word presentations sometimes acquire a high investment of energy (heightened cathexis) in schizophrenia, whereas there is insufficient investment of interest in objects. Differing from Federn, Freud ascribed this to an initiatory attempt at recovery, and an endeavour to regain the lost object.

THE BRAIN AND SCHIZOPHRENIA

Folk medicine down the ages sought and found herbal and animal substances, as well as inorganic matter, useful in elevating mood, galvanizing energies and alleviating pain. Since the 1950s from mainstream medical observations that reserpine and chlorpromazine were of value in the treatment of the psychoses, and subsequently that monoamine oxidase inhibitors and imipramine were useful as anti-depressants, there has been a burgeoning of the employment of psychotropic medications in the treatment of mental illness. Nowadays, over-medication and under-utilization of psychotherapy has become a problem. None the less, following thousands of double-blind trials, there is no doubt that the major tranquillizers are of great assistance, used judiciously, in the treatment and management of schizophrenia.

In the 1960s it became apparent that the phenothiazines were not only useful in tranquillization but in suitable doses they also had an anti-psychotic effect. As Murray (1979)[20] notes:

The latter property was attributable to them in the 1960s for two reasons. First, a number of studies revealed that the phenothiazines were significantly superior to phenobarbitone in the treatment of schizophrenia, and that although some phenothiazines had sedative properties, these effects did not seem to be central to their benefit. Secondly, a very influential study by Goldberg et al. (1965)[21] demonstrated the effectiveness of phenothiazines against what were considered particularly 'fundamental' symptoms ...

The finding that the phenothiazines and related drugs could ameliorate schizophrenia led to increased biochemical approaches to the study of schizophrenia, especially as earlier psychiatrists, including Bleuler, had supported the notion that a toxic complication was implicated in the schizophrenic process. Moreover, the experience of substances which could produce psychotic states, demonstrated especially by amphetamine abuse, spurred this biochemical research. There had been for decades, anyhow, the accumulation of evidence that the liability to schizophrenia was partly inherited, and that one possibility was of some biochemical abnormality in the neurotransmitters arising during some phase of the life-cycle under stress.

The *dopamine hypothesis* is based on the view that the anti-psychotic effects of the neuroleptics is due to the blockade of the dopamine receptors in the brain (Snyder et al., 1974[22]). Indeed there are now claims (Bird et al., 1977[23]) that there is increased dopamine in the limbic areas of the brains of schizophrenics at post-mortem. As Murray[20] notes: 'This could be a consequence of medication rather than schizophrenia, and there are other defects in the dopamine hypothesis (Crow et al., 1976[28]) but it is an area of great potential advance.'

Johnstone et al. (1976)[24] used computerized axial tomography (brain scan) to find that there was evidence of increased ventricular size in association with impaired cognitive functioning in many chronic schizophrenics. Here again it is possible that this was a consequence of heavy prolonged usage of phenothiazines, or of repeated ECT, but this may be a primary finding in some instances. Flor-Henry[25] suggests that when temporal lobe epilepsy is associated with schizophrenia, the lesion is in the dominant hemisphere, whereas when associated with affective psychosis, the epilepsy is related to the non-dominant hemisphere. Schizophrenia has often been found in people who are left-handed and Flor-Henry's suggestion reinforces the view that schizophrenia may be related to left hemisphere dysfunction. Gur (1977)[26] in comparing 200 schizophrenics with 200 normals on measures of laterality that included handedness, footedness, and eye dominance, found more motoric laterality imbalance in the schizophrenics.

In summary, the findings that those chemical agents which stimulate dopamine production in the brain exacerbate schizophrenic symptoms whereas those which have a dopamine blocking action have salutary effects in schizophrenia suggest that dopamine neurotransmission is pivotal in the schizophrenic process. Moreover, the neurological findings noted above are perhaps indications of the organic vulnerability to 'primary process' mentation of some schizophrenics.

There is further evidence that schizophrenia runs in families and that this has a geno-genic basis. Thus studies by Kety et al. (1973)[27] of biological and adoptive relatives of adopted children who later developed schizophrenia were compared for the presence of psychosis. There was a control group of the biological and adoptive relatives of non-schizophrenic adoptees. In the biological relatives of schizophrenic adoptees there was a much higher incidence of definite severe schizophrenia than among those of the control adoptees.

In general the evidence supports the occurrence of a genetic predisposition to the development of a biochemical, i.e. transmitter, defect in the aetiology of the schizophrenias as well as supporting the importance of psychosocial stress and mental conflict in the pathogenesis of these disorders.

REFERENCES

1. Voltaire (1763). *Traité sur la Tolérance*. London: Eloisa, Emilios.
2. Kierkegaard, S. (1849). *The Sickness unto Death*. Garden City: Doubleday (1954).
3. Garre, W. J. (1976). *The Psychotic Animal: A Psychiatrist's Study of Human Delusion*. New York: Human Sciences Press.
4. Skottowe, J. S. I. (1939). Shock therapy: a plea for proportion in psychiatry. *Proc. R. Soc. Med.*, **32**, 843.
5. Sawle-Thomas, J. C. (1940). Some clinical examples of 'dys-symbole': its relation to shock therapy. *J. Ment. Sci.*, **86**, 100.
6. Bleuler, E. (1911). *Dementia Praecox or the Group of Schizophrenias*. New York: Int. Univ. Press (1950).
7. Kant, I. (1790). *The Critique of Judgement*. In: *Great Books of the Western World* (ed. Hutchins, R. M., Adler, M. J. et al.), Vol. 42. London: Encyclopedia Britannica (1952).
8. Mill, J. (1829). *Analysis of the Phenomena of the Human Mind*. London: Baldwin and Cradock.
9. Herbart, J. R. (1816). *A Textbook in Psychology*. New York: Appleton (1897).
10. Freud, S. (1911). Formulations of the Two Principles of Mental Functioning. In: *The Standard Edition*, Vol. XII. London: Hogarth Press (1955).
11. Jung, C. G. (1918). *Studies in Word Association*. London: Heinemann.
12. Galton, F. (1883). *Inquiries into Human Faculty and Its Development*. London: Everyman Edition (1907).
13. Wundt, W. (1896). *Grundriss der Psychologie*. Leipzig: Kröner.
14. von Domarus, E. (1944). The specific laws of logic in schizophrenia. In: *Language and Thought in Schizophrenia* (ed. Kasanin, J. S.). Berkeley, Calif.: Univ. Calif. Press.
15. Schneider, K. (1959). *Clinical Psychopathology* (trans. Hamilton, M. W.). New York: Grune and Stratton.
16. Fish, F. J. (1966). *Schizophrenia*. Bristol: Wright.
17. Kant, I. (1764). *Versuch über die Krankheiten des Kopfes*. Konigsberg.
18. Federn, P. (1952). *Ego Psychology and the Psychoses*. New York: Basic Books.
19. Freud, S. (1915). The Unconscious. In: *The Standard Edition*, Vol. XIV. London: Hogarth Press (1955).
20. Murray, R. (1979). Schizophrenia. In: *Essentials of Post Graduate Psychiatry* (ed. Hill, P., Murray, R. and Thorley, A.), Chap. 11. London: Academic Press.
21. Goldberg, S. C., Klerman, G. I. and Cole, J. O. (1965). Changes in schizophrenic psychopathology and ward behaviour as a function of phenothiazine treatment. *Br. J. Psychiat.*, **116**, 107–17.
22. Snyder, S. H., Bannerjee, S. P., Yamamura, H. I. et al. (1974). Drugs, neurotransmitters and schizophrenia. *Science*, **184**, 1234–53.
23. Bird, E. D., Spokes, E. G., Barnes, J. et al. (1977). Increased dopamine and reduced glutamic acid decarboxylase and choline acetyl transferase activity in schizophrenia. *Lancet*, **2**, 1157–8.
24. Johnstone, E. C., Crow T. J., Frith, C. D. et al. (1976). Cerebral ventricular size and cognitive impairment in chronic schizophrenia. *Lancet*, **2**, 924–6.
25. Flor-Henry, P. (1976). Epilepsy and psychopathology. In: *Recent Advances in Clinical Psychiatry* (ed. Granville-Grossman, K.), Vol. 2. Edinburgh: Churchill Livingstone.
26. Gur, R. E. (1977). Motoric laterality imbalance in schizophrenia. *Arch. Gen. Psychiat.*, **34**, 33–7.
27. Kety, S. S., Rosenthal, D. and Wender, P. H. (1973). Mental illness in the biological and adoptive families of adopted individuals who have become schizophrenic. *Proc. Am. Psychopathol. Assoc.*, **63**, 147–65.
28. Crow, T. J., Deakin, J. F. W., Johnstone, E. C. et al. (1976). Dopamine and schizophrenia. *Lancet*, **i**, 563–6.

DIAGNOSIS II

CHAPTER 9

Differentiation of Hysteria from Schizophrenia and Borderline Conditions

In established cases of psychotic illness the clinical differentiation from neurotic disturbance presents little difficulty. The psychoses are characterized by a massive withdrawal from and distortion of reality which is reflected in such common symptoms as delusions, hallucinations and disfigurements of speech. Psychosis is the outcome of a disturbance in the relation between the ego and its environment (Freud, 1924[1]), whereas in neurosis the ego remains true to its allegiance to the outer world, and the conflict is localized in the struggle with instinctual demands.

In fully fledged cases of schizophrenia, the presence of delusions, hallucinations, dyssymbole (Thomas, 1940[2]; Skottowe, 1939[3]) and the generalization of automatization is clear evidence of gross damage of the *fonction du réel* and readily distinguishes the disease from hysteria. Early in a case of schizophrenia, however, the psychological resemblances to hysteria may result in a mistaken diagnosis. Jung (1906[4]) pointed out some of these resemblances: of the emotional indifference of many cases of dementia praecox to the *belle indifférence* of many hysterics, of the explosive excitements in dementia praecox to the explosive affects of hysteria, and the characterological abnormalities such as the tendency to embellishment which is shown in both diseases. He showed from a study of word association reactions that these symptomatic likenesses are accompanied by a similarity in psychological mechanism. The associations in both diseases are characterized by the presence of an abnormally strong complex that the psyche cannot overcome, but this psychological mechanism reaches deeper in dementia praecox, perhaps because of its toxic complications. Jung (1920[5]) also emphasized later, on the basis of his studies of psychological types, that personality factors were important in influencing the issue in both neurosis and psychosis. Thus he regarded schizophrenia as partly the result of an excessive degree of introversion, whereas hysteria, in many forms, shows an intensified extroversion. However, as noted previously (Chapter 7), a conspicuous feature of hysteriform borderline personality disorder is an exaggerated fear of being alone, and such people seek multiple superficial relationships to avoid loneliness. As Gunderson and Kolb (1978[6]) have noted, these patients are sometimes involved in very intense attachments which then become highly disturbed. The more superficial multiple relationships which characterize them as extroverted are thus an attempt to navigate between Scylla and Charybdis.

The following is an account of a case of hysteria that made the transition to a schizo-affective disorder.

Case 38. A young man was playing football when he lost consciousness and fell down. At the time he was standing up at rest away from the more active part of the game. On regaining consciousness he felt 'dizzy' but carried on. Later, during the course of the following months, he suffered six similar attacks, after each of which he complained of headache. During this time he was admitted to hospital for full investigation, which revealed no evidence of organic disease. It was noticed, however, that he appeared to be depressed and withdrawn, although his conduct was orderly and he replied relevantly to questions. He was considered a case of hysteria and referred for psychiatric examination. He objected to this and returned from the psychiatric clinic to the general hospital without keeping his appointment. Later it was noticed that he was standing about in fixed attitudes, and thereupon he was escorted for psychiatric examination. At interview he stared vacantly, and appeared dejected, with gross psychomotor retardation, although he occasionally drummed on the table with his fingers. He was mute at first and would not answer simple questions. Further attempts at conversation disclosed his belief that he was no longer alive, or that, if he were living, he was only two years old. He also believed that he had ceased to be a man and that his home was in hell. This was due, in his view, to his having provoked punishment by solitary masturbation. He proclaimed that he was a sex maniac, and in saying this contorted his face into a hideous expression. Further attempts to continue a difficult conversation resulted in his adopting a threatening pose and then, quite suddenly, walking out.

Following two electrically induced convulsions during the course of one week he became more accessible, though in a state of psychotic depression, as is adumbrated in the following letter, which he wrote at this time:

'Sir: I could never hope to clear my filthy ways, and the damage I have done to you, the staff, patients, and everyone here is too colossal to even have part of it forgiven, so will you please put an end to it all for the benefit of everyone as I have never been worthy of the slightest attention, and you have been doing everything for my own good and yet I was too blind and sinful to see it all. Also may I say what wrong I did when you gave me an opportunity to come in here a week or so before I did and yet I turned the offer down and therefore any punishment you care to give me will be less than I deserve. Please do not delay the end any longer for the benefit of you all.'

The onset of this illness was due to conflict over solitary masturbation. In conversation at one time he expressed the view that such activity led to a 'weakening of the brain and body'. So, during the football game he was overtaken by unconsciousness, thus dramatizing his inability to sustain vigorous exercise like his healthy coevals. This is a typically hysterical sequence, the deeper psychopathology of which can be inferred from analogous cases treated in prolonged intensive psychotherapy. Regression to auto-erotic activity is unconsciously equated with offence against the incest taboo, and in some cases the accompanying incestuous fantasies can be brought to light in analytic psychotherapy, as Abraham (1910)[7] elucidated from his work with 'hysterical dream-states'. It is largely on account of this that an inordinate sense of guilt and expectations of talion punishment arise. The castration complex may be worked out in the psychic sphere as an interference with possibilities of pleasure in recreation. This case, then, at first showed the usual hysterical structure as far as could be discerned, i.e. a conflict relating to genital wishes that had acquired a forbidden character found expression in the symptom.

During the time of his episodic losses of consciousness, the patient seemed adjusted to the outside world, was well conducted, and able to converse adequately with others, despite depression. Later, however, the process of introversion went deeper; his behaviour then excited comment on account of its eccentricity, and he seemed incapable of expressing his thoughts and feelings to others. These had then acquired an extravagantly fantastic content, and he had fallen victim to depressive delusions. His disease had developed from hysteria to a schizo-affective disorder.

In this case, further ECT sessions were followed by a remission at which time psychotherapy again became possible.

Case 39. A young woman became engaged to be married, whereupon she refused food, claiming loss of appetite. This persisted and led to a considerable weight loss. When first interviewed she was quite accessible, and was persuaded to take food. She spoke of her approaching marriage as being a suitable one, spoke highly of her fiancé, and insisted that she was looking forward to her wedding. Her fiancé seemed considerate and very much in love, but unable to explain her strange behaviour on any grounds except a possible physical illness. Tactful inquiry disclosed no untoward event during the courtship that might have caused a gross emotional upset. When I saw the patient later her behaviour had become quite disordered, alternating fairly rapidly between violent excitement and rambling incoherence. She had hallucinations, delusions and illusions. She was sometimes frightened by hallucinations of evil, threatening figures. She would proclaim periodically that she was Greta Garbo or some other famous actress, but these fleeting delusions of grandeur alternated with delusions of persecution in which she felt that all her friends were against her. She mistook me for Satan at first, and shouted obscene abuse; at a later stage she was on better terms with me, and spoke in a disconnected way about the Virgin Mary and her own sins. Tube feeding became necessary since throughout her illness she consistently refused food. She kept referring to the tube as a 'snake' entering her body, and refused to 'take it in', although it was noticed that after resisting she would yield with some signs of satisfaction, only to vomit the food forcefully. She was isolated, and her fiancé was not longer permitted to visit her. Further treatment resulted in remission.

This fragmentary account demonstrates the essential psychopathological features. The disturbance occurred at a time when genital heterosexuality had to be accepted. Her refusal to take food symbolized regressively her refusal to take in the phallus, and was at first on a hysterical level. As in *Case* 38, that of the patient who became unconscious after masturbating, further pathological events occurred that issued in incoherence, delusions and hallucinations. In such cases it may be assumed that the hysterical attempt to solve conflict was psychologically inadequate (Good, 1946[8]), or that there was a toxic complication as Jung (1906)[4] suggested; or both assumptions may be held. In any case the most important happening in the transition from neurosis to psychosis is extensive withdrawal from the outside world. Withdrawal from external reality occurs to some degree in neurosis, but it is not sufficiently massive to result in sustained delusional, hallucinatory, and dyssymbolic symptoms. These are evidence of a more serious disruption of object relationships.

In hysteria, introversion in fantasy to the infantile object is the rule; because of the possibility of arousing the Oedipus complex with its taboos this may result in conflict and symptoms. In schizophrenia, the withdrawal is further deepened toward the self (narcissism) (Freud, 1914[9]; Abraham, 1908[10]). This leads to further events in the early stages of a psychosis. The outside world is not so easily shut off in life, and the process of repression particularly suffers further disturbance. Under normal conditions the energy generated in consequence of metabolic processes is utilized in physical growth, in muscular movements directed towards the external world, and in general externalized interest. When an attempt is made to withdraw massively from the outside world, the disposal of energy in activities related to external reality is blocked. The repressive resistances are then faced with an energic drive that can no longer be withstood, and the consciousness is invaded with contents usually excluded (Jung, 1940[11]). Some of these continue to afford considerable embarrassment, and, repression being no longer effective, other mechanisms are emphasized in desperation. The chief of these is projection, the unwelcome contents are thrust out of the self upon the outside world. In this way withdrawal from reality is succeeded and accompanied by the distortion of reality shown in delusions and hallucinations. The pathogenesis of delusions and hallucinations is based upon the mechanism of projection, whereas the incoherence of schizophrenia is essentially based on withdrawal, words are no longer adequately invested with meanings in terms of objective realities. Important events in the genesis of psychosis may be summed up psychopathologically as the increasing narcissistic withdrawal, the increasing failure of repression, and the increasing use of projection. These relationships are diagrammatically represented in *Fig.* 9.1

Fig. 9.1 Schematic representation of the genesis of hysteria and schizophrenia

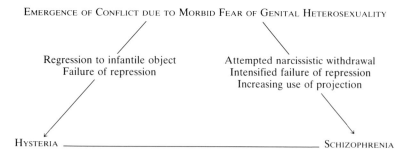

EMERGENCE OF CONFLICT DUE TO MORBID FEAR OF GENITAL HETEROSEXUALITY

Regression to infantile object
Failure of repression

Attempted narcissistic withdrawal
Intensified failure of repression
Increasing use of projection

HYSTERIA ——————————————————————— SCHIZOPHRENIA

Occasional Deeper Narcissistic Regression

Fig. 9.1 shows that schizophrenic psychosis may follow a hysterical phase (as in *Cases* 38 and 39) or may be otherwise initiated. An understanding of the basic psychopathological relationships enables one to form a judgement in doubtful cases as to the significance of the symptoms.

Incipient schizophrenia is often characterized by exaltation and hypochondriasis, both of which are directly due to the heightened narcissism (Freud,

1914[9]). Thus delusions of grandeur are an expression of the exaggerated increase of self-love. The anxiety that besets deeper introversion is worked out in hypochondriacal delusions of bodily derangement. These are, characteristically, more fantastic and bizarre than in hysteria, as was evident in the case of schizophrenia cited earlier (Chapter 8) in which the patient attributed abdominal pain to his possession of two stomachs, one male and one female, and declared that they periodically struggled fiercely, rising in his chest and pushing his lungs together. This patient also thought that the female was in the ascendant, and that he was likely to change his sex completely unless his doctors 'got on to' his case more energetically.

The content of this hypochondriacal delusion refers to the emergence of latent homosexuality, as is usual. During development into adulthood the phase of heterosexuality is preceded by phases of homosexuality and narcissism. In the process of withdrawal there is often a subjective experience of change or duality of sex. This patient also exhibited another symptom common in schizophrenia—perplexity; with his lessening contact with external reality, and the emergence of hitherto unconscious fantasies, the patient may be said to be living precariously in two worlds, in neither of which he is firmly settled, each of them presenting him with a set of contradictory data. This perplexity often expresses itself in a concern with metaphysical problems such as the nature of ultimate reality, the grounds of knowledge, cause and effect, etc. These speculations may become less and less clearly formulated. This symptom, like others, is also an expression of an attempt at healing, of reaching back to reality.

Schizophrenia is often ushered in with symptoms of hypochondriasis, exaltation and a peculiar over-ideation that becomes progressively more disconnected under unfavourable conditions. It is important to note such features since they suggest a dangerous velocity of deepening withdrawal, to stem which somatic methods of treatment might also become necessary (Abse, 1944[12]).

There are certain cases that present special difficulties for differentiation from psychosis. These are cases of hysterical puerilism, fugue, the Ganser syndrome and pseudo-dementia. In these there is a disturbance of psychotic degree in the sense of reality, but the psychotic excursion is usually temporary and non-progressive. The following case from many years ago is an example:

Case 40. A 30-year-old Indian hospital nurse complained of pains and took to her bed. Entirely satisfactory at work in the hospital for ten months, she became quarrelsome and capricious in her behaviour just before complaining of pains. No physical disability was found, but since she seemed depressed she was allowed to remain in bed. Soon after this, her conversation with her doctor and other visitors became aimless, whimsical and fanciful. When people lost patience and objected she refused to speak at all, and hid under the bedclothes. Her appetite as well as her behaviour was capricious, and since she continued hiding under the bedclothes she was referred for psychiatric examination. At first it was hard to make adequate rapport with her since she behaved like a sulky child. But she was persuaded to get up, and the childlike impression she made was emphasized by the luxury of her movements. Her conversation lacked seriousness; she was playful and inconsequential, turning aside playfully any attempt at anamnesis. She constantly spoke of the two nuns responsible for her upbringing, and wrote them childish letters. It later became apparent that she had received considerable instruction from the Italian nuns who had brought her up in the convent; on this basis she talked at length, discussing the plays of

Shakespeare and Shaw with adolescent enthusiasm. After a few such discussions it became clear that she was becoming more friendly and cooperative with other people. The occupational therapist was introduced to her, and soon she was spending considerable time in occupational therapy under her supervision, knitting and embroidering. She became greatly attached to the occupational therapist, who was able to influence her favourably. At this time she became very flirtatious towards any man she saw.

There was no doubt that she was 'growing up' again and was less a sulky child and more of a young adolescent, and it gradually became possible to discuss her situation in life and her history more realistically. An orphan of humble parentage, she had been taken as a young child to a convent where the nuns adopted her. When she was 21 she met a Muslim professor and left the convent to marry him, although she was a Christian. They lived together happily for several years and had two children. Her position in the household was unorthodox since she was an educated Christian, but her husband made concessions and she shared his life, including his intellecutal interests. They lived in a university circle, and she met and entertained her husband's associates and students.

It was with horror that after many such happy years she was forced to notice her husband's interest in another woman. Her husband then decided to marry this woman and add her to their household. The patient made it clear that she would not tolerate this, voicing her religious objections and her strong feelings about the position of women in society. She felt intensely jealous of the other woman, but in spite of her arguments her husband remained firm about his right to a plurality of wives. When the other woman arrived the patient took her children and left home. After placing the children in the convent in which she herself had grown up she joined the nursing service.

She had been successful in maintaining her independence and employment for nearly a year before the onset of the present illness. She had ignored her husband's letters, especially since he continued to insist on having at least two wives, and had made up her mind that reconciliation was impossible. She could not, sustain her heroic attempt at independent occupation and separation indefinitely, and became depressed, stopped working and took flight into illness, which was shortly translated into a complete denial in fantasy of her situation in life, and the reliving and dramatizing of her early days (*retour à l'enfance*).

This condition is sometimes known as 'hysterical puerilism' and involves a limited and usually temporary psychotic excursion. With denial provided by fantasy such an excursion is a transient defensive technique often utilized in childhood and, it must be admitted, one often carried over into adult life by many apparently well-adjusted people. In a similar way, hysterical pseudo-dementia and the Ganser syndrome are characterized by a shutting out of unpleasant realities. The patient is unable to answer simple questions with any accuracy (Ganser syndrome) and is sometimes incoherent and given to childish behaviour (pseudo-dementia).

The feigning of madness, not unusual among soldiers weary of the Army, sometimes leads to pseudo-dementia, which the patient is far from able to control. One patient learned that he was needed on the family farm where there had been insufficient work at the time he enlisted. With the rise of food prices, work on the farm promised greater economic advantage than staying in the Army, and this fact reinforced the patient's homesickness and made it unacceptable to stay. The need to withdraw from a current unpleasant situation is also a precondition of hysterical fugue and stupor.

It was formerly difficult to arrive at a diagnosis and prognosis in cases of stupor without organic basis unless observation was prolonged (Hoch,

1921[13]). The interruption of stupor by the slow intravenous injection of sodium amytal or pentothal often facilitates diagnosis and prognosis (Gottlieb and Hope, 1941[14]). In cases with a definite psychotic emphasis, the disinhibition caused by sodium amytal may result in the patient's expressing depressive delusions (depressive stupor) or delusions of persecution (paranoid state), or it may be that the patient expresses fantastic delusions or shows evidence of hallucinosis or impulsive excitement (catatonic stupor). In other cases it is easy to establish good rapport with the patient, who is enabled to express his thoughts and feelings lucidly, and to encourage him to awake. These cases are of a hysterical nature or, at the worst, show no fixed schizophrenic disorganization.

From this discussion it is clear that the differentiation of hysteria from schizophrenia is sometimes a difficult matter, especially when somatic symptom formation is the prelude to schizophrenic disorganization, or when an apparently hysterical illness is followed by a non-progressive and transient psychotic disturbance in reality adjustment. In nature, boundaries are not sharply demarcated, and in this differentiation the symptoms have to be evaluated on the basis of an understanding of psychopathology.

We have noted (Chapter 7) that transient psychotic episodes may develop in patients with hysteriform borderline personality disorder, especially when they are under stress or under the influence of alcohol or of street drugs. In psychiatric interviews such patients may display an intact formal organization of thought processes. However, as already considered, psychological testing, especially non-structured projective testing, as with the Rorschach, reveals the regressive tendency to primary process functioning. We have also noted (Chapter 2) that when hysterical symptoms also comprise convulsive seizures, or there is a history of such seizures, the gross regression of ego functioning periodically to primary-process-dominated discharges is self-evident. In psychotherapy, it becomes evident too that there is a confluence of pre-genital and genital drives under the overriding influence of strong oral and anal sadistic charges. Charcot, as already mentioned (Chapter 2), divided hysterical conditions into two groups, the convulsive and the non-convulsive. The former belong to the category of the hysteriform borderline personality disorders, and anamnesis in psychotherapy often reveals sexual molestation or brutal experiences in childhood. We have already detailed (in Chapter 7) the specific defensive operations of the traumatized immature ego which are habitually employed in borderline personality disorder. These include splitting, primitive idealization, projective identification, disowning projections, denial and omnipotent notions with devaluations of others. The early traumatic experiences impede adequately mature integration of the personality and the process of individuation. The defences employed are desperate efforts to prevent the submergence and collapse of the sense of selfness into the void of nothingness. Already in 1890, Rosse[15] had discussed the clinical evidences of *borderland* insanity and Lombroso (1878)[16] had previously discussed criminals who were not quite insane, though nearly so. These conditions of 'the borderland' often required prolonged observation, as well as psychodiagnostic testing, so that a definitive diagnosis cannot be reached in short contact work. The hysteriform borderline personality disorders, whether associated with convulsive seizures or not, have a tendency under stress to develop altered states of consciousness, which include fugues and somnambulisms, sometimes succeeded by a molar dissociation resulting in the syndrome of multiple personality.

REFERENCES

1. Freud, S. (1924). *Neurosis and Psychosis.* In: *The Standard Edition*, Vol. 19. London: Hogarth Press (1955).
2. Sawle-Thomas, J. C. (1940). Some clinical examples of 'dys-symbole': its relation to shock therapy. *J. Ment. Sci.*, **86**, 100.
3. Skottowe, J. S. I. (1939). Shock therapy: a plea for proportion in psychiatry. *Proc. R. Soc. Med.*, **32**, 843.
4. Jung, C. G. (1906). *The Psychology of Dementia Praecox.* New York: Nervous and Mental Disease Publishing Co. (1936).
5. Jung, C. G. (1920). *Psychological Types.* New York: Harcourt, Brace (1932).
6. Gunderson, J. G. and Kolb, J. E. (1978). Discriminating features of borderline patients. *Am. J. Psychiat.*, **135** (7), 792–6.
7. Abraham, K. (1910). Hysterical dream states. In: *Selected Papers.* London: Hogarth Press (1927).
8. Good, R. (1946). Depression. *Br. J. Med. Psychol.*, **20**, 344.
9. Freud, S. (1914). On Narcissism: An Introduction. In: *The Standard Edition*, Vol. XIV. London: Hogarth Press (1953).
10. Abraham, K. (1908). The psychosexual differences between hysteria and dementia praecox. In: *Selected Papers.* London: Hogarth Press (1927).
11. Jung, C. G. (1940). *The Integration of the Personality.* London: Kegan Paul.
12. Abse, D. W. (1944). Theory of the rationale of convulsion therapy. In: *Br. J. Med. Psychol.*, **20**, 33–50.
13. Hoch, A. (1919). *Benign Stupors: A Study of a New Manic-depressive Reaction Type.* Cambridge: Univ. Press (1921).
14. Gottlieb, J. A. and Hope, J. M. (1941). Prognostic value of intravenous administration of sodium amytal in cases of schizophrenia. *Arch. Neurol. Psychiat.*, **46**, 86.
15. Rosse, I. (1890). Clinical evidences of borderland insanity. *J. Nerv. Ment. Dis.*, **17**, 669–83.
16. Lombroso, C. (1878). *L'Uomo Delinquente.* Rome: Bocca Brothers.

CHAPTER 10

Hysteria and Hypnoid States

The Existence of Hypnoid States

In the course of history notions about and attitudes towards hysterical phenomena have been curiously and inextricably interwoven with views of the nature of hypnosis. At some times the art of hypnotizing was regarded as especially available to particular individuals, a divinely granted and sanctioned power or gift; at other times it was considered an instrument of dark powers and a force of evil. In these opposing beliefs we see a decomposition of the ambivalent feelings towards the ancient magician and priest, or towards the king endowed with supernatural power. In a peculiarly concentrated and evident way hypnosis has demonstrated the power for good or ill such an awesome person could exercise by intervening in the subject's psychic life. Similarly attitudes towards hysteria have also synchronously oscillated, hysteria being sometimes regarded with awe as a supernatural state in which prophetic utterance is possible, and at other times disdained as a state of demoniacal possession. Often the relationship between the art of hypnotizing and hysteria has become reciprocal when the good power of priest-physician was seen as capable of exorcizing the devil responsible for the hysteria. This association of hypnosis and hysteria in the mind of man through the ages—even long before these phenomena were described in such terms—is founded on a resemblance between them that is often immediately perceptible as peculiar alterations of consciousness. Sometimes some of these alterations are shared by the hypnotized and the hypnotizer, by the audience and the medium, and some elements are in a reciprocal relation.

In the early nineteenth century James Braid, the Scottish physician, eventually succeeded in obtaining recognition in orthodox medical circles for the facts of mesmerism (Bramwell, 1903[1]). He became convinced that it was essentially a narrowing of the attention, a 'mono-ideism', that ushered in the trance. He also began to understand something of the nature of the relation between hypnotist and patient, and of the effects of hypnosis on memory. After Braid's death in 1860 his discoveries were taken up in France. Soon there were two major schools of thought concerning hypnotism. The Paris school, under the leadership of Charcot, took the view that hypnotism was a phenomenon characteristic of hysteria, and one that could only be induced in persons suffering from, or at least prone to, that disease. The Nancy school, led by Bernheim and Liébault, followed up more closely the practice and theory of Braid. They believed that by suitable methods hypnosis could indeed be induced in nearly everyone, and they maintained that it was a phenomenon made possible by the general psychological trait of suggestibility. They tried to keep apart the problems of hysteria and hypnotism, disregarding Moebius's[2] dictum that 'Everyone is a little hysterical'.

The fact is that in both hypnosis and hysterical disease there are phases that show distinctive alterations of consciousness, although such alterations are more obvious at some times than at others, as will be discussed later. For the present we shall take into account the salient features of these alterations stressed by early scientific investigators. Janet (1907)[3] demonstrated that the restriction of consciousness pointed to by Braid as a prelude to trance is often characteristic of hysteria. The Paris and Nancy schools stressed the import-ance of suggestibility in both hypnosis and hysteria, although the two schools differed about general susceptibility to suggestion. They showed that the effects on memory of both hypnosis and hysterical disease may be either extraordinarily restrictive or amplifying. Moreover, the stages of hypnosis discussed by Charcot—lethargy, catalepsy, and somnambulism—can be seen quite independently of hypnosis as symptoms of hysteria. Janet (1907)[3] came to the important conclusion that in hysteria the integration of personality is imperfect and unstable, and that this results in dissociative phenomena. Identical dissociative phenomena, such as automatic writing, can be readily shown in persons in trance who exhibit no clinical evidence of hysterical disease in their daily life.

The conspicuous resemblances between hypnosis and hysteria discussed by these early investigators are then: restriction of consciousness, heightened suggestibility, alteration of memory function, and dissociative phenomena. These common features impressed Breuer and Freud in their subsequent work, and in a preliminary report (Breuer and Freud, 1893[4]) they repeatedly pointed out that in hysteria groups of ideas actually originate in hypnoid states. They wrote that the hypnoid states share one common feature, however much they may differ in other respects: the ideas that emerge in them are very intense but are cut off from associative communication with the remaining content of consciousness. Associations may take place between these hypnoid states, and their ideational content can in this way reach a high degree of psychic organization. Moreover, Breuer and Freud noted that the nature of hypnoid states and the extent to which they are cut off from other conscious processes vary, just as happens in hypnosis. They wrote in 1893:[4]

We have stated the conditions which, as our experience shows, are responsible for the development of hysterical phenomena from psychical traumas. In so doing, we have already been obliged to speak of abnormal states of consciousness in which these pathogenic ideas arise, and to emphasize the fact that the recollection of the operative psychical trauma is not to be found in the patient's normal memory but in his memory when he is hypnotized. The longer we have been occupied with these phenomena the more we have become convinced that *the splitting of consciousness which is so striking in the well-known classical cases under the form of* 'double conscience' *is present to a very rudimentary degree in every hysteria, and that a tendency to such a dissociation, and with it the emergence of abnormal states of consciousness (which we shall bring together under the term 'hypnoid') is the basic phenomenon of this neurosis.*

They presumed that these hypnoid states developed from reveries, so common in everyone: in a more leisurely time reverie no doubt went along with such quiet occupations as feminine needlework. It is familiar today to automobile drivers committed to long hours at the wheel of a virtually automatically controlled car.* In the *Studies on Hysteria* Breuer (1895)[5] emphasized the relationship of normative duplication of psychical functioning to pathological splitting in the following passage:

I suspect that the duplication of psychical functioning, whether this is habitual or caused by an emotional situation in life, acts as a substantial *predisposition* to a genuine pathological splitting of the mind. This duplication passes over into the latter state if the content of the two co-existing sets of ideas is no longer of the same kind, if one of them contains ideas which are inadmissible to consciousness—which have been fended off, that is, or have arisen from hypnoid states. When this is so, it is impossible for the two temporarily divided streams to reunite, as is constantly happening in healthy people, and a region of unconscious psychical activity becomes permanently split off. This hysterical splitting of the mind stands in the same relation to the 'double ego' of a healthy person as does the hypnoid state to a normal reverie. In this latter contrast what determines the pathological quality is amnesia, and in the former what determines it is the inadmissibility of the ideas to consciousness.

He observed of Anna O. that the girl seemed in perfect health, but had the habit of letting fantastic ideas flow next to her usual activities and that an anxiety affect entered into the day-dreaming and created a hypnoid state for which she had an amnesia. The hypnoid state repeated itself on numerous occasions, acquiring a richer ideational content alternating with states of normal consciousness.

Freud[67] wrote later in 1905 of the joint theory:

I have gone beyond that theory, but I have not abandoned it; that is to say, I do not today consider the theory incorrect, but incomplete. All that I have abandoned is the emphasis laid upon the so-called 'hypnoid state' which was supposed to be occasioned in the patient by the trauma, and to be the foundation for all the psychologically abnormal events which followed. If, when a piece of joint work is in question, it is legitimate to make a subsequent division of property, I should like to take this opportunity of stating that the hypothesis of 'hypnoid states'—which many reviewers were inclined to take as the central portion of our work—sprang entirely from the initiative of Breuer. I regard the use of such a term as superfluous and misleading, because it interrupts the continuity of the problem as to the nature of the psychological process accompanying the formation of hysterical symptoms.

Freud was more concerned with those unconscious genetics and dynamics of hysterical symptom formation that were more startling and at the same time more resisted in scientific circles, so he rejected or minimized the notion of 'hypnoid states'. He had elaborated the view that the body language of conversion reaction can be translated back to word language in the process of psychotherapy, and he had shown how partial failure of repressive defence had initially led to the conversion. At this time he turned away from giving due

---

*This may lead to 'highway hypnosis', and accidents (*see* Chapter 12).

consideration to obvious and marked fluctuations in the symbolizing, integrative, and adaptive functioning of the ego, and was especially occupied with defence functioning. This was, of course, before he turned his attention more definitively to ego psychology.

None the less, the intensity of his negative attitude towards the concept 'hypnoid state' that reduced to mere nominalism what is surely a phenomeno-logic definition may have been over-determined by inner factors related to his loosening relationship with Breuer in the kind of personal situation later repeated with Fliess.* Moreover Jones (1953)[6] notes that Freud himself had experienced

'spells where consciousness would be greatly narrowed: states, difficult to describe, with a veil that produced almost a twilight condition of mind'.†

Breuer (1895)[5] had previously remarked on Freud's interest in defence in the following noteworthy paragraph:

Freud's observations and analyses show that the splitting of the mind can also be caused by 'defence', by the deliberate deflection of consciousness from distressing ideas ... In normal people, such ideas are either successfully suppressed, in which case they vanish completely, or they are not, in which case they keep on emerging in consciousness ... I only venture to suggest that the assistance of the hypnoid states is necessary if defence is to result not merely in single ideas being made into unconscious ones, but in a genuine splitting of the mind. Auto-hypnosis has, so to speak, created the space or region of unconscious psychical activity into which the ideas which are fended off are driven.

Breuer and Freud were themselves struggling at this time to achieve a conceptual model that would relate the phenomena, and we must therefore make allowances for the language in which Breuer's statements are couched. We will later direct attention to the more sophisticated conceptual framework Freud achieved. Here Breuer suggests to me, however, that there is a place for understanding the hypnoid state as a possible way station during partial repression before conversion reduces the psychic tension. Considered thus, the concept of the hypnoid state does not interrupt the continuity of the problem as to the nature of the psychological process accompanying the formation of hysterical symptoms. Besides, the concept is based on an actual phenomenon—a striking change in the quality of consciousness, one that is important in understanding more adequately the vagaries of the hysterical personality.

The hypnotic trance is only one of a number of different kinds of trance (here called, following Breuer, 'hypnoid states'), similar in quality to some other forms of trance but different in its artificial outward characteristic and

---

*Freud himself discusses his childhood relationship with his nephew John, and its determining influence on his subsequent friendships in *The Interpretation of Dreams*, especially in relation to the 'non-vixit' dream.
†Such states are sometimes a phase in creative achievement.

the particular conditions of its emergence. Arnold M. Ludwig (1967)[7] points out that hypnoid or trance states may occur when an individual is absorbed in listening to music or dancing to it, engaged in artistic creation, prayer, reveries, or meditation, or in a hypnogogic or hypnopompic state. He writes:

> People may lapse into trance while driving on the road (highway hypnosis), standing at sentry duty, during watch in the crow's nest, or by continually staring at a radar screen. Almost any situation in which the individual is exposed to monotonous rhythmic stimulation, relative immobilization, fatigue, intense intellectual absorption, and the selective concentration on sensory stimuli to the exclusion of all other stimuli, might be conducive to the production of various depths of trance, whether it be in a solitary, interpersonal or group setting.

Thus trance phenomena—that is, qualitative shifts in mental functioning or altered states of consciousness—abound; it happens that hysterics are trance-prone, and readily develop pathological splitting, as Breuer noted.

Criteria for the Recognition of Hypnoid States

When Hubert S. Jennings[8] in 1906 confronted the question as to whether amoebae and paramecia have consciousness, he felt obliged to remark that if these organisms do not have consciousness they nevertheless behave very much as if they do. No doubt one is in the same basic philosophical quandary with all other living creatures inasmuch as one can only infer the presence of consciousness in others, the inference being partly based on one's own experience with oneself. Certainly a solipsistic position is clinically untenable; and certainly we have learnt that further inferences concerning unconscious psychic processes are very useful clinically in understanding ourselves and our patients. Despite the conceptual and epistomological difficulties involved, it is necessary to try to establish discriminate criteria for deviations in subjective experience and observable mental functioning from normative waking consciousness.

Once one takes the position that conscious and unconscious psychic processes exist, the way is open to evaluate through observation and inference the different levels of intensity of consciousness, and its qualities, one of which is concerned with the definition of the self in contradistinction to others. There is a complex relationship between consciousness and selfness. Introspection and the observation of other people quickly reveal diurnal variations in the intensity and quality of consciousness, variations which are often quite idiosyncratic in pattern but which generally include the alert waking consciousness, the dreaming consciousness, and such states of consciousness as the hypnagogic, the hypnopompic and the post-prandial. Such variations are statistically normal. In order to define criteria for identifying pathological hypnoid disturbance of consciousness, we will first contrast a common hypnoid state with another alteration of consciousness that is decisively pathological—depersonalization. This is clinically cogent, for in hysteriform borderline personality disorder the history often reveals an alternation of depersonalization with somnambulism or other hypnoid state; in hysterical personality disorder there is the occasional incidence of depersonalization.

The person afflicted with depersonalization complains that he is no longer the same; he has somehow changed, and is no longer himself. He may complain that he is a mere puppet, that things just happen around him, and that he has no joy or sorrow, hatred or love. He may feel dead, without hunger, thirst, or other bodily needs. The world also seems to have changed; it is somehow strange. From one viewpoint there is rejection of ego experience in the autopsychic, allopsychic, and somatopsychic spheres. However, as Schilder (1924)[9] stated:

All depersonalized patients observe themselves continuously and with great zeal; they compare their present dividedness-within-themselves with their previous oneness-with-themselves. Self-observation is compulsive in these patients. The tendency to self-observation continuously rejects the tendency to live, and we may say it represents the internal negation of experience.

Moreover, the depersonalized person observes not only his autopsychic function but also his own body; not only may he reject the experience of the body but he also continuously reports hypochondriacal sensations. And he not only reports estrangement from the external world but he gives a detailed account of the events he perceives taking place in the environment. There are in fact two conflicting directions in depersonalization, as Schilder emphasized, and these are sometimes condensed together in the reports of himself the patient offers in such profusion. The withdrawal from the external world—the narcissistic regression—is accompanied by defensive efforts to ward off objectionable perceptions of libidinal displacements within. At the same time, restitutional efforts to regain contact with the surrounding world are vigorously initiated. It is evident, of course, that in depersonalization we are dealing with a multiplicity of psychic events, but we are here concerned with only one aspect of these.

The paradoxical phenomenology of depersonalization becomes partly comprehensible from the viewpoint of defence and restitution. Here we have the compulsive cry of 'Wolf! Wolf!' before the wolf has yet descended on the fold. Depersonalization sometimes ushers in schizophrenic disorganization or other forms of ego loss or constriction. The patient begins talking as if already in some such state, but he also expresses intensified self-observation in the autopsychic and somatopsychic fields, and his heightened observation of what is going on around him. He samples, as it were, some degree of impoverishment of ego experience, and restitutionally observes himself and the world around him with sharpened vigilance. Besides, in this way he makes an appeal for help, just like the shepherd in the fable who suspects that his sheep are threatened by the wolf. He, too, is trying to summon help in order to prevent dissociation and to enable himself to maintain integration.

Wittels (1930)[10] emphasized that the hysteric has difficulty in attaining actuality as a grown-up human being, and that in consequence he confuses fantasy and reality, and allows the law of the id to enter the ego. Contrariwise, in the depersonalization syndrome the law of the super-ego enters the ego. The defensive self-observation with the internalized threat of negation of ego experience, the strangulation of affects, and the reversal of bodily sensations from pleasurable to unpleasant, are prominent features largely subtended by the increment in super-ego activity. The contrast becomes more startling when functional modalities of the id enter even more fully into the way the hysteric perceives himself and the world; for then the hypnoid state of consciousness, which has an almost completely different quality, emerges. Self-observation is deleted, ideation is intensely charged with affect, but vague and restricted in ways to be further explored. We will add here only that the ideational and verbal performance, unlike that in many instances of depersonalization, is inadequate, and symbol-making moves from the denotational toward the mythic mode (Spiegel, 1959).[11] Criteria looked for in making the diagnosis of common hypnoid states are thus essentially those connected with vague, restricted and affect-charged ideation, and with defective powers of self-observation, often associated with unadapted acting-out behaviour in the consequences of which the archaic super-ego, concealed from consciousness, once more reveals its ruthless and punitive power.

We have pointed out the antithetical nature of some qualities of consciousness in the depersonalization syndrome and in common hypnoid states. In the former, the phenomenological characteristics of heightened vigilance, limitation of affect and anhedonia are emphatic, whereas in the latter, a haziness of thought, a plethora of affect, and pleasurable excitement are often outstanding. In the former, self-observation reaches an excessive level, whereas in the latter it is grossly defective. However, these antitheses should not lead us to overlook one particular resemblance. In depersonalization, the loss of a feeling of selfness is complained about in one way or another. The patient may complain that he is nothing but a puppet, say 'I am no longer me', or in many other ways indicate that something is wrong with his ego-feeling, and at a self-directional, decisional and volitional level. Such complaints are absent in the hypnoid state, but observation reveals a lack of flexible social adaptability and a fixed focus as if the person were under a spell at the self-directional, decisional and volitional level. Depersonalized individuals and those in common hypnoid states resemble persons in hypnotic trance, and this likeness supports Farber's (1966)[12] thesis that 'hysteria is a particular disorder of will whose principal expression is willfulness'.

Walter Bonime (1972)[13] points out that depersonalization may briefly occur as a manifestation of improving health, and cites the depersonalization that sometimes signals progress in psychoanalytic treatment. The syndrome may then differ in three ways from that preceding personality disorganization: it tends to be brief (though it may recur over periods of weeks); it is often partly associated with pleasurable affect; and there is usually an increment of affective capacity. Although depersonalization may come to represent mainly an evasion of therapeutic work—may become resistance —it is in such instances the result of a new kind of personality functioning. The patient becomes anxious and 'depersonalized' as he becomes unfamiliar to himself in his assertion of an alien, but healthier, identity. One former alcoholic went through several periodic depersonalization crises while in analytic psychotherapy. These were painful at first, as he learned to deal with challenging situations by asserting himself more adequately and aggressively, and no longer resorted to being passive with the help of large doses of whisky.

Federn (1952)[14] believed that forms of intense estrangement (the perception of some objects in the real world as being no longer familiar) and of depersonalization can occur as intrinsic ego diseases, and can cease without leading to a fully developed neurosis or psychosis. In my experience, both such disturbances often occur in patients suffering from hysterical neurosis, and even more frequently among hysterical borderliners. Krohn (1978)[15] writes:

> The concept of a hypnoid state does, however, provide a quite valid, if rudimentary, description of some aspects of hysterical character or the hysterical ego that Abse (1959)[16] and Shapiro (1965)[17] later described. The hypnoid state described a state of consciousness in which ideas emerge with particular intensity, in which they fail to be brought into commerce with other ideas, in which conscious rational and objective processes of though fail to be brought to bear on the pathogenic thoughts and, most important, in which 'narrow fields of association' occur ... The concept, most probably Breuer's ... obscured Freud's most profound contribution in the early phase of his work—his understanding of the struggle to repress ... Nevertheless the hypnoid-state concept *does* embody later description of cognitive, characterological and ego psychological facets of the hysteric.

He goes on to enumerate the narrowed, restricted availability of ideation and fantasy, the proclivity to dissociate and repress, and the forgetting of troubling events habitual in the hysteric. It is perhaps now necessary to insist that Breuer's concept is founded on a recurrent phenomenon, and that this phenomenon exhibits in a periodically exaggerated way the hysteric's general style of processing and organizing information, as Shapiro (1965)[17] and Gardner and his associates (1959)[18] elaborated.

All human beings experience from hour to hour considerable fluctuations in alertness, self-observation, thought organization and other aspects of consciousness. Fatigue is an important influence on such fluctuation, and so is the social frame of reference. (A man's state of mind while engaged in professional activities during the day may contrast remarkably with what it is at a cocktail party later. The reality principle may loosen its hold even before alcohol effects the increasing influence of the pleasure principle.) In the hyponoic qualities of the hypnoid state the dominance of repetition compulsion becomes apparent. The state of mind is in one sense comparatively blind, and causes performance which is partly dissociated from what has been learnt previously in accordance with reality and the principles of pleasure and pain.

Consideration of such complexities can be deferred for now, to permit discussion of two aspects of thought organization, one relating to time perception, the other to the capacity for abstract thinking. When these aspects are neglected, clinical judgement can be seriously impaired.

Mild hypnoid states are admittedly hard to recognize against a background of normal fluctuations in the intensity of consciousness, and situational alterations in its quality, but a fugue state is usually readily detectable on psychiatric examination although it might escape casual observation. Apart from the restricted ideation and haziness of thought, and gross affective disturbance, there is an almost complete exchange of the present for the past in these extreme hypnoid states. Transference distortion is maximal, and object relations are characterized by mimetic caricature that is sometimes grotesque.

Kurt Goldstein (1946)[19] discussed the clinical significance of the abstract attitude and its relation to speech. From his work with brain-damaged patients he came to distinguish two ways of using words in connection with objects: *real naming*, which is an expression of the categorical attitude toward the world in general, and *pseudo-naming*, which is simply the use of remembered words. The incidence of pseudo-naming depends on the extent of the individual's verbal possessions. In it, words are used as properties of objects, just as other properties—colour, size, hue—are used: they belong to concrete behaviour.*

In the mild prolonged hypnoid states of some severe hysterical personalities, and in the more episodic hyponoic disturbances of others, verbal skills may remain apparently intact, and may not obviously reflect deficiencies in abstract thinking. Such searching investigation as is involved in psychoanalysis will, however, show that such patients are often unable to handle the abstract. Treatment must be modified accordingly to engage the patient's self-observation more fully, to impede the personality's total involvement in regressive events, and to monitor the affective flow. This is particularly important in respect to the analysis of the transference to the therapist. These patients often become completely and concretely involved in the transference without sufficient means to achieve any distance and sense of time that will help them to understand that they are caught up emotionally in reliving the past.

The Borderline Personality and the Hypnoid State

When Wilhelm Reich (1933)[20] described the outstanding features of the hysterical character he related them to fixation in the genital phase of infantile development and its incestuous attachment. He suggested that the hysterical character derives its strong genital aggression and its apprehensiveness from such fixation, and emphasized that such a character genitalizes everything; he called attention to 'the flooding of the genital with pre-genital libido' found in other character disorders. Marmor (1953)[21] emphasized deep-seated oral fixation in drawing attention to some clinical aspects of hysterical character disorder, especially its resistance to change, the immaturity and instability of its ego structure, and its close relationship to addictions, depression and schizophrenia. He regarded the fixations in the Oedipal phase of development as outgrowths of pre-Oedipal fixations, chiefly of an oral nature. Because of this view he dissents from the usual opinion that hysterical character neurosis is usually the most accessible of all the major clinical entities to pschoanalytic therapy.

Clinical experience indicates that there are two broad categories of hysterical kinds of character disorder and neurosis, one being generally accessible both symptomatically and characterologically to relatively brief analysis, the other, associated with marked orality and supported by

---

*The use of words held in memory and reproduced without appreciation of their abstract meaning appears in dreaming; the words are used in dream work for the disguised expression of latent dream thoughts. Freud pointed this out, and showed that whatever is clearly speech in a dream can usually be traced back to some real speech the dreamer has either heard or spoken himself. (Freud, 1900, in *Speeches in Dreams*, Chapter VI, Section F, iv.)

narcissistic ego disorder, requiring lengthy treatment. The latter enjoins considerable technical modification upon the analysis because of the psychotic mechanisms that become apparent, including severe transference regression phenomena, especially the protracted hypnoid states sometimes present. We have differentiated these latter disorders from hysterical personality disorder with the appellation 'hysteriform borderline personality disorder'.

In discussing 'the Borderline Case', Greenson (1956)[22] used the term 'borderline state' to denote a relatively stable clinical picture in which exist simultaneously indications of psychosis and neurosis, and healthy ego function. Zetzel (1956)[23] at the same panel discussion Greenson was addressing emphasized that, in some patients, psychotic problems were more clearly to be seen during the course of psychoanalytic treatment, and used the term 'borderline personality'. We have already noted that as early as 1891 George M. Beard[24] spoke of 'border-liners', and that Kernberg (1967)[25] later attempted a more general systematic account of the symptomatic, structural and genetic-dynamic aspects of the borderline personality. Shortly before Greenson and Zetzel took part in the panel at the meeting of the American Psychoanalytic Association, Reichard (1956)[26] had noted that two of the five patients reported in *Studies of Hysteria*, namely Anna O. and Emmy von N., showed schizophrenic features. She re-examined the cases Breuer and Freud had reported, applying to them current ego-psychological concepts and showing that they were not diagnostically an entirely homogeneous group. Others before Reichard—Noble in 1951,[27] Goshen in 1952[28] and Brill[29] in 1954—had commented on the psychotic elements in Freud's original patients. Reichard differentiated the cases of Anna O. and Emmy von N. from three other cases in the *Studies* on the basis of symptoms, family background, the outcome of treatment and dynamics, with particular regard for ego defect assessment. She claimed that only with such assessment could different types of hysteria be adequately classified. Easser and Lesser (1965)[30] similarly differentiated 'hysteroid' from the category of hysteria, and remarked especially on the painful masochistic elements in the fantasies of these more pregenitally orientated patients. The fact is that there are borderliners of hysteriform type.

We find psychotic patterns of defensive behaviour in these cases of hysteriform type, as well as outspokenly hysterical characterological features. Some such patients have shown denial, flight into activity or into passivity, projective distortion, and pathological lying. Conversion reactions have sometimes alternated with some of these features, and have also occurred along with massive flight into passivity. Sometimes these patients evinced depersonalization and hypnoid disturbances of consciousness. Women patients with extremely unstable love-object relationships have shown a compulsion to stage scenes, although they were avowedly phobic of such scenes. The scenes came about through their insidiously or blatantly provocative behaviour. The men involved by them were usually of a passive type, lending themselves to being controlled, but later, after a greater of lesser dose of symbolic phallic dismemberment, they became actively aggressive, usually engaging in the violent scene. A condensed formula would be: supportive feeding patterns of behaviour, with considerable sexual provocation, followed by controlling behaviour patterns, and then by castrating behaviour. Although they often overlapped to some extent, these patterns had a sequence with a typical tempo; the final acting-out before the disruption of the relationship typically occurred when the patient was in a hypnoid state. Analytic investigation of such character disorder showed, among other things, the genetic determination—early oral deprivation, with later successive identifications with the omnipotent feeding and soothing mother, the controlling mother, and the withholding mother—in a dramatic restaging of the patient's own early traumatic disturbance. This orally determined and unconsciously motivated behaviour complicated the unsurmounted penis envy and the Oedipal problems that were, of course, also involved in the re-enactment.

Fenichel (1945)[31] writes in Chapter XXI of his book about this kind of traumatophilia and traumatophobia:

The repetition is desired to relieve a painful tension; but because the repetition is also painful, the person is afraid of it and tends to avoid it ... There are many varieties of this mixture of fear of repetition and striving for it. When the striving is unconscious, the patients, in spite of a fear of upsetting experiences, experience upsetting things every day, they run from catastrophe to catastrophe; everything is disturbing and filled with emotion, there is never time, distance or relaxation enough for them to quieten down.

Obviously in such character disorder the elements of neurotic conflict and of trauma are simultaneously present. In these cases the defences against instinctive impulses are based on specific traumatic experiences. Flight into activity, denial, projective distortion, changes of identity and lying are often marked, but not to a degree that permits a clinical diagnosis of manic or schizo-affective psychosis to be made. The mechanisms are of the same order but less intense. Stengel (1945)[32] acquainted us with the obsessional repertoire of defences protecting against psychotic disturbance. We are less aware of low-keyed psychotic defences as a regressive evasion of neurotic problems related to the Oedipal phase. The exhibition of primitive pre-genital defences of course related not only to the arousal of the problems of the Oedipal phase of development, but also to early attempts to survive traumatic deprivation. The arousal of these pre-genital defences in hysteriform personalities is often associated with other regressive ego changes that lead to hypnoid states of consciousness.

Some Preliminary Metapsychological Considerations

In the theoretical section of *Studies on Hysteria*, Breuer (1895)[4] takes into account Moebius's previous discussion of hypnoid states. Moebius (1894)[2] had drawn attention to disturbances of consciousness in hysteria that resembled those artificially induced in hypnosis in that there was a 'vacancy of consciousness', or inhibition of the current of ideas so that emerging ideas met with no resistance from others. Breuer[4] himself emphasized the role of reveries that become complicated by strong affects, especially anxiety, and are thus transformed into spontaneous hypnoid states, citing the transformation of Anna O's 'private theatre' of imaginative products as an example. As for those hypnoid states that develop more suddenly, they are often consequences of an affect of great intensity, reactive to objective events that have stirred recollections. Freud's[4] case of Katherina—was an example: she was frightened when she witnessed a close relative's participation in a sexual affair which she only vaguely comprehended at first. Her disturbance of comprehension was explained by reference to the preliminary statement of Breuer and Freud (1895):[4] 'The affect itself created a hypnoid state whose products were then cut off from associative connection with the ego-consciousness.'

The hypnoid state is characterized by vague ideation restricted in associations and suffused with strong affects. Freud's (1926)[33] later formulations clarify that the emergent ideas are kept vague and restricted precisely because they can arouse anxiety. Anxiety is aroused when repression fails, either in a sudden confrontation that activates forgotten experiences and fantasies or because of day-dreams complicated by derivatives of unconscious fantasy in increasingly weakening disguise. Re-repression may then occur, and if this is inadequate, the defence may be supplemented by conversion. The genesis of a hypnoid state may, however, be a third temporary compromise, in which consciousness is occupied by ideational representations of unconscious fantasy, restricted in association from other ideas and in a preliminary stage of development themselves (Schilder, 1920[34]). The restriction of association, when marked, produces a splitting of consciousness, and anxiety is present in a variable degree although it is reduced by clouding of the ideas, that is, their lack of clarity. Sometimes the hypnoid state assumes forms recognizable clinically as fugue, puerilism, pseudo-dementia or the Ganser syndrome—forms that differ in emphasis on the state of development of ideas, the intensity of anxiety, the obtrusiveness of splitting and the direction and extent of acting out.

There are, of course, other dimensions in the formal characteristics of hypnoid states, especially the relative dominance of activity over passivity. For example, in an amok or similar state of fugue frenzied homicidal activity is dominant although suicide may ensue if death at the hands of those threatened is avoided. On the other hand, in latah a passive hypersuggestibility dominates as in artificially induced hypnosis, although copralalia combined with erotic hallucinosis may indicate the concomitant presence of active defiance. In these and other cultural variants of hypnoid states one should take into account their collective significance as a means of release and communication to the larger group. For example, in such ceremonial rites as those engaged in within the Voodoo cult, the trance state should be considered a sanctioned means of release and communication within that society. It is only when the activities in trance either originate outside the ritual or persist beyond its termination that they communicate pathology or sickness to other group members, however frenetic the roles and dances may be. Consideration of the transcultural diversity of hypnoid states leads to recognition of the need to discriminate between the culture-specific and the universal meaning of outwardly similar elements of communication and identity change.

Freud (1900)[35]* regarded consciousness as a sense organ for the perception of psychic qualities. Excitation flows in from two directions—from the perceptual system and from the interior of the psychic apparatus. In order to become

*In: 'The Unconscious and Consciousness—"Reality"'. Chapter VII, Section F. In: *The Interpretation of Dreams (see* ref. 35).

conscious, both internal and external perceptions require an additional cathexis of attention. In reverie the hypercathexis lending consciousness is of a lower intensity than that affording more alert waking consciousness; and in hypnoid states the cathexis is diminished still further. Moreover, in hypnoid states, countercathectic energy distributions that counteract unconscious drive representations in the process of repression have been weakened, and this may be true also of those that keep pre-conscious thought formations from reaching consciousness. It is also possible that word-symbol connections within the pre-conscious system, a stage through which thought development passes, are deranged, and that visual and acoustic imagery predominate. Such regression may account for the relative dominance of the concrete attitude over the abstract.

The lessening of the attention cathexis, together with the regressive separation of instinct representations from verbal images, deprives ideation of clarity and of associative connections within the pre-conscious system. These effects impede the 'associative corrections' of 'normal consciousness' discussed by Breuer and Freud in their peliminary paper. The failure of countercathexis results in heightened felt emotion, and in motor discharge, both inwardly (mien, affective expression) and outwardly, in action patterns that directly reflect unconscious themes.

There are, however, a variety of hypnoid states both acute and chronic, and some of them have an underlying homogeneity of pattern that contrasts with those varieties of depersonalization that show a restitutionally heightened attention associated with regressive narcissistic disorder. In 'The Unconscious and Consciousness' (Chapter VII), Freud (1900)[35] emphasized that the multiplicity of the problems of consciousness could be grasped only by analysis of the thought processes in hysteria. The dissociations of personality, which include phenomena of co-consciousness as well as of hypnoid states, have not been adequately scrutinized psychoanalytically thus far, although much has been accomplished by Morton Prince (1905)[36] and others (Erickson and Kubie, 1939[37], 1940[38]; Oberndorf, 1941[39]).

The nature of hypnosis itself requires further elucidation. Gill and Brenman (1961)[40] have shown that the induction phase of hypnosis is closely associated with bringing about a regressive movement that issues in a regressed state—the established hypnotic state. A subsystem within the overall ego structure becomes cathected in the induction phase and soon temporarily dominates ego functioning. The induction phase is generated by the combined operation of sensori-motor and ideational restriction, with concomitant evocation of an archaic object relationship with the hypnotist. As this phase develops it is characterized by the readier availability of ideas and affects that were previously repressed and of impressions the verbal or anatomical expression of which may be encouraged, blocked, or otherwise manipulated by the hypnotist. During this phase, spontaneous phenomena such as age regression and changes in the perceived body image may occur, whereas little of this sort is apt to happen once the hypnotic state is fully established.

Ronald E. Shor (1959)[41] has developed the theory that the usual state of consciousness is characterized by the mobilization of a structured frame of reference in the background of attention, which supports and gives meaning to all experiences the individual has. This frame is 'the generalized reality-orientation' of the person in question. Shor writes:

Perhaps the best way to explain what is meant by this proposition is to describe a state of consciousness in which the usual generalized reality-orientation is not mobilized in order to see more clearly the psychic functions that are imputed to it. Many experiences could be cited as illustrations—from literature, 'mystic experiences', or pathological states. The best of these have the quality of *merging* of self and world (as in the typical Nirvana experience) whereas the clearest illustration of our proposition would be an instance of the *loss* of self and world entirely.

He then gives the following personal account:

I had been asleep for a number of hours. My level of body tonus was fairly high and my mind clear to dream images so that I believe I was not asleep but rather in some kind of trance-like state. At that time I was neither conscious of my personal identity, nor of prior experiences, nor of the external world. It was just that out of nowhere I was aware of my own thought processes. I did not know, however, that they were thought processes or who I was, or even that I was an *I*. There was sheer awareness in isolation from any kind of experiential context. It was neither pleasant nor unpleasant, it was not goal-directed, just sheer existing. After a time a 'wondering' started to fill my awareness; that there was something more than this, a gap, an emptiness. As soon as this 'wondering' was set into motion there was immediately a change in my awareness. In an instant, as if in a flash, full awareness of myself and reality expanded around me. To say that 'I woke up' or that 'I remembered', while perhaps correct, would miss the point of the experience entirely. The significant thing was that my mind changed fundamentally in that brief instant. In rediscovering myself and the world, something vital had happened; suddenly all the specifications of reality had become apparent to me. At one moment my awareness was devoid of all structure and in the next moment I was *myself* in a multivaried universe of time, space, motion and desire.

Shor[41] maintains that the generalized reality-orientation 'does not maintain its regnancy' as the cognitive support structure in the background of awareness without active mental effort being constantly devoted to its maintenance, and he states, 'However, this active effort is not usually consciously directed.' When its supportive energy diminishes, the generalized reality-orientation fades into the more distant background of attention and becomes relatively non-functional. Shor holds that hypnosis is a complex of two fundamental processes—the construction of a special temporary orientation to a small range of preoccupations, and the relative fading of the generalized reality-orientation into non-functional awareness. In his 1959 essay he spoke of hypnosis as having two dimensions of depth: (*a*) the depth of *trance*, which is defined as the extent to which the generalized, everyday reality-orientation has sunk into non-functional unawareness; and (*b*) the depth of role-taking, which is defined as the extent to which the subject builds up a new, special orientation from the instructions of the hypnotist. In a later essay (1962),[42] he recognizes three dimensions of the depth of hypnosis, writing:

Gill and Brenman's (1959)[40] two intertwined induction phase factors correspond to two of our three dimensions of hypnotic depth. The first factor (sensorimotor and ideational deprivation leading to alterations in ego functioning) is our trance dimension.

The second factor (stimulation of an archaic object relationship onto the hypnotist) is our archaic involvement dimension. Also when the authors view the established hypnotic state as a regressed sub-system within the overall ego, they are referring in psychoanalytic terminology to what we have called profound hypnotic role-taking involvement; i.e. the complex of motivational strivings and cognitive structurings to be a hypnotized subject has become nonconsciously directive.

It seems to me that the factors of the provocation of archaic object relationships and 'profound hypnotic role-taking involvement' are inextricably meshed, the former as an unconscious transference dynamic, and the latter having drive derivatives at pre-conscious levels. However, Shor (1962)[42] argues that it is possible to reach a profound depth in hypnosis when archaic involvement is minimal, or may appear to be minimal. In general, Shor's argument—that appearing in his second paper—would seem to neglect problems raised by changed object relationships within the psyche that are not grossly projected onto the hypnotist in transference so he is not so obviously involved in the archaic regression. As for spontaneous hypnoid states such as are common in hysteria and hysteriform borderliners, a number of conditions found in artificial induction, such as monotonous rhythmic stimulation, visual fixation and relaxation, as well as the inner emotional turbulence associated with conflict that favours regression, may contribute to their emergence. Once the regressive movement has begun, the pathology of primitive internalized object relations exerts its further sway, and is partly expressed in accompanying behaviour. Internal dynamics concerned with the revival of parent/child relationships are mobilized, and the individual's archaic super-ego functions as the internalized representative of the parental imagoes of early infancy.

Further Metapsychological Considerations

Thus far we have considered hypnoid states in the context of hysterical character disorder and symptom neurosis, and in the related context of hysteriform borderline disorder. We have also contrasted hypnoid states with certain states of depersonalization. Other pathological disturbances of consciousness are available for comparison: schizophrenia, manic-depressive psychosis, or, for that matter, the closely related disorder of multiple personality where cleavage associated with a relatively high degree of integration of the separate partial personalities obtains. Also available for comparison are altered states of consciousness (ASCs, as they are now acronymically called) that are definitively normal, such as day-dreaming and the nocturnal dreaming consciousness. One among these, which is a remarkable alteration of consciousness, deserves scrutiny.

It has already been mentioned (p. 212) that, according to Jones (1953),[6] Freud experienced aberrations of the stream of consciousness, 'spells where consciousness would be greatly narrowed; states, difficult to describe, with a veil that produced almost a twilight condition of mind'. We know that such introverted disturbances of mentation are not uncommonly a prelude to creative thought, being as it were disturbances in the laboratory of the mind during the process of decomposition and recombination of the thought structures prior to the creative act, and sometimes attending it. This kind of disturbance of consciousness is not easily accessible to introspection; its counterpart, more frequently experienced by more of us—that state of heightened consciousness of life in the act of aesthetic appreciation—is more accessible.

Those aspects of the aesthetic experience that are relevant here are the rapt attention that may reach an extreme of fascination, the arousal of emotions and the ambiguity of ideas.* The following excerpt from Max Eastman (1938)[43] is pertinent:

> To me it seems obvious that such realization, or heightened consciousness of life, is desired for its own sake. It is not possible, perhaps, to have a 'pure' realization of anything—one quite unmixed with attitudes of action or of practical conception. Moreover, by deftly managing these attitudes, and by carefully selecting the kinds of things to be realized, the trance of realization can almost always be made to serve some end—as many ends as there are philosophies of art. But that men love art regardless of the attitude it inculcates, provided they are endowed with or instructed in the gift of loving it, and provided the attitude involved is not *too* sharply hostile to some quick passionate purpose in their hearts, is proven by innumerable facts. It was proven to us not long ago by the Rockefellers' patronage of Diego Rivera's painting. Almost all of Rivera's art is in its attitude, or motive, revolutionary, but that does not impede their admiration of it—not, at least, until a head of Lenin appears in a building where offices are to be rented. Lenin himself is described by all who knew him as the 'goal pursuing man', yet Lenin read all the Russian classics, Pushkin, Lyermontov, Turgenev, who had no leaning towards his goal, in preference to lesser artists who were bent on it. He read because he loved experience, not only knowledge, and not only action towards an end.

The state of consciousness that characterizes aesthetic appreciation is firstly one of heightened attention, though the attention is narrowed; this contrasts with some hypnoid states. Secondly, as Eastman amplified, there is definite suspension of action, which again contrasts with some hypnoid states in which there is flagrant neurotic acting out. Moreover, not only is the attention heightened, but the experience is emotionally rich. The consciousness of this richness is indeed connected with the delay in action, and the euphoric emotional experience is partly organized through the perception of the work of art. We must note that there can also be heightened and narrowed attention in some hypnoid states, and suspension of action; but often this is in the first phase of the hypnoid state, and is succeeded by a phase in which anxiety mounts before another change quickly brings reduced attention, diminished clarity of ideas, and ensuing action patterns in the prolongation of the hypnoid state. We understand this change to be part of the defence against dsyphoric affect, the signal function of which is exceeded when it fails to induce adequate repression.

As Plaut (1959)[47] noted, the phenomena of consciousness seem to be bound up with rhythmic alternations between focusing and defocusing. Focusing, or a high degree of awareness in one sector of the perceptual field, is accompanied

---

*The means whereby this satisfying experience is achieved—the excitation of sensuous pleasure, the relief of tension in vicariously solving conflict, the symbolic references of the work of art, the techniques of permitting the primary process to reappear—and the depths of emotion stirred do not immediately concern us. These means are discussed by Rickman (1940),[44] Fairbairn (1938)[45] and Kris (1952).[46]

by diminished attention to whatever is going on elsewhere. It reaches an unusual height in aesthetic appreciation. For example: a friend looking at a small classic Greek figure of a satyr seemed enrapt, and failed to respond to several signals. When called to account for the time he had spent before the figure he estimated that he had been standing there no more than a few moments, but the time had actually been 20 minutes. It is evident that many alterations of consciousness are involved in the process of extremely narrow focusing, and that one of them is the loss of the sense of passing time. In the face of these variables the problem arises concerning a narrowed focus of heightened attention in some hypnoid states. The subject's disregard of anything outside this field of concentration might lead to the conclusion that a generally reduced attention cathexis prevails, when attention is simply selectively heightened in one focal field at the expense of others.

We have noted that James Braid (1843)[48] was convinced that such narrowing of attention or 'monoideism' ushered in hypnotic trance. In the induction of hypnosis the subject gives narrowed and heightened attention to the operator and his instructions, and the persistence of this passive attention throughout the trance is partly responsible for the operator's ability to shift his subject's attention and gain remarkable results thereby, especially in the revival of memories. The hyperamnesia in hypnosis, including the possible reactivation of past events as in 'age regression', comes about not only because of the heightened, narrowed and 'shiftable' focus of attention, but also because of generalized regressive movements and the weakening of counter-cathectic energy distributions. Similarly, at the outset of spontaneous or chance development of hypnoid states, there is at first a heightened and narrowed attention in a phase of suspense during which there is often a lowering of attention cathexis prior to the full development of the hypnoid state. However, in some hypnoid states, as in somnambulisms, for example, there is a remarkable persistence of heightened attention *within a narrow focus*.

It is clear that the metapsychological assumptions considered thus far outline too static a model as far as problems of consciousness are concerned. We must concern ourselves in particular with rhythmic processes of focusing and defocusing. But this is not all, for in states of greatly narrowed focus and highly intensified concentration and absorption other alterations of consciousness take place. Anyone who has experienced this kind of extreme fascination in viewing a painting, for example, will recall a shift in attitude immediately afterwards, one in which curiosity about the period to which the work of art belongs is apt to be marked. Many other considerations also come to mind, including curiosity about the artist and his life, while the connoisseur is likely to think about the techniques used in producing the painting. This attitudinal shift after disunion with the work of art is not necessarily accompanied by any deliberate attempt to recall the aesthetic experience just enjoyed but it is possible to recall it in part and fleetingly. It should be noted that the aesthetic experience may fall short of the kind of sustained fascination we are concerned with here; there may be a rather rapid fluctuation of attitude from some degree of subjective involvement to some degree of objective detachment. It is a rather rare experience to have psychic distance so reduced as to bring about a state of fascination.

In a fully developed and well sustained experience of fascination, the usual background temporal orientation (part of the 'generalized reality orientation' noted by Shor[41]) is not simply impaired; it is deleted. Its later impairment, as the example shows, reflects temporary deletion of the time sense and the effort being made to restore it—an effort that seizes upon every perceptual cue. The more compelling the experience, the greater the tendency for the pendulum, so to speak, to swing to the other side of its arc as the person 'collects himself'. The viewer's conscious attitude changes from virtually total involvement in the object of his fascination to objective detachment; and the jolt given his time sense awakens a lively curiosity about the bygone world in which the artist lived, and the way he conducted his life within it.

Introspection, the fleeting recall of immediate past experience, and the sequence of considerations in which such opposition and displacement occur, confirm Bernfeld's (1928)[49] contention that the fascinated person loses his consciousness of his own separateness from the perceived object. There has been temporary alteration not only of the time sense but also of orientation in space. Greatly narrowed focus seems to be achieved only with this kind of primary identification, when the consciousness of self as well as the usual temporal and spatial orientation is more or less lost.* (Common speech acknowledges this in the expression 'I lost myself' in looking at, or listening to, a compelling aesthetic communication.) Moreover, in this kind of *engourdissement d'esprit* there is a reduction of countercathectic energies responsible for maintaining repression.

The variables so far briefly considered are diagramatically presented in *Table* 10.1.

In states of creativity and of aesthetic appreciation, as in other states of highly concentrated attention, the regressive events involved are utilized in the service of the ego. In hypnosis the therapist often attempts to help his patient to integrate some of these events in the course of his treatment. In hypnoid states they are later sequestered from normative waking consciousness by the intensified redeployment of mechanisms of repression and/or splitting.

Table 10.1 serves to show that hypnoid states characterized by deletion of self-observation and vague affect-charged and restricted ideation (Abse, 1961)[50] may shift to states of fascination, and vice versa. This relationship is clinically important in gaining a full appreciation of certain primitive kinds of erotic transference that are especially apt to develop in borderline personalities of the hysteriform type. According to Freud (1915),[51] among the more refractory in psychotherapy are those women

of elemental passionateness who tolerate no surrogates. They are children of nature who refuse to accept the psychical in place of the material, who, in the poet's words, are accessible only to 'the logic of soup, with dumplings for arguments'.

This kind of transference-love, like sustained primitive hostile transference, readily yields countertransference problems; the therapist himself may have a

---

*Keats's preoccupation with this kind of absorption of the poet in the creating process is expressed in his often-quoted 'Negative Capability' letter. *See* the excellent discussion in the biography by Bate, W. J. (1963). *John Keats.* Cambridge, Mass.: Harvard Univ. Press.

defensive alteration of consciousness and become involved in a hypnoid state. This can readily evolve from his evenly hovering attention as he listens, and can obstruct his necessary oscillation to alert focused understanding in the service of insight psychotherapy (see also Allen and Houston, 1959[52]).

The Defensive Aspects of Hypnoid States

As emphasized in this present text and earlier (Abse, 1961[50]), and especially in connection with automobile and industrial accidents (Abse, 1958[53]), the hypnoid individual's symptoms conform to the usual neurotic formula in being a compromise formation of instinctual demands and the counterforces resisting them. Robert Dickes (1965)[54] spoke of the defensive aspects of some hypnoid states, writing in an admirably succinct passage:

> The ego, subservient to the super ego, and executive organ of the psyche, then institutes the hypnotic defense in the service of repression. This requires one part of the ego concerned with the production of affect and memory as noted in consciousness. A successful defence indicates a hypnoid state of sufficient depth so that neither sexual nor aggressive responses are noted and access to the motor apparatus for direct expression is denied. Indirect expression of the drives may manifest itself, but is then a measure of the failure of defense. The hypnoid defence counters especially the unacceptable sexual impulses which are also directed towards the parents or their surrogates, which also must be countered.

Dickes (1965)[54] gives a number of illustrations in which his patients describe childhood events that offer clues to their proneness to hypnoid states. He indicates that in adult life the hypnoid state 'is often a repetition of a childhood hypnoid state which occurred as a means of warding off intolerable feelings due to overstimulation and abuse.' Dickes and Papernik (1977)[55] wrote later: 'We now believe that the hypnoid state can be used independently of repression and is not always an auxiliary defence.' I do not, however, see their statement as precisely accurate. Some hypnoid states with clearly evident instinctual derivatives permit access to the motor apparatus as in fugues and somnambulisms (*see* p. 270). Dickes and Papernik rightly criticize other investigators for confusing sleep and hypnoid states, but they themselves seem to include sleep as an altered state of consciousness. This could be misleading since sleep is a physiological state without consciousness. Of course, as Kubie noted (1943),[56] we are never totally awake nor totally asleep; parts of us are asleep in our waking moments, while all gradations of psychic consciousness, both active and inactive, lie along a spectrum. Dreaming consciousness is a normative alteration of waking consciousness, and some altered states of consciousness such as the hypnagogic experience described by Isakower (1938)[57], a regressive revival of oral-phase experiences and fantasies of gratification, are preludes to sleep (Abse, 1977[58]).

Dickes's (1965)[54] case material clearly shows the importance of drawing attention to the hypnotic evasion in the course of psychoanalytic treatment, and of encouraging the patient to collaborate in the search for insight into the origins of his defence. Such psychoanalytic work led Dickes to review the

Table 10.1 Diagrammatic 'representation' of the relationships between various psychic states.

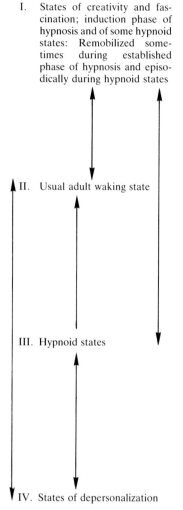

I. States of creativity and fascination; induction phase of hypnosis and of some hypnoid states: Remobilized sometimes during established phase of hypnosis and episodically during hypnoid states

A. Heightened and narrowed focus of attention (with lessened interval of defocusing)
B. Qualitative changes in consciousness:
   1. Deletion of self-consciousness
   2. Deletion of time orientation, impairment of space orientation
   3. Ideational ambiguity and plasticity
   4. Felt emotion heightened, but regulated
C. The above changes are related to the following:
   1. Identification with object structure
   2. Diminution of repression
   3. Partial regression from structured verbal symbols and interplay with visual and acoustic imagery

II. Usual adult waking state

A. Moderate concentration with rhythmic defocusing
B. Qualitative characteristics of consciousness:
   1. Dichotomoy of self and other
   2. Orientation in space and time
   3. Abstract thinking with ideational clarity
   4. Felt emotion, moderate and regulated
C. These characteristics achieved through maintenance of:
   1. Ego boundaries
   2. Repressive resistances
   3. Word-symbol connexions with object structures and instinct representations

III. Hypnoid states

A. Diminished attention cathexis (with longer intervals of defocusing)
B. Qualitative changes in consciousness:
   1. Deletion of self-consciousness
   2. Impairment of space and time orientation
3. Concrete thinking with ideational haziness
4. Flooding with emotion
C. These changes are related to:
   1. Failure of ego synthesis
   2. Diminution of repression
   3. Regression from verbal to visual and acoustic imagery

IV. States of depersonalization

A. Heightened attention cathexis (with lessened interval of defocusing)
B. Qualitative changes in consciousness:
   1. Heightened self-consciousness, especially of change in self
   2. Assertiveness of orientation in space and time
   3. Abstract thinking apparently intact but peculiarly over-ideational
   4. Excessive anxiety but devoid of pleasurable emotion

Table 10.1 (Continued)

C. These changes are related to:
1. Threat of failure of ego synthesis
2. Increased repression and strangulation of affect
3. Word-symbol connexions with object structures heavily invested, but impaired connexion with instinct representations. Regression to visual and acoustic imagery resisted

common occurrence of hypnoid states in various populations of the world. He notes that the Balinese culture is one in which trance is accepted in the way of life. Thus the Langiang dancers, groups of young girls who perform religious dances, are put into trance by chants and incense, and by concentrating on vibrating sticks from which puppets hang. When a girl grasps one of these sticks she is 'entered into by the Gods'. Dickes (1965)[54] wrote:

> The sexual connotation needs no elaboration. It should be understood that the dancing is entirely voluntary ... There is even dissociation among the various parts of the body which move in a disjointed fashion ... The ego state is one of deep regression, and there is complete loss of the normal state of awareness.

Hysterical convulsive seizures appeared in other Balinese dancing rituals. Belo (1960)[59] wrote:

> There is a universality about this strong seizure; it does not differ, apparently, from one culture to another, nor from one individual to another. It comes from too deep a level to be influenced by custom or by idiosyncratic trends of the personality ... The behaviour of the Langiang performer or the Kris dancer enacting his role is in this way comparable to that of the hypnotic subject in the somnambulistic state. In very deep trance, hypnotically induced or of the dramatic type we have been discussing, these cultural and individual patternings disappear; we are down to bedrock behaviour.

We have already noted that Janet (1907)[3] traced the connection between convulsive attacks and somnambulisms, and showed that the former were degraded forms of somnambulism in which appearance and behaviour are not classically somnambulistic. He connected such modification with a reduction of what we now call secondary process control, liable to occur when the ego apparatuses are constitutionally deficient, as in mental retardation. Convulsive phenomena are also apt to occur when a group sanctions the regression of its members and elevates collective experience over individuation. Such regression can be seen, for example, in the acceleration of excitement at meetings of the snake cult in the North Carolina mountains (see Fig. 14).

Fig. 14. Southern USA snake-handling cult. Preaching, guitar music, and singing induce 'shaking' reactions in some of the congregation and the preacher continues 'in unknown tongues'. Soon rattlesnakes are exhibited during escalating group excitement with the further development of trance states and clonic movements followed sometimes by catalepsy (*see 'They Shall Take Up Serpents'*, by Weston La Barre).

a: The exhibition of snakes. *b*, *c*: Accepting the snake. *d*, *e*: Developing the trance state. *[Continued overleaf.]*

f   g

h

(By courtesy of Dr Weston La Barre, Department of Sociology and Anthropology, Duke University, Durham, North Carolina, USA.)

Fig. 14. Southern USA snake-handling cult, *continued.*

f: Inducing cataclonus. *g*: Cataclonus. *h*: Catalepsy.

Collective Hypnoid States

As Dickes (1965)[54] rightly insists, the very ubiquity and generally ego-syntonic nature of hypnoid alterations of consciousness encourages us to underestimate their significance and to overlook their psychological implications. This is particularly the case in respect to the social and political influence of altered states of consciousness (ACSs).

Freud (1921)[60] pointed out the often striking similarities of the psychological relationship of the leader and the led and that of the hypnotist and his subject. The hypnotic relationship can be either of a maternal or paternal kind, or alternate between the two kinds. The former recalls the coaxing and soothing mother—a mother stroking and gently rocking her child as she sings a lullaby conveys a highly hypnotic effect. A paternal hypnotic relationship is a threatening one that requires obedience. According to Freud (1921):[60]

> The hypnotist awakens in the subject a portion of his archaic heritage which also made him compliant towards his parents and which he had experienced as an individual reanimation in his relations to his father; what is thus awakened is the idea of a permanent and dangerous personality, towards whom only a passive masochistic attitude is possible, to whom one's will had to be surrendered—while to be alone with him, to look him in the face, appears a hazardous enterprise.

In developing a maximally charismatic relationship with his followers, the leader is both intimidating and encouraging, rapidly alternating between these two ways of dealing with people. His charm is based on his inspiring both awe and love, and occasional glimpses of brutality only enhance his charm (see Abse and Jessner, 1962[61]).

Kohut (1976)[62] distinguishes between what he calls a charismatic leader and a Messianic one. He maintains that the former is an individual whose ego and grandiose self-images have merged, making him able to present himself as the object of the need others have to rediscover their own grandiose selves. The Messianic leader, on the other hand, induces a deeper regression. He is an individual whose ego and omnipotent 'self-object' have merged: the 'self-object' is not yet differentiated from the 'not self' but includes an unconscious re-use of the object, i.e. the mother or parts of the mother, as components of the self. Such an individual is then able to present himself to others as an object representing their own rediscovered omnipotent self-objects. Kohut (1976)[62] thus also stresses the importance of understanding the charismatic leader in terms of his relationship with others, as developed from his externalization of inner events that engendered grandiosity and omnipotent fantasies. Such externalization consists of a complex defensive and adaptive redeployment of his own unconscious infantile identifications, the whole process being of hysteriform nature. It is doubtful whether the distinction Kohut makes between the charismatic and the Messianic character can be maintained in the flesh, except in respect to emphasis. There are paranoid fluctuations in the depth of regression in the ongoing interactions of leader and led. In any case, the schematic distinction between the two types of leader seems artificial inasmuch as the charismatic person may often enact the role of the Messiah, and may periodically represent the potential incarnation of the glorified giving mother. Moreover, he may also symbolize the son or daughter who becomes in fact what the follower aspired in fantasy to be (Abse and Jessner, 1962[61]). Indeed, some of the dramatic changes initiated by the leader in relating to the led contribute powerfully to the fascination embedded in charisma (Abse and Ulman, 1977[63]; Ulman and Abse, 1983[64]). Glen Davis (1978)[65] writes:

... three basic approaches exist in the field of group political psychology: (1) the leader seen as the passive recipient of mass projections, who simply acts out these projections; (2) the Abse–Ulman formulation of interaction between the leader and the led; (3) the 'Great Man' theory, which minimizes the impact of the group, and maximizes the efficacy of the individual situation in a position of power ...

The interaction of the charismatic leader and his followers may be characterized from time to time by a hypnoid state shared by the leader and the led with reciprocal effect.

Table 10.1 shows that states of creativity and fascination are related to—and may, indeed, become—hypnoid states; they may also lead to depersonalization. Great group excitement can affect both the group and its charismatic leader. When the leader's consciousness, stimulated by the enthusiastic response of his audience, rises to ever more creative heights, the focus of his attention narrows and becomes more and more concentrated; his self-consciousness is swept away; and his emotions, although still under control, become increasingly fervid. He may, particularly if he is of a hysteriform borderline psychotic nature, become as disorganized intellectually as his audience and share its hypnoid state. Such hysterical frenzy may become clearly evident to the dispassionate observer at a mass meeting. The yield of such a phase of heightened creativity is not necessarily anything of real use in any substantive way, nor is it necessarily highly poetic; its quality will depend on the cognitive structure of the leader's ego and ego ideal, and the breadth of his empathy (Abse and Ulman, 1977[62]).

Ainslie Meares (1961)[66] emphasized the atavistic aspects of hypnosis and of hypnoid states, speaking of suggestion as being a very primitive function that has been superseded, somewhat unevenly, by the capacity for logical thought, a more recent evolutionary acquisition. He believes that in the period before it was acquired, 'prehuman man' accepted ideas entirely by the process of suggestion, and without critical evaluation, and he sees as the basic factor in hypnosis regression to this primitive mode of mental functioning. He writes (1961):[66]

On top of this basic regression is an overlay of psychological mechanisms. The regressive state favours hysteric mechanisms, such as hysteric defences, hysteric communication and dissociation. Identification and introjection are also conspicuous.

He makes interesting observations on the nature of yoga based on first hand experiences in India, Nepal, Kashmir and Burma, observations that accord with my own. From talking with yogis he came to see that their meditation differs from that often practised in the West.

It is neither prayer, nor concentration nor contemplation ... meditation in yoga practice is regarded as the experience of that part of all-pervading God that inhabits the individual.

He also points out that the affect in yoga is one of profound serenity. This has its counterpart in the developed and established hypnotic state in which patients so frequently comment on the calm they achieve; it contrasts with other hypnoid states in which, as noted, there is a suffusion and plethora of affects. Meares adds that

The hypnotized patient, left by himself and in the absence of any suggestions, drifts into this state of profound calm, which has obvious regressive or even fetal characteristics.

REFERENCES

1. Bramwell, J. M. (1903). *Hypnotism: Its History, Practice and Theory*, 3rd ed. London: Rider (1921).
2. Moebius, P. J. (1894). Über Astasie–Abasie. In: *Neurologische Beiträge*, Vol. 1. Leipzig: Meiner, Barth.
3. Janet, P. (1907). *The Major Symptoms of Hysteria*. New York: Macmillan.
4. Breuer, J. and Freud, S. (1893). On the psychical mechanism of hysterical phenomena: preliminary communication. In: *The Standard Edition*, Vol. II. London: Hogarth Press (1953).
5. Breuer, J. and Freud, S. (1895). *Studies on Hysteria*. In: *The Standard Edition*, Vol. II. London: Hogarth Press (1953).
6. Jones, E. (1953). *Sigmund Freud: Life and Work*, Vol. 1. London: Hogarth Press (1953).
7. Ludwig, A. M. (1967). The trance. *Comprehensive Psychiatry*, **8** (1), 7–15.
8. Jennings, H. S. (1906). *Behavior of the Lower Organisms*. New York: Macmillan.
9. Schilder, P. F. (1924). *Medical Psychology*. New York: Int. Univ. Press (1953).
10. Wittels, F. (1930). The hysterical character. *Med. Rev. New York*, **36**, 186.
11. Spiegel, R. (1959). Specific problems of communication in psychotic conditions. In: *American Handbook of Psychiatry* (ed. Arieti, S.). New York: Basic Books.
12. Farber, L. H. (1966). *The Ways of the Will*, pp. 99–117. New York: Basic Books.
13. Bonime, W. (1972). Depersonalisation as a manifestation of evolving health. *Psychiat. Spectator*, **8** (9), 9–16.
14. Federn, P. (1952). *Ego Psychology and the Psychoses*. New York: Basic Books.
15. Krohn, A. (1978). *Hysteria: The Elusive Neurosis*. New York: Int. Univ. Press.
16. Abse, D. W. (1959). Hysteria. In: *American Handbook of Psychiatry*, Vol. 1, pp. 272–92. New York: Basic Books.
17. Shapiro, D. (1965). *Neurotic Styles*. New York: Basic Books.
18. Gardner, R., Holtzman, P. S., Klein, G. S. et al. (1959). Cognitive controls: a study of individual consistencies in cognitive behaviour. *Psychol. Issues*, **1**, 1–186.
19. Goldstein, K. (1946). Naming and pseudonaming from experiences in psychopathology. *Word*, **2**, 1.
20. Reich, W. (1933). *Character Analysis*. New York: Farrar, Straus and Giroux (1972).
21. Marmor, J. (1953). Orality in the hysterical personality. *J. Am. Psychoanal. Assoc.*, **1** (4), 656–71.
22. Greenson, R. (1956). Panel Discussion, Meeting of American Psychoanalytic Association: The borderline case. *J. Am. Psychoanal. Assoc.*, **3**, 285.
23. Zetzel, E. R. (1956). Panel Discussion, Meeting of American Psychoanalytic Association: The borderline case. *J. Am. Psychoanal. Assoc.*, **3**, 285.

24. Beard, G. M. (1891). *Sexual Neurasthenia*. New York: Trent.
25. Kernberg, O. F. (1967). Borderline personality organisation. *J. Am. Psychoanal. Assoc.*, **15**, 641–85.
26. Reichard, S. (1956). A re-examination of studies in hysteria. *Psychoanal. Quart.*, **25**, 155–77.
27. Noble, D. (1951). Hysterical manifestations in schizophrenic illness. *Psychiat.*, **14**, 153–60.
28. Goshen, C. E. (1952). The original case material of psychoanalysis. *Am. J. Psychiat.*, **108**, 829–34.
29. Brill, N. Q. (1954). Discussion of: Jackson, D. Office treatment of ambulatory schizophrenics. *Calif. Med.*, **81**, 263–7.
30. Easser, B. R. and Lesser, S. R. (1965). Hysterical personality: a re-evaluation. *Psychoanal. Quart.*, **34**, 390–405.
31. Fenichel, O. (1945). *The Psychoanalytic Theory of Neurosis*. New York: Norton.
32. Stengel, E. (1945). A study on some clinical aspects of the relationship between obsessional neurosis and psychotic reaction types. *J. Ment. Sci.*, **91**, 166.
33. Freud, S. (1926). Inhibitions, Symptoms and Anxiety. In: *The Standard Edition*, Vol. XX. London: Hogarth Press (1955).
34. Schilder, P. (1920). On the development of thoughts. In: *Organisation and Pathology of Thought* (ed. Rapaport, D.). New York: Columbia Univ. Press (1951).
35. Freud, S. (1900). *The Interpretation of Dreams*. In: *The Standard Edition*, Vols. IV and V. London: Hogarth Press (1953).
36. Prince, M. (1905). *The Dissociation of a Personality*. New York: Longmans, Green.
37. Erickson, M. H. and Kubie, L. S. (1939). The permanent relief of an obsessional phobia by means of communication with an unsuspected dual personality. *Psychoanal. Quart.*, **8**, 471.
38. Erickson, M. H. and Kubie, L. S. (1940). The translation of the cryptic automatic writing of one hypnotic subject by another in a trance-like dissociated state. *Psychoanal. Quart.*, **9**, 51.
39. Oberndorf, C. P. (1941). Co-conscious mentation. *Psychoanal. Quart.*, **10**, 44.
40. Gill, M. M. and Brenman, M. (1961). *Hypnosis and Related States: Psychoanalytic Studies in Regression*. New York: Int. Univ. Press.
41. Shor, R. E. (1959). Hypnosis and the concept of the generalised reality-orientation. In: *Altered States of Consciousness* (ed. Tart, C. T.), Chap. 15. New York and London: Wiley (1969).
42. Shor, R. E. (1962). Three dimensions of hypnotic depth. *Int. J. Clin. Exp. Hypnosis*, **10**, 23–38.
43. Eastman, M. (1938). Art and the life of action. In: *The Enjoyment of Poetry with Anthology*. New York: Scribner (1951).
44. Rickman, J. (1940). On the nature of ugliness and the creative impulse. In: Rickman, J. *Selected Contributions to Psycho-analysis* (compiled by Scott, W. C. M.), London: Hogarth Press (1957).
45. Fairbairn, W. R. D. (1938). The ultimate basis of aesthetic experience. *Br. J. Psychol.*, **29**, 167.
46. Kris, E. (1952). *Psychoanalytic Explorations in Art*. New York: Int. Univ. Press.
47. Plaut, A. (1959). Aspects of consciousness. *Br. J. Med. Psychol.*, **32**, 239.
48. Braid, J. (1843). *Neurypnology, or the Rationale of Nervous Sleep Considered in Relation with Animal Magnetism*. London: Churchill.
49. Bernfeld, S. (1928). Ueber Faszination. *Imago*, **14**, 76.
50. Abse, D. W. (1961). Hysteria, hypnosis and the hypnoid state. In: *Proc. Third World Congress of Psychiatry*, Vol. 2, p. 856. Toronto and Montreal: Univ. Toronto Press and McGill Univ. Press.

51. Freud, S. (1915). Observations on Transference-love (Further Recommendations on the Technique of Psycho-analysis, III). In: *The Standard Edition*, Vol. XII. London: Hogarth Press (1953).
52. Allen, D. W. and Houston, M. (1959). The management of hysteroid acting-out patients in a training clinic. *Psychiat.*, **22** (1), 41–9.
53. Abse, D. W. (1958). The accident-prone individual. (Presented at the Governors' Conference on Occupational Health, N.C. Memorial Hospital, Chapel Hill.) *N.C. Med. J.*, **19** (5), 185–7.
54. Dickes, R. (1965). The defensive function of an altered state of consciousness: a hypnoid state. *J. Am. Psychoanal. Assoc.*, **13** (2), 356–402.
55. Dickes, R. and Papernik, D. S. (1977). Defensive alterations of consciousness: hypnoid states, sleep and the dream. *J. Am. Psychoanal. Assoc.*, **25** (3).
56. Kubie, L. S. (1943). The use of induced hypnagogic reveries in the recovery of repressed amnesic data. *Bull. Menninger Clin.*, **7**, 172–82.
57. Isakower, O. (1938). A contribution to the patho-psychology of phenomena associated with falling asleep. *Int. J. Psychoanal.*, **19**, 331–45.
58. Abse, D. W. (1977). The dream screen, phenomenon and noumenon. *Psychoanal. Quart.*, **XLVI**, 256–86.
59. Belo, J. (1960). *Trance in Bali*. New York: Columbia Univ. Press.
60. Freud, S. (1921). Group Psychology and the Analysis of the Ego. In: *The Standard Edition*, Vol. XVIII, London: Hogarth Press (1955).
61. Abse, D. W. and Jessner, L. (1962). The psychodynamic aspects of leadership. In: *Excellence and Leadership in a Democracy* (ed. Graubard, S. R. and Holton, G.). New York: Columbia Univ. Press.
62. Kohut, H. (1976). Creativeness, charisma, group psychology: reflections on the self-analysis of Freud. In: *Psychological Issues*, Vol. 9, Nos. 2/3 (Monographs 34/35) (ed. Gedo, J. E. and Pollock, G. H.). New York: Int. Univ. Press.
63. Abse, D. W. and Ulman, R. B. (1977). Charismatic political leadership and collective regression. In: *Psychopathology and Political Leadership* (ed. Robins, R. S.), Tulane Studies in Political Science, Vol. 16. New Orleans: Tulane Univ. Press.
64. Ulman, R. B. and Abse, D. W. (1983). The group psychology of mass madness: Jonestown. *Political Psychol.*, **4** (4), 637–61.
65. Davis, G. (1978). Review of: *Psychopathology and Political Leadership* (ed. Robins, R. S.). *J. Psychohistory*, **6** (1), 145–7.
66. Meares, A. (1961). The atavistic theory of hypnosis in relation to yoga and the pseudo-trance states. In: *Proc. Third World Congress of Psychiatry*, Vol. 1. Toronto and Montreal: Univ. of Toronto Press and McGill Univ. Press.
67. Freud, S. (1905). Fragment of an Analysis of a Case of Hysteria. In: *The Standard Edition*, Vol. VII. London: Hogarth Press (1955).

CHAPTER 11

Multiple Personality Disorder

In 1966, it was reported in the first edition of *Hysteria and Related Mental Disorders* that there were about two hundred accounts of cases of alternating and multiple personality disorder in the literature of psychiatry and psychology. Since this time, the number of cases reported in some detail has more than doubled, and many more psychotherapists have reported the existence of such cases in their practices. In a lecture at the National Institute of Mental Health, Bethesda, Maryland, USA, Putnam (1984)[1] offered the view that many patients go to different mental health services and are misdiagnosed, and thus inadequately treated. These patients are often secretive and most are unaware of their alternate personalities. Putnam[1] noted that when there is a time loss or a history of having been abused as a child, clinicians should consider multiple personality disorder (MPD) as a diagnosis, especially for those patients who have received a plethora of diagnoses or who have responded little or not at all to neuroleptic or antidepressant medications or to ECT.

In some of the cases reported in detail, the additional personality or personalities appeared only in the course of psychotherapy or hypnosis (Leavitt 1947[2]), but in others, more than one personality was manifested to other people by the individual in the course of daily life (Franz, 1933[3]).

As noted in Chapter 7, one of the main character traits of the hysterical personality, and more pronouncedly so of the hysteriform borderline personality, is the deployment of histrionic behaviour in a desperate attempt to assume a semblance of identity. Kuiper (1967)[4] uses the word 'ungenuiness' to describe the peculiar quality which infiltrates the interpersonal relationships of these patients, and he adds: 'I want to stress that I do not use "ungenuiness" here in the sense of conscious deception. I mean ungenuiness of feelings—which is phenomenologically quite different from deception and simulation.' The patients are not whole-hearted in their significant interactions with others, and some of them turn out to be afflicted with multiple personality disorder.

As outlined in Chapter 1, multiple personality occupies a nodal position in the history of the emergence of modern dynamic psychiatry from the exorcism embedded in the idiom of demonology and from mesmerism. A searching study of multiple personality was inaugurated in France by the publication in 1840 of the story of 'Estelle' by Antoine Despine (Pére).[5] Following this, the splitting of one personality into two was reported several times in nineteenth century medical literature. Among these cases was that of Félida X reported by Étienne Eugene Azam (1887),[6] whose account was published with an introduction by Charcot. Félida was a troubled young woman who had exhibited hysterical symptoms since puberty. One day she fainted, went into a brief lethargy and then became happy and assertive, grateful for having lost her feeling of sadness, which she recalled. After a few hours she had a similar episode which resulted in the return of her subdued personality. These switches recurred, sometimes days apart. Once, while in her second personality, she gave herself to her lover and became pregnant. When her drab personality returned, she was bewildered and unable to grasp what was happening as her pregnancy advanced and became obvious. But soon she appeared once more in her happy personality, and apologized to Azam for having caused him embarrassment in her ignorant confusion.

Félida X illustrates well how switching follows the clouding of consciousness, and also demonstrates that it is possible for one personality to be amnesic of the other although the second is aware of the experiences of the first. Personality A knew nothing about personality B, but B knew about herself and A also. This is a common pattern; it is usual for A to be a somewhat constricted personality and B to be considerably more carefree. Both Janet (1889)[7] and Ellenberger (1970)[8] identified the A of Felida as the sicker part of her personality, and thought of B as providing a short-lived opportunity for A to be healthier. *Simultaneous* partial personalities are more rare than the *successive* type illustrated by Félida. The simultaneous type is exemplified by St Augustine, who became aware from time to time of the vivid reappearance of the old pagan self he had abandoned. Similarly, in telling of his own experiences with mescaline, Giovanni Enrico Morselli (1944–5)[9] reports that he felt himself merging with a wild beast—like the lycanthrope of legend metamorphosed into a wolf—whose colour and scent he could momentarily perceive. The drug effect he noted suggests the fictive successive partial personalities of Jekyll and Hyde.

The medical literature offers many classifications of multiple personality. The following seems to cover better than most the protean forms seen in clinical practice:

1. Simultaneous partial personalities rarely well defined.
2. Those which may be (*a*) mutually cognizant, (*b*) mutually amnesic, or (*c*) one-way amnesic (like Félida X).
3. Clustered multiple partial personalities.

In regard to multiple clusters it should be noted that mesmerists eventually discovered that when people with dual personalities were magnetized, i.e., hypnotized, a third personality sometimes appeared. Janet (1889)[7] found multiple personalities emerging in his early experimental work with a hysterical patient known successively as Lucie, Leona and Rose. He emphasized the importance of naming in defining and developing one of these presences. 'Once baptized,' he wrote (1889),[7] 'the unconscious personality is more clear and definite, it shows its psychological traits more clearly.' However, personality clusters sometimes spontaneously develop sharp boundaries, although it has not been established thus far that in each such case reported the investigator was entirely uninvolved in the process. It is certain that hypnotic suggestion, whether conscious or unwitting, can prompt the multiplication and development of these revealing and revealed sub-personalities. In the course of treatment there is sometimes a proliferation of additional personalities in a patient whose psychic organization is susceptible to such cleavage. The case published as that of *Sybil* (Schreiber, 1973[10]) is one of a woman possessed by 16 different personalities, some of which seem to have come about from iatrogenic suggestion in the course of therapeutic interaction that dealt with the decomposition products. Gradually, however, there was a promotion of integration and more effective repression necessary for sound individuation. One must expect patients subject to the display of more than one personality to be exaggeratedly dramatic in some guises, spontaneously as well as in therapeutic circumstances.

Case Illustrations

Case 1. An absence of 'personal synthesis' is evident in this dialogue between myself (*M*) and a young woman (*P*) who became a patient after taking a bottle of chloral hydrate. (It was clear later that she was 'Olympia' when she swallowed the overdose.)
M: I gather Ronnie got his car stuck in the mud, became angry, and told you to leave; and you've been upset since then.
P: Olympia took my clothes out of the drawer and threw them on the floor and turned the bed upside down.
M: Olympia?
P: She is another person. She wants to die because Daddy beat her up so much and raped her when she was ten years old.
M: But Olympia is you, or part of you?
P: He used to beat me up all the time. One time he took a belt and put it around my neck and swung me around the room and let go bam! I was on the floor. One time I tried to stab him, and I knocked him down and broke his rib. He was a terrible man. He was an alcoholic. All of this is his fault. He made me like this and I hate being like this. I'm getting better, though ... I'm not getting as upset as I did. Olympia has come out only twice since February. They say she came out screaming in the shower. I don't remember that. Then another night she came out and turned over all the furniture. Nothing was standing except the TV set. She had set my clothes on fire and I had them on. That's what they told me. But I didn't do it. Olympia did. I didn't because I don't want to die. Olympia wants to die. I like living. I have Holly around, too. She's funny.
M: Holly?
P: Yeah. She's funny. She came out one night and performed for everybody, and it was fun. I knew what she was doing 'cause she let me see it, you know. She acted like a fool, running around, and laughed and sang songs.
M: Like a fool—you mean like a clown?
P: Yeah. She's been pretty smart.
M: I see. Why does she call herself Holly?
P: I don't know. I remember being conceived.
M: Conceived?
P: Yeah.
M: How do you mean?
P: Before I was a baby in Mama's stomach. Oh, I was waiting on the waiting line where little babies were.
M: Yes?
P: ... And I knew what my life was going to be through the whole time I lived and I didn't want to go into this life.
M: You didn't want to come in?
P: Uh uh. I wanted to go in for another family, but they wouldn't let me, whoever

created us. I don't know if there's a God or not. I think we're created by other beings.
M: I see. And you mean these other beings had you in the line-up for this particular family?
P: Yeah. I didn't like it.
M: And you wanted to get into another family. Where was your home?
P: Chicago.
M: All these terrible things happened there?
P: Yes. And he died there, after I left.
M: How old are you?
P: Twenty-two. I've been sick for ten years, but I was well for five of them.
M: How is that?
P: I felt well for five years when I was worshipping Satan and taking drugs, sixteen to twenty-one. I could have been the queen of the cult.
M: The queen of the cult?
P: He promised he'd get me into a good life. I worshipped him for two years and I could have been the queen of the cult. They liked me because I see auras and things like that. I hate to be punished for things. When I die I'll probably go to hell. God doesn't like me.
M: Is that why you turned to Satan?
P: Yes, He always causes bad luck for me.
M: Who caused bad luck?
P: God. I invited Him to my house one day, and He was perhaps too stuck up to come. He should have come. I got the right to know what He looks like. He thinks He can ruin me, and I don't even know Him. Sometimes I think He's a figment of people's imagination. They just got to have something to lean on. So they lean on ...
M: Don't you think that applies to Satan, that he could be a figment of people's imagination?
P: He was real. I saw him really, in another person's body.
M: Whose body?
P: Greg's.

   Case 2. A 14-year-old white girl named Patricia claimed at school that she was not Patricia. When asked who she was, she repeatedly asserted that she was 'Constance Hope Will'. Baffled, her teachers took her to the principal's office. Her mother was called, and she was soon admitted to the hospital, where she was amnesic about the episode on the following day, and unconcerned about it. She acknowledged having seen the story of *Sybil*, among others with a like theme, on the television. Her physical examination, with skull films, showed nothing pathological. When she was interviewed in the company of her parents and younger brother it became clear that the family was close, and that mother and daughter competed for the father's attention. The family was in the throes of deciding whether or not to return to California, where Patricia had spent her latency years. Patricia was clearly anxious about reaching the age of 15, when she would be expected to date; her longing to go back to California included a wish to return to the security she had enjoyed at the time her life was not yet complicated by having to relate to boys as a teenager. The name of her second personality indicated this, along with her determination to cope. She had complained at school of having found threatening notes in her locker, but the school authorities felt that she had written them herself. They noted that when she was 'Constance' she had spoken in a falsetto voice unlike her own. The 'Constance Hope Will' personality, dissociated and fragmentary, reflected her struggle with a faltering approach to growing up. In psychotherapy it became possible for her to integrate this attitude of the second personality in her efforts to adapt to the current demands of her situation. It was necessary to interpret this, and to give attention also to her regressive symptoms, including the use of a falsetto voice. The reduction of her anxiety concerning the heightened heterosexual libido of puberty was an important component of the subsequent psychotherapy.*

*This patient was carefully evaluated psychiatrically by Dr William Rheuban at the University of Virginia Hospital before she came to my notice.

Case 3. Melanie, 23 years old, black and married, had exhibited dramatic personality changes for ten months before she was referred to the hospital for treatment by Dr Susan Lazar. Her husband described abrupt changes in her associated with the dominance of 'others' who named themselves Marie, Carrie, Karen, Beth, Anna, Susan, Jane, Sharon and Bobbie. He perceived each one as different from the others, with a personality quite unlike his wife's. Melanie recalled nothing of this, but acknowledged having intervals of 'missing time' after a headache. Her husband had told her about 'the others' and about her differing modes of behaviour. She said she had heard threatening voices a few months before experiencing the 'missing times', and that when so spoken to she had sometimes seen 'a frightening red devil'.

She was the second child of nine born to a father who drank heavily and then became violent. At the age of two weeks she had had severe eczema, which led to her being taken off the breast at six weeks, and being confined in a hospital at the age of four years. During her bouts with this skin disease her parents had taken turns staying with her at night, stroking her to keep her from scratching. Since the family often moved, Melanie had few friends until she went to high school, but turned to her elder sister. The two girls believed that the elder sister was her godfather's illegitimate child. Melanie also had an imaginary friend she called Marie to play with when she was frightened by her parents' quarrels or deserted by her sister. The sister sometimes used the name 'Marie' in addressing Melanie as her 'playmate'.

Melanie remembered her father as abusive and partial to her elder sister. Her mother claimed that the situation owed much to Melanie's being mischievous and provoking after she got over the eczema and was no longer the object of her parents' special concern. The mother said she had never challenged Melanie's often expressed perception of her father as cold and unfeeling, but that she simply shared her resignation about what seemed unlikely to change. Melanie recalled sessions of 'sex education' her father had given the two sisters during Melanie's early adolescence. She had been alarmed but also excited by his warnings about sex. She saw intercourse between her parents when she was 12, and dreamed anxiously about it for some time. She claimed to have been raped by a gang of boys in an alley when she was 14, and said this event confirmed her contempt and hatred of men.

The family lived in Europe by the time she was 15, and it was there that she met her first boyfriend. Roy endeared himself to her by not rejecting her for her abusive and provocative behaviour. When she learned that she was pregnant with Roy's child she gave up a lesbian affair in which she had been engaged. She then had her first episode of amnesia, accompanied by changes in behaviour. She was told that she had skipped classes and fought in the schoolyard, although she could not remember doing so. She was jealous when Roy called her 'Marie' as she had asked him to do while in the 'Marie' personality, which had by then emerged. She was referred to a psychiatrist, who told her she was schizophrenic. She saw him only a few times.

Melanie's father was angry when he learned of her pregnancy, and forbade her to see Roy again. The family returned to the States, where Melanie bore her child, refusing to let her parents adopt it but permitting them to care for it. She continued corresponding with Roy, who had also returned to the States, but she married Jim after a courtship of four months. Her mother felt that this marriage reflected Melanie's resentment of Roy's having begun to date someone else. Although she continued to long for Roy, whom she still saw, a third man, Lew, appealed to her as being more caring, and she lived with him. They were happy at first, spending time with friends and overindulging in alcohol and drugs, particularly marijuana. Melanie was angry to discover that she was pregnant, and was able later to recall hating her unborn child for interrupting her hedonistic life. The infant, Danny, had an omphalocele at birth, spent months in intensive care, and underwent a number of surgical procedures. Melanie remembered vividly the appalling appearance of this child born two years before she entered the hospital for therapy. He was wasted, and his skin was so cracked and bleeding that he seemed to be rotting away.

She felt great guilt, and blamed his state on her use of drugs. Then she went with Lew and her parents to a primitive Baptist church where, moved by the preacher's words on the sinfulness of worldly pleasures, she felt possessed by the Holy Spirit, and publicly 'converted' to Christianity along with Lew. Danny improved, and she felt that this was due to her conversion and its attendant changes in her life.

Pregnant again, she was advised to have a tubal ligation and did have one after her infant, Denise, was born. But she felt that she had thereby lost her womanhood, and blamed Lew for not interceding. She felt that he had withdrawn from her, and she began trying to get his attention and reassurance. His best efforts to reassure her were insufficient, however, and it was then that her symptoms appeared. The first 'extra' personality was an angry 'Marie'. At first the 'extra' personalities would appear when Melanie awakened from sleep. Thinking she was possessed, Lew tried secretly to cure her by pressing a Bible to her body, but he finally told a preacher about the situation and was advised to have Melanie undergo a neurological examination. Her examination included an EEG and a CAT scan, but all results were negative. Lew did not insist that she keep her appointments with a psychiatrist; he had become fascinated with Melanie's different personalities, and even bribed some of them to do chores, enjoying his manipulation of them. But danger was indicated. 'Carrie' told Lew that one of the 'others' had taken his hunting knife and had hidden it to use against him, and he did find it in their bedroom. Then he came upon Melanie talking with 'Carrie', who was trying to persuade her not to hurt Lew. Lew also found sleeping pills hidden in a bathroom light fixture. He then insisted that Melanie seek psychiatric help.

It is interesting to note how effective personality-switching is in seizing the attention of witnesses. Although very few people who achieve real leadership exhibit multiple personalities to the pathological and obvious degree under discussion here, the hysterical charismatic person who becomes a leader often adds to the glitter of his persona by alterations of style not too remote from the multiple-personality syndrome (Abse and Ulman, 1977[11]). Such switches among MPD patients obviously serve the function of attracting the attention of others important to the patient, and they are on a smaller scale and involve fewer people than when similar phenomena appear in an unstable religious or political leader.

In his *Principles of Psychology* William James (1890)[12] gave an account of a famous case of double personality.

The Reverend Ansel Bourne disappeared from a Rhode Island town two months before a man calling himself A. J. Brown woke up in a fright asking where he was. He was in Pennsylvania, where he had rented a confectionary shop six weeks earlier. The confectioner then declared that his name was Bourne, that he was a clergyman, and that he knew nothing about the shop or Brown. His identity as Bourne was confirmed by relatives, but he was never able to explain this uncanny episode in his life.

T. W. Mitchell (1922)[13] began to perceive the temporal relation of certain multiple personalities to fugue states. He pointed out that

in the first fortnight of his absence from Rhode Island, Ansel Bourne's conduct conformed to that of ordinary fugue. *He forgot his personal identity* and wandered from city to city. For the next six weeks he led a quiet, respectable life as a small shop keeper, renaming himself and duly keeping accurate accounts and adhering to sensible routines. In this second state he had no recollection of his former life, and when he came to himself he had no recollection of his life during the second state (mutual amnesia).

Mitchell noted that:

The lost memories were, however, recovered during hypnosis, and the revelation so obtained of this frame of mind at the beginning of his fugue probably indicates the nature of the ideas that determined it. He said he wanted to get away somewhere—he didn't know where—and have a rest. When he opened his little shop, the fugue proper came to an end. The idea which determined his flight was about to be realized, and while it was working itself out, he lived the life of a secondary personality which was conditioned by the breach in the continuity of his memory, rather than by any great change in his character or conduct.

The fugue proper ended, as Mitchell wrote, and his behaviour indicated that as he settled into being a confectioner the definitive fugue state of consciousness tapered off.

Fugues are typically precipitated by a need to escape from some intolerable pressure. When James (1890)[12] hypnotized Ansel Bourne some three years after his escapade, the 'Brown' memory came back with surprising readiness and with such authority that while he was hypnotized it was impossible to make him remember anything about his normal life. He had heard of Ansel Bourne, but 'didn't know as he had even met the man'. When confronted with Mrs Bourne, he said that he had 'never seen the woman before!' In my own clinical practice the intolerable situations from which men had run away into fugue—one on a motorbike to the West Coast—were concerned with their respective wives. Each case was one in which frustrating marital tension had built up, and it became clear in psychotherapy that the husband was afraid of the activation of his extreme hostility in the presence of his wife.

Bourne's case was one of a fairly orderly flight to an orderly existence in his usual well-ordered way of life.

As expounded in Chapter 10, fugues are one of many kinds of *hypnoid states*. They are characterized by distinctive alterations of consciousness and share with some other hypnoid states vague ideation in a very restricted associational context, and a suffusion of consciousness with elated affect. *Table* 10.1 in Chapter 10, p. 228 is a diagrammatic representation of the relationships of various designated psychic states. It will be seen that in many hypnoid states there is a qualitative change in consciousness—the disappearance of self-consciousness; impairment of space and time orientation (in different ways in different hypnoid states); concrete thinking with ideational haziness and suffusion of emotion. In fugue, there is a purpose in what seems to be aimless wandering. The hazy thought processes are quite dissociated from the residual personality but are geared to the special purpose of a fragment of the personality that acts out, giving attention to relevant detail only. The divorced residual 'normal' personalities are paradoxically in the position in which Emily Dickinson saw the solitary cocoons of the mentally ill—

Safe in their alabaster chambers untouched by mourning
And untouched by noon.

The dissociated personality in fugue is acting out a wish-fantasy, and consciousness is suffused with feelings of well-being which replace the consciousness of frustration and the feelings of ill-being that precede the fugue. This contrasts with the somnambulistic hypnoid states in which—besides other differences—the painful past experience of stress is evoked in vivid imagery in an effort to alter and master it.

As already noted (Chapter 7), there is usually a special personality background that includes an habitual special cognitive style, when hypnoid alterations of consciousness occur. They are particularly apt to occur to persons whose usual mode of waking cognition is generally global, relatively diffuse, and impressionistic—the hysterical style of mentation described by David Shapiro (1965).[14] When such people are involved in marital conflict they can often escape into diminished awareness and the elimination of self-observation. For some, this opens the way for a previously unacknowledged fragment of the self to emerge into consciousness. Breuer (1895)[15] pointed out the importance of the hypnoid states from which most major and complex hysterias arise, and he acknowledged that Moebius 'had already said exactly the same thing in 1890.' Moebius (1894)[16] wrote:

> The necessary condition for the pathogenic operation of ideas is, on the one hand, an innate—that is, hysterical—disposition, and, on the other, a special frame of mind. It must resemble a state of hypnosis; it must correspond to some kind of vacancy of consciousness in which an emerging idea meets with no resistance from any other—in which, so to speak, the field is clear for the first comer. We know that a state of this kind can be brought about not only by hypnotism but by emotional shock (fright, anger, etc.) and by exhausting factors (sleeplessness, hunger, and so on).

The hypnoid state is certainly a stepping stone for the emergence into consciousness of a partial personality system. This sequence of events serves to illuminate Mitchell's statement about Ansel Bourne.

These considerations may also be applied to the other excerpts from cases cited. Thus Félida X was seen to lose consciousness in a fainting attack, then to be mentally only sluggishly responsive for a few minutes afterwards before showing a decisive character change. This startling metamorphosis contrasts with that of Ansel Bourne, who changed his occupational and nominal identity but retained his essentially modest and quiet character. In this case the safeguarding of the consolidated compulsive core features of his personality may indeed have been one of the deeper and more essential aspects of the purpose of the fugue, the amnesia and the second personality.

There always seems to be a suspension of the reflective self-representations in a hypnoid state before the vacuum is filled by the switch to a 'sub-personality' that is either very different or a restricted core. Roy Schafer (1968)[17] noted that

> young children and those adults whose ego development has been restricted may be said to have, at best, weak and inconsistently maintained reflective self-representations.

The reflective self-representation, in Schafer's use of the term, is the mental presentation of oneself as the thinker of the thought, the feeler of the feeling, and the impulse to action. He writes:

> In order for what is thought to be taken uncritically as an actuality, the reflective self

representations must be suspended. Their suspensions may be brief or long-lasting: they may be so weakly maintained that they make no significant or lasting difference; or they may be undeveloped. The thinker vanishes but the thought remains—now as an event, a thing, a concrete external reality, for there is no thinker to know it for what it is. Since it is the hallmark of primary-process ideation to take what is thought as reality, it follows that it is of the essence of primary-process ideation not to state or imply reflective self representations. This proposition conforms to psychoanalytic understanding of infantile subjective experience as lacking in clear self representations of any sort and as dominated by inadequate or absent differentiation between what is thought and what is real.

Hysterical fugue is one of a number of altered states of consciousness (the Ganser syndrome, pseudo-dementia, hysterical peurilism, etc.) which comprise a disturbance of psychotic degree in the sense of reality. The psychotic excursion is usually temporary and non-progressive. Sometimes, however, there is a dangerous velocity of deepening withdrawal and schizophrenia is ushered in with symptoms of hypochondriasis, exaltation and a peculiar over-ideation that under unfavourable conditions becomes progressively disconnected. Sometimes the hypnoid alteration of consciousness is followed by a massive hysterical conversion reaction, with clearing of the clouded consciousness, avoidance of schizophrenic fragmentation and a type of (partial) reality-adjustment. There are other paths that skirt schizophrenic disorganization, and one of these is that of multiple personality formation. These paths may lead away from psychosis, as they all do at first, and eventually lead to the restitution of a sense of reality and adequate psychic commerce with the external world, but some eventually prove merely detours winding around schizophrenia and sooner or later offering nothing but molecular disintegration.

The schizophrenic patient comes to 'molecular dissociation' in contrast to the molar or block dissociation found in hysteria and hysteriform disease. In molar dissociation large organized units of experience—memories and fantasies—are separated from other such units but remain basically intact in themselves, whereas schizophrenic dissociation occurs on the level of both perception and logic. Thus, words are separated from their references and affects are often disconnected from the strivings with which they had originally been associated, and this gives rise to incongruity of affect and ideation that conveys so weird an impression to the unsophisticated observer. In some cases the molar dissociation in hysteriform disease, including notably that found in multiple personality, protects the patient from further molecular disintegration; but in others it is a holding operation that becomes tragically merely a stage in the subsequent descent to florid schizophrenic disorder, as will later be illustrated here.

This case, which has been well studied and followed up, was treated at the University of Virginia Hospital under the supervision of Dr Ian Stevenson, and reported by Congdon, Hain and Stevenson[18] in 1961:

Case 4. The patient was a 23-year-old housewife whose primary personality we shall know as 'Betty', and who had suffered convulsive attacks following proceedings for divorce. In the hospital the patient recovered from the convulsive attacks and from depression and was then discharged and treated as an outpatient. During subsequent psychotherapeutic interviews the patient revealed that as a lonely child she had created an imaginery playmate whom she called 'Elizabeth'. About two months after discharge from the hospital, during one interview, when she was describing again her imaginery playmate, she suddenly sat bolt upright in her chair and then assumed a relaxed and friendly attitude unlike her usual self, and said: 'I think it's about time I started telling you about me.' The astonished therapist said: 'What do you mean?' and the patient replied: 'About me, not about her.' She then proceeded to describe herself (Elizabeth) and her career. From this time on until the disappearance of Elizabeth four months later it was possible for several observers to study both Betty and Elizabeth under a number of different circumstances. Psychological tests of the two personalities supplemented the clinical observations.

The characteristics of these two personalities may be described as follows. Betty showed restraint and primness at all times. She was polite and outwardly co-operative. She appeared dejected and rarely smiled. Exceedingly tense, her hands frequently trembled. Speaking in a low, even, over-controlled way, she sat stiffly and addressed the therapist formally. She ate daintily and sparingly and was extremely orderly and careful about her dress and belongings. She stayed by herself much of the time and socialized little. She complained of headaches, abdominal cramps and dysmenorrhoea; she fainted frequently.

Elizabeth, on the other hand, had a much more outgoing and friendly personality. She relaxed in her chair and talked informally. Her voice was pitched in a higher key and showed more inflexion and variety. She often used slang and was frequently humorous. More gregarious, she made friends easily. She felt healthy and made no complaints of bodily pain or discomfort.

For some months Betty had amnesia for Elizabeth's periods of dominance. Elizabeth, however, knew all that happened during control by Betty. Elizabeth adopted a scornful, patronizing air towards Betty, but was also sympathetic about her difficulties, especially those of her marriage; she completely denied that *she* was married.

Information gathered from the patient's family, notably her mother, revealed that for some time the patient's behaviour with her family had shown puzzling, abrupt, alternating contrasts. Ordinarily, her mother said, the patient was quiet and reserved and dressed in conservative style; but sometimes she would suddenly brighten, talk animatedly, dress gaily, and accompany her mother to the movies.

As already stated the first transition noted by her psychiatrist occurred as the patient was describing her imaginery playmate of childhood. Then the playmate emerged as the secondary personality. Subsequent change-overs could be induced on request of the psychiatrist; or they occurred during periods of stress, Elizabeth taking control during a time of stress for Betty. Instead of getting Betty into trouble, as some secondary personalities have done for their primaries, Elizabeth often saved Betty from difficult situations. For example, once Betty took a suicidal dose of sedative pills whereupon Elizabeth took control and vomited the pills. The observed transition took place quickly. Upon one personality being called during dominance of the other the patient would lapse into detachment for about ten seconds and the other personality would then appear.

The Rorschach test showed that Betty had a general personality structure strongly suggestive of hysteria. Her responses indicated emotional lability as well as much effort to control emotion, and a strong emphasis on adapting through conformity to social conventions. Elizabeth showed even more emotional lability and much less control, and a lack of social conscience and constraint suggesting egocentricity and an inability to delay immediate gratification of impulses for future gain. Despite these contrasts, other responses to Rorschach testing showed similarities: in their thought processes both attempted to be correct and accurate in a compulsive manner, and both lacked adequate capacity to be objective in their perception of the environment. Their reality testing was not gravely impaired but their perceptions were easily influenced by their emotions.

On the sentence completion test Betty showed overly strong needs to be good, passive and compliant. She appeared to think of herself as a little girl still under her grandmother's domination, a domination which, as we will see, was based on strict adherence to Victorian standards. She also seemed to have adopted some of her grandmother's rigidity, for she revealed an inflexible internalized set of rules. Most of Elizabeth's sentence completion reflected attitudes and needs opposite to those of Betty. Betty's completions reflected passivity and dependence while Elizabeth exhibited a need for rebellion and independence. Betty indicated that she valued being good but Elizabeth felt that being good was a bore. Betty's attitude towards marriage was negative while Elizabeth's was definitely positive. Betty derogated males but Elizabeth complimented them. Betty feared many things while Elizabeth stated defensively that she feared nothing.

Betty's associations to the word association test predominantly revolved around phobias and affects of fear and disgust. She exhibited major conflicts in sexual and social areas, with most of her ideation in these areas reflecting negative feelings. Elizabeth's associations were frequently diametrically opposite. In contrast to Betty's frequent associations of 'filthy', 'dirty', 'frightening' and 'sickening', Elizabeth gave more hedonistic associations such as 'pleasure' and 'happiness'. If not indicating pleasure her associations tended to be neutral. Many similarities of associations occurred, particularly for the more neutral stimulus words. A majority of the identical responses were popular ones. When away from sensitive topics such as sex Betty and Elizabeth for the most part showed similar associations.

As we will later discuss, these contrasting and alternating personalities consist of two ego–super-ego organizations partly dissociated from one another and partly overlapping. As Congdon, Hain and Stevenson (1961)[17] maintain, Elizabeth experienced a freedom of expression and enjoyment in some areas which was altogether unavailable to Betty. Sometimes her attempted compensation for Betty's disability went too far in the opposite direction, towards important loss of control. In spite of their differences the personalities were similar in areas not charged with anxiety.

During the course of psychotherapy the earlier history of the patient and of the origin and career of the secondary personality became clearer. Members of the patient's family corroborated the salient facts. Congdon, Hain and Stevenson (1961)[18] write:

The patient was an only child. She was reared in the home of her paternal grandparents, with whom her parents lived during their marriage. The patient's father committed suicide when he was 24 and she four years old. The patient's mother was an easy-going, but passive and rather ineffective woman who worked out of the home after her husband's death. She then soon entirely abdicated the direction of the patient's early life to her mother-in-law, the patient's grandmother. The latter was a formidable tyrant, of stern, unyielding morality based on strict adherence to Victorian standards. She completely outlawed sex as a legitimate pleasure and most other pleasures as well. The training administered by the patient's grandmother seems to have contributed extensively to the development in her personality of a very marked and indeed disabling shyness, especially with regard to members of the opposite sex. A neighbour added to her fears of sexuality by assaulting her sexually when she was five. As she reached adolescence, the patient attempted to suppress and conceal the signs of her developing womanhood by wearing baggy dresses and avoiding all make-up or other adornment. In her school years, she seems to have been a lonely child and her contacts with other children became reduced by her grandmother's snobbish disparagement of them as inferior to the patient. Despite the tremendous handicaps placed upon her social life, the patient managed to get along fairly well in school and eventually graduated from high school.

When the patient was about seven years old, she began to substitute for the satisfactions of real playmates the lesser ones of an imaginary playmate whom she called Elizabeth. Betty spent many hours in play with the fantasized playmate. Elizabeth was always allowed to do the things that she herself was forbidden to do, and always had the courage to undertake what the patient herself feared to do. The patient maintained this playmate well into high school. In grammar school, Elizabeth was the subject of fantasy adventures that the patient felt she dared not undertake herself. Throughout the school years the patient came to identify herself more and more with Elizabeth and to try out in life various little adventures while pretending that she was Elizabeth. For instance, as Elizabeth she would go to the local candy store to buy and eat some of the candy which was denied her as Betty. Social activities such as parties were usually forbidden her and on a few occasions when she was allowed to go she felt quite frightened at the prospect. So she extended the habit of pretending that she was Elizabeth and went to these parties as Elizabeth. As Elizabeth she could be more free and enjoy herself. This pattern became more and more firmly fixed in her senior year of high school. It seemed the only way for her to enter into any stressful situation outside of her own home.

At the time of her graduation from high school the patient had had very few dates, and only one boy had shown more than a passing interest in her. The patient took a position as a clerk-typist in a small business. At this time she fell even more under the dominance of her grandmother who now censored her mail and her chequebook and supervised the most minute details of her daily life. When her only suitor finally proposed to her, she seemed to have accepted him as much to escape from her grandmother as because of any attraction for him. They were married when the patient was 19. Almost immediately she discovered that her husband was a brutal ruffian and also a sexual deviant. The patient fled from the honeymoon but the grandmother forced her to return to her husband. The patient then managed to stay with her husband for three years, probably only because his frequent absences from home gave her respite from his cruelty. On one occasion when her husband behaved in a particularly cruel manner, the patient suddenly became unusually aggressive and chased him from the home. She (i.e., Betty) had amnesia for this episode (subsequently pieced together from the accounts of Elizabeth and relatives) in which she had asserted herself in the personality of Elizabeth. Elizabeth then remained in control for some six months. During this period she separated from her husband, had a brief affair with another man, and finally returned to live with her grandmother. She dressed in a more feminine style and showed the relaxed, friendly behaviour characteristic of Elizabeth. After a time 'things became dull again' and control lapsed to Betty. During the next few months, Elizabeth took control for brief periods of innocent play, but was never in control for long.

The patient's husband sued for divorce, charging the patient with adultery. The patient allowed the divorce to proceed without defending herself, although urged to do so by her lawyer. The stresses of renewed living under her grandmother's control (which Betty could not shake off) and of the divorce seem to have been precipitating factors in the occurrence of the hysterical convulsions which led to the patient's admission to the hospital previously mentioned.

Psychotherapy and subsequent course of the disorder

After the emergence of Elizabeth during the therapeutic interview, additional interviews with members of the family confirmed the existence of the alternating personality for some years back. The members of the patient's family had noticed the sudden shifts of her personality and attributed them to her being 'peculiar' without further understanding them. Elizabeth also supplemented the history since she had a full memory for the period of amnesia in Betty's life.

Shortly after the identification of Elizabeth as a secondary personality, the patient's divorce proceedings became more embroiled. A leakage of news in her community about the patient's affair with another man provoked a painful scandal which only subsided slowly. During the stressful period Elizabeth seemed to gain control more often and for longer periods. Betty, now having some awareness of the activities of Elizabeth (although no memory of them), became more depressed and made the suicidal attempt already mentioned.

The therapist gained the alliance of Elizabeth for the treatment of Betty. Whenever possible, the therapist talked with Betty. The therapist attempted to deal first with the patient's fears and guilt regarding sexuality, and second, with her lack of assertiveness. Success accompanied these efforts and Betty gradually recovered the memories of much of the periods during the dominance of Elizabeth. There then ensued a period during which, although the personalities continued to alternate, each had full awareness of the other. (This resembled somewhat the earlier period of conscious role playing.) After four months of therapy, Elizabeth dropped out altogether and Betty remained dominant. Although still susceptible to tension, depression, and physical symptoms related to these, Betty has remained dominant ever since (now two years) and her condition has gradually improved. She finally became independent enough to leave her grandmother's home and move to another town, where she is gainfully employed. Betty now recalls everything she did as Elizabeth and has insight into the value of the secondary personality in protecting her from severe stresses.

Discussion

In *The Ego and the Id*, Freud (1923)[19] writes:

> Although it is a digression from our theme, we cannot avoid giving our attention for a moment longer to the ego's object identifications. If they obtain the upper hand, and become too numerous, unduly intense and incompatible with one another, a pathological outcome will not be far off. It may come to a disruption of the ego in consequence of the individual identifications becoming cut off from one another by resistances; perhaps the secret of the so-called multiple personality is that the various identifications seize possession of consciousness in turn.

Freud goes on to explain that analytic experience shows that both a positive Oedipus complex and an inverted negative Oedipus complex of more or less equal strength exist. As the Oedipus complex dissolves, the four trends of which it consists—with a boy, an ambivalent attitude to his father and an affectionate relation to his mother, also an affectionate feminine attitude to his father and corresponding hostility and jealousy towards his mother—group themselves so as to produce a father identification and a mother identification. He writes:

> The father-identification will preserve the object-relation to the mother which belonged to the positive complex, and will at the same time take the place of the object-relation to the father which belonged to the inverted complex: and the same will be true, *mutatis mutandis*, of the mother-identification. The relative intensity of the two identifications in any individual will reflect the preponderance in him of one or other of the two sexual dispositions.

He emphasized that the broad general outcome of the Oedipus phase was the foundation of a precipitate in the ego of these two identifications in some way combined together, and that this modification of the ego, the part altered by the 'introjected parents' occupies a special position as a differentiating grade within the ego; it stands in contrast to the other constituents of the ego. To this component Freud gave the special name of 'super-ego'.

In the preverbal phases of development, there is domination of the pleasure-pain principle so that whatever is frustrating is felt as bad. It is projected outside the archaic ego whereas pleasure-giving animated part-objects are introjected; these psychic processes are modelled on the physiological functions of ingestion and excretion. As object representations develop further they become ordered into good and bad, that is, satisfying and frustrating, and primitive introjective and projective processes continue to operate, with much that is projected becoming re-introjected. The role of introjection in ego-building is momentous, as it also is in regard to forerunners of the super-ego. In relation to the child at the immediate post-Oedipal phase, the introjected parental imagoes are too magnificent, and the distance between them and the ego-feeling of the child is too great for their absorption into the rest of the ego. It is pertinent here that the early childhood in the case of multiple personality just described was fraught with complication during the Oedipal phase: following her father's suicide, her mother, a permissive but ineffectual woman, soon abdicated her care to a rigid, anhedonic and especially antisexual grandmother. These contrasting characters, we see at once, set the stage for incompatible introjects which could give rise to super-ego cleavage. In multiple personality it is often the internal regulator of ego functioning, the super-ego, which alternately functions permissively and harshly in different ways and to an extent which is excessively contrasting and beyond the range of normal fluctuations.

Freud (1923)[19] writes:

> The hysterical type of ego defends itself from the painful perception which the criticism of its super-ego threatens to produce in it by the same means that it uses to defend itself from an unendurable object-cathexis—by an act of repression. It is the ego, therefore, that is responsible for the sense of guilt remaining unconscious. We know that as a rule the ego carries out repressions in the service and at the behest of its super-ego; but this is a case in which it has turned the same weapon against its harsh task-master.

The literary fictional model of alternating personality, Robert Louis Stevenson's *The Strange Case of Dr Jekyll and Mr Hyde*,[20] shows just this kind of super-ego cleavage, an internal regulation which is strict resulting in a vulgar respectability, succeeded by phases during which this kind of regulation is altogether abandoned and antithetical sadistic behaviour is allowed to emerge.

In dual personality the ego oscillates from a position of major defence against id impulses and minor defence against super-ego pressures, to a position of major defence against super-ego pressures. Betty, in moving towards the second position, found herself to be Elizabeth, whose major defence system was to dissociate the grandmother introject and to allow herself to be regulated by the mother introject. At the age of 7 years the intimidated and lonely child attempted counterphobically and through play a ressurrection of the more adventurous and pleasurable phase of her earlier existence. In a little girl the early direct and immediate primary identification with her mother is reinforced by secondary identifications based on object love; later, with the dissolution of the Oedipus phase there is usually an intensified identification with the mother which contributes towards more robust feminine identity formation. In this case the actual loss of the father at four years of age and an actual seduction a year later seriously disturbed her sexual development, which was also impaired by the partial separation from her mother. The succeeding care by her grandmother, as we have seen, powerfully influenced super-ego development in a puritanical direction, and was also unusually harsh and restrictive. But the grandmother also emphasized sexuality: her words dwelt on the repulsiveness of sex, but smiles on her face as she talked betrayed the fascination and pleasure of the subject for her. In this way too then the patient had been paradoxically over-stimulated sexually. Without amplifying these aspects of the matter further the point is that Betty showed severe ego deficiencies. For example, in the psychological tests, impaired reality testing and severe anxiety in reaction to sexual stimuli were evident. Elizabeth too showed severe ego difficulties, including faulty reality testing and much less ability to delay impulse gratifications; although, through counterphobic defences, including the dissociation of the more or less parasitic introject of the grandmother, she showed less conflict in sexual and social areas. In other words, besides the conflicting identifications in the constitution of the super-ego as already emphasized, there are associated gross ego deficiencies which bring this case, like other cases of severe dissociative reactions, into the borderline category of hysteriform type already discussed in Chapter 7.

Fairbairn (1952)[21] held that the processes whereby independent psychic formations within the inner world of the growing child developed involved both superimposition and fusion of internal objects, that is, of part-object representations. He wrote: 'The extent to which the internal objects are built up respectively on a basis of *layering* and on a basis of *fusion* differs, of course, from individual to individual.'[21] Rinsley (1979)[22], in a reconsideration of Fairbairn's object-relations theory, points out that sometimes Fairbairn conflated 'Splitting' with 'Repression'. In Chapter 13 we shall discuss more fully the concept of dissociation.

Meanwhile, it may be repeated that Janet (1889)[7] contended that some hysterical symptoms can be related to the existence of split parts of the personality—subconscious fixed ideas endowed with autonomous life and development. Jung (1902)[23] later maintained that split off contents of the unconscious can take on the appearance of a human personality ('personification'). Later McDougall (1926),[24] extending theory to encompass repression as described by Freud, divided mental disorders into those where dissociation (splitting) was more emphatic and those where repression was operative to a major degree. Hart (1926)[25] interpreted molar dissociation not as a splitting into separate pieces but rather as connoting more or less independently acting functional units. Nevertheless the spatial metaphor employed by Janet has remained conceptually useful to psychopathologists, together with the concept of splitting as a vertical division of the mind and of repression as horizontally divisive. Laughlin (1956),[26] for example, lists separately side by side dissociation and the dissociation from consciousness of repression involved in amnesia. Both splitting and repression are operative in the psychopathology of multiple personality disorder (*see* Chapter 13).

The case of 'Olympia', in contrast to the predominance of incompatible super-ego maternal introjects described in the case of Betty/Elizabeth, represents predominance of an introject derived from adverse experience with a violent and destructive alcoholic father. Identification with the bad aggressor was a large part of the structure of an ego fragment. Yet in both cases the genetic importance of early traumatic experiences is to be noted. Indeed, such traumatic early experience constitutes a common background in cases of multiple personality. The case of the black young woman Melanie also outlines the traumatic problems she periodically had with a drunk, abusive and punitive father, on top of the rape in early adolescence by a gang of boys in an alley. The now well-known case of Sybil (Schreiber, 1973[10]) is remarkable for the traumatic experiences Sybil endured at the hands of a cruel psychotic mother. Schreiber writes:

In early 1957, the analysis unfolded a drama of cruelty, secret rituals, punishments and atrocities inflicted by Hattie on Sybil. Dr Wilbur became concerned that the taproot of Sybil's dissociation into multiple selves was a large, complicated capture-control-imprisonment-torture theme that pervaded the drama. One escape door after another from cruelty had been closed, and for Sybil, who was a battered child four decades before the battered child syndrome was medically identified, there had been no way out.

Schreiber (1973)[10] reported that Dr Cornelia B. Wilbur, Sybil's physician, had treated six cases of multiple personality in recent years—five females and one male.

Each corresponded to waking Sybil and alternating selves of which the waking self had no knowledge and for whose memories and experiences of the six cases there was a 'Vicky' character, who knew everything about all the selves and who served as a memory trace ...

According to Schreiber, as I have also observed, the hysterical personality may become multiple in order to assume identities that make it possible to escape from the cruelties and restrictive standards of an oppressive family milieu. For instance, a schoolteacher with four selves treated by Dr Wilbur at the University of Kentucky Medical School was the daughter of a mountain preacher of the fire-and-brimstone school. This bigot did not allow his children out of the house after dark because of his belief that when the sun went down, the Devil began stalking the hills. In many cases a cruel and restrictive family background is all too clear, but in others it may be more elusive retrospectively. As Schreiber insists, it is clearly substantiated that the escape into fragmentary personalities is undertaken without the awareness of the waking conscious self, and, far from being conscious, it is a strategy of the unconscious mind. It is also clear that the split-off selves often function as largely autonomous entities. It has been my experience that patients with multiple personality had an over-close attachment to one or both parents and a paradoxical deprivation of adequate and appropriate affection from them, absorbing instead considerable hostility from them. Such factors are, however, involved in varying degrees in the psychogenesis of hysterical and hysteriform personality disorders.

Ellenberger (1972),[27] analysing Breuer's (1895) original report of Anna O with the help of two further documents he discovered, has highlighted the desperate struggle for a consolidated identity represented in this woman's celebrated illness. He shows that her illness may be partly understood as a creation of her 'mythopoeic unconscious', a creation which was unwittingly encouraged by Breuer as an unconscious collaborator. He compares Anna O's (Bertha Pappenheim's) experience with Dr Breuer with that of Fredericke Hauffer with Dr Kerner who reported on his patient in his monograph, *The Seeress of Prévorst* (1829).[27] (This was actually the first recorded study in the field of dynamic psychiatry to be devoted to an individual patient.) The development of the Seeress under Kerner's observation is a paradigm of the psychotherapeutic situation of therapist and hysterical personality. It was out of such a situation that Bertha Pappenheim succeeded in eventually becoming the pioneer of social work and fighter for the rights of women.

As Breuer described her situation in one of the documents unearthed by Ellenberger, Anna O's personality at one phase of her illness was split into one conscious person, normal but sad, and another who was morbid, uncouth and agitated, and who spoke in an agrammatical jargon derived from four different languages. In a later phase, the sick and normal personalities coexisted but in a different time frame—the sicker personality living 365 days before the healthier one. Since her mother kept a diary of her illness, Breuer was able to ascertain that the events she hallucinated day by day had actually occurred one year earlier. She sometimes shifted spontaneously from the correctly time oriented normal personality to the other, and Breuer could also provoke the shift by showing her an orange. He had from time to time given her food and drink, including orange juice, and the orange, it would seem, symbolized the ever-flowing breast by means of which she could be soothed and made to be calmer. As in the case of Félida X reported by Azam, her personality switches were accompanied by a contrast in mood, but the boundaries of Anna O's partial personality system were not so clearly demarcated. It is noteworthy that her experience with Breuer, who for two years listened to her and cared for her assiduously, ultimately helped to integrate her personality in such a way that she became in turn able to listen to and care for the mentally disturbed. Although the famous abreactions in the course of therapeutic interaction were doubtless of considerable importance in the cure of many of her symptoms, it seems likely that profound processes of identification were not only at work then too, but influenced her later career.

The Psychotic Break Point and Restitution

Typical of many multiple personalities in my experience is the following vignette:

Case 5. This patient was first encountered in the Dorothea Dix State Hospital in a consultation to be followed by a teaching session. Her physicians included a senior psychiatrist and several residents in training. One of the latter gave an account of her history prior to interview, reading from the chart. The young woman had been in the hospital for three months. On admission she had been paranoid and hallucinating, and had been unable to give a coherent account of herself. She believed that she had been attacked by evil spirits; threatening voices she heard periodically made her feel that she continued to need protection from further attacks. From the medical notes it was apparent that she had improved in the hospital following psychotropic medication within a therapeutic milieu of considerable friendly support, so that she was now able to discuss her situation and problems more realistically, and to conduct herself appropriately, including participation in adjunctive therapeutic activities within the hospital. The history was of a well-adjusted, physically attractive young girl brought up with a fundamentalist type of religious background. She had done well academically at school and at college and had been a very obedient do-gooder who had pleased her parents consistently. While at college she had become friendly with a young man who led her into social activities with a group whose general behaviour included dancing and singing and rebellious political discussions, challenging the establishment. The college was not far from her home. Soon she ceased to visit home frequently, and this led to a disturbance in the family. At this point in her history she 'mysteriously disappeared'. In fact she went to New York and found a job as a shop assistant. At this time in New York, she had assumed another name and another personality and had forgotten about her home and background in North Carolina. In New York, she was vivacious and hedonistic, finding work modelling to support herself. She had numerous unstable heterosexual relationships there. Then one such friendship became more sustained. During the course of this developing relationship, the young man discussed living together. At this point, she became panic-stricken and confused and soon was hallucinating so that she was taken to the hospital. There, in New York, after some weeks, she recovered in the person of her previous personality. She came back to her family in North Carolina. Soon the secondary personality took possession of her again. She left her family and took a job in a larger city in North Carolina, where she again became heavily involved with a young man and again decompensated, leading to her present hospital treatment. Now in an interview, she was the modest, staid and obedient self who had knowledge of her other self only through hearsay.

Some Recent Studies

A case that has been studied carefully from a psychological viewpoint in recent years is found in Ludwig et al. (1972):[28]

Jonah, 27 years old, came to the hospital complaining of severe headaches often followed by amnesia. Observation revealed striking alternations of personality on different days, and further study showed four relatively stable personality structures. Jonah, the primary personality, designated 'the square', was an over-anxious, shy and retiring, polite and passive, and highly conventional type unaware of the secondary personalities. Sammy, 'the mediator', took over when Jonah needed legal aid. He first emerged at six years of age when Jonah's mother stabbed his step-father whereupon Sammy succeeded in persuading the parents never to fight again in front of the children, a reform that assuaged in some degree the fright Jonah experienced. King Young, 'the lover', emerged soon afterwards in response to Jonah's mother dressing him in girl's clothing—King Young from then on looked to Jonah's masculine sexual interests whenever these were threatened. Usoffa Abdulla, 'the warrior', was a cold, belligerent and angry partial personality system, who emerged at about the age of nine years following a fracas when a gang of white boys beat up the timid black Jonah. Whenever there was a physical threat Usoffa was apt to emerge, and he would fling caution to the winds and fight viciously and relentlessly.

The psychological studies showed the four personalities tested quite differently on all measures which were related to emotionally laden topics, but scored similarly on tests relatively free of emotion or interpersonal conflict, such as on intelligence and vocabulary tests. In this case, it was very clear that the split off personalities had important protective and defensive roles to ensure the continued existence of the terror-stricken Jonah, who, however, without considerable psychological help could not change himself sufficiently to absorb and integrate the other fragments of himself. These facets of himself were necessary for survival and growth of his individuality as a man in a stressful, complex and often hostile world.

Berman (1981)[29] has described the case of Veronica/Nelly which he invigilated for research purposes while she was treated by another therapist during a five month period in a psychiatric hospital.

Two months after admission, Veronica eloped from the hospital, and after three days called her therapist as Nelly, informing him that Veronica had died, and she was now a new whole person. Psychological tests conducted at that time pointed to some 'elements of integration', but soon the patient had to come into the hospital again as Veronica when a stormy transference ensued.

'Veronica expected her therapist to take care of her, at times calling him her father', writes Berman (1981),[29] 'and when he attempted to maintain the boundaries of therapy she became furious, and started making threatening telephone calls to his wife.' A period of chaos and turmoil, including several discharges and rehospitalizations, culminated in the termination of her therapy.

However, Berman noted in his long–term follow up of her that there was a gradual process of reintegration—therapy which appeared at first to be ineffective had had beneficial long–term effects.

In 1957, Thigpen and Cleckley[30] reported *The Three Faces of Eve*, the subject of which had been studied by Osgood and Luria using the semantic differential. Later, Osgood, Luria, Jeans and Smith (1976)[31] studied the three faces of another subject, Evelyn, using the same method. In both these cases a blind analysis of their personalities revealed their important differences, that is, without any access to the clinical phenomena. In 1975, the original Eve revealed her identity as Mrs Chris Sizemore, a fourth and further integrated self, through interviews with journalists, corroborating the usefulness of her earlier psychotherapy with Thigpen and Cleckley in a beginning of a more adequate process of individuation.

Another study of considerable interest is that reported by Benson et al., (1986).[37] They observed and treated two individuals with well-defined seizure problems. In each case a temporary aberrant personality was followed by the normal personality after a seizure. Thus a temporarily irritable and hostile personality pattern was succeeded by a placid and loving pattern. A generalized seizure restored the normal personality. Benson et al. confirm Charcot and Marie's view[38] that multiple personality is often associated with seizure disorder.

Intermittent and Sustained Alterations of Consciousness in Multiple Personality

In fugue, as we have noted, there is a purpose in what seems aimless wandering. Hazy thought processes quite dissociated from the residual personality are sometimes geared to the special purpose of setting the stage for the emergence of an alternate ego–super-ego organization. Fugue is but one of a variety of different hypnoid states (*see* Chapter 10). The dissociated personality, which may later emerge more starkly, in fugue is acting out a wish-fantasy, and consciousness is temporarily suffused with feelings of well-being, which replace the consciousness of frustration and its feelings of ill-being that preceded the fugue. This contrasts with the somnambulistic hypnoid states in which the painful past experience of stress is evoked in vivid imagery in an effort to alter and master it. A clear example of a somnambulistic state is the case of Irene, described by Janet[32] in 1907.

> Irene repeatedly rehearsed the death of her mother, experienced under especially stressful conditions. In her usual condition following the demise of her mother, she not only forgot all she had dramatized in the repeated somnambulisms, but she forgot the dire events themselves: 'I know very well my mother is dead', she stated, 'since I have been told so several times, because I see her no more and because I am in mourning, but I really feel astonished at it. When did she die? ...'

Hypnoid alterations of consciousness often occur in persons whose habitual cognitive style is global, relatively diffuse and impressionistic—the hysterical style of mentation described by David Shapiro (1965).[14] Thus when such people are involved in marital conflict they are apt to escape into diminished awareness without adequate self-observation, and this may permit an unacknowledged part of the self to emerge into consciousness.

Certainly a hypnoid state which comprises a suspension of reflective self-representations often precedes the switch to a very different personality or to a restricted core personality.

Traumatic Early Experience and Focal Attention

The genetic importance of early traumatic experience constitutes the common background of cases of multiple personality. The well-known case of Sybil, whose mother was afflicted with a psychotic character disorder and behaved cruelly towards her daughter (*see* p. 239), is paradigmatic in this respect. The analysis of Sybil, as Schreiber noted, unfolded a drama of cruelty four decades before the battered child syndrome was clearly identified in medical circles.

In order to set the optimal distance from another person in adult life flexibly, according to the time and nature of the interpersonal relationships, one must early achieve what Mahler (1975)[33] has called psychological birth. According to Margaret Mahler, the process of separation and individuation is concentrated in the first two-and-a-half years of life. She concurs with earlier analytic views, notably, Trigant Burrow's (1964)[34] about the importance of the early infant/mother relationship in respect to its providing a foundation for a sound sense of identity—or failing to do so. The infant is not at first aware of his mother, then during a period of symbiosis, he sees her as part of himself, the 'mothering half' of the symbiotic dyad. Later he comes to a terrifying awareness of his and her separateness, and in the *'rapprochement* crisis' experiences intense feelings of ambivalence. He longs to return to the comfort of symbiosis, but there is within him the thrust to strengthen a tenuously emerging sense of self. He (or she) wishes to be more independent, but is fearful of a greater vulnerability. Severe schizoid problems which loom in the background of cases of multiple personality are the result of unresolved and still intensely cathected conflicts originating in this early period. Because of the nature of the mothering, the symbiotic phase has then become *dyssymbiotic* inasmuch as it has become an impediment to growth. In later childhood there have been, characteristically, super-added sexually traumatic experiences. Multiple discrete formations of personality can be understood partly as attempts to master successive traumatic situations in which elements of the growing self have been impounded.

The language we use to describe and understand multiple personality is based on the analogy of physical force causing segmental fragmentation of a shaped material object. It is, for the most part, a useful analogy, inasmuch as there are psychic traumas and psychic shapes. Between the times of definitive fracture are intermittent phases of alteration of consciousness, the hypnoid states, as discussed above and in Chapter 10.

It is to be noted that the capacity for focal attention as it develops is linked to the emergence of reality-testing. This development during infancy and childhood is complex. Ernest G. Schachtel (1959),[35] in *Metamorphosis* states:

It is a change from (1) a diffuse total awareness of well- or ill-being, in which at first there is no distinction between the infant and the environment through (2) a diffuse, a more or less global awareness of an impinging environment to (3) a state in which distinct needs and feelings become increasingly differentiated and discrete objects emerge from the environment. Ultimately, these objects are conceived by the child to have an existence of their own that continues even when the object does not impinge on the child's receptors ...

The earlier states of consciousness adumbrated by Schachtel are regressively revived in the retreat from separation-individuation under traumatic stress before molar dissociation becomes established.

In this review of multiple personality, it must again be emphasized that nature does not always draw sharp boundaries.

For example, in a psychiatric interview during the admission into the hospital of a 25-year-old man in a profound depression, I mentioned to him the remarkable impression that he spoke with two voices. The contours of intonation were actually quite distinct for these two voices. In one, he spoke in a firm, deep bass, in the other in a bleating, whining falsetto. The history elicited included his repeated beatings by an alcoholic father up to the age of 15½ years. At this time, one evening coming home drunk, his father proceeded, as was his wont, to beat up his wife. The patient intervened and in the ensuing struggle with the ataxic father, two of the father's ribs were broken. The father never offered to beat the patient thereafter. As he recounted his biography the patient's voice changed back and forth each side of the historical caesura and in due course, as noted, I pointed this out. The patient stated that he was moody and that in conformity with these changes of mood, he and others had sometimes remarked on the considerable change in his voice. He acknowledged that he felt differently at these different times. His occupation was that of a medical technician in the emergency room of a large general hospital, assisting in the necessary surgery. At his work he had always felt masterful, as at some other times. On the other hand, there were times that he felt helpless and hopeless, when the falsetto voice emerged. However, in this case, the patient did not see himself as different personalities, but noticed changes in himself. Discussion of this, however, was rewarding in subsequent psychotherapy as the patient became aware of the deeper significance of his shifting ego-states.

Finally, from the above considerations it will be clear that multiple personality disorder with its aetiology in psychic traumas is, from one usually neglected viewpoint, related to narcissistic personality disorder, since splitting and active dissociation of mutually contradictory self and object representations is a central defensive mechanism of both. As pointed out by Akhtar and Thomson (1982)[36] there is greater cohesion of the self, and less risk of regressive fragmentation in those cases distinctively labelled narcissistic personality disorder.

REFERENCES

1. Putnam, F. (1984). *Psychiatric News* July 6, 1984. Washington, D.C.: Am. Psychiat. Assoc.
2. Leavitt, H. C. (1947). A case of hypnotically produced secondary and tertiary personalities. *Psychoanal. Revue* **34**, 274.
3. Franz, S. I. (1933). *Persons One and Three: A Study in Multiple Personalities.* New York: McGraw-Hill.
4. Kuiper, P. C. (1967). *On Being Genuine and Other Essays.* Menninger Clinic Monograph Series, No. 16. New York: Basic Books.
5. Despine, A. (Père) (1840). *De l'Emploi du Magnétisme Animal et des Eaux Minérales dans le Traitement des Maladies Nerveuses suivi d'une Observation très Curieuse de Guérison de Névropathie.* Paris: Germer, Ballière.
6. Azam, E. E. (1887). *Hypnotisme, Double Conscience et Altération de la Personalité.* (Préface de J. M. Charcot.) Paris: Ballière.
7. Janet, P. (1889). *L'Automatisme Psychologique.* Paris: Alcan.
8. Ellenberger, H. F. (1970). *The Discovery of the Unconscious: The History and Evolution of Dynamic Psychiatry.* New York: Basic Books.
9. Morselli, G. E. (1945). Mescalina e schizofrenia. In: *Revista de Psicologia*, Vols. 40–41, 1–23.
10. Schreiber, F. R. (1973). *Sybil.* Chicago: Regnery.
11. Abse, D. W. and Ulman, R. B. (1977). Charismatic political leadership and collective regression. In: *Psychopathology and Political Leadership* (ed. Robins, R. S.). Tulane Studies in Political Science, Vol. 16. New Orleans: Tulane Univ. Press.
12. James, W. (1890). *Principles of Psychology.* New York: Dover (1950).
13. Mitchell, T. W. (1922). *Medical Psychology and Psychical Research.* London: Methuen (1922).
14. Shapiro, D. (1965). *Neurotic Styles.* Austen Riggs Center Monograph Series, No. 5. (Foreword by Knight, R. P.). New York and London: Basic Books.
15. Breuer, J. (1895). In: Breuer, J. and Freud, S. *Studies on Hysteria.* In: *The Standard Edition*, Vol. II. London: Hogarth Press (1953).
16. Moebius, P. J. (1894). Über Astasie–Abasie. In: *Neurologische Beiträge*, Vol. 1. Leipzig: Meiner, Barth.
17. Schafer, R. (1968). *Aspects of Internalisation.* New York: Int. Univ. Press.
18. Congdon, M. H., Hain, J. and Stevenson, I. (1961). A case of multiple personality, illustrating the transition from role-playing. *J. Nerv. Ment. Dis.* **132**, 497.
19. Freud, S. (1923). The Ego and the Id. In: *The Standard Edition*, Vol. XIX. London: Hogarth Press (1955).
20. Stevenson, R. L. (1886). *The Strange Case of Dr. Jekyll and Mr. Hyde.* London: Longmans.
21. Fairbairn, W. R. D. (1952). *An Object Relations Theory of the Personality.* New York: Basic Books.
22. Rinsley, D. B. (1979). Fairbairn's object-relation theory: a reconsideration in terms of newer knowledge. *Bull. Menninger Clin.* **43**, 489–514.

23. Jung, C. G. (1902). *Zur Psychologie und Pathologie Sogenannter Occulter Phänomene. Eine Psychiatrische Studie.* Leipzig: Multze.
24. McDougall, W. (1926). *Outline of Abnormal Psychology.* New York: Scribner.
25. Hart, B. (1926). The conception of dissociation. *Br. J. Med. Psychol.* **6**, 241. (Reprinted 1962 in Vol. **35**, 15.)
26. Laughlin, H. P. (1956). *The Neuroses in Clinical Practice.* Philadelphia: Saunders.
27. Ellenberger, H. F. (1972). The story of Anna O: a critical review with new data. *J. Hist. Behav. Sci.* **8**, 267–79.
28. Ludwig, A. M., Brandseira, J. M., Wilbur, C. B. et al. (1972). The objective study of a multiple personality or are four heads better than one? *Arch. Gen. Psychiat.* **26**, 298–310.
29. Berman, E. (1981). Multiple personality: psychoanalytic perspectives. *Gutemotoral J. Psycho-anal.* **62** (3), 284–99.
30. Thigpen, H. and Cleckley, H. M. (1957). *The Three Faces of Eve.* New York: McGraw-Hill.
31. Osgood, C. E., Luria, Z., Jeans, R. F. et al. (1976). The three faces of Evelyn. *J. Abnormal Psychol.* **85**, 247–86.
32. Janet. P. (1907). *The Major Symptoms of Hysteria.* New York: Macmillan.
33. Mahler, M. S., Pine, F. and Berguran, A. (1975). *The Psychological Birth of the Human Infant.* New York: Basic Books.
34. Burrow, T. (1964). *Preconscious Foundations of Human Experience* (ed. Galt, W. E.). New York and London: Basic Books,
35. Schachtel, E. G. (1959). *Metamorphosis.* New York: Basic Books.
36. Akhtar, S. and Thomson, J. A. (1982). Narcissistic Personality Disorder: In: *New Psychiatric Syndromes: D.S.M. III and Beyond* (ed. Akhtar, S.), Chap. 2. New York: Aronson.
37. Benson, D. F., Miller, B. L. and Signer, S. E. (1986). *Arch. Neurol.* **43**, 471.

CHAPTER 12

The Accident-prone Individual

Vehicular Accidents

Bernard Hart (1912)[1] wrote:

> It has been pointed out that even the normal mind does not always present that undivided field of consciousness which we might be tempted at first sight to ascribe to it. Suppose, for example, I sit at the piano and play a piece of music. If I am a sufficiently expert performer it is possible that I may at the same time be able to carry on a complex train of independent thought, let us say the solution of some problem of conduct. My mind does not under these circumstances present a uniform stream of consciousness, but one divided into two parts or processes. Each of these processes requires a considerable expenditure of mental energy. The piece of music is perhaps one which I have never seen before, and it has to be played with appropriate and constantly varying expression—while the problem of conduct may be similarly complicated in its character. Each of these activities is almost entirely independent of the other, yet both can be carried on at the same moment. The field of consciousness must therefore be divided into two portions, in other words a certain degree of dissociation of consciousness must be present.

We have already noted (Chapter 10) that Breuer and Freud (1893)[2] recognized that from such normative dissociations of consciousness hypnoid states may readily develop. At that time, knitting, embroidery and other handiwork provided their women patients with much opportunity for reveries; and these had led into the development of hypnoid states saturated with wishful fantasies which came to have a forbidden character. Today, the automatic driving of motor vehicles offers an unusually liberal chance for normative dissociation which then can become dominated by primary process and transformed to a hypnoid state, so-called 'highway hypnosis'. During such an altered state an accident may be facilitated, often on the basis of a need for punishment, as the following example illustrates:

Case 41. A university freshman aged 18 years suffered multiple fractures following a motorcycle accident. He was recovering physically in hospital but had developed insomnia which led to psychiatric consultation and treatment. During the course of treatment it became apparent that he was in a state of considerable mental conflict shortly before the accident.

Anamnesis, as it was developed in psychotherapy, revealed a history of a very repressive tyrannical father who had subjected the patient to a curfew during his high school years. An ambience of fundamentalism with a very religious mother, to whom the patient was very attached, pervaded his childhood years. Leaving the small town in a rural area and coming to a large university where his coevals behaved and talked so differently from those in the group whom he had left behind resulted in his becoming very anxious. He attended some parties but did not succeed in initiating a date with a co-ed. Later he learned to drive a motorcycle which he greatly enjoyed. Soon after this he attended a party, and one of the young women gradually led him to a room in the house where they were alone. He became increasingly anxious and decamped, returning to the dormitory. Feeling exhausted he went into a deep sleep and later dreamed of beginning sexual intercourse. He awoke in fright at dawn and felt strongly that he had to ride his motorcycle. Taking off on a road into the country he soon collided with a truck coming in the opposite direction. His motorcycle had wandered just over the middle of the road and he had been thrown away from it.

In psychotherapy, it was found that in leaving the party early he had obeyed his father's curfew and was asleep by 10:00 pm. Asserting his masculine might on the motorbike after awakening, he countermanded castration anxiety—only to get himself severely punished and almost to get himself killed.

Myerson (1969)[3] has described a similar case. His patient, while driving an automobile, sometimes paid less attention to the road than to his rebellious, pleasurable involvement with speed and with the admiring women and the disapproving policemen who focused on him in his fantasy. His preoccupation with the imaginative derivatives and symbols of sadistic phallic wishes belonging to the Oedipal situation led him to reckless driving and once to bodily injury, indicating a primitive super-ego reaction.

Such cases as the above, and they are legion, seem to show that road accidents may often express a basic hysteria with mental conflicts predominantly related to the Oedipus complex. But the same is also true of present-day industrial accidents in general. In other words, accident-proneness is an alternative to illness-proneness including what Menninger (1938)[4] termed polysurgical addiction, in which surgical patients, often without road or industrial accidents, seek surgery as a means of punishment, sometimes as a way of escaping an imagined greater disaster by sacrificing part of themselves. In any event, the study of accident-proneness is of great importance in our industrial and technologically advanced society. Within the larger group of those who manage to incur an excess of accidents, there are a minority who need to expose themselves to danger and to avoid injury to 'prove' their invulnerability. Of course, they do get into repeated accidents, sometimes eventually fatal.

In one such case, a woman champion motorcyclist who was involved in more and more accidents, the first part of psychotherapy was necessarily devoted to helping her to relinquish her passion for racing which she had come to glimpse correctly as a death-threat.

Industrial Accidents

In a study of 3000 workmen, Marbe (1926)[5] showed that the probability of meeting with an accident at work is greater in the case of a person who has had previous accidents. Marbe was the first to demonstrate statistically the existence of an 'accident habit'. Since 1926 psychiatrists have directed attention to the psychology of those individuals who are involved in recurrent accidents in industry, and self-generated accident-proneness has been clearly demonstrated as an important factor.

First it is necessary to understand in general perspective the social setting in which the realization has come about that a high proportion of accidents are man-made and not machine-made, apart, of course, from the hard core of accidents which are the result of simple mechanical hazards.

Patterson and Willett (1951)[6] in the study of accidents in Scottish mines, found that the long term fluctuations in accident rates from mine to mine showed substantial correlation (+0·53), and that a similar positive correlation existed between two mines which they proceeded to study in detail. Since there were great differences in mechanical conditions in these two mines it seemed unlikely that the correlation could have been due simply to mechanical conditions. The depth of workings, underground travelling distances, the height of seams, roof, and other conditions differed considerably in the two collieries. Moreover, mechanization had progressed at different rates in the two mines. However, enforcement of safety regulations and medical facilities were much the same. Against this background they found not only the correlation in long term fluctuation in accident rates from mine to mine, as just stated, but a bifold annual cycle superimposed on a general uptrend in accidents in the two mines. Their observations led them to think that possibly an important factor in the increasing long term accident rate could be defined as a growing lack of cohesion in the working community, accentuated by long-wall face techniques in working the mines. In order to test this hypothesis they introduced a series of community steps aimed at increasing the cohesion of the working group in a particular section of a colliery. Off-the-job concerts, group trips to Glasgow and Edinburgh for football games, and various informal parties were fostered. On the job the same goal of increasing group cohesion was sought by emphasizing the interdependence of the workers, and by instituting a system of painting sections yellow to indicate to the man following on the job that all was left in good and safe order for him. In the first year of this experiment accidents were reduced to 54 per cent of the number predicted from the past curve and correlation between the mines, and there was evidence of change in the form of fewer improperly set supports for roofs and the like.

This study clearly showed the great importance of human relations—and, more particularly, of group morale and cohesion—in the field of safety and accident prevention.

In a study of 130 workers with a record of repeated accidents Alexandra Adler (1941)[7] concluded that a harmonious relation of the individual worker to his own job was a fundamental prerequisite of avoidance of accidents to himself and damage to his environment. The investigation of these workers had included the case history method of study, dreams, childhood recollection, emotional reactions to any accident, psychometric tests and general examination, noting in this the constitutional habitus.

Neither the psychometric tests of manual ability and reaction-time nor the constitutional classification revealed any significant difference between the control group and the accident-prone workers. The other components of the psychiatric evaluation, however, showed striking differential features which occurred with such frequency that it was possible to divide the subjects into eight groups, as shown in *Table* 12.1.

About the last three groups Adler comments as follows:

The alcoholics had definite signs of chronic alcoholism, such as continuous tremors. Many of them were intoxicated when they reported for work as can be seen from the rate of accidents occurring in the morning and afternoon. In the alcoholics, the accidents occurred more than twice as frequently in the morning as in the afternoon. In the other

Table 12.1 An analysis of 130 workers suffering repeated accidents*

Differential features by groups	Amercian workers		European workers	
	No.	%	No.	%
1. Revengeful attitude	4	13.2	56	56
2. 'Unlucky'	7	23.1	10	10
3. Longing to be pampered	6	19.8	6	6
4. Over-ambitious	2	6.6	4	4
5. Over-fearful	8	26.4	3	3
6. Alcoholics	1	3.3	12	12
7. Feeble-minded	1	3.3	7	7
8. Organic diseases	1	3.3	2	2
Total	30		100	

*After Adler, A. (1941), The psychology of repeated accidents in industry, *Amer. J. Psychiat.* **98**, 99.

groups the ratio was about equal. The feeble-minded had a very low grade of intelligence. They could not count or write more than their names. It is understandable that they were unable to follow the routine. In the other groups, the intelligence was equal to that in the general population. Of the three workers who had organic diseases, the American worker suffered from cerebral arteriosclerosis; one of the two European workers was subject to *petit mal* attacks, during which the accidents occurred, whereas the second suffered post-encephalitic Parkinsonism and his slowness of movement interfered with his work. The psychological structure in these 24 patients with organic disease or subject to chronic alcoholism was quite different from that found in the remaining accident-prone workers.

It is perhaps apparent from the foregoing that in the aetiological constellation responsible for accident-proneness in any one individual, social and physical factors *might* be operating forcefully in the current life situation of the individual. However, in order to understand more fully the vast majority of accident-prone individuals, such as those included in Adler's first five groups, we must take into account that *people take their pasts with them to their jobs*.

Case 42. Some years ago a middle-aged steelworker, following a series of minor accidents at his work, became involved in a car accident while being transported from one plant to another. He had suffered multiple fractures in the motor accident and had been regularly attending a physical rehabilitation clinic for several months. He had made a good recovery from his injuries but persisted in worrying about himself and in presenting himself to the doctor at the steelworks with all sorts of hypochondriacal complaints. One day the doctor spent more than his usual time with the patient and inquired into his domestic life. The patient became very disturbed emotionally and wept, saying that his wife was obsessed with the idea that he was going around with other women, and that she was making their home life so unbearable and turbulent that he could hardly get any sleep. Further inquiry disclosed that the patient had been impotent since the accident. He was referred for examination to a neurologist, who agreed with the works physician that the patient's impotence might be due to spinal concussion resulting from the accident. The neurologist reassured the patient, however, that, since there were no demonstrable neurological signs of any focal lesion, he had a good chance of recovering his *potentia coeundi*. The patient thereupon had told the neurologist that he was worried, not about his impotence, but about his wife's accusations and quarrelsomeness. On this account the neurologist advised referral to a psychiatrist as well as a conference between the works physician and the patient's wife.

I then saw this interesting patient, who apparently accepted his impotence cheerfully but complained about his wife. After two interviews, spaced a week apart, this patient was hypnotized on the third occasion and then was able to recall that when he was 40 years of age, two years previously, he had become depressed, thinking about his father who had died in his early forties. It was after this that the minor accidents had occurred at work and the impotence and arguments with his wife had started. In the final more serious accident in the car he had been sitting next to the driver whom he knew well. Becoming afraid as a big truck approached, though he knew that the driver was competent, he had suddenly seized the steering wheel. In the ensuing confusion the car left the road, hit a tree, and overturned, killing the driver and injuring the patient. The patient suffered considerable remorse about the loss of the driver and also in relation to the widow, towards whom in fact he had later been extremely helpful, even during his own rehabilitation from bodily injuries. In the waking state, however, he could recall no details of the accident or of his role in causing it. In the course of further psychotherapy this man was able to achieve domestic felicity, following the recovery of his sexual potency.

This case serves to illustrate the complex factors involved in unconsciously determined accident-proneness. In his past this man had surmounted a disturbed relationship with a punitive father and had made a good social, occupational, and sexual adjustment until the age of 40 years, when thoughts of his father's death made him think in terms of his own demise. Through repeated minor accidents he had unconsciously been punishing himself, much as he had in childhood received whippings from his father. He began, in short, to take disturbed elements of his past, previously dormant, to his job, culminating in a serious accident and loss of life and injury.

In *Table* 12.1 it is evident that revengeful attitudes figure prominently in the personality evaluation of European accident-prone individuals. Alexandra Adler (1941)[7] writes:

All of these showed a definitely bitter and revengeful attitude towards their parents or educators who were blamed by these workers for their unhappy life. They usually stated that their parents had forced them to take up an occupation which they did not like. Now, they said, the parents could see what the outcome was. If they had followed their original wishes to become artists or teachers, for instance, they wouldn't have become cripples. Their childhood was marked by difficulties in relation to school and relatives. One third of this group harboured serious ideas of suicide, which were not present in the remaining groups. But no actual attempt at suicide was admitted. We know from experience that suicidal persons usually have a revengeful attitude towards someone whom they want to punish through their suicide. In these workers, we may, therefore, consider the accidents as something like a substitute for suicide.

Not only, of course, are such people likely to incur accidents to themselves, but, as Marbe (1926)[5] pointed out, they also do the greatest damage to the machinery. This type of accident-prone individual, unlike the steelworker discussed above, has always felt considerably frustrated, regarding himself, through his parents' faults, as a square peg in a round hole. It is usually easy to understand that psychological decompensation in one form or another, revealed through accident-proneness or other symptoms, can occur when people feel frustrated and unhappy. But in *Case* 42 the man had been happily adjusted until the age of 40 years, and there were no outer circumstances to cause him to feel frustrated in any severe degree. It is perhaps more difficult to understand how this state of affairs—psychological decompensation, sometimes showing itself in accident-proneness—can overtake people who have achieved a good measure of success. Of course, the decompensation here also is related to inner causes connected with past experiences and fantasies *brought to the job*. It happens that such inner causes become activated sometimes in response to success.

The legend of Polycrates, told in one version by Herodotus, illustrates this peculiar situation of stress for some ambitious people.

> Polycrates, the tyrant of Samos, was so fortunate in everything that Amasis, King of Egypt, advised him to part with something he highly prized. Polycrates took the King's advice for he feared that the gods would become envious of his continuing successes in war and his further aggrandizement. He threw into the sea an engraved gem of extraordinary value, a favourite piece of booty. A few days afterwards a fish containing this very gem was presented to the tyrant. The gods thus showed their anger at the mortal's presumptuous ambition. Amasis, interpreting the matter just so, renounced all friendship with him as a man doomed by the gods. Soon a satrap, having captured the too-fortunate despot, put him to death by crucifixion.

This theme of 'pride going before a fall' projectively discloses a dominant fantasy in the minds of some people. As their ambitions are realized they begin to feel that something dreadful is now bound to happen. Attempting to forestall the catastrophe, like Polycrates, they make a sacrifice to appease the gods—gods resident, of course, only in their own guilty consciences.

In *Case* 42 the patient had begun to feel uneasy because, unconsciously, his success as a foreman in a steelworks represented the usurpation of the authority of his father with whom in life he had had a very ambivalent relationship and at whose death he had felt guilty for having wished to be rid of him. Reminded of his father's death by his approaching middle age he unconsciously sought self-punishment in accidents which, as we have seen, finally took a serious turn, and all this at a time when he was enjoying the fruits of the efforts of his youth. It is indeed sometimes difficult to discuss what constitutes 'stress' for a particular individual; frustration by outer circumstance, economic hardship, loss of love, setback in ambition, or other sources of misery are not the only conditions of stress for some, and one way of indirectly showing sickness of mind is by not avoiding accidents which only too often will then occur.

Some readers may remember that a fatal accident figures prominently in Thornton Wilder's strange story of human destiny, *The Bridge of San Luis Rey*.[8] Part I begins: 'Perhaps an accident', and Part V, in conclusion: 'Perhaps an intention'. Freud (1901)[9] showed at the turn of this century that common to everyday living are little accidents such as slips of the tongue or of the pen, and the forgetting of intentions or of names, leading to embarrassing situations. However, some of these so-called 'parapraxes' may be serious enough to lead to physical injuries or even to fatal results. These accidents demonstrate the existence of unconscious mental processes which are in conflict with the conscious ones; sometimes they compromise with the conscious intention and sometimes more blatantly replace it for a brief moment of dissociation. It is apparent that the first and last chapter titles of Thornton Wilder's novel acquire deeper meaning, because 'an accident' becomes only 'perhaps an accident' if a motive for its occurrence can be established. As for accidents in industry, unless the intention to avoid them is adequately carried through they only too easily occur. The intention to avoid an accident is sometimes forgotten because of a counter current in the unconscious processes.

Patients in Group 2 of Alexandra Adler's table, those who again and again called themselves the 'unlucky ones', showed very openly that they were bringing unconscious past sources of unresolved guilt to their current job. They reported that they had had 'bad luck' all their lives, starting from earliest childhood, and did not expect it ever to be different. Half of them had been illegitimate children—a significant finding.

They behaved, Adler reports, like persons who are courting blows. It is understandable that when people have deep-seated fatalistic notions that something dreadful, such as a mutilating accident, is about to happen regardless of any precaution taken, not much will be done to avoid it.

Case 43. A patient in prolonged intensive psychotherapy, who had been brought up in an orphanage and later adopted, showed that she had acquired an unusually severe and deep-seated sense of guilt based upon notions of possible 'bad seed'. This had considerably aggravated the usual and inevitable guilt-producing emotional problems of childhood. She had later oscillated between perfectionist attempts to get herself admired and involvement in humiliating minor accidents which were, prior to therapy, becoming of more and more serious proportions. Like the accident-prone 'unlucky ones' [of *Table* 12.1] she felt that these accidents were determined by the ill-favoured star under which she was born.

Because of guilt feelings connected with early childhood development patients such as the one described briefly above have a masochistic need for punishment. This constitutes a counter-current in the unconscious processes which sometimes results in physical accidents that temporarily relieve guilt feelings. Blaming fate, as such patients often do, helps further to relieve guilt and compensate for injured narcissism.

In contrast, Group 3 in *Table* 12.1 consists of those who always wished to be nursed and cared for. They had been pampered in their childhood and reacted to any setback in adult life by unconsciously seeking to renew this period of comparative bliss. They reported that the only time they felt really well, as they had during their happy childhood, was after an accident when they were sick and being taken care of. In these people too guilt about such wishes and self-punishment devices may lead to more catastrophic accidents.

Group 4 in *Table* 12.1 consists of six over-ambitious workmen. We have already discussed, with reference to *Case* 42, the guilty reactions producing a need for punishment which can complicate quite legitimate ambitions of adult life. These six workmen showed extreme ambition, as manifested, for example, by their repeated dreams of flying, common in individuals who want to be more powerful than others. They were interested in being ahead of the others, coming to work early, sometimes as much as two hours before the usual starting-time. This competitiveness and need to excel when pushed to such limits is often tied up with unresolved difficulties and can produce a self-damaging counter-current in unconscious processes sometimes leading to self-generated accident-proneness.

Group 5 in *Table* 12.1 are indeed often over-fearful just because of this self-damaging counter-current in the unconscious, and purposive accidents can be an expression of such self-destructive tendencies. In Alexandra Adler's study a substantial percentage of American workers fall into this category and are liable to dissociative reactions at work.

We might summarize as follows: While many accidents (and consequently the accident rate in any particular situation) are largely due to simple mechanical hazards, to personal reactions to social situational factors such as those connected with group morale, or to physical ill health, many of these and many others, especially those associated with an accident habit in the individual, require consideration of the fact that people take their pasts with them to their jobs. Unresolved anxieties and guilts, associated with the problems encountered by the individual in growing up, may sometimes set up self-damaging counter-currents in the unconscious forces of the psyche. These may issue in recurrent parapraxes on the job and self-generated accident-proneness. Accidents are thus nowadays common expressions of dissociative disturbances of hysteriform type.

Repeated Accidents Suffered by Children

Though the diagnosis of child abuse is often difficult, hospitals are developing procedures for detecting and handling suspected cases. No injury to a child, especially when injury is repeated, should be treated without regard for factors in the child and his environment that lead to accidents. Many accidents to young children are related to failure of the responsible caretakers to exercise reasonable control over the child-environment interaction prior to the accident. There are, of course, many community efforts to prevent childhood injuries, such as: burns, by legislation dealing with the flammable fabrics problem; poisoning, by making toxic chemicals and medications inaccessible to children; drownings, by enforcing safeguards; fractures, by means of mandatory seatbelts in cars; and there are many community educational programmes in which paediatricians take leadership. As severe problems from infectious diseases decline, injuries assume an obviously more prominent place in the statistics relating to childhood morbidity and mortality. This prominence is accentuated by the increasing availability of toxic chemicals, motor vehicles, inflammable fluids and other hazards to a child's life and limb.

A similar pattern exists world-wide: as a Third World country develops, the same hazards, with their impact on the statistics of child injury, occur, as in those countries which have passed through technological and socioeconomic revolutions. The universal appeal of rescuing children from avoidable hazards is very strong and can be utilized in education efforts.

Within this general context it is to be noted here that the following types of failures on the part of the mother to exercise reasonable control over the child-environment interaction are clinically observable: the mother feeling anxious and depressed abdicates control but fails to appoint a competent caretaker in her absence; failure of the mother's control of her own anger so that hitting the child occurs, or clumsy parapraxes, such as pulling the rug out beneath a standing baby or a toddler; failure to control the behaviour of other persons potentially dangerous to the child, such as offering provocations to a drunken husband; failure to protect the child from dangerous objects in the environment, such as metal heat radiators; leaving the child in an unsafe position, perhaps perched high on furniture. All such failures may readily result in droppings, fallings, collisions, or strikings. The child may be to a relative extent passively or actively involved in any of these circumstances. In some of the instances which have come to my notice the mothers have belonged to the category of hysteriform borderline personality disorder, with shifting ego states, hypnoid alterations of consciousness and destructive acting out. In several cases, the mother suffered a fainting attack with temporary loss of consciousness while carrying her baby.

In cases such as these, when there are repeated major maternal coping failures, it is obvious that effective intervention must include adequate psychotherapy for the mother.

REFERENCES

1. Hart, B. (1912). *The Psychology of Insanity*. Cambridge: Cambridge Univ. Press (1957).
2. Breuer, J. and Freud, S. (1893). On the psychical mechanism of hysterical phenomena: preliminary communication. *Studies on Hysteria*. In: *The Standard Edition*, Vol. II. London: Hogarth Press (1955).
3. Myerson, P. G. (1969). The hysteric's experience in psychoanalysis. *Int. J. Psycho.–anal.* **50**, 373–84.
4. Menninger, K. A. (1938). *Man Against Himself*. New York: Harcourt Brace.
5. Marbe, K. (1926). *Praktische Psychologie der Unfälle und Betnebsshaeden*. Berlin: Oldenbourg.
6. Patterson, T. T. and Willett, E. J. (1951). An anthropological experiment in a British colliery. *Human Organizations* **10**, 19.
7. Adler, A. (1941). The psychology of repeated accidents in industry. *Am. J. Psychiat.* **98**, 99.
8. Wilder, T. (1927). *The Bridge of San Luis Rey*. London: Longmans, Green.
9. Freud, S. (1901). *The Psychopathology of Everyday Life*. In: *The Standard Edition*, Vol. VI. London: Hogarth Press (1955).
10. Meyer, R. J. (1966). Monograph, 1966 Conference, University of Virginia. In: *International Symposium on Childhood Injury* (ed. Meyer, R. J.). Charlottesville: Univ. Press Virginia.

CHAPTER 13

The Concepts of Dissociation and Splitting

Dissociation in the form of splitting of the psyche became of predominant interest to psychotherapists in the nineteenth century following the work of Puységur (1809)[1] on lucid and somnambulistic possession states (Chapter 1). Despine (1840),[2] Azam (1887),[3] James (1890),[4] Hodgson (1891),[5] Flournoy (1900)[6] and Morton Prince (1906),[7] among others, paved the way for the work of Charcot and his associates at the hospital of the Salpêtrière.

As we have seen, from ancient times many physicians throughout the centuries, up to the nineteenth, had emphasized the role of frustration of sexuality in the pathogenesis of hysteria. Then in 1859 Briquet (1859)[8] confused this issue by denying the role of sex in his textbook on hysteria. Whereas most neurologists followed in the wake of Briquet (or at any rate in the wake of Charcot's modification of his views), gynaecologists since that time have held in general to a view that included the sexual psychogenesis of hysteria. Thus the American gynaecologist King (1891)[9] contended that hysterics were torn between two personalities—the 'reproductive ego' and the 'self-preservative ego'. He held that the rejection by a woman of the demands of reproductive functions resulted in her liability to develop hysterical symptoms, unless she became totally absorbed in the struggle for existence.

Among the neurologists there was one, however, who refuted Briquet's theory. Moritz Benedikt (1864)[10] found that hysteria definitely depended on functional sexual disorders. He further substantiated his views in 1868[11] with detailed clinical observations including male cases on the relationship of hysteria to disorders of the libido (as he named sex drive), and proclaimed the need for psychotherapy. In 1894[12] he described what he called the second life, the subliminal existence and importance of a secret means of escape for many people from the hardships of their routines, especially women. This secret life, just like the secrets it contained, was concerned with erotic notions, and became related to the onset of hysterical symptoms. He gave examples of severe hysterical disorders which were cured by confession of such 'pathogenic secrets'. It is now evident that these secrets of the fantasy life were but the partially concealed tips of icebergs.

It is also notable that splitting of the psyche was of considerable interest to novelists as well as psychotherapists for several generations prior to the work of Breuer and Freud. We have previously mentioned (Chapter 11) Robert Louis Stevenson's *The Strange Case of Dr Jekyll and Mr Hyde* (1886). This had been preceded by E. T. A. Hoffman's *Tom-Cat Murr* in 1820; this includes the story of Johannes Kreisler, surely a partial self-representation, who is a typical example of *Zerrissenheit*. Edgar Allen Poe's *Doppelgänger* tale, *William Wilson* is another example in the first-half of the nineteenth century. All such tales summon the theme that there is another darker and more impassioned self lurking in the shadows of the psyche. The short novel by Feodor Dostoevsky *The Double* (Dvoinik, 1846) illustrates this: Golyadkin, a lowly frustrated civil servant is repeatedly rebuffed in his ambitious but feeble efforts to gain the notice of the daughter of his superintendent. A strangeness begins to pervade his world wherein another Golyadkin, his physical double, emerges on the scene. Where the old Golyadkin fumbled, this one is both adroit and ruthless, and becomes favoured; however, perplexity and anxiety and disturbance in Golyadkin's relationships in reality result in his being taken away in a carriage to the madhouse. Otto Rank (1919)[13] regards Dostoevsky's treatment of the theme of the double as the most profound and moving of the many examples in imaginative literature which he adumbrates.

The novel shows the double as becoming more and more arrogant towards Golyadkin after first appearing as a humble supplicant. Golyadkin feels he is taken away from friends and ousted from his work by the double, who ultimately helps him into the carriage which takes him away. It becomes evident that the double in Dostoevsky's novel is the uncanny other self which, weak at first, takes over control later.

It should be noticed in passing that the great dramatic achievements of some of the playwrights of the nineteenth century included the portrayal of characters not composed of one solid unvarying personality, but composed rather of many incompatible facets to their respective personalities. Sometimes, as in Henrik Ibsen's dramas, we are shown how this multiplicity, already itself in conflict, is affected when it clashes with the fixed laws and conventions of society. Indeed, in large part due to Ibsen's influence, the drama of man's multiple schisms of personality was further developed in the earlier part of this century, especially by Luigi Pirandello. In Ibsen's plays the individual remains more or less unitary despite contending inner forces: for Pirandello there is a mass of dissociated and contradictory sentiments in individuals. Some of these are latent, but then erupt volcanically. This results in those incongruities which are the appanage of the *'Teatro del Grottesco'*.

Automatic Writing and Co-Consciousness: Somnambulism and Sequential Alterations of Consciousness

The phenomenon of automatic writing, often educed in cases of hysteria, illustrates a marked degree of dissociation or splitting and one which passes away from the control of the subject. While the attention of the subject is held in conversation by one observer another inserts a pencil in the subject's hand. Then this third person whispers questions and induces the subject to write his answers while the subject continues to discuss a different topic with the first observer. Under such circumstances it is sometimes found that the hysterical subject is, or becomes, only dimly conscious that his hand is writing and is, moreover, often altogether ignorant of the events he is recording. These events relate to episodes in his past life apparently forgotten on more direct questioning; thus such an experiment may be undertaken with the object of resuscitating these memories. It is obvious that in such an experiment a marked dissociation of the field of consciousness is elicited; one part of the field is engaged in conversation while the other comprises the systems of ideas which are finding expression in the automatic writing. Besides the dissociation of two separate, simultaneously present, systems of ideas finding conscious expression with greater or lesser clarity, there is another type of dissociation which is sequential. The somnambulism of Janet's patient Irene will serve to illustrate the second type.

This girl nursed her mother during terminal illness, at which time she toiled away also at a sewing machine in order to earn a livelihood. The mother died and Irene attempted to revive the corpse. The body slipped to the floor and she desperately attempted to drag it back into bed. Shortly after these events Irene began to have somnambulistic attacks. Janet (1907)[14] writes of these attacks:

> The young girl has the singular habit of acting again all the events that took place at her mother's death, without forgetting the least detail. Sometimes she only speaks, relating all that happened with great volubility, putting questions and answers in turn, or asking questions only, and seeming to listen to the answers; sometimes she only sees the sight, looking with frightened face and staring at the various scenes, and acting accordingly. At other times she combines hallucinations, words and acts and seems to play a singular drama.

Again, Janet writes of his patient between such attacks:

> We shall soon notice that even in these periods she is different from what she was before. Her relatives who conveyed her to the hospital stated: 'She has grown callous and insensible, she has soon forgotten her mother's death, and does not remember her attacks.' That remark seems amazing; it is, however, true that this young girl is unable to tell us what brought about her illness, for the good reason that she has quite forgotten the dramatic events that took place three months ago.

Janet concluded from cases of this kind that one series of ideas had become isolated from consciousness generally, in a process of dissociation. Thus, in the case of Irene, in the periods between attacks, she knew nothing of the events immediately preceding her mother's death, whereas during the attacks her consciousness was retracted and entirely occupied with the events leading to and including her mother's death. Then the train of ideas constituting the somnambulism would again abruptly disappear from consciousness and be replaced, equally abruptly, by the ideas and actions which had occupied her mind at the moment when the somnambulism began.

The dissociated system of ideas whose eruption into the field of consciousness is responsible for somnambulism (one variety of hypnoid state) pursues its own course without any obvious dependence upon the personality as a whole. Hart (1912)[15] defines dissociation as: 'the divorce from the personality of a system of ideas, the course and development of which are exempt from the control of the personality'. In our discussion of hypnoid states in Chapter 10 we referred to the distinctive alterations of consciousness involved, commonly, though not necessarily, the same in all dimensions: vague, affect-charged, restricted ideation, with defective powers of self-observation and often associated with unadapted acting-out behaviour. This description, as in many other instances of polyideic somnambulisms, does not tally with Irene's somnambulism, for during the attack there is a remarkable persistence of heightened attention within a narrow focus (*see Table* 10.1, Chapter 10). We have also shown that in some cases the dissociated system is far more extensive, including whole tracts of the patient's past life, and more completely developed, as in double personality (*see* Chapter 11). In such instances the behaviour when the dissociated system is in entire possession of the field may be reality adapted within variable limits; certainly a careful phenomenological analysis enables one to form an estimate of the degree to which the dissociated elements of the personality have access to consciousness, and the alterations in consciousness which contrast with usual waking conditions when consciousness is thus occupied. The fugue followed by amnesia discussed in Chapter 2 (*Case* 10) revealed a state of prolonged disturbed consciousness out of contact with the soldier's social reality, though he was sufficiently able to deal with ordinary physical hazards in his wandering. On the other hand, the parapraxes associated with serious accidents discussed in Chapter 12, and nowadays of much importance in connection with industrial and road traffic accidents, are associated with brief disturbances of consciousness during which reality testing of physical hazards is grossly impaired.

Fugue and Enactment of Wish Fantasies: Somnambulism and Compulsion to Repeat

The example of the soldier wandering at a seaside resort (*Case* 10) also demonstrates the purposive character of the fugue reaction. The present is exchanged for the past and is met as though indeed it were the past. The patient sought to return to a time and place when and where gratification was maximal, and to escape from the frustrational current situation in his life. Janet's somnambulic Irene combined hallucinations, words and acts in a dramatic re-living of the traumatic situation which precipitated her illness. This too demonstrates the exchange of the present for a remembered situation, in this case in an effort to master it. Indeed, when these somnambulic episodes are not spontaneous they may be evoked in hypnotherapy for the purpose of helping the patient to abreact the strangulated affects and to bring the memories to associative correction by drawing them into the normative stream of consciousness. In fugue the dissociation is dynamically related to a wish fantasy, with adherent feelings of well-being assuming dominance of consciousness and replacing consciousness of frustration and feelings of ill-being; whereas in somnambulism the painful situation of stress is evoked again, in an effort to alter it and to master it. Here is a clear analogy with the wish-fulfilling (manifest) dreaming consciousness on the one hand and the distressing dreaming consciousness on the other. The latter, in the traumatic neuroses, often ends in anxiety. Freud (1933)[16] asks, 'What conative impulse could possibly be satisfied by this reinstatement of a most painful traumatic experience?' It seems an attempt at mastery is often accompanied by an effort to disown pain; in the repetitions of somnambulisms the implied cry for help is also an important motive.

It is notable too that in the hallucinosis of somnambulisms (as in other hysterical dissociative reactions), thoughts, as in dreams, may be transformed into images, in spite of a sensory current flowing without interruption in a forward direction, a condition which is not present in sleep. Freud (1900)[17] in *Regression*, Chapter VII, Section B, gives a good instance of this. One of his youngest hysterical patients, a 12-year-old boy, was prevented from falling asleep by 'green faces with red eyes' which terrified him. The source of this phenomenon was a repressed, though at one time conscious, memory of a boy whom he had seen four years earlier. This boy had presented him with an alarming picture of the consequence of bad habits in children, including masturbation, for his mother had pointed out at the time that the ill-behaved boy had a greenish face with red-rimmed eyes. The drive-cathected idea (of punishment for a forbidden wish) was connected with an actual perception (of the sickly looking boy) and then was later symbolized in the hallucinatory images in which the forgotten perception was embedded. This is usually the dominant mode of hallucinosis in hysterical dissociative reactions; whereas in schizophrenic disorders the hallucinations are much further removed from actual perceptual experience. In the somnambulism of Irene, as in the many cases of somnambulism in soldiers who return from stress in battle or from stress in prisoner-of-war camps, the hallucinosis largely consists in revisiting actual painful experiences.

The Evolution of Janet's Concept

As Hart has made clear, Janet's concept of dissociation was formulated to describe, and partly to explain, a limited class of phenomena predominantly encountered in hysteria and hypnosis. Hart (1926)[18] writes:

Janet observed in these conditions definite evidence that mental elements and processes could preserve an independent existence apart from the main stream of consciousness. He showed, for example, that the sensations arising from the anaesthetic limb of an hysterical patient had not been destroyed, but were merely cut off from the central consciousness. Their continued existence could not only be inferred from certain facts in the patient's behaviour, such as the remarkable freedom from accidental injury enjoyed by the anaesthetic limb, but directly demonstrated by procedures which enabled the dissociated stream of consciousness to be tapped, hypnosis and automatic writing for instance.

There are, however, limits to the usefulness of Janet's concept of dissociation. It is cast in a spatial metaphor which implies the separation *en masse* of a number of mental elements from the greater aggregation of elements which constitutes the totality of the mind, a splitting into independent pieces. But this picture cannot be reconciled with the observed facts. To begin with, the same material may form part of each of the dissociated portions. Each of two dissociated personalities, for example, may possess the same memories. Or, as in the case studied at the University of Virginia Hospital and described in Chapter 11, while one (Betty) had amnesia for the other's (Elizabeth's) periods of dominance, the other (Elizabeth) knew all that happened during control by Betty. Moreover, despite the marked characterological differences, the personalities 'Betty' and 'Elizabeth' were similar in areas not charged with anxiety. Obviously the dissociation has here produced a barrier which in some respects is traversable, and in other respects—sometimes one of direction—is untraversable. Hart maintains that some of the difficulties in the application of the concept of dissociation disappear if we abandon the atomistic and spatial terminology which Janet employed. Dissociation does not connote, in Hart's interpretation, a splitting of the mind into separate pieces, but connotes more or less independently acting functional units. Hart (1926) writes:

> Instead of regarding dissociation as the splitting of conscious material into separate masses, it must be regarded as an affair of gearing, the various elements of mental machinery being organized into different functional systems by the throwing in of the appropriate gear ... With this conception, the difficulty in understanding how the same material can belong to several personalities, or how there can be a non-reciprocal amnesia between the normal and hypnotic consciousness, is largely overcome.

Certainly, Hart explores the limits of the spatial metaphor that Janet employed. Freud also had recourse to spatial metaphor in his metapsychology generally. An example of this is in his structural view of the psychic apparatus, the latter itself being also a spatial metaphor. Before language developed metaphor, especially faded metaphor, to buttress logical thought, it could not render a situation by any other means than a demonstrative indication of it in immediate experience, as Wegener (1885)[19] elucidated in his *The Life of Speech*. However, there is the hazard of impoundage in reification. This hazard has sometimes not been avoided in object-relations theory, especially in Melanie Klein's papers and early Kleinian writings, with a consequent marring of conceptualization.

It is of interest in the historical evolution of scientific concepts of mental orientation that while Freud was investigating aphasia, Breuer (with whom, Freud later collaborated in joint studies of hysteria), was investigating the semi-circular canals of the inner ear. Together with other somatic reflexes, Breuer found that these canals, placed in the three planes of space, make an important contribution to the orientation of the organism in space. As is now well-known, reflexes set up by changes of the position of the head in space, in concert with the effects of the otoliths of the labyrinths and tonic muscular reflexes, enable the achievement of equilibrium. All of these reflex activities in infancy underlie an eventual increasing awareness of orientation in the world developed in childhood. The asymmetric laterality of the body and of its functions gradually becomes more marked and by two years of age, there is usually a clearly dominant right or left hand. Observation of the development of children's concepts of right and left shows the association of the building of these concepts with increasing awareness of a differential in sensation and skills between the two sides of the body. It comes about that in general the ordering of spatial orientation is to a large extent in right-sided people subserved by the right cerebral hemisphere, whereas there is, in such people, the dominance of the left cerebral hemisphere in relation to speech. Of course in health there is continuous interaction between the hemispheres and other parts of the brain. None the less, the more concrete basis of spatial orientation is safeguarded by the right hemisphere. The semantic movement from the concrete to the abstract requires interaction between the right and left hemispheres to produce metaphoric symbolism. Cerebral laterality sets the stage phylogenetically for the enhancement of the level of metaphoric symbolism so important for the achievement of more advanced word language. Our orientation in our lifespace and in the cosmos is more finely tuned through language. Fully-fledged word language depends heavily not only on metaphoric symbolism but also on processes of emendation, which especially require an orderly arrangement of the elements of speech in time. These considerations have been more amply addressed elsewhere (Abse, 1971[20]). Here it is pertinent to show the way Freud (1923)[21] sustained a spatial metaphor in his diagram of the differentiated mental apparatus.

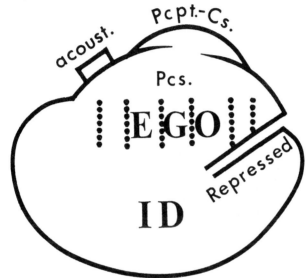

The differentiated mental apparatus as diagrammed by Freud. Pcpt.-Cs. = perceptual consciousness; Pcs. = preconscious; acoust. = special acoustic sensory perceptual supply to Pcs. (Reprinted by permission from *The Complete Psychological Works of Sigmund Freud* (ed. Strachey, J.), Vol. XIX, p. 24, © 1961, by Hogarth Press and the Institute of Psychoanalysis.)

Later, Freud (1933)[22] offered a second diagram to indicate the processes of the super-ego.

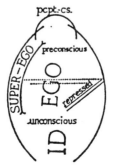

And Freud (1933)[22] warned as follows:

When you think of this dividing up of the personality into ego, super-ego and id, you must not imagine sharp dividing lines such as are artificially drawn in the field of political geography. We cannot do justice to the characteristics of the mind by means of linear contours.

Writing of dissociation in 1939, Henry V. Dicks (1939)[23] noted:

All we can say about it is that a hidden reservoir of mental function exists in various states of complexity in different people—comprising perhaps only one bodily process, or a whole side of the personality—which has been segregated by a more sudden and even more rigorous and effective force than repression from the main stream ... *At this level psychic tensions can discharge themselves direct* (hypobulically) into motor actions and can interpose barriers to the sensory representation of functions or systems and groups of functions among themselves or between them and that central experience—the ego. We may perhaps speak of *repression as a horizontal barrier* interposed between instinct impulse and its expression in egoic consciousness. *Dissociation might then be visualized as a vertical barrier*, or perhaps cleavage, sometimes within the repressed material itself ... [my italics].

In writing thus Dicks repeats in his own phraseology much that Janet had earlier expressed. Years later, Kohut (1971)[24] also discussed horizontal in contrast to vertical splits. In particular, he utilized the spatial metaphor to propound his theory of a normally separate agenda for the development of the self on the one hand and of object-relationships on the other.

Perhaps partly related to his need to emphasize the differences between his ideas and those of Janet, notably his need to develop the theory of the role of repression in the pathogenesis of hysterical symptoms, Freud for a long time overlooked vertical splits. He mentioned in 1924[25] the possibility of a cleavage or division of the ego as one means to avoid conflict, but it was not until 1927, in his paper on fetishism (1927),[26] that he explained that the fetishist consciously knows about female anatomy but, due to aroused castration anxiety, acts as if women had penises. In such cases there is a rift in the ego: disavowal on one track and acknowledgement on another. In the *Outline of Psychoanalysis*, Freud (1940)[27] further developed the concept of *the splitting of the ego*, stating that it applied not only in the psychoses, but 'to other states more like the neuroses and, finally, to the neuroses themselves'. Before writing the *Outline*, Freud had addressed himself to 'Splitting of the Ego in Defence' in an unfinished work (1940).[28] For the most part, insofar as Freud addressed the problem of splitting he dealt with high level splitting at the cognitive level. When this is marked, as in hysteriform borderline disorder, it betokens the vulnerability under stress to more primitive splitting at deeper regions of the ego. Volkan (1976)[29] writes:

The term splitting is applied in various ways; by qualifying it with the adjective 'primitive' I limit my reference to specific use. When memory traces of pleasurable— good—rewarding, and painful—bad—punishing experiences are organized and allo- cated to self–and object-representations, they provide 'all good' and 'all bad' self and object-representations. Primitive splitting is a defect in the integration of representa- tions of opposite quality; in the course of normal development the splitting no longer occurs and the representations coalesce; the split is mended. Primitive splitting can be used for defensive purposes, and, in fact, appears as the major defense of psychotic, borderline or narcissistic patients against primitive anxieties.

Volkan (1976)[29] described borderline patients' inclusion of the analyst in a cycle of introjective-projective relatedness. The representations of the analyst were saturated with several archaic object representations as the patient gradually established an 'analytic introject'. It was part of the analytic task to follow the changing nature of the projected fragments and their subsequent re-introjections. In the classification of character pathology, already discussed in Chapter 7, there is a continuum of a high level to a low level defensive repertoire: in the higher levels repressive defence predominates; whereas splitting is more prominent in hysteriform and narcissistic personality disorder.

Grotstein (1981)[30] has purveyed the notion that in its first hundred years psychoanalysis has had a history of developing the concepts of repression and displacement, whereas the future in the coming hundred years will lie in developing the concepts of splitting and of projective-identification. In this newer emphasis, as we have noted, psychoanalysis is assimilating the concepts generated by Janet, admittedly without anything but glancing acknowledgement. Moreover there were a few psychoanalysts who stressed the genetic importance of what is now the diffuse concept of 'projective-identification'. Thus Trigant Burrow (1918)[31] emphasized the pre-objective phase of individual development and 'the principle of primary identification', and Sandor Ferenczi (1909;[32] 1912,[33]) described both introjection as inclusion of objects in the ego and primitive forms of projection related to this, debating with Maeder his concept of exteriorization.

Dissociation, Identification, and the Body Image

Preyer (1882),[34] Bernfeld (1925)[35] and Schilder (1935)[36] have discussed the development of the body image: the psychic representation of the body, a core part of the mental ego. According to Preyer's observations the infant has in the beginning the same attitude towards the parts of his body as towards strange objects. He watches his arms and legs in motion just as he does a candle flame. The infant looks at his own grasping hand as attentively as at another person's moving fingers. He observes himself and touches himself in the bath, especially his feet (about the 39th week). He may bang his own head quite violently at the 41st week, and at about the 58th week he may bite his fingers, arms and toes, and then scream with pain. Early on he begins to press his hand on the table like a toy. This kind of intense observation of his own body diminishes in the second year. Preyer (1882) and Bernfeld (1925) draw the conclusion that a child has little knowledge of his body and has to learn to distinguish it from other objects by kinaesthetic, motor, and visceral data. Bernfeld (1925) states that it is a question of co-ordination of optic, tactile, and other sensations with motoric body experience. Preyer (1882) and Dix (1923)[37] have emphasized the importance of pain experience in this development, the latter reporting, however, that even in the tenth month the child's actions do not provoke the pain reaction expected by the adult. A

10-month-old child may bang his own head against a wall with little pain reaction and a bleeding skin wound may provoke little if any crying. At this age, however, pain reactions to disturbances in the internal organs, for example, colic, are much stronger. Preyer (1882) and Bernfeld (1925) also emphasize the importance of the obedience of the organ for creation of the body image. Schilder (1935) and Bernfeld (1925) agree that there is a nucleus of the body image from the beginning, and from the beginning some organs obey the needs of the body. This beginning nucleus represents especially the oral zone of the body. Schilder explains that, while we do not know in detail the development of the body image, we have reason to believe that there are inner factors given in the organism which determine this development, and that these maturational factors interact with individual experience.

In connection with the changing of the body image in the process of growing up and growing older, stages of this development, and decomposed elements of it, may sometimes be found projected and condensed with other symbolic references in mythological figures. The ancient Egyptians, for example, believed that every man has a *Ka* which is his exact counterpart or double, with the same features, gait and habitual raiment. Many of their monuments represent various kings confronting different divinities, while behind each king stands a little king. So exact is the resemblance of the manikin to the man, in other words, of the 'soul' to the body, that as there are fat bodies, thin bodies, long bodies, short bodies, so there are fat, thin, long and short corresponding souls. The *Ka* obviously bears a resemblance to the *homunculus*, the dwarf endowed with magic power, of later folk-lore. But the exact doubling in the *Ka* reveals less ambiguously, and less overlaid by other motifs, the central psychic representation of the body, the so-called 'body image'. On the other hand, there is a mental sense of vitality as part of ego experience, and this too was projectively reified in, to quote Frazer (1890),[38] an 'outward form of spirit'. The individual was believed to have a *Ba* which left the body at the moment of death. In the hieroglyphics this is often represented as a stork or as a bird with a bearded human head and a lamp, the latter referring to a very ancient belief that the *Ba* became a star. Whether it was the *Ba*, a symbol saturated with phallicism, which experienced the judgement of the dead and found happiness in the underworld in accordance with the laws of Osiris, or whether there was yet another entity, is not clear. The wandering soul was often referred to as the *Akh*, the radiant counterpart of the body as it was when alive. Lastly, the vital essence was sometimes referred to in the pyramid texts as the *Sekhem*.

This example from ancient Egypt illustrates the dissociation of the core body ego from the rest of the mental ego, with the remainders of the latter given varying emphasis, sometimes with body parts attached, to dramatize a continued sense of vitality. It seems that the Egyptians represented their orientation to the body predominately in terms of the *Ka*, and their orientation to the inner mental self in terms of the *Ba*, of the *Akh*, and of the *Sekhem*, which overlapped considerably. Since all spheres of human experience are mutually interactive their orientation to the world around them was pronouncedly coloured by their beliefs about themselves. As Marek (1949)[39] writes:

The pyramids of the Pharaohs—and only theirs, for persons of lesser degree contented themselves with mastabas, and the common man with a grave in the sand—were the fruits of a tremendously hypertrophied egocentrism, a point of view in which the interests of the community simply played no part ... the pyramids served the Pharaoh and none other; his dead body, his soul, and his *Ka*.

The megalomanic and narcissistic Pharaohs replicated and elaborated some of the ego experience of the first year of life when, as the observations of Preyer, Bernfeld and Schilder show, and as my own observations confirm, a considerable amount of attention is given to building up the representation of the body and separating this from the outer world.

As mentioned, Janet had shown, through hypnotic and automatic writing experiments, that the sensations arising from the anaesthetic limb of a patient had not been destroyed but were merely cut off from the central consciousness. In terms of Freud's more adequate theory these sensations were repressed along with other drive-cathected representations, and were no longer available for conscious and preconscious registration, and were thus dissociated (in a general sense) from the remainder of the body image. Sometimes there is a sudden integration of the body image, as the following example, one of several studied since World War II, illustrates:

Case 44. An ex-serviceman continued over several years to suffer a paralysed arm, anaesthetic to all tests periodically performed by medical examiners, after the healing of gunshot wounds. One day he was beginning to board an omnibus at a station in a city when the vehicle moved off suddenly; whereupon he jumped aboard with agility, grasping the rail with the hand of the paralysed member, much to his own astonishment. After this, sensation and movement came and went in his newly enlivened limb, so that he decided to seek medical attention again; following a few discussions, he recovered fully.

The important role of identification in the sociology of the body image is discussed by Schilder (1935).[36] He emphasizes that the postural model of the body is not static but in constant flux changing according to reactions to circumstances, a dramatic example of which is afforded by our brief description above. (*Case* 44). Usually, however, underlying all evident changes, there is a continuous process of construction, dissolution, and reconstruction of the body image. Processes of identification and dissociation are of considerable importance in bringing about such changes. In hysteria the mechanism of identification expresses the close relation of the patient to different postural models of different persons. Innumerable condensation of disturbed object relations may be expressed in a hysterical change in one organ of the body. As an example, Schilder draws attention to Freud's patient Dora. Dora developed a cough which was traceable to her observations of Mrs K.'s coughing attacks. Freud (1905)[40] showed that Dora unconsciously wished to put herself in Mrs K.'s position as the wife of Mr K., but felt guilty about her rivalry. She selected Mrs K.'s affliction as a point of identification, punishing herself for the forbidden Oedipal wish which also thus obtained expression. Her coughing attacks also expressed genital wishes to be infected and to take the place of her mother, who had vaginal catarrh.

As discussed in Chapter 4, pathological identifications account for the symptoms of hysteria often imitating those of prevalent organic disease, as well as accounting for certain forms of epidemic hysteria. As a simple example of the latter Freud (1921)[41] described a hysterical epidemic in a girls' school: one girl who received a love letter fainted, whereupon other girls fainted too. In this instance the motive for the identification was the girls' wishes for the same experience; they thus dramatized their forbidden wishes, accepting the punishment too. Anyone who offers some libido-economic advantage as a prototype at a time of heightened inner conflict and tension thus may be imitated.

Symptom observation may in itself also implicate dissociation, as in astasia–abasia or, again, as in the inability to speak the mother tongue accompanied by ability to speak a foreign language.

In short, it may be stated that pathological forms of identification and crass forms of dissociation figure prominently in somatic conversions as they do in 'psychic conversion' or so-called 'dissociative reaction'. In the *Diagnostic and Statistical Manual for Mental Disorders* (D.S.M. I) of the American Psychiatric Association (1952),[42] dissociative reaction is defined and discussed as follows:

> This reaction represents a type of gross personality disorganization, the basis of which is a neurotic disturbance, although the diffuse dissociation seen in some cases may occasionally appear psychotic. The personality disorganization may result in aimless running or 'freezing'. The repressed impulse giving rise to the anxiety may be discharged by, or deflected into, various symptomatic experiences, such as depersonalization, dissociated personality, stupor, fugue, amnesia, dream state, somnambulism, etc. The diagnosis will specify symptomatic manifestations.
>
> These reactions must be differentiated from schizoid personality, from schizophrenic reaction, and from analogous symptoms in some other types of neurotic reactions. Formerly, this reaction has been classified as a type of 'conversion hysteria'.

But, as we have seen, dissociation and identification processes figure prominently in the psychodynamics of somatic conversion reactions, just as they do in those reactions separated from them by the designation of 'dissociative reaction'. In the somatic conversion reactions the dissociation and identifications are concerned with the mental representation of the body, or the body image, and just as we have seen with multiple personality and other disorders of psychic identity, these dissociations and identifications are of a functional nature. Thus, to give a simple but instructive example, in astasia–abasia the patient cannot, as it were, find his legs and feet when the purpose is to stand and walk; otherwise he is able to feel his lower limbs as belonging to him. The point here is that if we use the term 'dissociative reaction' as indicated in the *Diagnostic Manual* mentioned above, then we must be careful to avoid the easy trap of semantic confusion: *What is distinctive in the so called 'dissociative reactions' is not dissociation as such but that this concerns the mental ego generally rather than being confined to that part of the mental ego we have discussed as the body image.*

Somatic conversions and psychic dissociation often occur together, though the emphasis in the symptom picture may be on one or the other. One, the somatic conversion, is predominantly concerned with autoplastic changes; the other issues more directly in alloplastic changes of behaviour. In those cases where somatic changes are accompanied by alterations of consciousness, and in those classified as Dissociative Disorders (as in D.S.M. III, 1980, of the American Psychiatric Association)[43] the personality is often of borderline type. These hysteriform borderline personality disorders differ from hysteria as we have seen (Chapter 7). They present at times transitions to psychotic disturbance, and, psychodynamically, the emphasis is in the direction of more pronouncedly pregenital character formations and more intensive masochism.

REFERENCES

1. Chastinet de Puységur, A. M. J. (1809). *Mémoires pour Servir à l'Histoire et à l'Établissement du Magnétisme Animal*, 2nd ed. Paris: Cellot.
2. Despine, A. (Père) (1840). *De l'Emploi du Magnétisme Animal et des Eaux Minérales dans le Traitement des Maladies Nerveuses suivi d'une Observation très Curieuse de Guérison de Névropathie*. Paris: Germer, Ballière.
3. Azam, E. E. (1887). *Hypnotisme, Double Conscience et Altération de la Personalité* (Préface de J. M. Charcot). Paris: Ballière.
4. James, W. (1890). *Principles of Psychology*, New York: Dover (1950).
5. Hodgson, R. (1891). A case of double consciousness. *Proc. Soc. Psychic. Res.* **7**, 221–55.
6. Flournoy, T. (1900). *From India to the Planet Mars: A Study of a Case of Somnambulism with Glossolalia*. New York and London: Harper.
7. Prince, M. (1906). *The Dissociation of a Personality*. New York and London: Longmans, Green.
8. Briquet, P. (1859). *Traité Clinique et Thérapeutique de l'Hystérie*. Paris: Baillière.
9. King, A. F. A. (1891). Hysteria. *Am. J. Obstet.* **24** (5), 513–32.
10. Benedikt, M. (1864). Beobachtung über Hysterie. *Zeitsch. Heilkunde.*
11. Benedikt, M. (1868). *Electrotherapie*, pp. 413–45. Vienna: Tendler.
12. Benedikt, M. (1894). Second life. Das Seelenbinnenleben des gesunden und kranken Menschen. *Wein. Klinik* **20**, 127–38.
13. Rank, O. (1919). *The Double: A Psychoanalytic Study* (trans. and ed., with an introduction by Harry Tucker, Jun.). Chapel Hill, N.C.: Univ. North Carolina Press (1971).
14. Janet, P. (1907). *The Major Symptoms of Hysteria*. New York: Macmillan.
15. Hart, B. (1912). *The Psychology of Insanity*. Cambridge: Cambridge Univ. Press (1957).
16. Freud, S. (1933). Revision of the Theory of Dreams. *New Introductory Lectures on Psycho-analysis*. In: *The Standard Edition*, Vol. XXII. London: Hogarth Press (1964).
17. Freud, S. (1900). *The Interpretation of Dreams*. In: *The Standard Edition*, Vols. IV and V. London: Hogarth Press (1953).
18. Hart, B. (1926). The conception of dissociation. *Br. J. Med. Psychol.* **6**, 241. (Reprinted 1962 in Vol. **35**, 15.)
19. Wegener, P. (1885). *The Life of Speech* (trans. Abse, D. W.). In: *Speech and Reason* (ed. Abse, D. W.). Charlottesville, Va: Univ. Press of Virginia; Bristol: Wright (1971).
20. Abse, D. W. (1971). *Language Disorder in Mental Disease*. In: *Speech and Reason* (ed. Abse, D. W.). Charlottesville, Va: Univ. Press of Virginia; Bristol: Wright.
21. Freud, S. (1923). *The Ego and the Id*. In: *The Complete Psychological Works of*

Sigmund Freud (ed. Strachey, J. in collaboration with Anna Freud), Vol. 19. London: Hogarth Press (1961).
22. Freud, S. (1933). The Dissection of the Psychical Personality. *New Introductory Lectures on Psycho-analysis*, Lecture 31. In: *The Standard Edition*, Vol. XXII. London: Hogarth Press (1964).
23. Dicks, H. V. (1939). *Clinical Studies in Psychopathology*, p. 99. London:Arnold.
24. Kohut, H. (1971). *Analysis of the Self*. New York: Int. Univ. Press.
25. Freud, S. (1927). Neurosis and Psychosis. In: *The Standard Edition*, Vol. XIX. London: Hogarth Press (1964).
26. Freud, S. (1927). Fetishism. In: *The Standard Edition*, Vol. XXI. London: Hogarth Press (1964).
27. Freud, S. (1940). Outline of Psycho-analysis. In: *The Standard Edition*, Vol. XXIII. London: Hogarth Press (1964).
28. Freud, S. (1940). Splitting of the Ego in the Process of Defence. In: *The Standard Edition*, Vol. XXIII. London: Hogarth Press (1964).
29. Volkan, V. D. (1976). *Primitive Internalized Object Relations*, p. 120. New York: Int. Univ. Press.
30. Grotstein, J. S. (1981). *Splitting and Projective Identification*. New York: Aronson.
31. Burrow, T. (1981). *Preconscious Foundations of Human Experience* (ed. Galt, W.). New York: Basic Books (1964).
32. Ferenczi, S. (1909). Introjection and transference. In: *Contributions to Psycho-analysis* (trans. Jones, E.). Boston: Badger (1916).
33. Ferenczi, S. (1912). On the definition of introjection. In: *Final Contributions to the Problems and Methods of Psycho-analysis* (ed. Balint, M.; trans. Mosbacher, E.). New York: Basic Books (1955).
34. Preyer, T. W. (1882). *Die Seele des Kindes*. Leipzig: Voss.
35. Bernfeld, S. (1925). *The Psychology of the Infant*. London: Kegan Paul (1929).
36. Schilder, P. (1935). *The Image and Appearance of the Human Body*. New York: Int. Univ. Press (1950).
37. Dix, K. W. (1923). *Körperliche und Geistige Entwicklung eines Kindes*. Leipzig: Wunderlich.
38. Frazer, J. (1890). *The New Golden Bough*. New York: Criterion Books (1959).
39. Marek, K. W. (1949). *Gods, Graves, and Scholars*. New York: Knopf (1956).
40. Freud, S. (1905). Fragment of an Analysis of a Case of Hysteria. In: *The Standard Edition*, Vol. VII. London: Hogarth Press (1955).
41. Freud, S. (1921). *Group Psychology and the Analysis of the Ego*. In: *The Standard Edition*, Vol. XVIII. London: Hogarth Press (1955).
42. D.S.M. I (1952). *Diagnostic and Statistical Manual of Mental Disorders*, 1st ed. Washington, D.C.: Am. Psychiat. Assoc.
43. D.S.M. III (1980). *Diagnostic and Statistical Manual of Mental Disorders*, 3rd ed. Washington, D.C.: Am. Psychiat. Assoc.

CHAPTER 14

Dissociation and Communication

Molar and Molecular Dissociation

Both Kraepelin (1913)[1] and Bleuler (1911)[2] endeavoured to distinguish between the fragmentation or molecular dissociation of schizophrenia and block, or molar, dissociation characteristic of hysterical conditions. As noted in Chapter 7, molar splitting in 'Dissociative Disorders' (as designated in D.S.M. III) frequently occurs in hysteriform borderline personality disorder. Noble (1951)[3] emphasized that there were often hysterical manifestations in schizophrenic disease, so that both forms of dissociation noted by Kraepelin and Bleuler can occur together phenomenologically. In previous chapters, it has been shown that molar dissociation is indicative of the presence of severe mental conflict and has the significance of a defensive reaction to incompatible forces within the psyche independently seeking expression on what would otherwise be a collision course. In order to understand the nature of dissociative phenomena from a structural as well as from a dynamic viewpoint it is necessary to explore more fully the meaning of dissociation in terms of ego disorder.

In *A Psychoanalytic Approach to the Classification of Mental Disorder*, Edward Glover (1932)[4] offers theoretical constructions which are germane. Glover maintains that any psychic system, which (*a*) represents a positive libidinal relation to objects or part-objects, (*b*) can discharge reactive tension, i.e., aggression and hate, against objects, (*c*) can in one or other of these ways reduce anxiety, may be termed an 'ego-nucleus'. Thus an oral ego nucleus, which includes representation of the oral body zone, as discussed in Chapter 13, gratifies instinct on a part-object (mother's nipple); can exert aggression against the nipple (sucking, pulling, biting); and is in these ways tension-reducing in effect. As it evolves the primitive ego is polynuclear in the sense of being a series of relatively independent organizations. These become more coherent and integrated as the anal-sadistic level of libido organization is reached. Oral elements dominate the first primitive nucleus during the phase of oral primacy, but this nucleus also represents other erotogenic zones in increasingly active function—cutaneous, respiratory, alimentary, excretory, and muscular—as well as the muscular reactive systems which discharge aggressions. This oral nucleus is thus itself a cluster formation of ego nuclei. As the anal phase of development evolves, further ego nuclei which show an increasing degree of organization represent the anal body zone and related drives. The first cluster and immediately succeeding nuclei locate the fixation points of the psychoses, whereas the last-organized nuclei, including the anal-sadistic and phallic representatives, locate the fixation points of the obsessive-compulsive and hysterical neuroses. Multiple fixation points in the oral-anal boundary as well as at the phallic phase, to which regression takes place in the face of later frustration, determine the emergence of borderline states and dissociative reactions.

This brief account may suffice to clarify Glover's suggestion that, besides the usual descriptive clinical standard, a standard based on the historical modifications of ego structure needs also to be taken into account in the classification of mental disorder. This developmental standard is closely related to the qualitative 'reality-sense' clinical criterion discussed in Chapter 6. Diagnostic evaluation may be based on these three sorts of criteria: the descriptive, the developmental, and that of reality testing. It also usefully includes study of the repertoire of ego defences exhibited. These observations and inferences then operate as a system of checks, one upon another.

Glover (1932)[4] states that the 'decomposition products' of schizophrenia require careful study; in the case of primitive ego nuclei the object is invariably a 'part-object', and in schizophrenic regression it becomes so once more. Elsewhere I have discussed these considerations (Abse, 1955[5]), including observation of a case of schizophrenia at the Dorothea Dix State Hospital at Raleigh, North Carolina. Here is an account of a psychiatric interview with a patient suffering from paranoid schizophrenic disorder, selected because of the especial clarity of the manifest 'decomposition products':

Case 45. A 33-year-old divorced woman, diagnosed as a case of paranoid schizophrenia, was interviewed in the hospital. The patient appeared pale and undernourished. Her facial expression was blank (poker-faced), and she spoke in a monotonous voice without adequate affective expression. She was disorientated as to time and person but not as to place. She stated that she felt that her soul was trying to hold her body together with difficulty. But there were many souls, some of which she feared were escaping her. In the event of this happening she felt that she would break into pieces. Some of these souls were against her whereas some were nice and struggled against the others. Her body, she felt, had been severely punished without reason and one soul was murdered in this business. She spoke then of a 'Theresa' who tried to get inside her, and with her eyes to teach her body to put the mouth to the vagina or to the rectum. At one time Theresa was taken out, but she had remained a nuisance, sometimes getting back in. One time her rectum was lanced to get her out. At this time the patient interrupted her conversation to talk to a soul which she instructed to keep her rectum free from saliva and to hold her together from right to left. The patient went on to discuss disconnectedly her feeling that she had left parts of herself all along the way from New York to California. She spoke again, more connectedly, about her mother-in-law who, she thought, was responsible for sexual perversions and for killing the President of the USA. She described her mother-in-law as a 'sexual maniac', saying that she kept trying to put her vagina into the mouth of one of her souls (at this point slapping her right buttock, as if to locate the soul involved). Further conversation with this patient led to her talking about her father. She stated that her father's first body was attempting to put its penis into one soul's mouth, and this was terrible. She then related her difficulty with her saliva, stating that she felt that her mouth and rectum should be dry, and that she had to spit all her saliva out. She continued that her mother-in-law had killed the President, and when amplification of this detail was requested, explained that she had killed Franklin D. Roosevelt by cutting his main artery. She further explained that her mother-in-law killed all Presidents who are not elected and that she had informed the doctors how to put the artery back together. On request, the patient gave her married name but stated that her present self or body was different, again giving her single name at the end of interview.

This interview material represents the content of the patient's remarks to a very large extent; whereas only a hint is afforded of the more formal elements involved in her efforts at communication. In fact, the patient exhibited very considerable difficulty with abstract thinking, neologisms were frequent, blocking was evident from time to time, and her attention could not be focused for the purpose of history-taking. Any attempt at anamnesis resulted in apparently irrelevant replies, and tangentially she would discuss the ideas outlined above; she was then encouraged to do this.

It is with these ideas that we may concern ourselves for the purpose of this discussion. At once it is obvious that the patient is communicating her perception of a disintegrating personality process. This is not unusual in schizophrenic psychosis, but it is often overlaid and obscured by other events. In this particular case this aspect is unusually clearly demonstrable.

One may state briefly that the clinical features in a case of schizophrenia are referable to two categories of events: one of these is due to the regressive process and the other to restitutional efforts (Freud, 1915[6]; Jung, 1906[7]). Thus in dementia praecox simplex the patient presents a clinical picture of quiet disintegration for the most part; whereas the reactive efforts at restitution are much more to the forefront in paranoid schizophrenia. It is, of course, a matter of emphasis as far as the clinical picture is ultimately concerned, because the regressive process and reactive attempts at reclaiming reality relation are contemporaneously present; at one or another moment one or the other may be more in evidence. In addition to this entanglement of categories of events, various results ensue, more or less contemporaneously, from the regressive process and from the restitutional process respectively. Thus, events resulting from the regressive process alone may evince themselves at various levels simultaneously or consecutively during a short time. So the clinical picture is both confused and confusing. This state of affairs may in itself lend support to clinical diagnosis, but from the interpretive viewpoint it may well be all the more difficult to understand what is going on. In this particular case, however, the patient's attempts at restitution are very largely devoted to formulating what is going on regressively within. She is attempting to gain control by thinking over her experience with herself, an attempt at mastery which happens to be allied with our own efforts to understand. It is occasionally the case that the regressive process is thus reflected almost directly in conscious formulations which are communicated, albeit in 'schizophrenic language', and that this reflected ego feeling is the main focus of the patient's preoccupation, comparatively unobscured by other events. A case such as this one thus offers a very opportune instance of more than usually direct reporting from the patient of her experience associated with personality disintegration.

To repeat, it would seem at once obvious that the patient is communicating her inner perception of a disintegrating personality process. She remarks:

1. That her soul is trying to hold her body together with difficulty.
2. That in the event of some souls escaping she will break into pieces.
3. That she feels that she has left parts of herself all the way from New York to California.
4. That she has informed the doctors (i.e., she knows) how to put the artery back together.

These remarks express her experience of threatened and actual disintegration as well as attempts to resist the process. Destructive impulses are partly projected upon her mother-in-law, and then, as reported in the last remark (4), she obtains delusional satisfaction that she knows better than the doctors how to bring about repair.

Her delusions also express her experience of an internal drama of struggling souls. Some of these she describes as 'nice', and these struggle against the others. It is evident that some of these dissociated partial personality systems belong to approved levels of ego functioning and some to disapproved levels. But how approved and disapproved? The patient supplies part of the answer, for she states that some of them are against *her*; and *she* makes the judgement value of 'nice' about others. Psychoanalytic theory has identified the super-ego with an inwardly directed scrutinizing function (Freud, 1933[8]), and in this patient it is clear that ego feeling has become largely invested in the super-ego as part of the total defensive operation. The patient strives to identify herself with the super-ego fraction of her total personality, and to a very large extent, one might say to a pathological extent, she succeeds. It is this achievement which enables us to share her scrutiny of what goes on within, for in her own way she formulates and communicates this scrutiny.

One disapproved soul particularly bothers the patient. This she calls 'Theresa', someone who had tried to lead her into temptation—anatomically transgressive sexual pleasures. Evidently this temptation is recurrent, for Theresa sometimes succeeds in getting into her again following expulsion. Theresa represents oral–anal homo-erotic strivings, and it is these urges, reawakened in the process of regression, against which the patient vigorously defends herself. In the first place it is a strenuous attempt to identify herself completely with her super-ego and thus to dissociate from herself those psychic systems which represent forbidden libidinal urges. Of course, the total defence is more complex than this, and this dissociation of ego nuclei is obscured by processes of introjection and projection (Foulkes, 1937[9]; Knight, 1940[10]). However, it is not sufficiently obscured in this case, so that we cannot discern the sequestration of unmanageably charged ego nuclei. The more general implications of the patient's remarks point up clearly her perception of loss of synthesis in ego functioning.

The specifically paranoid aspect of the illness is represented in her accusations against her mother-in-law, for example, that she is a sexual maniac. In this way a disowning projection of forbidden urges upon a woman with whom she is in relation is typically accomplished (Ferenczi, 1912[11]). Other remarks indicate a forbidden oral father-penis-incorporation wish and a defence in spitting out. Oral wishes and fantasies, originally perhaps connected with her sucking and biting experiences at the nipple, show up in the operation of the primitive oral ego nucleus; and the defence in spitting out, coeval with this early phase of ego structure (Freud, 1915[6]), is the anlage of the later-formed paranoid defence.

For the purpose of this discussion it is sufficient to point out that Glover's conceptual model corresponds with the verbal reportings and the implications thereof of certain patients suffering from schizophrenic psychosis. In a disconnected way such patients work over ideational derivatives from the operation of disintegrate primitive ego nuclei established at oral–anal, auto-erotic and homosexual phases, as well as reporting on the total experience of the disintegrating process (Scott, 1951[12]; Palombo and Bruch, 1964[13]; Volkan, 1964[14]).

In severe schizophrenic disorganization not only is there evidence of the operation of relatively independent and disintegrated ego nuclei in a way which betokens a kind of 'comminuted fracture' of the ego into multiple small fragments, but dissociation is evident in many other respects. In Chapter 8 we discussed the contribution of dissociation to thought disorder and to certain forms of affective disorderliness; notably, the usual congruity of ideation with affect, and of affect with drive, is sundered as part of the generalized dominance of the primary process.

In obsessional neurosis this kind of dissociation is shown differently: certain ideas become supervalent, substitutes for others which are heavily drive-cathected and affect-laden, and unwelcome to the personality as a whole; these ideas are isolated from the affect appropriate to the operative anal-sadistic drive. Thus Freud described the case of a lady who had an overwhelming need to examine meticulously the number of every banknote which came into her possession. The sight of the banknote aroused a compulsive need to know the number, a compulsive development of thought and action which the patient was quite unable to control, much to her distress. Here too is a system of ideas separate from and relatively independent of the main body of consciousness, indeed of the major dominant ego nucleus, though the personality is aware of the existence of a dissociated system. But the dissociation especially takes the form of isolation of affect connected with underlying drives, and only pain is reactively experienced. In obsessional disorder the personality is aware of the existence of a dissociated system, aware of the ideas as foreign intruders, but is unaware of the more significant meanings. As such patients often say: 'The idea forces itself into my mind', or: 'I feel compelled to repeat this silly action'. In such instances both molar and more molecular forms of dissociation are evident.

We have noted the molar type of dissociation which occurs in such dissociative reactions as multiple personality and a variety of hypnoid states. In these latter, evidence of altered consciousness is often phenomenologically stark, but different from those alterations characteristic of fundamental symptoms of schizophrenia inasmuch as consciousness is occupied by a *homogeneous* constellation of ideas and emotions. Though alien to, and dissociated from, the usual character of the personality, the ideas and emotions show in themselves a consistent organization. The ideation may be vague and restricted and consciousness suffused with strong emotion; or ideation may be very restricted but plastic and especially clear within a narrow focus. At the same time temporal and spatial orientation and the consciousness of self may be deleted or diminished, as discussed in Chapter 10.

Ecstatic Religion and Glossolalia

Apart from fugue states, severe amnesias, depersonalization syndromes, alternating personalities, or common somnambulisms, altered states of consciousness amounting to hypnoid disturbance may be heavily though transiently involved in aesthetic peak experiences and in states of creativity, as we have already described (Chapter 10).

They are also involved in certain religious experiences which, from a clinical point of view, resemble more closely, and sometimes become identical with, pathological hysteriform conditions. This association is clinically cogent if only because such experiences are often elicited in the history of individuals who apply for psychiatric treatment on account of disabling somatic or mental symptoms. We are therefore bound to notice these molar dissociations as much for their pathological import as for their intrinsic interest. These dissociative reactions are for the most part transient, though sometimes the issue is in a conversion reaction or psychotic disturbance. Paradoxically, sometimes a conversion reaction abates following a hypnoid state induced through group religious excitement.

In well-integrated societies ostentatious ceremonies accompany and mark an individual's life crises. There is organized community support and participation in the crucial events of his life cycle, including notably the losses he suffers of his relatives and of outstandingly important figures in his society. Van Gennep (1909)[15] focused on the *rites de passage*. He distinguished and examined in terms of their order and content three major phases in the activities associated with such ceremonies: *Séparation* (separation), *Marge* (transition) and *Aggrégation* (incorporation). Rites of separation are prominent in funeral ceremonies, rites of incorporation at marriages, whereas transition rites predominate in pregnancy, betrothal and initiation. However, all three elements are present in every set of ceremonies though not equally developed, and they all may be reduced to a minimum as in remarriage or adoption. Van Gennep (1909)[15] also applied this analysis to the ceremonies associated with changes of the seasons. New Year ceremonies include rites of expulsion of winter and incorporation of spring: the one dies and the other is reborn. At such ceremonies there is generally a focus and a measured emotional flow exhibited by the participants, though there are times of intensification of passion with more decisive alterations of consciousness and rhythmic movements. Chapple and Coon (1942)[16] distinguish between those ceremonies associated with the seasonal changes and other regular occurrences and those related to the crises in the individual's life cycle which, for him, do not recur.

Ritual in such crises is a response to an intensified emotional problem which it symbolizes and for which it attempts an amelioration, which is of benefit both to the affected individual and to the community: it helps to ensure continued group cohesion and adaptation as well as affording relief of anxiety and depression in the individual. Sometimes the emphasis is upon an individual's definitive disease, especially one which may become disruptive for the group if not treated in a healing rite.

A vivid example of this is afforded by Harris (1957)[17] in her description of *Saka*, a 'possession hysteria' of women in an East African tribe. Following strong indications of hysteroid dysphoria a woman becomes convulsive with jactitations of the shoulders and rhythmic movements of the head from side to side. In an altered state of consciousness, the woman then performs repetitive acts, sometimes seizing others' goods. The illness is described as 'wanting and wanting', and in fact follows her wanting something, something belonging to her husband, or something that the husband has refused to buy for her, for example, sugar. The healing is accomplished in a group ceremony when the spirit who possesses the woman is appeased by being given various objects she has craved, usually items associated with men's activites. During the ritual, she wears male garb and carries a walking stick. The husband provides cigarettes and bananas and manufactured cloth in the appeasement ceremony during which there is drum beating and frenzied dancing.

It is significant that in this culture women's rights are sharply limited. Men have access to work, and have cash to spend in the village. As for the mainstays of tribal life, land and cattle, these are inherited by the men. The primitive phallic symbolism in the ceremonial ritual facilitates release of strangulated affects of anger, envy and jealousy, and the fantasy enacted is one of turning the tables on the privileged men.

Around the world, the most commonly oppressed group is women, and ecstatic phenomena are more likely to be found in cultures where there is a rigid division between the sexes and in which men are clearly quite dominant, as in the East African tribe of the previous example. Bennett Simon (1979)[18] writes:

While such a formulation [oblique defiance of customarily enforced submission and obedience] hardly constitutes an exhaustive explanation of these phenomena, it is an important component. These group rites can involve men as well, particularly groups of men within the culture who are in marginal and subservient positions. There is no doubt but that these experiences not only provide a release but that they accord importance and dignity to otherwise disenfranchised groups. In the ritual these oppressed groups seem to obtain (symbolically, or in more literal form) something of what the dominant group possesses. Thus the women in the *Bacchae* take on male functions and male powers, especially as warriors. They leave their looms and their children, taking up arms and defeating men in the field of combat. They carry the thyrsus, which symbolizes the disembodied phallus.

Such are the folk customs which allow periodic temporary switch from masochistic victim to identification with the aggressor, in controlled rites. I. M. Lewis (1971)[19] has emphasized a similarity between these marginal or peripheral cults and the central possession religions. In these too, he holds, the circumstances which encourage the ecstatic response in religious ceremonies are precisely those where men feel themselves constantly threatened by exacting pressures which they do not know how to combat or control, 'except through those heroic flights of ecstasy by which they seek to demonstrate that they are the equal of the gods'.

Within Western culture, *glossolalia* is currently of special interest since it has become a frequent manifestation of a dissociative reaction, one which has moved from the extreme fundamentalist Christian sects to the more mainstream and traditional churches. Sometimes, as with other similar dissociative phenomena, the ecstatic glossolalic response is aided and abetted by group interaction which includes ingestion of hallucinogenic mushrooms, or, in more sophisticated cults, such synthetic drugs as *d*-lysergic acid diethylamide.

About a quarter of a century ago, speaking in tongues, previously confined to a few extremely conservative religious sects, began to appear in mainline Protestant churches. With the increase within Episcopal, Lutheran and

Presbyterian congregations, it lost some of its more intensely ecstatic character, and became a quieter way of relaxation and communion. In many of these churches, there is a feeling that the gift of receiving the Holy Spirit manifest in glossolalia is incomplete without someone who can interpret the tongues. John P. Kildahl (1972)[20] notes that there is a belief that there is a relationship between speaking in tongues and other charismatic gifts, including interpretation, prophecy and healing. All these are held to be gifts of God utilizable for special purposes; but it is also recognized that there can be abuses. Not all glossolalia appears to be directed by the Holy Spirit, but can be allied to false prophecy and be a snare of the devil. Such contrasting attitudes have a lengthy history.

Early Egyptian writings recount the occurrence of ecstatic utterances in religious ceremonies, and ecstatic crises of verbigeration were sometimes part of the mystery religions of Ancient Greece. Occasionally they are mentioned in the Old Testament. The best known example in our Western culture is, however, the Pentecostal experience recorded in the Acts of the Apostles. The disciples 'were filled with the Holy Ghost and began to speak with other tongues as the Spirit gave them utterance'. The observation of their happy excitement and strange loquacity led some in the crowd to decide that 'these men are full of new wine'. But Peter told them: 'These are not drunk as you suppose, seeing it is but the third hour of the day.' Saint Paul claimed to speak in tongues 'more than you all', and indeed began speaking sometimes in sounds which were not in any known language at all. This 'lalling' Paul praised as a way to edify the spirit of the speaker in private prayer, or as a sign to impress the unbelievers, and he permitted the use of the 'tongues' in church if it were followed by interpretation. Yet Paul worried about its abuse and later, in the second century, the Church decided that possession by the Holy Spirit in this extraordinary way was no longer permissible. When the phenomenon of the tongues occasionally cropped up in later centuries it was considered either of demoniacal origin, a devilish counterfeit of the gift of the Holy Ghost, or a symptom of insanity. But this attitude did not everywhere prevail, and in the nineteenth century, as again more recently, many sects revived the early Christian practice.

According to Cutten (1927),[21] who described fundamentalist church meetings in Chicago at the beginning of this century:

> The meetings began with singing, praying and testimonies, increasing gradually in loudness and excitement until motor automatisms appeared in the form of jerking of the body, loud shouting, high jumping, and then speaking with tongues ... sometimes sensory automatisms in the form of visions and hallucinations of hearing. Not infrequently some member of the congregation fell to the floor unconscious, and if one form of physical manifestation appeared in a meeting ... it was spread through the well-known phenomenon of psychic contagion.

Many fundamentalist sects, including the Ranters and the Shakers, have continued to manifest the verbigerations and motor disturbances in rural areas throughout the Christian world, and recently these practices have been revived in more traditional churches in California.

Kildahl (1972)[20] provides an excellent illustration from his records of how the ability to speak in tongues typically begins.

Following an ordinary evening church service, interested members of the congregation were invited to stay on to discuss the gift of tongues. One of a dozen who did, Bill Jones, remembered praying: 'Lord, fill me with your spirit. Use me to do your will. Open my life to your leading.' The preacher began to pray in tongues and Bill later reported: 'I felt, as I listened to him praying in tongues, as if there were an electrifying charge in the air.' The leader asked him to make an effort to move his lips in a free and relaxed manner and he said to Bill: 'Say after me what I say, and then go on speaking in the tongue the Lord will give you: AISH NAY GUM NAY TAYO ...' prayed the preacher and Bill tried to repeat the same sounds and go on with his own: AISH NAY GUM NAY ... ANNA GAYNA ... AYNA GANNA KEENA ... KAYNA GEENA ANNA NAYNANNA ...' Bill had begun to speak in tongues.

Audition of the glossolalic, from a developmental perspective, reveals that the subject reverts to the actual pre-stages of word language, babbling and lalling; and conversation with him later often shows that he felt suffused with omnipotence and was speaking effectively in many languages, including Hebrew and Greek, despite the evident babyish performance.

Pre-Stages of Language

The pre-stages of language are embedded in the general development of childhood, in both libidinal and aggressive development and in the associated early building of the image of the body which becomes invested with 'ego feeling', that gradually achieved personal feeling of unity and continuity, of contiguity with others, and of causality.

In 1905 Freud[22] described the progressive shifts in body zones most responsive to and most actively interacting with the environment and outlined oral, anal and phallic phases of development. These observations were later (1913) incorporated in the concept of successive but overlapping libidinal organizations in each of which different drives dominate. As René A. Spitz (1946)[23] has emphasized, libidinal development paves the way for all developments, and this certainly includes that of speech. The oral-cannibalistic phase dominated by the drive to incorporate is followed by the sadistic-anal phase in which the child's strivings to master his body, and all obstacles encountered, are paramount.

Peller (1964)[24] writes:

In the first phase mouth and skin are most highly libidinized; in the second phase skeletal muscles and the ring muscles of the body openings (mouth, anus, urethra) are the executive organs. Each phase can be characterised by the changes which occur between its start and its end. At the beginning of life, the infant cannot differentiate which sensations come to him from the outside and which from the inside of his body; he only knows his comfort and discomfort. Toward the end of the oral phase, he can remember the agent related most often to the relief of tension and to positive pleasure; he has an image of his own self ... He comes to perceive whatever has the greatest impact on his search for comfort-augmenting or reducing the pleasure. Through the highly libidinized incessant and tremendously repetitive motor and sensory activites of the sadistic-anal phase, the child comes to develop further the images of his body self and of his body functions. His activity creates for him the world of things contained in three dimensional space, and it is during this period that he forms attachments to his family ... In the third organization, the Oedipal-phallic phase, the child's component drives and his cognitive achievements are focussed in such a way that he can conceive of his parents as persons.

Throughout these developments, as Peller (1964)[24] points out, the infant seems to experience and exhibit differing forms of megalomania, of feelings and ideas of vast power and importance, only subsequently considerably indented by the exigencies of living with reduced maternal protection. It is necessary in this connection to grasp the profound importance of unconscious identification upon which imitation is based. All is not so simple as the phrase 'an instinct of imitation' might lead one to think: identification is achieved by the child on account of a need to survive and to master, to take into himself the powers of the protecting parents in order to combat the feelings of helplessness which give rise to anxiety at the time that ego differentiation is taking place in the anal phase. At this time, about 18 months of age, the child learns to utter words like those uttered around him. Soon, from 24 to 30 months, there is a veritable 'naming explosion', so that from a few words at about 18 months and a few more until about 2 years, he comes to acquire a vocabulary of about a thousand words and understands about twice as many uttered around him.

Peller (1964)[24] enumerates some important developments which precede language, the intensity of which are species-specific:

1. A prolonged helplessness which fosters strong attachment to the mother.
2. The early interest in and understanding of facial expressions.
3. The intense pleasure derived from the functioning of the vocal apparatus.
4. Extensive playful activity which brings about contact and motor interaction with the human and nonhuman environment. [In this connection Peller rightly emphasizes the pleasure derived from responding to self-created stimuli.]
5. The great reliance which comes to be placed on the distance receptors of sight and hearing.
6. The readiness to become aware of similarities between himself and others which, itself gradually built-up, then prepares the ground for the ability to put the self into the place of the other, and even to see oneself from a distance.

All these widely different developmental features of the human infant precede language, and some in turn through language are themselves greatly enhanced. Throughout childhood development there is this dynamic circular process which consists of feedback and feed-forward processes in a network. Thus the vocabulary explosion noted above is as much the result of the newly arising activities of the infant as of the maturation of cerebral mechanisms. Prior to this, there is one type of play where the feedback character is obvious, namely, babbling and lalling. At about six months the vowel-like cooing (which has become interspersed with occasional consonantal sounds) gives place to babbling and to lalling which more clearly resemble single syllables. The deaf child soon gives up this babbling—presumably because there is insufficient feedback, no accompanying enjoyment engendered by hearing his own voice or any other. Normally this babbling and lalling play goes on for hours of every day during many months. As the Sterns (1907)[25] pointed out, it may continue even in the dark. Peller (1964)[24] writes:

Indispensable as this self-stimulation is, it is not enough. The infant must listen to other humans speaking—or the formative period for speech will come and go and language will not develop ... Incidental observations indicate that the child listens intently to his mother's voice and that it is this listening which enhances his babbling.

The mother's talking and the child's listening display but one facet of their mutually nurturing bond, a bond which when impaired results in the child's failure to thrive in many aspects of growth and development. It is certainly of profound significance that we speak of our 'mother tongue', the language that eventually evolves from our cries when in need and our coos when satisfied. The coos emerge later than the cries, at about the sixth to the eighth week of extra-uterine life, often following the smiling response.

The babbling and lalling which occur in the second half of the first year of life are often replaced by a periodic 'blathering'—the recurrent protrusion and withdrawal of the flattened relaxed tongue through the lips while phonating. Blathering is also occasionally evident in the second year of life. This oral libidinal activity provides the pleasurable foundation for free tongue and lip movement, that is to say, the self-pleasing early functioning of the tongue, including blathering, becomes a means also of imitating sounds heard and later embedded in verbal communication.

W. Clifford M. Scott (1955)[26] has given a brief account of a blathering episode in the setting of an early maternal transference situation engendered during the treatment of a 35-year-old woman.

The tongue has been 'overlooked', as Bonnard (1960)[27] insists, in its role as a primal organizer of the self in the early oral phase of libidinal development. The tongue is a means of finding and scanning the outside, and by its movements and sensations the baby begins to discriminate between the inside and outside surfaces of the mouth. It achieves, indeed, a high degree of precision and versatility of movement ahead of any other part of the body. Moreover, the tongue always returns to its fixed, midline base, presumably aiding early orientation. Bonnard (1960)[27] states:

> If we watch young children attempting a troublesome balancing or integrative task, including learning to write, we can often observe the tongue protruded to serve like the offsetting combination of the rudder and the centre board of the boat, i.e. as the body's centering point.

Corresponding with its vast importance in the early orientation of the self in the world, the area of representation of the tongue in the human cerebral cortex is very large compared with that of other parts of the body. It is probable that the overlooking of the primal importance of the tongue in the early development of the baby is due to its later major role in speech. However, this overshadowing function, this harnessing to the requirements of speech, is prepared for in its earlier orientating functions; phylogenetically this speech function follows the adoption of the erect posture.

Early on the tongue is an important sensory bridge from inside the self to the outside and to the initial experience of external objects. Similarly the movement from self-pleasuring auto-eroticism to knowing and loving other people and the world we inhabit together is promoted by the acquisition of the mother tongue. From his cries meant to restore pleasure and remove pain, from his enjoyment of babbling and lalling, to his *monoreme* his one-word sentence, the infant makes a momentous transition: he recognizes the need, for his own purposes, to speak the language of those around him. In the word explosion which soon follows, he is like Adam, whom God allowed to share in the creation by naming each living creature. If at first in his magical thinking he glories in the borrowed omnipotence, yet this uniquely human capacity to conceptualize objects and to fix the concepts with names is a really potent instrument for constructing the world and finding himself and his place in it.

Glossolalia is a dissociative phenomenon in which the lalling which occurred in the transition from infancy (Latin *in* = not + *fans, fantis*, part of *fari* = to speak) to childhood is regressively revived.

Janet (1907)[18] traced the connection between convulsive hysteria and somnambulisms, showing that convulsive attacks were merely degraded forms of somnambulism where the outer expression of the somnambulic ideas in physiognomy, attitude, and act was no longer clear. In the phenomenon of glossolalia we see the more gradual development of this degradation of word language until there is, usually, a release of motor automatisms in an ecstatic crisis. There is a gradual dominance of primary process in the escalation of group excitement, and, as part of this invasion by primary process, magical thinking is generated, including fantasies of identification with the omnipotent Godhead. All this is facilitated by group resonance and unconscious interaction. That aspect of glossolalia concerned with the degradation of word language, the development of hyponoic formations, and the emergence of motor automatisms takes us to the heart of the problem of hysterical symptom formation, and, indeed, to the origins of the science of psychoanalysis.

Putting aside for the present problems of the highest levels of abstract conceptual thinking, and descending to the next rung of the ladder to levels of thinking still high in the hierarchy, which comprise denotational and propositional thinking concerned with action, we find that, even without the power of speech, pantomimic movements of gesture may serve the purposes of communication. One who finds himself among an alien people, say a Greek among barbarians who speak a totally unrelated tongue, discovers that communication can often be established for practical purposes by means of deliberately executed movements of a high propositional content. Besides these pantomimic movements there are other movements too, notably those expressive movements of appeal and of other important emotions. Some of these are expressed by the so-called 'voluntary musculature' and others belong to vasomotor, pilomotor, and secretomotor modalities of expression, such as the cutaneous phenomena of blushing and of 'gooseflesh'. The studies of Darwin (1872)[29] showed that emotionally expressive movements and secretions, such as those of physiognomy, are widely diffused phenomena, so consistent in character as to be readily recognized by all mankind, whatever the language, culture or education. Emotionally expressive movements, including those of gesture, are in general less voluntary and more automatic than those of pantomime, and communicate at a comparatively high level of efficiency among all people. Now, in conversion phenomena along with other movement complexes which we will shortly discuss, there are both denotational propositional pantomimic movement and emotionally expressive gesture. However, these, with other movement complexes, are involved *in a distorted and condensed way*, much as Freud showed that the visual imagery of dreaming consciousness was a condensed expression, with distortion due to displacement and disguise through symbolism, of wishes unacceptable to waking consciousness.

The language of gesture has preceded human speech in phylogenetic and ontogenetic development, and in adults normally accompanies speech in varying degrees, emphasizing and embellishing or especially adorning speech which is heavily charged with emotion. Macdonald Critchley (1939),[30] through a study of communication between deaf-mutes, came to realize that there exists among the deaf and dumb a gestural system of speech which is independent of racial and linguistic barriers and which is largely instinctive. A striking similarity has been found between this system of gestures and the sign talk practised by some aboriginal communities. In conversion reactions too, though in a distorted and condensed way, there is resort to language more primitive than speech, namely, body language, which substitutes for word language, and the meaning of which, in its most significant aspects, is dissociated from the awareness of the communicant. He imparts information of which he is defensively unaware, or which he defensively misinterprets, to one able to perceive, and in the mutual enterprise of psychotherapy more and more adequate information becomes available. To this aspect of psychotherapy we will later return. Meanwhile, it is to be noted that glossolalia represents a halfway house between the loss of valid word language and motor automatisms. Indeed, glossolalia appears in the setting of hypnoid disturbance of consciousness and usually issues in motor automatisms.

REFERENCES

1. Kraepelin, E. (1913). *Textbook of Psychiatry* (English trans.). (Section on dementia praecox.) Edinburgh: Livingstone (1919).
2. Bleuler, E. (1911). *Dementia Praecox or the Group of Schizophrenias*. New York: Int. Univ. Press (1950).
3. Noble, D. (1951). Hysterical manifestations in schizophrenic illness. *Psychiat.* **14**, 153.
4. Glover, E. (1932). A psychoanalytic approach to the classification of mental disorders. *J. Ment. Sci.* **78**, 819.
5. Abse, D. W. (1955). Early phases of ego-structure adumbrated in the regressive ego states of schizophrenic psychosis, and elucidated in intensive psychotherapy. *Psychoanal. Rev.* **42**, 229–38.
6. Freud, S. (1915). Observations on Transference-love. (Further Recommendations on the Technique of Psycho-analysis, III.) In: *The Standard Edition*, Vol. XII, p. 159. London: Hogarth Press (1955).
7. Jung, C. G. (1906). *The Psychology of Dementia Praecox*. New York: Nervous and Mental Disease Publishing (1936).
8. Freud, S. (1933). The Dissection of the Psychical Personality. *New Introductory Lectures on Psycho-analysis*. In: *The Standard Edition*, Vol. XXII. London: Hogarth Press (1964).
9. Foulkes, S. H. (1937). On introjection. *Int. J. Psychoanal.* **18**, 269.
10. Knight, R. P. (1940). Introjection, projection, and identification. *Psychoanal. Quart.* **9**, 334.
11. Ferenczi, S. (1912). On the part played by homosexuality in the pathogenesis of paranoia. In: *Contributions to Psycho-analysis*. Boston: Badger (1916).

12. Scott, R. D. (1951). The psychology of the body image. *Br. J. Med. Psychol.* **24**, 254.
13. Palumbo, S. R. and Bruch, H. (1964). Falling apart: the verbalisation of ego failure. *Psychiat.* **27**, 248.
14. Volkan, V. D. (1964). The observation and topographic study of the changing ego states of a schizophrenic patient. *Br. J. Med. Psychol.* **37**, 239 (1964).
15. Van Gennep, A. (1909). *The Rites of Passage* (trans. Vizedom, M. B. and Caffee, G. L.). (Introduction by Kimball, S. T.) Chicago: Univ. of Chicago Press (1960).
16. Chapple, E. D. and Coon, C. S. (1942). *Principles of Anthropology.* New York: Holt.
17. Harris, G. (1957). Possession hysteria in a Kenya tribe. *Am. Anthropol.* **59**, 1047.
18. Simon, B. (1979). Hysteria—the Greek disease. In: *The Psychoanalytic Study of Society* (ed. Munsterberger, W. and Boyer, L. B.), Vol. 8, Chap. 5, pp. 193–4. New Haven: Yale Univ. Press.
19. Lewis, I. M. (1971). *Ecstatic Religion.* Harmondsworth: Penguin Books.
20. Kildahl, J. P. (1972). *The Psychology of Speaking in Tongues.* New York and London: Harper and Row.
21. Cutten, G. B. (1927). *Speaking with Tongues: Historically and Psychologically Considered.* New Haven: Yale Univ. Press.
22. Freud, S. (1905). Three Essays on the Theory of Sexuality. In: *The Standard Edition*, Vol. VII. London: Hogarth Press (1953).
23. Spitz, R. A. (1946). *The Smiling Response.* In: *Genetic Psychology Monographs*, Vol. 34.
24. Peller, L. E. (1964). Language and its Prestages. *Bull. Philadelphia Assoc. Psychoanal.* **14** (2).
25. Stern, C. and Stern, W. (1907). *Die Kindessprache.* Leipzig:
26. Scott, W. C. M. (1955). A note on blathering. *Int. J. Psychoanal.* **36**, 348–9.
27. Bonnard, A. (1960). The primal significance of the tongue. *Int. J. Psychoanal.* **41**, 301–7.
28. Janet, P. (1907). *The Major Symptoms of Hysteria*, 2nd ed. (Fifteen lectures given in the Medical School of Harvard University.) New York: Macmillan (1920).
29. Darwin, C. (1872). *The Expression of the Emotions in Man and Animals.* London: Murray.
30. Critchley, M. (1939). *The Language of Gesture.* London: Arnold.

CHAPTER 15

The Syndrome of Gilles de la Tourette

Until Tourette's paper in 1885[1] describing a special syndrome of motor tics, which he named *maladie des tics compulsifs avec coprolalie*, inco-ordinate movement disorders were usually all diagnosed as *chorea*, a Greek word for 'dance'. Even then, Tourette did not conclude that he had found a disorder distinct from other choreas. Bockner (1959)[2] emphasized organicity since many of his patients had previously been suffering from rheumatic chorea in childhood. Bing (1925)[3] provided the first post-mortem report, on a patient with the syndrome who had committed suicide. He came to the conclusion from meningitic thickening and adhesions in the region of the facial nerve that psychogenic and organic factors were inextricably intertwined.

In childhood, tics are frequent and often evanescent. The development of the Tourette syndrome is much less frequent. In this syndrome the compulsive swearing and sometimes the repetitious performance of obscene gestures which develop in the course of the disease open a door psychologically to the more usually inaudible and completely sequestrated anal-sadistic meanings of *habit tic*. It must of course be remembered that, while various tics may show psychogenic impulse components, many develop on a somatopsychic basis, as, for example, after an encephalitis, presumably through damage to the brain basis of the controlling and integrative capacity of the ego.

Gilles de la Tourette syndrome consists of the onset in childhood, usually between the ages of 6 and 10 years, of multiple tics, followed later by compulsive swearing. Often accompanying these primary symptoms are various echo phenomena, including echolalia (the repetition of words or phrases spoken by others, to an excessive degree, i.e., beyond the repetitions usual in the process of learning, or achievement of ego mastery, in childhood), echopraxia (the repetition of motor acts performed by others, again to an excessive degree), and pallilalia (the repetition with increasing rapidity of words or phrases used by the afflicted individual himself). As stated, copropraxia (the repetitious performance of obscene acts or gestures) occasionally develops.

The disorder may begin insidiously or follow an obviously precipitating traumatic event. The tics usually begin in the face, neck and arms, and may spread to involve the trunk and legs. They disappear in sleep and in the waking state can be partially or completely suppressed for brief periods by conscious effort. Often they are migratory, for example, occurring first in the muscles of eye and jaw. They may disappear from these muscles and then involve those of the trunk and shoulders. At some time in the development of the syndrome the

297

muscles of phonation and of respiration become affected, and the subject begins to make peculiar grunting and barking sounds. Later the sounds become clearly formed words, assuming an obscene character. In the majority of instances the explosive vocal utterances are emitted at the peak of a burst of motor jerks. Both Guinon (1886)[4] and Gilles de la Tourette (1899)[5] observed a peculiar alteration of consciousness of a vaguely anxious and depressive kind accompanying the syndrome.

Itard (1825),[6] famous as the author of *The Wild Boy of Aveyron* (1894),[7] first described such a case—a French noblewoman who displayed both choreiform movements and obscene vocalizations. He noted:

> Thus in the middle of an interesting conversation suddenly, without being able to avoid it, she interrupts what she says or hears by horrible cries and extraordinary words which make a deplorable contrast to her distinguished manner. These words are mostly rude, offensive oaths, and obscene adjectives which are no less embarrassing for herself than for those listening ...

Gilles de la Tourette believed that both sexes were equally affected, but later evidence indicates that males are affected more often than females (Mahler and Luke, 1946;[8] Eisenberg, Ascher, and Kanner, 1959[9]). Most patients are destined to go through life displaying some of the stigmata of the disorder though now much reduced in intensity with adequate pharmocotherapy and psychotherapy. Gilles de la Tourette stated that, while exacerbations and remissions were the rule, he knew of no cases in which all symptoms disappeared concomitantly. Sometimes a patient with the syndrome develops a schizophrenic psychosis (Heuscher, 1950;[10] Michael, 1957[11]). In some few cases the disorder spontaneously disappears before adulthood.

Gilles de la Tourette read accounts of the syndromes of *latah* of Malaya, *myriachit* of Siberia, and of the *Jumpers* (Shakers) of Maine, and identified his syndrome with these other disorders. These bizarre disorders include imitative behaviour, coprolalia and a marked startle reaction, but are limited to certain ethnological groups, and the similarities to *maladie des tics* do not extend to the tics themselves.

Consistent physical findings have not so far been adduced. Balthasar (1956)[12] in one post-mortem found the ratio of small to large neurocytes in the striatum to be twice that of a control specimen, a ratio similar to that found in the striatum of a 1-year-old child. However, when he re-examined another specimen obtained by DeWulf and van Bogaert, who had found no pathological changes in the central nervous system, he found the cell counts within normal limits.

Multiple tic syndromes have often been reported following rheumatic chorea. In this connection, even in regard to the chorea itself, it must be remembered that, in a child, the diagnosis between a relapse of Sydenham's chorea and a hysterical mimesis is sometimes extremely difficult; certainly it is impossible on the basis of symptom observation alone. Not uncommonly hysteria is responsible for evanescent hyperkinesis definitely choreiform in type in young children. In such children an impression of choreiform movements may have been previously produced by an attack of rheumatic chorea, or the child may have observed such an attack in one of his siblings.

Turner and Critchley (1925)[13] described a variety of tics, particularly respiratory, following encephalitis lethargica, both in the acute phase and as late sequelae. Kanner (1957)[14] states: 'In recent years, tics in postencephalitic patients were referred to lesions in the striapallidal system.'

Pacella (1944–5)[15] found that the electro-encephalograms of *tiqueurs* showed the same incidence of abnormalities as other children in the primary behaviour disorder group, namely, about 30 per cent. He speculated that perhaps in *tiqueurs* a frustrating experience or series of experiences, associated with inhibition of consciously directed kinetic activity, results in a suppression of cortical dominance over such activity, redirecting some of the cortically controlled energy into lower levels of functional organization and integration.

The physical findings in Gilles de la Tourette's syndrome are thus nebulous at present; whereas the findings for *tiqueurs* in general, including this syndrome, suggest a neurological deficit in many instances. Anyway, the combination of the migratory nature of the tics in this syndrome, the remissions, the hypnoid disturbances of consciousness, the coprolalia and the generally expressive nature of this and other symptoms has led to the investigation of psychogenic factors. Ascher (1948),[16] for example, concluded that 'the echolalia and coprolalia appear to be related to certain attitudes the patient had towards one or both parents, and also constituted an attempt to suppress their expression'. Mahler and co-workers (Mahler and Rangell, 1943;[17] Mahler, 1944;[18] Mahler, 1944–5;[19] Mahler et al. 1945;[20] Mahler, 1949[21]), in regard to tic syndromes generally, came to the view that there is a crucial conflict between the child sufferer's aggressive expansive impulses and the restrictions of the environment, with the restriction later becoming internalized. The tic represents 'provocative erotic aggression towards mother or father as aggressor' (Mahler, Luke, and Daltroff, 1945[20]). Bonnard (1957)[22]* described children who had been witnesses of quarrelling parents and interpreted their tic-like gestures as testificatory and related to autoplastic re-enactment of traumatic scenes. The gestures showed a condensation of identifications with the aggressor and the aggressed-against adults.

Many workers have thought that hostility lies behind the tics and coprolalia in Gilles de la Tourette's syndrome, and some have implied that limited verbal skills also play a part in the development of the syndrome in some instances. According to this view the subject cannot for one or another reason achieve verbal outlets for aggressive feelings, and the tics and gestures are substitutes for verbal elaboration. The coprolalia, under hyponoic conditions, achieves a primitive verbal discharge of this hostility, as is evident in the case described below, studied and treated at the University of Virginia Hospital by Doctors D. J. Polites, D. B. Kruger and Professor Ian Stevenson (1965).[23]

History of the Illness: The patient was admitted to the neurology service of the University Hospital in November, 1961, at the age of 15 years. His chief complaint was 'jumping and jerking of my legs—sometimes my whole body jumps'. He was unaware of

*Augusta Bonnard's paper, 'Testificatory gestures of children', delivered at a Research Meeting, Department of Psychiatry, University of North Carolina, Chapel Hill, NC, 1957.

any abnormal movements until 10 years of age, when one of his teachers asked why he was twitching his face and neck muscles. Shortly thereafter he began shrugging his shoulders and nodding his head repetitively. Around the age of 12 years he began saying 'tut, tut, tut' and 'tsk, tsk, tsk', repetitively. When 13 years old, he began saying 'hell' and 'damn' on occasion. A year later outbursts of repetitive swearing commenced. Pallilalia, echopraxia and copropraxia were denied by the patient and were not observed by others. Except for partial remission lasting a few weeks at 12 years of age the symptoms had shown a progressive course; in the year prior to admission he had had frequent total body tics, which were sometimes very severe jactitations. A few weeks prior to admission, according to his mother, he had expressed the fear that people were trying to harm him and he slept with knives under his bed.

He had been taken at different times to several physicians who had diagnosed rheumatic fever and 'St Vitus's Dance'. One attempted to confine the patient to bed for 6 months, but then his tics grew markedly worse and he was unable to adhere to the regimen.

Growth and Development: The patient's mother had much nausea and vomiting during his gestation, but he was delivered at term without complications. At birth he weighed 8 pounds and was apparently normal in every respect. He was breast-fed for only a short time because his mother's milk was not 'rich enough nor plentiful'. His mother denied any problems with his toilet training which was completed before the age of 2 years. He talked at 16 months, but walking occurred later (his mother could not recall the time of this). She stated that he was 'fat and clumsy' as a small child. The patient maintained that he had been over-active all his life. He had had mumps and chicken-pox but none of the other usual childhood illnesses. However, he is said to have had many sore throats with pyrexia until his tonsils were removed at the age of 5 years. No significant head traumas could be recalled. The patient stated that he had often started fights with other boys at school but had stopped doing this at sometime around 9 years of age. The tics began at 10 years of age, about 1 year after his family moved to the town in which they are now living. At this time he had to change to a new and larger school. The patient had performed satisfactorily at school but required tutoring in the sixth and ninth grades because a doctor, believing that the patient had Sydenham's chorea, kept him out of school from time to time.

Family History and Social Situation: Both parents were poor sources of information. The mother showed blunted affect and sometimes giggled inappropriately; there was frequent thought blocking in her conversation. The father drank excessively and had managed his money so poorly that his income was turned over to his wife's management after she had threatened court action. The marriage was manifestly unhappy. The mother frequently told the patient that she did not love his father and that she had been in love with another man before her marriage. The patient often pleaded with his mother to divorce his father but she had not done so; she would not do this as long as she had responsibilities at home. The patient consciously despised his father but professed great love for his mother.

The patient was the youngest of four children. The oldest, 24 years of age at the time of the patient's admission, had had three separations from her husband. The second sibling, a brother, was probably the most emotionally disturbed of the four. He was 21 years old, had never dated or held a job, and had remained at home avoiding people. He had been rejected from army service when called by the draft. He steadfastly refused to see a doctor. The third sibling, also male, was 19 years old and in the Navy. He and the patient had fought frequently earlier in life but had later become closer to one another. When this brother left home the patient's condition had worsened. The patient frequently spoke of his fondness for this brother and his loneliness without him.

Observation and Examination of the Patient: The patient was of ungainly appearance, going through puberty. His presence never failed to attract attention in the hospital. He would run up and down the halls boisterously, talking loudly and oblivious of the usual social amenities. His tics were frequent and severe, involving almost every skeletal muscle in the body during his waking hours. Often he would have a severe jactitation, hurling himself in the air and striking the floor with a loud thud. His speech was liberally interspersed with grunts. Occasionally, when annoyed by others in the ward, he would launch into a stream of obscenities, consisting of repetitions of 'hell', 'shit', 'damn', or 'son-of-a-bitch'. Environmental events and worsenings of symptoms did not always correlate, but when his parents visited him his hyperactivity would increase and his tics would become more severe. He was rude to both, usually in a semi-jocular way, but he was sometimes solicitous of his mother.

No significant general physical or neurological abnormalities other than the tics were found. The mental status examination revealed appropriate affect, no gross abnormalities in thought processes or content, and no hallucinations or delusions. His sensorium was clear. Further interviews, however, revealed a high level of magical thinking and preoccupation with hostile and destructive thoughts which he diluted with humour. A need to reduce authority figures in order to feel more confortable with them was shown by constant humorous efforts to call various doctors 'Mr' or to refer to them by their first names.

Laboratory examinations, including skull films, showed no abnormalities except for the EEG, the report of which read: 'No definite seizure discharges were seen in this record, but the occasional, spontaneous, bi-synchronous rhythmic, 4 per second occipital theta activity would suggest the possibility of an instability in electrogenesis at subcortical levels, of a potentially epileptiform nature.'

In reporting the results of psychological tests done early in his case (November, 1961), the psychologist stated: 'the motor tics may be expressions of obsessive-compulsive mechanisms and of over-controlled and repressed aggressions. It is felt that the patient has a strong potential for psychosis.'

Treatment: Several treatment approaches were tried consecutively in this case; these sequential treatments are discussed fully by Polites, Kruger and Stevenson (1965).[23] Here is a brief summary of the more important approaches.

In one phase of treatment an attempt was made to influence the symptoms through hypnotic suggestion. The authors report: 'He was a difficult patient to hypnotize, but after several sessions he was able to enter a medium trance in which he experienced hyposthesias and paraesthesias, hallucinated odours and carried out post-hypnotic suggestions. During the hypnotic trances, his tics became much less frequent and severe, sometimes ceasing altogether until he was aroused. In this phase, we gave the patient simple suggestions that he would feel better on coming out of the trances. The patient had twenty-two sessions of this type extending over seven weeks. No discernible improvement outside the hypnotic sessions themselves occurred during this phase.'

Later, in hypnotherapy, temporal localization of the tics was attempted. While under hypnosis the patient was told that for a certain period during the day he would find his ability to control his jerks strengthened, that his ability to concentrate on controlling his jerks would improve and that the 'urge to have jerks' would be weaker. At first aimed at a special one-hour period during the day, this was expanded to a two-hour special period. Further 'special periods' were later added. The tics improved about 70 per cent during the special periods themselves, and about 40 per cent in intervening periods. Most dramatic was the reduction of total body tics. Later the patient was given 10 mg of trifluoperazine (Stelazine) daily, whereupon further symptomatic improvement took place. However, he resisted return to school as long as any tics persisted.

Another approach was then decided upon. He was given a series of drug interviews over a 2-month period (10 sessions; in each session usually about 600 mg of amytal and 10 mg of methylamphetamine were administered). The emotionally charged contents of these abreactive sessions were concerned chiefly with sexual and hostile wishes and guilty and sinful feelings. Hostile wishes and fantasies were concerned for the most part with his parents and his eldest brother. His guilty and sinful feelings were found to be especially closely related to emerging heterosexual longings associated with compulsive masturbation, as well as murderous wishes directed against his brother. He felt that his illness was in part a punishment for his sins. He connected his coprolalia with thoughts of cursing his parents and eldest brother—thoughts which he could not control. During these interviews the tics increased. At one stage, between the seventh and ninth abreactive sessions, the tics also increased markedly outside the treatment sessions. At this time the patient sought and received a good deal of attention from the nursing staff. Moreover, he began to make a better adjustment in group activities on the ward. At this time too, as after completion of all drug interviews, he became more dependent on his therapist, who responded with support and encouragement. The patient began to write poetry in the hospital. He stated that he had desultorily attempted this at home but had kept this activity concealed from his family; he had felt that none of them would appreciate his poetic efforts. At the time of his final discharge from the hospital he was having long periods of complete freedom from symptoms, and it was estimated that he was 90 per cent free of tics. Further outpatient treatment was arranged.

Arthur K. Shapiro (1978)[24] gives a brief account of his initial interest in the syndrome when he overheard a young woman in a bookshop making peculiar noises which initially sounded like 'shi, pi, fu'. Soon, with shaking and spasmodic jerking movements she vociferated 'Shit, piss, fuck'. Well-dressed in a conventional seal fur coat, she showed this extraordinary behaviour while she was browsing through a book of the collected poetry of John Keats.

Robinson (1972)[25] has reported on the anatomical and physiological contrasts between human and other primary vocalizations. His studies led him to infer that two distinct levels of the nervous system are involved in speech and language behaviour. The first well-known cortical level consists of Broca's area: the left inferior frontal gyrus, Wernicke's auditory speech area in the first temporal convolution and the Superior Cortical or Supplementary Speech area within the mid-sagittal fissure just anterior to the Rolandic motor foot area. This level which is unilateral has undergone considerable development in humans and provides a brain basis for the control and production of speech and language behaviour. The second level, which Robinson maintains is another bilateral system, older from the evolutionary viewpoint, lies at the rostral end of the limbic system, terminating in the cingulate gyrus, and it provides the basis for emotive speech and language behaviour. The areas of the cerebral cortex of the first level function semi-autonomously from, and usually dominate, the second limbic system level, modulating emotional expression and elaborating language formulations (compare Secondary and Primary Processes discussed in Chapter 2). It is easy to surmise that in poetic expression the two systems are brought into intimate balance whereas in the prosaic mode there is more suppression of the limbic system under the domination of cortical control. In the Tourette syndrome gross dissociation of the two neural components which are the bases of human speech and language is evident. There is an organic impairment of the capacity for integration of the two systems which renders the patient peculiarly vulnerable under the stress of profound compliance–defiance mental conflict to the emergence of vocal tics. As was noted by Gilles de la Tourette (1885)[1] many of these patients are highly intelligent. Some of them seek to mend their disability through an especially emphatic interest in poetry.

Murray (1982)[26] has recently discussed Samuel Johnson, the great lexicographer—'Dictionary Johnson' as he came to be known—with regard to his habitual tics and gesticulations, involuntary vocalizations and compulsive behaviour. He suggests that these symptoms constituted an affliction with Tourettism. Boswell (1791)[27] in *The Life of Samuel Johnson L.L.D.* quotes Sir Joshua Reynolds:

> Those motions or tricks of Dr. Johnson are improperly called convulsions. He could sit motionless, when he was told to, as well as any other man. My opinion is, that it proceeded from a habit which he had indulged himself in, of accompanying his thoughts with certain untoward actions, and those actions always appeared to me as if they were meant to reprobate some part of his past conduct. Whenever he was not engaged in conversation, such thoughts were sure to rush into his mind; and for this reason, any company, and employment whatever, he preferred to being alone. The great business of his life (he said) was to escape from himself; this disposition he considered as the disease of his mind which nothing cured but company.

Thus two centuries ago Reynolds laid emphasis on psychogenesis. So did Lord Brain in 1949,[28] noting that there was no evidence of organic neurological disorder at autopsy. Hitschmann (1945)[29] stated:

> As predisposition for his compulsive neurosis and the tic, we find aggression and anality of the same high degree. We do not yet know enough about the psychogenesis of tics, but it is sure that the movements ward off or express hostile and anal impulses.

Johnson's mother was 40 years old at his birth and he was nursed by a hireling. It is likely that the wet-nurse was suffering from tuberculosis and that this resulted in his scrofula, and had some organic relation too to his chronic tics and convulsive movements. As in so many cases of Tourette disease, there is a series of psychosomatic and somato-psychic sequences involved in a dynamic circular aetiological process. Meyer (1984)[30] notes that Johnson suffered severely from fear of death and castration anxiety, and he adds:

> He revered his 'governess' Hester Thrale, but his misogyny reveals itself in his pieces for *The Idler* and *The Rambler*, and he alluded to women as hypocritical, emasculating and unclean, suggesting a revulsion towards the female genital.

His mighty labours with the English Dictionary, his poetry and prose and his witty conversations reveal a preoccupation with words and their precise meanings, presumably in a creative effort to overcome and to master his basic speech and language difficulties. It is notable that coprolalia was absent from his involuntary mouthings which took the form of moans and groans, blowings, whistlings and heavy sighings; but there were periodic repetitions of phrases from literature such as snippets from Shakespeare, and especially from the Lord's Prayer which may have been successful efforts to countermand profanities.

Joseph Bliss (1980),[31] himself a patient with a 62-year history of Tourette syndrome, has given an account of sensory signals preceding each movement. The movement, which gives some relief, he regards as a voluntary capitulation to a demanding and relentless wife. He believes the abnormal movement only seems altogether involuntary because of the instant capitulation to an unrecognized sensory stimulus. Thus the view has been developed that sufferers must learn to manipulate these first tentative 'subjective feelings of imminence', sometimes by rerouting them into less embarrassing areas. As regards vocalization, it would seem that Dr. Johnson accomplished this by substituting prayers for blasphemies. Of course, voluntary muscles are only relatively voluntary as compared to those that are relatively involuntary.

It seems evident that, in the syndrome of Gilles de la Tourette, as in other hysterical and hysteriform conditions, there is a pronounced tendency for a reversal of the natural history of words to their somatic foundations of inaudible gesture, sometimes via vocalizations. Indeed, as noted earlier, Breuer and Freud (1895)[32] re-reversed this reversal, finding that their psychotherapy worked through abrogating the pathogenic efficacy of the original non-abreacted ideas by affording them and associated strangulated affects an outlet in speech, and through bringing them to 'associative correction by drawing them into normal consciousness', i.e., by the work of integration into consciousness with the supportive and guilt-reducing efforts of the psychotherapist. However, in this syndrome the compulsive swearing and more denotative obscene gestures, occurring usually under hyponoic conditions of consciousness, are a bridge to the more recondite condensations of identifications, to the sexual symbolic references of body movements, to the expressions of anger and of appeal, and to the fantasy connotations involved in the multiple tics and severe jactitations. Identifications, sexual and hostile wish fantasies, and associated mixed emotions are embodied in a highly compressed form in dissociated efforts at communication in the tics and jactitations. These efforts achieve more and more clarity in the peculiar grunting and barking sounds, and then in the compulsive swearing, though consciousness itself comprises diminished awareness at such times of more open conflict.

We have already noted in Chapter 14, when discussing glossolalia, that similar manifestations including degradation of words to less apparently meaningful sounds, tic-like gestures, and convulsive crises, occur under conditions of excessive group excitement. In all these hysteriform conditions regressive ego functioning is of central importance. This regressive functioning is a response to continued *repression* which counters the expression in more evolved formulated thought and language of forbidden wish fantasies. It is to be borne in mind that the communicative disorder evident in Gilles de la Tourette's syndrome may sometimes develop partly as a somatopsychic sequence, as already stated, on account of organic damage to the brain basis of the controlling and integrative capacity of the developing ego. Bockner (1959)[2] first introduced phenothiazine (chlorpromazine) medication as part of the treatment of this condition, and such medication may be a necessary part of the total treatment and management of *maladie des tics*.

Shapiro and Shapiro (1982)[33] conclude from their chemotherapeutic studies that haloperidol improves about 86 per cent of patients, with 14 per cent discontinuing treatment because of side effects. However, Van Woert, Rosenbaum and Enna (1982)[34] maintain that while haloperidol provides excellent symptomatic control without significant side effects in only about 25 per cent of Tourette syndrome patients, it has many disabling side effects (along with some other neuroleptic medications), such as depression, dysphoria, extrapyramidal signs, cognitive impairment and interference with motivation and learning. There have been several reports that clonidine ameliorates Tourette syndrome, and other drugs, such as pimozide, are now on trial (Cohen et al. 1980;[35] Debray et al. 1972[36]). In haloperidol–resistant patients, or in those with adverse side effects, other medication approaches are thus now available. The beneficial therapeutic response to dopamine receptor blockers such as haloperidol, and the adverse effect of drugs that increase dopamine activity, have led to the view that overactivity of the dopaminergic system in the basal ganglia of these patients is a characteristic of Tourettism. Van Woert, Rosenbaum and Enna (1982)[34] suggest that though this hypothesis has been useful in stimulating research, it should not discourage investigations of other neurotransmitter abnormalities in Tourette syndrome.

It has been repeatedly reported that there is a prevalence of tics, multiple tics and Tourettism in the families of patients afflicted with the syndrome (Eldridge et al. 1977[37]). Kidd et al. (1980)[38] mailed self-report questionnaires to a random sample of the national membership of the American Tourette Syndrome Association. Part of the questionnaire was designed to encourage information regarding the incidence of Tourette syndrome and/or tics in the relatives of the respondents. Of 75 questionnaires returned, 66 provided data on relatives. Because of the small size of this pilot sample (231 relatives among the 66 families), only borderline statistical significance existed for many of the differences that were found. However, the patterns of the frequencies of the syndrome itself and/or tics in the respondents' relatives did suggest the following:

1. Within these families, multiple tics are related to Tourette syndrome.

2. The disorder (the syndrome or tics) is transmitted from parent to child.

3. The sex difference in the prevalence of Tourette syndrome is real because it was found among relatives of both male and female probands.

4. The sex difference may be considered a threshold phenomenon related to transmitted susceptibility.

The combination of an apparently significant increase in the frequency of affected relatives over the general population frequency and the significance of parental classification (a higher frequency of multiple tics among siblings existed when at least one parent also had the syndrome or multiple tics) provides strong evidence for the existence of vertical transmission of some factors that confer susceptibility to Tourette syndrome and to multiple tics.

In his essay 'On Obscene Words', Ferenczi (1911)[39] makes the point that these words have a peculiarly compelling power, vividly evoking the excremental or sexual organ or function in substantial actuality. Their impact may be felt by some as assualtive and, as a result, resisted in disgust. This special character of arousing memory traces of a primitive hallucinatory and motor quality is related to their 'arrest' in the context of concrete thinking. At the same time as the psychic counterforces—disgust, shame, and guilt—against sadistic infantile sexuality are being formed, the impulse develops to utter and draw obscenities, which is a preliminary stage in the inhibition of visual sexual curiosity and exhibitionism. Later, with the advent of the latency period, there is a wave of repression against sexual fantasies and activities, even as manifested in the weakened form of speech. Thus the 'obscene word images' are repressed, as Ferenczi surmises, at a time when speech is still characterized by a highly regressive tendency and a vivid 'mimicry of imagery'. In consequence, the repressed verbal signs remain at a primitive developmental stage, whereas the rest of the vocabulary for the most part gradually outgrows its hallucinatory and motor character and is thus made suitable for abstract thought activities. In this light, the compulsive swearing in the syndrome of Gilles de la Tourette acquires a special significance in the periodic severely regressive ego functioning evident in the disease. The utterance of obscene words shows, in high degree, what is scarcely indicated with most words, their original source in pretermitted action (Stone 1954;[40] Abse, 1955[41]).

REFERENCES

1. Gilles de la Tourette, G. (1885). Étude sur une affection nerveuse caracterisée par de l'incoordination motrice accompagnée d'écholalie et de coprolalie. *Arch. Neurol.* **9**, 19–42, 158–200. (English translation: Study of a neurological condition characterised by motor incoordination accompanied by echolalia and coprolalia (jumping, latah, myriachit) (trans. Goetz, C. G. and Klawans, H. L.) In: *Gilles de la Tourette Syndrome* (ed. Friedhoff, A. J. and Chase, T. N.). New York: Raven Press (1982).
2. Bockner, S. (1959). Gilles de la Tourette's disease. *J. Ment. Sci.* **105**, 1078–81.
3. Bing, R. (1925). Über lokale Muskelspasmen und Tics. *Schweitz. Med. Wochenschr.* **6**, 993–7.
4. Guinon, G. (1886). Sur la maladie des tics convulsifs. *Rev. Méd.* **6**, 50–80.
5. Gilles de la Tourette, G. (1889). La maladie des tics convulsifs. *Sem. Méd.* **19**, 153–6.
6. Itard, J. M. G. (1825). Mémoire sur quelques fonctions involontaires des appareils de la locomotion, de la préhension et de la voix. *Arch. Gén. Méd.* **8**, 385–407.
7. Itard, J. M. G. (1894). *Rapports et Mémoires sur le Sauvage de l'Aveyron.* Paris: Bureau du Progrès Médical.
8. Mahler, M. S. and Luke, J. A. (1946). Outcome of the tic syndrome. *J. Nerv. Ment. Dis.* **103**, 433–45.
9. Eisenberg, L., Ascher, E. and Kanner, L. (1959). A clinical study of Gilles de la Tourette's disease (*maladie des tics*) in children. *Am J. Psychiat.* **115**, 715–23.
10. Heuscher, J. E. (1950). Beiträge zur Ätiologie der 'Maladie Gilles de la Tourette' und zum Regressions-Problem. *Schweiz. Arch. Neur. Psychiat.* **66**, 123.
11. Michael, R. P. (1957). Treatment of a case of compulsive swearing. *Br. Med. J.* **1**, 1506–8.
12. Balthasar, K. (1956). Über das anatomische Substrat der generalisierten tic-Krankheit (maladie des tics, Gilles de la Tourette). Entwicklungshemmung des corpus striatum. *Arch. Psychiat. Nervenkrank.* **195**, 531–49.
13. Turner, W. A. and Critchley, M. (1925). Respiratory disorders in epidemic encephalitis. *Brain* **48**, 72.
14. Kanner, L. (1957). *Child Psychiatry.* Springfield, Ill.: Thomas.
15. Pacella, D. L. (1944–5). Physiologic and differential diagnostic considerations of tic manifestations in children. *Nerv. Child*, **4**, 313.
16. Ascher, E. (1948). Psychodynamic considerations in Gilles de la Tourette disease. *Am. J. Psychiat.* **105**, 267–76.
17. Mahler, M. S. and Rangell, L. (1943). A psychosomatic study of maladie des tics. *Psychoanal. Quart.* **17**, 579–603.

18. Mahler, M. S. (1944). Tics and impulsions in children: a study of motility. *Psychoanal. Quart.* **13**, 430–44.
19. Mahler, M. S. (1944–5). Introductory remarks. *Nerv. Child.* **4**, 307.
20. Mahler, M. S., Luke, J. A. and Daltroff, W. (1945). Clinical and follow-up study of the tic syndrome in children. *Am. J. Orthopsychiat.* **15**, 631–47.
21. Mahler, M. S. (1949). A psychoanalytic evaluation of tics: a sign and symptom in psychopathology. In: *The Psychoanalytic Study of the Child* (eds. Eissler R.S., Freud, A., Hartmann, H. et al.), Vols. 3–4. New York: Int. Univ. Press.
22. Bonnard, A. (1957). Testificatory gestures of children. Lecture, Department of Psychiatry. Chapel Hill, N.C.: Univ. of North Carolina.
23. Polites, D. J., Kruger, D. B. and Stevenson, I. (1965). Sequential treatment in a case of Gilles de la Tourette's syndrome. *Br. J. Med. Psychol.* **38**, 43–52.
24. Shapiro, A. K. (1978). Introduction. In: *Gilles de la Tourette Syndrome* (ed. Shapiro, A. K., Shapiro, E. S., Brunn, R. D. et al.). New York: Raven Press.
25. Robinson, B. W. (1972). Anatomical and physiological contrasts between human and other primate vocalisations. In: *Perspectives on Human Evolution* (ed. Washburn, S. L. and Dolinhow, P.), Vol. 2, pp. 438–43. New York: Holt, Rhinehart and Winston.
26. Murray, T. J. (1982). Dr Samuel Johnson's abnormal movements. *Gilles de la Tourette Syndrome* (ed. Friedhoff, A. J. and Chase, T. N.). In: *Advances in Neurology*, Vol. 35, pp. 25–30. New York: Raven Press.
27. Boswell, J. (1791). *The Life of Samuel Johnson L.L.D.* Everyman's Edition. London: Dent (1949).
28. Brain, W. R. (1948). Some reflections on genius. *Lancet* **1**, 661–5.
29. Hitschmann, E. (1945). Samuel Johnson's character, a psychoanalytic interpretation. *Psychoanal. Rev.* **32**, 207–18.
30. Meyer, B. C. (1984). Some observations on the rescue of fallen women. (Lecture recorded by C. Sarner). *Newsletter New York Psychoanal. Soc. and Inst.* **21** (4), 2.
31. Bliss, J. (1980). Sensory experiences of Gilles de la Tourette syndrome. *Arch. Gen. Psychiat.* **37**, 1343–7.
32. Breuer, J. and Freud, S. (1895). *Studies on Hysteria.* In: *The Standard Edition*, Vol. II. London: Hogarth Press (1955).
33. Shapiro, A. K. and Shapiro, E. S. (1982). Tourette syndrome: history and present status. *Gilles de la Tourette Syndrome* (ed. Friedhoff, A. J. and Chase, T. N.). In: *Advances in Neurology*, Vol. 35, pp. 17–23. New York: Raven Press.
34. Van Woert, M. H., Rosenbaum, D. and Enna, S. J. (1982). Overview of pharmocological approaches to therapy for Tourette syndrome. *Gilles de la Tourette Syndrome* (ed. Friedhoff, A. J. and Chase, T. N.). In: *Advances in Neurology*, Vol. 35, pp. 369–73. New York: Raven Press.
35. Cohen, D. J., Detlor, J., Young, J. G. et al. (1980). Clonidine ameliorates Gilles de la Tourette syndrome. *Arch. Gen. Psychiat.* **37**, 1350–6.
36. Debray, P., Messerschmitt, P., Lonchap, D. et al. (1972). L'utilisation de pimozide–pédo-psychiatrie. *Nouv. Presse Méd.* **1**, 2917.
37. Eldridge, R., Sweet, R., Lake, C. R. et al. (1977). Gilles de la Tourette's syndrome: clinical, genetic, psychological and biochemical aspects in 21 selected families. *Neurol. (Minneap.)* **27**, 115–24.
38. Kidd, K. K., Prusoff, B. A. and Cohen, D. J. (1980). The familial pattern of Tourette syndrome. *Arch. Gen. Psychiat.* **37**, 1336–9.
39. Ferenczi, S. (1911). On obscene words. In: *Contributions to Psychoanalysis.* Boston: Badger (1916).
40. Stone. L. (1954). On the principal obscene word of the English language; an inquiry with hypothesis, regarding its origin and persistence. *Int. J. Psychoanal.* **35**, 1.
41. Abse, D. W. (1955). Psychodynamic aspects of the problem of definition of obscenity. *Law and Contemporary Problems.* **20**, 572.

CHAPTER 16

Regression and Semantic Speech

The basic mental process of naming was well discussed in Plato's *Cratylus*[1] many centuries ago. Plato, although he pushes the idea to absurdity, suggests also in the *Cratylus* that words do not arise from the arbitrary choice of the gods but have a natural origin. DeSaussure (1916)[2] in his course in General Linguistics shows that what emerges as a word—in his terms a linguistic sign—is a union of signifier and signified. Yet he considered that the linguistic sign is in general quite arbitrary, that is to say, with no inner relationship of sound image, thought and signified thing. Only by immersion in the realms of onomatopoeia, of synaesthesia, or kinaesthesia, and of animistic thought in early development can one refute DeSaussure's tendentious view that the linguistic sign, or name of the thing, person, process, relation, etc., is quite arbitrary. Actually, more words in a particular language's vocabulary than one would normally appreciate remain anchored through intrinsic qualities to their references. Further, despite the effects of phonetic drift, including consonant shifts and many other complex factors in the natural evolution and social dynamics of language which so often obscure the earliest origins of words and which make them seem to be merely 'arbitrary' linguistic signs, despite that is, a complex process of seeming 'denaturalization', a great many phonetic symbols are still not divorced from the formative activity of the speaker and the listener. Here is but one example of a parallelistic connection mainly kinaesthetic between word and 'thing-meant': the 'oo' sound as in 'room', 'tube', 'loop', that is to say, as used in words denoting something enclosed, tubular, or rounded, is brought about by lip movements which before phonation already imitate the form of the object names.

In 1812, Samuel Taylor Coleridge[3] commented cogently:

> I wish our clever young poets would remember my homely definitions of prose and poetry; that is, prose—words in their best order; poetry—the best words in their best order.

It is indeed in poetry that the 'best' words, those that somehow retain essential links between word and thing, most often occur, and there is much admired poetry to demonstrate the point. Compare this with Ferenczi (1916),[4] who, in his essay 'On Obscene Words' made a counterpoint that the 'worst' words too have a peculiar compelling power, vividly evoking the excremental or sadistic sexual function in substantial actuality. This special character of arousing memory traces of a primitive hallucinatory and motor quality is related to their 'arrest' in the context of concrete thinking.

As we have noted in Chapter 14, in glossolalia, the subject reverts to the actual prestages of word language, babbling and lalling, and at the same time generates an omnipotent notion of effectively speaking in many languages, despite the evident babyish performance. Sometimes in a hysterical pseudo-dementia a *'retour à l'enfance'* includes an inability to name objects as a prominent symptom, thus imitating some organic dementias, in which, even when there is not an extensive nominal aphasia, a 'word-need' is often a distressing symptom.

It is of course by progressive increase in size and complexity of the brain that the primates emerge from amongst the mammalia, and that man in turn transcends other primates. This basic phonetic symbolic representational power with its special brain basis was somehow acquired by our primate ancestors. We may name them the 'Linguistic Primates'. But how did they, or we, develop further once *that* fateful step in evolution was accomplished? Wegener (1885)[5] suggests two further principles of linguistic development namely, *Emendation* and *Metaphor*. Beyond the original use of language in naming, fixing and conceiving objects even in their absence from immediate perception, Wegener's principles of emendation and metaphor clarify many of our clinical problems. Both these processes have their foundation in more primitive symbolism and use extensions of it in response to fulfilling the need for increasingly more adequate communication.

Emendation

In order to understand these principles, it is necessary first to focus on that early phase of language development which Buhler (1934),[6] basing his views on Wegener's work, designated 'empractic'. To illustrate empractic language Buhler offers the example of a patron in a restaurant. In such a situation empractic language is an effective means of communication. The fact that he enters the restaurant, sits down at a table, peruses a menu, and so forth, is ample evidence as far as the watching waiter is concerned that the patron intends to eat and/or drink something. Let us suppose in this instance that when the waiter approaches, he says only: 'Coffee'. Now he has spoken one word at the moot point in his otherwise tacit, intelligible behaviour. He inserts just one word at this point, and any elements of ambiguity in the total situation are, from the waiter's standpoint, sufficiently removed. This demonstrates the essentials of the empractic use of language and is a particularly good example, evoking the customer's infancy when following vocal cries he was fed by his mother. For the most part in the empractic stage of language, to which it is *sometimes* economical and effective to revert for practical purposes, adequate communication is possible with few words, maybe one only, inserted into a particular physical and social context. Susanne K. Langer (1942)[7] writes of this:

The context is the situation of the speaker in a setting visible to the hearer; at the point where their thinking is to converge, a word is used, to fix the crucial concept. The word is built into the speaker's action or situation, is a diacritical capacity, settling a doubt, deciding a response.

A word such as 'coffee' when inserted into the illustrated context is really, in meaning, a one-word sentence. That is to say , here it means at least 'Bring me a cup of coffee!'; perhaps additionally it implies much more: 'I entered this particular restaurant because I wish to have a cup of coffee here.' In this way, of course, we are now substituting a verbal context for the visible physical and social context, unnecessary in the actual situation depicted, but important for a further discussion of Wegener's principles of development of speech.

At this point, it is apposite to relate this empractic phase of language development to the conversion phenomena of hysteria. It will suffice to mention that the essential messages in a conversion reaction are embodied cryptically in the somatic symptoms, which do not involve primarily any words at all, and only relatively infrequently the laryngeal apparatus. Word language is reduced and compressed in inaudible symbols of a more primitive character, in such a way that the subject is unware of their essential meaning, and his reference group very likely misled. We have, of course, the concepts of repression and of the unconscious (of the repressed unconscious) as well as of regression to aid us in our quest for understanding. The disorder of expression and of communication, internal and external, is indeed a function of pathological repression and regression as we have learned from Freud.

As already outlined in Chapter 14, Peller's work (1964)[8] emphasizes that the whole story of the beginnings of semantic speech includes events in the pre-verbal phase of development, a phase which antedates and prepares the ground for the empractic phase of language development. Towards such a developmental understanding of language beginnings, hysterical disorders afford us many a clue. The following six categories into which the embodied messages of conversion reactions fall constitute a guide to such clues:

1. Sexual symbolic references.
2. Distorted affect expressions—e.g. of appeal, of anger, of resentment, of joy, of sadness, etc.
3. Condensation of identifications.
4. Associated connotations relating to fantasies: wish-fulfilling and self-punitive.
5. Denotational propositional—pantomimic movements—often truncated, or with reversals in sequence, or other disguises.
6. Metaphoric embodiments.

We will later return to the last on this list in discussing Wegener's second principle of language development, namely, metaphor. As regards, empractic speech, the young child's assumption that with a word or two mother will understand holds up in a favourable maternal environment remarkably well. If we tried this way of speech in situations that are more ambiguous than that of the patron in the restaurant, we would be likely to frequently find ourselves very disappointed. Wegener (1885),[5] confronting this ambiguity, expounded the growth of explicit statement from a matrix of key words, eked out by pointing in the setting of an obvious situation. Wegener shows us a natural process brought about by the necessity of being adequately understood, and by the need to avoid misunderstanding. All discourse, he saw, involves two aspects, namely the context and the novel statement in this context which the speaker wants to communicate. Where the physical and social context does not give sufficient direction, the novel assertion would remain ambiguous; so the speaker is impressed by the necessity to set forth this context verbally in more detail in order to clarify the meaning of the novel predication. The lone noun or verb is supplemented with demonstratives, like 'his' or 'that'. From such syllables, added as supplements to the one word sentence, arise inflections. More and more vocables are gradually needed to modify the original expression, to accompany and emphasize gestures and bodily expressed attitudes. The 'word-sentence',* being insufficient, is thus supplemented by more and more words. Appositives and then relative clauses, and so on, are added as corrections of deficient presentations. Thus grammatical structure evolves by emendation of an ambiguous assertion. All these auxiliary utterances Wegener sees as the exposition of the one-word sentence, providing in part or whole, a verbal context to supplement or substitute for the implicit context which is deficient as far as the listener is concerned. It is by this process of emendation that fully fledged speech begins to emerge.

Kraepelin (1905)[10] commented on that aspect of the disfigurements of speech in schizophrenia which he called *agrammatic disturbance*. Confusion is caused, as far as the listener is concerned, by the fact that ideas indicated by correctly chosen words are distorted by the structure of a sentence, by the juxtaposition of sentences which do not seem logically to belong together and by the fact that topics are introduced without adequate exposition (lacking in verbal context). This aspect of speech disfigurement represents the abrogation of Wegener's first principle of support to enable fully fledged speech. The grammatical structure has not evolved sufficiently by emendation of an ambiguous expression to support purposeful dialogue. All those auxiliary utterances, evolved in the process of exposition of the one-word sentence, which provide a verbal context to substitute for the deficient implicit context, are conspicuously absent in very many samples of the speech of patients suffering schizophrenic disorder. In this respect it is as if the patients had reverted to the notion that few speech indications must be sufficient as far as the listener is concerned. The impression created in the unsophisticated auditor in such instances is that excessive brevity is the soul of witlessness.

All discourse, according to Wegener, involves the verbal or practical context and the 'novelty' presented by the speaker. It is in connection with this novelty that we encounter his second principle, namely, metaphor.

Metaphor

When a precise word is lacking to designate an experience, to name a thing, a process, a relation, a characteristic of a person, or a feeling, when, put another way, there is a lack of a conventional phonetic symbol with adequate representational power, some word is then created for the new denotational purpose. Now usually this word already denotes something else, and is dredged up on the basis of some analogy suggested by this other reference. The context makes it clear that the word is not referring to the first thing, that

*An earlier vocal unit as described by Antoine Grégoire is the *monoreme* (*see* Chapter 14, p. 293), close to the interjection, but a one-unit referential pattern which precedes an actual word (*see* Werner and Kaplan, 1963[9]).

this is not literally denoted; hence the word must mean something else. Consider the following series of statements:

1. The man *runs* to the village.
2. The brook *runs* swiftly past the farmhouse.
3. The rumour *runs* through the town.
4. The fence *runs* around the yard.

In the second example, the word 'runs' does not indicate actions of the legs as it does in the first example; it indicates a rippling flow. There is, a moment's reflection discloses, an audible rippling flow in the audition of the morpheme 'run' and in the kinaesthetic impressions of its enunciation. With its phonetic symbolic representational origins, however, we are not immediately concerned. We are concerned with the fact that in the second meaning in this second example it has moved from its naming of a specific bodily activity, that of the legs moving more quickly than in walking, to this indication of a rippling flow. Aristotle[11] already recognized the concept which is the reference of the word 'metaphor' (*meta*-change and *phora*, from the root 'to carry'). Metaphor signifies to carry change. This change of meaning of a word or phrase functions by means of replacement of a part for the whole or a whole for the part; usually it is a shared part or common attribute that is involved in the transfer of the word to denote another process, relation or object. The context makes it clear what the word is referring to. In the last example, there is not a denotation of changing place, of movement in space by the fence, whatever the associated connotations. Metaphor essentially consists in a semantic movement.

To give another example, one might say of a fire: 'It flares up.' One might say too: 'his anger flared up'. In the second use of the word 'flare' we know that this does not refer to the physical flame but indicates the idea of 'flaring up' as a symbol for what his anger is doing. As Langer (1942)[7] writes of this instance:

> The expression 'to flare up' has acquired a wider meaning than its original use, to describe the behaviour of a flame; it can be used metaphorically to describe whatever its meaning can symbolize. Whether it is to be taken in a literal or metaphorical sense has to be determined by the context.

Wegener shows that if metaphor is often used, it fades to a literal significance. We take the word to mean that which all its applications have in common. Constant figurative use generalizes its sense. It comes to have again a literal significance, but a different one from its original specific meaning before it went through a figurative sense. He shows that general words are derived from specific appellations by metaphorical use, so that our literal language is a repository of faded metaphors.

The structure of language grows from the one or two word sentence by gradual emendation, as Wegener noted; but, he points out that another essential aspect of discursive language, namely generality, is achieved through the fading of metaphor. Before language acquired faded metaphors to buttress logical thought, it could hardly do more than represent needs and feelings by a demonstrative indication of them in immediate experience. The process of fading of metaphors is one bridge on the complex pathway from the early empractic phase of semantic speech to the developed phase of discursive exposition. It is to be noted that since in metaphorical usage it is the context which guides the newer meaning, it follows that the context itself must always be expressed literally, because it has not, in turn, a context to define its sense. Only the novel predication can be metaphorically lively; the context may of course have many words which have faded in their earlier predicational use.

As reflection always reveals, metaphoric symbolism is derived from the sensori-motor foundations of experience, both from that of perceptually differentiated sensori-motor experience and from the very early pre-verbal undifferentiated synaesthetic and kinaesthetic experience of infancy. The progressive differentiation in development of the different sense modalities, and of the auto-psychic from somato-psychic spheres, is often selectively disrupted in conversion hysteria, with a regression of some metaphoric speech to its somatic foundations in childhood, as will be shown here in one example. In schizophrenia, there is a complex disturbance of metaphoric symbolism in thought and language, and there may also be an infiltration with more primitive cryptophoric symbolism. This complex disturbance in metaphoric symbolism is ultimately due to the ease of regression in the usually maintained differentiation of the mental self, both the auto-psychic from the somato-psychic and the self from the non-self, the allo-psychic.[12] In addition to this, an infiltration with more primitive symbolism occurs due to the partial failure to maintain the boundary of the auto-psychic from the somato-psychic, a partial regression to the early infantile beginnings of ego-formation. As in regression generally, this regression in the ego does not simply replicate the earlier state of affairs but contaminates the earlier with distortions of later acquired functions, especially that of semantic speech. Some examples of disturbance of metaphoric symbolism and of infiltration with cryptophoric symbolism in schizophrenia are also offered here.

In contrast to the role of faded metaphor in the development of *generality*, more lively metaphor is heavily involved in *affective* communication. In hysteria this is often excluded from conscious expression in speech by the process of repression generated by conflict. However, metaphor often finds its outlet within the dramatic somatic symptoms through regression to its somato-psychic foundations.

Case 46. An example is provided by Jessica B., a white, single, 42-year-old elementary-school teacher who came one evening to the emergency room of the university hospital and was admitted to the hospital as an inpatient. Three weeks earlier, a week after her mother had been admitted to the hospital for congestive heart failure and a day after an argument with her landlady over a rent increase, she had awakened from sleep with numbness of the head and pains in her legs. Disturbed by these symptoms, she spent five days in her community hospital where a physical examination that included X-rays, blood studies and ECG disclosed no abnormalities. Her symptoms were described as functional and she was discharged. Three days afterward, feeling that her condition was worsening, she reported to the emergency room of the university hospital with the complaint that the numbness of her head had given way to 'peculiar sensations' and that when she walked her legs were even more painful than before.

After being sedated and having a night's sleep the patient disclosed in a psychiatric interview that she had recently been reprimanded before her colleagues by the principal of her school. She felt that the reprimand, which accused her of lax discipline with her pupils, was undeserved. She was out of sympathy with the principal's stringent disciplinary policy, but offered neither rebuttal nor defence. She insisted in the interview that she respected the principal, who although very strict, had never before been unfair. However, she thoughtfully conceded that the principal brooked no argument, and added that disagreement with her could result in her being dismissed as a former colleague had been in similar circumstances. It was clear that the patient was a dedicated and conscientious teacher who had given herself wholeheartedly to her work with children.

It was then mentioned that the principal was black. Jessica B. had grown up in a family strongly prejudiced against 'uppity' blacks, although she insisted that her college education had erased the racial prejudices of her early training.

Further discussion of Jessica's symptoms revealed that in spite of her efforts to keep her mind on her work her thoughts often turned to the incident of the reprimand and her silent humiliation, and that every time they did her head became numb. She then expressed the fear that she might 'blow her top' in a confrontation with the principal and ruin her career in doing so. Because of this she avoided running into her in any way as she moved about the school on her daily concerns, and this avoidance was becoming increasingly difficult as getting around became more and more tortuous and fraught with tension.

Interpretations were offered relating to the lack of usual sensation in the top of her head to her notion of 'blowing her top'; it was as though the untoward absence of feeling were a punishment embodying the notion. The pain of her legs in walking was interpreted as representing her feelings of discomfort over having to be about her business without encountering the principal. She appreciated with some surprise in further discussion the extraordinary way in which metaphors failing to gain verbal expression with appropriate emotion had 'gone underground' in a mute bodily manifestation. She was then able to discuss the anxiety and guilt associated with the mental conflict occasioned by the arousal of hate towards her black superior.

In subsequent psychotherapy the roots of her predisposition to hysterical conversion were found to be embedded in the nexus of her experience with her family as a child. Outwardly compliant, she had experienced bitter feelings of hostile rebellion against her mother, who had become gravely ill only recently. She had always been afraid to express herself at home, but when growing up she had inwardly felt herself superior to her uneducated, sensual, and tyrannical mother. Her individuation had, in fact, been built upon a 'negative identity'.

Metaphors are indeed not merely ornaments of speech. They may mediate the direct unreflective expression of strong feeling on the one hand, and, on the other, they are an essential part of the development of discursive exposition. As Sir Charles Sherrington pointed out in his Gifford lectures (1941),[13] where knowledge falters, the mind has recourse to metaphor. In fact, analogical thinking conveyed through metaphor is a basic requisite in the acquisition of knowledge; again and again as knowledge falters, metaphor is enlisted. To object to arguments because they are based on 'metaphorical thinking' is unjust; we have certainly at the least to use faded metaphor to keep our thinking afloat at all in discursive language. Anyway the question remains whether the metaphors employed represent useful similarities with conse-quent adequate reference to things, processes and relationships. As for the sort of metaphoric language which functions largely to convey feelings, its adequacy depends upon how well it performs this function. Often in the preliminary retranslation of hysterical somatic symtpoms to metaphoric language, it performs this function usefully.

The point to be made here is simply this: sometimes, a preliminary retranslation of part of the meaning of somatic symptoms to metaphoric language facilitates access to the emotions of the patient, especially those emotions associated with repressed drive derivatives which, together with these derivatives, are defended against because they come into conflict with how the patient thinks he *ought* to be motivated, how he *ought* to feel and to behave. It is to be noted that in the process of unconscious defence, the patient loses effective communication *within the self*, so that both inner self-related means of expression and communication and the outer expressive and communicative efforts become progressively more distorted—beneath a shell of rationalization which, together with the somatic symptoms, are eventually offered to the physician for his consideration.

The somatic symptoms of conversion hysteria condense a variety of messages, the emphasis differing in various symptomatic expressions. The following example will illuminate this statement:

Case 47. A middle-aged black woman whose life had become one of increasing hardship, economically, socially and sexually, developed a clouded (hypnoid) mental state associated with peculiar movements of the arms and fingers. She was referred for neurological investigation for the possible determination of brain tumour or a presenile organic dementia. This investigation, which was quite thorough yielded no positive pathological findings. The resident conducted a conversation with her while she was in amytal narcosis, at which time she discussed in a vague and disconnected way her father's encouragement of her education and her once-upon-a-time interest in the piano. At first sight of this lady, the psychiatrist said to the resident who had reported the ramblings of the patient in amytal narcosis, 'But she is now playing the piano.' In the ensuing short interview, the patient, with initial direction, went into considerable and vivid detail about her father's looking at her admiringly as she was playing the piano, and about how proud he was of her at this time during her school years—all described by the patient in the present tense.

In brief, in response to adverse life circumstances, this patient had retreated to a time of maximal happiness in her life, a time effectively symbolized by her piano playing with an encouraging, admiring, affectionate father at her side, with whom she confused the psychiatrist. Clinically, this case was a hysteriform borderline state, the conspicuous features being a hysterical pseudo-dementia, and apparently weird movements of the arms and fingers. These movements were in fact pantomimic in their essential nature. In discussing hysterical symptomatic attacks in 1909 Freud[14] wrote:

When one psychoanalyses a patient subject to hysterical attacks one soon gains the conviction that these attacks are nothing but fantasies projected and translated into motor activity and represented in pantomime.

As an example of disordered metaphoric symbolism in schizophrenic thought and language it is interesting to reconsider the case of paranoid schizophrenia so ably reported by Carl G. Jung in *The Psychology of Dementia Praecox* (1906).[15] The patient was investigated partly by use of the word-association tests which Jung had then recently invented. A middle-aged seamstress, she spontaneously verbalized fleeting delusions of grandeur and persecution. Thus she claimed to be a millionairess, and complained that in the night her bed had been filled with needles. In 1888, a year after admission to the Burghölzli Hospital, Jung described her speech as becoming 'more and more disconnected and her delusions less understood'. Nevertheless, he understood that she felt she had a mysterious 'monopoly' and by the aid of peculiar gestures eked out by a few words, he gleaned that a certain Rubinstein from St Petersburg sent her large sums of money. He commenced simple word-association tests and to the first item in the first of these, to the stimulus word 'Pupil', the patient responded with 'Now you may write: "Socrates".' Jung thought this was 'a quite striking reaction for a seamstress', and that it looked very affected and pointed to a complex of emotionally accentuated ideas. In regard to this response, as well as to others, including neologisms such as 'Groundpostament' (given as the 67th *stimulus* item on a later occasion), Jung attempted to learn what the patient had meant. This attempt was a failure, for in response to requests for explanation the patient produced a series of fresh neologisms comprising a word-salad, though she 'spoke in a self-confident tone, as if she were perfectly clear about the meaning of her words, and seemed to think what she said was an explanation'. Thereafter, Jung moved to the method of continuous associations in order to try to elucidate the meaning of her strange responses. He asked the patient to say all that came to her mind when he presented her successively with her own responses as fresh stimuli. Her response when thus presented with 'Socrates', is given below. Jung states that: 'As the patient spoke very slowly in reference to her delusions and was constantly disturbed by "thought-deprivations", her production could readily and literally be transcribed.' He therefore reproduced the tests verbatim omitting, however, the repetitions.

Socrates—scholar—books—wisdom—modesty—no words in order to express this wisdom—it is the highest *groundpostament*—his teachings—had to die on account of bad people—falsely accused—sublimest sublimity—self-satisfied—that is all Socrates—the fine learned world—no thread cut—I was the best tailoress, never had a piece of cloth on the floor—fine artist world—fine professorship—is *doubloon*—twenty-five francs—that is the highest—prison—slandered by bad people—unreason—cruelty—excess—rudeness.

There was apparently a long pause before 'no thread cut'. Jung[15] writes as follows:

The thoughts did not follow smoothly, but were constantly inhibited by 'thought-deprivation' which the patient designated as an invisible force which always takes away just what she wishes to say. Thought-deprivation appeared especially whenever she wished to explain something conclusively. The conclusive thing was the complex. Thus we see from the above analysis that the essential element appears only after having been preceded by a number of obscure analogies. The object of the test was, as the patient knew, to explain the neologisms. If it took her so long to reproduce the important phrase ('no thread cut') her imaginative faculty must have suffered from a peculiar disturbance which can be best designated as a *deficiency in the faculty of discrimination between important and unimportant material*. The explanation of her stereotype 'I am Scorates' or 'I am Soctratic' lies in the fact that she was the 'best seamstress' who never cut a thread and 'never had a piece of cloth on the floor'. She is an 'artist', a 'professor', in her line. She is tortured, she is not recognized as a world proprietress, etc. She is considered sick, which is a slander. She is 'wise' and 'modest'. She has performed the 'highest'. All these analogies to the life and end of Socrates. She therefore wishes to say 'I am and suffer like Socrates'. With a certain poetic licence, characteristic in a moment of strong affect, she says directly 'I am Socrates'. The pathological part of this lies in the fact that her identification with Socrates is such that she cannot free herself from it. She takes her identification somehow as self-evident, and she assumes so much reality for the metonymy that she expects everybody else to understand it. Here we distinctly see a deficient capacity to discriminate between two ideas. Every normal person can still differentiate between an assumed role or a metaphoric designation and his real personality, even if a vivid fantasy, i.e, an intense feeling-tone will for a time firmly adhere to such a dream or wish-formation. The connection does finally come with a reversal of feeling and with it a re-adaptation to reality ...

From Jung's account, it would seem that the patient became involved, at any rate fleetingly, in the false belief, the delusion, that she actually was Socrates. From her standpoint (as long as we assume as seems evident from Jung's report that she had read about the historical or Platonic Socrates' prosecution and death), Socrates, like herself, was a perfectionist; he too (*but metaphorically*) did not cut the thread, for he adhered to his commitment to pursue the truth by his dialectic method however much he was threatened. His exalted status as a philosopher likewise is analogous, from her standpoint, with her exalted position as 'World Proprietress', as having performed 'the highest', etc. She and he are alike in being in captivity and slandered, as she sees it. Her imaginative faculty is disturbed in a way that can be specified more narrowly than in Jung's assertion that the deficiency is 'in the faculty of discrimination between important and unimportant materials'. Certainly, it is important that Socrates was a man, and that he died in the year 399 B.C.; these two conditions are different from her own, but in her mind, they are overridden by the important respects in which she feels she resembles him. It is, of course, in the *completeness* of the identification that her imaginative faculty is disturbed. The trial identifications, part of the experiments of thought, which are controlled and integrated in the total process of reality-testing, often become quite uncontrolled in schizophrenia under the influence of strong emotion. In particular, as Freeman et al. (1959),[16] following Federn (1952),[17] have elaborated, there is a basic shakiness of ego boundaries so that ego-feeling may become invested heavily in one of these identifications. A regression to primary identification, to that sort of identification which preceded the formation of ego boundaries, then readily occurs under conditions of arousal of strong emotion.

Harold F. Searles (1965),[18] in discussing the increasingly stable thought differentiation in two treated and recovered schizophrenic patients, states:

Thus, although it is correct to say that without the establishment of firm ego boundaries, a differentiation between metaphorical [figurative] and literal meanings cannot take place, it would seem equally correct to say that metaphor, at least, could never develop if there had not once been a *lack* of such ego boundaries—if there had never been, as we believe there always has been, in infancy, a relatively unimpeded flow between the areas of experience which come, later, to be felt as inner world and outer world ...

The regression in schizophrenia which leads to profound disorder of metaphoric symbolism, constituting an important element in the varieties of disarray of thought and speech in the disease, is partially to a developmental phase which normally in its due season, is essential for the growth of semantic speech. One may add that the same kind of regression occurring in regulated quota is one element in creative thought. The poet John Keats designated this creative element as that of 'negative capability' (see Bate, 1963[19]).

In some forms and phases of schizophrenia the failure in repression and the regression in the psychic part of the total mental ego results not only in general disturbance of metaphoric symbolism but in an infiltration of that kind of symbolism which normally, after the repressive barrier has been established, is only evident in dreaming consciousness, that is, an infiltration of cryptophoric symbolism. The cryptophoric symbolism of dreams often replaces a part or function of the body by the visual image of an external object. Thus the male organ may be replaced by a snake or airplane, the female breasts by peaches, the female genitals by a jewel case. Indeed the visual cryptophoric symbolism of dreams pertains, to a very large extent, to the expression of sexual strivings and anxieties, the symbols substituting for sexual objects and relations. However, cryptophoric symbolism may also represent other parts of the body with images of other things, and sometimes may represent one part of the body by another part of the body.

In his essay on 'The Unconscious', Freud (1915)[20] discusses a patient suffering from schizophrenia who provides an example of the diffuse infiltration of cryptophoric symbolism into conscious thinking, though Freud does not designate the phenomenon in this way. He writes:

A patient whom I have at present under observation has allowed himself to be withdrawn from all the interests of life on account of a bad condition of the skin of his face. He declares that he has blackheads and deep holes on his face which everyone notices. Analysis shows that he is playing out his castration complex upon his skin. At first he worked at these blackheads remorselessly; and it gave him great satisfaction to squeeze them out, because, as he said, something spurted out when he did so. Then he began to think that a deep cavity appeared whenever he got rid of a blackhead, and he reproached himself most vehemently with having ruined his skin forever by 'constantly fiddling about with his hand'. Pressing out the content of the blackheads is clearly to him a substitute for masturbation. The cavity which then appears owing to his fault is the female genital ...

REFERENCES

1. Cratylus. In: The Dialogues of Plato (trans. Jowett, B.). In: Great Books of the Western World, Vol. 7. London: Encyclopedia Britannica (1952).
2. DeSaussure, F. (1916). Course in General Linguistics. New York: Philosophical Library (1959).
3. Coleridge, S. T. (1812). Lectures on Shakespeare and Milton. London.
4. Ferenczi, S. (1916). On obscene words. In: Contributions to Psychoanalysis. Boston: Badger.
5. Wegener, P. (1885). The Life of Speech (trans. Abse, D. W.). In: Speech and Reason (ed. Abse, D. W.). Charlottesville, Va: Univ. Press of Virginia; Bristol: Wright (1971).
6. Buhler, K. (1934). Sprachtheorie. Jena: Fischer.

7. Langer, S. K. (1942). *Philosophy in a New Key*. Cambridge, Mass.: Harvard Univ. (1957).
8. Peller, L. E. (1964). Language and its Prestages. *Bull. Philad. Assoc. Psychoanal.* **14,** 55.
9. Werner, H. and Kaplan, B. (1963). *Symbol Formation*. New York: Wiley.
10. Kraepelin, E. (1905). Über Sprachstorungen in Traume. *Psycholog. Arbeit.* **5,** 1.
11. Aristotle. *On Poetics*. In: *The Works of Aristotle* (trans. Bywater, I.). Chicago, Ill.: Univ. of Chicago Press (1952).
12. Wernicke, C. (1906). *Grundriss der Psychiatrie*. Leipzig: Barth.
13. Sherrington, C. (1941). *Man on his Nature: The Gifford Lectures*, 1937–38. Cambridge: Cambridge Univ. Press.
14. Freud, S. (1909). Some General Remarks on Hysterical Attacks. In: *The Standard Edition*, Vol. IX. London: Hogarth Press (1959).
15. Jung, C. G. (1906). *The Psychology of Dementia Praecox* (trans. Brill, A. A.). New York: Nervous and Mental Disease Publishing Co. (1936).
16. Freeman, T., Cameron, J. L. and McGhie, A. (1958). *Chronic Schizophrenia*. London: Tavistock.
17. Federn, P. (1952). *Ego Psychology and the Psychoses* (ed. and trans. Weiss, E.). New York: Basic Books.
18. Searles, H. F. (1965). The differentiation between concrete and metaphorical thinking in the recovering schizophrenic patient. In: *Collected Papers on Schizophrenia and Related Subjects*. New York: Int. Univ. Press.
19. Bate, W. J. (1963). *John Keats*. Cambridge, Mass.: Harvard Univ. Press.
20. Freud, S. (1915). The Unconscious. In: *The Standard Edition*, Vol. XIV. London: Hogarth Press (1957).

CHAPTER 17

Symbols, Affects and Language

Symbolization and Communication

We have tried to show that in hysteria, disturbances in interpersonal relationships provoke, or are the result of, intrapsychic conflicts. These disturbances and conflicts are then circularly aggravated and are subsequently, sooner or later, causally related to the onset of conversion reactions. In any particular case of hysterical conversion reaction the symptoms, as symbols, condense wishful and punitive fantasies. Moreover, inasmuch as these wishes and punitive fantasies are related to other people, both those in the patient's current life situation and those in his past, the symptoms, as symbols, also condense identifications with others of significance. The wishes are invariably of an intrapsychically forbidden character because of unconscious involvement with strivings and feelings of the early family drama embedded in memory. The symptoms, and symbols, also condense emotional expressions of appeal and sometimes of other emotions, such as anger or remorse. We have also tried to show that, besides connotations of wishes and fantasies and affects, denotational propositional pantomimic movements, or even secretions, may be involved, describing in a truncated and distorted way past experiences of import. These feats of condensation accomplished in the symptoms through unconscious symbolism are only elucidated gradually through word symbolism in the treatment process. It is then that we are confronted by the 'over-determination' of the symptoms, the corollary of condensation in the symptoms. The word symbols of communicative speech, unlike conversion symptoms (which we call a 'body language'), in general tend in the direction of clarifying and separating the elements of thought, relating them more logically and in terms of time and place, and expressing pertinent associated emotions more punctuately. For the patient, as for a naive observer, what is intelligibly communicated by the symptoms is essentially sickness, suffering and a need for help. The meanings may extend beyond this uncertainly in many directions, such as a notion that the illness is a condign punishment and a particular organic disease. The important point is that symbolization at the level of more primary process is of a different order from that at the level of secondary process, though the latter is constantly drawing on the former in verbal communication to a varying extent in prose, poetry and song.

As noted in Chapter 16, in discussing hysterical symptomatic attacks, Freud (1909)[1] wrote:

When one psychoanalyses a patient subject to hysterical attacks one soon gains the conviction that these attacks are nothing but fantasies projected and translated into motor activity and represented in pantomime. It is true that these fantasies are unconscious, but otherwise they are of the same nature as those that may be observed directly in day-dreams or revealed by an interpretation of nocturnal dreams.

He discusses the condensation of several fantasies, the multiple identifications, the antagonistic inversion of innervation, and the reversal of sequence of events in the movements of the attack, as well as the libidinal cathexes involved in the ideational content (fantasy). The symptoms in hysterical attacks, as in persistent somatic conversions, consist of condensed and otherwise distorted expressions which thus only indirectly represent, i.e., symbolize, the conflictual defence struggle of the patient.

Sapir (1933)[2] writes:

Many attempts have been made to unravel the origin of language, but most of these are hardly more than exercises of the speculative imagination. Linguists as a whole have lost interest in the problem ... It is probable that the origin of language is not a problem that can be solved out of the resources of linguistics alone but that it is essentially a particular case of a much wider problem of the genesis of symbolic behaviour and of the specialization of such behaviour in the laryngeal region, which may be presumed to have had only expressive functions to begin with.

In the symptoms of conversion hysteria there is this *expressive* function in which instinctual impulses that previously were repressed, and defences against them, are symbolized. In the passage from Freud's early essay (1909),[1] the defences are represented by the antagonistic inversion of innervation and the reversal of sequence of events in the movements of the attack, amongst other features of distortion, which include the dominance of primary process, namely, condensation and displacement. It is this very upset in the usual ratio of primary to secondary process which is the source of the initial unintelligibility of the symptom picture; later in the translation to word symbols the ratio is shifted, though here too the defensive aspects of communication assert themselves and the total defence struggle of the patient is only gradually unmasked.

The symptoms, then, consist in an autoplastic attempt at expression which is in the direction of discharging tension associated with intrapsychic conflict. Drive and defence are simultaneously symbolically expressed, short-circuiting conscious perception of conflict related to the early family drama. This expression in the ego-alien symptoms, reducing inner tension, is the so-called 'primary gain' of the illness. The secondary gain consists in the sequential utilization by the ego of the perceived symptoms to communicate to others (usually in a more or less transparent attempt at manipulation), and also to rationalize for the self. Such sequential manoeuvres, based as much on misinterpretation of the meaning of the experienced symptoms as on interpretation of them, may be elaborated in speech as part of the effort to manipulate other people and, through them, the current life situation. Thus the attention-attracting functions of the symptoms may be emphasized by associated non-verbal behaviour and verbal communication. Similarly, sympathy-, dominance- and compensation-gaining functions of the symptoms may be elevated into the foreground and justified non-verbally and verbally. The fact that this secondary gain is accomplished through more secondary-process associated ego activity does *not* mean that such gain is a matter of secondary importance to the patient emotionally. In the complex stratification of the psychic life these strivings are derivatives of frustrated oral-dependency needs for narcissistic supplies, and of anal-manipulative needs for mastery. The importance of secondary gain in the psycho-economy of the patient is maximal in instances in which there is heavy quantitative loading of pregenital fixation. These considerations are of considerable importance in treatment, as will be discussed later. It might also be noted here that, while in conversion hysteria genital wishes from the realm of the Oedipus complex find a distorted expression in the symptoms of somatic disorder, in some instances pregenital fixation may actually determine the selection of the organ involved in disordered function. There are also *pregenital conversions*, where the unconscious impulses expressed symbolically in the symptoms are predominantly pregenital; in such instances the clinical picture is hysteriform. The inner nature of the symptoms is still of a symbolic character and translatable into word language.

To be noted here are expression and communication—the partially separable aspects of the general process of symbolization. These expressive and communicative aspects are, of course, mutually interactive. Both are involved in evolved speech where the communicative aspect is more emphatic.* In early pre-stages of speech, as in the important lalling phase in the transition from infancy to childhood, the expressive aspects are dominant.

Fenichel (1945)[4] in Chapter XII of his book states: 'In conversion, symptomatic changes of physical functions occur which, unconsciously and in a distorted form, give expression to instinctual impulses that previously had been repressed.' He adds: 'Any neurotic symptom is a substitute for an instinctual satisfaction. However, conversion symptoms are not simply somatic expressions of affects but very specific representations of thoughts which can be retranslated from their "somatic language" into the original word language.' As just outlined, the condensed expressive symbolism of the symptoms may be translated into the more adequate communication afforded by word symbols. Ziegler et al. (1960),[5] Ziegler and Imboden (1962)[6] and Ziegler et al. (1963)[7] stress the social-communicative aspects of the symptoms, and, for the most part, pay attention to secondary process ego activity as this is related to secondary gain, rather than to the core-condensed expressive symbolism as this may be elucidated in psychoanalysis. The social-communicative aspects are indeed of considerable importance, related as these are to the pregenital problems of the patient and, distortively, to the core-condensed expressive symbolism in so far as this results from oral–anal determinants. But it is possible to overlook genital sexual symbolic aspects of hysterical

*In the 'Project for a Scientific Psychology' written in 1895, Freud (1950)[3] already suggested that the social function of speech is a secondary acquisition. The innervations of speech, he considered, were at first a discharge mechanism for the stored excitations in the retentive neurons; this path of discharge then acquired the highly important secondary function of establishing human contact. The infant screams and thus attracts attention to his distress; thenceforward the cries serve to bring understanding with other people and are gradually absorbed into speech associations.

symptoms with this kind of focus, especially as these are related to Oedipal problems. Often the resistance of the patient to the translation of incestuous wishes and castration anxiety involved in symbolic expression is heavier than to over-dependency problems.

Rangell (1959)[8] emphasizes, in accord with these views, that the somatic changes of conversion represent defensive forces as well as libidinal and aggressive impulses. As we have seen, Freud had already paid considerable attention to these defensive forces. Rangell also emphasizes that conversion can exist at any level of psychosexual development, from the phallic level of the hysterical personality to a primitive pregenital state, as for example, in the catatonia of schizophrenic disorder. We have seen that Jung (1906)[9] had early emphasized both the symptomatic resemblances in hysteria and schizophrenia and the dependence of these resemblances on a similarity in psychological mechanism. It should be noted, however, that in very primitive pregenital states, though the symptoms may be highly symbolic and massively defensive, and though it may be possible to translate them into word language, this cannot often be a matter of re-translation in any degree. For the defences and strivings represented in these symptoms are often grounded in preverbal experiences and reactions which have never achieved connection with preconscious word symbols. Perhaps rather, in some of these psychotic somatic symptoms, we can decry an anlage of neurotic conversion phenomena.

It was mentioned that the highly condensed symbolic process encountered in conversion phenomena is of a different order from the symbolic process employed in waking thought and language. The short quotation from Freud's essay, 'Some General Remarks on Hysterical Attacks', shows that early on he was impressed by parallels between the nature of hysterical symptoms and the dream. The dream is indeed the first member of a series that includes the hysterical symptom, the obsession, and the delusion. It is differentiated from the others by its transitory nature and by the fact that it occurs under conditions that are part of normal life. In patients with conversion reactions the connecting links between their dreams and their symptoms may be very clear (Abse, 1959[10]). As Freud states in his essay, not only are the forces producing the distortion and the purpose of the distortion of the expression of wishes the same as those we are familiar with from the interpretation of dreams, but the technique of the distortion is similar. In particular, the type of symbolism employed in symptom formation resembles that employed in manifest dream formation.

Ella Sharpe (1937)[11] writes of the latter: 'The dream then has a twofold value; it is the key to the understanding of unconscious fantasy and it is the key to the storehouse of memory and experience. The unconscious wish and fantasy have at their disposal all experiences from infancy.' As an approach to the mechanisms that make the manifest dream out of latent thoughts and the unconscious store of experience and impulse, she first details the principles and devices of poetic diction, since these principles show the impress of the same origin as dream mechanisms. She indicates the help to be obtained in elucidating dreams 'from the simple fact that the bridges of thought are crossed and recrossed by names, that the basis of language is implied metaphor and that we all learned our mother tongue phonetically'.

Some Further Aspects of Language Development and the Conversion Process

In Chapter 16, we discussed some views concerning the origin and acquisition of language. We stressed the imitative aspects, not only in terms of imitation of conventional sounds—phonetic imitation of the words used in the immediate milieu of the learner—important as this is, but of the original selection of words in terms of imitation of natural sounds emanating from animate and inanimate objects around (onomatopoeia) and, more than this, in terms of sounds which otherwise suggest the sense through associations grounded in the very matrix of perception, itself genetically synaesthetic and sensori-motor. The word 'onomatopoeia' literally means 'name-making' and name-making requires a mental fusion of word and thing.* The significance of the word 'water', for example, burst upon Helen Keller (1902),[14] when the stream gushed over her hand, not before, when she had simply needed water and attempts had been made to exploit the need to teach her the name. There is a primitive process of transient identification of word and thing and self involved, so we think, in the complex processes of language acquisition which ramifies into more superficial forms of imitation. In the acquisition of verbal language by an individual the 'lalling stage' of babyhood is of great importance. Thus Latif (1934),[15] quoted by Langer (1942),[16] states:

"Many more sounds are produced by the infant during this period than are later used, at least in its own language ..." Yet the passing of the instinctive phase is marked by the fact that a great many phonemes which do not meet with response are completely lost. Undoubtedly that is why children, who have not entirely lost the impulse to make random sounds which their mother tongue does not require, can so easily learn a foreign language, and even master several at once ... [She later states] There is an optimum period of learning, and this is a stage of mental development in which several impulses and interests happen to coincide: the lalling instinct, the imitative impulse, a natural interest in distinctive sounds, and a great sensitivity to 'expressiveness' of any sort.†

As we noted, Bühler (1934),[19] called attention to an elementary stage in the development of language which he designated as 'empractic'. A child may use one word to his mother and, just as he confidently expects, she will respond by her extended understanding of the request. For example, when my

---

*Freud (1891)[12] found that some aphasic disorders suggested a divorce between word and thing presentations. Thus in some cases of aphasia patients show a severe word-need though retaining ability to respond appropriately to the corresponding thing, indicating differential damage to the brain bases subserving 'word' and 'thing' functions.

De Saussure, in his *Course in General Linguistics* (1916),[13] shows that what emerges as a sound image or word—in his terms, a linguistic sign—is a union of 'signifier' and 'signified'. But, unlike the view here propounded, he considers, as did Aristotle in contradistinction to Plato, that the linguistic sign is quite arbitrary, i.e., with no inner relationship of sound image, thought, and signified thing. He writes: 'Because the sign is arbitrary, it follows no law other than that of tradition.' I have tried to show earlier that it is not *only* a question of onomatopoeia; otherwise, of course, all languages would use the same imitative words.

†*See also* Laffal (1964)[17] and Peller (1964).[18]

small son used to say, 'Outdoors!', his mother would respond by gathering the appropriate toys and taking him with them to his sandbox in the yard. Certainly many of a child's complex requests are couched in one-word imperatives. The word is inserted, as it were, into a situation diacritically, creating a response which changes the situation. Bühler writes: 'Where a diacritical verbal sign is built into the action, it frequently needs no surrounding framework or other verbal indicators.' He cites the example of the patron in a restaurant—that he intends to eat is understood by the waiter, and he speaks only at the crucial point in his otherwise tacit intelligible behaviour, as a diacritical sign: 'He inserts it, and the ambiguity is removed; that is the *empractic* use of language'* Wegener (1885),[20] as we have outlined in Chapter 16, expounded the growth of explicit statement from such a matrix, namely the communication by key words eked out by pointing in an obvious situation or context. Many have found themselves in an analogous situation when in a foreign country with only a meagre available vocabulary. Wegener also adduced two important principles of further linguistic development: emendation and metaphor.

It was stated earlier in this chapter that symbolization at the level of predominantly primary process activity is of a different order from that at the level of predominantly secondary process, though secondary process activity is constantly drawing on primary process activity in speech communication. More than this, in the history of the group creative process in which language has evolved to the developed phase of discursive exposition there has been a continuous interplay of primary and secondary process, periodically reaching greater intensity in certain individuals and accelerating the evolution of

---

*The empractic use of speech is evident when an adult in a situation of obvious emergency employs only the key word, 'Help!' Of course, under conditions of disease, the empractic use of language even in emergencies can become deranged. For example, a student suffering from diabetes mellitus, falling into hypoglycaemia while working in his room, attracted the attention of his landlady by loud cries. She found him in his room mixing flour and treacle and pouring the concoction over his coat. His disordered behaviour led to the summoning of a physician whose efforts, however, to administer sugar were resisted by the student; shortly he was rushed to the hospital for necessary attention. The disordered behaviour of loud shouting and mixing of flour and treacle were based on the student's knowledge of his illness inasmuch as, in a hyponoic state, he unconsciously demonstrated the mess he was in on account of impaired carbohydrate metabolism; but he was also expressing his rage about his illness which was a handicap to his work; moreover, he was expressing denial of his illness in his transactions with the physician who first came to his assistance. Certainly, in such instances of disordered consciousness, the utterances, like other aspects of the behaviour, are meaningful but more or less undecipherable expressions (though the trained investigator-observer, as in this instance, may discover their meaning); being thus cryptic communications, they serve in the situation only to heighten its ambiguity. This ambiguity is part and parcel of the sufferer's conflictual motives and feelings; he has not, at this level of thought formation, reached a clear conscious intention unimpeded by countercurrents within himself. Frequently in alcoholic intoxication, the empractic use of words serves to increase the ambiguity of emitted messages, because fundamental ambivalences are being expressed. Usually, under conditions of clearer consciousness, key words help to resolve the external ambiguities in the setting of a more or less obvious situation which includes motor behaviour, and help to clarify the intentions of the speaker for those addressed.

language, and thus of human thought. In the novel predication where metaphor becomes a must, the processes of primitive identification, condensation and displacement are harnessed to and controlled by logical thought. In the thought experiments of reasoning inappropriate condensations and displacements are rejected, and those that are appropriate emerge as logical analogies by means of which metaphors and other figures of speech are achieved. A word symbol formed by transient identifications in perceptual experience is displaced from its original referent and condensed with another. We might add too, briefly here, that in the fading of these metaphors the original referents often come to be subdued or repressed. The general words come to provide a basis for the abstract attitude.*

In mental diseases, especially in schizophrenia, there is a complex disturbance of abstract thinking, the complexity of the disturbance partly showing itself in a retrogressive direction of thought formations accompanied and overlaid by strange over-ideational restitutional efforts. This disordered thinking is reflected in disfigurements of speech. In hypnoid alterations of consciousness among other features there is a sharp tendency towards an empractic use of language.

Ella Sharp (1937)[11] discusses how an awareness of the phonetic acquisition of language and of its development via metaphor can help us to realize the import of words in terms of human experience. To take full advantage of this in investigative psychotherapy we need to remember that words acquire secondary meanings and convey abstract ideas, but they do not lose the concrete significance experienced in their first hearing and use in the unconscious storehouse of the individual's past. The historical past of words is often enough involved in the historical past of the speaker, and even when it is not, the word is always connected with the speaker's historical past. As three examples among many to illustrate the fact that, apart from other psychical values that follow from self-expression as such, the very language used in self-expression will itself yield up significance, Ella Sharp gives the following; the first is one of phonetic or clang association:

*In the complex process of interplay of primary and secondary processes, condensation is used more discriminatively to achieve identification. Displacement in also used more discriminatively under the regulative reality principle. The upshot of regulated condensation, identification, and displacement emerges as another order of symbolic activity. This kind of transformation is involved, of course, in sublimation in which instinctual strivings are compelled to detours whereby desexualization is accomplished. The aims of the strivings are changed through endopsychic displacements and more discriminate identifications, i.e., there is a symbolic reorganization of experience. To give two brief clinical examples recently encountered: the speleological interests of a young man were found to be derived from preoccupation with and anxious perplexity about the female genitals, and part of the defence to surmount severe castration anxiety associated with an unconscious current of resistance against recognizing that women do not possess penises; in another case, in the course of decompensation, a microbiologist became the victim of compulsive peeping—a major sublimation became reduced to its original source in sexual curiosity. So far, the process of sublimation is inadequately discussed in the psychoanalytic literature, despite phrases such as 'neutralization'. It is to be noted here that there is a gradient in the unconscious symbolic reorganization of experience, so that sublimated activities come to be of a different order from their sources in unconscious primordial symbolism.

An inhibition in connection with reading the daily paper was illuminated for me by a patient bewailing the fact repeatedly, 'I have not read the paper this week. I don't know what is happening. I haven't looked at the paper at all.' During the course of the analytical hour, her seemingly chance associations brought her to the fact that she was menstruating. Then the theme with which she opened came to my mind: 'I have not read the paper. I don't know what is happening.' I realized then that the sound 'red' will be first known by a tiny child in conjunction with a colour sensation, and that the later use of 'read' as the past tense or past participle of 'read' will carry with it also its first significance. Thus I was put on the track of an actual experience, namely that of seeing menstrual blood in a lavatory [paper] when the sight had aroused anxiety. So we can understand a deeper significance in 'I don't know what is happening in the world'.

Another patient reports a dream: 'You were sitting in a deck-chair wearing a sailor hat.' Sharpe writes:

Let us forget unconscious symbolism for the moment and pursue only this device of metonymy. 'A sailor hat', said my patient with the ingenuousness of the direct child, 'will be a hat belonging to a sailor, and as you were sitting in a deck-chair it means you represent a sailor.' 'What kind of sailor?' I queried. 'Well, I once told my mother you looked like a pirate.' 'Which pirate?' I asked. 'Oh, Captain Hook, I'm sure.' We were then launched on a wealth of fantasy concerning the nefarious practices of pirates in comparison with which the bald interpretation of a sailor hat as unconsciously meaning a phallus could have been barren indeed.

The above example is especially good for its bearing on the practice of psychotherapy and the importance of reaching the emotions of the patient.

In Chapter 2, the symptom of bent back or camptocormia in soldiers was briefly discussed, and in this discussion we mentioned that to describe lack of courage and stability common speech utilizes metaphoric phrases which denote impairment of the erect posture. We hear of people who 'lack backbone', of the 'spineless' and, in a directive context, this conveys to us vividly the powerlessness of these people to stand up for themselves. Such comparatively unfaded metaphor conveys sometimes more vividly than phrases which include 'courage' (a more faded metaphor from the Latin *cor* = heart) or 'stability' (from the Latin *stare*, to stand) the meaning of cowardice (from the Latin *cauda* = tail). This metaphoric language, which in verbal context is a novel predication, is embodied in the conversion symptom in a non-verbal context of the military situation; the symptom is equivalent to a word used empractically. We notice too that the less vivid, or rather faded, metaphors of the words 'courage' and 'stability' and 'cowardice',* useful as they are as generalizations about certain qualities of character, are themselves derived from body parts and functions. Indeed it is usually the case that metaphoric language derived from adverse or pleasurable sensuous bodily

---

*Freud (1910)[21] notes that, as in dreams, contraries are not kept apart, so philologists have found in the oldest languages contraries such as 'strong-weak', 'light-dark', 'high-deep' were expressed by the same word. Remains of this original double meaning seem to have survived even in highly developed languages; thus, in Latin *altus* = 'high' and 'deep', and *sacer* = 'holy' and 'accursed'. This antithetical sense of primal words, which could be given one direction in context, may help to explain the derivation of the word 'cowardice' from a word denoting 'tail'.

experience and involving the body image itself more than the outside world, is involved in the re-translation of the symbolic somatic symptom into words. In camptocormia the unconscious symbolism of castration, or reduction to passive homosexual impotence, is reached only after an excursion into this metaphoric language which more easily mediates emotional expression, being less deeply repressed. At the deeper level we reach the primary type of symbolism, namely, the equating of one part of the body with another; the spine, the tail and the posture of the body in general depicting the phallus in its erect or flaccid condition.

The symptom of camptocormia ('the functional bent back') is discussed by Simons (1964)[22] in a case of overt schizophrenic disease. In this case the patient himself offers concretistic, magical and paranoid explanations for his disability, some of which, however, seem to be secondarily elaborated from the symptom which partially failed in its conversive defensive function of displacement of instinctual pressures from psyche to soma.

In the symptoms of conversion hysteria verbal messages are reduced to wordlessness, a regression which partakes of the qualities of the one-word sentence in the empractic use of language. For example, the soldier with bent back is in a situation where there are expectations concerning his behaviour which arouse conflict in him. These expectations, sufficiently clearly embedded in the military situation, are unacceptable to him because of a nostalgic countercurrent against compliance. Since discipline does not permit a clearly negative response verbally or non-verbally, he had to find a moot point significant of ambiguity in the clearly established setting; this he finds in the proviso that only sickness provides an adequate excuse for non-compliance. Thus the situation is rendered somewhat ambiguous and he then inserts his symptom in order to resolve the ambiguity. The symptom which dramatizes a broken back is thus of social-communicative value in the here-and-now of the total situation which includes his experience and that of those relating to him. Indeed, when in psychotherapy we attempt to clarify this situation, the symptom is apt to 'join in the conversation' in a way suggesting the insistence on repeating the word 'sick'. The bent back will bend even lower under such circumstances; similar exacerbations of symptoms are frequent in the early phases of psychotherapy with many cases of conversion hysteria. In Chapter 2 we discussed the case with hyperhidrosis of the wrist as an example. The hyperhidrosis increased in severity *pari passu* with a heightening of the patient's resistances at the beginning of psychotherapy; the symptom, in this way, joined in the dialogue, attempting to resolve again the ambiguity which the psychotherapy was reviving, and to resolve it, of course, in a flight into illness.

The symptoms are thus, at this (social-communicative) level, a substitute for words in an empractic use of language. The social-communicative aspects to which Ziegler et al. (1960),[5] Ziegler and Imboden (1962)[6] and Ziegler et al. (1963)[7] have paid so much attention are largely concerned with this, and the further secondary elaboration of this demonstrative indication of the patient's plight in his current experience. We can, of course, put into our words what at this level is communicated symptomatically, and further elaborated in the course of time both verbally and non-verbally, and addressed to family members, the doctor, and others involved in the patient's life space; it would be a 'novel predication' like this: 'I am physically sick, and need help, sympathy, and special consideration on this account in this particular situation.' What is actually expressed in the symptoms is, however, both *more* than this and, in important aspects, *different* from this; this *more* and this *different* are, of course, excluded from the awareness of the patient but may be recovered in analytic psychotherapy. Briefly and roughly it can be said that the immediate social-communicative aspects of the symptoms are to a large extent equivalent to the empractic use of language, and also to a large extent refer to secondary gain; whereas more extensive novel predications are recovered in the further efforts in psychotherapy to elucidate the inner meanings of the symptoms, and to bring these meanings, which inlcude primary gain, to expression in discursive language.

Freud (1911)[23] showed that, in a case of paranoia, as far as the unconscious homosexual wish fantasy was concerned, delusions could all be represented as contradictions of the proposition: 'I (a man) love him (a man).' This predication had to be excluded from the awareness of the patient and was replaced by delusions of persecution. In the first place, the contradiction becomes 'I do not love him—I hate him'; then the latter proposition becomes transformed by projection into 'He hates me', which justifies the patient in his hate. Several authors who have since discussed the Schreber case point out that the judge suffered severe traumatic experiences in childhood.* Then, at a certain stage in his life cycle, and following precipitating stresses, his mental disorder began and included delusions of persecution based on homosexual wish fantasies which had become heavily cathected. What is of pertinence here is that aroused unconscious strivings and feelings, in a provoking situation and in a vulnerable personality, pressed for conscious representation as 'I (a man) love him (a man)'. This was replaced by another (preconscious) novel predication before an acceptable version found ideational and feeling representation consciously. In paranoid disorder this replacement process occurs in the psychic sphere. In conversion reactions the ultimate replacement is in the somatic symptom. The preconscious penultimate novel predications are repressed after achieving word connection and then are embodied in the symptom. Thus are embodied in the symptoms of conversion hysteria the metaphors of these novel predications concerned with drive-cathected interpersonal realtionships, and in these embodiments are also the more primitive versions from which the metaphoric replacements themselves are derived. We here reconstruct a course of events which in practice, in investigative psychotherapy, is in the reverse direction. For we are gradually enabled to retranslate the symptoms from their cryptic symbolism into these ideational representations; and first of all to those which have acquired word connections, often in a metaphoric language which is affect-laden.

In this description, inadequate notice has been taken of those counter-cathecting defensive forces which are the basis of censorship of the emerging

---

*The following are among the writers who have notably contributed towards an understanding of the Schreber Case and of paranoid ideations: Freud (1911),[23] Baumeyer (1956),[24] Fairbairn (1956),[25] Friedmann (1905),[26] Gierlich (1928),[27] Greenspan (1964),[28] Katan (1950),[29] MacAlpine and Hunter (1955),[30] Niederland (1951,[31] 1959a,[32] 1959b,[33] 1960[34]), Salzman (1960),[35] Volkan (1976),[36] White (1961).[37]

predications. For example, paranoid perceptual distortion of external reality is based also on an initial defence against affect, a pleasurable affect accompanying homo-erotic wish fantasies which itself would otherwise convey some degree of subjective awareness; in other words, a signifying emotion is, in the total defence, replaced by misperception which justifies an affect (disgust) of opposite signification.

Affect Symbolism
The Stream of Consciousness and the Expression of Feelings

A river is always flowing. It may move slowly and peacefully over most of its reaches, and then suddenly the stream-bed falls rapidly and the river hurries along in a turmoil of broken water. The individual consciousness is also in perpetual flow, moving perhaps slowly and peacefully within the close confines of particular circumstances of life until these change drastically and the movement becomes a turmoil. Often the clinician, for example, witnesses the fate of the obsessive-compulsive woman at the climacteric, when the changes of outer circumstances and of somatic conditions result in an agitated (involutional) melancholia. More usually, to paraphrase William James (1890)[38] conscious experience is a teeming multiplicity of objects and relations and feelings in constant flow, constantly changing more or less rapidly, and sometimes there is a narrowing or broadening of the stream or a changing of direction and velocity. From this immediately given introspective general picture of our own experience, for each one of us is, so to speak, a more or less separate 'river', clinical observation reaches outward to enable inferences about and comparisons of the stream of consciousness, of the characteristic qualities of segments of individual experience, in disease. The individual experiences in different diseases may be compared not only with one another—as in Chapter 10 we compared some hypnoid alterations of consciousness with some depersonalization disturbances—but with spontaneously occurring shifts of consciousness in health, as in Chapter 10 too, when we described the shifts in aesthetic experience, or as may also be attempted by study of the dreaming consciousness, reveries and hypnagogic states. Moreover, artificially induced shifts in the flow of consciousness are also available for study; those induced by drugs or by hypnosis often reveal dramatic changes.

Rapaport (1957)[39] suggested the following criteria as aids in defining the varieties of thought organization that characterize different states of consciousness: the use of visual imagery, the use of verbalization, the awareness of awareness, explicitness or implicitness, differentiation and the recruitment of connotative enrichment by means of condensation, displacement and symbolism. These and other aspects of thought organization have been briefly considered in these pages as they arose for consideration from clinical experience of different disorders of consciousness in hysteria and hysteriform diseases. It has been observed that the qualities of thought organization vary in a remarkable way with variations in both the quality and intensity of the affective and conative ground in which the thinking is embedded. Bleuler (1906)[40] first endeavoured to relate supervalent ideas to a basis in a chronic affect which had arisen in response to actual experience. In this way he breached the ramparts which kept the alienist with his patient remote from the realm of unconscious orexis anchored in memory.

Not only do the phenomenologic characteristics of a disturbed state of consciousness require careful clinical observation as was emphasized in the work of Kraepelin, but these characteristics require to be related to the total defensive struggle of the individual patient as was emphasized in the work of Freud. The formal characteristics of thought organization, the thought content, the affective experience and expression, the felt impulses and the evident activity, all these, as observed, reported and inferred, are inter-related and related to unconscious determinants. Only by grasping these relationships can we understand the phenomena in depth, in the framework of maladaptation and the defensive struggle against ego-alien impulses and affects.

McDougall (1923)[41] rightly insisted that conative experience is the felt impulse to action and is prominent in experience in proportion to the strength of the working of the impulse. Such felt impulse is present in all emotional experience. When, for example, we are afraid we feel the impulse to retreat or to escape from the object which frightens us; when we are angry we feel the impulse to attack the object which angers us; when we are curious we feel the impulse to draw nearer to the exciting object. We become more easily introspectively aware of the impulse when we do not give ourselves up to it, but, suspending it, turn our attention from the object to ourselves. McDougall states:

> If the conative factor could be subtracted from an emotional experience, without other change, that experience would be radically altered. We might still think of the object, and our thinking would still be coloured by the emotional quality: but the whole experience would be profoundly different; it would seem to lack its very essence, to be empty and unreal.

As originally pointed out by Charles Darwin (1872)[42] and developed by McDougall (1923),[41] the expressions of the emotions are essentially adaptations of the body to modes of instinctive activity. Thus, when the 'instinct' of escape is excited the impulse vents itself and attains its goal, primarily by swift locomotion. But in order that these locomotory movements (running, flying or swimming) shall attain the highest possible effectiveness there are secondary adjustments of the body, 'serviceable associated reactions', as Darwin called them. These adaptations of the body are importantly mediated by the autonomic nervous system supplemented by endocrine secretions. Thus, in flight the heart and lungs work more rapidly; the blood-flow is shunted from the digestive tract and skin to be concentrated in the lungs, muscles and brain; the pupils of the eyes are dilated so that as much light as possible is admitted from the field of vision; the bladder and intestine may even be emptied. As McDougall states:

> It is the sum of these effects which we call the expression of the emotion of fear—the dilated pupil, the staring eye, the dry mouth, the arrested digestion, the pallor of the skin, the rapid pulse and breathing, the voiding of urine, all these are symptoms of fear—together they constitute the unmistakeable expression of fear.

Darwin also emphasized the contraction of the facial risorium and the platysma of the neck, drawing the corners of the mouth and lower part of the cheeks downward and backward and ridging the sides of the neck, with widely open eyes and mouth, at a certain intensity of fear. He pointed out that sometimes part of the expression of an emotion, though currently purposeless, was originally of use to our forebears. He amplifies this by reference to tame animals. Thus the Sheldrake duck feeds on the sands left uncovered by the tide and when a wormcast is discovered 'it begins patting the ground with its feet, dancing as it were, over the hole, and this makes the worm come to the surface. Now Mr St. John says that when his tame Sheldrakes came to ask for food, they patted the ground in an impatient and rapid manner.' But he also points out the former usefulness to ancestral types of apparently unserviceable associated involuntary movements. Moreover, he introduced his 'principle of antithesis': certain emotional states lead to habitual movements which were primarily, or may still be, of service; but when a directly opposite emotional state is induced there is a strong and involuntary tendency to the performance of movements of a directly opposite nature though these have never been of any service. Finally, of pertinence here, Darwin alluded to the human importance of the expression of the emotions even when their primary biological utility was lost in the sands of time:

> The movements of expression in the face and body, whatever their origin may have been, are in themselves of much importance for our welfare. They serve as the first means of communication between the mother and her infant; she smiles approval, and this encourages her child on the right path, or frowns disapproval. We readily perceive sympathy in others by their expression; our sufferings are thus mitigated and our pleasures increased; and mutual good feeling is thus strengthened. The movements of expression give vividness and energy to our spoken words. They reveal the thoughts and intentions of others more truly than do words, which may be falsified.

Affects and Subjective Awareness

One result of ignoring development during childhood and infancy may be lists of instincts, as postulated, for example, by McDougall. For review of development often shows that what later appears on the basis of goal seeking to be a discrete adult activity is originally derived from the same instinct source as another adult activity. On the other hand, the sexual instinct has been shown by developmental studies to have many components. In short, without a developmental viewpoint which includes the events of infancy it is only too easy to make false assumptions in instinct theory. These criticisms, like others based on psychoanalytic knowledge, should not, however, lead us to ignore McDougall's important work, especially the evidence with which he develops his view that emotions are essentially indicators of the working of derivatives of instinctive impulses. He shows that fear, anger, disgust, tender feelings, lust, distress (feeling of helplessness), elation, loneliness and other feelings have a cognitive function; they signify to us primarily, not the nature of things, but rather the nature of our impulsive reactions to things. They are the cognitive bases of self-knowledge and self-control. In this sense they are subjective rather than objective in function, primarily subserving cognition of the state of activity of the organism. With this view, he modifies the Lange–James theory of emotions. Thus, he states (McDougall, 1923[41]):

We are now prepared to consider the famous Lange–James theory of the emotions, and to understand in what sense it is true, and in what respects erroneous. The essence of the theory is the assertion that the 'emotions' are essentially of the same nature as 'sensations'; that 'an emotion', as felt or as an emotional quality, is a mass or complex of confused sensory experience arising from the sensory impressions made by the processes going on in the various organs of the body, and that each distinguishable quality of emotion owes whatever is specific or peculiar in its quality to the specific conjunction of bodily impressions made by a specific conjunction of bodily activities, the visceral organs playing a predominant part in this sensory stimulation. If this statement is modified or supplemented by recognizing that, just as the sensory qualities of the special senses are duplicated in imagery, the sensory qualities of the visceral or bodily senses are also duplicated in imagery, we must, I think, accept it as substantially true.

And he goes on to criticize severely the over-statement of James which results in the largely false paradox that emotion is the consequence of bodily activities; so that, for James, we feel sorry only because we cry, instead of its being largely the other way around. James had ignored the fact that sensational qualities may be centrally excited in the form of imagery, independently of immediate external stimulation, or, to quote Spinoza (1677),[43] a man is as much affected pleasurably or painfully by the image of a thing past or future as by the image of a thing present.

The view that emotion can lend cognitive steer was overlooked to a considerable extent following Kant's categorization of knowing, feeling, and striving in the eighteenth century. It appears that Kant had an excessive, one might say obsessional, distrust of emotion, regarding it as destructive to logical thought (see, for example, *The Critique of Judgement*, written in 1790[44]), which indeed it can be, especially when there is *emotional flooding*. We have already discussed some aspects of this in relation to schizophrenic thought disorder (Chapter 8). Earlier, Spinoza (1677)[43] (*see also* Meerloo, 1965[45]) had noted the cognitive values of affects. At the same time too, especially in his essay on 'Human Bondage or the Strength of the Emotions' he clearly expatiated on the theme of human infirmity in moderating and checking the emotions. Freud came to a turning point in his attitude towards emotion, indeed to a revolution in his own thinking, when he recognized the signal function of anxiety and the ego's capacity to reduce anxiety for its defensive and adaptive functions. This recognition was developed considerably in *Inhibitions, Symptoms and Anxiety* (Freud, 1926[46]).

In the early days of psychoanalysis affect was equated with the quantity of operative psychic energy in a temporal segment of mental activity. As the instinctual sources of psychic energy were later elaborated conceptually this equation became tantamount to the equation of affect with the quantity of drive cathexis, an equation which, we have seen above, McDougall disputes, partially separating the felt strength of drive as he does from the accompanying emotion. Breuer and Freud (1893)[47] write that the therapy 'brings to an end the operative force of the idea which was not abreacted in the first instance, by allowing its strangulated affect to find a way out through speech'. Later, such ideas were explicitly regarded as derivatives of cathected drives. In 1900 Freud shifted attention to affective experience as the psychic reflection of discharge processes of energies of instinctual somatic origin, thereby, as Brierly (1951)[48] indicates, ranging affects on the efferent rather than on the afferent pathway of the instinctual arc. But this is actually a complementary proposition since the development, realization, and recession of an emotion take place in time and comprise from inception circular efferent–afferent processes which become integrated into the complex of experience. And Freud (1926)[46] later, as just noted, laid emphasis on the relation of affective experience to executive, adaptive, and defensive aspects of ego functioning. Previously, in 1900, he had recognized that one of the concomitants of the development of the secondary process and of reality testing was the taming of affects by their transformation into signals, a reduction normally only partially maintained, and a quarter of a century later he elaborated on this signal function.

When Fenichel (1941)[49] reviews these considerations he points out that children and neurotic persons have more frequent emotional spells than mature adults. A mature adult, of course, does not lack emotion but he does not have overwhelming emotional spells. The ego's increasing strength enables damping of the affects at the moment of arousal. The ego is no longer overwhelmed by something alien to it, but it senses when this alien something begins to develop, and simultaneously upon this recognition it re-establishes its mastery, binding the affects, using them for its purposes, 'taming' them.* 'To be sure', Fenichel (1941)[49] writes, 'even the most adult ego can [only] do this to a certain degree.' He then describes a stage of development in which the ego is weak and the affect dominant, followed by another stage in which the ego is stronger and has learned to use the affects for its purposes. He notes that a third stage is always possible in which once more an elemental affect may overwhelm the organism. The genuinely stronger ego is, one should add, more open to emotional experience, does not require the rigid checks which detract from the psychobiological value of signal function, and is consequently less brittle and less liable to overwhelming affective experience. In schizophrenic patients, for example, the hyperexic defence against affect breaks down frequently and has far-reaching and protracted effects. In itself this defence is already pathological inasmuch as experience is impoverished and self-realization through ensuing integration of felt experience is impeded. In those liable to schizophrenia the breakdown of rigid defences results in far-reaching disorganization of executive and adaptive ego functions, including perception, memory, and thinking.

Psychoanalytic affect theory remains incomplete and suffers from lack of contact with the views of philosophers and with the evidence, hypotheses, and considerations raised by other psychologic approaches. Here it is relevant to draw attention to this facet of the function of affects, namely, their cognitive

---

*It is this taming of affects beyond mere signals into felt emotion which is not overwhelming, which especially justifies, I think, the use of the term 'affect symbol' in the general sense. A once-serviceable associated reaction is suspended and abbreviated and the part-reaction is utilized at another level to inform the self; also it often communicates effectively to others. As expounded later affect symbolism is distorted in psychophysiologic disorder so that its cognitive value is diminished or deleted.

value. Jung (1920)[50] in his typology has discussed the importance for some people, the so-called 'predominantly feeling types', of orientating themselves both subjectively and objectively on the basis of their feelings. Rignano (1911)[51] has contributed some important views, especially in regard to the fundamentally mnemonic nature of affective tendencies. Twenty years ago, Alexander and Isaacs (1964)[77] discussed this function of affect. We will now address ourselves to the supplementary cognitive steer afforded by affects in relation to the changing situations of outer reality.

Affects and Calculation of the Probability of 'Good' and 'Bad'

McDougall (1923)[41] designates emotions which accompany specific modes of instinctive striving as primary. When multiple instinctive modalities are simultaneously in operation, the accompanying emotions are described as secondary, or fused, or blended, and he gives many instances. Of these instances we will repeat only those of admiration and awe.

Admiration, he maintains, is a complex affective state and not merely a pleasurable perception or contemplation. There seem to be two primary emotions essentially involved, namely, wonder and negative self-feeling or the emotion accompanying the instinct of submission. Wonder is revealed by the impulse to approach, characteristic of the instinct of curiosity. But the approach is hesitant. We do not simply proceed to examine the admired object as we should one that provokes merely curiosity and wonder. We also have the impulse to shrink together, to be still and to avoid attracting his attention; that is to say, the instinct of submission is excited, with its corresponding emotion of negative self-feeling, by the perception that we are in the presence of a superior power. As an example of the further complication of an emotion McDougall considers the nature of our emotion if the object of our admiration is also of a threatening and mysterious nature and therefore capable of exciting fear—a tremendous force in action, such as the Victoria Falls, or a display of the Aurora Borealis, or a magnificent thunderstorm. The impulse of admiration to draw near humbly and to contemplate the object is countered in some measure by an impulse to escape. We are kept suspended in the middle distance, neither approaching very near nor going quite away; in short, admiration, itself a blended emotion, is blended with fear, as we experience the emotion we call 'awe'.

There is another class of emotions which McDougall describes and with which we must now concern ourselves, namely, the derived emotions. An emotion of this class is not constantly correlated with any one impulse or tendency, but rather may arise in the course of any strong impulse or tendency and is the product of the influence of a new cognition concerning the object to which that impulse is directed. McDougall (1923)[41] writes:

> The force or energy which literary convention and common speech attribute to such emotions as hope or anxiety or joy is in reality the energy of the desire from which the derived emotion springs; this energy is reinforced in hope and joy by the pleasurable anticipation of success; moderated or checked in anxiety and despondency by the anticipation of failure; and rendered painful in sorrow by the baffling of all action.

The primary emotions largely owe their specific qualities to the visceral sense impressions made by the bodily changes accompanying instinctive strivings. In the developed mind every excitement of a primary emotion or of blended emotion involves conation and also cognition of the probability and degree of failure or success of conation. Hence, in all concrete experiences of emotional quality these are partly coloured by derived emotions or feelings; they are tinged with hope, anxiety, joy, sorrow, surprise, or simple pleasure or pain.

Anxiety

Writing of emotion, McDougall (1923)[41] states:

> We all know what it is to be emotionally excited. And we know that the experience of being emotionally excited is not always of the same quality; we experience emotional excitements of many distinguishable qualities. We confidently use a large number of words to describe these experiences. Most of these words are used in both adjectival and substantival forms, and some are used also as verbs, transitive and intransitive. We say 'I was angry or afraid' (adjectival), or we say 'I felt anger or fear' (substantival); or again we say 'I raged' or 'I feared him' (verbs). The substantival form may be used as the name of an agent as when we say 'I was moved by anger or impelled by fear', or 'curiosity carried me away', or 'anger overwhelmed me, or gave me strength' or 'fear lent wings to my feet'. The last usage is the most forcible; it is appropriate to poetical and romantic description. The poets legitimately personify these emotional experiences and speak of them as personal powers and agents. Plato set this fashion long ago, when he described Reason as striving to control the Passions, which drag us along like a team of spirited horses. It results from this usage that psychologists commonly speak of 'the emotions' or of 'an emotion', just as they speak of 'sensations' or 'an idea'.

McDougall goes on to write of our natural tendency to reify whatever we name and to advise that the adjectival form is scientifically preferable whenever possible, and that the use of a substantive does not imply a thing or agent but always a mode or quality of experience.

Important among the varieties of emotional experience is anxiety. What part does this quality of emotional experience play in our mental life? What is its function? Under what conditions, internal and external, do we feel this qualitative variety of emotional experience? Does this kind of emotional experience contribute towards the achievement of our natural goals? These are questions which philosophers and psychologists have posed for centuries, and it is also clear that man concerned himself with measures to alleviate the intensity of this emotion for ages before. Magical and magico-religious security measures of the most irrational kind are part and parcel of recorded history; indeed they can be reconstructed imaginatively from the artifacts of ancient cultures long before any written record.

McDougall classifies anxiety with the 'prospective emotions of desire'. He writes (McDougall, 1923[41]):

> Let us consider first the following five emotions: confidence, hope, anxiety, despondency and despair. All these presuppose the operation of some strong impulse or desire: and, since they presuppose also a certain level of development of intelligence, namely that level upon which the goal of impulse is more or less clearly imagined and

impulse takes the form of desire, we may say that they presuppose desire and arise only in the course of activity prompted and sustained by desire. The desire itself is independent of, and must come into operation before, the rise of these emotions. And during the working of any one strong desire (no matter what may be the nature of the instinctive impulse at work and what the nature of the object or goal to which it is directed) all these five emotions are apt to be experienced. They are, in fact, only so many named points in a scale of feeling or emotion of which confidence and despair are the two extremes.

Illustrating the transition from one point in the scale to another, McDougall describes a party of polar explorers tormented by desire for a good meal:

Let us take this type of crude but strong desire, springing directly from an instinct, and develop imaginatively the emotional experience of such a party; we may suppose it to have used up its supply of food, while returning on foot from the Pole and still separated by fifty miles of snow-covered ice from a store of food, deposited on the outward journey. All members of the party strongly desire to reach this store of food. The strong desire springs primarily from the food-instinct; but it is reinforced by the intellectual understanding that the survival of the party depends upon their reaching this goal; for this understanding brings to the support of the primitive hunger-impulse many remote desires, the desire to see wife and child again, to report the scientific results of their labours, to announce their success to an admiring world; in fact, all those desires which together constitute what common speech calls 'the love of life' or 'the fear of death'. All members of the party are strong, the weather is good, the snow underfoot is hard, the position and distance of the food-store are well known. Impelled by strong desire they tramp on with *confidence*. That is to say, they see no reason to doubt their ability to reach their immediate goal, the store of food, which means not only a good meal but also safety.

When they have travelled but halfway to their goal, an adverse wind springs up, bringing clouds and a threat of snow. Each man knows that, if the wind should blow stronger and the snow fall thickly, they will need all their strength to achieve their goal. Success no longer seems certain. Their confidence is no longer sure and untroubled. But they *hope* for the best. That is to say, the prospect of possible failure converts confidence to hope.

As they march on hopefully, the adverse wind grows stronger, and the snow falls more thickly. Each man secretly becomes a prey to *anxiety*. He still does his best to be and to appear hopeful. But now his desire prompts not only the imagination of a good meal and of a successful issue to all their labours, but also a careful consideration of all the possibilities and chances of failure as well as of success. During the phases of confidence and of hope, their striving was sustained and reinforced by the pleasurable anticipation of success; perhaps they joked about the enormous meal they were presently to enjoy. Now if they converse at all, it is only to discuss the prospect of the wind and snow abating; and the painful contemplation of possible failure depresses their energies. But the transition from confidence to hope and to anxiety is gradual; hope and anxiety alternate with every veering of the wind and every gust of snow; there is no sharp line to be drawn between the two states. We might recognize finer divisions of the emotional scale by speaking of anxious hope and hopeful anxiety.

The weather grows still worse; the men feel their strength ebbing; every step is a painful effort. At length one blurts out: 'We shall never make it!' And all in their hearts know that there is but too good ground for his remark. 'Oh! Shut up!' they say, 'We must make it.' And they trudge on. But now anxiety passes into *despondency*. Presently they agree to sit on their sledge awhile; and the attitude of despondency is clearly expressed by each relaxed figure, the bent back, the dropping head, the eyes staring vacantly. Their imaginations are now filled with painful depressing anticipations of final failure.

They rise and struggle on, with utmost exertions of will-power.

But now they come upon a wide opening in the ice, stretching indefinitely far in either direction across their course. Now they know that they cannot reach their goal. In consequence, despondency passes into *despair*; and they fall on the snow, content to pass into that last sleep which will end their labours (McDougall, 1923).

Concerning Scott's South Polar expedition, on the basis of which McDougall wrote this tragic story, there is much information in the explorer's diaries. Scott (1912)[52] wrote: 'We are already beyond the utmost limit to which man has attained, each footstep will be a fresh conquest of the great unknown. Confident in ourselves, confident in our equipment, and confident in our dog team, we can but feel elated at the prospect before us.' However, as is well known, later the explorers came across Amundsen's cairn, indicating that the Norwegian expedition had preceded them and thus had become the official discoverers of the South Pole. The ebullience of the passage in the diary quoted above contrasts with Scott's disappointment as he contemplates the inevitable agonizing return: 'Well, we have turned our backs on the goal of our ambition with sore feelings. And must face 700 miles of solid dragging— and goodbye to most of the day-dreams! Great God! This is an awful place.'

Deprived of the energizing triumph that being first to the South Pole would have provided, Scott and his companions faced the ordeal of their return, an ordeal which they hoped to endure successfully so that they could return to their homes and loved ones. Adverse winds and threats of snow turned hope to anxiety, and as conditions worsened, with high winds and heavy snow impeding their reaching their next food store, despondency began to dominate the group. A month after reaching the pole, Evans dies, and the weakened Oates, realizing that he was another impediment, and hoping by this desperate sacrifice to save his companions, quietly stepped from the tent into a blizzard and was never seen again. Weakened by the intense cold, the continuous struggle and diminishing supplies, Scott wrote a letter to his 'widow' in which he states that the few survivors had disavowed suicide, and intended to persevere to the last. Finally, after eight days of impenetrable storm, only eleven miles from the next depot and possible survival, Scott wrote in despair: 'It seems a pity, but I do not think I can write more ... For God's sake look after our people.' Thus the march of Scott's depression issued ultimately in his feelings of utter helplessness.

We are all engaged in the journey through life, as so often our dreams portray, and in the course of this journey we must deal with the emotions highlighted in Scott's factual account, if only in lesser intensity. Thus Scott's diaries and McDougall's interpretation of them have considerable figurative value. They show how strong desire and data-scanning can interact to change feelings concerned with the chances of success—or failure. The representational world of our emotional life is inescapably a product of the events, favourable or unfavourable, in the external world as much as those evoked inwardly by fantasy.

McDougall's sad story depicts the five derived emotions named by A. F. Shand (1921)[53] 'the prospective emotions of desire', for all of them imply desire that looks forward to a goal. In the instance recounted these emotions occur in great intensity, for the desire from which they derived was of great strength and urgency. Here, in this view, anxiety is considered in its setting alongside other emotions which also have their reference to the future. The anxious patient is concerned with future catastrophe whereas the severely depressed patient, as will be more fully discussed later, is also preoccupied with the loss he feels he has sustained. Of the five prospective emotions derived from the interaction of desire and of judgement of probabilities of success or failure, three (when confidence and hope are smitten that is), anxiety, despondency and despair, belong to the sphere of dysphoria. There are also retrospective emotions in the developed mind, which belong to the dysphoric end of the spectrum, namely regret, remorse and sorrow, allied to which is grief. These retrospective emotions are also 'derived' in the sense that they are incidental to the evocation in memory of conative–affective experiences, rendering these memories painful or reinforcing their painful elements. Like all emotions, these are the result of a differentiation of the fundamental forms of feeling, pain and pleasure, in the differentiated psyche.

It is to be noted that McDougall's description of anxiety and the other prospective emotions of desire is anchored in reality. Appraisal of the future probabilities of gratification of needs is wholly pre-empted by considerations relating to changes in the personal and physical environment. This is exactly what we call 'common sense'. After all, why should anyone be afraid, let us say, of not securing food when the likelihood is that there will be plenty available when his phasic need for nourishment asserts itself? However, this is the essence of *morbid anxiety*. It is apparently lacking in common sense and we require more than common sense to understand it.

The Indian Sage of Ishopanishat says: 'It moves. It moves not. It is distant. It is near.' This statement is lacking in common sense but it makes sense of another order. Naked-eye observation assures me, as I briefly observe the heavens on a clear night, that the stars stand still. Scientific observation has resulted in the argument that if I think the stars are still, that shows only that I am too far from them. On the other hand, when I was sure that the earth was flat scientific observations corrected this view, indicating that the near view was incomplete. The evolution of new techniques of observation results in new convictions. Sigmund Freud reached novel conclusions following new techniques of observation. From his analyses of adult patients he had drawn inferences about the general occurrence of the Oedipus complex in childhood, of castration anxiety, and the significance of extragenital erotogenic zones of the body. He checked the inferences in the famous 'Little Hans Case', an analysis of a phobia in a 15-year-old boy (Freud, 1909[54]).

Little Hans refused to go out into the street because he was afraid of horses. Investigation showed that what he was suffering from was not a vague fear of horses but a quite definite apprehension that a horse was going to bite him.

Freud (1926)[46] writes:

> We shall not make any headway until we have reviewed the little boy's psychological situation as a whole as it came to light in the course of analytic treatment. He was at that time in the Oedipus position, with its attendant feelings of jealousy and hostility towards his father whom nevertheless—except insofar as his mother was the cause of estrangement—he dearly loved. Here, then, we have a conflict due to ambivalence: a firmly rooted love and a no less well-grounded hatred against one and the same person.

Little Hans's phobia must be an attempt to solve this conflict. Conflicts of this kind due to ambivalence are very frequent and they can have another typical outcome, in which one of the two conflicting feelings (usually that of affection) becomes enormously enhanced and the other vanishes. Only the exaggerated degree and compulsive character of the feeling that remains betray the fact that it is not the sole one in existence but is continually on the alert to keep the other feeling under suppression, and enables us to postulate the operation of a process which we call repression by means of reaction-formation (in the ego). Cases like Little Hans show no traces of reaction-formation of this kind. There are clearly different ways of egress from a conflict of ambivalence.

Meanwhile we have been able to establish another point with certainty. The instinctual impulse which underwent repression in Little Hans was a hostile one against his father. Proof of this was obtained in the analysis while the idea of the biting horse was being followed up. Hans had seen a horse fall down and he had also seen a playmate, with whom he was playing at horses, fall down and hurt himself. Analysis justified the inference that he had a conative impulse that his father should fall down and hurt himself as his playmate and the horse had done. Moreover his attitude towards someone's departure on a certain occasion makes it probable that his wish that his father should be out of the way found a less hesitating expression. But a wish of this sort is tantamount to an intention of putting the father out of the way oneself—is tantamount, that is, to the murderous impulse which is one component of the Oedipus complex.

So far there seem to be no connecting links between Little Hans's repressed instinctual impulse and the substitute for which we suspect is to be seen in his phobia of horses. Let us simplify his psychological situation by setting on one side the elements of infancy and ambivalence. Let us imagine that he is a young servant who is in love with the mistress of the house and has received some tokens of her favour. He hates his master who is more powerful than he, and he would like to have him out of the way. It would then be eminently natural for him to be afraid of his master and to dread his vengeance—just as Little Hans was frightened of horses. We cannot, therefore, describe the anxiety belonging to this phobia as a symptom. If Little Hans, being in love with his mother, had shown fear of his father, we should have no right to say that he had a neurosis or a phobia. His emotional reaction would have been entirely comprehensible. What made it a neurosis was one thing alone: the replacement of his father by a horse. It is this displacement, then, which has a claim to be called a symptom, and which, incidentally, constitutes the alternative mechanism which enables a conflict due to ambivalence to be resolved without the aid of a reaction-formation. Such a displacement is made possible or facilitated at Little Hans's early age because the inborn traces of totemistic thought can still be easily revived. Children do not as yet recognize or, at any rate, lay such exaggerated stress upon the gulf that separates human beings from the animal world. In their eyes the grown man, the object of their fear and admiration, still belongs to the same category as the big animal who has so many enviable attributes but against whom they have been warned because he may become dangerous. As we see, the conflict of ambivalence is not dealt with in relation to one and the same person; it is circumvented, as it were, by one of the pair of conflicting impulses being directed to a vicarious figure.

We started from McDougall's story of the polar explorers who found themselves separated from their food store and who experienced increasing difficulty in reaching the food. During the course of this stress, the men suffered from *objective anxiety*, a condition of increased sensory attention and motor tension or 'anxiety preparedness'. Freud showed that in this development there is a repetition of an old traumatic experience restricted to a signal, in which case the rest of the anxiety reaction can adapt itself to the new

Fig. 17.1 Anxiety

'Prospective Emotions of Desire' (Shand, 1921[53]).

        a. Confidence
        b. Hope
        c. Anxiety
        d. Despondency
        e. Despair

———

1. OBJECTIVE ANXIETY

2. NEUROTIC OR MORBID ANXIETY

| Free-floating as in anxiety neurosis | | Firmly attached to ideas or situations as in the phobias |

THE SEVERE ANXIETY ATTACK

Accompanying other symptoms or occurring independently in many severe neuroses or psychoses (e.g., hysteria, schizophrenia, paranoid states)

3. MORAL ANXIETY

(Often a variety of neurotic anxiety or contributing to it)

———

MOTIVES FOR THE DEFENCE AGAINST INSTINCT
        a. Super-ego
        b. Objective anxiety
        c. Anxiety due to the strength of instinct
        d. Need for synthesis

situation of danger by flight or fight. If, however, the old traumatic experience gets the upper hand a state of unadapted paralysis develops. In Freud's view, the process of birth which comprises characteristic modifications of the heart's action and of respiration due to efferent innervations, is the prototypical anxiety experience. In later life, under conditions of danger, a perception of similar autonomic events is usefully restricted to a signal.*

Neurotic anxiety may be observed in three forms as indicated in *Fig.* 17.1 below: as a general apprehensiveness or free-floating anxiety ready to attach itself to any new possibility, as firmly attached to certain ideas in what are called the 'phobias' as in the horse phobia of Little Hans, or as a severe attack. Freud asked two questions at the outset: 'What are people afraid of when they

———

*As already noted, the restriction may not be so severely implemented so that instead of dysphoric affect signalling, there is felt affect adequately modulated. This then may acquire positive cognitive value, without flooding and consequent cognitive disorganization. Thus the felt affect is available as a symbol, signifying a relationship between subjective reaction and a type of external situation.

have neurotic anxiety?' and, 'How can one bring this kind of anxiety into line with objective anxiety felt towards an external danger?'

We saw in the case of Little Hans that his hostility to his father was uncovered in the process of treatment and that only then did his anxiety about being bitten by horses become comprehensible in terms of the little boy's emotional situation. Ideas relating to his hostility to his father had been repressed, i.e., excluded from his conscious awareness, but the affect of anxiety relating to his hostile wishes was perceived and attached by displacement to horses. The first neuroses of children are indeed phobias—conditions, that is to say, in which one can see quite clearly how what began as anxiety development due to ideational representatives of hostile or erotic wishes is replaced by symptom formation. We see clearly in the infantile phobias that the danger is an internal one instead of an external one as in objective anxiety, and that the internal danger is not consciously recognized. The same situation exists for neurotic anxiety in adults. To make an analogy, we might compare the situation in children to that of the archaeological situation of Pompeii, and that in adults to Herculaneum. Herculaneum was covered by a depth of hardened lava of 65 feet. Pompeii, on the other hand, lay under a blanket of *lapilli*, small fragments of glassy volcanic rock, not too resistant to light tools, and not nearly so deeply buried as its sister-city Herculaneum. It often takes longer to uncover the internal danger relating to the neurotic anxiety of adults.

To return to the first question then: What are neurotically anxious people afraid of? We are familiar with the division of the mental personality into super-ego, ego and id. It is, of course, the ego which is the locus of perception, and, in particular, the perception of anxiety. The three main varieties of anxiety—objective anxiety, neurotic anxiety, and moral anxiety—can easily be connected with the dependent relations of the ego: on the external world, on the id, and on the super-ego. The internal dangers relate to the id and to the super-ego. Here, taking as illustration the phobia of Little Hans in order to simplify the situation, we perceive that the internal danger consisted of his hostile wish against his father, though he had externalized this in terms of an emotional fear of a horse biting him. The boy was afraid of a wish derived from an instinctual demand or id impulse and he thus suffered neurotic anxiety. But he was obliged to renounce this id impulse and to distort the source of the anxiety because it would have involved an external danger situation, namely conflict, and a losing conflict, with his father. In other words, the internal instinctual danger is only a half-way house to an external and real danger situation. Psychoanalytic investigation has found this to be the answer to the second question: How can neurotic anxiety be brought into line with objective anxiety?

The real danger which the boy fears as a result of the complex of Oedipal wishes is the punishment of castration, or, to be medically more precise, the loss of his penis.

Freud (1933)[55] writes:

> Naturally you will object that after all that is not a real danger. Our boys are not castrated because they are in love with their mothers during the phase of the Oedipus complex. But the question cannot be so easily dismissed. It is not primarily a matter of

whether castration is really performed; what is important is that the danger is one that threatens from without, and the boy believes in it. He has some grounds for doing so, for, not infrequently, threats of his penis being cut off are made during his phallic phase, at the time of his early masturbation; and no doubt allusions to such a punishment will always find a phylogenetic reinforcement on his side. We have conjectured that, in the early days of the human family, castration really was performed on the growing boy by the jealous and cruel father, and that circumcision, which is so frequently an element in puberty rites, is an easily recognizable trace of it. We are aware of how far removed we are from the common point of view in saying this, but we must maintain our position that fear of castration is one of the most frequent and one of the strongest motives of repression, and therefore of the formation of the neuroses. The analysis of cases in which, not, it is true, castration itself, but circumcision, has been performed on boys as a cure or as a punishment for masturbation (a thing which was by no means of rare occurrence in English and American society) has provided proof ... Fear of castration is naturally not the only motive for repression; to start with, it has no place in the psychology of women; they have, of course, a castration-complex, but they cannot have any fear of castration. In its place, for the other sex, is found fear of the loss of love, obviously a continuation of the fear of the infant at the breast when it misses its mother. You will understand what objective danger-situation is indicated by this kind of anxiety. If the mother is absent or has withdrawn her love from the child, it can no longer be certain that its needs will be satisfied, and may be exposed to the most painful feelings of tension. There is no need to reject the idea that these conditions for anxiety fundamentally repeat the situation of the original birth-anxiety, which, to be sure, also implied separation from the mother. Indeed, if you follow a line of thought suggested by Ferenczi, you may add fear of castration too, to this series, for the loss of the male genital organ results in the impossibility of a reunion with the mother, or with a substitute for her, in the sexual act.

This example of phobia indicates that children defend themselves against their instinctual demands when these entail conflict with those who are responsible for their care and upbringing. It is anxiety which sets the defensive process going. There are in general three powerful motives for defence against instinctual demands, and a fourth which is strong in some adults. These are detailed in *Fig*. 17.1.

The defensive struggle with which psychiatrists and psychoanalysts are longest familiar is that which forms the basis of neurosis in adults. Here one is confronted with a situation in which a wish seeks to enter the field of consciousness and to achieve gratification. The ego is not averse to the admission of this wish but the super-ego protests. The ego submits to the demands of the super-ego and initiates struggle against the wish, itself, of course, a derivative of instinctual impulse. Defence is, in a word, motivated by super-ego anxiety. Often the super-ego demands a degree of sexual renunciation and restriction of aggression incompatible with psychic health. The ego becomes thus deprived of its independence, hostile to instinct, and incapable of enjoyment. Study of the defence struggle in adults often impels the therapist to pay attention to the analysis of the super-ego in order to modify its severity and so reduce the anxiety it sets up. For this anxiety often proves on scrutiny to be out of proportion to the legitimate demands of adult reality, and remote from adult ethical standards. It is embedded in a savage matrix long since alien to the conscious appraisal of the patient himself. Often enough in this work we have to penetrate a depth of 'hardened lava', as it were, to reach the elusive introjective defence system from which is derived the archaic core of the super-ego. In this work exuberant fantasies associated with particular early experiences of the patient are often unearthed. The same sort of results in neurosis are produced in adults by anxiety of conscience as castration anxiety produces in young children.

The ego of a little child does not always combat instinctual impulses of its own accord. Defence is prompted by anxiety in relation to the parents or their surrogates who bring the child up and who have forbidden gratification on pain of restriction or infliction of punishment. We discover that objective anxiety is *ultimately* responsible for the development in children of the same sort of phobias, obsessional neuroses, hysterical symptoms and neurotic traits as occur in adults in consequence of super-ego anxiety.

We now come to the third motive for the defence against instinct. In the very process of differentiation of ego from id, including progress from primary to secondary process and from pleasure principle to reality principle, a mistrust of unhampered gratification of instincts is set up. Suffice it to say here that, if the demands of instinctual impulses become excessive, mistrust of instinct is intensified to the point of anxiety. It is as though the ego fears destruction of its own organization. In psychiatric practice we see this sort of anxiety in the forefront of the clinical picture, or more emphatically revealed, whenever an access of instinctual energy threatens to upset the balance of the psychic institutions; physiologically at puberty and the climacteric, pathologically at the beginning of one of the periodic advances which occur in psychosis.

Finally, in many people anxiety which springs from the ego's need for synthesis is often apparent. No doubt this is related to the anxiety just discussed. The adult ego requires some degree of harmony of the impulses it is ready to acknowledge and express, and some harmonious development in the goals it seeks to reach. Alexander's work (1933)[56] on instinctual conflict is pertinent here—the conflict between homosexuality and heterosexuality, passivity and activity, which the ego seeks to settle on account of the anxiety generated by widely opposing tendencies. Greenacre (1958)[57] has described primitive body disintegration anxiety especially as it occurs in patients suffering from faulty development of the body image for which there are sometimes early actual physical determinants.

Hysteria, Depression and Affect Equivalents

Ziegler, Imboden and Meyer (1960)[5] in a study based on systematic clinical observation of patients at the Johns Hopkins University Hospital who were referred for psychiatric consultation found a high prevalence of depressive symptoms alongside conversion reactions in 40 of 134 patients. They inferred from careful history reviews, that in many of the patients the conversion symptoms served to mask depressive disorder whereas in others the conversion reactions only partially masked depression. In older patients, severe bodily pains partially or completely concealed depression. Similarly, McKegney (1967)[58] comparing 144 patients with conversion reactions to other psychiatric patients found that 22 per cent suffered evident depression whereas 43 per cent of those without conversion reactions were overtly depressed. On the other hand, covert depression was inferred more frequently in conversion hysteria (35 per cent compared to 18 per cent in other psychiatric disorder).

Lazare and Klerman (1970)[59] reported a five year study of a woman suffering depression who in the course of her disorder developed camptocormia. They had previously described in 1968[60] the frequency of conversion symptoms among a group of hospitalized depressed women. Lazare and Klerman support the view earlier outlined by Abse (1966)[61] that depressive affects, consciously perceived and the readiness for them unconsciously perceived, precipitate conversion defence. It is evident that the signal function of depressive affects has been overshadowed by concentration on that of anxiety with which they are so often alloyed.

Other studies show that hysterical personality disorder increases the risk of depression. Slavney and McHugh (1974)[62] comparing male and female patients with a primary or secondary diagnosis of histrionic personality disorder as defined in D.S.M. III with a mixed control group found that the hysterical group showed significantly more overt depressive symptoms: 79 per cent of the hysterical personality inpatients, 32 per cent of the control patients in hospital for psychiatric disorder. In this study, 50 per cent of the index patients had made an attempt at suicide before care in hospital whereas only 16 per cent of the other psychiatric patients were in hospital on account of an attempt at self-destruction.

McDougall (1923)[41] writes:

> The very type of sorrow is the emotion of the mother bereft of her much-loved child. Imagine the emotions of a mother who loses her child through a fatal sickness. During the course of the sickness she will pass through all the prospective emotions of desire, the desires of love to protect, to relieve, to preserve its object. At the time of the fatal issue, distress may be the dominant emotion; the mother, having exhausted all her resources in vain gives herself up to weeping and to crying on God and man for help. This phase soon gives place to pure sorrow or tender regret; the tender emotion and impulse of her love bring its object frequently, almost constantly, to mind; and in imagination she dwells upon all that she would do, if the object were still with her, and on all she might have done before she lost it. All such retrospective desires are painful, because they are necessarily thwarted.* The name 'Grief' is properly used to denote an emotion closely allied to sorrow, but differing from it in that, in the sentiment from which it springs, the tender protective impulse is subordinated to the impulses of extended self-regard.

In discussing mourning and comparing this with melancholia Freud (1917)[64] explained that the painfulness in the work of mourning, in the gradual detachment from the lost loved one, is in this 'thwarting' mentioned above and in the struggle to accept the reality of loss which the thwarting keeps pointing up. Human beings, Freud insists, are always unwilling to abandon any 'libido position' so that the demands of reality cannot be fully met immediately. The object detachment has to take place piecemeal, step by step, from memories of the lost one, the task requiring time and energy. In time, with the expression of grief, of the feeling that the world has become poor and empty, the bereaved person becomes gradually once more free and uninhibited. In contrast, in

---

*See Lewis (1963)[63] for a personal account of bereavement.

melancholia the accent is more on the person himself as having become poor and empty. He feels worthless and morally despicable and is suicidal.

As we have noted above there are retrospective derived depressive affects, incidental to the evocation in memory of painful conative–affective experiences, as well as prospective depressive emotions, as confidence and hope are disrupted and anxiety gives place to despondency and despair. Mental depression signifies a sense of ill-being, and, as Mendelson (1960)[65] sagely remarks, 'There is now ample evidence that the term "depression" covers a variety of affective states which differ not only overtly but subjectively.'

The causes and occasions of a sense of ill-being from within and from without are so common that it is not possible for anyone to avoid the experience altogether. Clouston (1883)[66] defines 'mere melancholy' as a sense of ill-being and a feeling of mental pain with no real perversion of the normal reasoning power, no morbid loss of self-control, no uncontrollable impulse towards suicide, the power of working not being destroyed, and the ordinary interests of life being only lessened, not abolished. He defines pathological depression or 'Melancholia' as mental pain and sense of ill-being usually more intense than in 'mere melancholy', with loss of self-control, or insane delusions, or uncontrollable impulses towards suicide, with no proper capacity to follow ordinary avocations, with most of the ordinary interests of life destroyed, and commonly with marked bodily symptoms such as loss of appetite and constipation.

Abraham (1911)[67] stated that anxiety and depression are related to each other in the same way as are fear and grief. In the light of our brief discussion of the 'derived' emotions, we now see that this rough statement opposes fear to the retrospective depressive emotions only, with which, certainly, pathological forms of depression are usually heavily involved; that we fear a coming evil and that we grieve over one which has occurred illustrates this opposition in time. Depression is usually the aftermath of loss or disappointment in reality—or in fantasy. It sometimes happens that a minor actual loss or disappointment may be followed by pathological depression as a result of distortion produced by unconscious fantasy. The nature of depression can indeed be assessed as pathological not only on account of its intensity and persistence or on account of its issue in disordered behaviour as Clouston emphasized, but also on account of its not being objectively warranted.

Good (1946)[68] drew attention to two broad groupings of severe depression. The first group consists of patients who have lost contact with reality, are retarded, and complain in a low monotonous voice of having committed unforgivable sins and of being destined to endure the tortures of hell. Such patients reproach and vilify themselves; they may refuse food or demand to be annihilated. Patients in the second group may, on the other hand, appear deceptively alert, and retain the ability to smile and to communicate adequately, giving a good account of themselves. They may complain that life does not seem worth while or that the joy has departed from living, or else, perhaps, remark, 'I feel as though I had a big disappointment, only it lasts.'

From the practical point of view in all cases of depression the danger of suicide requires to be assessed; in this connection, particularly in regard to the second group of patients mentioned above, it is a dangerous though prevalent fallacy that those who threaten suicide never actually attempt it. In fact they often do, as often as those who do not overtly and directly express suicidal intentions.

Freud (1917)[64] showed, in some forms of melancholia, that careful attention to the rebukes and complaints which the patient makes about himself logically apply more accurately to the 'lost object', lost through rupture of the relationship, perhaps through death. Unlike what happens in normal grief, and in mourning, the libidinal attachment is apparently rapidly withdrawn. The released libido is, however, not free to seek fresh attachments, nor is it a simple matter of return of the libido to the self. There is, instead, an intimate identification of the self with the image of the person to whom the patient was attached, albeit very ambivalently; this primitive process is designated 'introjection'. Now the hatred, formerly not so obvious in the ambivalent attachment, is turned against the part of the self fused with the introjected lost object.

Abraham (1924)[69] showed that in melancholia there were certain preconditions, namely, fixation at the oral-sadistic level, a severe injury to infantile narcissism brought about by early deprivation by the mother, and the occurrence of the first great disappointment in love before the Oedipus wishes were successfully mastered. He showed that repetition of this latter disappointment in later life was the precipitating situation. Freud (1917)[64] had also noted the regression to pregenital fixation in melancholia, attributing importance to the anal-sadistic phase as the basis for many clinical features. Beck (1974)[70] lists the following signs and symptoms of pathological depression:

Emotional: sadness or apathy; crying spells, self-dislike; loss of gratification, loss of feelings of affection; loss of the sense of humour.

Cognitive: negative self-concept; negative expectations; exaggerated view of problems; attribution of blame to self.

Motivational: increased dependency; loss of motivation; avoidance; indecisiveness; suicidal wishes.

Physical and vegetative: loss of appetite; sleep disturbance; fatiguability; loss of sexual interest.

Both Beck (1974)[70] and Lichtenberg (1957)[71] have emphasized the 'cognitive triad'—a negative view of oneself, a negative view of experience one has had or is having, and a negative view of the future. All three can be activated by what may be really only a minor setback. This evokes fantasy formation that distorts perception. The depression-prone person is vulnerable as a result of his own enduring negative concepts.

Fenichel (1954)[4] characterized these depression-prone individuals whom Beck has described as dominated by an underlying negative self-concept as 'love addicts'. They are constantly having problems in everyday life with the regulation of self-esteem. Depression is often exaggerated by these people in an attempt to coerce others into providing narcissistic supplies, protection, forgiveness, security and love. Bibring (1953)[72] similarly emphasized the loss of self-esteem in the pathogenesis of depression. The wish to be loved and valued, the desire to be strong and the wish to be loving and good are relentlessly pursued by the depression-prone, and depression results when these wishes are not realized as often they cannot be. As we have noted in Chapter 7, this aspect of depression is prominent in some hysteriform borderline personality disorders. These patients whose borderline disorder approaches affective rather than schizophrenic decompensation are liable to conversion reactions and dissociative phenomena along with depression. Often the conversion and dissociative reactions serve to protect them from experiencing severely depressive affects.

According to Mendelson (1960)[65] the term 'manic-depressive equivalent' was coined by Foster Kennedy in 1944 to designate somatic complaints following a periodic course in the absence of or with mood changes. Before this, though the term 'depressive equivalent' may not have been used, it was known that somatic symptoms, such as fatigue and anorexia, were complained of by patients who denied depression but gave non-verbal indications of it. Such cases were investigated by Landauer (1925),[73] who termed them 'equivalents of mourning'.

After pointing out Freud's description of anxiety equivalents in his earliest work on anxiety neuroses, Fenichel (1945)[4] writes in Chapter IX of his book:

> It cannot be doubted that all other affects can likewise be replaced in a similar way by equivalents of somatic sensations. It is characteristic of certain compulsive personalities that when analysis has successfully attacked their affect blocking, they begin to complain of certain changes in body sensations, without realizing their psychic significance. Before they can again experience the affects fully, they first find the road to affect equivalents.

Fenichel also notes that Schreber's somatic 'basic language' consists of affects reduced to body sensations. Alexander (1950)[74] cites many instances of psychosomatic disorders occurring after object loss when one might have expected depressive feelings to become manifest. Finally in this connection it is to be noted that cases have been reported in which remission of psychosomatic disorder is followed by the development of overt psychosis, and vice versa. As well as depressive syndromes paranoid schizophrenic disorders have been observed to occur in these alterations (Grinker and Robbins 1954, Chapter 2, Case 2[75]). In these latter cases the general proposition of the severe depressive: 'I hate myself'—represented, however, non-verbally and in terms of severe inferiority feelings—is changed by further defence to feelings which may be represented as 'Everybody, or some significant person, hates me'.

A greater or lesser loss of self-esteem is always the resultant of the underlying complex dynamics of depression. This inner loss, in clearly reactive depressions, is initially due to the loss of external supplies of affection. To a greater or lesser extent this becomes complicated by loss of internal supplies from the 'protective super-ego' and/or vilification by the 'punitive super-ego'. These disturbances are not so intensive in neurotic depressive reactions as in psychotic depressive disorder.

Both in conversion phenomena and in psychophysiological disorder it might be conceived that one or another physical mode of suffering is sought unconsciously or stumbled upon and held as a lesser evil than severe dysphoric affects of anxiety and of a depressive order; in other words, that the defence in mental representation of physical suffering is ultimately the result of a defence against becoming conscious of severe dysphoric feelings. This, however, is an incomplete view, because it ignores the inextricable association of these feelings with unconscious strivings. Just as ideas distantly related to forbidden unconscious strivings may be pleasant or innocuous and yet defended against in order to avoid the awakening of pain through their associations in the drive organization of memory, so affect representations of a pleasurable kind may be inadmissible. These too, in the context of a particular situation, may serve to awaken pain through memory. Freud's essay 'On Transience' (1916)[76] gives a forceful illustration of this. On a walk through a smiling countryside with a young poet it became evident that the sensitive young man could feel no joy in the beauty of the scenery. He was disturbed by the thought that all that beauty was fated to extinction, that it would vanish when winter came, like all human beauty and all the splendour that men have created or may create. Freud came to the conclusion that the associated idea of transience was arousing a foretaste of mourning which caused a recoil against pleasurable involvement. It should be added that the painful emotional character of detachment of libido from its objects is the counterpart of the libido striving to cling to them.

REFERENCES

1. Freud, S. (1909). Some General Remarks on Hysterical Attacks. In: *The Standard Edition*, Vol. IX. London: Hogarth Press (1953).
2. Sapir, E. (1933). Language. In: *Selected Writings of Edward Sapir*. Berkeley, Calif.: Univ. of California Press (1958).
3. Freud, S. (1895). Project for a Scientific Psychology. In: *The Standard Edition*, Vol. I. London: Hogarth Press (1957). Also in: *The Origins of Psychoanalysis*. New York: Basic Books (1954).
4. Fenichel, O. (1945). *The Psychoanalytic Theory of Neurosis*. New York: Norton.
5. Ziegler, F. J., Imboden, J. B. and Meyer, E. (1960). Contemporary conversion reactions: clinical study. *Am. J. Psychiat.* **116,** 901–10.
6. Ziegler, F. J. and Imboden, J. B. (1962). Contemporary conversion reactions, II: Conceptual model. *Arch. Gen. Psychiat.* **6,** 279–87.
7. Ziegler, F. J., Imboden, J. B. and Rodgers, D. A. (1963). Contemporary conversion reactions, III. *J. Am. Med. Assoc.* **186,** 307.
8. Rangell, L. (1959). The nature of conversion. *J. Am. Psychoanal. Assoc.* **7,** 632–62.
9. Jung, C. G. (1906). Dementia praecox and hysteria. In: *The Psychology of Dementia Praecox*, pp. 70–98. New York: Nervous and Mental Disease Publishing (1936).
10. Abse, D. W. (1959). Hysteria. In: *American Handbook of Psychiatry* (ed. Arieti, S.), Vol. 1, pp. 272–92. New York: Basic Books.
11. Sharpe, E. F. (1937). *Dream Analysis*. London: Hogarth Press.
12. Freud, S. (1891). *On Aphasia*. New York: Int. Univ. Press (1953).
13. De Saussure, F. (1916). *Course in General Linguistics*. New York: Philosophical Library (1959).
14. Keller, H. (1902). *The Story of My Life*. Garden City: Doubleday, Doran.
15. Latif, I. (1934). The physiological basis of linguistic development and the ontogeny of meaning. *Psychol. Rev.* **41,** 55.
16. Langer, S. K. (1942). *Philosophy in a New Key*. Cambridge, Mass.: Harvard Univ. Press (1957).
17. Laffal, J. (1964). Freud's theory of language. *Psychoanal. Quart.* **33,** 157.
18. Peller, L. E. (1964). Language and its prestages. *Bull. Philadelphia Assoc. Psychoanal.* **14,** 2.
19. Bühler, K. (1934). *Sprachtheorie*. Jena: Fischer.
20. Wegener, P. (1885). *The Life of Speech* (trans. Abse, D. W.). In: *Speech and Reason* (ed. Abse, D. W.). Charlottesville, Va: Univ. Press of Virginia; Bristol: Wright (1971).
21. Freud, S. (1910). The Antithetical Meaning of Primal Words. In: *The Standard Edition*, Vol. XI. London: Hogarth Press (1955).

22. Simons, R. C. (1964). A case of camptocormia (conversion in a schizophrenic process). *Arch. Gen. Psychiat.* **11**, 277.
23. Freud, S. (1911). Psycho-analytic Notes upon an Autobiographical Account of a Case of Paranoia (Dementia Paranoides). In: *The Standard Edition*, Vol. XII. London: Hogarth Press (1955).
24. Baumeyer, F. (1956). The Schreber case. *Int. J. Psychoanal.* **37**, 61.
25. Fairbairn, W. R. D. (1956). The Schreber Case. *Br. J. Med. Psychol.* **29**, 113.
26. Friedmann, M. (1905). Contributions to the study of paranoia. In: *Studies in Paranoia: Nervous and Mental Disease*. (Monograph No. 2.) Washington: Nervous and Mental Disease Publishing (1908).
27. Gierlich, N. (1907). Periodic paranoia and the origin of paranoid delusions. *Studies in Paranoia: Nervous and Mental Disease*. (Monograph No. 2.) Washington: Nervous and Mental Disease Publishing (1908).
28. Greenspan, J. (1964). The original persecutor—a case study. *Bull. Philadelphia Assoc. Psychoanal.* **14**, 13.
29. Katan, M. (1950). Schreber's hallucinations about the little men. *Int. J. Psychoanal.* **31**, 32.
30. MacAlpine, I. and Hunter, R. A. (1955). *Daniel Paul Schreber: memoirs of my nervous illness*. London: Dawson.
31. Niederland, W. (1951). Three notes on the Schreber case. *Psychoanal. Quart.* **20**, 579.
32. Niederland, W. (1959*a*). The 'miracled-up' world of Schreber's childhood. In: *The Psychoanalytic Study of the Child* (ed. Eissler, R. S. I., Freud, A., Hartmann, H. et al.), Vol. 14. New York: Int. Univ. Press.
33. Niederland, W. (1959*b*). Schreber: father and son. *Psychoanal. Quart.* **28**, 151.
34. Niederland, W. (1960). Schreber's father. *J. Am. Psychoanal. Assoc.* **8**, 492.
35. Salzman, L. (1960). Paranoid state—theory and therapy. *Arch. Gen. Psychiat.* **2**, 679.
36. Volkan, V. D. (1976). In search of a 'living' archaic structure. In: *Primitive Internalised Object Relations*, Chap. 1. New York: Int. Univ. Press.
37. White, R. B. (1961). The mother conflict in Schreber's psychosis. *Int. J. Psychoanal.* **42**, 58.
38. James, W. (1890). *Principles of Psychology*. New York: Dover (1950).
39. Rapaport, D. (1957). *Cognitive Structures in Contemporary Approaches to Cognition*. Cambridge, Mass.: Harvard Univ. Press.
40. Bleuler, E. (1906). Affectivity, suggestibility, paranoia. *N.Y. State Hosp. Bull.* **8**, 481 (1912).
41. McDougall. W. (1923). *An Outline of Psychology*. London: Methuen (1936).
42. Darwin, C. (1872). *The Expression of the Emotions in Man and Animals*. London: Murray.
43. Spinoza, B. (1677). *Ethics*. In: *Great Books of the Western World* (ed. Hutchins, R. M., Adler, M. J. et al.), Vol. 31. London: Encyclopedia Britannica (1952).
44. Kant, I. (1790). *The Critique of Judgement*. In: *Great Books of the Western World* (ed. Hutchings, R. M., Adler, M. J. et al.), Vol. 42. London: Encyclopedia Britannica (1952).
45. Meerloo, J. A. M. (1965). Spinoza: a look at his psychological concepts. *Am. J. Psychiat.* **121**, 890.
46. Freud, S. (1926). Inhibitions, Symptoms and Anxiety. In: *The Standard Edition*, Vol. XX. London: Hogarth Press (1955).
47. Breuer, J. and Freud, S. (1893). On the psychical mechanism of hysterical phenomena: preliminary communication. In: *The Standard Edition*, Vol. II. London: Hogarth Press (1953).
48. Brierly, M. (1951). *Trends in Psycho-Analysis*. London: Hogarth Press.
49. Fenichel, O. (1941). The ego and the affects. In: *Collected Papers, Second Series* (ed. Fenichel, H. and Rapaport, D.). New York: Norton (1954).

50. Jung. C. G. (1920). *Psychological Types*. New York: Harcourt Brace (1923).
51. Rignano, E. (1911). On the mnemonic origin and nature of affective tendencies. *Monist* **21**, 321.
52. Scott. R. F. (1912). *The Diaries of Robert Falcon Scott*. London: Methuen (1929).
53. Shand, A. F. (1921). *The Foundations of Character*, 2nd ed. London: Methuen (1929).
54. Freud, S. (1909). Analysis of a Phobia in a Five-year-old Boy. In: *The Standard Edition*, Vol. X. London: Hogarth Press (1955).
55. Freud, S. (1933). Anxiety and Instinctual Life. *New Introductory Lectures on Psychoanalysis*. In: *The Standard Edition*, Vol. XXII. London: Hogarth Press (1955).
56. Alexander. F. (1933). The relation of structural and instinctual conflicts. *Psychoanal. Quart.* **2**, 81.
57. Greenacre, P. (1958). Early physical determinants in the development of the sense of identity. In: *Emotional Growth*, Vol. 1, pp. 113–29. New York: Int. Univ. Press (1971).
58. McKegney, F. P. (1967). The incidence and characteristics of patients with conversion reactions: 1. A general hospital consultation service sample. *Am. J. Psychiat.* **124**, 542–5.
59. Lazare, A. and Klerman, G. L. (1970). Camptocormia in a female: a five year study. *Br. J. Med. Psychol.* **43**, 265–70.
60. Lazare, A. and Klerman, G. L. (1968). Hysteria and depression: the frequency and significance of hysterical personality features in hospitalized depressed women. *Am. J. Psychiat.* **124**, 48–56.
61. Abse, D. W. (1966). *Hysteria and Related Mental Disorders. An Approach to Psychological Medicine*. Bristol: Wright.
62. Slavney, P. R. and McHugh, P. R. (1974). The hysterical personality: a controlled study. *Arch. Gen. Psychiat.* **30**, 325–9.
63. Lewis, C. S. (1963). *A Grief Observed*. Greenwich, England: Seabury.
64. Freud, S. (1917). Mourning and Melancholia. In: *The Standard Edition*, Vol. XIV. London: Hogarth Press (1953).
65. Mendelson, M. (1960). *Psychoanalytic Concepts of Depression*. Springfield, Ill.: Thomas.
66. Clouston, T. S. (1883). *Clinical Lectures in Mental Disease*. London: Churchill (1904).
67. Abraham, K. (1911). Notes on the psycho-analytical investigation and treatment of manic-depressive insanity and allied conditions. In: *Selected Papers of Karl Abraham*. London: Hogarth Press (1927).
68. Good, R. (1946). Depression. *Br. J. Med. Psychol.* **20**, 344,
69. Abraham, K. (1924). A short study of the development of the libido, viewed in the light of mental disorders. In: *Selected Papers of Karl Abraham*. London: Hogarth Press (1927).
70. Beck. A. T. (1974). Depressive neurosis. *Adult Clinical Psychiatry*. In: *American Handbook of Psychiatry*, 2nd ed. (ed. Arieti, S.), Vol. 3, Chap. 4. New York: Basic Books.
71. Lichtenberg, P. (1957). A definition and analysis of depression. *Arch. Neurol. Psychiat.* **77**, 516–27.
72. Bibring, E. (1953). The mechanism of depression. In: *Affective Disorders* (ed. Greenacre, P.), pp. 13–48. New York: Int. Univ. Press.
73. Landauer, K. (1925). Aequivalente der Trauer. *Int. Z. Psychoan.* **11**, 194.
74. Alexander, F. (1950). *Psychosomatic Medicine*. New York: Norton.
75. Grinker, R. R. and Robins, F. P. (1954). *Psychosomatic Case Book*. New York: Blakiston.
76. Freud, S. (1916). On Transience. In: *The Standard Edition*, Vol. XIV. London: Hogarth Press (1955).
77. Alexander, J. M. and Isaacs, K. S. (1964). The function of affect. *Br. J. Med. Psychol.* **37**, 231.

CHAPTER 18

Some Egregious and Gregarious Aberrations Periodically Sustained by Hysteriform Borderliners

The Gaslighting Syndrome

Calif and Weinshell (1981)[1] in describing some noxious products of projective-identification, not at all uncommon in my experience, point out that inwardly potentially painful unconscious conflicts of a very regressive nature belonging to one person can be unloaded onto a vulnerable second person who partially incorporates the projection, and comes to fear becoming mentally deranged. One illustration they offer, surely familiar to many psychiatrists, is that of an extremely anxious married woman who felt herself to be on the verge of insanity. The term coined for this syndrome—gaslighting—arose from the popular film *Gaslight* based on Patrick Hamilton's 1939 play *Angel Street*, which tells the story of a wife in just such a situation. In Calif and Weinshell's case, the patient thought of her husband as being stable and competent whereas she thought of herself as being scatterbrained. Her husband and, through his powerful influence, her children had developed a consensus that she was very sick and totally responsible for the prevailing domestic chaos. Here is a typical example of the husband's behaviour in producing severe stress and then proclaiming his wife's mental inferiority and instability: once he nonchalantly drove through busy city streets at high speed, repeatedly warning his wife to keep watching out for the police, and seemingly quite unconcerned about safety. His wife, panic-stricken, pleaded with him to take care and slow down whereupon he berated her for irrational concern.

In therapy, the wife's self-image improved and she became more self-assertive at home. The husband then stepped up his denigrations. Failing to browbeat her into subjection, he withdrew all interest in her but then he became symptomatic physically, soon suffering a brief psychotic decompensation. Subsequently, there was a divorce; the husband later married a young woman who apparently was content to be quite subservient, much as the patient had been. The patient herself remarried and functioned well without excessive anxiety.

352

The concept of communicated mental disease, which is based on the stark phenomena of contagion of psychotic delusions, has a long history, some of which is outlined below in connection with so-called 'hysterical psychoses' and 'collective hysteria'. Lasègue and Falret (1877)[2] described seven examples of *la folie à deux (ou folie communiqué)* and 65 years later Gralnick (1942)[3] was able to review one hundred and three cases in the medical literature. Cases of *folie à trois* and *à plusieurs* (S. M. Coleman and S. L. Last[4]) have also been described. In such cases there is flagrant psychosis initiated by an overt psychotic, whereas in the gaslighting syndrome an hysteriform borderline character disorder avoids psychotic disengagement from social reality by the domination of an hysteriform passive partner who is driven to the verge of psychotic disorganization or into it. Already in 1877, Lasègue and Falret had stated: 'The main therapeutic indication is to separate the two patients. Then one of them might recover, especially the second, since he is cut off from the source of delusions.' While this may also be salutory in cases of the gaslighting syndrome where there is an effort to drive the other person crazy, often more active psychotherapeutic intervention is beneficial. Harold F. Searles (1959)[5] scrutinized the painful re-enactment of such a struggle with the therapist, and examined the problems this sets up for the appropriateness of the therapist's responses in the treatment situation.

In the gaslighting syndrome more narrowly defined there is an endopsychic perception quickly negated and partially repressed of irrationality amounting to insanity within the perpetrator who then disowns this notion and projects it upon the submissive partner. The latter in the setting of a dyssymbiotic relationship resists the interactional projective-identification with difficulty and becomes very anxious in the process. This pathological interactional process has been evident in several hysterical women (spouses of compulsive physicians) who have been in analytic psychotherapy with me. In two such cases, there was an attempt to persuade the grossly neglected wife that it was quite abnormal for her to want sexual intercourse at all! A remarkable novella published in 1892 and written by Charlotte Perkins Gilman entitled the *The Yellow Wallpaper* ironically delineates such emotional and intellectual violation with clinical precision and aesthetic tact. The writer had had the experience of treatment of her hysterical nervous disorder by the renowned psychiatrist S. Weir Mitchell whose method routinely consisted of enforced rest and reduction of external stimulation. The story she afterwards wrote concerns a woman who has been taken to the country by her husband, a physician, in an effort to cure her of nervous disorder. The doctor is presented as kindly and well meaning but it becomes apparent that his treatment of his wife is guided by those same nineteenth century attitudes towards women which had already been an important source of her affliction. Inadvertently, he is thus a vicious abettor of her sickness. As Elaine R. Hedges (1973)[6] writes:

Here is a woman who, as she tries to explain to anyone who will listen, wants very much to *work*. Specifically, she wants to write (and the story she is narrating is her desperate and secret attempt both to engage in work that is meaningful to her and to retain her sanity). But the medical advice she receives, from her doctor/husband, from her brother, also a doctor, and from S. Weir Mitchell, explicitly referred to in the story, is that she do nothing. The prescribed cure is total rest and total emptiness of mind. While she craves intellectual stimulation and activity, and at one point poignantly expresses her wish for 'advice and companionship' (one can read to-day respect and equality) in her work, what she receives is the standard treatment meted out to women in a patriarchial society. Thus her husband sees her as a 'blessed little goose.' She is his 'little girl' and she must take care of herself for his sake. Her role is to be 'a rest and comfort for him.' That he often laughs at her is, she notes forlornly and almost casually at one point, only what one expects in marriage.

And Hedges[6] writes further:

> Increasingly she concentrates her attention on the wallpaper in her room—a paper of a sickly yellow that both disgusts and fascinates her. Gilman works out the symbolism of the wallpaper beautifully, without ostentation ... Inevitably, therefore, the narrator, imprisoned within the room, thinks she discerns the figure of a woman behind the paper. The paper is barred—that is part of what pattern it has, and the woman is trapped behind the bars, trying to get free. Ultimately in the narrator's distraught state, there are a great many women behind the patterned bars, all trying to get free.

The Hysterical Psychoses

Hollender and Hirsch (1964)[7] consider that hysterical psychosis is the most serious manifestation of hysterical disease. They note that such a psychosis is marked by a sudden and dramatic onset temporally related to a profoundly upsetting event or circumstance; that manifestations include hallucinations, delusions, depersonalization and grossly unusual behaviour and that the acute episode seldom lasts longer than one to three weeks. They also note that affectivity, if altered, is in the direction of volatility, not flatness, and that thought disorder when it occurs at all is sharply circumscribed and very transient. This description accords for the most part with the D.S.M. III label of *Brief Reactive Psychosis* which quaintly remarks that 'the psychotic symptoms appear immediately following a recognisable psychosocial stressor that would evoke significant symptoms of distress in almost anyone' (1980).[8] Presumably, it would also be negatively symptomatic if there were no symptoms of distress in anyone thus stressed. In regard to the notion that this psychotic excursion is the most grave manifestation of the hysterical process, it would seem more accurate to regard it as the outcome of failure of the usual repertoire of defences employed in hysteriform character disorder, but that there remains a remarkable ego resilience so that in a short time and with support these defences may be reinstituted.

Richman and White (1970)[9] note that in regard to the central importance of situational and interpersonal precipitating factors the disorder is associated with intense anxiety relating to death or destruction or actual experience of object loss. Martin (1971)[10] perceived hysterical psychosis as an extreme means of escape by hysterical women from disturbed symbiotic relationships in marriage rather than confrontation of the challenge of separation-individuation.

There is a group of hysterical psychoses among circumpolar peoples which have frequently occurred from pre-contact periods to the present, and are now known as the *Arctic Hysterias*. There are two types: one imitative and excited, the other quite frenzied and dissociated. The imitative type is confined to Siberia, whereas the more frenzied dissociative style occurs in Siberia, Alaska, Canada, Greenland and Lappland. Characteristic of both types is suddenness of onset, and according to Edward F. Foulks (1972)[11] who has written a comprehensive monograph of outstanding value, this onset is brought about by fright, followed by a short-lived period of bizarre behaviour and a return to normality with the cessation of acute symptoms. Aberle (1952)[11] points out that similar sudden frenzied dissociative states frequently occur in diverse societies, as in Mongolia, Malaya, North Africa, Siam, Bengasi and the Philippines.

The imitative types in Siberia characteristically occur in females during late adolescence and at the menopause. Symptoms include shouting obscenities, echopraxia, echolalia, heightened suggestibility, wild dancing, and sometimes jumping into water or into a fire. Foulks (1972)[11] notes:

> The behavior in general is stereotyped and repetitive, the performer being in a hypnotic-like state. Among the Ainu a woman would perform automatic acts of cursing her husband or some other man. This was one of the only occasions when she could do so without retribution. In many of these cases, the precipitating event was a sudden startle. In the case of the Ainu the startling object was both specific and perhaps symbolic of the underlying conflict. Ainu women greatly fear snakes, which are regarded as having supernatural powers. An encounter with a snake in a dream or in actuality would precipitate the automatic behavior ...

Usually such an episode is regarded as spirit possession. It is evident that such a spirit is one of protest.

Frenzied dissociative types of 'arctic hysteria' are given different names: they are called *olonism* by the Samoyed; *miryachit* by the Tungus (Yap, 1951,[12] 1952[13]). These disorders are commonly seen in young women and in nervous types of young men aspiring to become shamans. According to Foulks (1972)[11] symptoms include loss of appetite, headache, apathy and indifference to surroundings, which continue for several days. Then quite suddenly, the afflicted person becomes wild-eyed, and with an air of exaltation begins to chant or speak 'in tongues'. Arms and legs are often waved about, jactitations occur and often a seizure. Novakovsky (1924)[14] noted that sexual expression was manifest in the hysterical attack with erotic utterances. He felt that the high incidence of such disorders in the early spring was attributable to rising sexual tension. Aberle (1952)[11] cited cases of women who reported that the onset of their attacks was precipitated by sexual dreams of being attacked by men or male genitalia.

The frenzied dissociative types of arctic hysteria are discussed in the literature on the Eskimos as *pibloktoq*.

Robert Peary (1910)[15] while residing among the Polar Eskimos of Greenland, on his way to attempt to attain the North Pole observed:

There exists among these people a form of hysteria known as *pibloktoq* (the same name as given to the well-known madness among their dogs), with which women, more frequently than men are affected. During these spells, the maniac removes all clothes and prances about like a broncho. In 1898, while the Windward was in winter quarters off Cape D'Urville, a married woman was taken with one of these fits in the middle of the night. In a state of perfect nudity she walked the deck of the ship; then, seeking still greater freedom, jumped the rail, onto the frozen snow and ice. It was some time before we missed her; and when she was finally discovered, it was at a distance of half a mile, where she was still pawing and shouting to the best of her abilities. She commenced a wonderful performance of mimicry in which every conceivable cry of local bird and mammal was reproduced in the throat of Inaloo. This same woman at other times attempts to walk the ceiling of her igloo; needless to say, she has never succeeded.

It is apparent that Peary's observation is consistent with Martin's view of some hysterical psychoses representing an extreme means of escape from a frustrational marital relationship. It also seems to exhibit similar dynamics to those so eloquently outlined in *The Yellow Wallpaper* novella discussed above when a woman of an active activity type seeks companionship, and freedom to follow her avocation but feels walled-in. Of course, one can sympathize with the existential plight of Eskimos hemmed in by darkness and extreme cold, and sometimes exhausted by the struggle for survival in an environment so hostile to human life, conditions which no doubt augment the effect of 'psychosocial stressors'.

The famous early translator of Freud, A. A. Brill (1913)[16] interviewed Peary's lieutenant, Donald MacMillan, regarding his observations of the Eskimos and *pibloktoq* during the attempt to reach the North Pole. MacMillan remarked that *pibloktoq* reminded him of a little child discouraged and unhappy because he imagined that no one loved him or cared for him and therefore runs away. Brill concluded that: 'This plainly shows that just as in civilized people, it is love that plays the great part in the causation of the malady ...'

The emphasis on love deprivation in the multiple causation of *pibloktoq* and related mental disorders of the Eskimos such as hermiting behaviour or *qivitoq*, is replaced by some medical investigators by emphasis on dietary deprivation. Several articles have suggested that arctic hysterias may be closely associated with lack of adequate dietary calcium and low levels of vitamin D synthesis during the long winter (Hoygaard, 1941;[17] Wallace, 1961[18]). Edward F. Foulks (1972)[11] states that several serological surveys of the North Alaskan Eskimo 'do not support the notion that this population is unable to maintain normal calcium levels'. He adds: 'Serum total calcium determination of ten Innuit who manifested arctic hysteria-like behaviours revealed normocalcaemic levels during all seasons of the year. However, several subjects demonstrated calcium levels which were decidedly on the low side of normal,' and he writes further: 'Our studies, therefore, indicate that the behaviours seen in the arctic hysterias are not accompanied by states of chronic hypocalcaemia. This finding does not exclude the possibility, however, that hyperventilation with anxiety, or alterations in calcium rhythms, might play a role in precipitating the attacks, especially in view of low normal serums in several subjects.' No doubt the calcium hypothesis was suggested initially by the carpo-pedal spasms, the tetany and other dystonic features of *pibloktoq* which in this way, as others, is similar to manifestations of the *grande hystérie* described by Charcot.*

Parker (1962)[19] pointed out that Eskimo societies, as some other highly hysterogenic societies, had the following characteristics:

1. Early high gratification of dependency needs and minimal repression of sexual drives.

2. Emphasis on communalistic values and a great amount of face-to-face cooperative patterns, with high expectation of mutual aid.

3. Considerable disadvantage involved in the female role with low self-esteem requiring much bolstering.

4. Prevalent beliefs in supernatural possession and 'hysteric-like' behaviour models provided in institutionalized religious practices.

In such societies group opinion to create shame is the main method used to maintain socially acceptable behaviour. The super-ego is thus poorly structured internally and social control is maintained for the most part by ridicule-shame methods. Parker emphasizes that the shamanistic practices of the Eskimo provide a socially-sanctioned outlet for hostility and, at the same time, the very role model for hysterical behaviour when such an outlet does not suffice.

Among the Eskimos who live in the Hudson Bay area there is a variant syndrome known as *whitico*. The same syndrome is known as *windigo* among the Ojibwas of Southeastern Ontario. The illness is ushered in with gastro-intestinal disturbance, anorexia, nausea, vomiting and diarrhoea. These symptoms are no doubt related to defences against cannibilistic fantasies which are later more directly expressed by the affected individual as they are in the folklore. At the time of anorexia, the patient is morose and anxious, ruminating concerns about transmogrification into a 'whitico'. The *whitico* is an animated giant skeleton made of ice which devours human beings. The patient becomes more agitated and sleepless and the alarmed family calls upon a good *shaman* to counteract the bad *shaman's* spell, since this is what they consider to be the source of the evil. Meth (1974)[20] writes: 'Most often the patient improves after appropriate magic is applied but at times, particularly in remote areas where no 'good' *shaman* is available, the patient may coldly kill one or more members of his family and eat them.'

It seems likely that the *whitico* patient conflates the life saving properties of cannibilism during extreme famine—for cannibilism has been a means of survival among Eskimos—with an imputed value in an extreme

---

*David Landy, Professor of Anthropology, University of Massachusetts, enlarges the aetiologic constellation of *pibloktoq* by implicating vitamin A intoxication. Hypervitaminosis A may indeed be involved in some hysterical reactions of Innuit peoples. Eskimo nutrition provides abundant sources of vitamin A and lays the probable basis, according to Landy, for hypervitaminosis A through ingestion of the livers, kidneys and fat of arctic fish and mammals where the vitamin often is stored in poisonous quantities. Landy discusses a variety of ecological, nutritional, biological-physiological, psychological-psychoanalytic, social structural and cultural explanatory classes and recognizes that: 'It should be obvious that these factors are not mutually exclusive, and two or several may transact with each other' (personal communication).

emotional emergency caused by a gross depletion of narcissistic supplies. As Meth (1974)[19] pungently remarks: 'the stark, cruel arctic environment must create a feeling of utter isolation in its inhabitants, who must crave for the relief of their loneliness, and what could offer greater closeness than the incorporation of another human being?'

In Malay *latah* signifies 'love madness'. Kraepelin (1909)[21] and Bleuler (1936)[22] both considered the syndrome to be a 'primitive hysteria'. It consists of echopraxia, echolalia, and coprolalia; sometimes there is only evidence of mimicry and automatic obedience, but it is basically compounded of defiance and compliance. Thus it has features in common with the altered states of consciousness and of behaviour evident in arctic hysterias though first described in the steaming jungles of Malaysia. It is widely distributed geographically, and has been reported in Japan, Lapland, the Philippines, Mongolia, Thailand, India, Terra del Fuego and the State of Maine, under different names annotated by Friedmann recently (1982).[23] It is usually exhibited by middle aged or older women. In its milder forms, which may be quite short lived, the Malays regard it as a behavioural quirk rather than a disease.

In much of the late nineteenth and early twentieth century medical literature, Gilles de la Tourette's syndrome (*see* Chapter 15) is placed in the same group of disorders as *latah*. However, the earliest and most striking manifestations of Tourettism are the tics. Tics do not occur in *latah* whereas the imitation phenomena are always salient. On the other hand, echopraxia may be lacking in *maladies des tics*. Often coprolalia occurs in both syndromes.

J. J. Abraham (1912)[24] pointed out that *latah*, which usually seizes women, has its counterpart in *amok*, which is overwhelmingly a male phenomenon. *Amok* (or *amuck*) is so-named from the reference in agglutinative Malay to furious embattlement. After hours or days of withdrawal into solitary and quiet isolation, the amok person (*pengamok* in Malay) suddenly runs out and attacks all who are around—his family and acquaintances, and any strangers who might appear on the scene. The homicidal behaviour persists for hours, or rarely, days, until the man is restrained or killed. In the event of survival he then falls into a stupor for some hours or a few days. Upon regaining alert waking consciousness, he is usually depressed and irritable but amnesic for the assaultive episode. Reconstruction of the prodromal period and elucidation of the evidence for the post-morbid amnesia for the *amok* events in a recent study by Schmidt et al. (1977)[25] in general confirms the detailed descriptions and the impressions reported by numerous occidental travellers to the Malay Archipelago during this past century. Social withdrawal and emotional disturbance were present in 17 of 20 subjects and total amnesia in 15 of them, and in 5 to a partial degree. In recent decades, the term *amok* has been applied to sudden similar outbursts of unexpected violence that occur among other peoples. Joseph Westermeyer (1982)[26] has written a detailed account of the syndrome; he also made earlier observations in Laos (1972).[27] Other reports have been based on observations in New Guinea and Papua (Burton-Bradley, 1968[28]), the Philippines (Zaguirre, 1957[29]), the United States (Lion et al., 1969[30]) and the Arctic (Kloss,

1923[31]). As noted by Westermeyer (1982),[26] similar forms of sudden assault, but with a different label (*berserk*) have been described among mediaeval Scandinavians. Meth (1974)[20] interprets that the *pengamok* attempts a conflict solution by repression of his hostility but this begins to fail. He makes a desperate prodromal attempt at withdrawal, then a last-ditch attempt at survival against the forces of inner disintegration by externalizing his destructiveness and killing others. Often this too fails, as in the events which follow, he is killed.

The surviving *pengamok* whose amnesia is partial seems to have experienced a vivid hallucinatory state. This together with the amnesia betokens an acute hysteriform dissociative reaction, more or less culture-bound in the form of Malay *amok*. However, difficulties in expressing anger in the setting of hysteriform borderline personality disorder are world-wide and more or less culture-independent. Thus the sudden and unexpected outburst of violent behaviour publicly displayed, and non-specific in regard to any other human beings who just happen to be around the scene of bloodshed, occurs in all countries. The ready availability of hand guns and other lethal weapons in some countries aggravates the gravity of the problem of amok-like disordered behaviour. For centuries in Malay *amok*, the weapon used was the short sword or *kris*. This imposed some limits on the scale of mass murder. The difficulties of restraint and protection against sudden violent behaviour have increased enormously with the availability of modern lethal weapons.

The following case illustrates some amok-like features and is not an unusual example nowadays in my experience in the USA.

Case 48. A 38-year-old white married businessman was admitted to hospital. He appeared fatigued and dishevelled. There was a large bruise over the left eye which he indignantly ascribed to 'police brutality'. Coherent and relevant with no evident psychotic disturbance, the patient gave a fair initial account of himself. He had been getting progressively more depressed during the past four months, he complained, and had been entertaining thoughts of suicide. During the past ten days he had been drinking beer heavily, and four days prior to admission he had been involved in a shooting affair, and had been in gaol on criminal charges. He had shot at a moving vehicle, he now understood, and had wounded the driver. Moreover, he had been told that he had fired shots into a store, and had endangered several peoples' lives therein. He was dejected, and could not remember what had happened. He had been driving his car several miles away from his home and he had had a semi-automatic hunting gun in his car, now confiscated by the police. At the time of admission, the patient also came to complain that his father was wanting to control his life, and that his mother was afraid of his father. The past medical history included several surgical interventions for peptic ulcers and for hernia repairs, appendectomy, cholecystectomy and tonsillectomy. He denied any drug allergies or any drug taking, except alcohol and prescribed medications. He was a cigarette smoker.

The psychological evaluation included the Rorschach, Bender-Gestalt, Draw-a-Person and Beck Depression Inventory. In summary, the patient had a personality disorder, and was presently experiencing a pathological mood disturbance along with some breakdown of reality testing, suggesting some mild-degree of thought disorder. There was a markedly oral character structure with considerable suppressed hostility. On the Rorschach, there was an explosive type of content, suggesting that he was the kind of individual who impulsively acts out, particularly when his control threshold is lowered by alcohol.

The examining internist reported in summary that the physical examination revealed a white male appearing his stated age, short of stature, with a contusion of the left eye. Scattered rhonchi were noted. The blood pressure was 128/70 with a pulse of 76 and respirations of 16. Multiple old scars were present, slightly tender in the right upper quadrant of the skin of the abdomen. Deep tendon reflexes were 1+ to 2+. Laboratory findings were within normal limits.

The diagnostic impression after these examinations was of atypical bipolar psychosis and borderline personality disorder. At first during his hospital stay the patient was profoundly depressed and anxious. However, he became cooperative in distributive discussions. He was first treated on a closed unit and medicated with Eskalith (lithium carbonate) capsules 300 mgm q.i.d. and with Xanax (alprazolam) 0·5 mgm t.i.d. He developed diarrhoea for which he was treated with Mitrolan (calcium polycarbophil) tablets 2 p.o. q.i.d. It became evident that the bowel disturbance was largely psychosomatic as worsening occurred when he was facing some of his problems in psychotherapy.

After three days the patient was moved to an open unit where he continued to cooperate, although he also continued to complain of loss of appetite and lethargy. Nevertheless, he became involved in therapeutic activities including working out in the gymnasium and working in the green-house. He remained anxious but his depression diminished. He was able to explore more dimensions of his problems in a realistic way. Soon he started to attend the substance abuse classes and also entered into bioenergetic therapy as a group experience. He gradually continued to improve in response to these measures, his anxiety diminishing. As he improved interviews took place with his father and mother, and later joint interviews with the patient and his wife. He continued to be a very active member of the bioenergetics and psychotherapeutic groups and he became much less tense. He worried about his legal problems and was anxious about seeing his lawyer repeatedly. His depression abated and he began to sleep more adequately. He also was sedulous in attending adjunctive therapeutic activities, and these then also included ceramics. It was thought, following conferences with personnel concerned with his therapy, that though he remained mildly anxious and periodically mildly depressed after four and a half months of inpatient treatment that he had at last become well enough to leave the hospital, but could continue to make good use of some of the hospital services, including bioenergetics, group therapy and ceramics, while attending in psychotherapy as an outpatient. Though anxious about this the patient during two more weeks worked through in individual psychotherapy some of his anxious feelings before discharge from hospital, and he agreed to further outpatient psychotherapy.

In the discharge summary of his hospital stay the following statements were made in accordance with D.S.M. III.

Final Diagnosis:

Axis I   Atypical bipolar disorder

Axis II   Borderline personality disorder

Axis III Small incisional hernias. Chronic ulcer disease, now in remission
          (treatment in past has included subtotal gastrectomy)

Allergies: None known

Condition on discharge: The patient is mildly anxious and very concerned about his legal situation. He is no longer despondent and remains cooperative in psychotherapy and prepared for further efforts in this regard.

Disposition: He left to live locally and to attend the hospital for various activities and to attend for outpatient psychotherapy.

Prognosis: The prognosis is favourable with continued outpatient psychotherapy and continued lithium medication.

Recommendations: Eskalith medication (300 mg, one capsule t.i.d.). Lithium levels to be taken every two weeks. Continued medication with Entozyme (2 tabs after each meal) and Mitrolan tabs 2 q.i.d. He should attend for further group bioenergetic therapy and individual psychotherapy on an outpatient basis.

In the psychiatric report which I was ordered by the court to submit 9 months later, I included the following remarks in the last two paragraphs:

The patient has been in weekly outpatient psychotherapy since discharge from hospital, as well as attending for bioenergetic therapy weekly. Moreover he has attended group therapy and AA meetings regularly. In addition he has continued with psychotropic medications under my prescription. With this strenuous therapeutic programme he has fully cooperated and, in my opinion, has improved considerably, notably with better integration of his personality, including improved self-control. He has abstained from alcohol, and there have been no further episodes of alteration of consciousness associated with bizarre and disordered behaviour. He continues to suffer from psychosomatic disorder, now much milder than heretofore, and disturbances of sleep, and these are associated with his present legal plight.

He is no longer a danger to himself, to his family, or to society at large. This improvement is likely to be maintained and to be enhanced, by continued outpatient psychotherapeutic work which should continue for another year.

During the course of psychotherapy the patient remembered drinking at a bar in a tavern in a small nearby town through which his father often travelled on his way to and from work. At another time he recalled the shattering glass of the store, and being stopped by a police car behind him at the side of a reservoir. At the time he did not know where he was and blacked out again after opening the door of his car on command. He awakened in a prison cell with no bed and nothing in it except a commode, lying on the floor, face 'all bruised up and sore'. He was faced with the facts that he had wounded the driver of a passing car, a stranger motoring through by whom he was being sued, as he was by the storekeeper whose window had been shattered and whose customers had been frightened. He was thankful, however, that no one had been killed and that the passing driver of the car was recovering from his wound.

In further analytic psychotherapy, the patient was able to give an account of his struggles with a tyrannical father which also became represented in transference. He was the only son, having three older sisters, and he had felt put down all his life and ordered around by his father. Shortly before the *amok*-like episode he had attempted to go into business on his own, had attempted to retrieve a large sum of money he had made through separate business deals and had entrusted to his father. The latter had characteristically refused to release the money and insisted that he had to have regard for the welfare of the family, and that the patient was incapable of looking out for himself.

It became apparent to the patient that his running off in his automobile and firing his hunting gun had been inspired by a forceful patricidal wish, and that the passing motorist had been his father in fantasy. It was of interest too that there had been an incubation period of several days after the confrontation with the father about releasing his money, just as is reported in the *amok* syndrome. During this time he had been ruminating about his sufferings and humiliations at the hands of his overbearing father down the years, remembering in particular an episode when his mother had gone on a hunger strike in order to make her husband yield on an issue and had almost died in the unsuccessful attempt. During this solitary period he had been drinking beer heavily. In the course of the psychotherapy, the aggravation endured by the patient from the benevolent tyrant of the family, including his interventions with the patient's successive wives—he had been divorced twice—were associated with his recurrent ulcers and diarrhoea problems.

In Chapter 10 the various qualitative features of hypnoid alteration of consciousness were discussed, including those in fugues and somnambulisms and states of depersonalization. In those which are id-dominated as in the *amok*-like syndrome adumbrated above, it is evident that the murderous genie suddenly emerges out of the bottle. Akhtar and Brenner (1979)[32] attempt a differential diagnosis of fugue-like states including hysterical fugue, epileptic fugue, those associated with non-epileptic organic conditions such as head trauma, cerebrovascular disease and mental retardation, as well as those alcohol and drug related. In clinical practice, several such conditions may be involved in the pathogenesis of fugue-like states; in those with organic complicity, psychodynamic factors are usually also quite evident. Thus in regard to 'organic fugues', Akhtar and Brenner note that these fugues 'can be viewed as a variety of "catastrophic reaction", outbursts of impulsive behaviour and affective discharge during stressful, usually anger provoking situations.' As in the case described above there is a period of build-up of accumulated resentment and of heightened conflict before sudden decompensation. The regressive features of ego functioning are viewed by Luparello (1970)[33] as a partial reversion to the state where differentiation between the mother and child has not yet taken place, amplifying an hypothesis proposed earlier by Geleerd (1956).[34] Luparello emphasizes in a case report of a patient in psychoanalysis the intense separation anxiety and the suicidal and murderous impulses. He writes:

> The fugue as a regression to the early mother-child phase of development may well function to regain the lost object and simultaneously defend against the murderous impulses arising out of the turning away of the love-object. The suicidal tendencies may simultaneously express a wish to join the lost object and serve as a deflection of rage from the object to the self.

In this case too depressive problems were evident. As noted by Fenton (1982)[35] an underlying depressive illness is common as well as personality disorder. He points out also that in contrast to other hysterical phenomena, fugues are more common in men and more likely to occur in people who have previously experienced episodes of altered consciousness, such as following a head injury or heavy drinking.

The Ganser Syndrome and Hysterical Pseudo-dementia

In his original papers Ganser (1898,[36] 1904[37]) described a 'peculiar hysterical state' characterized by the inability of the patient to answer simple questions correctly; instead the patient passes over ('*vorbeigehen*') the appropriate answer and selects one that is approximate though incorrect, or the patient often gives an absurd reply. Moreover the patient displays episodic anxiety and hallucinosis, and lastly he shows the stigmata of hysteria. He described 24 patients, as well as the four symptoms mentioned which have since become known as the Ganser syndrome. All of these patients were on remand in gaol at the time of examination. Many of the patients obviously had a clouding of consciousness: in one case an almost complete analgesia to pin-prick was present, in another shifting zones of hyperalgesia and analgesia were evident. After a few days the patients gained 'a state of clarity', were able to answer questions correctly and had no memory for their earlier eccentric replies. 'This state of clarity', he added, 'did not last but was periodically interrupted by a deep depression in which, besides the reappearance of hallucinations and the return of hysterical sensory disturbances, one also observed the confirmation of the previously described reaction to elementary questions.' In all the cases the syndrome was 'preceded by trauma which can be regarded as a strongly operative precipitating factor'.

The following case came to my notice 35 years ago.

Case 49. A hardworking and conscientious middle-aged carpenter of good repute astonished everyone in the Welsh village in which he lived by breaking into a shop, stealing a bicycle and resisting arrest when caught in the act. He presented a picture of the Ganser syndrome, giving approximate replies only to simple questions, and these not concerned with the night of the felony. He did not remember anything concerned with the breaking-in episode. He appeared anxious and absent-minded, sometimes apparently preoccupied with visions, and it was difficult to get his attention for long. He was quite unable to give a coherent account of himself.

In brief, in the events which followed, I advised the court that he was temporarily unfit to plead. My report was disregarded. At the assizes, which I attended as an expert witness, the prisoner anxiously replied over and over, 'Guilty and not guilty' when asked how he would plead. He was sentenced to 18 months' imprisonment in spite of my insistence that he was ill. Within three weeks, because his erratic behaviour in prison disturbed others, including his custodians, he was sent to the mental hospital in Abergavenny where I then worked.

His condition improved greatly with rest, sedation, careful feeding and support under prolonged observation in a friendly milieu; it then became possible to pursue the investigative aspects of his treatment. He had abstained from sexual intercourse for the previous five years, after his wife underwent pelvic surgery that left her an invalid. For some time he had hoped for her improvement but had subsequently become reconciled, partly with the help of prayer, to sexual abstinence. What he conceived of as wicked thoughts intruded, especially at the sight of young women in church, and later he became involved in a struggle with solitary sexual stimulation and sadistic sexual thoughts which were soon accompanied by blasphemous muttering. The actual crime of breaking in to steal a bicycle to ride on while ringing its bell symbolized and resymbolized in one detail superimposed on another a savagely defiant and sadistic phallic penetration. The interdiction of sexual intercourse had resulted in his undergoing a libidinal regression accompanied by a strengthening of the anal-sadistic component instinct and the overthrow of his usual defensive repertoire, including even consolidated reaction formations and isolation of affect. In the actual violent episode the usual complex defence was replaced by a gross regression in ego functioning and hysterical and psychotic warding off mechanisms.

It became apparent in this case, as sometimes occurs, that the patient's capacity for enjoyment and expression of warm and tender emotions had been considerably limited throughout his life, and that his family had suffered from his compulsive personality disorder as much as they had benefitted from his being a good material provider. When the compulsive defences were ruptured then there was resort to hysterical symbolic discharge and primitive denial and splitting defences.

According to Whitlock (1982)[38] the Ganser symptoms of approximate answers, talking past the point and regressive metonymy occur in a number of different psychiatric settings not all of which involve a clouding of consciousness. He[37] gives two examples of regressive metonymy: one of his patients stated of a drawing he had made of a house that it pictured 'an amalgamation of building materials'; another, asked where he was, replied he was 'in a Department of Education in illness', by which phrase he presumably designated the teaching hospital he was in. Such Ganser symptoms together with this kind of pretentious grandiloquent metonymy are sometimes manifest in florid schizophrenia in my experience.

Curran, Partridge and Storey (1976)[39] distinguish hysterical pseudo-dementia from the Ganser syndrome on the basis of the absence of clouding of consciousness. Certainly, as they state, hysterical pseudo-dementia is 'particularly prone to occur in those of subnormal mentality when under stress which has led them to suggest themselves into being more stupid than they really are'. In this way, as so often occurs in hysterical exaggerations, a weakness is converted to a manipulative strength. Trethowen (1979)[40] notes, 'in some instances it may be difficult to differentiate such behaviour from pure simulation'. There are many cases when the Ganser syndrome is exhibited as part of a hysterical pseudo-dementia. Thus Anderson and Mallinson (1941)[41] discuss the case of a 42-year-old naval stoker of limited intelligence. On examination he gave both approximate and absurd answers to questions and manifested a degree of ignorance about the elementary mechanics of living which would prevent him from adjusting to the service or to leading a self-reliant life outside the Navy. The authors concluded that in this case there was a resort to hysterical exaggeration and exploitation of his inadequate intelligence.

'Psychose Passionelle' of De Clérambault

De Clérambault (1942)[42] described five cases of women afflicted with the 'conviction of being in amorous communication with a person of much higher rank, who has been the first to fall in love and was the first to make advances'. Usually there was a sudden and explosive onset and the conviction was held in a state of heightened and clear consciousness. One of his cases, a 53-year-old milliner believed that King George V was in love with her. She felt she received messages from sailors and tourists who were visiting in France. She persistently pursued the King, paying several visits to London, and waiting for him outside Buckingham Palace. She once saw a curtain move in one of the palace windows, and this she interpreted as an amorous regal signal.

This kind of erotic delusional disorder was known to many earlier psychiatrists including Clouston (1887)[43] and Kraepelin (1921).[44] It was regarded as a form of paranoia. In 1956, Balduzzi[45] discussed the case of a 26-year-old married woman who developed an ardent passion for the married physician who attended her abortion. She pestered him with telephone calls and daily messages, frequently visiting his home. Her own marriage was an unhappy one in which she had lost interest. Indeed she neglected her young daughter, was preoccupied, and would talk of little but the doctor. She stated that when she had first encountered him, 'I felt changed into another person—Until then I had not lived'. The doctor, she maintained, had 'reciprocated several times with an ardour even more pronounced than her own'. Finally the doctor's wife pushed her out of her door and there were also further scenes which included the physician. She then declaimed, 'He acts like that only because, for reasons I am not yet able to understand, he is compelled to assume attitudes entirely contrary to his feelings, because he does not want others to understand his real passionate love; in fact, I have noticed that he has shown himself more aggressive to me verbally, when that woman, who passes for his wife, is present.' These and similar observations of *psychose passionelle* reveal that the experience of the patient is one of intense fascination with much heightened and narrowed attention, as in one phase of states of creativity, as noted in Chapter 10. In this kind of falling in love archaic features are heavily accentuated and the feeling of the little 'I' and the big 'you' becomes instead: 'I become everything again by being part of your greatness', with consequent expansion of ego boundaries. Moreover there is gross impairment of the erotic sense of reality in as much as consideration for and of the object is severely distorted. Freud (1921)[46] pointed out the resemblance of some features of 'falling in love' to some hypnoid states following hypnosis. In *psychose passionelle* the most primitive aspects of this altered state of consciousness endure and are uncorrected by intermittent secondary process thinking.

Enoch, Trethowan and Barker (1967)[47] report the case of a well-spoken, unmarried young woman aged 20.

Her mother had died when she was four years of age and she was raised by an anxious and overprotective father, whom she had always despised, and by a strict grandmother. Her first sexual experience was with an elderly man when she was 17 years of age. Later there were several short lived affairs with other older men, all bitterly opposed by her father. The writers found no obvious psychotic features, but found that she did not strictly adhere to the truth. Her complaint was of excessive lethargy. For two years she had become infatuated with a bachelor aged 53 years, socially and intellectually her superior. He was in her office where she was a clerk. 'As soon as he spoke to me I felt I had known him all my life, and it frightened me ... this was the man I was intended to love—from that moment to this I have never been the same.' Her work suffered and she was dismissed. Before leaving she confronted her 'lover' and declared her feelings towards him. He was astonished, not realizing how she felt, and became extremely embarrassed when she flung her arms around his neck and passionately kissed him in the office.

At interview after her dismissal he admitted being flattered by her attentions and was not, at first, averse to their association. He always emphasized the difference in their ages, however, and repeatedly assured her that there was no future for them and that marriage was impossible. Occasionally he persuaded her to stop pestering him, but soon she telephoned again to arrange a further meeting.

He advised her to associate with a man of her own age. She then had intercourse with a youth, who did not attract her, and returned to her lover declaring triumphantly that the experiment had failed and that he was the only man for her.

On another occasion she presented him with contraceptives which he declined. They both denied having intercourse, although he undoubtedly encouraged her initially by 'heavy petting'. Frequently she telephoned him at the office several times a day or sent telegrams to his home, until in desperation he promised to see her 'just one more time'. After admission a meeting was arranged in hospital between the patient and her lover. He reiterated that there was no future for them. She exclaimed that it was unfair that she had to suffer so much while he 'got off Scot free'. She then hit him smartly across the face, but at the same time held his hand with her other one. She broke down and said there was nothing left for her but suicide. While in hospital she continued to telephone him and write excessively and her letters were mixed with love, abuse and threats of suicide. Chemotherapy, E.C.T. and insight-directed psychotherapy were all ineffective. Although she claimed to be overcoming her passion, on being pressed it was apparent that she still believed that he was attracted to her.

De Clérambault had noted that if hope for reciprocated love is repeatedly shattered, a phase of spite and grievance may ensue; negative reactions took place concomitantly in this case reported by Enoch, Trethowan and Barker. Arieti and Bemporad (1974)[48] found that such cases were 'not too rare'. In my experience milder variants nowadays follow attempts at sexual therapy, as the following case illustrates.

Case 50. The patient and her husband had been in many sessions with a pair of psychologist sex therapists trained in techniques advocated by Masters and Johnson. The patient suffered from frigidity and her husband from premature ejaculation. Her husband improved considerably, and the patient too had made some progress sexually, though not to the point of enjoying orgasm. However, the patient later became progressively more disturbed, soon refusing attempts at intercourse by her husband and finally revealing that she was in love with the male psychologist therapist. She expressed the view that they had a 'spiritual understanding', and that they had met in a former life, about which she had some dreams. She made many attempts to communicate with the psychologist who refused to see her, probably on account of the extravagant ideas she purveyed on the telephone. However, she maintained that he had shown in many ways that he knew of their former life together and that he would arrange in due course for a divorce, and then resume his relationship with her. She maintained that this was because he was 'an honourable man' and this was the only reason why he would not see her at present. It became evident in psychotherapy that she had developed a transference psychosis of an hysteriform nature.

The background which gradually emerged was of early defective mothering—her mother was a cold character—and then a turning to her father for affection which she at first received. He later turned away from her following the birth of her brother, four years her junior. As she grew up she had enviously watched them both having a very close relationship, going fishing together, etc. whereas she felt ignored by her father. It became clear that the former life alluded to her earlier warm relationship with her father, and that the work involving sexuality and its acceptance with the therapist was translated into spiritual union with him. Later she insisted on his 'provocations' and his and the other therapists' failure to relate her problems to her early family drama. Both of these criticisms, though much exaggerated and elaborated, had a reality-foundation in my opinion. Her prudish antisexual repressive attitudes had landed her in trouble in her marriage, but the attempt at rescue in couples' sex therapy propelled her into a hysterical psychosis, from which she emerged with considerable difficulty during analytic psychotherapy.

The Couvade Phenomenon and Syndrome

The widespread custom of couvade acknowledges the husband's deep involvement in his wife's pregnancy. In its extreme form, the mother return to her work as soon as possible after birth and then waits on the father. Thus the roles of the sexes are temporarily reversed. The word 'couvade', derived from the French *'couvaison'* meaning 'brooding time', refers to the established rite when the husband takes to bed just before, during, or shortly after, the time of his wife's labour. He may refrain from food, may groan with mock pains, and receive a good deal of attention as shown to a woman at the time of childbirth. The term 'couvade' is sometimes reduced to 'half-couvade' when the restrictions on the father though insistent are ritually much lighter at the time of child-birth; such restrictions together with some mild injunctions are almost universal among primitive and ancient peoples. In former times, the full couvade was observed by Marco Polo in Chinese Turkestan, in more recent times in Californian tribes of Amerinds, in the Congo, and many other places. Anthropologists generally have recognized its social function to emphasize the role of the father in reproduction.

In 1919, Reik (1919)[49] noted that an important tendency permeating both initiation rites and couvade ceremonies of primitive societies is an endeavour to counter and thus to modulate the cathexis of Oedipus wishes, that is those for father-murder and mother-incest. Reik found that those peoples who practised the full ritual were acting on the conviction that the basis of the powerful attraction for the mother that boys had was the physical fact of birth. One essential aim of both initiation and couvade ceremonies was thus to mitigate this physical fact and to establish a modifying fiction that the boy at any rate has been reborn by the father, thus attempting to diminish his incestuous and patricidal wishes and fantasies.

According to Malinowsky (1937)[50] there is another element involved, namely that of sympathetic magic: the husband attempts to absorb some of the suffering, thus relieving the parturient woman's pain. Reik later (1931)[51] also viewed the couvade ritual as based on ambivalence as well as identification. Further insight has been afforded by psychoanalytic clinical experience with men suffering symptoms occurring outside an established rite but coinciding with the pregnancy and parturition of their spouses. This experience indicates that womb-envying current within a polyphony of thoughts and fantasies concerning birth are heavily involved in the world wide practice. Edith Jacobson (1950)[52] outlined the development of a wish for a child in boys, and no doubt frustrated male creativity is of general importance in the origins of the rite.

Trethowan (1965)[53] and Trethowan and Conlon (1965)[54] compared the physical and mental health of 327 husbands during their wives' pregnancies with 221 men whose wives were not pregnant, and had not been so during the previous year. They found that a significantly greater number of expectant fathers suffered more often from loss of appetite, toothache and nausea and vomiting: common symptoms which together often constitute a couvade syndrome. Occasionally, as shown in Fig. 6, a couvade syndrome includes conversion phenomena which take the form of crude emulation of the pregnant condition. Besides gastro-intestinal symptoms—nausea and vomiting and bloating—this male patient exhibited hysterical pseudocyesis while his wife was approaching full term.

It has been pointed out by both Jacobson (1950)[52] and Boehm (1930)[55] that a persistent envy of the procreative power of women, often concealed by a countermanding machismo, is generated by the birth of a younger child at the peak of castration conflict. 'These men,' writes Jacobson (1950),[52] 'seem to be unable to renounce or to sublimate their wish to grow children themselves.' She notes also that creative work quite normally is the main sublimatory channel for such a wish.

The couvade syndrome, sometimes mimicking the wife's distress during pregnancy and/or labour, is a striking example of the fact that quite severe pain may be generated through the mechanism of over-identification and from the force of fantasy. The frequency of toothache in couvade symptomatology is sometimes due to the pregnant wife having actual dental problems, and offering the over-identifying and anxious husband, as it were, somatic compliance, in this case in the body of his spouse. The choice of the afflicted organ is, however, fundamentally due to its lending itself to the symbolic expression of the pain of losing male potency, partly the result of frustration of aggressive genital sexual wishes during the latter part of pregnancy, and partly expressing the feelings of shared helplessness connoted in the metaphor of 'having one's teeth drawn'. Enoch, Trethowan and Barker (1967)[47] cogently suggest too that a symbolic relation exists between the extraction of teeth, which sometimes the husband's toothache results in, and the extraction of a baby during childbirth.

Even more densely condensed birth fantasies account for the extraordinary association of styes and tarsal cysts suffered by expectant fathers reported by Inman (1941).[56] Here the process of pathological formation is quite sequestrated from the mainstream of experience, and one can only marvel at the plastic power of unconscious fantasy which so often issues in psychosomatic disease. In the case of styes and tarsal cysts suffered by husbands during their wives' pregnancies, the disorder is time-limited and the ocular symptoms soon abate.

The Münchausen Hospital Addiction Syndrome

Asher (1951)[57] clearly described a hospital addiction syndrome which previously had received but scant attention in medical literature. However, for many decades, physicians had briefly mentioned its existence and commented on its peculiar features. The syndrome is characterized by repeated admissions to hospitals of patients apparently in dire physical distress requiring acute care, but investigations disclose no significant organic abnormality to account for the emergency. Such patients have medical histories coloured by dramatic complaints and repetitive visits to physicians, clinics and hospitals. They often cooperate in undergoing elaborate diagnostic studies and receive potentially dangerous and risky therapies. In due course, they are found to have deceived other physicians (who are angry with them) at different hospitals. Frequently they discharge themselves against medical advice, perhaps during an argument with the doctors and nurses which had been provoked; sometimes they depart before surgical incisions have adequately healed. Inspection of the abdomen usually reveals multiple scars.

One such case was studied by Drs B. Robert Ashby and John Whelan and myself, while these psychiatrists were in training at the University of Virginia

Hospital. It happened that Dr Ashby had seen the patient at another hospital three years previously. He rendered this report of his previous experience with this patient.

Case 51. While serving as the duty intern in the Emergency Room of the Charleston County Hospital in Charleston, South Carolina, in November 1965, I was summoned to see a patient who had just entered the emergency ward. There I encountered a large-framed, muscular, middle-aged white male who was in a half-sitting, half-reclining posture on his bed. The patient was perspiring profusely. His respirations were rapid and appeared laboured. An oxygen mask was already in place. Several patches of discolouration were noted on the patient's shirt and appeared to be fresh blood.

Upon asking for a history of his difficulty, the patient was able to reply in short sentences between gasps in his breathing. In contrast to his unkempt appearance, as evidenced by his need for a shave and haircut and his dirty and ragged clothes, he spoke very fluently, intelligently, and with the hint of a New England accent. He briefly recounted that he had been a passenger that day on a bus from Florida to Boston. Several miles south of Charleston, he developed the abrupt onset of right-sided chest pain, accompanied by difficulty in breathing. Upon arriving at the Charleston bus terminal, he disembarked from the bus to seek medical assistance. As he was searching for directions to the nearest hospital, there was an increase in the severity of the chest pain, the development of more difficulty in breathing, and onset of coughing—productive of at least 'half a cup of liver-like bloody material'. His distress was noted and he was rushed by ambulance to the Emergency Room.

He continued that he had been working as a circus cook in New Orleans until two weeks previously. About two weeks prior to that, he had been treated by the circus physician for severe 'thrombophlebitis' of both lower extremities. He had continued on subcutaneous heparin until leaving the circus in New Orleans, a job which was lost due to severe damage to the circus as a result of heavy flooding of lower Louisiana that autumn. He stated that he made his way to Florida, where he did part-time work for several days. He developed bilateral leg pain again. He failed to seek medical attention, but decided instead to return by bus to his home town of Boston.

He reported that he had had a similar episode of thrombophlebitis six years previously, but denied any past history of chest pain or dyspnoea.

The physical examination revealed a normal blood pressure. The pulse was rapid, but regular and strong. The chest examination revealed loud, harsh breath sounds throughout. The heart was normal. The abdomen had multiple healed surgical scars and several ecchymotic areas. The extremities had areas of induration and there were ecchymoses of both arms. The lower extremities were markedly oedematous bilaterally. They were reddened, appeared inflamed, and were warm to touch. There were changes of chronic stasis dermatitis and Homan's sign was present bilaterally.

The immediate impression was pulmonary embolism secondary to thrombophlebitis of the lower extremities.

While admission arrangements were being made, the patient was asked about any drug allergies. He promptly replied that he had had 'a bad reaction to MS' which was an unusual response from a layman.

It was at this point that the patient asked for an honest assessment of his condition. He was told that his condition was essentially stable at the moment; but, that, in all frankness, it was stressed that his illness had serious implications because it was likely that a blood clot had passed from his legs to his lungs—a situation which could have very serious consequences.

He responded to this report that he was Catholic and asked if a priest could be called as soon as possible, for he had 'some matters to confess'. He was assured that his request would be met.

As he was being taken from the Emergency Room for admission, he repeatedly thanked the staff for their kindness to him—actually being overly ingratiating in his manner.

After arriving on the medical ward, he gave essentially the same history. He ascribed his abdominal surgical scars to procedures for appendicitis, hernia repair and 'adhesions'. Little additional information about his background was obtained except that he was a native of Boston, was an orphan without any family, and was a bachelor. He gave his age as 52.

Soon after arriving on the medical ward, he 'took a turn for the worse'. He appeared more dyspnoeic and coughed up small amounts of 'bright red blood'—which was witnessed by the medical resident and intern.

Appropriate studies and therapy were initiated and elaborate precautions were taken to prepare for treatment of shock or any serious complication. An emergency surgical consultation was requested. The surgeon recommended that, should any deterioration occur or evidence of additional embolization appear, emergency embolectomy and/or ligation of the inferior vena cava would be indicated immediately.

Within several hours, the patient's condition had apparently stabilized and he appeared more comfortable. On subsequent review of all of his hospital chart records, no abnormality of his vital signs was found during his hospitalization except for a rapid rate of respiration and a rapid, regular pulse.

When the priest arrived, the patient requested and received the last rites of the Church.

The following morning, almost 24 hours after admission, the patient began to become uncooperative without any apparent reason. He repeatedly pulled out his intravenous tubing, refused to take any medication, and became verbally hostile toward the staff and other patients. He suddenly announced: 'I am getting out of this damn place.' He refused to listen to reason and demanded to leave. He was advised that he would be leaving against medical advice and would be required to sign the standard discharge against medical advice release form. He refused initially to sign the form, but abruptly changed his mind, signed the form, and stormed out of the hospital.

As word of this patient's behaviour and sudden walkout spread throughout the hospital, many of the staff believed that the 'poor ignorant fool' would probably collapse and be brought back to the hospital dead on arrival before he reached the city limits of Charleston.

It was learned later that the patient found the priest, who had given him the last rites, and had borrowed funds from him, allegedly to use for bus transporation to Boston.

In March 1966, I was reading the current issue of the *AMA News*. The following paragraph brought back vividly the experience with this patient: 'Leo Lamphere, who has faked his way into hospitals for a number of years as a leading example of the 'The Baron Münchausen Syndrome', showed up again in Dayton, Ohio, several weeks ago and received a 30-day sentence at the Correction Farm. Lamphere limped on swollen legs, sometimes spit blood and complained of symptoms which suggested a pulmonary embolus when he appeared at three hospital emergency wards. Under an alias, Leo Leon, he was admitted to one of the hospitals for a period of six days. He was arrested on the suspicion of seeking drugs and sentenced in Municipal Court to the Correction Farm.' The alias, Leo Leon, was the same name used by the patient who was admitted to the Charleston County Hospital.

The brief article concluded with a reference to an article in the *Journal of the American Medical Association* by Chapman in 1957[58] which described his experience and knowledge about this same patient.

Chapman (1957)[58] wrote that his acquaintance with Leo Leon began in 1954, when for a period of 40 days, 'the medical wards of the State University of Iowa Hospitals were kept in a state of turmoil by the extraordinary behaviour of a single patient.' By various means, Chapman had been able to trace back as early as 1943 the bizarre hospitalizations of this one patient. His history indicated countless, probably several hundred, hospitalizations over the years throughout the United States and even in Canada. The patient almost always presented with the same story and complaints that were given in Charleston. In spite of repeated efforts to discover the source of the blood which he is able to cough, its true source has not been found. The patient had undergone almost every diagnostic study known, some on more than one occasion, and has undergone exploratory surgery, as well as specific procedures, such as surgical ligation of the inferior vena cava.

In 1968, as stated, this patient was admitted to the medical service of the University of Virginia Hospital. Following two psychiatric interviews, in consultation, he signed out abruptly, apparently disgusted with the nature of the psychological line of inquiry, and presumably afraid of his cover being blown.

A common feature of these patients is that they are usually socially isolated and without family ties or any close personal relationships. There is a background of gross lack of parental nurturing in early life, and a fragile ego fundament results.

In two cases seen in state psychiatric hospitals, there was a history of negligent mothering and a generally aloof father who, however, when periodically drunk would become interested in his son and then often physically abusive. These patients were both seeking attention from and repeating a struggle with a sadistic father. Moreover, it was evident that before the crises severe anxiety had been mounting and that their desperate and factitious efforts, although they knew what they were doing, were motivated by an attempt to be somebody, preferably someone who could outwit doctors, so that extinction of ego-feeling could be avoided, as the psychotic breakpoint was approached. The behaviour to signal a somatic emergency is fundamentally a desperate restitutive measure, one to make contact and to interact with and relate to other human beings, to be cared for and recognized, without which schizophrenic disorganization impends. The medical setting is the stage upon which this primarily unconscious driven restitutive process is acted out. These patients have thus some likeness to those Menninger (1934)[59] describes as polysurgical addicts. They have come to need and to enjoy pity, as well as to resent it; and 'the doctor or surgeon represents a parent whose ministrations can be enjoyed only if they are painful'.

Spiro (1968)[60] insists rightly that these patients should have a primary psychiatric diagnosis with the additional qualifying phrase 'with chronic factitious symptomatology'. Even though Asher (1951)[57] thought the syndrome to be common and many case reports followed his initial one, it is likely that it only seems so because a single patient is seen so often by so many. This view is at any rate partly supported by Ireland, Sapira and Templeton (1967)[61] who found that only 59 different patients had then been described, 39 from the United Kingdom and 8 from the USA. It was found too that men outnumber women in a ratio of three to one, and that the mean number of times admitted to hospital was 24.

Barker (1962)[62] studied seven patients during an 11-year period in Britain and came to the conclusion that 'by far the most remarkable characteristics shared by this group of patients was their marked capacity for relentless self-destruction'. This thanatotic element is accompanied by a thanatophobia which stimulates desperate restitutive measures, dramatized in the peculiar and complex behaviour of these patients *vis-à-vis* doctors and hospitals. With high technology, and psychophobic physicians, the drama is often heightened and much elaborated.

Post-traumatic Stress Disorder: Acute, Chronic or Delayed

In his Introductory Lectures (1917),[63] as in other contexts, Freud purveyed the concept of a complementary series of conditions which give rise to neurotic disturbance. These conditions comprise a disposition based on heredo-constitutional endowment and unconscious early childhood frustrations and conflicts as well as external precipitating situations of stress. Experiences that precipitate neuroses disturb the psychic equilibrium achieved between warded-off impulses and the warding-off forces of repression and other defences. Early in his work with hysteria, Freud (1896)[64] pointed to two external conditions the presence of which calls for the consideration that the symptoms are possibly of a functional nature. For this consideration to be positive the traumatic power of the externally produced disturbance must be strong enough to be held accountable; and its determining quality must be appropriately related to the specific symptoms exhibited.

In Chapter 2, it was noted that in war neuroses in general the actual stress and resulting current mental conflict are prepotent whereas in peacetime neurosis the unsettled childhood conflicts which had been triggered by current events in the life of the patient assume greater aetiologic importance. In neurosis, as in other sicknesses, there is always an aetiologic constellation of conditions within the field of medical observation, as Halliday (1943)[65] so lucidly outlined. In one case of neurotic disturbance, the relative conditions concerned in pathogenesis may obtain more in constitution or in developmental maladjustments, and in another in the degree of stress to which the patient was subject before the onset of symptom formation. When there is death-threat involved in gross overstimulation as happens with man-made catastrophes of battle or natural disasters of peacetime, the designation *Traumatic Neurosis* is appropriately applied to indicate the overwhelming importance of the influx of disorganizing stimulation, and to draw attention to an identifiable psychiatric syndrome including hypervigilance, phobias, sleep disturbances (with recurrent nightmares repeating some of the terror of the precipitating events) and spells of disorientation, sometimes with anxiety-ridden hallucinosis ('flash-backs') besides other symptoms of an hysterical nature.

From their clinical work with Vietnam veterans within Veterans Administration Hospitals in the United States, Horowitz and Solomon (1978)[66] noted that the florid manifestations of stress response syndromes may not appear until after termination of environmental stress events, and sometimes only after a latency period of apparent abatement of acute symptoms of anxiety. Post-traumatic stress disorder (PTSD) may thus be more or less delayed. Whenever they arise, the symptoms fall into two categories though some symptoms are composed of both intertwined. One category consists of intrusive ideas related to the precipitating situation, compulsive repetition of trauma-related behaviour and attacks of related stormy affects. Contrarily, there is a negative category of symptoms consisting of emotional avoidance, denial, splitting and repression, in a massive unconscious attempt to conceal underlying conflicts and to protect against the arousal of primitive destructive impulses and terror. In discussing the 'psychical mechanism of hysterical phenomena', Breuer and Freud (1893)[67] had already pointed out these two categories of symptoms, often simultaneously present, and they stated: 'Both of these conditions, however, have in common the fact that the psychical traumas which have not been disposed of by reaction cannot be disposed of otherwise by being worked over by means of association ...' and they added: 'It may therefore be said that the ideas which have become pathological have persisted with such freshness and affective strength because they have been denied the normal wearing-away processes by means of abreaction and reproduction in states of uninhibited association.'

The long-term difficulties, chronic and delayed, of Vietnam veterans as they were gradually, and reluctantly, recognized, intensified interest in post-traumatic stress disorders. No doubt this accounts for the introduction of PTSD as a nosological entity in the latest edition of *The Diagnostic and Statistical Manual of Mental Disorders*, D.S.M. III (1980).[68] There has also been renewed interest in severe stress disorder generally, that is, that following traumatic events outside the range of those that can be coped with adequately by human beings. Comparisons have been made of the post-combatant patterns of disorder in American, Australian, Russian and Israeli veterans, as well as of the symptoms suffered later by released prisoners of war, Iranian hostages, victims of rape, fire and a range of other catastrophes. Shatan (1982)[69] maintains that the effects of man-made catastrophic stress are much more persistent and disabling than those following a sudden 'act of God'. He points to common features of Vietnam veterans and K-Z (concentration camp) or death-camp survivors. The meanings which the victim comes to ascribe to his traumatic experiences are of the utmost importance as he elaborates them both consciously and unconsciously, and they require elucidation in psychotherapy. Hendin, Pollinger, Singer and Ulman (1981)[70] show that following similar traumatic experiences the victims of combat neurosis display differences in their reactions as well as core similarities, and these differences need to be taken into account.

Fenichel (1945)[71] insists that there is no traumatic neurosis without psychoneurotic complications. He writes:

> After the individual has experienced too much influx, he is afraid, cuts himself off from the external world and therefore blocks his discharges; and experience of a trauma creates fear of every kind of tension, sensitizing the organism in regard even to its own impulses. If, on the other hand, discharges are blocked (psychoneurotic defence) a little influx, otherwise harmless, may have the effect of one much more intense, creating a flooding. A neurotic conflict creates fear of temptations and punishments and also sensitizes the organism in regard to further external stimuli. 'Trauma' is a relative concept ...

Following World War I there were many victims of chronic traumatic neurosis and Abram Kardiner (1947)[72] explored the discombobulations of ego function evident in these chronic cases. He emphasized the attempts at adaptation, and the attempts of the organism to achieve psychic equilibrium, after trauma. He wrote: 'The traumatic experience can precipitate any of the well-known types of neurotic or psychotic disorders. However, irrespective of the nature of the resulting clinical picture, the distinctive features of traumatic neurosis are always present.' This view is in accord with that expressed more recently by Krystal and Niederland (1968),[73] who recognized a syndrome resulting from massive psychic trauma characterized by persistence of symptoms of withdrawal from social life, insomnia, recurrent nightmares, chronic depressive and anxiety reactions and far-reaching somatization.

In discussing the war neuroses, Freud (1921)[74] referred to 'parasitic doubles of the super-ego' which for a time could usurp the power of regulation of the super-ego acquired in childhood. Not only does a 'war super-ego' permit the expression of impulses otherwise forbidden, but it may even make demands which continue to be tempting, which the reinstated super-ego of peacetime may find difficulty defending against.

Both Jung (1928)[75] and McDougall (1920)[76] pointed out the limited therapeutic value of abreaction in the traumatic neuroses engendered in the 'unique psychic atmosphere of the battlefield', to quote Jung. The dramatic rehearsal of the traumatic moment, its emotional recapitulation in the waking or in the hypnotic state certainly often has a beneficial therapeutic effect. On the other hand, McDougall pointed out that in quite a large number of cases simple abreaction could worsen the patient's neurotic disturbance. He argued that in such refractory cases, an essential factor, that of dissociation, had been overlooked. It is this dissociation in the psyche, and not only the existence of a highly charged affective complex that has to be reckoned with in treatment, and the therapeutic task must include the facilitation of integration. As Jung (1928)[75] observed: 'the typical traumatic affect is represented in dreams as a wild and dangerous animal—a striking illustration of its autonomous nature when split off from consciousness.' Abreaction is itself an attempt to reintegrate the autonomous complex, but this attempt at incorporation, and belated mastery, by reliving the traumatic situation repeatedly, can be effected adequately often only with the active support, and in the presence of the doctor; and as Jung insisted, this curative process requires something more than a feeble rapport. These considerations amply demonstrate the application of key concepts forged during decades of psychotherapeutic work before World War I and afterwards. The work of the therapist in such instances may be stated figuratively: his loving attention to the patient enables them both to face those terrible moments, and this serves to exorcize their lingering traumatic power, while acknowledging their powerful role in shaping what he has become.

At the onset of World War II, the concepts of dynamic psychiatry were much better understood and accepted, and further studies such as those of Grinker and Spiegel (1945)[77] extended our knowledge of the effects of trauma upon the ego. Later the effects of prolonged traumatic experiences were also explored. In their account of clinical observations on the Survivor Syndrome, Krystal and Niederland (1968)[73] show that the problems of survivors of massive destructive assault are many and complex. They describe far reaching disturbances of personality which can be directly traced to the oppressive threatening milieu in which the survivors were forced to dwell for so long. An identification with the bad image attributed to them by their oppressors ('devil-identity') may become a life-long burden—or a reversal and reprojection may sometimes take place as in the 'white devils' theory of the American Black Muslims. Commonly, however, the victim assumes a 'slave' identification or a 'slave house-boy' identity. The former involves a constriction of human capabilities, the latter an ambivalent ingratiating stance associated with a turning against fellow-sufferers. These authors discuss the consolidated masochistic and paranoid character deformations engendered by the need to maintain repression of reactive hostility, including murderous rage, towards their oppressors for a prolonged period.

Krystal and Niederland (1968)[73] further introduce consideration of the dimension of social pathology, especially the later formation of abnormal families and communities. For besides such symptoms as hypervigilance, conversions, phobias, sleep disturbances, disorders of memory, spells of disorientation, dreams merging into hallucinosis and dream-like experiences in the waking state, muscle tensions and other psychosomatic disorders, much serious schizoid and paranoid and depressive disorder was engendered in these survivors of prolonged stress, and their families and communities were later adversely affected. Robert Jay Lifton (1970)[78] also emphasizes social pathology, including the dehumanization of invaders and those invaded in war.

It is obvious that the concepts developed from the early treatment of individual traumatic neuroses can only convey some hints of what may be necessary for people who have been exposed to extreme situations for long periods, often *en masse*, including 'death immersion'. Of course, wars between nations now create conditions which quickly facilitate collective regression attitudes—dehumanization of the enemy, disowning projections on to him, rationalizations and licence to murder him. Some of these regressive mental changes stick with many of the survivors in the ensuing peace with distressing social consequences.

In 1973, van Putten and Emory[79] discussed, and gave case histories to illustrate, the earlier ignoring of traumatic neuroses in Vietnam returnees. These patients, because they reject authority and mistrust institutions, came for medical help to the Veteran's Hospital only out of desperation, years after discharge from service. Explosive aggressivity, 'flashbacks' of combat scenes, and phobic problems of a paranoid type had led to mistakes in diagnosis such as psychomotor epilepsy, schizophrenic disorder, or attribution entirely to substance abuse. Such patients in my experience have not received early effective treatment with emphasis on cathartic psychotherapy. On the contrary, they received, while in Vietnam, treatment which emphasized massive psychotropic medication, followed by crowding out with sundry recreational activities, any focus on their essentially traumatic and pathogenic experiences. Such temporarily suppressive treatment invited the reinforcement of dissociation, though it may have worked during the period while the soldier was on active service overseas. Van Putten and Emory (1973)[79] rightly insist that early recognition of the syndrome is really essential. Even in these cases, with delayed recognition of combat neurosis, appropriate treatment resulted in much genuine improvement. As they state, 'The current emphasis on the "here and now" in psychotherapy, in conjunction with the combat veteran's reluctance to discuss his traumatic experiences and the therapist's wish to be done with the war, may easily create a tacit agreement between therapist and veteran to avoid the subject.'

Indeed it is in cases of delayed post-traumatic stress that all too often a military history had never been taken from a veteran, and other diagnoses mistakenly applied. Often enough, the same is true of the story of a survivor from a Nazi concentration camp. As Horowitz (1974)[80] has emphasized, a treatment strategy is required to prevent either extreme denial which impedes both emotional and conceptual processing or extreme intrusive-repetitiousness which might cause panic states of increased avoidance manoeuvres. Within these parameters, however, the magnitude of the traumatic events must gradually be approached. As Shatan (1982)[69] observes, 'With this approach, we will eventually hear stories of war and persecution, for veterans and survivors need to repair their torn fabric of faith in other human beings.'

Figley (1978)[81] following review of many studies of stress disorders among Vietnam veterans, concluded that veterans who had been exposed to the most extreme degree of stress in combat showed a greater incidence of later neurotic disturbance than those who had not been so exposed. Of the approximately four million American soldiers involved, eight hundred thousand of them were assigned to actual combat in Vietnam and proved to be at greater risk for developing delayed post-traumatic stress disorder, including chronic or intermittent psychosis-like symptoms and severe life impairment.

It may require emphasis that psychoneurotic problems with their seeds in childhood interact with the later engrafted trauma of battle experience. Moreover, just as unresolved and unfinished residuals of childhood trauma may be apparently symptomless until a challenge occurs at an adult phase of development when an outbreak of symptoms ensues, so with delayed post-traumatic stress disorder. Thus it may make itself acutely manifest at the usual time of mid-life crisis. The following case illustrates that manifest behaviour disorder may be triggered in peacetime by a disappointment in the love life of a combat veteran.

Case 52. This was the first psychiatric admission for this 38-year-old unmarried white male from Kentucky. He was brought in on commitment after being jailed three days previously for crashing the gate of the local electric power plant with his truck, and threatening security guards with a gun.

The patient has not had any difficulty in the past with the law except for minor traffic violations. Three weeks prior to his admission here his woman friend aged 25 years refused to marry him. She refused to explain why, but spoke of his being overweight. For the three weeks before admission he went on 'a crash diet', losing about 20 pounds. He also had stopped drinking his usual half-a-dozen cans of beer daily. The patient maintains that he was feeling well on the day before the incident for which he was arrested by the police when it came to his notice that his woman friend was dating someone else. He became very angry, drank several beers, got into his truck, and then heard his CB radio tell him to go down and crash the gate at the power plant. He obeyed the order.

History of Present Illness: The patient states he moved from New York about one year ago with his father because of lack of work. He spent two tours in Vietnam in the Army from 1966–70 and talked of killing and seeing his friends dying. He states he has been living with 2 other men but has never been close enough to anyone to share his problems or feelings. 'I just get away from them.' He was trained as an electrician during the years of 1971–76, did not find work in New York, and at the age of 37, was still living with his father. He and his father decided to move the patient to Virginia where his union found him a job at the power plant, and his father went on to Florida. The patient states he was engaged to a girl during the time he was in Vietnam, quit hearing from her, and returned home to find that she had been killed in an automobile crash. Another engagement ended because 'we just didn't agree'. He denies any usage of illicit drugs.

Mental Status Exam: The patient is a middle-aged, muscular male who is dressed casually. Speech is slightly pressured, circumstantial and tangential. Motor activity is increased and he complains of difficulty talking because of tightness in his jaw muscles which in subsequent interviews resembled a dystonic reaction but occurred obviously from increased anxiety. He states he feels anxious and sad and appears somewhat depressed although he laughs frequently inappropriately. He also makes hostile remarks, i.e., 'I've been asked that question a lot already, I don't give a damn' and was especially hostile when discussing his unsuccessful relationships with women. Cognitive functions were within normal limits but slowed. He has several thoughts with a paranoid flavour: He felt the power plant was going to blow up, made constant references to things that could occur tragically, stated that people were watching him when he was on the job, and had a general fear of things going wrong. He states the policeman searched him and his possessions in search of a bomb at the time of the incident and fears someone is after him and caused all this trouble. He was stated to have threatened the County Sheriff with blowing up the jail with a bar of soap if he wasn't released and he felt he was being brought to the hospital so he could be X-rayed, 'In search of a bomb in my body'. He feels that the radio has given him messages. He became perplexed in further interviews and wondered 'whether someone made me crash the gate or not' and he made reference to 'a very sinister person' stating that he had seen the devil in the fireplace. Proverbs were interpreted concretely. Insight and judgement were severely impaired.

Family History: The patient's mother died of pneumonia when he was age 2 and he grew up with his paternal grandmother and father. His grandmother died in 1968 while he was in the Army. He has a one year older brother whom he hasn't seen in 8 years because of a family argument. His father who is disabled for the past 15 years from rheumatoid arthritis and back pain now lives in Florida. The father states that the patient was a quiet child, without friends and he spent much of his time alone. His brother often chose to fight with him, once even hitting him in the back with a shovel. His older brother also made better grades than the patient, and in other ways made him feel inadequate. It seems that during schooling he had difficulty sometimes distinguishing himself as being a separate individual from his brother, by which means he was able to generate feelings of well-being.

Personal History: The patient finished junior high school, went to trade school, and then joined the Army, was later discharged and became an electrician's apprentice. He states he had his first sexual intercourse in the Philippines at age 20 and hasn't had any intercourse in the past 7 years because 'I got the clap once and if I got it 3 times I would have been dishonorably discharged'. One year ago the patient felt he had appendicitis which was not confirmed by a physician, and he became very angry, thought he might die and at that time he heard threatening voices on the CB radio. The physical examination was within normal limits.

Laboratory Data: SMAC CFA, glucose, CBC with Diff. and U/A all within normal limits, except for urobilinogen elevated up to 4. MMPI has manic and schizophrenic high points.

Hospital Course: The patient was put on Haldol 5 mg b.i.d. He developed some akathisia and the medication was changed to Navane which was increased up to 30 mg q.h.s. His thought disorder gradually disappeared but an excited affective component still remained. During the first week of his hospitalization it was noted that his motor activity was markedly increased and he had difficulty distinguishing himself from other patients. He seemed to fuse readily with almost any other patient during community meetings. He has now individuated much more, has better controlled thought processes and is an engaging person, pleasant to talk to.

Impression: Recent trauma in a form of a breakup with one woman friend, the death of a fiancée and traumatic battle stresses are felt to have precipitated his present illness which is compatible now with a schizoaffective disorder.

Follow-up psychotherapy revealed potency problems since embattlement, and the acting out behaviour was obviously of a sexual-symbolic nature involving sadistic notions of coitus of which he was frightened. It also revealed his anger and fear of powerful authorities and his need to obtain constant reassurance from his father following demobilization. It became clear that he had a vague notion of seizing power when he crashed the gates of the power plant where he had a job as a minor factotum which he resented. It gradually emerged that he had suffered disturbed sleep with recurrent nightmares and that his father had ministered to him during the nights these occurred after his leaving the army. These terrifying dreams were of scenes of bloody violence when he had entered 'Viet-Cong Villages'. Many were massacred, including small boys, some of whom had hurled grenades and killed several of his companions. They were thus regarded as especially dangerous. He had seen and saw, in these dreams, the dismembered limbs of children. (These horrible scenes were also representations of his shattered self which he was trying to repair.) He had made efforts to be friendly with his uncle. Once driving his truck with his uncle beside him, his uncle became afraid and, probably correctly, criticized his reckless driving. The patient stopped the vehicle and during the subsequent altercation became belligerent. His uncle stalked off, found his own way back home and was subsequently unfriendly. This incident became of importance in the transference transactions.

Harvey J. Schwartz (1984)[82] has discussed the necessity and difficulties in building a trustful relationship in such cases. This is achieved only by means of great patience and quiet perseverance. These patients suffer from deep-seated guilt and anxiety related to the unconscious mobilization of primitive, destructive fantasies and they are apt to disown and project the wish to destroy upon the therapist, making the handling of the transferences a difficult but not usually insurmountable problem. Only as more positive dependent transference is developed can the patient gradually recover memories of traumatic events, discuss their meanings for him and his feelings and notions about his own involvement, and so gain progressive integration.

It is well-known that in the traumatic neuroses, whether the result of an industrial accident or of exposure to violence in battle, or whatever severe stress, secondary gain motivation often assumes an increasingly dominant sway. The anxiety symptoms demonstrate to the patient and his reference group a measure of helplessness which may readily become exaggerated in order to secure help such as was available when hurt in childhood. This element of secondary gain is vastly amplified in some victims of PTSD, and sometimes leads to unjustifiable estrangement of medical advisors who suspect malingering and consequently neglect the suffering which is actually present. Of course, financial compensation has symbolic value as love and protection as well as actual advantage. However, on the contrary, many Vietnam veterans only very reluctantly seek help. As noted by John Ingram Walker (1981),[83] the Vietnam veteran may be symptomatic for months, even years, before seeking a physician, and even then he is often coaxed into treatment by relatives, friends, counsellors or parole officers. When he does show up for help, there is usually a recent precipitating stress, such as divorce or loss of job, so that the underlying post-traumatic stress disorder may not be detected. This tardiness, this hesitation in seeking help is itself symptomatic and is accounted for by the unique circumstances, of the Vietnam War. In *No Victory Parades* Polner (1971),[84] a social historian, concludes that 'the theme of alienation and betrayal comes to mind again and again as we reflect on [the communications of] the veterans of this study', and he observes that regardless of whether the veteran became anti-war, pro-war or neutral he felt it terribly unfair to be sent into Vietnam and then to hear so much criticism of the war by many of the influential leaders and publications in America. As Lipkin, Blank, Parson and Smith (1982)[85] note, individuals with PTSD experience a profound shattering of basic concepts of self and humanity. They are victims of what Lifton (1980)[86] called 'the broken connection'—severe anguish by exposure to mutilation, meaningless misery, and death which have weakened or broken their links to the civilized community. In the case of the Vietnam veteran for a long time afterwards the countervailing social forces were quite inadequate as Lipkin et al. (1982)[85] emphasize in the following passage:

> The final assault on the soldier's ability to cope with the experience of Vietnam often came when he or she returned to the United States. In contrast with previous wars, soldiers arrived in Vietnam in small groups of strangers, served there for 12 or 13 months, and often returned home alone. Most World War II veterans came home with friends on troop ships. They were able to spend days or weeks making a gradual transition from combat to peacetime, and were greeted by cheering crowds, parades and a grateful public. Vietnam veterans commonly came back by plane, in less than 48 hours, to a hostile, embarrassed or indifferent welcome. They were jumpy, dazed and uncommunicative. The hyperalert vigilance needed for survival seemed bizarre to family and friends used to automobile backfires, crowds and city noises.
>
> The powerful political and social antagonism toward the war made veterans question their participation and denied them the social support necessary to integrate death, destruction, and killing into a terrible but legitimate aspect of a soldier's life experience. Almost every returning veteran learned quickly and painfully to be secretive about his or her experiences, reactions and activities in Vietnam. Nobody wanted to hear about Vietnam. Family and friends welcomed the returnee but overtly or covertly rejected the military experiences that had become a part of his or her identity.
>
> The United States has been profoundly affected by the Vietnam War. Family and friends of those who went to war, and of those who did not, have spent years adapting to changes in their lives. For some individuals, psychiatric disorder has been part of the struggle to adapt.

The traumatic neuroses of Vietnam veterans highlight the problems of post-industrial societies in our present turbulent world. Kriegman (1983)[87] has discussed the prevalence of entitlement dysfunctions in our society. The individual is significantly affected psychologically by the fulfilment, or nonfulfilment of what he considers his entitlements. Such dysfunction looms large in cases of post-traumatic stress disorder. Some patients have unrealistically grandiose expectations of their entitlement, whereas others do not feel entitled to say or do or procure what our democratic society has sanctioned. Post-traumatic stress disorder is also part of the increasing problem of suicide and homicide, including terrorism. The victims of PTSD often have exaggerated responses to international crises. Thus the 1982 Anglo-

Argentine Falklands war evoked flashbacks in Vietnam veterans, some of whom became so disturbed that they again required supervision and support in hospital. In many of the cases which require treatment in hospital it is evident that these disappointed veterans are loaded with murderous rage. The patient discussed above (*Case* 52) who thought he was brought to the hospital so that he could be X-rayed 'in search of a bomb in my body' expressed eloquently in physical terms the brewing tumult in his psychic inner world which could so readily be activated.

From the considerations raised above, it is readily understandable that 'rap groups' for Vietnam veterans proved so beneficial for many of them. The social interaction and relationships built outside the family with their peers with a common service background often afforded sufficient support for ventilation of feelings and the voicing of constructive criticism concerning their own self-defeating and self-destructive behaviour as well as allowing a grappling with the social, political and ethical issues raised by the folly of a society which hurled them into a futile war in Asia. However, in my experience, those among the Vietnam returnees who have been exposed to combat also require individual psychotherapy. Indeed, sometimes involvement in a rap group has resulted in symptomatic exacerbation or destructive acting out so that treatment in hospital became necessary before outpatient individual therapy could be initiated.

Collective Hysterical Psychoses

The transition from consideration of the effects of military involvement in Asia to that of collective hysteriform outbreaks is not difficult. Charles Mackay (1841)[88] gave an account of the state of public feeling in Europe towards the end of the eleventh century when Peter the Hermit preached the holy war which instigated the First Crusade. At the time adverse circumstances resulted in attitudes and feelings conducive to such an instance of what Mackay dubs 'The Madness of Crowds'—here we can leave such considerations to the social historian and economist. We cannot, however, forego the important contribution—the critical contribution—made by the psychopathology of leadership and of the group dynamics in such deranged mass movements. The experience of the behaviour of Adolf Hitler and his Nazi cohorts has especially sensitized psychiatrists and social scientists to the concepts of charisma, of pathology in political and religious leadership and of collective psychological regression. In the recent American aberration, the ageing leadership, with problems of sustaining grandiosity and multipotence against emerging castration anxieties, and suffused with unconscious filicidal and vengeful fantasies, eventually tipped the scale, with disastrous consequences for the invaded country and for so many citizens of the USA. Of course, many returnees among non-combatants sailed on nonetheless, despite the turbulent waters, without damage to the gunwales.

There are minor historical examples of the phenomena of mass madness less recondite than those of the Holocaust or of the Vietnam War which lend themselves more readily to investigation, and which thus provide useful insights. One such recent example is that of the Reverend Jim Jones and his followers in the People's Temple who were plunged into group madness and suicide. (Cf. R. B. Ulman and D. W. Abse, 1983.[89])

In the study of the madness which engulfed the inhabitants of Jonestown, Guyana, as in other recent psychoanalytic studies, including those of Hitler and Stalin (Abse and Reckrey, 1970;[90] Waite, 1971;[91] 1977;[92] Ulman, 1979;[93] Langer, 1972;[94] Bychowski, 1971[95]), there is evidence that the pathological charismatic leader is of intensely narcissistic personality type, the result of early severe traumatic experiences which injured the normative regulation of self-esteem. As Kohut (1976)[96] suggested the charismatic leader of this kind has allowed the grandiose self so to dominate his personality that others are able to rediscover their own archaic grandiose selves in the leader and thus acquire the means to diminish the anxiety aroused in times of mass panic. Within the mind of the leader, a fusion of ego and grandiose self has occurred in an effort to compensate for earlier frustrations of narcissistic needs and a resulting sense of inferiority, which is thus split off from awareness. The charismatic leaders described in the studies just cited have gravitated to the political or religious arena protesting against an unjust state of society and affirming an ideal ethic of some sort. Yet, in their various ways within this context, they have sought to gain a new personal identity suffused with a feeling of power in order to mend fragmented psyches beset by feelings of helplessness. Once in the political or religious arena, their need for power in action has merged with the people's need for a saviour.

Unlike the floridly psychotic patient who has become a failure in society, the charismatic leader has found an audience to save him or her from approaching this fate and through which archaic fantasies can become partially enacted. The course of events during and after the leader's achievement of power often raises the question as to whether the attraction of followers was the means for a time of forestalling or preventing a break with reality. Sometimes, despite a prolonged exhibition of apparent strength of fanatical and fabulous dimensions under certain adverse conditions (which vary from leader to leader), vulnerability becomes obvious before an evident disintegration of personality. At other times, the leader seems to need to generate a crisis not only to preserve momentum with followers but as reassurance of his ability to cope with and to overcome difficulties; it appears that some severely traumatized individuals periodically require a traumatic situation to endure and surmount.

Following the establishment of leadership and group formation, the question arises as to whether the regression to archaic levels of experiencing and functioning mark the beginning of constructive or destructive behaviour. With the deepening and intensified relationships of leader and led, the interaction of their respective subjective worlds decides the issue. Sometimes a leader is expelled to prevent a massively destructive and explosive course of action. On the other hand, in a highly disturbed society, with a modal personality vulnerable to deep regression, a poorly integrated and fragile character can continue to dominate as leader.

Collective Regression

Freud (1921)[97] emphasizes the attachments of the members of the group to the leader, and the resulting attachments to one another. The attachment to the leader is partly expressed in an intense identification with him or her, an identification that becomes internalized so that a group member unconsciously comes to replace or modify his or her operative ideals to accord with those of the leader. This process of introjection results in each individual member seeking all the more fiercely to mould himself or herself in accordance with this inner model, a model that the leader, of course, continues to project. In brief, the identification of the individual member with the charismatic leader involves profound alterations in the central self and object configurations which structure the member's inner subjective world (Stolorow and Atwood, 1979;[98] Stolorow and Lachmann, 1980[99]). The secondary identifications with other group members characteristically leads to ties and attachments to them, that is, to a bond or union to each one of them and to the group as a whole. All these ties composed of both identifications and mutually dependent attachments constitute an unconscious current manifesting itself in various ways, including a common ideology.

The identifications and attachments that unconsciously structure a group have a narcissistic dimension, an aspect with vicissitudes in parallel with the life of the group, its successes and its failures. The charismatically led group readily develops a 'group self' (Strozier, 1982[100]) of hyperbolic quality; the group self becomes easily endowed with the glory and awesomeness of the numen enjoyed by the leader. The group's conscious and unconscious images of itself often coalesce in a grandiose and exhibitionistic group self. Thus emerge a vastly enhanced group self-esteem, intensified empathic bonds between group members, a shared elevated conception of themselves as a group, and a shared group fantasy of merging with the omnipotent leader.

The identification of the individual with the leader of the group and attachment to the leader and bonds with other members limit the outlets for intragroup aggression and hostility. In the charismatically led group these limits are very restrictive. In order to gain the leader's support, masochistic submission to the latter's will and ideas are essential in a measure that may be massive (Ulman, 1979[101]). Yet, the individual is often also in revolt against such a real or fantasied submission to the leader; besides, the leader may also prohibit divisiveness within the group. The individual thus incurs a submissive cost for membership within such a group.

Following the demands and dictates of an authoritarian charismatic leader often generates some secret hostility and rage within the individual group members. The resulting conflict of ambivalence may become so severe that under certain circumstances destructive rage may be directed against the leader. For the most part, however, the ties of the members of a mass movement may be preserved, and destructive hostility displaced onto other groups, or individuals outside the group, or some scapegoats may be found within, and sacrificed. One or more of these courses may be explicitly encouraged at different times by the leader and may be part of an official ideology. There may also be collusion or connivance in order to preserve the cohesion of the group and the leader's authority.

While the more or less successful displacement of group anger and narcissistic rage may prevent group dissolution, it may also readily lead to group paranoia. The group comes to imagine that the objects of displaced anger and rage seek retaliation and revenge; at the least, provocations from outside become grossly exaggerated; at the most, mutual provocation becomes escalated with real danger resulting from paranoid groups on a collision course. In any event, an outside group (or groups) assumes the role of the group's unconsciously established persecutors. Anxiety may reach paranoid psychotic proportions, or the group may experience and be overwhelmed by depressive anxiety.

Freud (1921)[97] suggested that the psychological state existing between the leader and the led resembles the condition existing between a hypnotist and subject. He argued that the hypnotist awakens in the subject a portion of his archaic heritage which also makes him compliant towards his parents and which he has experienced as an individual re-animation in his relation to his father; what is thus awakened is the idea of a paramount and dangerous personality, towards whom only a passive-masochistic attitude is possible, to whom one's will has to be surrendered—while to be alone with him, 'to look him in the face', appears a hazardous enterprise.

Thus the charismatic leader weaves a hypnotic spell over the members of a mass movement. Under such a 'mass hypnosis', the members of a mass movement may blindly follow the orders of the charismatic leader as in a day dream or trance. If they are ordered to perform acts of great heroism, they obey willingly. If, on the other hand, they are ordered to perform acts of savage barbarism, they carry out their duties without apparent signs of conscience, guilt, or shame. In other words, the charismatic leader may utilize 'mass hypnosis' as a means of mobilizing collective forms of archaic psychic functioning. As Jung (1946)[102] noted, a pathological leader like Adolf Hitler becomes a 'possessor' (*Ergreifer*: one who seizes), while the individual members of a mass movement, like the Nazi movement, become 'possessed' (*Ergriffener*: one who is seized).

Abse and Jessner (1962)[103] point out that the main weapon (and armour) of the charismatic leader is charm. This charm conveys not only magic power but the leader's own delicate need for love and protection. There is an especially marked trend in such persons to turn to activity in relation to others in order to avoid anxiety. Encouraging others may be very reassuring, indicative of the kind of treatment wished for by him but vigorously defended against so much of the time. On the other hand, the successful intimidation of others also provides reassurance by its clear indications of power. The need to intimidate or to encourage others in such cases stems from the unconscious identification with an extraordinarily powerful aggressor or an omnipotent provider, originally the early parental imagoes. The charismatic leader is among those character types that are habitually intimidating and encouraging, and often rapidly alternating between these polarities. Their charm is based on inspiring both awe and love. This charm is often highlighted by an intermittent and sudden outright brutality.

Schiffer (1973),[104] like Abse and Jessner, suggests that the charismatic leader represents not only an early paternal imago, but an early maternal imago as well. According to Schiffer, individuals spend their lives attempting to rediscover the early imago of the mother in an effort to save themselves from the terror associated with the increasing responsibilities and the progressive independence involved in maturing. Thus, in addition to a group's need for hope and salvation, the charismatic leader also fulfils the followers' need for an early maternal imago to assuage never fully surmounted archaic fears. The suggestibility of individuals is of varying degree. Hysteriform borderliners who are excessively suggestible are readily enlisted as followers by a charismatic leader, himself or herself afflicted by hysteriform borderline personality disorder.

High suggestibility is very largely the result of uncontrolled processes of unconscious identification and is associated with a fragile ego fundament; sometimes a hyperexic defence against vulnerability to suggestion includes an emotional detachment. Even in the latter eventuality, however, the impact of events in a group may rupture such a massive defence.

In the formation and maintenance of groups, primitive processes of unconscious identification may become very active and may escalate beyond the control of many people. Moebius' dictum that everyone is a little hysterical is frequently illustrated by behaviour in groups. We can but briefly consider here simple crowds and highly organized groups, but there are, of course, many varieties of grouping of human beings. The character of both simple crowds and more permanent organized groups also varies considerably. Often, the individual in becoming one of a crowd loses in some degree his self-consciousness and he may even become depersonalized. Enveloped and overshadowed and carried away by forces he is powerless to control, he may fail to exercise self-criticism, self-restraint, and more refined ideals of behaviour. It is often the case, too, in simple crowds that the order of reasoning employed is that of the lowest common denominator, and this facilitates suggestibility. A further ground of heightened suggestibility in a crowd is the prevalence of emotional excitement. The kinds of regression in the collective ego adumbrated above are, of course, contingent upon many factors, including the type of leadership. In the highly organized group, with its greater control of impulses and with a continuity of direction of activity, with a differentiation and specialization of the functions of its constituents, emotional excitement may be periodically evoked, with accompanying hysterical excrescences. The hysterical phenomena are then apt to occur in a setting of group paranoid formations, which serve to enhance group narcissism and to direct hostility outwards. We are, of course, here considering only the pathological aspects of group functioning, often associated with pathological, especially hysterical and paranoid, leadership, and frequently with the occurrence of hysterical phenomena.

In the ceremonial rites of religious groups as, for example, in the Voodoo cult in Haiti, the trance state is a sanctioned means of release and communication within the group. Only when the activities generated during the hypnoid state persist beyond, originate outside, or exceed the ritual, do they communicate anything abnormal, or sickness, to other members of the group. In particular, the phenomenon of possession usually occurs within the context of ritual exhibition, as the dances and roles become increasingly frenetic; often, the priest himself enacts the spirit-role, sometimes another member of the group does so. However, this socially sanctioned mode of behaviour is occasionally made use of in an individual attempt to express and reduce mental conflict. Such cases have been reported in many parts of India where an individual so 'possessed' may be designated as a patient and brought to a psychiatric clinic (Teja et al., 1970).[105] The phenomenon has been encountered mostly in young women of low socioeconomic and educational class. Such symptoms of possession, of governance by a strange soul, occur alone in hysterical instances, and the abnormal behaviour is readily understandable as a response to a frustrational life situation. In other instances, the symptoms of possession form only a minor part of the total clinical picture of schizophrenia or of mania. The authors of the Indian study separate 'hysterical psychosis' from the major psychoses.

In the USA extremist political meetings and avant-garde encounter group therapy sessions also precipitate their quantum of hysterical acting-out, and of subsequent conversion and dissociative reactions.

In 1278, a couple of hundred dancers gathered on a bridge on the Rhine at Utrecht. The bridge collapsed and many perished. Survivors were treated at a chapel dedicated to Saint Vitus, and thus the dancing mania acquired his name.

Ferrio (1948)[106] reported on outbreaks of epidemics of St Vitus Dance, of dancing and singing in the vicinity of churches until collapse, sometimes after seizures.

Arieti and Bemporad (1974)[48] observe of the psychic epidemics which repeatedly occurred in the Middle Ages, that they were of a hysterical nature, 'induced by the effect the crowd had on the predisposed person.'

Of all the collective hysterical psychoses, perhaps lycanthropy has maintained the greatest historical grip and occurs, it is said, even now in some mountain villages of Italy. People feel themselves transformed into animals, especially wolves, in this affliction, and then commit sundry transgressions. Henri S. Boguet, the superior judge of the town of Saint Claude in the department of Jura in France left an account of his judicial proceedings in a book first published in 1602. Witchcraft as interpreted by this judge was frequently complicated by demoniacal possession and lycanthropy. He condemned to death about six hundred people suffering from lycanthropy during an epidemic in France in the sixteenth century, and his account is rendered with an extraordinary lack of compassion.

REFERENCES

1. Calef, V. and Weinshell, E. M. (1981). Some clinical consequences of introjection: gaslighting. *Psychoanal. Quart.* **50**, 44–66.
2. Lasègue, C. and Falret, J. La folie à deux (ou folie communiquée). *Ann. Med.-psycholog.* **XVIII** (Novembre 1877). English trans. Michaud, R. Supplement to: *Am. J. Psychiat.* **121** (4) (October 1964).
3. Gralnick, A. (1942). Folie à deux—the psychosis of association. *Psychiat. Quart.* Part I, **16**, 230; Part II, **16**, 491.
4. Coleman, S. M. and Last, S. L. (1939). A study of folie à deux. *J. Ment. Sci.* **85**, 1212–23.
5. Searles, H. F. (1959). The effort to drive the other person crazy—an element in the aetiology and psychotherapy of schizophrenia. *Br. J. Med. Psychol.* **32**, 1–18.
6. Hedges, E. R. (1973). Afterword. In: Gilman, C. P. *The Yellow Wallpaper*. New York: Feminist Press.
7. Hollender, M. H. and Hirsch, S. J. (1964). Hysterical psychosis. *Am. J. Psychiat.* **120**, 1066–74.

8. D.S.M. III (1980). *Diagnostic and Statistical Manual of Mental Disorders*, 3rd ed. Washington, D.C.: Am. Psychiat. Assoc.
9. Richman, J. and White, H. A. (1970). A family view of hysterical psychosis. *Am. J. Psychiat.* **127**, 280–5.
10. Martin, P. A. (1971). Dynamic considerations of the hysterical psychosis. *Am. J. Psychiat.* **128**, 745–8.
11. Foulks, E. F. (1972). The Arctic Hysterias of the North Alaskan Eskimo. In: *Anthropological Studies*, No. 10 (ed. Maybury-Lewis, D. H.). Washington, D.C.: Am. Anthropolog. Assoc.
12. Yap. P. (1951). Mental diseases peculiar to certain cultures: a survey of comparative psychiatry. *J. Ment. Sci.* **97** (407), 313–27.
13. Yap. P. (1952). The Latah reaction: its psychodynamics and nosological position. *J. Ment. Sci.* **98** (413), 515–62.
14. Novakovsky, S. (1924). Arctic or Siberian hysteria as a reflex of the geographic environment. *Ecology* **5**, 113–27.
15. Peary, R. (1910). *The North Pole*. New York: Stokes.
16. Brill, A. A. (1913). Pibloktoq or hysteria among Peary's eskimos. *J. Nerv. Ment. Dis.* **40**, 514–20.
17. Høygaard, A. (1941). Studies on the nutrition and physio-pathology of Eskimos. *Skrifter Utgitt Av Det Norske Videnskaps-Akademi I Oslo. Mat-Natury. Klasse*, No. 9.
18. Wallace. A. F. C. (1961). Mental illness, biology and culture. In: *Psychological Anthropology* (ed. Hsu, F.). Homewood, Ill.: Dorsey Press.
19. Parker, S. (1962). Eskimo psychopathology. *Am. Anthropol.* **64**, 74–96.
20. Meth, J. M. (1974). Exotic psychiatric syndromes. In: *American Handbook of Psychiatry*, 2nd ed., Vol. 3, Chap. 32. New York: Basic Books.
21. Kraepelin, E. (1909). *Lehrbuch der Psychiatrie*. Leipzig: Barth.
22. Bleuler, E. (1936). *Text-book of Psychiatry*. New York: Dover.
23. Friedmann, C. T. H. (1982). The so-called hystero-psychoses. In: *Extraordinary Disorders of Human Behaviour* (ed. Friedmann, C. T. H. and Faguet, R. A.), Chap. 13. New York and London: Plenum Press.
24. Abraham, J. J. (1912). Latah and amok. *Br. Med. J.* **1**, 438.
25. Schmidt, K., Hill, L. and Guthri, G. (1977). Running amok. *Int. J. Soc. Psychiat.* **12**, 264.
26. Westermeyer, J. (1982). Amok. In: *Extraordinary Disorders of Human Behaviour* (ed. Friedmann, C. T. H. and Faguet, R. A.), Chap. 10. New York and London: Plenum Press.
27. Westermeyer, J. (1972). A comparison of amok and other homicide in Laos. *Am. J. Psychiat.* **129**, 703.
28. Burton-Bradley, B. G. (1968). The amok syndrome in Papua and New Guinea. *Med. J. Australia* **1**, 252.
29. Zaguirre, J. C. (1957). Amuck. *J. Philippine Federation Private Medical Practice* **6**, 1138.
30. Lion, J. R., Bach-Y-Riat, G. and Ervin, F. R. (1969). Violent patients in the emergency room. *Am. J. Psychiat.* **125**, 1706.
31. Kloss, C. B. (1923). Arctic amok. *J. Malaya Branch Royal Asiatic Soc.* **1**, 254.
32. Akhtar, S. and Brenner, I. (1979). Differential dignosis of fugue-like states. *J. Clin. Psychiat.* **40**, 381–5.
33. Luparello, T. J. (1970). Features of fugue: a unified hypothesis of regression. *J. Am. Psychonanal. Assoc.* **18**, 379–98.
34. Geleerd, E. R. (1956). Clinical contribution to the problem of the early mother–child relationship. In: *The Psychoanalytic Study of the Child*, Vol. II, pp. 336–51. New York: Int. Univ. Press.
35. Fenton, G. W. (1982). Hysterical alterations of consciousness. In: *Hysteria* (ed. Roy, A.), Chap. 16. Chichester and New York: Wiley.

36. Ganser, S. J. M. (1898). Über einen eigenartigen, hysterischen Dämmerzustand. *Arch. Psychiat. Nerven Kranken* **30**, 633. English trans. Shorer, C. E. (1965). *Br. J. Criminol.* **5**, 120.
37. Ganser, S. J. M. (1904). Über einen hysterischen Syndrom. *Arch. Psychiat. Nerven Kranken* **38**, 34.
38. Whitlock, F. A. (1982). The Ganser syndrome and hysterical pseudo-dementia. In: *Hysteria* (ed. Roy, A.), Chap. 14. Chichester and New York: Wiley.
39. Curran, D., Partridge, M. and Storey, P. (1976). *Psychological Medicine*, 8th ed. London: Churchill.
40. Trethowen, W. H. (1979). *Psychiatry*, 4th ed. London: Ballière, Tindall.
41. Anderson, E. W. and Mallinson, W. P. (1941). Psychogenic episodes in the course of major psychoses. *J. Ment. Sci.* **87**, 383–96.
42. De Clérambault, G. G. (1942). Les psychoses passionelles. In: *Œuvre Psychiatrique*. Paris: Presses Univ.
43. Clouston, T. S. (1887). *Clinical Lectures on Mental Diseases*, 2nd ed. London: Churchill.
44. Kraepelin, E. (1921). *Manic Depressive Insanity and Paranoia*. Edinburgh: Livingstone.
45. Balduzzi, E. (1956). Un caso di erotomania passionata pura secundo Clérambault. *Riv. Sper. Freniat.* **80**, 407.
46. Freud, S. (1921). *Group Psychology and the Analysis of the Ego*. In: *The Standard Edition*. Vol. XVIII. London: Hogarth Press (1955).
47. Enoch, M. D., Trethowan, W. H. and Barker, J. C. (1967). *Some Uncommon Psychiatric Syndromes*. Bristol: Wright.
48. Arieti, S. and Bemporad, J. R. (1974). Rare, unclassifiable and collective psychiatric syndromes. In: *American Handbook of Psychiatry*, 2nd ed., Vol. 3, Chap. 31. New York: Basic Books.
49. Reik. T. (1919). *The Psychological Problems of Religion*. New York: Farrar (1946).
50. Malinowsky, B. (1937). *Sex and Repression in Savage Society*. London: Kegan Paul.
51. Reik. T. (1931). *Ritual*. London: Hogarth Press.
52. Jacobson, E. (1950). Development of the wish for a child in boys. In: *The Psychoanalytic Study of the Child*, Vol. 5, pp. 139–52. New York: Int. Univ. Press (1952).
53. Trethowan, W. H. (1965). Couvade. *Mother and Child Care* **1**, 53.
54. Trethowan, W. H. and Conlon, M. F. (1965). The couvade syndrome. *Br. J. Psychiat.* **111**, 57.
55. Boehm, F. (1930). The feminity-complex in men. *Int. J. Psychoanal.* **11**, 444–69.
56. Inman, W. S. (1941). The couvade in modern England. *Br. J. Med. Psychol.* **19**, 37–55.
57. Asher, R. (1951). Munchausen syndrome. *Lancet* **1**, 339.
58. Chapman, J. S. (1957). Peregrinating problem patients: Munchausen syndrome. *J. Am. Med. Assoc.* **165**, 927.
59. Menninger, K. (1934). Polysurgery and polysurgical addiction. *Psychoanal. Quart.* **3**, 173.
60. Spiro, H. R. (1968). Chronic factitious illness: Munchausen's syndrome. *Arch. Gen. Psychiat.* **18**, 159.
61. Ireland, P., Sapira, G. D. and Templeton, B. (1967). Munchausen's syndrome. *Am. J. Med.* **43**, 579.
62. Barker, G. C. (1962). The syndrome of hospital addiction (Munchausen syndrome). A report on the investigation of seven cases. *J. Ment. Sci.* **108**, 167.
63. Freud, S. (1917). *Introductory Lectures on Psycho-analysis*. In: *The Standard Edition*, Vol. XVI. London: Hogarth Press (1955).
64. Freud, S. (1896). The Aetiology of Hysteria. In: *The Standard Edition*, Vol. III. London: Hogarth Press (1953).
65. Halliday, J. L. (1943). Principles of aetiology. *Br. J. Med. Psychol.* **19**, 367.

66. Horowitz, M. J. and Solomon, G. F. (1978). Delayed stress response syndromes in Vietnam veterans. In: *Stress Disorders among Vietnam Veterans: Theory, Research, and Treatment* (ed. Figley, C. R.). New York: Brunner-Mazel.
67. Breuer, J. and Freud, S. (1893). On the psychical mechanism of hysterical phenomena: preliminary communication. *Studies on Hysteria*. In: *The Standard Edition*, Vol. II. London: Hogarth Press (1953).
68. D.S.M. III (1980). *Diagnostic and Statistical Manual of Mental Disorders*, 3rd ed. Washington, D.C.: Am. Psychiat. Assoc.
69. Shatan, C. F. (1982). The tattered ego of survivors. *Psychiat. Ann.* **12** (11), 1031–8.
70. Hendin, H., Pollinger, A., Singer, P. et al. (1981). Meanings of combat and the development of posttraumatic stress disorder. *Am. J. Psychiat.* **138**, (November).
71. Fenichel, O. (1945). *The Psychoanalytic Theory of Neurosis*. New York: Norton.
72. Kardiner, A. (1947). *War, Stress and Neurotic Illness*. New York: Hoeber.
73. Krystal, H. and Niederland, W. G. (1968). Clinical observations on the survivor syndrome. In: *Massive Psychic Trauma* (ed. Krystal, H.). New York: Int. Univ. Press.
74. Freud, S. (1921). Psychoanalysis of War Neurosis. In: *The Standard Edition*, Vol. XVII. London: Hogarth Press (1955).
75. Jung, C. G. (1928). The therapeutic value of abreaction. In: *Contributions to Analytical Psychology*. London: Routledge and Kegan Paul.
76. McDougall, W. (1920). Discussion of the revival of emotional memories and its therapeutic value. *Br. J. Psychol.* Medical Section, **10**, 35.
77. Grinker, R. and Spiegel, J. P. (1945). *Men Under Stress*. Philadelphia: Blakiston.
78. Lifton, R. J. (1970). *History and Human Survival*. New York: Random House.
79. Van Putten, T. and Emory, W. H. (1973). Traumatic neuroses in Vietnam returnees: a forgotten diagnosis? *Arch. Gen. Psychiat.* **31**, 768–81.
80. Horowitz, M. J. (1974). Stress response syndromes: character style and brief psychotherapy. *Arch. Gen. Psychiat.* **31**, 768–81.
81. Figley, C. R. (1978). *Stress Disorders Among Vietnam Veterans*. New York: Brunner-Mazel.
82. Schwartz, H. J. (1984). An overview of the psychoanalytic approach to the war neuroses. Introduction to: *Psychotherapy of the Combat Veteran* (ed. Schwartz, H. J.). New York: Spectrum Publications.
83. Walker, J. I. (1981). The psychological problems of Vietnam veterans. *J. Am. Med. Assoc.* **246** (7), 781–2.
84. Polner, M. (1971). *No Victory Parades: The Return of the Vietnam Veteran*. New York: Holt, Rhinehart and Winston.
85. Lipkin, J. O., Blank, A. S., Parson, E. R. et al. (1982). Vietnam veterans and posttraumatic stress disorder. In: *Hosp. Commun. Psychiat.* **33** (11), 908–12.
86. Lifton, R. J. (1980). *The Broken Connection*. New York: Simon and Schuster.
87. Kriegman, G. (1983). Entitlement attitudes: psychosocial and therapeutic implications. *J. Am. Acad. Psychoanal.* **11** (2), 265–81.
88. MacKay, C. (1841). *Extraordinary Popular Delusions and the Madness of Crowds*. New York: Page (1932).
89. Ulman, R. B. and Abse, D. W. The group psychology of mass madness: Jonestown. *Political Psychol.* **4** (4), 637–61.
90. Abse, D. W. and Reckrey, R. (1970). Politics and personality. *Br. J. Social Psychiat.* **4**, 1–16.
91. Waite, R. G. L. (1971). Adolph Hitler's anti-Semitism: a study in history and psychoanalysis. In: *The Psychoanalytic Interpretation of History* (ed. Wolman, B. B.). New York: Basic Books.
92. Waite, R. G. L. (1977). *The Psychopathic God. Adolph Hitler*. New York: Basic Books.

93. Ulman, R. B. (1979). Review of R. G. L. Waite's *The Psychopathic God: Adolph Hitler Psychohistory Rev*. **8**, 77–8.
94. Langer, W. (1972). *The Mind of Adolph Hitler: The Secret Wartime Report*. New York: Basic Books.
95. Bychowski, G. (1971). Joseph V. Stalin: paranoia and the dictatorship of the proletariat. In: *The Psychoanalytic Interpretation of History* (ed. Wolman, B. B.). New York: Basic Books.
96. Kohut, H. (1976). Creativeness, charisma, group psychology: reflections on the self-analysis of Freud. *Freud: The Fusion of Science and Humanism* (ed. Gedo. J. E. and Pollock, G. H.). In: *Psychological Issues*, Vol. 9. New York: Int. Univ. Press.
97. Freud, S. (1921). *Group Psychology and the Analysis of the Ego*. In: *The Standard Edition*, Vol. XVIII. London: Hogarth Press (1955).
98. Stolorow, R. D. and Atwood, G. E. (1979). *Faces in the Cloud: Subjectivity in Personality Theory*. New York: Aronson.
99. Stolorow, R. D. and Lachmann, F. M. (1980). *Psychoanalysis of Developmental Arrests: Theory and Practice*. New York: Int. Univ. Press.
100. Strozier, C. B. (1982). *Lincoln's Quest for Union: Public and Private Meanings*. New York: Basic Books.
101. Ulman, R. B. (1979). Jim Jones and the People's Temple: a study of the interaction between a pathological leader and his followers. Paper presented at Annual Meeting of American Psychological Association in New York.
102. Jung, C. G. (1946). Civilisation in transition. In: *The Collected Works of C. G. Jung* (Bollinger Series XX). New York: Princeton Univ. Press (1964).
103. Abse, D. W. and Jessner, L. (1962). The psychodynamic aspects of leadership. In: *Excellence and Leadership in a Democracy* (ed. Graubard, S. R. and Holton, G.). New York: Columbia Univ. Press.
104. Schiffer, I. (1973). *Charisma: A Psychoanalytic Look at Mass Society*. New York: Macmillan.
105. Teja, J. S., Khanna, B. S. and Subrahmanyan, T. (1970). 'Possession states' in Indian patients. *Indian J. Psychiat*. **12**, 71–87.
106. Ferrio. C. (1948). *La Psiche e i Nervi*. Turin: Utet.

DIAGNOSIS III

Differentiation of Conversion Hysteria from Psychophysiological Autonomic Disorder

Psychological Stress

The traumatic neuroses which follow, after a greater or lesser interval, exposure to the threat of death remind us that Ferenczi (1933)[1] brought to light the traumatic factors in childhood which are involved in the pathogenesis of the psychoneuroses, including hysteria, in adult life. He especially laid emphasis on the characterological mal-developments and psychoneuroses brought about by premature grafting of oppressive forms of passionate sexual love riddled with guilt onto a still immature child yearning for tenderness. As Masson (1984)[2] in his highly controversial book correctly notes:

> Perhaps never before had anyone spoken for the abused child with such sympathy and eloquence. The ideas which Freud had propounded to a sceptical medical world in his 1896 papers were here repeated, but expanded by the knowledge gained by analysis in the years after 1896.

As previously noted in Chapter 2, oral deprivation is frequently of aetiological importance in hysteria, and when it is severe its traumatic effect is evident in hysteriform borderline disorder. When severely traumatic situations of early oral deprivation do not offset the birth trauma, and when maternal care is insufficient and complicated by sexual over-stimulation in childhood, the seeds of later hysteriform disease are sown in plenty. Ferenczi (1933)[1] emphasized both early maternal love deprivation and sexual molestation by the father, and it is evident that many of his women patients had been so afflicted, and that these aetiological factors influenced his therapeutic technique, as is discussed in Chapter 20.

Later, psychological stresses at different phases of the life cycle are often evident triggers of psychoneurotic symptom formation. Harold Wolff (1953),[3] following contemporary usage in physics, defines stress as the internal resisting forces which the organism activates in dealing with noxious external forces. These—the stressors, as Selye (1950)[4] designates them—are usually understood as situations which comprise such events as separation from significantly related persons (death, divorce, retirement from work, etc.), or as the entry of new persons into the patient's life space with the attending need for a new adaptation (birth of child, in-laws moving into home, appointment of

393

a new supervisor, etc). or as loss of self-esteem through failure (in college, in business, etc.). These contingencies are certainly common among stressors precipitating mental and psychosomatic illness. But matters are not always so obvious. As Ernest Cassirer (1944)[5] writing of man as user-of-symbols, has put the point: man cannot escape from his own achievement; no longer in a merely physical universe, he lives in a symbolic world. Indeed, it is not only the changing situations, but what man makes of his experience of them which counts for good or ill. The following case excerpt provides a suitable illustration:

Case 53. A 50-year-old physician who came to psychiatric interview prefaced his account of his symptoms and of himself by stating that he thought his visit would necessarily turn out to be a waste of time. His symptoms, he explained, were the result of raised blood-pressure, and following medication he was considerably improved. The colleagues who had thoroughly examined him, and with whose advice and treatment he was cooperating, were satisfied with his improvement, but one of them had suggested that, in order to leave no stone unturned, he should explore any possibilities of stress in his personal life. There were ideas around, I gathered during the further course of explanation, that connected hypertension with mental stress, and he wanted to talk about this. However, he could find no stresses in his life at present. On the contrary, never had his life been so free from mental stress. Twenty-five years earlier he had started the solo practice of medicine in a rural area. There he had remained and prospered. For years he had worked very hard for very little material reward; then, as economic circumstances improved, many more of his patients paid their bills. He married and had several children. His ambition had been to provide adequately for his family and to set the stage for considerably more leisure and recreation by the time he was fifty. In this he had succeeded. For the past year he had had two young doctors as partners in his practice and now he was often on the golf course in the afternoon and had much more time to spend with his wife and children. Everything had, as he amplified, worked out as planned, and for the past six months as far as he was concerned he could not have been in a happier situation. It was six months ago when he had been attending a medical meeting—during the past year he had had more time for such meetings—that he first developed symptoms which led to the check on his blood-pressure. A searching history disclosed, among other facts, that during his last year as a medical student his father, a farmer who had supported him by dint of hard work through his college years and through medical school, became sick. Soon, the father requested him to come home to help on the farm, work which he had undertaken periodically as opportunity permitted through his school years. At this time, in his final year as a medical student, he felt he could not risk his career; and, indeed, his father recovered. However, the following year, during his time as an intern, his father suddenly died. During his first interview it became clear that he still blamed himself for his father's death at 55 years of age. It also became clear that his fixed idea of lessening the load for himself before he was 50 was based on a wish to avoid his father's fate, which he felt was somehow connected with his father's persistent hard work on the small farm.

The legend of Polycrates has already been discussed with reference to the motor-car accident which 'befell' the steelworker (*Case* 42). As psychotherapy revealed, unconscious symbolism had made of my physician-patient's success the realization of a forbidden and guilt-ridden wish to supersede his father ruthlessly.

Flanders Dunbar (1943)[6] contrasts patients suffering from hypertensive cardiovascular disease, coronary occlusion, and the anginal syndrome with patients with bone fractures; she writes:

Sherrington's analysis of the mind as essentially subserving an inhibitory function in relation to motor behaviour is of interest in this connection. The greatest relief of tension is provided by action, the least by fantasy and thought, whereas speech stands halfway between. If tension is expressed directly in action, the action is likely to be ill-considered, and to create situations injurious to the patient. If, on the other hand, all action is repressed or entered upon only after considerable thought and the suppression of emotion, the development of a different type of psychic or somatic symptomatology or both is favoured.

In criticizing the evidence for this kind of unconscious symbolic activity in the case of Little Hans (see p. 339), Joseph Wolpe and Stanley Rachman (1960)[7] maintain that Freud's claim of 'a more direct and less roundabout proof' of his theories, including that of unconscious symbolism, is not justified by the evidence presented. Obviously, what is *unconscious* cannot be observed and reported directly by the subject; much less by the investigator dependent upon communication with the subject. Freud was alluding to the confirmation of theory by a lesser degree of inference from data than was usual in work with adults. This view is ignored by Wolpe and Rachman, who appear to think that unconscious symbolic activities should be observable data rather than inferred from data. Apart from this flaw in logic distributed over their entire discussion of unconscious dynamics, these authors also ignore the weight of inferences from case investigations in general and from the study of dreams and parapraxes. These inferences converge in the view that patients unconsciously—and idiosyncratically, in terms of their former experiences, wishes, anxieties, and guilts—extract a meaning from outer events side by side with the general consensus as to the meaning. For Little Hans, of course, the horse was a horse—and also represented aspects of his feeling experiences related to his father. It is, indeed, this kind of unconscious symbolic elaboration of actual events, unconsciously linking the perception of them with latent but readily triggered intrapsychic conflicts, which is so often heavily involved in the precipitating situations of mental and psychosomatic disorder.

Eysenck (1965)[8] attempts to explain Hans's phobia in terms of conditioning, citing analogy with Watson's conditioning of Little Albert. Certainly Hans had been warned to avoid horses lest they bite, by the father of Hans's friend. A. V. Conway (1978)[9] also notes that weight is put upon the injury another friend of Hans suffered when they were playing horses, and he points out that this would have necessitated the ideational transposition from friend to horse, whereas the very notion of Hans' forming such an identity in his mind between a human and a horse is explicitly ridiculed by Eysenck. Similar logical inconsistencies, as well as gambits of quoting Freud out of context in these misleading critiques, are shown to illustrate the dictum: 'When we cannot understand something, we can always fall back on abuse.'

In the case of the physician (*Case* 53), the situation of success into which he moved reactivated a readiness for dysphoric emotions (anxiety and guilt) connected with an unresolved conflict of ambivalence concerning his father. The reactivation of this unconscious conflict was decisive for the elevation of his blood-pressure. We have previously shown in Chapters 2 and 4 (see also *Table* 10.1, p. 228) that in the conversion process, the somatic symptoms themselves were related to the conflicts aroused by changes in the patient's life situation. It is now necessary to add that in psychophysiological disorder also the changes in the life situation are often symbolically elaborated unconsciously before the pathological reaction becomes manifest. As for the symptoms in psychophysiologic disorder, we will consider the nature of symbolism involved in them shortly.

With regard to the case described above, we understand that the word 'success' symbolized the physician's conscious assessment of the situation in life he had achieved. Moreover, this view of his readily fitted in with our assessment too as we discussed the nature of his conscious intentions and values. The order of referential symbolism belonged to secondary process thinking and was reality orientated. He also elaborated the symbol unconsciously as a threat of disaster, and this made his success a pathogenic stressor situation. In thus relating stress to intrapsychic conflict, we do not overlook stressors which of themselves are frustrating or threatening—there are situations which are in themselves frustrating of vital strivings and thus are inherently stressors. There is in fact a continuum of frustrations involved in external physical reality, in interpersonal relationships or social reality, and in intrapsychic conflict. Instinctual strivings may meet frustration not only from within but from other people or from adverse outer physical or social factors. People encounter starvation, physical injury, sleep deprivation, maternal rejection and loss of those they love. Such stressors require recognition; and we are also required to search for the extended subjective and unconscious meanings by suitable techniques so that we are enabled to understand more fully the reactions to them in the inner world of the patient.

There are many subtle aspects of stressor situations commonly encountered clinically. From the viewpoint of his reference group, a man's situation in life may seem to offer no major frustrations, whereas from his own point of view, perhaps secretly, it may offer considerable obstacles to the satisfaction of his wishes or to the attainment of his ideals. Thus too, in some cases, feelings of deprivation may not be consciously experienced, but the patient's preconscious expectations of life at a particular phase of his life-cycle may be grossly jarred by the actual situation he finds himself in. In such instances, the expectations may have powerful unconscious determinants. Erik H. Erikson (1950)[10] has attempted to bridge the gaps in our knowledge of the relationships between psychosexual development and social growth. These extensions of theory to include endopsychic displacements at a psychosocial level involve the study of adaptive crises at different phases of the life-cycle, including adulthood. For example, 'generativity' is a critical development pervading psychic life as a stage of growth in a healthy adult personality. People who have reached this stage, in contradistinction to those who have never developed it, may become frustrated and regress to a need for pseudo-intimacy, perhaps with a sense of stagnation. Such an issue may set the stage for psychosomatic disorder.

Psychophysiological Disorder

Alexander (1950)[11] states that the similarity between hysterical conversion symptoms and vegetative responses to emotions lies in the fact that both are reactions to psychological stimuli. In the last section we have elaborated upon this similarity. Before proceeding to consideration of the differentiation of conversion reactions from psychophysiologic autonomic disturbances we will first discuss the salient psychodynamics of the latter.

In summing up and attempting to integrate the contributions of Alexander (1950),[11] Dunbar (1938),[12] Lindemann (1944),[13] Wolff (1950),[14] Engel (1953),[15] Mirsky (1957)[16] and other workers, Edward Kollar (1961)[17] offers the following propositions:

The psychological stimuli which evoke a state of stress arise from situations which the individual interprets to mean that a source of gratification either is threatened or is lost. If the individual feels his source of gratification is threatened the response is excitatory (fight or flight). If the individual passively experiences this state of excitation, it is called anxiety. Should the excitatory state be actively directed against the source of danger, it is called aggression (rage or anger). If the individual feels he is deprived of gratification the response is depression (grief). Anxiety, aggression and depression are psychobiological states with characteristic patterns of autonomic activity. Anxiety and aggression are expressed mainly through adreno-sympathetic mechanisms. Anxiety is accompanied by an adrenal pattern of autonomic activity, and aggression with a nonadrenalin pattern [Funkenstein, 1955;[18] Ax, 1960;[19] Silverman and Cohen, 1960[20]]. Depression is expressed physiologically at least in part through para-sympathetic mechanisms.

Kollar (1961)[17] makes these propositions schematic, as in *Fig.* 19.1. These statements are, of course not inclusive enough; since as we have discussed here, varieties of emotion and mixed emotions frequently occur, and these are not adequately included in these statements and in the schema. Nevertheless,

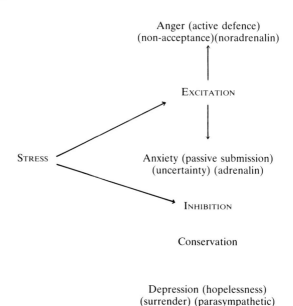

Fig. 19.1 Kollar's schema (*after* Kollar, 1961[17]).

despite the over-simplification which is thus built in, and of which we should be aware, these statements are extremely useful in orientating ourselves from the stressor situations to those psychophysiologic reactions which are basically different from conversion reactions in their psychodynamics and physiology.

In my view, the hallmarks, psychodynamically speaking, of psychophysiologic autonomic reactions are these: there is a partial but deep regression (deeper than in hysteria and hysteriform disorder) to the oral 'psychosomatic unit' or de-differentiated mouth-breast-visceral body ego; the part-regression is *dissociated* from the differentiated psyche, including the preconscious ego system, which thus is enabled to function relatively conflict-free; repression thus does not fail, as in hysterical disease; this regressively activated and dissociated oral-ego nucleus remains persistently hyperexic since it can only find tension-reduction very indirectly, if at all.

The Two Stages of the Oral Phase and Synergistic Confluence

As a result of his analyses of manic-depressive patients Abraham (1916,[21] 1924;[22] *see also* 1924[23]) differentiated two stages in the oral phase of development: early infantile urges to be nursed at the breast with the pleasures of sucking were later overlaid by cannibalistic urges with pleasure in biting, these becoming pronounced at the time of eruption of the milk teeth. In manic-depressive patients a major point of fixation is within this later biting period, and to this substage regression occurs characteristically in the illness. Freud (1913)[24] had been led by the analysis of obsessional neuroses to postulate a pregenital phase in the development of the libido which he called the 'anal-sadistic phase'; later (1915)[25] he described the oral-sadistic phase. Abraham (1916,[21] 1924[22]) was able to show that, during periods of quiescence, cases of manic-depressive psychosis characterologically resembled those of obsessional neurosis. He wrote (1924):[23]

As far as my experience goes, at any rate, it does not seem possible to make a hard and fast distinction between the melancholic and the so-called 'obsessional character'. In their 'free interval' patients suffering from circular insanity exhibit the same characteristics as psychoanalysis has made us acquainted with in the obsessional neuroses—the same peculiarities in regard to cleanliness and order; the same tendency to take up an obstinate and defiant attitude alternating with exaggerated docility and an excess of 'goodness'; the same abnormalities of behaviour in relation to money and possessions.

This similarity in the characterological patterns of patients suffering from obsessional problems with those suffering periodic mania or depression exemplifies a situation also known to exist in compulsive characters and in somatic reactors as well as in other connections. The oral-sadistic fixation of the manic-depressive patients comes later to reinforce the anal-sadistic phase resulting in characterologic defences similar to those employed by compulsive characters, whose primary fixation is in the anal-sadistic phase. Of course, in many patients there are multiple points of fixation, and associated with this and with manic modes of defence there are obsessional neuroses which periodically remit symptomatically. The *synergistic confluence* of instinctual cathexes in its benign aspects was especially emphasized by Abraham (1925).[26] In 1925 he wrote:

> The final [genital] stage of character formation shows traces everywhere of its association with the preceding stages. It borrows from them whatever conduces to a favourable relation between the individual and his objects. From the early oral stage it takes over enterprise and energy; from the anal stage, endurance, perseverance and various other characteristics; from sadistic sources, the necessary power to carry on the struggle for existence ... And a considerable portion of his sadistic instincts is employed no longer for destructive but for constructive purposes.

This harmonious synergistic confluence may be contrasted with excessive oral-sadistic–anal-sadistic confluence which sets the stage for conflict and hyperexic character formations, such as severe obstinacy and perpetual delaying, or heightened suggestibility and extreme impatience. In other words, characteristics derived from a satisfied sucking period may coincide in important repsects with others derived from the final genital phase; whereas deprivation or over-indulgence at the sucking period with resultant enhanced oral sadism issues in a more fixed anal sadism and a more pronouncedly sado-masochistic adult character (Goldman-Eisler, 1948–51[28]).*

Of course, among a larger number of admixtures of synergistically confluent stages of libidinal organization and stages of object love, together with correlative and variable defences, we have here singled out a polarity—but it is one of considerable clinical significance. The point here is that many sorts of more or less compulsive characters, when confronted with a frustrating life situation, regress to a *more heavily charged* sadistic position with which their inner defences can no longer cope; further (deeper) regression then occurs and is equally untenable. This activated mouth–breast–visceral ego nucleus is dissociated and finds expression in psychophysiologic autonomic disorder.

In order to see more clearly—from the inside as it were—what is being dissociated and expressed psychophysiologically, we will here have recourse to an excerpt from the therapy of a schizophrenic patient from whom it was possible to learn:

Case 54. A 27-year-old white male graduate student in linguistics had been in psychotherapy for 3 years following an acute paranoid schizophrenic illness when he offered the following material in interview. He opened the session by relating a dream which he claimed had occurred first at the age of 2 years and occasionally recurred thereafter: 'There were shiny, silvery birds: very bright, like shiny butterflies in a slick darkness. They were gliding along effortlessly with a perfect smoothness.' The patient went on the speak of 'light' as the strongest of all symbols used throughout art. Light, he said, always contrasts with darkness, and darkness is even more desirable than light. A mere spark in a black void would be ecstasy. In paintings of the Madonna and Child the Christ-child shines. 'Child and mother,' said the patient, 'after this, what is there left.'

The patient next complained of sensations that he experienced every time he entered the therapist's office: 'a feeling of dryness inside as well as outside. The air here is too sharp, acute, and drying. My nose runs and drinks fluids.' The patient explained that coming into the office his 'autonomic system is no longer under control'. He could not

---

*Ferenczi's *Thalassa* (1924)[27] gives this extended significance, including discussion of the phylogenic roots of such confluences.

control this when he saw the therapist. Then he went on complaining that the therapist put too many demands on him to do things; hence all these sharp smells and unpleasant sensations. People should do things for him—he could not do things for himself as well as others. He did not want any demands. He did not want to talk.

This patient—whose intense interest in linguistics stemmed partly from an attempt to master and to countermand a powerful regressive surge to the preverbal infantile phase of being, a regressive trend that was readily activated by frustration or narcissistic injury even of minor degree—was, at the time of this interview, in the throes of intense mother-dependent transference. In the dream the patient had depicted the effortless smooth sensations of the satisfied infant with his nursing mother. This was followed by an account of unpleasant sensations associated there and then with the therapeutic situation which was frustrating, particularly on account of the implicit demand to talk.

The student of linguistics was expressing a longing for the satisfaction possible in the preverbal period of life. Passive-dependent (sucking) oral wishes were afforded fulfilment in a visual transformation of previsual bodily sensations in the dream. He reported the antithesis of these sensations in expressing his frustration in the therapy situation; he also reported involuntary somatic efforts to rid himself of these dry and uncomfortably sharp sensations—'My nose runs and drinks fluids'.

There are occasions in psychotherapy when such bodily sensations are reported or are indirectly offered in a dream. These bodily sensations belong to the archaic oral phase of development. In writing of the modality of primal perception, René A. Spitz (1955)[29] contends that in the newborn the sensations of skin discomfort are indistinguishable from discomfort in the passages of the mouth, nose, larynx, and pharynx. The intra-oral sensations are combined with sensations from the hand, skin, and labyrinth. This perceptual experience is inseparable from need tension and need gratification, the former expressed by the affective manifestations of unpleasure, the latter leading to quiescence. As already mentioned (*see* Chapter 14), Felix Deutsch (1954)[30] discusses the value of verbalization, not only of thoughts and feelings, but of bodily sensations or sensory perceptions in analytic psychotherapy. He especially recommends research into the chronologically preverbal phase of development through their scrutiny. The primordial 'unity of the senses' has also been discussed (Chapter 14) and the view that this mode of sensation is superseded but not entirely replaced during maturation and development. In the dream imagery of the shiny silvery birds 'gliding along effortlessly with a perfect smoothness', the patient (*Case* 54) described experience of gratification of a suckling which resulted in pleasurable quiescence. On the other hand, his antithetical sensations by day in the therapy situation represented a revival of frustrational experience attached to the oral phase, and he described involuntary events which combated these unpleasurable sensations.

Such glimpses into the nature of archaic oral-ego strivings are also afforded in psychotherapy when a patient reports the Isakower phenomenon; vague sensations of something soft filling the mouth, at the same time felt on the outside surface, and visually shadowy and round, sometimes growing enormous in size before shrinking, are described by some patients as predormescent experiences (Isakower, 1938[31]). In addition to this kind of evocation of early experience at the breast in a hypnagogic state, Lewin (1946)[32] has described the dream screen, the surface on to which dreaming sometimes appears to be projected, as a 'memory of the breast'.*

The ego is in its beginning stage following birth. The organism emerges at birth from a highly protected and quiet environment into a flood of excitation without an adequate defence apparatus, a situation which Freud described as the 'model for all later anxiety'. Fenichel (1945),[33] in Chapter IV of his book, writes:

> Probably this being flooded by excitation is highly unpleasant and evokes the first mental tendency, namely, the tendency to get rid of the state of tension. When the outside world succeeds in helping the infant cope with these stimuli satisfactorily, he falls asleep. New stimuli, such as hunger, thirst, cold, awaken him. The first traces of consciousness do not differentiate between ego and non ego but rather between greater and lesser tension; at this time relaxation is concomitant with a loss of consciousness. If every need could be immediately taken care of, a conception of reality would probably never develop.

Benedek (1952)[34] sums up: 'Normally crying is a signal for the mother to take care of the baby. The rhythmically returning course of events is this: arising need—disturbances of sleep—crying—gratification—sleep again.'

If, as a result of frustration in adult life, a part-regression takes place to this early infantile phase, the dependent longings and the de-differentiation are threatening to the rest of the organized ego—especially in the compulsive personality with predominantly counterphobic and affect-isolating defences, with a perfectionistic ego ideal and thus readily aroused shame anxiety; so then a massive defence against feelings of helplessness and rage is instigated. This defence results in the dissociation of the mouth–breast–visceral body ego, and persistent discharge occurs via the autonomic nervous system.

Neurophysiologic evidence (Gerard, 1959[35]) supports the view that cognition is to a large extent a function of the cerebral neocortex, whereas phylogenetically older structures, especially the limbic system and hypothalamus, are involved in feeling experience and patterns of behaviour associated with fight, flight, food and sex. The distinction made by psychologists between cognition, on the one hand, and orexis (including both affects and conation), on the other, corresponds to some extent to a physical difference of function between major portions of the brain. However, in health, as was shown previously (*see* Chapter 17), the cognitive functions are aided and abetted by

---

*Lewin (1948,[37] 1953[38]) has developed his ideas concerning the dream screen in subsequent articles. Spitz (1965[39]) considers that, while the nipple forms part of early perception, this is *contact* perception; the observation that the nursing infant stares unwaveringly at the mother's face as soon as his eyes are open makes this probably the first visual element in early perception. At this stage of life stimulation in one system of the body is responded to in other systems, so that it is likely that the sensations in the oral cavity of the nursing infant are inseparable from tactile and other sensations, including vision of the mother's face, in undifferentiated perception.

Clinical experience indicates that the dream screen appears in the dreams of schizophrenics at times when the wish to look at the primal scene is heavily cathected; it then functions to reduce associated anxiety. Thus the dream screen has a protective function in diminishing the intensity of aroused affects, and the dream in which it appears also fulfils a regressive means of escape from threatening sadistic phallic sexuality (Abse, 1977[40]).

the integration of feeling and striving experience. Thus in health the brain basis works as a whole. It is possible that in severe psychophysiologic disorder the dissociation has its neurophysiologic basis in the partial separation of the functions of the neocortex from those of phylogenetically older brain structures. Or, perhaps more precisely, the mutual influences of the more recently acquired and older brain structures are grossly impeded.

From the psychological viewpoint what is expressed autonomically takes the form of distorted affect symbolism, primarily removed from the possibility of ideational development, which can only become elaborated later following the perception of disturbed organ function. Garma (1950)[36] seems to mistake this secondary ideational development for primary idea symbolism.

The Differentiating Features

The discussions of symbols, affects and language (Chapter 17), of regression and semantic speech (Chapter 16) and of dissociation and communication (Chapter 14), are of help in the exploration of Alexander's view of the difference between conversion symptoms and vegetative neurosis. In the course of this exploration and critical evaluation of Alexander's view, some tentative hypotheses are suggested, the extent of the general value of which remains to be tested by further clinical investigation.

Alexander (1950)[11] states:

A conversion symptom is a *symbolic* expression of an emotionally charged psychological content: it is an attempt to discharge the emotional tension. It takes place in the voluntary neuromuscular or sensory-perceptive systems whose original function is to express and relieve emotional tensions. A vegetative neurosis is not an attempt to express an emotion but is the physiological response of the vegetative organs to constant or to periodically returning emotional states. Elevation of blood pressure, for example, under the influence of rage does not relieve the rage but is a physiological component of the total phenomenon of rage ... it is an adaptation of the body to the state of the organism when it prepares to meet an emergency. Similarly, increased gastric secretion under the influence of emotional longing for food is not an expression or relief of these emotions; it is the adaptive preparation of the stomach for the incorporation of food.

The first part of the statement seems to imply that the conversion process takes place *only* in the voluntary neuromuscular and sensory-perceptive systems, and is excluded from organs innervated by the autonomic nervous system. We must consider, however, that voluntary movements are themselves only relatively voluntary, and that vegetative functions such as breathing, coughing, urinating, vomiting and defecating are subject to considerable influence from the conscious will, reflecting anatomical and physiological connections of the higher levels of the central nervous system with innervations of organs subserving vegetative functions. Regression within the ego may result in its more direct involvement with vegetative functions which the more differentiated adult ego has ceased to influence directly. For example, in hypnotic regression, simple commands of the hypnotist may influence many more functions than the usual working conscious will. Thus the command: 'Your right hand is cold!' can result in vasoconstriction and reduced temperature of the designated body part. The simple imagery of coldness of the hand is in this instance sufficient to give rise to actual coldness, i.e., a hyperfunctioning has become possible in a regressive ego state. More than this, however, a seeming hyperfunctioning may be induced under hypnosis through more indirect suggestions employing imaginative situations. The suggestion, say, that the right hand is being thrust into ice-cold water as part of a trial by ordeal is obviously of a different character from a simple command which does not portray such an emergency situation, and does not provide the same kind of evidence for hyperfunctioning in a regressive ego state. It does, however, show how hysterical fantasy may involve autonomic functions indirectly. From these considerations it may be assumed that the conversion process is unlikely to be excluded from organs innervated by the autonomic nervous system. And, indeed, many disorders involving derangement of organs thus innervated are of a hysterical nature; a common example is enuresis without demonstrable organic cause. As illustrations too are cases of hysterical pseudocyesis, or of hyperhidrosis, such as the case shown in *Fig.* 6 and *Case* 5 in Chapter 2. Alexander's apparent restriction of conversion to the voluntary neuromuscular and sensory-perceptive systems, though inaccurate, does approach an important point of distinction between conversion and psychophysiologic autonomic disorder, as will be discussed shortly.

Again, we need to pause to consider the statement that a vegetative neurosis is not an attempt to express an emotion. Here there is an implicit disregard of any distinction between instinctual strivings and accompanying affects. In the preceding pages we have indicated, on the model of the reflex arc, that instinctual strivings, like outer perceptions, at first occupy the afferent side of the arc; then, *with affect*, on the efferent side of the arc, they are discharged. The affects are ranged on the efferent side of the arc, i.e., they are essentially motoric. Of course, there is feedback from the motoric manifestations, that is, the efferent paths have their own afferents, and it is these latter which are *perceived* as emotions, especially those which are of visceral origin. Alexander's statement has the further disadvantage of disregarding the cognitive functions of the affects. I would alter the statement to: 'A vegetative neurosis attempts a partial discharge of dissociated archaic instinctual impulses, and the accompanying emotions are primarily blocked from the differentiated ego.'

If we consider the dissociation of the primitive ego nuclei which represent the defended-against supplicant strivings and rage reactions as a piece of drastic psychic autotomy for the purpose of preventing any possible repressive failure on the part of the more organized remainder of the ego, we will make an important conceptual step. Since the dissociated strivings have access to discharge only through autonomic channels, and the efferent innervations do not lead to integration of emotion with cognition, the autotomy does not prevent a state of damming up of the organism. The more organized remainder of the ego, with its extensive preconscious system, is thus bound to note secondarily this damming up, this state of emergency, despite attempts at denial and despite its divorce from the sources of this tension. Typically we thus have primitive ego nuclei with access to discharge only through autonomic channels, and the more organized remainder operating with signal anxiety in a state of emergency. Thus, in psychogenic essential hypertension the elevation in blood-pressure results both from the general state of emergency and from autonomic discharges appropriate to rage expressing the activity of the sequestrated primitive oral-sadistic nucleus. The rage reaction is also inhibited in its development, for what was sequestrated at the beginning is again defended against in the feedback from the discharges: the visceral sensations are not integrated as emotions in the preconscious ego system. Similarly, increased gastric secretion under the influence of oral longings is complicated by the effects of anxiety on gastric functioning, and the emotional significance of the visceral discharges remains uninterpreted subjectively. Beyond all this, at more organized ego levels, a mask of imperturbability may altogether disguise the emotional turmoil, as happens in individuals with consolidated obsessional-compulsive defences. The specific dynamic patterns which Alexander (1950)[11] delineates in connection with gastric hyperfunction and with essential hypertension become all the more comprehensible if the splitting in the ego system is given more weight, and if the affects of helplessness, anger and anxiety are seen as failing in greater or lesser degree in their cognitive functions.

The essential differentiation from conversion reactions is to be sought dynamically in the divorce of both primitive strivings and their affects from the preconscious ego system. This divorce is much more complete and of a different nature from the simpler repressive defence in hysterical conversion reactions. The basic conflicts in psychophysiologic disorder, the defence struggle against primitive strivings, have never reached the level of preconscious word symbolism, whereas in conversion hysteria the preconscious word connections have been made and then secondarily excluded through the process of repression, and these word connections may be sought in de-repression at a metaphoric level. In conversion hysteria the conflicts represented in the symptoms are embedded in experiences when speech was already emergent, whereas in psychophysiologic disorder the basic conflicts belong to the period of preverbal archaic experience. In conversion reactions, as the ideation is recovered through word symbolism the affects readily find appropriate connections. In psychophysiologic disorder the affects have completely failed in their cognitive functions, and the patient is alienated from his emotions much more drastically.

Thus, Alexander's dictum that conversion reactions are concerned with the voluntary neuromuscular and sensory-perceptive systems, as they frequently are, should more properly read: 'concerned with the preconscious ego system, the chief domain of which is the voluntary musculature and sensory-perceptive apparatus'. But the preconscious ego may become more directly involved with autonomic functions too, reassuming more control, some of which had been delegated during differentiation. The essential dynamic considerations are concerned with the conflicts which issue in conversion; these had original connections with the preconscious ego system. Alexander's statement that a vegetative neurosis is not an attempt to express an emotion must be interpreted in terms of the failure of emotional expression to become cognitively integrated. In psychophysiologic disorder the emotions accompanying dissociated primitive archaic strivings are inhibited in their development and isolated as much as possible from the preconscious ego system.

The following case study illustrates criteria used in differential diagnosis, as well as its difficulty:

Case 55. A 26-year-old married white woman was admitted to hospital for psychiatric consultation complaining of painful hands and feet. She stated her hands and feet tingled then 'burned' until she was frantic, and she claimed that her only relief was in putting her hands and feet in cold water. Physical examination showed atrophic skin changes, oedema and severe blistering of the hands and feet, with no other objective findings in the skin, nervous system, or elsewhere. Six weeks prior to admission attacks of burning pain had started in the extremities. These attacks had lengthened in duration and increased in frequency and severity despite treatment based on successive views of her condition as Raynaud's disease and erythromelalgia during the course of extensive medical consultations. She had been referred for psychiatric help because of the onset of insomnia and because there had been an apparently delirious episode at night when she was repeating: 'They have brought two in,' which frightened her husband considerably. The attacks had started two weeks after the birth of her second child.

The patient was described as usually happy and gregarious and seemed afraid only of staying at home alone at night. She was the third of six siblings, had a high school education, and did well at school. Her early childhood was described as normal. At 20 years of age she married her present husband; married life was described as 'adequate and well-adjusted' in the medical reports until the onset of this illness. Since the beginning of her present condition the patient had been 'neglecting her children and only did work that was absolutely necessary at home', according to her husband. He said that she had spent all day every day recently soaking her hands and feet in cold water, acting depressed and unhappy, and that she did not improve with medication. Her husband was a hard-working farmer and the patient had assisted him with his work as well as attending to her housework prior to the onset of this illness.

Discussion with the patient quickly brought to the fore hard conditions in her marriage, and her husband's dissatisfaction because her illness had put him in debt, so he said, and slowed up the farm work. Four years previously when she had had her first baby she was off extra work (on the farm) for two weeks, and she had expected the same degree of indulgence after her recent parturition. Then her illness had started and prevented her from undertaking *any* work. In further discussions it became clear that the patient was of masochistic but resentful disposition, feeling that it was her duty to help her husband to her limits, but resenting his grumbling, especially recently after the second birth when he obviously wanted her to start work on the farm as quickly as possible. Her mother had been hard-working too, only prevented periodically from doing all she otherwise could on account of attacks of rheumatoid arthritis. During the course of these further discussions the patient acknowledged that with all the work and the difficulty (as it would seem from her husband's account) of making ends meet on the farm, she had been worried about a second pregnancy. And she said that she was afraid that 'another child would land me in hot water'—meaning she felt as extended as her resources allowed with her one child and efforts to please her husband. It later also became apparent that she had worried about 'getting into hot water' before marriage when she had occasionally participated in sexual intercourse. Moreover, soon after marriage and then after each delivery the patient had been treated for urinary infection, during the course of which, briefly, she had suffered from burning pains on urination.

In this case the elucidation of a stressor situation and conflict, associated with symptomatology comprising vasomotor disturbance of the extremities, at first suggested psychophysiologic disorder (Obermeyer, 1955[41]). Discussions revealed, however, once she was sufficiently involved in psychotherapy and her defences reduced, that the patient had recourse to metaphoric language which was already the beginning of retranslation of her bodily disorder back to the word symbolism of her thoughts before the somatic disorder began. Moreover, when she was helped to make connections between her verbal utterances and her bodily symptoms her affective responses were cumulative, enabling her to express her feelings more and more adequately as the conditions of her existence and her experiences in the past were reviewed. The 'getting into hot water' had been somatically dramatized as well as the wish to delete the experience by actual cold-water immersion. Her sense of duty, masochistically exaggerated, and her resentful feeling against being exploited like her mother were in conflict; the conversion accomplished a compromise solution causing her suffering but getting her off the job. The conflictual strivings and their affects were not so distant from the preconscious ego system that a pathway could not be quickly opened up. However, it must also be acknowledged that in such cases there may also be a psychophysiologic basis for the choice of symptoms. Dissociated dependent longings and rage reactions resulting from their frustration could issue in vasomotor instability which may be readily utilized by an incubating conversion reaction. Its refinements then raise symptoms to another level of symbolism, one beyond the autonomic responses of the preverbal infant. For the conversion process may complicate any somatic disorder, including other kinds of psychogenic somatic disorders. The impaired organ provides the somatic compliance, the major alteration in the body image which may be readily symbolically elaborated. In the differentiation of conversion hysteria from psychophysiologic autonomic disorder, as from organic disease (*see* Chapter 4), it is thus necessary to avoid an 'either–or' frame of reference.

Alexithymia

This explication of the problem of the differentiation of conversion defence from psychophysiologic disorder, including the miscarriage of the cognitive function of affects in the latter, is a repetition of that offered in the first edition of this book in 1966. In 1967 Sifneos[42] drew attention to a cluster of cognitive traits found in some patients suffering from a variety of psychosomatic diseases. He named this cluster of traits 'alexithymia'. Nemiah (1977),[43] who has developed the concept, states that alexithymic characteristics consist essentially in marked difficulty in expressing feelings in words and absence of fantasies appropriate to or expressive of feelings, with thought content being dominated by the details of the events in the immediate external environment. Obviously these characteristics are consistent with the deep splitting (autotomy) of the activated mouth–breast–visceral ego nucleus with access to discharge only through autonomic channels and loss of access to the preconscious ego system where word connections whereby heightened self-awareness becomes possible is normatively effected.

Harley C. Shands (1975)[44] drew attention to the correlation of the alexithymic cognitive style to Bernstein's 'restricted code' (Bernstein, 1964)[45] of the working class in England in contrast to the 'elaborated code' of the middle-class. Shands (1975)[44] wrote:

Bernstein shows again and again how much the problem is that of (1) developing the kind of code which affirms membership through the unspoken (unconscious) habits which describe a single universe as opposed to (2) the training in adopting and using multiple points of view characteristic of middle-class education ... Bernstein has pointed specifically to the difficulty of carrying out the psychotherapeutic 'game' with working-class members—and the recent rise of family therapy is presented by some of its proponents as a partial answer to the difficulty in involving working-class persons in the abstract operations of 'insight' or 'dynamic' psychotherapy.

Sifneos, Nemiah and Shands, with others, acknowledge that somatic reactions also occur among those who are not alexithymic. A case excerpt might indicate clues to a theoretical solution of this apparent paradox.

Case 56. A middle-aged upper-middle-class cultivated woman was in prolonged psychotherapy for severe colitis which improved with medications (antispasmodics, cortisones, etc) from the gastroenterologist as well as while in psychotherapy. This first improvement may be roughly assessed as from severe, when it was life-threatening, to moderate, when she found it necessary to visit the toilet about a dozen times a day and was on a special diet. Although ordinarily affectively expressive, she wore a mask of imperturbability whenever she came face to face with her divorced husband in social situations in which she could not avoid the confrontation, and was impassive whenever she spoke in treatment of current interaction with him. She carefully nursed an image of herself as a poised and gracious woman, which she was, and she rejected any possibility that she entertain any hostile jealous impulses and feelings. Her narcissistic adherence to this picture of herself and to a posture of well mannered behaviour was always maintained. One day, after 2 years of psychotherapy, her ex-husband's second wife left him. Her colitis abruptly disappeared when she heard this. The temporal connection, and the relationship of her colitis to her hostile jealousy became gradually apparent to her during further interpretive work of the kind that had been quite ineffective previously. Moreover, she was able to explore her feelings about her social reference group, which, she felt, would appreciate from his second wife's defection how 'impossibly difficult' her ex-husband was to live with. In this way, she became able to approach guilt-feelings and the self-punishing aspects of some of her symptoms, including the colitis, all of which were internal reactions to fierce death-wishes.

In regard to the psychotherapy of alexithymic somatic reactors, my experience is similar to that of Heinz H. Wolff (1975)[46] as expounded in his important article: 'The Contribution of the Interview Situation to the Restriction of Fantasy Life and Emotional Experience in Psychosomatic Patients'. In the case cited above, however, the patient was not alexithymic in general and usually richly expressive in her fantasy life and emotions. Nor was I bored in the sessions, though admittedly perplexed at times by the plateau of improvement reached without adequate symptom abatement before the news of the collapse of her ex-husband's second marriage. Understanding here led us to a split-off part of herself analogous to that which occurs in dual or multiple personality. Often in such cases (cf. Chapter 11) there is a one-way amnesic situation. The alter ego, or one of the fragmentary personalities, knows about the usual self, but the usual self is oblivious to the split off fragment or fragments. In other words the mental barrier is traversible in only one direction. In this case of the woman with ulcerative colitis the barrier was immediately traversible by certain deeds and could not be breached by words. To be brief, under certain circumstances in some patients who are not alexithymic by definition, psychosomatic disorder occurs as a result of resort under stress to localized but deep splitting; though psychosomatic integration had been achieved previously, and was maintained for the most part between thought and feeling and mind and body, an important regressive exception developed under stress which led to bodily symptoms.

Some Further General Considerations

In his paper on psychogenic disturbances of vision Freud (1910)[47] drew attention to the fact that 'neurotic' disturbances of organ functioning were not necessarily of the same order as hysterical conversion phenomena. Unfortunately his terminology in this essay is both misleading and confusing, restricting as he does 'psychogenic' to hysterical disorder whereas the physiological disturbances of organ functioning he discusses are also psychogenic. The essay, however, implied that between histogenic and hysterical disorders there is a large field of functional disorders, those now designated psychosomatic. Fenichel (1945)[33] recognized four classes of these functional disorders. These are:
   1. Affect equivalents.
   2. Results of changes in the chemistry of the dammed-up person.
   3. Physical results of unconscious attitudes or unconsciously determined behaviour patterns.
   4. All kinds of combinations of these three possibilities.
Moreover, as emphasized repeatedly in Chapters 2 and 4, hysterical elaboration of these psychophysiologic functional disorders often takes place secondarily. We have already noted many examples in these pages of complex psychogenic functional disorders with hysterical elaborations—the case of paroxysmal tachycardia presented in Chapter 4 (*Case* 21), that of hemiparesis (Case 29), that of transient hypertension with iatrogenic hypochondriasis (*Case* 30). We also have discussed the 'affect equivalents' as being *affect symbols* inasmuch as they represent a state of feeling cryptically. Often they can be shown to be the remnants of movements once possessing biological utility or of the antitheses of such residual movements, as Darwin's study of emotional expression and communication illuminated (*see*, Chapter 17, pp. 331–2).

In his Presidential Address to the Royal College of Psychiatrists, W. Linford Rees (1975)[48] furnished a synthesis of the action and interaction of causative factors in psychosomatic disorders based on studies of hundreds of patients suffering from diseases such as asthma, vasomotor rhinitis, hay fever, urticaria, thyrotoxicosis, peptic ulcer, premenstrual tension, migraine and colitis. He found that in all psychosomatic groups compared with control groups certain traits of personality were more common including general instability, timidity, lack of self-assertion, anxiety-proneness marked sensitivity and obsessional attributes. He stated: 'The aetiology of psychosomatic disorders can best be understood as the dynamic interaction of intrinsic and extrinsic factors, many of which have additive effects in producing the response of the target organ.' Rees discussed numerous psychosocial stressors, especially bereavement, threat to the security of a loved person, family and marital and sexual conflicts, sudden traumatic experiences and severe problems at work or of a financial nature, and he also emphasized the role of genetic constitutional factors. He also supported the proposition that life changes of sufficient magnitude whether apparently distressful or not, even when associated with success and apparently pleasant, may have 'stressful power' for the individual. In this regard, Rees refers to the work of Holmes and Rahe (1967).[49]

Holmes and Rahe attempted to quantify the impact of life events on the individual by means of a social readjustment scale which they validated in several thousand cases. Each life event was given a score to indicate the relative stressful power of the event. Thus death of the spouse was found to have the highest score. From these scores the life experience of a person over a period of time is assessed by Life Change Units, and can be used for the study of individuals and groups. Holmes and Rahe (1967)[49] were able to show that life changes had additive effects and taxed the adaptive capacity of the individual. It is evident in all this that sometimes, for a particular individual, the hazards of prominence and power are considerable and such a person may seek, but not find, the security of obscurity. The method has been used to study correlations between life changes and various illnesses in both retrospective and prospective studies. These studies have shown that all forms of disease, medical and surgical as well as definitively psychosomatic in the special sense, tend to occur in a person's life associated with life changes of sufficient magnitude in the two years preceding the onset of illness.

These findings support the view expressed in 1845 by Ernst von Feuchtersleben who gave articulate expression to the principle that man is a psychophysical totality in his *Lehrbuch der Artztlichen Seelenkunde* (1845).[50] Indeed, for this reason he is often regarded as the founder of psychosomatic medicine as a systematic discipline. Alexander (1950)[11] emphasized that nature does not know such strict distinctions as 'functional' versus 'organic', and he pointed out that functional disorders when prolonged could lead to organic disorder with morphological changes—the functional disorder of a vegetative organ associated with emotional disturbance of any kind may lead to tissue changes and later to irreversible organic disease. In more recent years Claus B. Bahnson and Marjorie Bahnson (1964)[51] and C. B. Bahnson (1980)[52] have developed the view that the rapid growth of neoplastic de-differentiated tissue may be partly a regressive organic mode of replacing a personal loss, the associated grief being energetically defended against at a psychic level.

In accordance with this view of the multifactorial determination of organic disease, as of psychosomatic disorder in the narrower sense, and in accordance too with systems theory which encompasses feed-back and feed-forward interactions at various levels, including somatopsychic as well as psychosomatic sequences, two studies of night-time smoking and its relationship to lung cancer were accomplished at the University of Virginia Hospital, and summarized in the *1974 Year Book of Cancer*[53] below:

Self-Frustration, Night-Time Smoking and Lung Cancer. D. Wilfred Abse, Marilyn M. Wilkins, Gordon Kirschner, Don L. Weston, Robert S. Brown and W. D. Buxton (University of Virginia Hospital, Charlottesville) report two studies in which 36 lung cancer patients and 29 patients with other diseases of the chest were interviewed concerning their smoking habits and patterns. The first study revealed that cancer patients are generally older, have smoked for a longer period of time and tend to smoke more often at night after intending to retire. Cancer patients also differed from control patients in terms of their sensitivity to the interviewer's own smoking habits: 10 of 12 cancer patients questioned by a smoking interviewer admitted to smoking at night but only 2 of 11 cancer patients questioned by a non-smoking interviewer disclosed night-time smoking habits.

Study 2 was designed to reduce the patients' sensitivity to the interviewer variable so that a more accurate account of the night-time smoking habits, particularly among cancer patients, could be obtained. A concerted effort was made to establish ease and rapport with the 17 patients who were interviewed at length. In this group of patients, 9 reported a history of night-time smoking and all 9 were later diagnosed as having lung cancer. Of the 8 men interviewed who did not smoke at night, only 4 had lung cancer. While the lung cancer patients had smoked during the day for a longer period of time and smoked roughly twice as much as the cancer-free patients, these factors did not seem to account for their practice of night-time smoking. In fact, cancer patients who smoked at night reported less daytime smoking (1·3 packs) than did cancer patients who did not smoke at night (2·8 packs).

When data from both studies were combined, night-time smoking and patient age emerged as significant variables: of the patients under 53 who did not smoke at night, 29 per cent later were diagnosed as having lung cancer; of those under 53 who smoked at night, 67 per cent; of those over 53 who did not smoke at night, 75 per cent; and of those over 53 who smoked at night, 86 per cent. Hence it seems possible that night-time smoking is not only linked with the incidence of lung cancer, but that it may also influence the age at which the patient is likely to develop lung cancer. It is obvious that night-time smoking provides further irritation to tissues already cumulatively insulted over a long period of time by the day-time smoking. However, patients with chest diseases other than lung cancer occasionally reported night-time smoking, especially if they were heavy day-time smokers. That the lung cancer patient's practice of night-time smoking was not related to the length of time he had been smoking nor to the amount he smoked daily suggests that cancer patients who smoke at night differ from smokers who do not develop cancer.

Descriptions of the lung cancer patient indicate a significant impairment in his ability to discharge emotional tension.[54] His general inexpressiveness is accompanied by a rather stoic attitude in which the fulfilment of basic needs is notably absent. Such characteristics, occurring within the context of increasing discouragement and depression, may contribute to the cancer patient's reported sleeplessness and tendency to smoke at night. Night-time smoking, particularly during the later part of middle-age, may indicate an incipient though uncomplaining form of neurotic decompensation for several years before emergence of lung cancer symptoms.

In conclusion, in regard to the complex relationships of hysteriform and depressive disorder and organic disease, it is to be noted that published investigations indicate an association between immune response alteration and the severity of depressive symptoms (Schleiffer et al., 1985[55]).

REFERENCES

1. Ferenczi, S. (1933). Confusion of tongues between adults and the child (the language of tenderness and of passion). In: *Final Contributions to the Problems and Methods of Psycho-analysis* (ed. Balint, M.; trans. Mosbacher, E. et al.). New York: Basic Books (1955).
2. Masson, J. M. (1984). *The Assault on Truth*. New York: Farrar, Straus and Giroux.
3. Wolff, H. G. (1953). *Stress and Disease*. Springfield, Ill.: Thomas.

4. Selye, H. (1950). *Stress*. Montreal: Acta.
5. Cassirer, E. (1944). *An Essay on Man*. New Haven: Yale Univ. Press.
6. Dunbar, F. (1943). *Psychosomatic Diagnosis*. New York: Hoeber.
7. Wolpe, J. and Rachman, S. (1960). Psychoanalytic 'evidence': a critique based on Freud's case of Little Hans. *J. Nerv. Ment. Dis.* **130**, 135.
8. Eysenck, H. J. (1965). *Fact and Faction in Psychology*. London: Penguin.
9. Conway, A. V. (1978). Little Hans: misrepresentation of the evidence? *Bull. Br. Psychol. Soc.* **31**, 285–7.
10. Erikson, E. H. (1950). Growth and crises of the 'healthy personality'. In: *Personality in Nature, Society and Culture* (ed. Kluckhohn, C., Murray, H. A. and Schneider, D. M.). New York: Knopf (1953).
11. Alexander, F. (1950). *Psychosomatic Medicine*. New York: Norton.
12. Dunbar, F. (1938). *Emotions and Bodily Changes*. New York: Columbia Univ. Press.
13. Lindemann, E. (1944). Symptomatology and management of acute grief. *Am. J. Psychiat.* **101**, 141.
14. Wolff. S. (1950). Discussion. *Res. Publ. Ass. Res. Nerv. Ment. Dis.* **29**, 476.
15. Engel. G. L. (1953). Homeostasis, behavioural adjustment and the concept of health and disease. In: *Mid-century Psychiatry* (ed. Grinker, R.). Springfield, Ill.: Thomas.
16. Mirsky, I. A. (1957). The psychosomatic approach to the etiology of clinical disorders. *Psychosom. Med.* **19**, 424.
17. Kollar, E. J. (1961). Psychological stress: a re-evaluation. *J. Nerv. Ment. Dis.* **132**, 382.
18. Funkenstein, D. H. (1955). Physiology of fear and anger. *Sci. Am.* **192**, 74.
19. Ax, A. F. (1960). Psychophysiology of fear and anger. *Psychiat. Res. Rep. Am. Psychiat. Assoc.* **12**, 167.
20. Silverman, A. J. and Cohen, S. I. (1960). Affect and vascular correlates to catechol amines. *Psychiat. Res. Rep. Am. Psychiat. Assoc.* **12**, 16.
21. Abraham, K. (1916). The first pregenital stage of the libido. In: *Selected Papers*. London: Hogarth Press (1927).
22. Abraham, K. (1924). A short study of the development of the libido, viewed in the light of mental disorders. In: *Selected Papers*. London: Hogarth Press (1927).
23. Abraham, K. (1924). The influence of oral erotism on character-formation. In: *Selected Papers*. London: Hogarth Press (1927).
24. Freud, S. (1913). A Disposition to Obsessional Neurosis. In: *The Standard Edition*, Vol. XII. London: Hogarth Press (1953).
25. Freud, S. (1915). Instincts and Their Vicissitudes. In: *The Standard Edition*, Vol. XIV. London: Hogarth Press (1957).
26. Abraham, K. (1925). Character-formation on the genital level of libido-development. In: *Selected Papers*. London: Hogarth Press (1927).
27. Ferenczi, S. (1924). *Thalassa: Theory of Genitality*. New York: Psychoanalytic Quarterly (1938).
28. Goldman-Eisler, F. (1948–51). Breastfeeding and character formation. In: *Personality in Nature, Society and Culture* (ed. Kluckhohn, C., Murray, H. A. and Schneider, D. M.). 2nd ed., Chap. 11. New York: Knopf (1953).
29. Spitz, R. A. (1955). The primal cavity: a contribution to the genesis of perception. In: *The Psychoanalytic Study of the Child*. (ed. Eissler, R. S., Freud, A., Hartmann, H. et al.), Vol. 10. New York: Int. Univ. Press.
30. Deutsch, F. (1954). Analytic synesthesiology. *Int. J. Psycho-anal.* **35**, 293.
31. Isakower, O. (1938). A contribution to the patho-psychology of phenomena associated with falling asleep. *Int. J. Psycho-anal.* **19**, 331–45.
32. Lewin, B. D. (1946). Sleep, the mouth and the dream screen. *Psychoanal. Quart.* **15**, 419–34. Reprinted in: *Selected Writings of Bertram D. Lewin* (ed. Arlow, J. A.). New York: Psychoanalytic Quarterly (1973).

33. Fenichel. O. (1945). *The Psychoanalytic Theory of Neurosis*. New York: Norton.
34. Benedek, T. (1952). Personality development. In: *Dynamic Psychiatry* (ed. Alexander, F. and Ross, H.). Chicago: Univ. Press.
35. Gerard, R. W. (1959). Neurophysiology: brain and behavior. In: *American Handbook of Psychiatry*. New York: Basic Books.
36. Garma. A. (1950). On the pathogenesis of peptic ulcer. *Int. J. Psycho-anal.* **31**, 53.
37. Lewin, B. D. (1948). Inferences from the dream screen. *Int. J. Psycho-anal.* **29**, 224–31. Reprinted in: *Selected Writings of Bertram D. Lewin* (ed. Arlow, J. A.). New York: Psychoanalytic Quarterly (1973).
38. Lewin, B. D. (1953). Reconsideration of the dream screen. *Psychoanal. Quart.* **22**, 174–99.
39. Spitz, R. A. (1965). *The First Year of Life: A Psychoanalytic Study of Normal and Deviant Development of Object Relations*. New York: Int. Univ. Press.
40. Abse, D. W. (1977). The dream screen: phenomenon and noumenon. *Psychoanal. Quart.* **46**, 256–86.
41. Obermeyer, M. D. (1955). *Psychocutaneous Medicine*. Springfield, Ill.: Thomas.
42. Sifneos, P. E. (1967). Clinical observations on some patients suffering from a variety of psychosomatic diseases. *Proc. 7th European Conf. Psychosomatic Research*. Basel: Karger.
43. Nemiah, J. C. (1977). Alexithymia: theoretical considerations. *Proc. 11th European Conf. Psychosomatic Research* (Heidelburg, 1976). In: *Psychother. Psychosom.* **28**, 199–206.
44. Shands, H. C. (1975). How are 'psychosomatic' patients different from 'psychoneurotic' patients? *Psychother. Psychosom.* **26**, 270–85.
45. Bernstein, B. (1964). Social class, speech systems, and psychotherapy. *Br. J. Sociol.* **15**, 54–64.
46. Wolff, H. H. (1975). The contribution of the interview situation to the restriction of fantasy life and emotional experience in psychosomatic patients. *Psychother. Psychosom.* **26**, 290.
47. Freud, S. (1910). The Psycho-analytic View of Psychogenic Disturbance of Vision. In: *The Standard Edition*, Vol. XI. London: Hogarth Press (1955).
48. Rees, W. L. (1975). Stress, distress and disease. *Br. J. Psychiat.* **128**, 3–18.
49. Holmes, G. H. and Rahe, R. H. (1967). The social re-adjustment scale. *J. Psychosom. Res.* **11**, 213–18.
50. von Feuchtersleben, E. (1845). *The Principles of Medical Psychology, being the Outlines of a Course of Lectures* (trans. Lloyd, H. E.; revised and ed. Babington, B. G.). London: Sydenham Society (1847). (Originally published as: *Lehrbuch der Arztlichen Seelenkunde*. Vienna: Gerold (1845).)
51. Bahnson, C. B. and Bahnson, M. B. (1964). Cancer as an alternative to psychosis: a theoretical model of somatic and psychologic regression. In: *Psychosomatic Aspects of Neoplastic Disease* (ed. Kissen, D. M. and LeShan, L. L.). London: Pitman Medical (1964).
52. Bahnson, C. B. (1980). Stress and cancer: the state of the art. *Psychosom.* **21** (12), 975–80; **22** (3), 207–20.
53. Clark, R. L., Cumley, R. W. and MaCay, J. E. (ed.) (1974). *The Year Book of Cancer 1974*. Chicago: Year Book Medical.
54. Kissen, D. M. (1966). The significance of personality in lung cancer in men. *Ann. N.Y. Acad. Sci.* **125** (3), 820–6.
55. Schleifer, S. J., Keller, S. E., Sims, S. G. et al. (1985). Depression and immunity. *Arch. Gen. Psychiat.* **42** (2), 129–33.

CHAPTER 20

Psychotherapy

Principal Types of Psychotherapy and Their Indications

Wolberg (1954)[1] wrote of the varieties of psychotherapy:

> If he [the patient] decides to get professional help, he will be no less confounded, particularly if he lives in a large city where there are many representative types of therapy. If such is the case, what should he do? Should he choose a therapist who practices the 'common sense' method of Adolf Meyer? Should he find an orthodox Freudian psychoanalyst? Or should he get an adherent of a deviant psychoanalytic school; and, if so, of what school—that of Adler, Jung, Stekel, Rank, Horney or Sullivan? Is a therapist to be preferred who knows the techniques of hypnosis or narcosynthesis; or one who employs short-term therapy, such as described by Alexander and French; or of psychiatric interviewing, like that elaborated by Finesinger; or the non-directive therapy of Rogers; or psychodrama, such as advocated by Moreno and his group? Should he pay credence to the enthusiastic claims of an acquaintance who is getting inspirational group therapy; or to one who is being 'cured' by sitting in an orgone box; or the more recent acquaintance who is all agog about 'conditioned reflex therapy'?

Plato felt that in rhetoric and poetry language was often used as a means of putting images between men's minds and the facts. There are today many more schools of psychotherapy than Wolberg mentioned with so little announced intersubjective consensus as to the facts that it is natural to wonder whether a good many misleading images are not being purveyed simply for the purpose of gaining a victory in argument. In the future it is likely that the developing science of psychoanalysis, which has already enabled us to understand so many of the factors involved in different forms of psychotherapy, will encompass an understanding of many more, especially those involved in the present prolific family and group therapies, and so make possible clearer indications for their utilization or avoidance.

Historically the utilization of mental or moral influence upon an individual or group of individuals for the purpose of healing sickness is as old as communication between human beings. It is a variety of communication distinguished by the fact that one or more persons are benevolently concerned about another's disease. If we think in terms of the etymology of the word 'disease', and if we are impressed with the fact that another persons's benevolent concern, however represented in attitude, word, or deed, whenever it is accepted by a sick person, has some effect upon his recuperative capacity, we perceive that it is a futile undertaking to look for a beginning of psychotherapy in recorded history. Innumerable examples of it can be found even in very ancient records. Thus the inscriptions of the Egyptians made many thousands of years ago contain pertinent examples of priest-physicians healing by means of chanted incantations, ritual performances, and offerings to the gods or forces of nature, so that these seemed to intervene in the direction of restoration of health.

As Frazer (1890)[2] details in *The Golden Bough*, the priest-physician was one of a class of functionaries; the existence of such a class already represents a considerable political and religious evolution of savage society. The magician of former times had ceased to be merely a private practitioner and had risen to a position of much influence and repute; indeed, beyond that of priest, he often enough attained to that of chief or king. Frazer shows that in this evolution from magician to priest the operation of spirits is postulated and elaborated, and attempts are made to win their favours by prayer and sacrifice. In other words, magic and religion become alloyed.

However, magic itself, when unalloyed, assumed that in nature one event follows another necessarily, without spiritual intervention—an assumption in accord with the scientific conception of the world. The flaw in magic is, of course, not in this general assumption of a sequence of events determined by natural law, but in a total misconception of the nature of the particular laws which govern that sequence. At any rate in savage society the magician was supposed to understand the laws of nature, and it was to him that men turned when they were sick. As we now understand this he effected his cures largely by means of one method of psychotherapy, namely, suggestion.

Suggestion has been defined by McDougall (1926)[3] as

a process of communication resulting in the acceptance with conviction of the communicated proposition in the absence of logically adequate grounds for its acceptance.

Suppose a magician advises a savage woman to give her sick baby sugar candy to suck and to put glue on his palms, so that the child will thrive and grow up to speak sweet words and have precious things stick to him. Suppose that the woman accepts this advice and believes in its efficacy. The suppositions are not so far-fetched, for in Samarkand such events actually did occur (Frazer, 1890). This is an example of suggestion as defined by McDougall and the magical thinking involved (like produces like) is of the homoeopathic sort.

Modern psychotherapy had its beginnings in the remote past, in the matrix of magical thinking, when man was first attempting to control the forces of nature directly. In these attempts reality testing was overshadowed, as the above example shows, by wishful thinking, which included notions of the omnipotence of thought and the assimilative projection of man's own association of ideas, even the manner of the association of his ideas, on to the external world. The attempts were thus limited in their efficacy, and so far as success obtained it was dependent upon both the fortuitous amount of reality basis and the force of suggestion. Yet here we can discern not only the beginnings of science but the spirit of the healer striving to help his fellow. Without this relationship there is no effective psychotherapy.

We have already detailed in Chapter 1 (pp. 6–8) the links which Franz Anton Mesmer and his disciple the Marquis de Puységur established between magical methods of treatment and modern psychotherapy. Mesmer believed that an impalpable fluid saturated with 'animal magnetism' could be manipulated by the human will to cure disease. Puységur found that instead of the mesmeric crisis a trance-like state he called 'somnambulism' could be induced during which the subject was highly suggestible, and he used this trance to further the cure. As noted by Hippolyte Bernheim (1891)[4]:

Animal magnetism had only one value: it gave birth to the discovery of induced somnambulism. In 1819, the Abbot Faria first redeemed this phenomenon from the swaddling clothes of the magic and idle fancy which had obscured its nature. He showed that everything was the subject's imagination ... Magnetism was discredited but it was reborn with Braid and became a scientific doctrine (under the name of hypnotism) boiled down to what it really is—an induced sleep with heightened suggestibility ... It remained for Dr Liébault, in our times, to establish the doctrine of therapeutic suggestion openly and definitively. Contrary to the old and ridiculous practices of animal magnetism, the methods of modern hypnotism constitute appropriate ways to augment suggestibility and intervene therapeutically by verbal suggestion.

During his first years of practice as a neurologist, Sigmund Freud was constantly preoccupied with the imperfection of his therapeutic methods. He wrote of this (1925):[5]

My therapeutic arsenal contained only two weapons, electrotherapy and hypnotism, for prescribing a visit to a hydropathic establishment after a single consultation was an inadequate source of income. My knowledge of electrotherapy was derived from W. Erb's textbook which provided detailed instructions for the treatment of all the symptoms of nervous diseases. Unluckily I was soon to see that following these instructions was of no help whatsoever and that what I had taken for an epitome of exact observations was merely the construction of fantasy. The realization that the work of the greatest name in German neuropathology had no more relation to reality than some 'Egyptian' dreambook, such as is sold in cheap book-shops was painful, but it helped to rid me of another shred of the original faith in authority from which I was not yet free. So I put my electrical apparatus aside ...

But then he found he was unable always to induce the hypnotic trance, or else not deeply enough. Furthermore he found that improved patients often remained free from symptoms only as long as they were in contact with, and on good terms with, the physician. This was often also the case for treatment utilizing suggestion in the waking state. Already while he was with Charcot, Freud had found that hysterical contractures and paralyses did not fit with any anatomical distribution of the peripheral nerves, but corresponded to an image, a mental representation of the arm or the limb. In the *Étude Comparative des Paralysies Motrices Organiques et Hystériques*, written and published in French (1893),[6] he noted that

hysteria behaves in its paralyses and other manifestations as though anatomy did not exist, or as though it were totally ignorant of it.

This was obviously a step towards his later conception of the symbolism involved in hysterical symptoms. Meanwhile, at Nancy with Bernheim, he learned that hysterical patients were often unaware of situations connected with their illnesses which both hypnosis and waking suggestion sometimes helped them to remember.

In Vienna, Freud gave up hypnosis as a means of treatment because of its relative unreliability and because his mind, now prepared, enabled him to rethink the observations on a hysterical patient about whom Josef Breuer had kept him informed.

Eventually, Freud, as noted in Chapter 1, discovered that communicated propositions were accepted with conviction because of the prestige with which the therapist was endowed through the *transference* of emotion to him from prestige-endowed parental figures of the past. He came to show that, in the dependency relationship so characteristic of hypnotic rapport, the patient reverts mentally to the earliest couple of years of life, when he felt that his parents were omnipotent. In this way the patient experiences reparticipation in the lost omnipotence of his own earliest months of life. When active mastery of his own problems fails hypnosis provides the possibility of a passive-receptive mastery. This, though less intensely, is what all other methods of suggestion provide in some measure.

At the beginning of this century, Dubois (1904)[7] stressed the efficacy of persuasion as a method of treatment.* In persuasion the patient is offered rational grounds for the acceptance of communicated propositions; there is an appeal to reason. Suggestion is present too in persuasion treatment, i.e., a transference relationship has been established on the order of the same conscious over-valuation of the therapist. In the patient's mind he takes over the role of the early powerful protective parent who knew best. The essence of persuasion is that the patient should get well because it is proved to his satisfaction that there is no cause (anatomical, pathophysiological, etc.) to prevent it, whereas the essence of direct suggestion is that the patient will get well because the physician says that he will. It follows from this that the more clearly logical reasons are communicated in persuasion the more it is effective. It also follows that the more the lack of reason behind suggestion gets the attention of the patient, the less likely it is to succeed. Brief psychotherapy is weighted in one way or the other, and it requires considerable skill to know where to put the weight. In regard to this an understanding of the patient's needs and operational intellectual powers are involved. As Rado (1956)[9] has noted, some patients approach the therapist evincing a predominantly magic-craving attitude, others with a parentifying attitude less magically coloured; still others are co-operative on a more adult level in their approach to the therapist.

In sharp contrast to suggestion and persuasion therapies, psychoanalysis comes to demonstrate to the patient the nature of his transferred emotions and drives. This understanding of transference can be traced back to Freud's preoccupation with Breuer's case of Anna O. (Bertha Pappenheim), as he worked with similar cases. For a long time, Freud was struck by the obscurities which clouded the history of Breuer's case, including those connected with the hasty termination of treatment. Ernest Jones (1953)[10] in his biography of Freud writes:

> Freud has related to me a fuller account than he described in his writings of the peculiar circumstances surrounding the end of his novel treatment. It would seem that Breuer had developed what we should nowadays call a strong countertransference to his interesting patient. At all events he was so engrossed that his wife became bored at

---

*For a later exposition, see Jerome Frank (1973),[8] *Persuasion and Healing*.

listening to no other topic, and before long she became jealous. She did not display this openly, but became unhappy and morose. It was a long time before Breuer, with his thoughts elsewhere, divined the meaning of her state of mind. It provoked a violent reaction in him, perhaps compounded of love and guilt, and he decided to bring the treatment to an end. He announced this to Anna O. ..., who was by now much better, and bade her good-bye. But that evening he was fetched back to find her in a greatly excited state, apparently as ill as ever. The patient, who according to him had appeared to be an asexual being and had never made any allusion to such a forbidden topic throughout the treatment, was now in the throes of an hysterical childbirth (pseudocyesis), the logical termination of a phantom pregnancy that had been invisibly developing in response to Breuer's ministrations. Though profoundly shocked, he managed to calm her down by hypnotizing her, and then fled the house in a cold sweat ...

In a study of the therapeutic revolution from hypnosis to psychoanalysis, Léon Chertok and Raymond de Saussure (1979)[11] pointedly contrast Breuer's panic in the Anna O. case with Freud's coolness in the face of similar erotic provocation from women patients. Without questioning the validity of Freud's discovery of transference, they find that there was a defensive aspect, namely a depersonalization of the therapeutic relationship, interposing a third person between the patient and the physician, like the nurse who is present during the gynaecologist's examination.

Bernheim had demonstrated that a patient when awakened from a hypnotic trance could then be induced to remember what had happened during the time of the trance if the physician firmly insisted upon it. Freud tried similar coercion on his patients and eventually found that without using hypnosis he could succeed none the less in achieving catharsis of past traumatic experiences as well as in integrating these experiences in the setting of adequate rapport. He first dispensed with hypnosis in a case refractory to trance, that of Fräulein Elisabeth von R., in the autumn of 1892 (1895).[12] He tried a so-called 'concentration' technique. The patient, lying down with closed eyes, was directed to concentrate her attention on a particular symptom and to try to recall events from which it might have originated. Freud would press her forehead with his hand and suggest that thoughts and memories would come to her. As this worked, he came to give the strict injunction to ignore all censorship and to express every thought even if she considered it to be irrelevant, unimportant, or too unpleasant. This was his first step towards the method of free association. Ernest Jones (1953)[13] writes of this:

Freud was still given to urging, pressing and questioning, which he felt would be hard but necessary work. On one historic occasion, however, the patient, Frl. Elisabeth, reproved him for interrupting her flow of thoughts by his questions. He took the hint and thus made another step towards free association.

At this time, and for a considerable period afterwards, Freud continued to use the symptoms as starting points, and then he used sequential segments of patients' dreams similarly. His discussion of psychotherapy in the *Studies* (1895)[14] shows the inception of the psychoanalytic method which he there called 'psychical analysis' modifying Breuer's 'cathartic method'. It was in his chapter on psychotherapy that he stated the often quoted: 'Much is won if we succeed in transforming hysterical misery into common unhappiness.' As for Elisabeth von R., she had been able to abreact many painful experiences including those punctuating her devoted nursing of her father during his terminal illness, those concerned with her mother's increasing ill-health, those of her first brother-in-law's callousness and of the quarrels between her two brothers-in-law. She was also able to recall her thoughts and feelings of disappointment related to her first love during the time of her father's illness. As Freud (1895)[12] noted it was a tale of suffering enjoining sympathy, and he added: 'But what shall we say of its relations to her painful locomotor weakness, and the chances of an explanation and cure afforded by our knowledge of these psychical traumas?' Indeed the patient came to share in the investigative psychotherapy. It became evident that there were connections between the forgotten pathogenic scenes and the symptoms. Elisabeth von R. was finally able to remember her guilt-ridden fleeting wish to marry her (second) brother-in-law, a wish which had come to her unbidden at the deathbed of her sister. This memory, together with those of other misfortunes, had been converted to the painful astasia–abasia. There were associations between her painful mental impressions and the bodily pains, the latter symbolizing the former. Moreover, they symbolized her eventual difficulty, following sustaining terrible personal losses, in 'standing alone'. Freud considered that some connections between the experiences and the symptoms had been originally asymbolic and embedded in associations of simultaneity of events. Moreover he found that conversion did not take place in connection with her painful impressions when they were fresh, but in connection with her memories of them. 'I believe,' he wrote (1895),[12] 'that such a course of events is nothing unusual in hysteria and indeed plays a regular part in the genesis of hysterical symptoms.'

As Erikson (1956)[15] has pointed out, this approach involved for Freud the relinquishment of the usual doctor role, that of the all-knowing father, which was at the time quite safely anchored in the whole contemporary cult of the paternal male as the master of every human endeavour except in the nursery and the kitchen. Indeed, already in the *Studies on Hysteria* (1895) an evolutionary change in the doctor-patient relationship is irregularly and gradually adumbrated. Breuer and Freud, from the beginning of their studies, were bound to respect the sometimes outstanding talents and characters of their patients, rather than to lose themselves in the prevalent global notion of degeneracy as the hallmark of hysteria (Nordau, 1895[61]). Bram (1965),[17] in 'The Gift of Anna O.', tries to show that the primordium of psychoanalytic thinking and technique did not develop simply as a matter of chance, but was involved in the patient's intensive relationship with Breuer in which she participated in joint creative activity with him. Breuer stopped the treatment because of the resulting assault at that time on his own sense of identity and his fear of departing so far from the orthodox doctor-patient relationship. It remained for Freud to offer the patient a conscious and direct partnership, making the healthy part of the mind of the patient a partner in the joint understanding of the unhealthy parts. Thus was established a basic principle of psychoanalysis which may be stated in the words of Erikson (1956):[15] 'One can study the human mind only by engaging the fully motivated partnership of the observed individual, and by entering into a sincere contract with him.'

In various types of psychotherapy the gold of analysis is alloyed with the copper of suggestion and the silver of persuasion in various proportions. Associated with these three elements are the following factors:

1. The development of a personal relationship between the physician and the patient.
2. 'Abreaction' or the verbal expression of the emotional difficulties and emotionally toned experiences and fantasies of the patient, within the framework of this relationship.
3. The communication of propositions to the patient in an attempt to strengthen his personality by insight.

The transference aspects of the relationship between physician and patient remain unanalysed in suggestion and persuasion therapy. The communication of insight is most effectively accomplished by means of prolonged transference analysis. Briefly in direct suggestion under hypnosis the exaggerated dependency relationship to the physician enables him to communicate positive notions which the patient accepts. On account of the diminished resistance which characterizes the state of hypnosis the therapist is able alternatively, or first of all, to induce considerable abreaction. In waking suggestion and in distributive discussions with a patient, derivatives of the warded-off impulses and emotions find expression in the patient's communications—that is to say, abreaction is more gently induced. It is possible too, on the basis of the material communicated by the patient, to offer interpretations which convey insight of one sort or another. This insight may relate to his real situation in life or to his current conflicts (his defence against wishes), or it may be concerned with the influence of his childhood experiences on his current difficulties. Generally speaking, in the psychoneuroses a single or a few abreactive sessions, even if in the waking state and accompanied by attempts to convey insight, are necessarily of limited efficacy; such sessions cannot accomplish as much of a solution of the defence struggle as the 'working through' in analysis eventually may, as we shall see.

There is a popular dichotomy which categorizes psychotherapies into 'covering' and 'uncovering' types, a categorization which supplements the divisions into suggestion, persuasion and analysis. Just as these latter divisions are not necessarily mutually exclusive in practice, so the dichotomy into 'covering' and 'uncovering' psychotherapies is not so sharp as is sometimes imagined. Fenichel (1945)[18] writes: 'The neurotic conflict is the basis of every psychoneurosis. Only a change in the dynamic relations of the constituents of this conflict can change the neurosis. In principle, this can be done in two ways: either by an increase or by an annulment of the defence', that is, by a covering or uncovering type of psychotherapy. Since, however, an undoing of a repression might be used for the intensification of another repression, a psychotherapy may be wittingly or unwittingly 'covering' or 'uncovering' in varying proportions. In brief psychotherapy, in the setting of the support offered by the relationship to the physician, 'abreaction' may be restricted to recent disturbing events, and 'interpretation' mainly directed towards the detection and relationship of repetitious patterns of behaviour and to the tasks in reality with which the patient is currently confronted. (It may be considered better to speak of 'clarification' rather than 'interpretation' in so far as the procedure does not engage in the elevation to awareness of unconscious defences, strivings and fantasies.) Attempts at more deep-reaching psychotherapy may often defeat the avowed purpose in that the interpretations, though correct as deductions concerning unconscious dynamics and genetics, and even effective and in some measure ego strengthening, are *interceptive*, blocking the fuller development of the transference neurosis and the fuller illumination of the defence struggle which this affords. Psychoanalytically orientated psychotherapy, using the conceptual tools of psychoanalysis, including repression, unconscious infantile sexuality, and derivative theory, may wittingly modify the technique in order to make analysis possible in at least some measure, or in order to avert a severe regression or psychotic eruption. It may also be necessary to limit the goal of a psychoanalytically orientated psychotherapy to symptom relief; this decision will be based on the nature of the disorder, its particular phase, and an evaluation of the personality of the patient and his life situation.

The neuroses may be roughly classified according to their accessibility to psychoanalysis and psychoanalytically orientated psychotherapy in the following order: hysteria, compulsion neuroses, neurotic depressions, character disturbances, perversions, addictions, and impulse neuroses. Many promising psychotherapeutic efforts in recent decades have been devoted to schizophrenic patients (Volkan, 1976[19]). Regarding prolonged and intensive psychotherapy of psychosis, we need more information about the variations from the 'model' technique of psychoanalysis and their relationship to the genetics and dynamics of the disease process (Abse and Ewing, 1960;[20] Will, 1961;[21] Searles, 1961;[22] Burnham, 1961;[23] Karon and Vandenbos, 1981[24]).

As Fenichel (1945)[18] wrote:

Classification is of general value only. Complications may make the analysis of a hysteric especially difficult or of a schizophrenic relatively easy. Many other circumstances must be considered in making the prognosis: the general dynamic relationship between resistances and the wish for recovery, the secondary gains, the general flexibility of the person.

It is not only the structure of the neuroses but the personality of the patient and his particular life situation that need to be taken into account. Psychotherapy is a mutual enterprise and time and money are consumed in prolonged and intensive forms of it. When possible, with younger people the diagnoses mentioned above are indications for psychoanalytic psychotherapy. With older people more regard than is often shown should be paid to their life situation. Briefer psychoanalytically orientated methods judiciously employing suggestion and persuasion should be considered. For some people a trial period in psychoanalytic therapy may demonstrate a severity of regression which is not confined to the analytic situation, and which eludes confinement within the treatment sessions. In such instances considerable modification of technique may be necessary in order to avoid disruptive events in the life situation. The aphorism that one cannot make an omelette without breaking eggs is a poor consolation for the patient and his reference group when the situations produced during a chaotic phase are irretrievable.

In a subsequent section of this present chapter, the complementary functions of group analysis and psychoanalysis are discussed. Meanwhile, it is to be noted that group-analytic psychotherapy as pioneered in the United Kingdom by S. H. Foulkes and colleagues (1948,[25] 1964,[26] 1965[27]), properly conducted, affords support and promotes abreaction, reality testing and the acquisition of insight; access to unconscious dynamics, though less pronounced than in individual analysis, is often secured. In general there is less danger of a partial dissolution of so-called 'autonomous ego functions', and for this reason borderline states and severe character neuroses often respond favourably without seriously adverse events in their life situation. Certainly this method of psychotherapy promises the possibility of dealing more adequately with some patients who are unamenable in individual psychotherapy. Moreover, the group-analytic experience sometimes reaches into areas of personality functioning otherwise unexplored in individual forms of treatment, and sometimes with considerable benefit for patients who have previously been in prolonged analysis.

Now it is as well to mention that psychotherapists of all schools have from time to time reported remarkable changes in patients within a short period of treatment. The least explored aspect of this concerns those self-curative forces which sometimes are mobilized through suggestion by the therapist. Sometimes these announce themselves if not prevented from doing so by clumsy therapy. This is one of many reasons why the public needs safeguards against the deluge of those without specialized knowledge and experience who bungle the delicate tasks involved in psychotherapy. After all, there may be only two kinds of psychotherapy: good and bad. But this also is not a simple matter, for a therapy may afford symptom relief at the same time that it suppresses the potentials for self-discovery and self-development.

The Dora Analysis Revisited

In the dyadic psychoanalytic situation established gradually by Freud, free association came to be used as a substitute for the direct memory recall enjoined in hypnosis. In hypnotic sessions, recollection of repressed events was utilized both to reconstruct aetiology and to discharge those emotions linked to past traumatic experiences. In the replacement of the cathartic-hypnotic sessions by those of relaxation and free association, Freud remained convinced of the therapeutic importance of the discharge of emotion. The patient in the free association sessions was led to recall the past gradually, and simultaneously to express verbally the formerly repressed feelings associated with the painful events of the past. Free association differed from cathartic-hypnosis in that the patient's recollections and discharge of emotion took place in smaller quantities over a longer period. This differed from the former more dramatic hypnotic sessions with their attendant massive abreactions.

Eventually, Freud perceived the cardinal importance of enabling the patient to make such changes in his or her ego which allowed for remembering painful experiences and for coping with emotional constellations which had previously been unbearable. Ego resistance required reduction by bringing about substantial changes in defences rather than by rendering the ego well-nigh defenceless through hypnotic trance.

The Dora (Ida Bauer) case occupies an important historical transitional position in Freud's work as he began to create the psychoanalytic situation. It is not only a link between his theory of dreaming and the theory of libidinal development, but it also illustrates a way-station between symptom-analysis and transference analysis. In the Prefatory Remarks, Freud (1905)[28] wrote:

At that time [the time of the *Studies on Hysteria* 1893–1895], the work of analysis started out from the symptoms, and aimed at clearing them up one after the other. Since then I have abandoned that technique, because I found it totally inadequate for dealing with the structure of the neurosis. I now let the patient himself choose the subject of the day's work, and in that way I start out from whatever surface his unconscious happens to be presenting to his notice at the moment …

Later, in the Post-Script, he plainly acknowledged that he 'did not succeed in mastering the transference in good time,' that the transference took him 'unawares, and because of the unknown quantity—one which reminded Dora of Herr K—she took her revenge on me as she wanted to take her revenge on him, and deserted me as she believed herself to have been deceived and deserted by him. Thus she acted out an essential part of her recollections and fantasies instead of reproducing it in the treatment …' Freud suspected that the 'unknown quantity' which stimulated excessive transference distortion may have had to do with money and with jealousy of another patient who had kept up relations with the Freud family after her recovery.

Dora's parents were unhappy in their marriage. Their friends, Herr and Frau K., were also in a situation of marital tension and discord. Dora's mother developed a *Hausfrau* neurosis, partly as a means of revenge against her husband. Dora's father resorted to a liaison with his friend's wife, Frau K. This lady also enriched her life with a warm relationship with Dora. Herr K. paid Dora much attention for several years too, and then when she was almost 18 years old, began a speech at an outing with her at a lake, avowing his love and the hope of marrying her after divorce. Dora, however, struck him in the face, fled, complained to her parents and clamoured for the family relationship with this other couple, her former friends, to be entirely broken off. She also suffered a recurrence of nervous coughing and aphonia, and of depression, from which she had suffered at times from her eighth year. She had also suffered from the age of 8 dyspnoeic attacks and, from the age of 12, attacks of headache.

Two Family Dynamics: Doubling and Splitting

The dynamics of the relationships within and between members of the two families in the Dora case are described by Freud. His remark that maybe Dora's unspoken jealousy of another patient who had kept up relations with the Freud family after her recovery contributed to the demoost exclusively composed of her family and the K. family in transaction. We receive an impression of individual neurotic characters in interaction with members of their own family and with members of the other family, and of Dora being finally precipitated into Freud's office as the 'identified patient'. A kind of doubling of the family had gradually occurred from the starting point of Frau

K.'s nursing of Dora's father through a long illness; and from this overt participation in the cure of physical illness, covert attempts at cure of neurosis took place in the intimate friendships of members of the two families. *Pari passu* with the doubling of the family are obvious splitting defensive measures within individuals at different levels. These range from the level of clear hypocrisy and deceit, of attitudes, strivings and feelings and actions about which silence is enjoined and secrets kept (or, on challenge, rationalizations deployed) to those at an unconscious ego level. These comprise both an acknowledgement and disavowal of wishes, fantasies and actions, and the solution of conflicts of ambivalence by means of regression with the projection of 'good' and 'bad' object representations on to this or that member of this or the other family. All these defensive struggles are accomplished in the context of allegiances and divided allegiances, of affiliations and disaffiliations within the clanship of the two families, ending up with Dora's insistence on a rupture of the double family situation into its two separate family constituents. To be brief, some of this, which is illustrated time and again in the material which Freud presents, can be shown by one of Dora's father's speeches reported by Freud:

I have no doubt ... that this incident [the erotic proposal by the lake] is responsible for Dora's depression and irritability and suicidal ideas. She keeps pressing me to break off relations with Herr K. and more particularly with Frau K., whom she used positively to worship formerly. But that I cannot do. For, to begin with, I myself believe that Dora's tale of the man's immoral suggestions is a fantasy that has forced its way into her mind; and besides, I am bound to Frau K. by ties of honourable friendship and I do not wish to cause her pain. The poor woman is most unhappy with her husband, of whom, by the way, I have no very high opinion. She herself has suffered a great deal with her nerves, and I am her only support. With my state of health I need scarcely assure you that there is nothing wrong in our relations. We are just two poor wretches who give one another what comfort we can by an exchange of friendly sympathy. You know already that I get nothing out of my own wife. But Dora, who inherits my obstinacy, cannot be moved from her hatred of the K.'s. She had her last attack after a conversation in which she again pressed me to break with them. Please try to bring her to reason.

Freud had explained earlier that Dora's older brother (later a famous politician) used to try as far as he could to keep out of the family disputes; but when he was obliged to take sides he would support his mother. The compulsive mother was occupied all day long in keeping the house clean; and Dora criticized her mercilessly, and had 'withdrawn completely from her influence'. Freud notes that 'the usual sexual attraction had drawn together the father and daughter on the one side and mother and son on the other'. This amounted to the 'perverse triangle' now discussed by family therapists, certainly in Dora's case, and yet another seems to have existed for her brother in his childhood. So far as we know there were no highly significant counter-players for him in the K. family, whereas for Dora, Mr and Mrs K. and their two children were all involved in her efforts to replay and rework her intrafamilial conflicts.

Freud points out that Dora's reproaches against her father, which had come to the foreground before the treatment was instituted, had a 'lining' of self-reproaches. While she was right in thinking that her father did not wish to look too closely into Herr K.'s behaviour towards her for fear of being disturbed in his own love-affair with Frau K., Dora had previously made herself an accomplice in the affair and had dismissed from her mind every sign of its true character, until after the adventure by the lake. Indeed there had been someone in the house who had been eager to open her eyes to the nature of Frau K.'s relationship with her father and to induce her to take sides against her. This was her own last governess, and later there was another governess in her double family drama, the governess of the two children in the K. family. Both these governesses were heavily involved in inflicting narcissistic injuries which had considerable aetiologic importance in the origin and exacerbation of Dora's neurosis. Freud amply describes some aspects of her wounded pride without elaborating on its theoretical salience as would no doubt be done today.

The Dreams and Transference

As Jones (1955)[29] states, Freud's main object in publishing this case was to illustrate the value the interpretation of dreams has for analytic treatment. The analysis of the dreams revealed Dora's sexual love for her father, for Herr K. and for his wife, all of which had been repressed. The dreams also revealed a complicated interplay of hatred, disgust and jealousy connected with these plural sexual interests and demands for attention.

In connection with the final repetitive dream (which starts with a house on fire and to which, on the next day after first reporting it to Freud, Dora brought the addendum of smelling smoke after awakening) it became apparent that she knew that her father had fallen ill through a venereal infection before marriage, and that she ascribed her mother's later abdominal pains and vaginal catarrh to venereal infection from her father. Moreover, 'symptomatic acts and certain other signs' led Freud to trace her dyspnoea at the age of 8 to her overhearing her father breathing hard during sexual intercourse. The synthesis of this first dream included revealing her feeling that she had been recently threatened with a serious danger. The dream indeed first occurred following Herr K.'s proposal at the lake, and his later intrusion into her bedroom. The synthesis also included her intention to depart with her father; further it expressed a childhood wish to be rescued by her good affectionate father from her bad father (who had anyway in fact brought her into this danger situation) and who was now represented by the sexually aggressive Herr K. All this is elaborated by Freud and the 'synthesis' is buttressed by many details derived from items of behaviour of other family members, as, for example, Dora's mother's tormenting passion for cleanliness, and by a number of conjectures, some based upon Freud's experience with other patients.

One has the impression generally, evident in his discussion of switch words and switch phrases ('catarrh', 'leave the room') and of antitheses such as 'fire' and 'wetness', that Freud was very active in his work with Dora, and this in the teeth of high resistance, and in directions which were likely to evoke in her much anxiety. In a footnote related to interpretations of sexual symbolism and of incestuous wishes which he had offered to Dora, Freud writes:

I added: Moreover the re-appearance of the dream in the last few days forces me to the conclusion that you consider that the same situation has arisen once again, and that you have decided to give up the treatment—to which, after all, it is only your father who makes you come. The sequel showed how correct my guess had been. At this point my interpretation touches for a moment upon the subject of transference—a theme which is of the highest practical and theoretical importance, but into which I shall not have much further opportunity of entering in the present paper.

However, Freud discusses the transference problem at length in the Post-Script. He was going far too rapidly in terms of dream content generally with Dora, and he was catching up rapidly with himself in regard to the transference aspects. As for Jones's (1955)[29] statement that Freud's main object in publishing this case was to illustrate the value the interpretation of dreams has for analytic treatment, it should be added that in this case the transference aspects had been largely neglected, with the consequent premature termination of the treatment by the patient. The smoking analyst was not immediately aware of the fire that had been kindled in the analytic room.

Freud notes the speech made by the father ('I refuse to let myself and my two children be burnt for the sake of your jewel-case') in the first dream and states his belief that such speeches are regularly constructed out of pieces of active speeches which have either been made or heard. According to Freud (1900)[30] there is thus no creation of speeches in dreams, and they are to be regarded as speeches which the dreamer has actually heard (or read) in reality, usually within the preceding day. The speeches may undergo, in the course of the dreamwork, distortions, condensation and secondary revision. A portion of a speech actually heard may be selected and another omitted, or fragments originally unconnected may be put together. Robert Fliess (1953)[31] suggests that the appearance of a speech in a dream comprises a representation of the super-ego, and that the conditions laid down by Freud for speeches to occur in dreams are not invariable. Sometimes there is affirmation of an ideal ego through a speech in a dream. This may be the case in this dream wherein Dora achieves multiple identifications. It seems to me that one fundamental meaning is related to the primal scene: mother wanted to stop and save her jewel-case but father insisted that fertilization must occur, despite the sacrifice. Thus a primitive masculine ideal is ruthlessly asserted, and reveals the depth of Dora's sadomasochistic wish-fantasies and terror. There are, of course, many ramifications of this fundamental theme: Dora's knowledge of her father's luetic infection before marriage led her to feel he ought not to have married and infected her mother though then two children would not have been born; thus he protected himself and his two testicles (his children), but the children had consequent nervous vulnerabilities, as she thought (so did Freud though he did not give voice to this). Thus there is a double view of the father (of the good and bad father) which gets into a tangle in her thoughts which are infiltrated with notions of phallic cruelty to which she is both drawn and aversive.

Freud's preoccupation with switch words and phrases, his repetitions of 'no smoke without fire' seem to *partly* represent his unexamined countertransference to Dora's ambivalent sadomasochistic erotic transference. He spends a great deal of time in his presentation of the Dora case justifying disregard of the usual considerations of discretion, quoting from Richard Schmidt's book *Essays on Indian Eroticism*, and this seems also to be *partly* a displacement of countertransference feelings generated in the analytic situation with Dora. Freud (1900)[30] had already expressed some of his guilty emotional reactions to implied reproaches of indiscretion (loose tonguedness) and sadistic piercing looks, for example, in passages of the 'Non Vixit' dream analysis, a dream actually concerned with the topic of his own ambitions. Working with Freud on these two dreams must have seemed to the already coerced Dora as further evidence of a man's coercion of her, that she was being treated as a specimen in the service of his wishes (ambitious wishes in Freud's case). Rescue or assistance are rejected in the second dream entirely, and vengeance is completed with the final addendum that while the others were at the cemetry burying her father, she 'not the least sadly' began reading a big book on her writing table. It is evident that the transference message that she would run away, unless she was loved and not treated merely as a vehicle for other people's purposes, erotic or ambitious, was embedded in both dreams. Freud asks the question as to whether he might have kept her in treatment if he had shown 'a warm personal interest in her', and we can also wonder whether if his investigative zeal concerned with dreams had been tempered by a greater regard for and analysis of the transference, and by a reduction of inexpedient defences of his own in the analytic situation, this warm personal regard may not have sufficiently emerged—as it did, of course, with patients in later work. But after all, Freud had to learn the hard way too; indeed his was the hardest task of all!

In his monograph on scopophilic-exhibitionistic conflicts, David W. Allen (1974)[32] emphasized that in the psychoanalytic psychotherapeutic process the therapist must feel free to look, and to show what he has seen. This is especially true of transference phenomena. Reciprocally the patient gains the freedom to show himself or herself and to observe both inwardly and outwardly. In regard to Freud's psychoanalytic work, Allen dwells instructively on Freud's successfully sublimated scopophilia and exhibitionism. This success followed a phase of less resolved conflicts broadly hinted at in his presentation of the case of Dora. It is necessary to pay heed to those who have criticized the efforts of Sigmund Freud in his psychotherapeutic work with Dora, especially those concerned with turmoil in adolescence. Erikson (1962)[33] writing, as others, from the vantage point of more than half a century of evolution of psychoanalysis as therapy, stated:

> How many of us can follow today without protest Freud's assertion that a healthy girl of 14 would, under such circumstances, have considered Mr. K.s advances 'neither tactless nor offensive'. The nature and severity of Dora's pathological reaction make her the classical hysteric of her case history; but her motivation for falling ill, and her lack of motivation for getting well, today seem to call for development considerations.

Peter Blos (1972)[34] comments:

> As we consider Dora's disruption of her analysis in developmental terms, we could say today that the consolidation of her neurotic defences had been aggravated by the fact that her analysis was being conducted as if an adult neurosis already existed. As a consequence, the adolescent ego became overwhelmed by interpretations it was unable

to integrate, and it simply took to flight. If there is one thing adolescent analysis has taught us, it is that ill-timed id interpretations are unconsciously experienced by the adolescent as a parental—that is, incestuous—seduction.

Arnold A. Rogow (1978)[35] has noted:

Perhaps no other case of Freud's, not excluding that of Schreber or the Wolfman, has received so much comment and criticism from such a variety of sources, including in addition to psychoanalysts and psychiatrists, sociologists, historians, psychologists, political scientists, literary critics, and novelists. The vicissitudes of Dora's analysis and questions about Freud's treatment of his adolescent patient, the importance of the case in the evolution of psychoanalytic theory and technique, the relevance of Dora to an understanding of manners and morals in *fin-de-siècle* Vienna, Dora's place in the long history of women's efforts to liberate themselves from male oppression, even the status of the case as, in Steven Marcus's words, 'a great work of literature'—these aspects of Dora do not exhaust the range of interests and viewpoints to which the case lends itself. Clearly Dora's three months with Freud have a significance far beyond the clinical aspects of psychoanalysis.

There is another clinical aspect which is relevant here. It has been discussed lucidly by Russell Meares (1976)[36] who points out that the revelation of secrets lies at the core of uncovering varieties of psychotherapy, and that the notion of 'the secret' can therefore be regarded as critical to an understanding of the psychotherapeutic process. As Breuer and Freud (1893)[37] acknowledged in their preliminary communication, they found the nearest approach to their theoretical and therapeutic views concerning hysteria in those propounded by Moritz Benedikt (1864)[37] who first formulated the concept of the pathogenic secret. The Dora case is obviously replete with guilty family secrets. Meares (1976)[36] draws attention to the way that secrets are disclosed with care in a developing dialogue with another who can be trusted to share and respect them. 'They then become the coins of intimacy and the currency of its transactions,' he writes. But the need to confess and expiate guilt is more or less obstructed by fear of condemnation or rejection or betrayal. And the need for an intimate relationship by sharing secrets is thus also counterbalanced by a fear of ensuing damage to the self-system. Both secrecy and the sharing of secrets in an intimate relationship are invariably unconsciously entangled with sexuality.

Maurice Apprey (1983)[87] has emphasized the high degree to which fathers have blatant incestuous strivings towards their troubled adolescent daughters, a fact which becomes apparent during psychotherapy. He writes:

Sadly, Freud rejected the idea of father as the source of the traumatogenic incestuous strivings in his theory of neurosis in Letter 69 written on September 21st, 1887, (S.E. 1: 259–160). Nevertheless, we can see in our clinical work how incestuous feelings in parents persist and how they are reciprocated by the resurgence of Oedipal strivings in the adolescent.

Apprey (1983)[87] provided group therapy to these fathers to facilitate the transformation of their incestuous strivings into non-sexual affirmation of their daughters' emergence into womanhood. He suggests that psychotherapy of these young women requires a two-pronged Janusian approach.

One face looks toward the adolescent liminars who have to negotiate in their ambiguous place such issues as their incestuous strivings and their sexual organization. The other face looks at the task of the parents of adolescents as they transform their own incestuous strivings toward their children into a non-sexual parental affirmation ...

Apprey thus identifies adolescent pathology as often a crisis simultaneously in the family life cycle and in the adolescent's individual development. These considerations have an obvious bearing on the family drama in which Dora had her troubled existence at the time of her psychotherapy with Freud.

Short-Term Dynamic Psychotherapy

Writing almost 50 years ago Wilhelm Stekel (1938)[38] contended that ...

orthodox analysis has reached a crisis which betokens that the end is near, that collapse is approaching. Clinical records of its successes count for nothing now. The happy days of interminable analyses are gone for ever. The public has awakened, and there are few countries nowadays in which people can afford such luxuries. Analysts must adapt themselves to the idea of short periods of treatment ...

It is evident that ever since Freud's method led to longer and longer analyses, efforts were made to curtail the length of treatment so that it could be applied to more people, and so that analytic psychotherapy could be in the currently overused phrase 'cost-effective'. Yet psychoanalysis of years' duration has continued to flourish side-by-side with the briefer psychotherapies, despite financial difficulties and its detractors. Indeed, as has occurred in my own practice during several decades, many psychiatrists use both long and short-term methods of treatment as is feasible and practical. There are, of course, enthusiastic protagonists who exclusively utilize one or the other type of psychotherapy. David H. Malan (1980)[39] writes:

In patient after patient it can be demonstrated that improvement begins immediately following certain types of events in therapy, particularly the open acknowledgement of hostility in the transference, followed by an interpretation linking patterns in the transference relationship with similar patterns in current and past relationships. Davanloo refers to this as a T-C-P interpretation and has demonstrated time and again, with audiovisual proof, the impact of such interpretations on the patient, both during therapy and in the initial interview itself.

Although I do not share many of the views propounded by Wilhelm Stekel in his *Technik der Analytischen Psychotherapie*, I benefited from his book 40 years ago and have applied his technique with success in work with many patients, with modifications over the years, and this technique is essentially that now advocated by Davanloo and treated as a brilliant new discovery by Malan. What is certainly new is the use of audiovisual monitoring apparatus and the drastic curtailment of time spent with the patient to the few sessions required by the majority of hypnotherapists who followed in the wake of Hyppolyte Bernheim at the turn of the century.

As Malan (1980)[39] indicates, all the analysts who made attempts to develop a brief method realized that more activity, and less passivity, on the part of the therapist was required in the psychotherapeutic enterprise if the length of time was to be effectively shortened. Following in Stekel's path were Ferenczi and Rank (1925)[40] and Alexander and French (1946).[41] Stekel first pointed out that lengthy analyses entailed certain risks; he became concerned with 'an analytically inculcated infantilism' and an 'analytically induced brooding-obsession'. Alexander and French (1946)[41] discussed not only the lengthiness but the frequency of interviews which could gratify some patients' dependent needs more than was desirable, and could in some cases, exercise a seductive influence on some patients' regressive and procrastinating tendencies. Ferenczi and Rank recommended as one active measure that a term should be set to the treatment, but soon Ferenczi (1925)[42] declared that setting a term had proved a ticklish matter in some cases, and that with some patients he found it necessary to continue the analysis, achieving success only in prolonged treatment.

Sifneos (1972,[43] 1979[44]) has more recently claimed that there are patients suffering from circumscribed problems based on the male or female Oedipus complex who can be substantially helped in a maximum of 15 sessions. Malan (1963,[45] 1976[46]) claims that there are often categories of patients in whom longstanding character problems can be substantially relieved in a maximum of 40 sessions.

The Corrective Emotional Experience

Alexander (1956)[47] propounded the view that both in psychoanalysis and in briefer psychoanalytically orientated types of psychotherapy, an essential element consists of the patient's corrective emotional experience. The central therapeutic element is an experience of difference in the relationship with the therapist from that which characterized the childhood relationship with the parents. The therapist's reaction, and his responses, to the patient's fantasies and feelings emphasize a difference from the attitudes displayed by the parents during his formative years. In shortening therapy, the therapist requires to be more active in generating a climate that allows the patient to experience the difference between the present attitude of the therapist and the past attitude of the parents where similarities in the psychological situation of the patient are repeated in the transference. In all forms of aetiological psychotherapy, according to Alexander, the basic therapeutic principle is the same: to re-expose the patient, under more favourable circumstances, to emotional situations which he could not handle in the past. The patient, in order to be helped, must undergo a corrective emotional experience suitable to repair the traumatic influence of previous experience. Just because the therapist's attitude is different from that of the authoritative person of the past, the patient has an opportunity to face again and again, a revival of emotional situations, formerly unbearable, in a more favourable context.

Writing of battle neurosis, Alexander and French (1946)[41] note that a graphic illustration of such a corrective experience is afforded by the procedure of narcosynthesis. Under mild narcosis, the patient re-lives in vivid imagery the dangers of combat which he had been unable to master in reality. The pharmacological effect of the narcotic and the presence of the therapist in whom he has confidence reduce the intensity of anxiety, and the patient is thus able to face the revived situation in fantasy more adequately, the very one to which he had succumbed formerly. We have already discussed some aspects of such therapy in Chapter 1 (p. 17). Entailed is a *therapeutic regression*, and this is an essential element in every type of psychoanalytic psychotherapy, long or short. In discussing his research project utilizing psychedelic drugs as adjuncts to analytic psychotherapy, John Buckman (1969)[48] alludes to the corrective emotional experience involved. He remarks:

> LSD is here used in order to bring to full consciousness and with great emotional impact forgotten or poorly repressed memories, fantasies and conflicts many of which have origins in the patient's childhood or even infancy and some of which are obviously archetypes shrouded in a good deal of magical and superstitious thinking. The advantage of using LSD is that with suitable doses the patient is able, with minimal clouding of consciousness, to gain very vivid access to some of the more primitive illogical recesses of his mind. The fact that he may be able after prolonged preparation and in an atmosphere of trust and support to relive these conflicts may produce for him what is called a corrective emotional experience, as a result of which there may be considerable modification of internalised early figures, especially those consolidated within a punitive archaic super-ego.

As Alexander (1956)[47] repeatedly pointed out, though he has been grossly misunderstood and misrepresented in this regard, the corrective emotional experience is a necessary part of the cure even in the case of the analyst who comes out from his shell of observational reserve only when absolutely necessary to interpret resistance and transference. However, in some cases, a special climate is usefully cultivated to emphasize the difference of the current from the past experience. In some quarters nowadays, and from another theoretical standpoint, the Kohutian therapist strives to repair early narcissistic injuries by emulation of a responsive-empathic maternal self-object during therapeutic regression and revival of primitive relatedness. The emphasis, that is, by the psychoanalytic self psychologist is placed on 'the stunted self' and its need for a self-object in order to complete its development (Kohut, 1971,[106] 1977[107]).

Psychoanalysis and Group Psychotherapy

F. W. Graham (1984)[49] points out that it is mistaken to view group analysis quite apart from psychoanalysis proper, and he discusses the resistances so often shown by psychoanalysts to participation in and understanding of group-analytic psychotherapy. As Graham emphasizes, the essence of both psychoanalysis and group-analytic psychotherapy resides in the management of resistance and transference. 'Management' is, of course, a blanket term covering many analytic activities, especially verbal interventions, including interpretation of defences, the elucidation of fantasies, notably those of the transference and the recovery of memories. Victor H. Rosen (1975)[50] proposed a schema of interventions in psychoanalytic therapy. He included nine categories, eight besides that of the crucial interpretative nature. All the interventions by the analyst are the means whereby he contributed to the working alliance, towards the goal which Graham (1984)[49] defined so well as 'the retrieving of split-off parts of the self, expanding of ego functions, an increased capacity to bear tensions and to mourn adequately, and a libidinal shift towards a strengthening of the genital character position.' How comparatively successfully can the quest be pursued in the group and individual modalities, that is, how useful is each method as a means to reach the goals? Moreover, how complementary are these two methods and to what extent may one interfere with the other? As Dr Graham indicates, such questions have been but seldom addressed.

I recently attempted to explore these problems, including the paradox in group-analytic psychotherapy of greater access to narcissistic resistances but fewer possibilities for their detailed exploration compared with individual analysis (Abse, 1983[51]). Furthermore, the end-phase in group-analytic psychotherapy has limitations related to and overlapping with that of frequency of sessions. The group member exhibiting separation anxiety, depressive emotions and idiosyncratic fantasies because of the momentous impact of the group's impending dissolution will have much less time in each session for considering termination phenomena than in individual analysis. Similar difficulties of 'working through' obviously also apply to short-term dynamic psychotherapy of the dyadic type discussed above.

The analyst in the psychoanalytic situation has to demonstrate to the patient again and again the pathogenic defence and help him recognize and then elucidate the unconscious impulse and fantasy. Freud (1914)[52] noted that working through describes that 'part of the work which effects the greatest changes in the patient and which distinguishes analytic treatment from any kind of treatment by suggestion'. Sedler (1983)[53] usefully emphasized that working through is accomplished only with the active participation of the patient striving for recovery from the neurotic illness: he criticized the one-sided focus in the literature on the analyst's point of view. He quotes Fenichel (1945):[54]

> Systematic and consistent interpretive work, both within and without the framework of the transference, can be described as educating the patient to produce continually less distorted derivatives, until his fundamental instinctual conflicts are recognizable. Of course this is not a single operation, resulting in a single act of abreaction; it is, rather, a chronic process of working through, which shows the patient again and again the same conflicts and his usual way of reacting to them, but from new angles and in new connections.

Sedler (1983)[53] lays more weight on the patient's task in the working through process. It is a labour to be accomplished by the patient which the neurosis has, for so long, served to postpone. It is the labour of transformation that makes possible the shedding of the neurotic encumbrance and its symptomatic trappings in favour of a healthier, more rewarding adaptation. Freud (1893)[55] had early on discussed 'working over' in the context of the trauma theory of hysteria. His 'Preliminary Communication' maintained that the traumatic situation could have been rendered relatively harmless by an immediate energetic reaction 'from tears to acts of revenge'. However, when in the nature of the situation such action was precluded, speech availed to abreact the strangulated affects 'almost as effectively'. Failing these responses of action and/or speech, the traumatic event retained its pathogenic power. In the same year Freud defined 'working over' as a means to deal with the affects generated by the psychical trauma even when adequate motor and speech reactions had been absent. In this early formulation, 'working over' consists in the production of various associations, 'including contrasting ideas', in the company of which painful recollections and other associations no longer exert so monolithic a pathogenic force. In the context of consideration of his continuing experience of investigative psychotherapy of hysterical patients, Freud (1895)[14] further elaborated the concept of 'working over' to include the gradual exposure of hidden memories of pathogenic events which intensified abreaction instead of diluting the forcefulness of affect. In this second way, by gradually dispensing with the veil of intermediate associations, core conflicts were approached and thus too the therapeutic problem of recurrence of symptoms. Gradually, following this beginning, the concept of 'working over' became absorbed into that of 'working through', with its basis in the opposition (and sometimes collaboration) of remembering and repeating.

As is well known, in all well-integrated societies ostentatious ceremonies ratify the changes involved in an individual's life crisis. There is organized community support for the individual and participation in crucial events of his life cycle, including the losses he suffers of his relatives and friends. Van Gennep (1908)[56] focused on these *rites de passage* and distinguished three major phases when the activities associated with such ceremonies were examined in terms of their order and content: *séparation* (separation), *marge* (transition) and *agrégation* (incorporation). Rites of separation are prominent in funeral ceremonies and rites of incorporation at marriages, whereas transition rites predominate in pregnancy, betrothal and initiation. However, all these elements are present in every set of ceremonies though not equally developed, and they all may be reduced to a minimum, as in remarriage or adoption.

It has become clear that such rituals are a response to emotional upheavals which they symbolize and they are attempts to alleviate distress for the benefit of both the individual and his community, ensuring continued cohesion and adequate group adaptation. Sometimes the emphasis is on an individual's disease, especially one which may become disruptive for the group if not treated in a healing rite.

These institutionalized rites of passage are by and large adapted to the immediate purpose of 'working over' (in Freud's sense), and this is not to be confused with the full process of 'working through' in psychoanalysis, though one may posit that 'working over—working through' is on a conceptual continuum. Many forms of group therapy have more to do with 'working over' whereas group-analytic therapy aspires, as in psychoanalysis, to full 'working through'. It implements this, in my opinion, to a lesser degree than does a 'successful' individual psychoanalysis. However, a closer approach to the typological ideal is achieved when individual analysis is followed by group analytic psychotherapy. Also, there are individuals whose psychological-mindedness is so deficient that only an experience in a group that breaches their armour can ready them for psychoanalysis. Thus the sequential utilization of psychoanalysis and group-analytic psychotherapy may further the process of thorough 'working through'. It should be emphasized that individual analysis also has its limits, so that analysis may become interminable, and that group-analytic therapy may result in the further 'working through' of otherwise refractory resistances.

Problems in Evaluation of Psychotherapy

For theoretical and practical reasons, notably those related to economic and political considerations, many mental health professionals, including psychiatrists, continue to debate the effectiveness of psychotherapy. In the USA the system of third-party payments for sickness benefits by private insurance corporations has resulted in much bureaucratic ado, raising among other issues the legitimacy of the widespread utilization of psychotherapy. In response, there have been renewed efforts to clarify its indications and its efficacy, without, however, substantial yield of further knowledge which is especially lacking in the desired credible quantification. Julian Meltzoff and Kornreich (1970)[57] whose review of the psychotherapy research literature overlapped with that of Bergin and Strupp (1972)[58] came to the conclusion that the effectiveness of psychotherapy has been amply demonstrated. They weighed the evidence from the controlled experiments of one hundred outcome studies with a wide variety of patient types treated by 'journeymen therapists'. Bergin and Strupp (1972),[58] more dubious, insisted that their criteria for the acceptibility of evidence differed from those of Meltzoff. They noted incidentally that in an earlier review (Bergin, 1967;[59] Dittman, 1966[60]) had scrutinized 14 outcome studies, 10 of which yielded positive results whereas their own analysis of the same 14 studies revealed only 2 strongly indicating favourable results. However, they added: 'We have been fortunate to know a few psychotherapists whom we consider masters of the art, which is precisely our reason for rejecting the more pessimistic side of Eysenck's view'.

In another study, Strupp, Fox and Lessler (1969)[61] addressed the type and quality of therapy, and concluded that the most important ingredient in the therapeutic encounter was the warmth of the relationship established. Many of the patients who reviewed their psychotherapy reported that they had experienced a hitherto unknown degree of acceptance, understanding and respect, and within a framework of benevolent concern and warmth they had been able to look into some of the most troublesome aspects of their behaviour and attitudes. Strupp et al. (1969)[61] write:

> This experience provided a sharp contrast to other human relationships they had known. It could be set up against the criticism, exploitation, and dependency which they had either encouraged themselves or of which they had been the victims, it permitted expression of shameful, anxiety-provoking and painful feelings; and it supplied them with a professional helper who insisted that they examine some of the problems in their lives and work out—on an emotional as well as cognitive level—viable solutions.

Luborsky et al. (1975)[62] in making tallies of outcomes of controlled comparisons of different types of psychotherapies with each other found as had Meltzoff and Kornreich (1970)[57] that most patients in psychotherapy benefitted. They found only significant differences in proportions of patients who improved in different types of individual and group therapy, long term and short term. Moreover, their findings included, (i) that the alleviation of a variety of psychosomatic conditions was accomplished more frequently by a combination of psychotherapy and medication, and (*ii*), that behaviour therapy may be especially suited for the treatment of circumscribed phobias.

In regard to this last finding, the following case illustrates several such sequences noted in clinical practice; of course, these patients are a self-selected group.

Case 57. A middle-aged dentist found himself unable to enter the room where he conducted his work. He had been in practice for many years with increasing success. Over a couple of months he became increasingly distressed by his phobia. He heard about the cures obtained by Dr Joseph Wolpe and following discussion with his physician he was referred to the celebrated psychiatrist. He was put through the usual paces prescribed by Wolpe and emerged cured of his symptom, resuming work promptly and efficiently. Six months later he became depressed, sleepless and this time his physician referred him to me. In psychotherapy, it became increasingly evident that he was enraged with his much younger brother, a prominent physician. He had been unable to afford to go to medical school. Later when in practice he had helped his brother financially to become a physician. His brother now worked in a large and grand professional building opposite where he worked, and he could see this building from his office window. He was ashamed of his jealousy, and had kept it a secret (with associated ambitious fantasies) until in this psychotherapy. Until the year of his sickness he had periodically entertained notions of going to medical school himself and becoming famous as a maxillofacial surgeon. He had begun to address the reality of its being too late, at a time when his brother had become so busy with patients and committees that he had little time to fraternize.

There is no doubt that the behaviour therapy had enabled him to get over the work hump, but it will be apparent that further psychotherapy was necessary. It should be added that in many cases getting back to work after such immobilization often enough initiates a benign cycle as restoration of self-esteem takes places. However, there are cases such as this one briefly described where further psychotherapeutic efforts are obviously necessary.

Strupp and Hadley (1977)[63] have noted that there may be *negative effects* following a psychotherapy which relieves the presenting symptoms:

An illustration of this outcome would be a person who entered some form of highly directive therapy aimed at the modification of maladaptive behaviour such as nail biting or insomnia. As a result of therapy, the individual might learn to master the problem and experience a greater sense of well-being. Such a person would be rated by himself and society as improved. The therapist would likewise consider the therapy a success. However, a more dynamically orientated or broadly trained mental health professional might judge that the patient had achieved the behavioural changes at the cost of increased rigidity and compulsivity. This, in turn might render the patient more susceptible to exacerbations (e.g. depression) at a later period in his life. Such outcomes are by no means uncommon, and they may occur as a function of training programs in assertiveness, self-control etc.

It is also to be noted that following psychotherapy, there may be quite considerable beneficial effects that are delayed.

It is evident that we have entered a thorny thicket, and one which is obviously further complicated when we take into consideration 'maintenance psychotherapy.' Here is a brief report of an experience in psychotherapy doubtless familiar to many practising psychotherapists.

Case 57. In the course of psychotherapy a young woman lost her schizophrenic symptoms and instead showed those of obsessional neurosis. Attendance in psychotherapy became limited to once a week. Under these conditions she was able to work as a secretary for an important business executive, live away from her family, and to a limited extent enjoy some friendships and social pleasures. She herself often wished to terminate the psychotherapy, but whenever I attempted to reduce further the frequency of visits, symptoms of schizophrenic disorganization became evident. She would, however, weather my absences due to conferences or vacations, quite well. When I left my London practice she was transferred to the care of a colleague who had a similar experience with her. She continued at work with minimal symptoms of an obsessional neurotic kind, provided in general she attended once weekly for psychotherapeutic sessions. In her case, in other words, psychotherapy had become part and parcel of her vital psycho-economy, and without this routine ominous indications of commencing schizophrenic disorganization would shortly appear. One memorable symptom of this highly intelligent, personable and cultivated young woman was that, in walking up Wimpole Street from business offices in the West End of London to my consulting room she would almost invariably find one or more silver coins of the realm on the pavement. Often I walked down this street, and, despite the greatest alertness on several occasions, was never able to find any lost coins. This young woman was very concerned about social status, prestige and wealth, and her regained interest in money was partly responsible for this exceptional perceptivity.

H. J. Eysenck (1965)[64] may not be very impressed with this as an effect of psychotherapy, but the young woman in question certainly valued her psychotherapy despite her ambivalence, promptly paying her monthly bill; and objectively it was clear that the psychotherapy enabled her to be a 'going concern', to avoid a good deal of suffering, and to enjoy life to a limited extent.

The question posed here is this: is it necessary to lose all sense of clinical reality, not to mention a sense of proportion, in attempting a scientific appraisal of the results of psychotherapy? Leaving aside those pseudo-scientific studies which so cleverly ignore basic clinical experiences and observation of change in psychotherapy, there is nevertheless an obligation to try to determine the effectiveness of different methods of psychotherapy. Not only do we need to know more about the gross changes in the patient due to the psychotherapy, but the minutiae of the processes of the particular psychotherapeutic enterprise under study require to be fully explored. Only in this way can we aspire to bring together the suitable patient, the suitable disease, the suitable therapist and the suitable method.

C. Knight Aldrich (1975)[65] insists that the precise indications for therapeutic use of uncovering insight-producing psychotherapy should be clarified and that this clarification should include whether long- or short-term psychoanalytic psychotherapy is preferable. He contends that attempts to answer these questions have not had enough controls or enough scope, and perhaps that there has not been enough willingness to face the consequences of the answers. He is especially concerned to know whether iatrogenic disability may indeed result from long-term psychotherapy, and, if so, to what extent and under what circumstances; and also to know whether psychoanalytically orientated treatment is more applicable to lower-class patients than has been assumed.

Rosenbaum et al. (1956)[66] reached tentative conclusions from a study of the gross changes in patients in a 12-month period of psychotherapy with residents training in dynamic psychiatry. Approximately 70 per cent of the entire group of 210 patients experienced appreciable improvement with treatment. The group of 'much improved' patients had had significantly better 'childhood environments'. Ability to develop interpersonal relations at the time therapy was started was significantly associated with improvement in therapy. Good sexual adjustment, high social status, and a favourable financial situation were significantly associated with 'much improvement' in therapy. No significant associations could be established between the pre-treatment marital adjustment, work adjustment, insight or housing facilities, and improvement with therapy. Religious activity was associated to a significant level with lack of change in treatment. Improvement, when it occurred, was found mainly in marital and work adjustment, with less in financial status, sexual adjustment, and interpersonal relations. It was noted that patients more frequently dropped out of therapy with less experienced residents. If the patient continued in therapy, however, he was likely to improve with a less experienced resident as with one who was more experienced. There was an association between intensity of therapy and improvement. However, the authors note that more intensive therapy may have been recommended at the 'intake' conference because the patient had sufficient ego strength to undergo 'uncovering' therapy. These patients would, of course, have been initially more likely to improve.

The picture presented in this evaluation of results in psychotherapy would be considerably further illuminated, it seems to me, if a study similarly conducted with similar rating scales and definitions were carried through with more experienced and highly trained psychiatrists, and if the frequency of visits were increased as considered desirable, so that both the study and the psychotherapists would have more scope.

Watterson (1954)[67] describes the work done up to 1954 in connection with the programme of psychotherapy research at the Menninger Clinic. He discusses three 'observation windows' opened on to the stream of study, and the follow-up study. Attempts were made, and were continued, to bring into line the kinds of data collected at the time of initial evaluation, of termination of treatment, and of follow-up. He gives a short account of an instrument used called the 'health-sickness scale'. The continuum of this scale ranges from a state of ideally good mental health at one end to a state of total personality disintegration at the other. The criteria incorporated into the scale are largely descriptive in nature, with the exception of the second which is largely inferential. They are:

1. The patient's need to be protected and/or supported by the therapist or hospital versus the ability to function autonomously.
2. The seriousness of the symptoms, e.g., the degree to which they reflect personality disorganization.
3. The degree of the patient's subjective discomfort and distress.
4. The patient's effect on his environment: danger, discomfort.
5. The degree to which he can utilize his abilities, especially in work.
6. The quality of his interpersonal relationships.
7. The breadth and depth of his interests.

Gross changes in the patients are evaluated in terms of these criteria and may then be used to answer such questions as: How effective is psychotherapy? To what extent does it promote healing in this or that disease, and in what kinds of patients? Of course, it would be helpful, if possible, to compare the natural history without formal psychotherapy of similar diseases in similar patients.

Then there is the question of the attitude of the physician.

Case 59. A woman who suffered severe stomach ache was taken to hospital and there treated by a gastro-enterologist. After thorough physical investigation he relieved her distress in due course by dosing her suitably with antispasmodic medication. During one of his visits to her bedside the woman complained of her domestic situation, but he took little notice of this. On another occasion the woman stated that she had come to think that her problems with her husband might have something to do with her sickness. The doctor again took little notice. On yet another visit the woman told the physician that she had a great deal of confidence in him and wanted to discuss with him her emotional disturbance which had arisen as a result of her husband's infidelity. The doctor told her that he was not the man to discuss such things with; he found such talks upsetting, and besides she might be upset by his attitudes—he could not be 'non-judgemental' about such events; she should see a psychiatrist who was trained to listen to such matters in a 'non-judgemental' way; anyway her illness was responding to the medication and everybody was upset sometimes, etc. The patient, however, remained adamant in her insistence that she wanted to talk to him: she had confidence in him and did not want to see a stranger. The doctor later became upset by the patient's insistence and referred her to me as an outpatient. In interview the patient was initially unresponsive and obviously reluctant to talk. Eventually she asked me what was the use of her talking to me. She believed that, as I had been trained to be 'non-judgemental', she would be unable to find out anything of value to herself in her discussion of her husband's infidelity and her reactions to it. It was at this point that I learned the details of the encounters with the gastro-enterologist. In our discussion I found it necessary to point out to this patient that no one was 'non-judgemental', that like everyone else I had been reacting in terms of 'good' and 'bad' since I was born. After this we made headway in our talks.

The fact is that, though my attitudes and reactions continue to differ in important respects from those of that particular gastro-enterologist, there is an important way in which we are alike. When a patient comes to a physician he comes for help: he is in some distress. My attitude from the beginning is partly the traditional medical attitude reflected in the questions: 'How far, and in what respects, is this patient deviating from health?' and 'How did this come about?' The answers, of course, come to comprise the diagnosis, and the job is to help that patient to move in the direction of health. These days, just as psychiatrists are supposed to be 'non-judgemental', so we are expected to be quite 'objective' and not to permit ourselves value judgements in regard to 'improvements' (I have never learned that we should ignore worsenings), but only to consider 'changes' in the patient. According to this view this is the way to be scientific. It is easily understood that certain people require a bulwark of an apotheosis of a 'non-judgemental' attitude, however feigned this really is, in order to protect themselves from a massive counter identification both threatening to themselves and noxious for the patient. The manoeuvre might well be useful sometimes in supportive types of psychotherapy of brief duration involved in social help for the patient. Similarly, there is obvious need for an insistence on scientific objectivity in assessing change in psychotherapy. It is, however, doubtful if this is ever arrived at by a pretence of deletion of 'value judgements'. The most important in-built controls in the psychotherapeutic situation are the therapist's consciousness of his own reactions and their meaning for him in the therapeutic situation, their subordination to the goals of treatment, and their analysis and consideration when it comes to the scientific assessment of change in the patient.

Now health is, of course, a typological ideal, but this does not mean that we have to get lost in an excessive relativistic culturalism. A medical training helps to protect one from such confusion. In both physical and psychological medicine we are confronted by disease processes which impede growth and create pain, and we have to try to understand these processes so that we can do something useful about the situation. This 'something useful' does not necessarily involve immediate total abolition of pain, for there are situations in which this would be noxious for growth or have other disabling long-term effects such as interfering with later adequate treatment, and a later higher level of freedom from discomfort. Jones (1942)[68] affirmed three attributes of mental health: happiness, adaptation to reality, and, related to both of these, efficiency. When these are impaired it is due to the triad of fear, hate, and guilt. He also states that psychoanalysis, when it works effectively, not only removes manifest psychoneurotic symptoms, but so deals with the fundamental conflicts and complexes as to bring about a considerable freeing and expansion of the personality leading to changes of a general order in the character and intellect, notably in the direction of increased tolerance and open-mindedness. Thus, as he states, it constantly happens in the course of analysis that the patient receives what might be called 'bonuses' in addition to the actual benefit he expected in coming for treatment. Often the goal set by the therapist is more advanced than the symptom-relief that the patient craves, and the therapist in analytically orientated methods tries to safeguard the bonuses referred to by Jones. These bonuses are related both to obviating in large measure the need for future symptom formation, and the promotion of self-realization. It is clear that we are here concerned with the quality of recovery from neurotic disability, which is often overlooked in part or in whole in comparative mensuration of different methods of psychotherapy.

Another aspect of recovery too is often overlooked in cross-sectional studies through an observational window at one period of the patient's life. Goethe, in referring to a period of sadness through which he had passed, spoke of this disease in retrospect as a measure of his health. Inability to experience grief or other painful emotion may be far otherwise than a measure of health; a deadening of reactivity may secure relief from symptoms but at a great price to personality, as we know from some drastic physical methods of treatment of mental disorder. But such a price can also be exacted in repressive methods of psychotherapy. Sometimes, of course, the price may have to be paid; the point is that where possible it should be avoided in order to achieve recovery which includes not only symptomatic and social improvements but a progressive change psychosexually as well.

Train (1958)[69] discussed another pitfall in the evaluation of psychotherapy related to these considerations. Flight into health may occur when the inexpediently protective neurotic structure is threatened with dissolution and the 'return of the repressed' is imminent. For certain patients this mobilization of defence may be the best available treatment. However, a false sense of achievement may be shared by the therapist. In some instances, of course, serious problems may later arise for the patient. At a later age, worsening relapses may occur, with the patient at that time less flexible and so less amenable to more radical treatment.

Finally, to get into the thorniest part of the thicket, there is the problem of controls in the evaluation of psychotherapy. Rogers and his associates (1951)[70] in their studies of client-centred psychotherapy, have employed the method of self-controls, a method marred by the promise of treatment but none the less of considerable interest. Watterson (1954)[67] outlined a more ambitious possibility so far unrealized. He envisaged precisely stated hypotheses concerning the association between the presence or absence of various elements in the treatment and ensuing changes in the patient. He writes:

> We might, for instance, develop working hypotheses relating the occurrence of characterological change to the amount or kind of insight or to the recovery of the infantile amnesia, or relating certain attitudes on the part of the therapist to changes of a favourable or unfavourable kind in the patient ... When that point is reached, it should be possible to make testable predictions that a certain technical manoeuvre or a particular therapist will be associated with a given change in the patient owing to the presence or absence of some specific element of technique or personality factor respectively. Experimental and control groups could be brought into being to test out such specific hypotheses. Neither patient nor therapist would know what hypotheses were actually being tested, that is, which therapy or therapist was deemed by the investigators to promote (or to fail to promote) this or that change in the patient.

One of Freud's greatest achievements was to devise a unique method of therapy and investigation, the psychoanalytic situation, and to explore its essential ingredients. Later workers have increasingly attempted to refine our knowledge of these ingredients (Strachey, 1934;[71] Sterba, 1934;[72] Alexander, 1956[73]). However, the part played by the psychotherapist's contribution remains to be more fully explored. In this respect the work of Hans. H. Strupp (Strupp, 1960;[74] Strupp et al., 1963,[75] 1964[76]) has been seminal. Gradually, through continuing work of this kind we may draw nearer the point envisaged by Watterson, when it will be possible to explore more exactly the minutiae of the processes of a particular psychotherapeutic enterprise (Wallenstein and Robbins, 1958;[77] Luborsky, 1962;[78] Horowitz, 1977[79]).

Walter V. Flegenheimer (1982)[80] attempts to compare the various brief therapies, in regard to their indications, especially the matching of the style of the patient, of the therapist and of the technique. He compares the time-limited psychotherapy of Mann (1973),[81] the intensive brief psychotherapy of Malan (1976),[46] the broad-focus short-term dynamic psychotherapy of Davanloo (1978),[82] the short-term anxiety-provoking psychotherapy of Sifneos (1979),[44] the eclectic short-term psychotherapy of Wolberg (1980)[83] and Alexander's techniques of brief psychotherapy (1965).[84] In particular, Flegenheimer, basing his views on the work of Burke, White, and Havens (1979),[85] considers that there is a good developmental fit for young hysterics in the techniques advocated by Sifneos (1979),[44] insofar as they are suitable for short-term psychotherapy in other respects. Sifneos limits his patients to those with an Oedipal focus, of above average intelligence and who already have an ability to understand phenomena in psychological terms, as well as the curiosity and willingness to explore themselves.

Edmund Neuhaus and William Astwood (1980)[86] for the most part concern themselves with once weekly individual psychotherapy on an outpatient basis. The authors are much influenced in their approach to neurotic distress by the concepts mined by Harry Stack Sullivan from his work with schizophrenic patients. They emphasize that psychotherapy to be effective requires an intimate and sharing relationship between patient and therapist, and that the quality of the patient-therapist interaction deeply influences the healing process. While they discuss 'techniques', they cite Bach on piano-playing to the effect that key-board players whose main asset is mere technique are at a disadvantage as compared with the gifted. They insist that there are quite skilled therapists who leave the patient untouched emotionally and that, after all, psychotherapy remains an art.

Metaphoric Speech and Fractional Catharsis in the Psychotherapy of Conversion Hysteria

We have already discussed in Chapter 16 the role of faded metaphor in the development of generality in discursive thought and language in contrast to the presence of lively metaphor in verbal communication expressive of emotion. In conversion hysteria such affective verbal communication is often excluded by repression. However, metaphor often finds an outlet without access to speech within the dramatic somatic symptoms through regression to its somato-psychic foundations. Many examples have previously been offered, including *Case* 46 in Chapter 16. Here is another illustrating some elements of the basis of a common complaint.

Case 60. A middle-aged married business man was referred with recent depression and disturbed sleep following several therapeutic efforts to cure severe backache which he had suffered for 2 years. He had been investigated and treated by a series of healing practitioners, including an orthopaedic surgeon, a neurosurgeon, a chiropractor and an osteopath. However, the backache persisted, though it had been temporarily relieved following treatment by each of the practitioners he had applied to for help. During the first few psychotherapeutic sessions he displayed some angry emotion which increased considerably in the further course of psychotherapy. This anger became evident in discussing frustrations endured during certain business dealings. Eventually he noted of a business associate: 'He smiles while he slips the knife into your back, so you don't know what's happening til later'; and, on another occasion of the same individual: 'He keeps getting my back up'. During the first year of his association with this particular counter-player in his business life he had suffered from peptic ulcer for which his family physician, who recently had referred him to me, had treated him with cimetidine medication with favourable response. He no longer suffered from any gastrointestinal symptoms, but had begun to get backaches soon after such symptoms had subsided.

This is quite a typical sequence, with the typical medical history of a compulsive competitive character who comes to suffer backache of a combined psychophysiologic and hysterical conversion nature. So is his history of iatrogenic reinforcement, following many thorough investigations and verbal interactions with medicos and other therapists. Nowadays, indeed, the commonest bodily pains and aches of a functional kind are headaches and pains in the neck and back, and those with these complaints have outstripped in frequency those presenting to a psychiatrist for ulcer-like pains, or with demonstrable peptic ulcer. As repeatedly noted, Breuer and Freud (1895)[14] early recognized the therapeutic importance of speech in affording more adequate affective expression, whereas joining in merely intellectual games with a hysterical patient does not promote recovery.

In the usual social-communicative focus of dialogue, whereas attention is usually paid to the *intended* meaning in the context of discursive language, some of the literal referents are subdued and others quite repressed. Under certain social conditions, it is true, attention is shifted to literal and concrete referents sometimes through accompanying gestures or through a play on words, for the sake of comic effect. (This aspect of joking is considered in Freud's *Jokes and their Relation to the Unconscious* (1905).[88]* In psychotherapy, to garner the possible literal referents requires 'listening with the third ear', to borrow Reik's (1948)[89] phrase. This involves the therapist's oscillation between focused knowledgeable understanding and 'free-floating' or, as Freud expressed this, 'evenly-hovering' attention. Then these literal referents of metaphoric language become available to the therapist so that his response may be more adequate in the treatment process.

Early in the course of his investigations with Breuer, Freud (Breuer and Freud, 1895[14]) came across a series of metaphoric expressions which his patient Frau Cäcilie M. invoked and which connected with different symptoms. (This patient, incidentally, he had got to know far more thoroughly, so he writes, than any of the other patients mentioned in *Studies on Hysteria*.) In one phase of his work with her she reached the recollection of the scene of her quarrel with her husband when the symptom of facial neuralgia was concomitantly reproduced. She described this conversation and her husband's remark which she had felt as a bitter insult. Suddenly she put her hand to her cheek, gave a loud cry of pain, and said: 'It was like a slap in the face.' At this time Freud was concerned with association by simultaneity of events, such as a painful scene and some current somatic organ compliance, but was coming to realize the part played also by symbolization in conversion phenomena. At another time this patient was afflicted with a violent pain in her right heel, a shooting pain at every step she took, which impeded walking. Freud (Breuer and Freud, 1895[14]) writes:

Analysis led us in connection with this to a time when the patient had been in a

---

*In discussing the 'manifold applications of the same material', Freud gives as one example the witticism of Dr Johnson, who said of the University of St Andrews in Scotland, which was then poor in purse but prolific in the bestowing of graduate honours: 'Let it persevere in its present plan and it may become rich by degrees.' Other instances of double meanings may be clearly based on metaphoric and literal referents, as in another of Freud's examples: A medical colleague of Freud's, well known for his wit, once said to the writer, Arthur Schnitzler, 'I am not at all surprised that you became a great poet. Your father had already held up the mirror to his contemporaries.' The mirror used by the writer's father, the famous Dr Schnitzler, was the laryngoscope.

sanatorium abroad. She had spent a week in bed and was going to be taken down to the common dining room for the first time by the house physician. The pain came on at the moment when she took his arm to leave the room with him; it disappeared during the reproduction of the scene, when the patient told me she had been afraid at the time that she might not 'find herself on a right footing' with these strangers.

Similarly, a series of her experiences were accompanied by a stabbing sensation in the region of the heart ('it stabbed me to the heart'). Moreover, the pain that occurs in hysteria as if nails are being driven into the head (clavus) was in this case related to incoming unwelcome thoughts ('Something's come into my head'). Pains of this kind with this patient were always cleared up as the problems involved were adequately discussed. In the case of Fraulein Elizabeth von R., who suffered pain in the legs associated with astasia–abasia, metaphoric speech gave access to her feelings. The symptoms were found to be related to a mental conflict concerning her love of her sister's husband based on a former warded-off incestuous attachment to her father, and the impasse created by this unconscious conflict was expressed by the patient in her feeling that she found 'standing alone' painful and that she could not progress in her life, could not 'take a single step forward'. Thus the ways in which the patient expressed her feelings about her psychological plight related to her symptoms and were portals through which her repressed conflicts could be approached in discussion. Moreover, in these sessions the symptoms would 'join in the conversation' as memories connected with these repressed conflicts were aroused.

As Freud writes, in taking a verbal expression literally and in feeling the 'stab in the heart' or the 'slap in the face' after some slighting remark as a real bodily event, the hysteric is not taking liberties with words but is simply reviving again the sensations to which the verbal expression owes its justification. Both hysteria and linguistic usage draw their material from a common source, a source, that is, in early sensorimotor experience.

Ella Freeman Sharpe (1940)[90] discusses the employment of metaphors by the patient in the course of psychotherapy as indicative of the revival of typical early experiences; some of these are of common occurrence in infancy and have conditioned metaphors in the development of language. Metaphor has evolved, she thinks, alongside the control of the bodily orifices, and emotions which had originally accompanied bodily discharge find verbal images in the preconscious which themselves are based on repressed psychological experiences. 'Affective language' is easily distinguishable in simple words and phrases expressing emotion, such as 'damn!', 'blast!', 'Oh God!'; these are psychical discharges which represent what in infancy and early childhood would have been bodily ones. Metaphor continues to reflect in its literal meanings the infantile situation in which the earlier prelinguistic discharge of affect took place. In the psychotherapy of hysterical states our listening must also allow for the physical basis and experience from which metaphorical speech springs.

In recent years much attention has come to be paid to the role of figurative language in human development and communication. Billow (1977)[91] has usefully reviewed the burgeoning psychological literature. As Hoffman (1984)[92] notes recent experiments on memory, and on the comprehension of poetic metaphor, proverbs and idioms, have significantly advanced our knowledge concerning the flexibility of learning. However, there is not a commensurate further study of the role of metaphor in the psychotherapeutic process or of the disturbance of metaphoric symbolism in emotional disturbance and mental disease. The psychological approach to the scientific exploration of language initiated by Wilhelm Wundt (1896)[93] at the turn of the century in laboratory studies of the association of ideas has been well maintained and developed. Wegener (1885),[94] unlike Wundt, observed language as an experiment of nature without the encumbrance of artificial conditions in the laboratory. His lead in the careful and painstaking observation of the expansion of thought and language of the growing school child remains to be more adequately followed. In the domain of psychopathology, the psychoanalytic method by intensifying the therapeutic process evokes metaphoric responses from the patient. Voth (1970)[95] considers the value at the appropriate time, of directing the patient's attention to these metaphoric expressions and asking for associations to them, as is customary to a dream. He states:

> Unless there is a clear contraindication to especially focused analytic work, such as excessive anxiety or impending disorganization, and if the timing is right, I believe the therapist should interrupt the patient's flow of associations and ask him to associate to what he has just said or, later, at a more opportune moment remind the patient of what he said and then ask him to reflect on it. The opportunity has arrived for the therapist to expose those meanings in appropriate doseage and in such a way as to make them maximally usable to the patient in a way congruent with the patient's ability to grasp, tolerate and use new insight in the context of ongoing development in the treatment.

Treatment

From the considerations raised in previous chapters concerning the aetiology and psychopathology of hysteria and hysteriform conditions, it will be apparent that the approach to treatment is not simply directed by the diagnosis of hysterical symptom-formation. More extended investigation of the patient is required in order to determine the approach to therapy, an investigation concerned with his ego assets and character structure, with his life situation, including his age and position in the life cycle, with his general physical health including factors of somatic compliance, and with the particular genetics and dynamics, including the defences, insofar as these can be inferred in preliminary investigative psychotherapeutic sessions. There are many cases of hysteria of relatively sound basic personality structure, without excessively pronounced oral ego orientation and psychotic patterns of defensive behaviour, of good intelligence and educational status, and sufficiently youthful, who are both symptomatically and characterologically accessible to formal psychoanalysis of relatively short duration. The faultily repressed memories and fantasies and associated strivings are in these cases afforded an outlet in less and less disguised derivatives with affective discharge through speech, and through the continuing work of interpretation, with ensuing ego integration. However, there are other cases less amenable to analysis, where analysis requires modification, or where 'covering' types of psychotherapy may result in amelioration.

In cases complicated by the exhibition of psychotic mechanisms, psychoanalytically orientated psychotherapy, with modification of the usual techniques of psychoanalysis, especially to discourage undue regression, may sometimes be possible. In such *hysteriform conditions* an important goal of psychoanalysis may still be preserved, namely, considerable personality change—to a degree which substantially reduces the need for symptom formation in response to frustrational life situations. Important modifications often required are: the patient is seen face to face, comfortably seated for conversation, and free association is abandoned or not insisted upon; the patient is confronted as soon as possible, and repeatedly when necessary, with the transferred origins of hostile feelings; the patient is offered more support, carefully, than is customary generally in psychoanalysis. In regard to the latter, in psychoanalysis need gratification is at a minimum, the frustration being a preliminary step to interpretation; however, borderline patients often require more support and cannot usefully adapt themselves to such technical strictures (Knight, 1953[96]). Over-much support, or other need gratification, can, of course, enhance regression and is to be avoided, but the balance of frustration–gratification has to be shifted towards more gratification in order that insight therapy can proceed at all with many of these patients, especially in the earlier phases of treatment.

In any case various conditions may indicate the suggestive and cathartic methods of treatment for relief of symptoms, and others may contraindicate psychoanalysis. Immediate help may be mandatory, as for example, in anorexia with bodily emaciation, or when anxiety and confusion dominate the clinical picture in acute hysteria. Consideration of such cases for psychoanalysis must wait until symptoms have been relieved and the patient is calmer. Advanced age, exceptionally great secondary gain, and feeble-mindness are contraindications to analysis. In instances of conversion reaction or dissociative reaction which follow a severely stressful precipitating situation, the simpler supportive and expressive methods of psychotherapy may suffice for recovery to the *status quo ante*. The question of psychoanalysis may, in such cases, be raised by the patient himself and may be best left to his own consideration and decision.

There are some cases of conversion reaction with an unfavourable prognosis, no matter what treatment is attempted. The conversion reaction may be the only possible emotional solution for the patient because of the real life situation which excludes healthier possibilities of gratification. Such cases may not ever recover from valetudinarianism, attended by a 'favourite' physician who is apt to be changed from time to time. Other cases, which used to be designated 'chronic degenerative hysteria', deteriorate into a massive form of emotional dependence, even parasitism, upon others. When the victim or victims separate or are separated from such patients, institutionalization may be necessary, sometimes because of a supervening psychotic disorder of depressive or paranoid type.

Perley and Guze (1962)[97] arbitrarily restricting the diagnosis of hysteria retrospectively to those patients with 'a dramatic or complicated medical history beginning before the age of 35' and with a minimum of 15 symptoms distributed among various organ systems, exclude other 'conversion' symptoms 'which may be found in many different disorders (psychiatric, neurologic and medical)'. These authors, relying entirely on symptom descriptions, ignore the limitations of symptom observation just as they ignore its essential usefulness in hysterical disorder from a psychodynamic viewpoint. Of course, if some symptoms are selected from the vast array of possible hysterical conversion phenomena—an array which incidentally, as we have seen, includes almost anything conspicuously exhibited in organic disease, due to the mechanism of identification—we are already apt to ignore the symptoms or combinations of symptoms which may be manifestations of hysteria. If, as in this study, selection is based upon a pitifully small sample, in terms not only of numbers but of places and times, error is compounded. Then if, as in their study, the groups of symptoms are only slightly less than one-third of the number of patients' charts studied, we are invited to further errors to be further compounded by statistics. There is an alchemist in Goethe's *Faust* who concocts within his crucible a *homunculus* which cannot survive outside of it; that is, when faced with the facts of life its materiality evaporates and we suspect that it was after all only a spiritual invention of its creator. However, whatever may be the value of these authors' abstractions, the women patients finally decanted as suffering from hysteria retain their materiality; as the authors' study shows, their symptoms persisted essentially unchanged over a period of 6–8 years; some of them may belong to the group of the inadequately treated; more of them probably belong to those chronic hysterias discussed above whose symptoms sometimes mask and protect them from psychotic disorder.

In selected instances of conversion hysteria, following adequate investigation, hypnotherapy continues to find a place, and some therapists utilize hypnosis for 'uncovering' types of psychotherapy (Wolberg, 1945[98]). Meldman (1960)[99] pointed out and illustrated the hazards of hypnotic symptom removal. As emphasized here repeatedly, an adequate history and an extended diagnosis, including the appraisal of the psychodynamics involved and the general personality background, are essential if unwarranted risks in hypnotherapy are to be avoided. Sometimes a readiness for cure occurs in the passage of time; then hypnotherapy can dramatically facilitate recovery, as the following brief case excerpt illustrates:

Case 61. A man, 45 years of age, had been in analytic psychotherapy (for 18 months) up to the preceding year, when therapy was terminated by the patient. He continued to suffer spastic paralysis of his legs and was able to get about only in a wheelchair, a condition which had persisted for 5 years following disputes at his business. When first encountered, the patient displayed remarkable insight in regard to his current and recent personal relationships, with the exception of his relationship with the analyst who had worked with him previously. Inferred from two interviews with this patient was a considerable unconscious hostility transferred to the analyst, although he spoke at length about this doctor's patience and perseverance with him; it also seemed likely that he was now ready to get well, although he could not let this happen as an outcome of the analytic treatment as far as it had proceeded before termination. Following the induction of a hypnotic trance with relaxation of his limbs, and direct suggestions of full power of movement on awakening, he was able clumsily to get on his feet and move around. Following exercises with an attendant over a period of a few days he left hospital to return to his work, walking around freely and easily.

It is necessary to acknowledge that the standard classical procedure of psychoanalysis, which aims at the complete reconstruction of the patient's development and the basic structural change of his personality, has limited therapeutic range. However, those ingredients of psychotherapy which have been identified in psychoanalytic work are utilized in every analytic psychotherapy; and indeed are present in every psychotherapeutic transaction whether acknowledged or not. The corrective emotional experience emphasized by Alexander (1956)[47] encompasses many elements: the monitoring of an optimum emotional flow (fractional catharsis) in a setting of benevolent concern; a process of relinquishment of inexpedient defence with derepression; a lifting of the veil obscuring memories of childhood and interpretation of the transference repetition with recall or reconstructions of genetic pathogenic traumata; the elucidation of unconscious fantasies related to the defence struggle (the dynamics of conflict); time for working over and working through. Thus is the unconscious made gradually conscious and more amenable to control, and insight achieved in variable measure.

It is beyond the scope of this volume to discuss in more detail psychoanalytic therapy and the unique psychoanalytic situation evolved by Freud from his studies of hysteria, which within a relatively rigid framework, permits the greatest possible freedom of self-revelation and of self-expression verbally. Fenichel (1939),[100] Glover (1955),[101] Stone (1961)[102] and Greenson (1967)[103] have produced valuable treatises on the technique and practice of psychoanalysis. In more recent years the problems of countertransference have been highlighted. Among the problems of impediments to therapeutic progress narcissistic resistances of the therapist have an important place. Ulman and Stolorow (1985)[104] have discussed this aspect of noxious countertransference from an intersubjective viewpoint. In an analysis of a series of dreams of a patient and therapist, they illustrate that transference and countertransference continually shape one another in a specific pattern of reciprocal mutual influence. An understanding of the vicissitudes of this intersubjective system is indeed always crucial if the therapeutic process is to be facilitated.

REFERENCES

1. Wolberg, L. R. (1954). *The Technique of Psychotherapy*. New York: Grune and Stratton.
2. Frazer, J. (1890). *The New Golden Bough*. New York: Criterion Books (1959).
3. McDougall, W. (1926). *Outline of Abnormal Psychology*. New York: Scribner.
4. Bernheim, H. (1891). *Bernheim's New Studies in Hypnotism* (trans. Sandor, R. S.), p. 16. New York: Int. Univ. Press (1980).
5. Freud, S. (1925). An Autobiographical Study. In: *The Standard Edition*, Vol. XX, p. 16. London: Hogarth Press (1955).
6. Freud, S. (1893). Some Points in a Comparative Study of Organic and Hysterical Paralysis. In: *Collected Papers*, Vol. I. London: Hogarth Press (1924).
7. Dubois, P.-C. (1904). *The Psychic Treatment of Mental Disorders*. New York: Funk and Wagnalls (1909).
8. Frank, J. D. (1973). *Persuasion and Healing: A Comparative Study of Psychotherapy*. Baltimore: Johns Hopkins Univ. Press.
9. Rado, S. (1956). *Psychoanalysis of Behaviour: Collected Papers*. New York: Grune and Stratton.

10. Jones, E. (1953). *The Life and Work of Sigmund Freud*, Vol. 1, pp. 224–5. New York: Basic Books.
11. Chertok, L. and de Saussure, R. (1979). *The Therapeutic Revolution: From Mesmer to Freud*. New York: Brunner/Mazel.
12. Breuer, J. and Freud, S. (1895). *Studies on Hysteria*. Case 5 (Freud). In: *The Standard Edition*, Vol. II. London: Hogarth Press (1955).
13. Jones, E. (1953). *The Life and Work of Sigmund Freud*, Vol. 1, pp. 243–4. New York: Basic Books.
14. Breuer, J. and Freud, S. (1895). *Studies on Hysteria*, Chapter IV: The psychotherapy of hysteria (Freud). In: *The Standard Edition*, Vol. II. London: Hogarth Press (1955).
15. Erikson, E. H. (1956). The first psychoanalyst. In: *Insight and Responsibility*. New York: Norton (1964).
16. Nordau, M. (1895). Introduction. *Degeneration* (2nd ed.; trans. Mosse, G. L.). New York: Fertig (1968).
17. Bram, F. M. (1965). The gift of Anna O. *Br. J. Med. Psychol.* **38**, 53.
18. Fenichel, O. (1945). Therapy and prophylaxis of neuroses. In: *The Psychoanalytic Theory of Neurosis*, Chap. 23. New York: Norton.
19. Volkan, V. D. (1976). *Primitive Internalised Object Relations. A Clinical Study of Schizophrenic, Borderline and Narcissistic Patients*. New York: Int. Univ. Press.
20. Abse, D. W. and Ewing, J. A. (1960). Some problems in psychotherapy with schizophrenic patients. *Am. J. Psychother.* **14**, 505.
21. Will, O. A. (1961). Process, psychotherapy and schizophrenia. In: *Psychotherapy of the Psychoses* (ed. Burton, A.). New York: Basic Books.
22. Searles, H. F. (1961). The evolution of the mother transference in psychotherapy with the schizophrenic patient. In: *Psychotherapy of the Psychoses* (ed. Burton, A.). New York: Basic Books.
23. Burnham, D. L. (1961). Autonomy and activity–passivity in the psychotherapy of a schizophrenic man. In: *Psychotherapy of the Psychoses* (ed. Burton, A.). New York: Basic Books.
24. Karon, B. P. and Vandenbos, G. R. (1981). *Psychotherapy of Schizophrenia*. New York and London: Aronson.
25. Foulkes, S. H. (1948). *Introduction to Group-analytic Psychotherapy*. London: Heinemann.
26. Foulkes, S. H. (1964). *Therapeutic Group Analysis*. New York: Int. Univ. Press.
27. Foulkes, S. H. and Anthony, E. J. (1965). *Group Psychotherapy. The Psychoanalytic Approach*. London: Penguin Books.
28. Freud, S. (1905). Fragment of an Analysis of a Case of Hysteria, pp. 12, 118, 119. In: *The Standard Edition*, Vol. VII London: Hogarth Press (1953).
29. Jones, E. (1955). *The Life and Work of Sigmund Freud*, Vol. 2. New York: Basic Books.
30. Freud, S. (1900). *The Interpretation of Dreams*. In: *The Standard Edition*, Vols. IV and V. London: Hogarth Press (1953).
31. Fliess, R. (1953). *The Revival of Interest in the Dream*. New York: Int. Univ. Press.
32. Allen, D. W. (1974). *The Fear of Looking or Scopophilic-exhibitionistic Conflicts*. Charlottesville, Va: Univ. Press of Virginia.
33. Erickson, E. H. (1962). Reality and actuality. *J. Am. Psychoanal. Assoc.* **10**, 456.
34. Blos, P. (1972). The epigenesis of the adult neurosis. In: *The Psychoanalytic Study of the Child*, Vol. 27, p. 130.
35. Rogow, A. A. (1978). Dora and her brother. A further footnote to Freud's 'Fragment' of a case of hysteria'. *J. Am. Psychoanal. Assoc.* **26**, 331.
36. Meares, R. (1976). The secret. *Psychiatry* **39** (3), 258–65 (quote from p. 259).
37. Benedikt, M. (1864). Beobachtung über Hysterie. *Zeitsch. für Practische Heilkunde* (1964), **20**, 127.

38. Stekel, W. (1938). *Technik der Analytischen Psychotherapie*. Berne: Medizinische Verlag Hans Huber. (Quote from Preface, p. xiv: *Technique of Analytical Psychotherapy* (trans. Paul, E. and C.). London: John Lane, Bodley Head (1939).
39. Malan, D. H. (1980). The most important development in psychotherapy since the discovery of the unconscious. In: *Short-term Psychotherapy* (ed. Davanloo, H.), Chap. 2, p. 19. New York and London: Aronson.
40. Ferenczi, S. and Rank, O. (1925). *The Development of Psychoanalysis*. Monograph No. 40. New York: Nervous and Mental Disease Publishing.
41. Alexander, F. and French, T. (1946). *Psychoanalytic Therapy*. New York: Ronald Press.
42. Ferenczi, S. (1925). Contra-indications to the 'active' psycho-analytical technique. In: *Further Contributions to the Theory and Technique of Psycho-Analysis* (compiled Rickman, R.; trans. Suttie, J. I.). New York: Basic Books (1960).
43. Sifneos, P. E. (1972). *Short-term Psychotherapy and Emotional Crisis*. Cambridge, Mass.: Harvard Univ. Press.
44. Sifneos, P. E. (1979). *Short-term Dynamic Psychotherapy*. New York: Plenum Press.
45. Malan, D. H. (1963). *A Study of Brief Psychotherapy*. London: Tavistock Publications.
46. Malan, D. H. (1976). *The Frontier of Brief Psychotherapy*. New York: Plenum Press.
47. Alexander, F. (1956). *Psychoanalysis and Psychotherapy*. New York: Norton.
48. Buckman, J. (1969). Psychedelic drugs as adjuncts to analytic psychotherapy. In: *Psychedelic Drugs*, pp. 210–16. New York: Grune and Stratton.
49. Graham, F. W. (1984). Psychoanalysis and group psychotherapy. *Group Analysis*. **17** (1), 3–11.
50. Rosen, V. H. (1975). The nature of verbal interventions in psychoanalysis. *Psychoanal. Contemp. Sci.* **3**, 189–209. New York: Int. Univ. Press.
51. Abse, D. W. (1983). Some complementary functions of group-analytic psychotherapy and individual psychoanalysis. In: *The Evolution of Group Analysis* (ed. Pines, M.), pp. 17–28. London: Routledge and Kegan Paul.
52. Freud, S. (1914). Remembering, Repeating and Working Through. (Further Recommendations on the Technique of Psycho-Analysis, II.) In: *The Standard Edition*, Vol. XII. London: Hogarth Press (1955).
53. Sedler, M. J. (1983). Freud's concept of working through. *Psychoanal. Quart.* **52**, 73–98.
54. Fenichel, O. (1945). *The Psychoanalytic Theory of Neurosis*, p. 31. New York: Norton.
55. Freud, S. (1893). On the Psychical Mechanism of Hysterical Phenomena: A Lecture. In: *The Standard Edition*, Vol. III. London: Hogarth Press (1953).
56. Van Gennep, A. (1908). *The Rites of Passage* (trans. Vizedorn, M. B. and Caffee, G. L.). Chicago: Univ. of Chicago Press (1960).
57. Meltzoff, J. and Kornreich, M. (1970). *Research in Psychotherapy*. Chicago: Aldine and Atherton.
58. Bergin, A. E. and Strupp, H. H. (1972). *Changing Frontiers in the Science of Psychotherapy*. Chicago: Aldine and Atherton.
59. Bergin, A. E. (1967). An empirical analysis of therapeutic issues. In: *Counseling and Psychotherapy: An Overview* (ed. Arbuckle, D.). New York: McGraw-Hill.
60. Dittman, A. T. (1966). Psychotherapeutic processes. In: *Annual Review of Psychology* (ed. Farnsworth, P. R., McNemar, O. and McNemar, Q.), Vol. 16, pp. 51–78. Palo Alto: Annual Reviews.
61. Strupp, H. H., Fox, R. E. and Lessler, K. (1969). *Patients View Their Psychotherapy*. Baltimore: Johns Hopkins Press.

62. Luborsky, L., Singer, B. and Luborsky, L. (1975). Comparative studies of psychotherapies. *Arch. Gen. Psychiat.* **32**, 995–1008.
63. Strupp, H. H. and Hadley, S. W. (1977). A tripartite model of mental health and therapeutic outcomes. *Am. Psychol.* **32** (3), 187–96 (quote from p. 192).
64. Eysenck, H. J. (1965). The effects of psychotherapy. *Int. J. Psychiat.* **1**, 97–178.
65. Aldrich, C. K. (1975). The long and short of psychotherapy. *Psychiat. Ann.* **5**, 12 (December).
66. Rosenbaum, M., Friedlander, J. and Kaplan, S. M. (1956). Evaluation of results of psychotherapy. *Psychosom. Med.* **18**, 113.
67. Watterson, D. J. (1954). Problems in the evaluation of psychotherapy. *Bull. Menninger Clin.* **18**, 232.
68. Jones, E. (1942). The concept of a normal mind. *Int. J. Psychoanal.* **23**, 1.
69. Train, G. J. (1958). Flight into health: a pitfall in the evaluation of psychotherapy. *Int. Record Med.* **171**, 111.
70. Rogers, C. R. (1951). Studies in client-centered psychotherapy. *Psychol. Service Center J.* **3**, 47.
71. Strachey, J. (1934). The nature of the therapeutic action of psychoanalysis. *Int. J. Psychoanal.* **15**, 127.
72. Sterba, R. F. (1934). The fate of the ego in analytic therapy. *Int. J. Psychoanal.* **15**, 117.
73. Alexander, F. (1956). *Psychoanalysis and Psychotherapy*. New York: Norton.
74. Strupp, H. H. (1960). *Psychotherapists in Action*. New York: Grune and Stratton.
75. Strupp, H. H., Wallach, M. S., Jenkins, J. et al. (1963). Psychotherapists' assessments of former patients. *J. Nerv. Ment. Dis.* **137**, 222.
76. Strupp, H. H., Wallach, M. S. and Wogan, M. (1964). Psychotherapy experience in retrospect: questionnaire survey of former patients and their therapists. In: *Psychological Monographs, General and Applied* (ed. Kimble, G. A.), Vol. 78, No. 11. Washington, D.C.: Am. Psychol. Assoc.
77. Wallenstein, R. S. and Robbins, L. L. (1958). Further notes on designs and concepts. In: 'The Psychotherapy Research Project of the Menninger Foundation, Second Report.' *Bull. Menninger Clin.* **22**, 117.
78. Luborsky, L. (1962). The patient's personality and psychotherapeutic change. In: *Research in Psychotherapy* (ed. Strupp, H. H. and Luborsky, L.), Vol. 2. Washington, D.C.: Am. Psychol. Assoc.
79. Horowitz, M. J. (1977). Structure and the processes of change. In: *Hysterical Personality* (ed. Horowitz, M. J.), Chap. 6. New York: Aronson.
80. Flegenheimer, W. V. (1982). *Techniques of Brief Psychotherapy*. New York and London: Aronson.
81. Mann, J. (1973). *Time-limited psychotherapy*. Cambridge, Mass.: Harvard Univ. Press.
82. Davanloo, H. (1978). *Basic Principles and Techniques in Short-term Dynamic Psychotherapy*. New York: S. P. Medical and Scientific Books.
83. Wolberg, L. R. (1980). *Handbook of Short-term Psychotherapy*. New York: Thieme–Stratton.
84. Alexander, F. (1965). Psychoanalytic contributions to short-term psychotherapy. In: *Short-term Psychotherapy* (ed. Wolberg, L.), pp. 84–126. New York: Grune and Stratton.
85. Burke, G. D. Jun., White, H. S. and Havens, L. L. (1979). Which short-term psychotherapy? *Arch. Gen. Psychiat.* **36**, 177–86.
86. Neuhaus, E. C. and Astwood, W. (1980). *Practising Psychotherapy*. New York and London: Human Sciences Press.
87. Apprey, M. (1983). Liminality as metaphor in adolescent psychotherapy and psychoanalysis. *J. Psychoanal. Anthropol.* **6** (1), 3–16 (quotes from pp. 5–6 and 4).
88. Freud, S. (1905). *Jokes and their Relation to the Unconscious*. In: *The Standard Edition*, Vol. VIII. London: Hogarth Press (1953).

89. Reik. T. (1948). *Listening with the Third Ear*. New York: Farrar and Strauss.
90. Sharpe, E. F. (1940). Psycho-physical problems revealed in language: an examination of metaphor. *Int. J. Psychoanal.* **21**, 201.
91. Billow, R. (1977). Metaphor: a review of the psychological literature. *Psychol. Bull.* **84**, 81–92.
92. Hoffman, R. R. (1984). Recent psycholinguistic research on figurative language. In: *Discourses in Reading and Linguistics* (ed. White, S. J. and Teller, V.). New York: N.Y. Acad. Sci.
93. Wundt, W. (1896). *Grundriss der Psychologie*. Leipzig: Kröner.
94. Wegener, P. (1885). *The Life of Speech* (trans. Abse, D. W.). In: *Speech and Reason* (ed. Abse, D. W.). Charlottesville, Va: Univ. Press of Virginia; Bristol: Wright (1971).
95. Voth, H. M. (1970). The analysis of metaphor. *J. Am. Psychoanal. Assoc.* **18** (3), 599–621 (quote from p. 601).
96. Knight, R. P. (1953). Management and psychotherapy of the borderline schizophrenic patient. In: *Psychoanalytic Psychiatry and Psychology* (ed. Knight, R. P. and Friedman, C. R.), Vol. 1. New York: Int. Univ. Press (1954).
97. Perley, M. J. and Guze, S. B. (1962). Hysterical—the stability and usefulness of clinical criteria. *New Engl. J. Med.* **266**, 429.
98. Wolberg, L. R. (1945). *Hypnoanalysis*. New York: Grune and Stratton.
99. Meldman, M. J. (1960). Personality decompensation after hypnotic symptom suppression. *J. Am. Med. Assoc.* **173**, 359.
100. Fenichel, O. (1939). Problems of psychoanalytic technique. *Psychoanal. Quart.* **7**, 421–42; **8**, 57–87, 164–85, 303–24, 438–70.
101. Glover, E. (1955). *The Technique of Psycho-analysis*. New York: Int. Univ. Press.
102. Stone. L. (1961). *The Psychoanalytic Situation (An Examination of its Development and Essential Nature)*. New York: Int. Univ. Press.
103. Greenson, R. (1967). *The Technique and Practice of Psychoanalysis*. New York: Int. Univ. Press.
104. Ulman, R. B. and Stolorow, R. D. (1985). The 'transference–countertransference neurosis' in psychoanalysis. An intersubjective viewpoint. *Bull. Menninger Clin.* **49** (1), 37–51.
105. Kohut, H. (1971). *The Analysis of the Self*. New York: Int. Univ. Press.
106. Kohut, H. (1977). *The Restoration of the Self*. New York: Int. Univ. Press.

Subject Index

Author Index

Major authors and associated topics are also referred to in the subject index.